D0782247

MONOGRAPHS OF THE HEBREW UNION COLLEGE — NO. III

EUPOLEMUS
A STUDY OF JUDAEO-GREEK LITERATURE

EUPOLEMUS
A STUDY OF JUDAEO-GREEK LITERATURE

by

Ben Zion Wacholder

HEBREW UNION COLLEGE–JEWISH INSTITUTE OF RELIGION

Cincinnati, New York, Los Angeles, Jerusalem

1974

Library of Congress Catalog Card Number: 0-87820-401-6
Manufactured in the United States of America

M. DWORKIN and Co.
New York / Jerusalem

TO MY FATHER

ר׳ פנחס שלמה ב״ר מנחם מענדיל זצ״ל

Who taught me how to study

TABLE OF CONTENTS

Page

Preface   x

Chapter One   LIFE AND WORKS   1
                   Name   4
                   Date   5
                   Life   7
                   Works   21

Chapter Two   THE TRADITION   27
                   First and Second Maccabees   27
                   Second Maccabees   38
                   Ptolemy of Mendes   40
                   Alexander Polyhistor   44
                   Josephus   52
                   The Church Fathers   57

Chapter Three   THE HELLENIZED MOSES – JEWISH AND PAGAN
                   (Fragment One)   71
                   1. The First Wise Man   74
                   2. The Inventor of Alphabet   77
                   3. The First Written Law   83
                   4. Hecataeus of Abdera and the Origin of the Hellenistic
                      Moses   85

Chapter Four   HELLENISTIC BIBLICAL CHRONOLOGIES
                   (Fragment Five)   97
                   First Stage––Reconciling Biblical Dates   98
                                The Septuagint   99
                                Demetrius   100
                   Second Stage––Fusion of Biblical and Greek Myth   104
                                Pseudo-Eupolemus; Artapanus   104
                   Third Stage––Fusion of Bible with World Chronicles . . .   106
                                Eupolemus   107
                                Graeco-Phoenician Chronicles   110
                                Date of the Exodus   111
                                Hellenistic World Chronicle   113
                                Biblical Dates in Heathen Chronicles   117
                                Anti-Judaean Biblical Chronology   125

Chapter Five   FROM MOSES TO DAVID (Fragment Two)   129
                   1. Joshua-Samuel-Saul   129
                   2. David's Campaigns   131
                   3. David Chooses Site for the Temple   139
                   4. David Provides for the Temple   145

TABLE OF CONTENTS (Continued)

Page

Chapter Six   KING SOLOMON (Fragment Two) 151
1. Coronation 151
2. Correspondence 155
3. First Year 170

Chapter Seven   THE TEMPLE OF SOLOMON (Fragment Two) 173
Foundation and Walls 175
Pillars 181
Lamps 183
Gates 186
Portico 187
Laver 190
King's Platform 193
Altar 194
Scarecrow 196

Chapter Eight   JERUSALEM 203
Hierosolyma 205
Dedication of Temple 208
Expenditures of Temple 213
Gifts for Egyptians and Phoenicians 215
Yahweh's Gold in Zeus' Temple: Theophilus 217
Shields. Solomon's Death (Fragment Three) 223

Chapter Nine   THE FALL OF JERUSALEM (Fragment Four) 227
Worship of Baal 228
Nebuchadnezzar's Campaign 230
The Armies 234
The Conquest of Jerusalem 235
Jeremiah Saves the Ark 237

Chapter Ten   THE SOURCES 243
Hexateuch 246
Kings and Chronicles 248
Style 254

Chapter Eleven   THE GRAECO-PALESTINIAN LITERATURE 259
Priestly Origin 259
Pseudo–Hecataeus 262
Pseudo-Hecataeus I 266
Palestine and the Septuagint 274
Graeco-Biblical Palestinian Tradition 280
Philo's *Jerusalem* 282
Samaritan Syncretistic Biblical History 287
Qumran Texts and the Graeco-Jewish Tradition 291

TABLE OF CONTENTS (Continued)

Page

Chapter Eleven   Political Writings 293
         Pseudo-Alexander 293
         The Tobiad Saga 295
         Herod's Memoirs 296
         Anti-Herodian Diatribe 297
         Justus of Tiberias 298
         Justus and Josephus 304

APPENDIX A   The Fragments of Eupolemus 307

APPENDIX B   The Fragments of Pseudo-Eupolemus 313

INDEX   1. Passages 315
         2. General 326
         3. Modern Authors 329

Preface

This work is the first book-length study of the surviving Greek fragments of Eupolemus, including an analysis of the man and his time. A doctoral dissertation, *Eupolemi Fragmenta* (1840) by Carolus Kuhlmey argued that Eupolemus was not a Jewish but rather a pagan historian; this view was brilliantly refuted by Jacob Freudenthal. In this study, however, Eupolemus' history of the Jews from Moses to 158 B.C. serves as a springboard to explore the nature of a Graeco-Judaen literature that flourished in Palestine from the second century before the Christian era to the time of the death of the last Jewish King Agrippa II, about A.D. 93.

Eupolemus emerges as a significant figure of the once numerous but now forgotten Jewish Hellenistic writers. His style bridged the diverse literary traditions of history writing of the Greeks and the Hebrews. A native of Jerusalem and a member of the priestly clans that officiated in the Temple, Eupolemus devoted a lengthy section of his work to a minute, if fanciful, description of the Solomonic sanctuary, fragments of which survive. Eupolemus' father had negotiated the Seleucid occupation of Jerusalem in 200 B.C.; some four decades later Eupolemus brought back a promise from the Roman Empire to aid Judah Maccabee and his faltering rebels against the Seleucid rulers.

This book offers a documentation that some members of Jerusalem's priestly Hellenists favored the Maccabean rebellion. Eupolemus' fragments serve as a counterfoil to the accounts in the First and Second Books of Maccabees which depict that struggle as being strictly between "paganized" Hellenizers and traditionalist defenders of the ancient Jewish faith.

Chapter One traces Eupolemus' somewhat blemished priestly ancestry, the tradition of diplomatic service, and the works attributed to Eupolemus. Chapter Two examines the evidence that the passages ascribed to Eupolemus are in fact his writings. It delineates his influence upon ancient and Byzantine chroniclers, assembling passages which, albeit unacknowledged, possibly or probably are remnants of Eupolemus' history. The next two chapters analyze the Hellenized image of Moses and the date of the exodus from Egypt found in Eupolemus' fragments. Like other pagan and Jewish writers, Eupolemus modeled his description of Moses after the accounts of Egypt written by an immensely popular historian-philosopher, Hecataeus of Abdera (300 B.C.). The view that Moses was an unknown figure to pagan intellectuals before the advent of Christianity is shown to be incorrect, since ancient universal historians and chroniclers normally incorporated a section devoted to the Jewish lawgiver.

Chapters Five through Nine present a commentary on Eupolemus' account of Solomon's Temple. Although written in Greek, Eupolemus' work appears to be a continuance of the traditions of the Books of Kings and Chronicles. The concluding two chapters describe Eupolemus' sources and style and the emergence of the Graeco-Judaen literature.

Professor John Strugnell graciously annotated an early draft of the first four chapters. His erudite and perceptive notes have not only removed many errors, but have also inspired new avenues of investigation. Professor Nikolaus Walter kindly sent me a draft of Eupolemus' fragments in preparation of a new collection of Jewish-Greek remnants. Frequent chats with my colleague and friend, Samuel Sandmel, have added clarity and focus to the treatment of many complex discussions. I alone, however, am responsible for the points of view expressed as well as for the errors and misinterpretations in this study.

I am deeply indebted to my friend and colleague Stanley Chyet for his valuable assistance in editing the book. My daughter Faye (Nina) has removed quite a number of obscure and infelicitous expressions. Under the direction of Mrs. Rissa Alex, the typing staff of the College, and especially, Miss Yetta Gershune, has performed a remarkable job in typing and retyping barely legible manuscripts.

My profound gratitude goes to the Hebrew Union College-Jewish Institute of Religion, President Alfred Gottschalk, Dr. Jacob Marcus, and the Committee of Publications for issuing this book under the imprint of Hebrew Union College Press.

B.Z.W.

Chapter One

LIFE AND WORKS

Chapter One

LIFE AND WORKS

The rather curious name Eupolemus (Brave Warrior) appears three times in Graeco-Jewish texts:

1. The First and Second Books of Maccabees record that in 161 B.C. Judah Maccabee dispatched an embassy to Rome to negotiate a treaty between the Hasmonean rebels and the Roman Republic. "Eupolemus, the son of John, the son of Akkos, and Jason the son of Eleazar" were the members of the Jewish delegation.[1]
2. The name Eupolemus appears in Josephus' list of apparently heathen historians whose allegedly erroneous treatment of Jewish affairs resulted from ignorance rather than from malice.[2]
3. The Church Fathers, Clement of Alexandria (died before 215) and notably Eusebius of Caesarea (died in 339), quoted from the writings of Eupolemus extensive excerpts dealing with Jewish history during the biblical period.[3]

Were these authorities referring to different men by the same name or was there only a single individual called Eupolemus? Some scholars (Hody, Kuhlmey, Willrich, Dancy) have maintained that Eupolemus the ambassador and Eupolemus the historian were not identical.[4] A somewhat larger group of

---

1 I Macc. 8:17; II Macc. 4:11; Josephus, *A.J.*, XII, 415 (paraphrasing I Macc. 8:17); Jacoby, *FGrH* 723 T 1. The sources mention no date but 161 is assured not only from the context of I Macc. Chapter 8, but also from *A.J.*, XIV, 233, where the Consul Fannius is said to have given the envoys, evidently Eupolemus and Jason, a letter of recommendation to the magistrates of Cos (see below page 18).

2 Jos. *C. Apionem*, I, 218; Euseb. *P.E.*, IX, 42, 3 (secondary) = *FGrH* 723 T 3.

3 Clement Al., *Stromata*, I, 153, 4 (723 F 1b); I. 130, 3 (723 F 2a); I, 141, 4 (723 F 4; Walter, Eup. F 5). Eusebius, *H.E.*, VI, 13, 7 (723 T 2); *P.E.*, IX, 25, 4 (723 F 1a); IX, 30-34, 18 (723 F 2b); IX, 19 (723 F 3); IX, 39 (723 F 5; Walter, F 4). Jerome, *De vir. ill.*, 38, is based on Clement and Eusebius, as are the medieval texts (cited below, p. 68).

4 H. Hody, *Histoire Critique* (Paris, 1711), I, 29; C. Kuhlmey, *Eupolemi Fragmenta* (Berlin, 1840), 10-26, citing the older literature; H. Willrich, *Juden und Griechen* (Göttingen, 1875), 157-161; *Judaica* (Göttingen, 1900), 71f., 111, 117; *R.E.* "Eupolemos" No. 9, VI (1907), col. 1227; J.C. Dancy, *A Commentary on I Maccabees* (Oxford, Basil Blackwell, 1954), 129.

scholars (Vossius, Freudenthal, Schürer, Jacoby, Abel, Walter) have defended the common identification.[5] Still others (Krauss, Bévenot, Pfeiffer,
Turner) have remained uncommitted, pointing out that the evidence is not
decisive one way or the other.[6]

Carl Kuhlmey, the author of the only monograph on Eupolemus,
presented a comprehensive defense of the view that the texts were referring
to two men by the name Eupolemus—one a Jew and the other a heathen.[7] He
cited Josephus' testimony that Eupolemus was a heathen,[8] bolstering it with
internal evidence. Errors found in the fragments of Eupolemus (for example,
that David was the son of Saul) and extreme syncretistic tendencies (for
example the identification of Atlas with Enoch[9]) would suggest that the
author of the fragments was not a Jew. Since Judah Maccabee's envoy to
Rome was certainly a fellow Jew, Kuhlmey reasoned, he could not have been
the one also known to us as the writer.

Kuhlmey's seemingly tight case, however, falls apart on close scrutiny.
Josephus' testimony here is equivocal. After listing a sample of nine pagan
authors who misrepresented Jewish affairs partly out of malice but mostly
out of ignorance of Scripture, Josephus adds: "But Demetrius of Phaleron,
the elder Philo, and Eupolemus do not stray far from the truth, their errors
being excusable, as they could not follow our writings quite accurately."[10]

---

5   I. Vossius, *Antiquité des temps rétablie et défendue contre les juifs* (Paris,
1687), 44; J. Freudenthal, *Hellenistische Studien: Alexander Polyhistor* (Breslau, 1875),
127; E. Schürer, *Geschichte des jüdischen Volkes* (Leipzig, 1909) III[4], 475 f., who cites
the older literature; F. Jacoby, *R.E.*, "Eupolemos" No. 11, VI (1907), cols. 1227-1229;
F. Susemihl, *Geschichte der griechischen Litteratur in der Alexandrinerzeit* (Leipzig,
1891-92), II, 648-652; O. Stählin, in Christ, *Griechischer Litteraturgeschichte* (Munich,
1920), II[6], 1, 589 f.; F. M. Abel, *Les livres des Maccabées* (Paris, Librairie Lecoffre,
1949), 153; N. Walter in his forthcoming publication of the Graeco-Jewish writers.

6   S. Krauss, in *The Jewish Encyclopedia*, V (1903), 296; R. H. Pfeiffer, *History
of New Testament Times* (New York, Harper & Brothers, 1949); H. Bévenot, *Die beiden
Makkabäerbücher* (Bonn, 1931), 104; 201; N. Turner, in *The Interpreter's Dictionary of
the Bible* (New York, Abingdon Press, 1962), II, 181; Jean Starcky, in a note, *Les livres
des Maccabées* (La Sainte Bible), by F.-M. Abel (3rd ed., Paris, Cerf, 1961), 148.

7   Kuhlmey, *Eupolemi Fragmenta*, 10 ff.

8   *C. Apionem*, I. 218.

9   Euseb., *P.E.*, IX, 30, 1, p. 538, 13 f. = 723 F 2b, p. 673, 5. *P.E.*, IX, 17, 9, p.
504, 7 f. = 724 F 1, p. 679, 18 f.

10   *C. Apionem*, I, 218: ὁ μέντοι [Φαλερεὺς] Δημήτριος καὶ Φίλων ὁ πρεσβύτερος
καὶ Εὐπόλεμος, οὐ πολὺ τῆς ἀληθείας διήμαρτον. οἷς συγγιγνώσκειν ἄξιον οὐ γὰρ
ἐνῆν αὐτοῖς μετὰ πάσης ἀκριβείας τοῖς ἡμετέροις γράμμασι παρακολουθεῖν (723 F 3).
The brackets are supplied by Jacoby (723 T 3, p. 672, 8 = 737 F 1), who evidently
retracted from his earlier position that the reference was to pseudograph (*FGrH*, IID, p.
653, on 228 F 51). The excision, however, is justified. Eusebius, whose text of Josephus
contained the word (*P.E.*, IX, 42, 3), nevertheless identified Demetrius with the historian
ignoring the epithet "Phalerean" (*H.E.*, VI, 13, 7).

In his *Textes d'auteurs grecs et romains relatifs au Judaïsme* (Paris, 1895), 217, note
1, Théodore Reinarch argued that our passage is an interpolation. It interrupts the flow

Aside from the identification of Demetrius, as hailed from Phalerum, generally agreed to be an inadvertent error, scholars have interpreted this passage, because of its context, to mean that Josephus labeled these men as heathens. However, the naming of the elder Philo, who is to be distinguished from the younger Philo of Alexandria mentioned elsewhere in Josephus, indicates that this is a misinterpretation of Josephus. Moreover, although Josephus criticizes their minor errors, he grants that as a rule their interpretations are accurate. The solution to this apparent contradiction seems to be that although Josephus implied that Demetrius, Philo and Eupolemus were heathens, he was careful not to say so directly. Josephus, who quotes pagan writers voluminously but not Jewish ones, was implying that he himself was the first Jew to write in Greek. To the knowledgeable, it would appear that he was only criticizing the Graeco-Jewish writers for their ignorance of Hebrew. This is evidently the oldest criticism of the dependence on the Septuagint text. Kuhlmey's deduction from Josephus that Eupolemus was a heathen is misleading. A contrary inference could perhaps be justified just as well.

There remains the internal evidence of the fragments, adduced by Kuhlmey, as tending to show that these texts were written by a heathen. But Freudenthal has effectively rebutted Kuhlmey's case. The fragment which displays strong syncretistic tendencies was shown by Freudenthal to have been written by someone other than Eupolemus.[11] The author of the syncretistic fragment was a Samaritan, whereas the other fragments which had come down to us in the name of Eupolemus were composed by someone extremely loyal to the temple of Jerusalem. The Samaritan author, now referred to as Pseudo-Eupolemus, was a syncretist; the Jerusalemite, a patriot who was barely influenced by heathen thought.[12] The great devotion to the temple of Jerusalem displayed in the fragments shows conclusively that, contrary to Kuhlmey, Eupolemus was a Jew.[13]

That Eupolemus the writer was not a heathen, however, does not necessarily indicate that he was identical with the Eupolemus mentioned as

---

of the narrative and, moreover, Josephus knew better than to label Jewish historians as pagans. But in a note to this passage in the Budé edition of *Contra Apionem* (Paris, 1930), 41, Reinach has abandoned this thesis, commenting only that Josephus mistakenly assumed that Demetrius, Philo, Eupolemus were Greeks since he knew them only from the writings of Alexander Polyhistor.

11 Freudenthal, *Hellenistische Studien*, 82-103.

12 Freudenthal's view (see previous note) is now generally accepted. Jacoby assigned Pseudo-Eupolemus (Anonymous) No. 724 FF 1-2. See Wacholder, "Pseudo-Eupolemus' Two Fragments on The Life of Abraham," *HUCA*, XXXIV (1963), 83-113, who follows Freudenthal and Jacoby on Assigning the anonymous passage of Eusebius, *P.E.*, IX, 18, 2, to Pseudo-Eupolemus. However, N. Walter, in *Klio*, XLIII-XLV (1965), 184, has questioned the view that the Anonymous and Pseudo-Eupolemus are identical.

13 See below pp. 145ff.

Judah Maccabee's envoy. Krauss and Dancy have taken the position that there is no reason to identify the two as one and the same.[14] Nevertheless, a close analysis of the evidence points strongly to the view that Judah's envoy to Rome was also the author under whose name Greek extracts have been preserved. The evidence rests on a) the name; b) the date; and c) the content of the fragments.

NAME

Eupolemus was an unusual, if not a rare, name, in antiquity.[15] Other than in the passages under discussion here, no other Jew by such a name is attested in the literary, epigraphical, or papyrological remains of antiquity.[16] The Jews in the Hellenistic period, like those of subsequent generations, tended to borrow from their environment popular and typical names, favoring those associated with royalty and aristocracy. Since Eupolemus was not a common name among Greeks and otherwise unheard of among Jews, the burden of proof rests on those who argue that there might have been two famous Jews with such an appellation.

The question of identity is a rather common problem in Hellenistic Jewish literature and is not limited to Eupolemus. Extracts from a philosophical commentary on the Pentateuch have been preserved by a certain Artistobulus, sometimes dubbed the Peripatetic.[17] It has been frequently asked whether or not the first known biblical commentator was identical with the Aristobulus who, in II Macc. 1:10, was described by the Jews of Jerusalem as "of the family of anointed priests, teacher of Ptolemy the king." Two writers by the name of Aristeas are known in the Hellenistic literature: one, the reputed author of the so-called Letter of Aristeas; and the other, author of a work *On the Jews,* from which a fragment dealing with Job has been preserved.[18] Were there one or two men named Aristeas? Attempts have been made to identify Jason of Cyrene, whose work in an abridged form is now known as the Second Book of Maccabees, with one of the several Jasons recorded during the second or first century B.C.[19] Similarly, there is the

14   See above, n. 6.

15   W. Pape, *Wörterbuch der griechischen Eigennamen*[3] (Braunschweig, 1831-70), III, 417; F. Preisigke, *Namen* (Heidelberg, 1922), s.v. "Eupolemos."

16   A possible but unlikely exception is the name אבטולמוס, found in M. Eruvin, III, 4; Genesis Rabbah 85, p. 1038, 8, which Jastrow, *s.v.,* explains: "probably Πτολεμαῖος or Εὐπτόλεμος = Εὐπόλεμος." But there is no ground to emend the name to be read Eupolemus.

17   The main passages of Aristobulus: Euseb. *H.E.,* VII, 32, 16-18; *P.E.,* VIII, 10-17; XIII, 11-16; Clement, *Strom.,* I, 72, 4; 150, 1; V, 97, 7.

18   Euseb., *P.E.,* IX, 25, p. 518, 6-22 = 725 F 1.

19   II Macc. 2:19-31 182 T 1. A. Schlatter, *Jason von Kyrene* (Munich, 1891); Schürer, *Gesch. des jüd. Volkes,* III[4], 485.

problem of whether Theodotus, the author of a historical poem on Shechem, was the same person mentioned by Josephus, or rather a Phoenician historian.[20] There is no single answer that would apply to all cases. Each identification must stand on its own. In the case of Aristobulus, the evidence suggests that the "teacher" of Ptolemy was identical with the Peripatetic philosopher.[21] It is generally agreed that the author of the Letter of Aristeas was not the same as the one who wrote on Job.[22] This question, however, is still problematic, since Alexander Polyhistor, writing in the middle of the first century B.C., apparently thought that these two were the same.[23] Curiously, the vast literature dealing with the Letter of Aristeas takes no account of this evidence. All attempts to identify Jason of Cyrene, the original author of the Second Book of Maccabees, have been unsuccessful.

But the name Eupolemus differs from common appellations such as Aristobulus, Aristeas, or Jason. Because of its rarity among Jews, it is conceivable that Eupolemus was a Greek pseudonym or dual name adopted during the Maccabean rebellion against the Syrians. Nevertheless, all that is known of Hellenistic nomenclature tends to suggest the view that there was only one Eupolemus.

DATE

I Macc. 8:17 reports that in 161 B.C.[24] Judah Maccabee dispatched Eupolemus as ambassador to Rome. The date of Eupolemus, the historian,

20   C. Apionem, I, 216 737 F 1. Tatian, Ad. Graec., 34 = 784 T 1; 794 F 5d. Euseb. P.E., IX, 22, p. 512, 11-516, 10 = 732 F1; A. Ludwich, De Theodoti Carmine Graeco-Iudaico (Königsberg, 1899). See also the problem whether the name Theophilus, mentioned in C. Apionem, I, 216, is identical with the Theophilus of Euseb. P.E., IX, 34, 19 = 733 F 1.

21   See ,L. Valckaner, Diatribe de Aristobulo Judaeo Philosopho Peripatetico Alexandrino (Leiden, 1809); N. Walter's thorough study, Der Thoraausleger Aristobulos (Berlin, Akademie-Verlag, 1964). Identification is denied, however, by S. Sandmel, in The Interpreter's Dictionary of the Bible (Nashville, Abingdon Press, 1962), I, 221.

22   Freudenthal, Hell, Studien, 141 f.; P. Wendland, in The Jewish Encyclopedia, II, 92; R. Tramontano, La lettera di Aristea a Filocrate (Naples, 1931), 44 ff.; M. Hadas, Aristeas to Philocrates (New York, Harper and Brothers, 1951), 4.

23   Passage on Job (P.E., IX, 35 = 625 F 1) and describing Jerusalem's temple (P.E., IX, 38, 2-11) both are attributed to Aristeas. Since the latter passage is derived from the Letter of Aristeas (88-90), it follows perhaps that the former was also taken from the same author, or that, at least, Eusebius assumed that they were identical. Freudenthal's argument that the historian Aristeas wrote a wretched Greek, while the so-called Pseudo-Aristeas' style was that of an educated man (see previous note) is not convincing. It must be kept in mind that the style of relating a biblical story such as Job's called for a Septuagintal Greek while an independent account such as the Letter of Aristeas was usually written in the literary style in vogue at the time. See Jacoby, FGrH, 725 F 1, p. 680, app. crit. to lines 1-2.

24   For the date see W. Kolbe, Beiträge zur syrischen und jüdischen Geschichte (Berlin, 1926), 37; note 1. Cf. also B. Niese, in Festschrift für Nöldeke (Leipzig, 1906), II, 817 f. where A.J., XIV, 233, is cited to determine the date.

can be deduced from his own chronological summary, as reported by Clement of Alexandria: "Also Eupolemus, in a similar treatment [to that of Philo], says, 'From Adam to the fifth year of the reign of Demetrius, when Ptolemy ruled Egypt in the twelfth year—make a total of 5,149 years.' . . . From that time to the Roman consuls Gaius Domitius and (Gnaius) Asinius [?], add up to 120 years."[25]

A number of learned papers have been written to explain the meaning of this passage. In the nineteenth century, scholarly opinion maintained that Eupolemus was referring to Demetrius II Nicator (145-139/38), whose fifth regnal year occurred in 141/40 B.C.[26] The difficulty of such a dating is that it does not synchronize with the other clues—the twelfth year of a Ptolemy and 120 years before the Roman consuls Domitius and Asinius. There is no Ptolemy whose twelfth year of reign would fall in the year of 141/40. Therefore, scholarly opinion, since Kuhlmey and Freudenthal, now believes that Eupolemus was dating his chronology during the reign of Demetrius I Soter (162-150), whose fifth year occurred in 158/7 B.C.[27] This almost, but not quite, tallies with the twelfth year of Ptolemy VIII Euergetes II Physcon, who had become joint ruler of Egypt on the 5th of October, 170 and whose twelfth year is to be dated in 159/8 B.C. The names of the Roman consuls are somewhat corrupt, but if slightly emended the reference here could be to Consuls Dometius and Assinius Pollio, whose term of office was in 40 B.C.; 120 years before that date yields 160 B.C.[28] The three clues of Clement's testimony yield three different years, but the differences are minor, attributable to common errors.

Thus we find that the date of Eupolemus' mission to Rome in 161 B.C. is very near the time when a writer of the same name was engaged in writing a biblical history, constructing a chronology from Adam to his own day. Is it not reasonable to assume that the ambassador and the writer are the same person? This synchronism, however, is open to other serious objections, which are discussed below (Chapter Two, pages 40-44). But we can anticipate

25   Clement, *Strom.*, I, 141, 4; 723 F 4 (F 5). The names of the consuls are corrupt in the Ms. and we follow here the emendation of Kuhlmey, *Eupolemi Fragmenta,* 34; Freudenthal, *Hell. Studien,* 230, 15. (See also below n. 28.)

26   M. Niebuhr, *Geschichte Assur's* (Berlin, 1857), 354; C. Mueller, *FGH*, III, 208; Graetz, *MGWJ*, XXVI (1877), 61; *Geschichte act Juden* (Leipzig, 1906), III[5], 601-04, the latter defending his dating against Freudenthal's.

27   Kuhlmey, *Eupol. Fragm.,* 27-35; Freudenthal, *Hell. Studien,* 133-25, 214, Schürer, *Gesch. d. jüd. Volkes,* III[4], 476, Jacoby, *R.E.* "Eupolemos" No. 11, VI (1907), cols. 1227 f; Y. Gutman, *The Beginnings of the Jewish-Hellenistic Literature* (Jerusalem, Mosad Bialik, 1963), 76 f. [in Hebrew].

28   The Ms. reading of *Strom.* I, 141, 5, is γαίοῦ δομετιανου κασιανοῦ.Following *A.J.* XIV, 389, where Josephus recorded the consulships, this text was amended by Kuhlmey (p. 34); and Freudenthal (215). γναίου δομετίου καὶ ἀσινίου; Sylburg read, καίσαρος δομετιανου καὶ σαβίνου; Gutschmid, γναίου δομετίου καὶ ἀσινίου ὑπὸ κασιανου,which is the most plausible text. But see below, pp. 40-41.

the results of our discussion here by saying that whatever these objections, they in no way affect the conclusion that Eupolemus the historian dated his work in 158/7 B.C.

In addition to the name and the date, the contents of the fragments attributed to Eupolemus tend to confirm the assumption that Eupolemus the ambassador was identical with the historian of the same name. As is shown below, the Jewish emissary to Rome was a member of one of the leading priestly families of Jerusalem. The Greek texts reveal that their author claimed expertise in the architecture of the temple. The author's devotion to Jerusalem and to the biblical tradition centered around Mount Zion.[29] When name, date, and content of the fragments all point in the same direction, there is good reason to believe that Judah Maccabee's ambassador to Rome was identical with the author of works on biblical history, fragments of which have survived.

LIFE

During the Hellenistic period, for the first time in the history of literature, the owning and writing of books became a common practice. It was also then that authors became personalities worthy of some of the recognition usually reserved for royal figures. Although the custom of writing books had spread also among the Jews, for a long time they resisted the trend to honor a man purely for authorship. The book mattered, not the author—a view which persisted among Jews until the nineteenth century and doubtless goes back to the very roots of Hebrew culture. Thus Jewish literature produced during the intertestamental period remained by and large either anonymous or pseudonymous.[30] It is not an accident, therefore, that only a few names of the once numerous Graeco-Jewish writers have survived: Aristeas, Aristobulus, Artapanus, Cleodemus-Malchus, Demetrius, Eupolemus, Ezechiel the Tragedian, Jason of Cyrene, Philo the Elder, Theodotus, and Theophilus.[31] Unfortunately, our knowledge of most of these men is extremely limited.[32]

---

29   See below, p. 140.

30   Ecclesiasticus by Ben Sira is the only Apocryphal work of which the author is known. Cf. the collections: *Apokryphen und Pseudepigraphen des Alten Testaments,* edited by E. Kautzsch (Tübingen, 1900); *Apocrypha and Pseudepigranha,* edited by R. H. Charles (London, 1913); *Altjüdische Schrifttum,* edited by P. Riessler (Augsburg, 1928).

31   For a more complete list of Graeco-Jewish writers, see Freudenthal, *Hell. Studien;* Jacoby's grouping in *FGrH,* IIIC, 2, Nos. 722-37 ("Juden") and below, *passim.*

32   For recent treatments of Ezekielus, see J. Wieneke, *Ezechielis Judaei....fragmenta* (Münster, 1931); and of Aristobulus, N. Walter, *Der Thoraausleger Aristobulos (Texte und Untersuchungen zur Geschichte der altchristlichen Literatur* [Berlin, Akademie-Verlag, 1964]).

Eupolemus, however, is an exception, and the reconstruction of his life assumed significance not only because it sheds light on a public figure in Jerusalem during the Maccabean rebellion, but also because it offers us a glimpse into the world of Graeco-Jewish writers during the second century B.C.

I Macc. 8:17 records that Eupolemus was "the son of John, the son of Haccos."[33] The mention of a patronymic in ancient Jewish texts frequently suggests a man of distinguished rank. I Macc. 2:1, for example, described Mattathias, the organizer of the Hasmonean insurrection, as "the son of John, the son of Simeon, a priest of the sons of Joarib, who had moved from Jerusalem to Modim." The author of the First Book of Maccabees tailored the formula of descent to accord with the relative importance of the figure. Mattathias was given a lengthy description, and Jason, Eupolemus' associate, a mere patronymic; Eupolemus himself received something between the two. John, Eupolemus' father, is said to have been the son of Akkos. As has been pointed out, although it might indeed have been the name of John's father, Akkos was mentioned primarily to indicate descent from the famous Aaronite clan, known in the Hebrew Biblical texts as Hakkoṣ (הקוץ) and in Greek as Ἰκώς or Ἀκκώς.[34]

The Hakkos clan had a stormy history. Its relative social standing in the establishment can be gauged from Chapter 24 of First Chronicles. There the twenty-four divisions of the priestly hierarchy are ascribed to David, listed presumably in descending order of importance. The clan of Joarib heads the list and that of Hakkos is the seventh. Some scholars, however, believe that Chapter 24 of I Chronicles should be regarded as a late addition intended to raise the standing of the Hasmoneans.[35] If so, I Chr. 24:10, recording the clan of Hakkos, in fact describes Eupolemus' social position during the second century.[36]

The pedigree of Hakkos' family, however, was not faultless. After their return from the Babylonian exile the descendants of Hakkos served in the Temple at Jerusalem. But a branch of the clan was banned from touching the holy of holies (including the right to occupy the office of high-priesthood) because of intermarriage with Barzillai, a priest from Gilead. Despite this

---

33   Εὐπόλεμος υἱὸν Ἰωάννου τοῦ Ἀκκώς (I Macc. 8:17); A reads Ἀκχώς.

34   See previous note; I Chr. 24:10; Ezra 2:61; Neh. 3:4, 21; I Esdras 5:38.Cf. . also Abel, Les livres des Maccabées, 153.

35   See W. Rudolph, Chronikbücher (Handbuch des Alten Testament, Erste Reihe, Tübingen, Mohr, 1955), 161, who regards not only the reference to Joiarib in I Chr. 24:7 as a Maccabean interpolation, but I Chr. 9:10; Neh. 11:10; 12:6, 10 as well. Ezra 8:16 lists a certain Joiarib who is not a priest.

36   It is conceivable though that even if Joiarib (I Chr. 24:7) was placed at the top of the list by a Maccabean reshuffler, 24:10 may reflect an ancient tradition, although a Maccabean house-cleaning may nevertheless have reshuffled the order to place Joiarib first. See the Qumran list, in Vetus Testamentum, 4 (Supplement 1954), 24 f.

blemish, the Hakkos clan continued to officiate in the Temple during the week of Pentecost until the destruction of the edifice. The name of Hakkos was evidently in the partly preserved calendar of priestly courses found among the Dead Sea Scrolls. In the rabbinic and in medieval literature, Hakkos continued to be mentioned as being associated with a certain locality *ylbon,* in Galilee, apparently because the family owned property there.[37] The evident similarity in the backgrounds of the Joarib (Hasmoneans) and the Hakkos (Eupolemus) clans is remarkable. It is reasonable to presume that, in addition to the political association, the two families shared similar religious and social views of the world. Many of the prejudices reflected in Eupolemus' fragments may have been to a large extent also those of Judah Maccabee.

The background of Tobiads also resembles that of the clan of Hakkos. The home of the Tobiads was Arak el-Emir, where archaeologists have dug up a family mausoleum dating perhaps back to 175 B.C. and a Hebrew inscription "Tobiah" of circa 500 B.C.[38] Ezra 2:59-61 (Neh. 7:62f.) couples the descendants of Tobiah and Hakkos as stained because of a possible intermarriage. In part the blemish of the Tobiads appears to have been political. Nehemiah was angered because the high priest Eliashib had reserved a chamber of Jerusalem's Temple for the Tobiads. Elsewhere, Nehemiah labels Tobiah as "the Ammonite slave." This clan figures prominently in the archives of the Zenon papyri, in which the name "Tubias" appears six times. Two of Tobias' letters, dated in 257 B.C. and addressed to Apollonius, the minister of Ptolemy Philadelphus, have survived. The correspondence records the purchase of slaves and cattle, but it is clear that Tobias ruled Transjordan on behalf of Egypt.[39]

---

37   Neh. 3:4, 21: "Meremoth the son of Uriah, son of Hakkoz," assists the high priest Eliashiv in the rebuilding of Jerusalem's walls. "Also, the sons of the priests: the sons of Haviah, the sons of Hakkoz, the sons of Barzillai, who had taken a wife from the daughters of Barzillai the Gileadite...sought their registration among those enrolled in the genealogies, but they could not find them, and so they were excluded from the priesthood as unclean. And the governor told them that they were not to partake from the most holy food, until there should be a priest to consult Urim and Thummim" (Ezra 2:61-63; Neh. 7:63-65; cf. I Esdras 5:38). For the Qumran fragment of the Priestly list, see previous note. Cf. also Samuel Klein, *Beiträge zur Geographie und Geschichte Galilaeas* (Kirchhain, 1909); *Sefer Hayishuv* (Jerusalem, 1939), 162-65; *Galilee* (Jerusalem, Mosad Harav Kuk, 1968), 181-92. According to S. Abramson, *Tarbiz,* 15 (1943-44), 52, the clan of Hakkos officiated in the Temple on the week of the festival of Pentecost, in the beginning of the month of Sivan.

38   See H. C. Butler and E. Littmann, *Publications of the Princeton University Archaeological Expedition to Syria,* Division II, Section A; Division III, Section A, Part I (Leiden, 1904-1908). See also *Corpus Inscriptionum Iudaicarum,* No. 868, II (Vatican City, Pontificio Instituto di Archeologia Cristiana, 1952), 105.

39   See *Corpus Papyrorum Judaicarum,* I, Nos. 1-17, esp. No. 1, 8, 14; 2d, 15 (Cambridge, Mass., Harvard University Press, 1957), I, pp. 115-46.

Although sheik of Transjordan, Tobias maintained close links with Jerusalem. He had married the daughter of the high priest Simon the Just. His son Joseph, by outwitting and outbidding all the other more prominent tax farmers, became the chief collector of royal revenue of Coele-Syria. Most of the monies deposited at the Temple of Jerusalem during the first decades of the second century B.C. belonged to Hyrcanus, either the son or grandson of Joseph. When Coele-Syria became a bone of contention between Syria and Egypt, the Tobiads favored the latter, while Eupolemus' father John sides with the former. Like those of Eupolemus, remnants of a Tobiad history have survived (see below, pp. 295-96). But unlike Eupolemus, who sided with Judah Maccabee, the Tobiads seem to have led the faction which advocated the Hellenization of Judaea. The clan suffered heavily when the Seleucids conquered Palestine, and its disappearance seems to have followed the rout of the Hellenizers.[40] It is instructive that by family background the Hakkos clan was, on the one hand, part of Jerusalem's highest priestly authorities and, on the other hand, paralleled the half-foreign and heavily Hellenized ruler of Transjordan.

Eupolemus' father, John, had a reputation as an accomplished diplomat. II Macc. 4:11 credits him with securing the charter for Judaea from Antiochus III in 198 B.C. when the king succeeded in wresting Coele-Syria from Egyptian hegemony. The letters are preserved in Josephus and, if genuine, show that John's reputation as an extraordinarily skillful diplomat was well deserved.[41] Antiochus III's charter granted the Jews the right to govern themselves in accordance with their ancestral laws.[42] In other words, the king reasserted the status quo ante, the right of the priests to exercise exclusive power.[43] A generous subsidy to the temple, originally offered by King Cyrus, was now renewed. Gentiles were prohibited by royal decree from trespassing

40   On the Tobiads, see A. Büchler, *Die Tobiaden und die Oniaden* (Vienna, VI. Jahresbericht der Israelitisch-Theologischen Lehranstalt, 1899), 8-143; A. Momigliano, "I Tobiadi nella preistoria del moto maccabaico," *Atti della reale Accademia delle Scienze di Torino,* 67 (1932), 165-200; R. Marcus' notes on *A.J.,* XII, 154-236; V. Tcherikover, *Hellenistic Civilization and the Jews* (Philadephis and Jerusalem, The Jewish Publication Society and the Magnes Press, 1959), 127-42, 430-34.

41   *A.J.,* XII, 138-156. For Willrich's challenge of these documents (*Urkunden-fälschung in der hellenistisch-jüdischen Literatur* [Gottingen, 1924], 18-24) and the scholarly response to this challenge, see the works listed by R. Marcus, in the LCL edition of Josephus, Vol. VII, Appendix D, 743-66. See now M. Stern, *Hate'udot lemered Hahashmona'im* (Jerusalem, 1965), 28-46.

42   κατὰ τὸν ἐπιχώριον νόμον   (*A.J.,* XII, 140; cf. XII, 142, Ezra 7:14, 25-26). It is interesting to note that, as far as I know, historians and encyclopaedias have ignored John and his work.

43   Incidentally, *A.J.* XII, 142, asserts that the Gerusia in 200 B.C. consisted of both the priests and the scribes of the Temple.

within the inner walls of the Temple.[44] It is not known whether John was also involved in the resettlement of the 2,000 Babylonian Jewish families from Babylonia to Phrygia (as reported by Josephus).[45] We do know, however, that John was the representative of the Gerusia (Council of Elders) of Jerusalem, which, in the words of Josephus, "assisted the king in the expulsion of the Egyptian garrison" from Jerusalem and eagerly welcomed the Syrians.[46] Conceivably, John not only executed the policies of the Gerusia, but was also one of those who led the faction which preferred the relatively mild rule of the Seleucids to the heavy-handed economic exploitation of the Ptolemies.

In siding with the Seleucids against the Ptolemies, John and his fellow priests could not predict the catastrophe that was to result under Antiochus IV. But Jerusalem's theocratic rulers evidently exhibited the same tendencies as did aristocrats elsewhere. The common people, however, according to Polybius (V, 86, 10), preferred the Macedonian dynasty of Egypt to the one of Coele-Syria. As far as we know, no Ptolemaic king ever interfered with the religious practices of his subjects. The Ptolemies, however, imposed higher taxes on the more prosperous classes than did the Syrian kings. Antiochus III's subsidy to the Temple of Jerusalem was in fact a subvention to the priests. The Seleucid faction in Jerusalem acted in their self-interest, but lacked the foresight to perceive the impending disaster.

As the representative of Jerusalem's Gerusia before the king, John must have known Greek. Hebrew and Aramaic were part of his training, which no doubt also included knowledge of ancient Jewish lore and practice in the priestly duties. But Hellenizing elements were dangerously infiltrating Jerusalem's theocratic circles and it was perhaps natural that the cosmopolitan-minded priests were affected first. John's choice of the name Eupolemus for his son is the first recorded case of a Greek name given in Jerusalem. In fact, if Daniel 11:14 is taken literally, the faction that supported the entry of the Seleucids into Jerusalem had been favoring Hellenization as early as the beginning of the second century B.C.

As to the chronology of Eupolemus' life, we have three dates:

1. John, Eupolemus' father, represented Jerusalem's Council of Elders at the court of Antiochus III about 200 B.C.[47]

---

44 *A.J.*, XII, 138-46; cf. Ezra 6:3-12. On the prohibition of entrance, see M. Kelim, I, 8; *A.J.*, XV, 417; *B.J.*, V, 194; J.-B. Frey, *Corpus Inscriptionum Iudaicarum*, II, 329 f.

45 *A.J.*, XII, 147-52.

46 *A.J.*, XII, 138: "King Antiochus to Ptolemy, greeting. Inasmuch as the Jews, from the very moment when we entered their country, showed their eagerness to serve us and, when we came to their city, gave us a splendid reception..." (R. Marcus' translation in L.C.L. edition. Cf. E. Meyer, *Ursprung und Anfänge des Christentums* (Stuttgart and Berlin, 1921), II, 121-28.

47 II Macc. 4:11. Cf. C. L. W. Grimm's comments on this verse in his *Kurzgefastes exegetisches Handbuch zu den Apokryphen*, II (Leipzig, 1857), 81 f.

2. Judah Maccabee dispatched Eupolemus to Rome in 161.[48]
3. In 158/7 Eupolemus computed the age of the world to have been
5,149 years (from Adam to the fifth year of King Demetrius).[49]

It must be assumed that John was already a mature man in 198 when he
represented Jerusalem before the Syrian king. His son Eupolemus complained
in 161 that the journey to Rome had been arduous, perhaps indicating old
age.[50] It follows that Eupolemus was probably born during the third century,
possibly during its last decade, but more likely somewhat earlier.

Eupolemus, it can be assumed, received a traditional priestly education,
plus some of the training becoming fashionable as the Hellenizing winds
began to penetrate Jerusalem. The high priest at the time of Eupolemus'
youth was Simon II, surnamed the Just. A lengthy encomium of this high
priest is available in the writings of Ben Sira, who flourished circa 190 B.C.,[51]
but Simon the High Priest and Ben Sira represented by and large a generation
that was hardly affected by Hellenization. The Ptolemies were primarily
interested in collecting exorbitant taxes rather than in bringing "enlightenment"
to the barbarians. Ben Sira's grandson, however, who migrated from
Jerusalem to Alexandria in 132 B.C., had mastered enough Hellenistic culture
to translate his grandfather's proverbs into Greek.[52] Another resident of
Jerusalem, Lysimachus, rendered the Book of Esther at the beginning of the
second or first century B.C. into idiomatic Greek.[53]

Eupolemus grew up in Jerusalem when the leading families were bitterly
divided between those who favored the *ancien régime* of Egypt and those
who welcomed the new garrison of Syrians. For his father the victory of the
latter represented a personal triumph. More significantly, despite the doubts
raised by Tcherikover, there is no question that the gates of Jerusalem were
more open to Hellenism during the Seleucid period than during Egyptian
rule.[54] In the fragments of Eupolemus' writing we can assess the degree of
Greek one prominent Jerusalemite had taught his son. Freudenthal, whose
arguments will be discussed below, correctly felt that Eupolemus' Greek was
very defective,[55] but Freudenthal was judging in terms of classical Greek.
Certainly, Eupolemus never completely mastered the language; nevertheless,

48   I Macc. 8:17; 723 T 1.
49   Clement, *Strom.*, I, 141, 4; 723 F 4 (Walter, F 5).
50   I Macc. 8:19. See below, p. 16.
51   Ecclus. 50:1-21; *Cf.* M. Avot, I, 2.
52   Prologue to Ecclus.
53   See colophon to LXX Esther; and E.J. Bickerman, *JBL,* 63 (1944), 339-62;
"The Septuagint as a Translation," *Proceedings of the American Academy for Jewish
Research,* 28 (1958), 1-39. See below, 255-58.
54   V. Tcherikover, *Hellenistic Civilization and the Jews* (Philadelphia, 1959),
88 and passim.
55   Freudenthal, *Hell. Studien,* 109.

his Greek was in places superior to that of the Septuagint translators of I Kings who were describing similar subject matter.[56] The Greek education of Eupolemus is of great significance since from him we can learn what kind of training was received by the Hellenizing priests at the turn of the second century B.C.[57]

From the sources utilized by Eupolemus we also learn something about the cultural milieu of Jerusalem at the turn of the second century B.C. Eupolemus was aware of the debate then going on in Alexandria as to whether or not Greek philosophy was taken from the East: We can deduce that he made use of the works of Herodotus, Hecataeus of Abdera, Ctesias of Cnidus, who spent many years in the Persian court as the doctor of Artaxerxes II Mnemon (404-359), Manetho, the high priest of Heliopolis (c. 280 B.C.), and Greek histories of Phoenicia.[58] This is quite a respectable list of Hellenistic sources in view of the fact that only a fraction of Eupolemus' work has survived.

Although it is conceivable that Eupolemus received his Greek education in Alexandria, sent there as a youth by his wealthy father, there is no evidence to support such a hypothesis. It is unlikely, moreover, that a prominent participant in the expulsion of the Egyptian garrison would have sent his son to Alexandria. If, on the other hand, Eupolemus received all of his training in Jerusalem, his use of Herodotus, Ctesias, Hecataeus, Manetho, and others testifies to the existence of a Greek historical library in Jerusalem at the turn of the second century B.C. Apparently Greek tutors trained the artisocratic youth of Jerusalem in the "wisdom of Yavan."

Because of their novelty, the Hellenistic elements of Eupolemus' education have been stressed. It should not be forgotten, however, that the major part of his training was concentrated in the priestly lore. Even his Greek words reveal Hebrew phrasing and a sentence structure akin to those of the Books of Kings and Chronicles. A lifelong study of Hebrew and Aramaic was but little affected by the Greek that he acquired from a tutor. Judging by his writings, the Pentateuch formed the center of his training, with the prophetic and historical books taught only for edification. Of course, the sections of the Pentateuch dealing with the priestly service and the sanctuary were given precedence, followed by the legal parts.[59] The imagination was given free rein in the "aggadic" portions. In general, it would seem that Eupolemus' mastery of Jewish lore differed little from that of the authors of the Book of Jubilees, of the Genesis Apocryphon, or of the Biblical Antiquities, falsely attributed to Philo.

---

56 See below, p. 251.
57 See below, p. 35.
58 Freudenthal, *Hell. Studien,* 110 ff., but see below, p. 168.
59 See 723 FF 2-3, and below, p. 247.

Eupolemus apparently grew up in a relatively peaceful, if not free, environment. At the turn of the century, the fighting between the Ptolemaic garrison and the invading armies of Antiochus III interrupted a long era of quiet. Finally the invaders, with the assistance of some priests, breached the walls of the city. Meanwhile, the priests jostled for positions, but the word of the High Priest Simon the son of Onias had both divine and legal sanction. The taxes imposed by Egypt had been heavy, but the new Seleucid overlords eased the burden somewhat, at least temporarily. Jerusalem remained a prosperous city, primarily because of the flow of gifts from fellow Jews in places such as Alexandria and Antioch.

In 167 Antiochus IV Epiphanes revoked the charter which had been granted by Antiochus III to the Jews through the intercession of Eupolemus' father.[60] Soon the new king commenced the forcible Hellenization of Jerusalem. Originally, Hellenization had found supporters among the priestly classes, who had even requested that the king convert the Holy City into a Greek polis.[61] The Jewish Hellenizers had not, however, advocated the abrogation of the Torah, the basic legal code of the land since the days of Ezra.[62] But this abrogation was precisely what Antiochus IV now decreed. While some of the Hellenizers submitted willy-nilly to the wishes of the king, others felt compelled to assist either passively or actively those who responded to the persecution of their ancient faith by taking up arms. Thus Hellenization, which had begun to penetrate the priestly classes peacefully and imperceptibly, became the focal point both of the revolt against the occupying power and of a civil war. For the first time since Solomon some eight centuries earlier the high priestly Zadokite clan was confronted with both a political and a religious crisis.

Where did Eupolemus stand in this struggle? The fact that Judah Maccabee dispatched him to Rome to represent the rebels indicates that he probably never belonged to the faction advocating the conversion of Jerusalem into a polis.[63] It is unlikely, however, that Eupolemus could really be classified as an opponent of Hellenism. The fact that he was a native of the Holy City who bore a Greek name and wrote in Greek is by itself no indication of pro-Hellenistic tendencies.[64] But two hints in the fragments do suggest that Eupolemus' views were not completely orthodox, although the evidence is

60   II Macc. 4:11.
61   II Macc. 4:7 ff.
62   *Cf*, E. J. Bickerman, *Gott der Makkabäer* (Berlin, Schocken Verlag, 1937), 59-89; Tcherikover, *Hellenistic Civilization,* 117 ff.
63   Josephus, *A.J.,* XII, 415, labels Eupolemus and his fellow envoy Jason as Judah's friends; he took this for granted, on the basis of I Macc. 8:17.
64   Possibly, though, the fact that these are the first Hellenized names does suggest pro-Hellenizing sympathies. The custom of having two names, one Hebrew and another Greek, attested from the line of the Hasmonean Kings, no doubt antedates the Hasmonean revolt. What was Eupolemus' Hebrew name?

not quite conclusive. In 158/7, a decade after the inauguration of the persecution and four years after his mission to Rome, he still indirectly acknowledged the Syrian sovereignty over Judaea, by dating the age of the world from Adam to the fifth year of Demetrius I.[65] One wonders whether a member of the Hasidim sect or a Hasmonean zealot would have mentioned the king's name without damning him. It is conceivable, though, that in 158/7, because of the dismal military outlook for the rebels and because of a more flexible policy of the king, the Hasmoneans were inclined to make peace with Demetrius I.

The second indication of Eupolemus' stand on the main issue of the day is more complicated. As a rule his writings are free from anything which might have been objectionable to the most pious.[66] There is, however, a significant exception. Eupolemus reports that King Solomon shipped the surplus gold of the Temple to Tyre, where the Phoenician king used the gold to construct a pedestal for a statue of Zeus.[67] While there is no evidence in the Jewish tradition for this, it is significant that, according to II Macc. 4:18-20, a similar incident occurred when the Hellenizing High Priest Jason was installed in office. Jason dispatched a gift of 300 drachmas to Tyre in honor of Heracles on the occasion of the Tyrian quintennial Olympic games. En route, the envoys thought it abominable to use the Temple's money for an idolatrous sacrifice and requested instead that the donation be designated for a more worldly purpose—the construction of a trireme.

Since Eupolemus ascribed to Solomon the sending of the Temple's surplus gold for the Tyrian Zeus, he is unlikely to have been very indignant about a minor gift for Heracles. Certainly, Eupolemus found the whole action less objectionable than did Jason of Cyrene, the author responsible for the account of the embassy to Tyre. In fact, as suggested below (page 222), it is not impossible that Eupolemus invented the story of Solomon's gift for Zeus to defend the high priest's dispatch of the gift to the Tyrian Olympics. It is also conceivable, although unverifiable, that Eupolemus himself was personally involved in the scandal. The Greek term used here to describe the envoys is $\theta\epsilon\omega\rho oi$, which Zeitlin-Tedesche render as "sacred ambassadors."[68] This translation may be somewhat too strong, but the text does suggest, what is otherwise reasonable, that the envoys were priests. Since we find that both John and his son Eupolemus were used as ambassadors, it is possible that

65   Clement, *Strom.*, I, 141, 4; 723 F 4 (Walter, F 5).

66   See, however, P. Dalbert, *Die Theologie des Hellenistisch-jüdischen Missions-literatur unter Ausschlus von Philo und Josephus* (Theologische Forschung, IV, Hamburg, 1954), 42; and Gutman, *Beginnings of the Jewish-Hellenistic Literature*, I, 85.

67   Euseb., *P.E.,* IX, 34, p. 544, 15-20 723 F 2a, p. 677, 9f. Theophilus, 733 F 1.

68   (II Macc. 4:19). Technically, $\theta\epsilon\omega\rho o\varsigma$ means a spectator, i.e., one delegated to see the Olympic games; cf. Liddell, Scott, Jones, s.v.; S. Zeitlin, *The Second Book of Maccabees* (Dropsie College-Harper, 1954), 134.

Eupolemus was one of those sent by Jason to Tyre.[69] This would explain why Eupolemus, writing later, may have indirectly defended his action. In terms of the author of the Second Book of Maccabees, Eupolemus could be regarded as sympathizing with the Hellenizers. This sympathy was apparently retained even after his friendship with Judah because his history was written in 158/7, several years after the leader's death. It is possible, though, that the description of Solomon's shipment of gold for Zeus was written when the Hellenizers dominated the country.

If Eupolemus' participation as Jerusalem's delegate at the Tyrian games is only a matter of speculation, his prominent role in the Maccabean quest for foreign allies cannot be questioned. II Macc. 4:11 identified John, the Jewish envoy to Antiochus III in 198 B.C., by his son Eupolemus, "who went as an ambassador to make a treaty of friendship and alliance with Rome." The background, the names of the ambassadors, and the text of the treaty are reported in I Macc. 8:17 ff.:

> So Judah chose Eupolemus the son of John, son of Haccos, and Jason the son of Eleazar, and sent them to Rome to establish friendship and alliance, and to free themselves from the yoke; for they [the Romans] saw that the kingdom of the Greeks was completely enslaving Israel. They went to Rome, a very long journey;[70] and they entered the Senate chamber and spoke as follows: 'Judah, who is also called Maccabee, and his brothers, and the people of the Jews, have sent us to you to establish alliance and peace with you, that we may be enrolled as your allies and friends.'
>
> The proposal pleased them. And this is the copy of the letter which they wrote in reply, on bronze tablets, to Jerusalem to remain there as a memorial of peace and alliance.
>
> May all go well with the Romans and with the nation of Jews at sea and on land forever, and may sword and enemy be far from them. If war comes first to Rome or to any of their allies in all their dominion, the nation of the Jews shall act as their allies wholeheartedly as the occasion may indicate to them. And to the enemy who makes war they shall not give or supply grain, arms, money, or ships, as Rome has decided and they shall keep their obligations without receiving any return. In the same way, if war comes first to the nation of the Jews, the Romans shall willingly act as their allies, as the occasion may indicate to them. And to the enemy allies shall be given no grain, arms, money, or ships, as Rome has decided; and they shall keep those obligations and do so without deceit.

69   Both the embassies of Eupolemus and his father John are mentioned immediately before, in II Macc. 4:11. The Vulgate, it is true, renders the passage as if to imply that the delegates were sinners (peccatores), but this no doubt is a corruption of "spectatores," and does not absolutely impute any wickedness to the messengers.

70   The journey was indeed long if, as explained above in note 1, the itinerary led through the island of Cos, off the Ionian coast. This would have been a roundabout way, possibly taken because the ambassadors had to travel surreptitiously to avoid becoming known to the Syrian authorities. Conceivably, also, Eupolemus traveled during the winter (161-60), which made the journey difficult.

Thus on these terms the Romans make a treaty with the Jewish people. If after these terms are in effect both parties shall determine to add or to delete anything, they shall do so at their discretion, and any addition or deletion that they may make shall be valid.

And concerning the wrongs which King Demetrius is doing to them we have written to him as follows: 'Why have you made your yoke heavy[71] upon our friends and allies the Jews? If now they appeal again for help against you, we will defend their rights and fight you on sea and on land.'[72]

If genuine, this was a rather astonishing document. Envoys of outlaws operating in the fringes of the Seleucid empire brought back a treaty of friendship and alliance between the politically non-existing "People of the Jews" and Rome. Eupolemus and his colleague must have been men endowed with unusual powers of persuasion.[73]

The text of this treaty has been subjected to a searching analysis by leading nineteenth and twentieth century scholars. Those who have questioned the historicity of the alliance point to its title: "Treaty of Friendship and Confederacy ($\phi\iota\lambda\acute{\iota}\alpha$ $\kappa\alpha\grave{\iota}$ $\sigma\upsilon\mu\mu\alpha\chi\acute{\iota}\alpha$)," in Latin, *amicitia ac foedus.* Such an alliance, it has been argued, between the mightiest power and hunted rebels is inconceivable; especially since the former sat with her hands folded while King Demetrius routed the rebels and almost succeeded in quelling the uprising.[74] The consensus of scholars, however, now disregards these objections, believing rather that it was not a real *foedus,* an alliance, but a declaration of friendship, which in the course of translation from one language into another assumed a broad formula not in the original Latin text.[75]

---

71 Note the Hebraism -- rather strange words purportedly coming from a Roman. See note 79.

72 For a technical commentary on the treaty, see E. Taübler, *Imperium Romanum* (Leipzig, 1913), 239-54; for a general commentary, see Abel, *Les livres des Macc.,* 152-57.

73 Zeitlin (*I Book of Macc.,* 152) is somewhat picayune, when he points out that the wording of the treaty tended to be more favorable to the Romans than to the Jews.

74 J. Wellhausen, *Israelitische und jüdische Geschichte*[4] (Berlin, 1914), 250, 1; Willrich, *Judaica,* 61-85, denied not only the treaty, but also any diplomatic relationship between Rome and the Jews at that time. Mendelssohn, *Rheinisches Museum,* 30 (1875) 428-35; Niese, *Gesch. d. griech. u. mak. Staaten* (Gotha, 1903), III, 254 f.; Graetz, *Gesch. d. Juden,* III[5] 657-60, among others, deny only the treaty itself, Graetz ascribing it to the time of Simon; R. H. Pfeiffer, *History of New Testament Times* (New York, Harper and Brothers, 1949), 16, also denies the authenticity of the covenant.

75 , F. Ritschl, *Eine Berichtigung der republikanischen Consularfasten* (Bonn, 1873); C. L. Grimm, *Zeitsch. für Wiss. Theologie* 17 (1874), 231-38; E. Taübler, *Imperium Romanum,* 29-54, O. Roth, *Rom und die Hasmonäer* (Leipzig, 1914); E. Schürer, *Gesch. d. jüd. Volkes,* I[4], 220; Meyer, Ursprung; II, 246 f.; Abel, *Les livres des Macc.,* 153; D. Bévenot, *Die Beiden Makkabäerbücher* (Bonn, 1931), 105; S. Zeitlin, *I Book of Maccabees,* 39f.; R. Marcus in L.C.L. edition of Josephus, VII, 218 n. a. The historicity of the treaty is defended by Giovannini and Müller, *Museum Helveticum,* 28 (1971), 156-71; Fischer, *ZNW* 86 (1974), 90-93.

Logically, those who argue against the historicity of the alliance have the upper hand. Factually, however, the treaty between Judah and Rome appears to be historical. The authenticity of the title is confirmed in the body of the text ("if war comes to the nation of the Jews, the Romans shall act as their allies.") and independently by II Macc. 4:11. That Rome later ignored the alliance is no proof that it had never existed. Timarchus, who proclaimed himself in 161 B.C. as the "King of Babylonia" and was confirmed by Rome, provides a parallel to what happened in Judaea.[76] Rome did nothing when the rebel was hunted down by Demetrius and slain. Rome, in the words of Justin, pursued a policy to aid the Jewish cause in the belief that whatever weakened the Hellenistic kingdoms strengthened the Roman Republic.[77] Circumstantial evidence for the historicity of the Judaeo-Roman treaty, as alluded above, can also be deduced from *Antiquities,* XIV, 233, where Josephus preserved the following document: "Gaius Fannius, son of Gaius, proconsular praetor, to the magnistrates of Cos, Greetings! I would have you know that envoys had come to me from the Jews, asking to have the decrees concerning them, which were passed by the Senate. These decrees are herewith appended. It is my wish, therefore, that you take thought and care for these men in accordance with the decree of the Senate, in order that they may safely be brought through your country to their homes."[78] Although Josephus does not say to whom and when this decree was granted, and although there is much scholarly dispute on this matter, it is reasonable to suppose that the reference is to Eupolemus' mission; for it is recorded that in the year 593 of Rome (161 B.C.) Fannius Strabo was the consul who treated with Demetrius I. If so, the care taken by the Roman authorities that the Jewish envoys return home safely may have been normal procedure. Possibly, though, fear that Seleucid agents might have heard of the mission somehow required special security.

Although the alliance is historical, it does not mean that each and every phrase of the treaty as preserved in I Macc. 8:23-32 is necessarily accurate.[79]

---

76   Two similar cases are recorded: The one is that of Timarchus of Babylon who rebelled against Demetrius I; the other is the so-called "Foedus Astypalaeense" of 105 B.C., in *Corp. Inscr. Graec.,* No. 2485; Roth, *Rom und die Hasmonäer,* 10-13. Here Rome made a treaty with the small island to secure a naval base against pirates.

77   Justin, XXXVI, 3, 9.

78   B. Niese, in *Festschrift für Nöldeke,* 817-29; Marcus' note *c* to *A.J.,* XIV, 233 (Loeb Classical Library Edition); E. J. Bickerman, *Chronology of the Ancient World* (Ithaca, New York, Cornell University Press, 1968), 178.

79   The numerous Hebraisms in the treaty point to substantial changes: I Macc. 8:23: $\epsilon \grave{\iota} \varsigma \ \tau \grave{o} \nu \ \alpha \grave{\iota} \hat{\omega} \nu \alpha$ = עד עולם = forever; 8:28: $\kappa \alpha \acute{\iota} \ \phi \upsilon \lambda \acute{\alpha} \xi o \nu \tau \alpha \iota \ \tau \grave{\alpha} \ \phi \upsilon \lambda \acute{\alpha} \gamma$-$\mu \alpha \tau \alpha \ \tau \alpha \hat{\upsilon} \tau \alpha$ = שמר ישמרו אותם = and they shall keep the stipulations; 8:25: $\kappa \alpha \rho \delta \acute{\iota} \alpha \ \pi \lambda \acute{\eta} \rho \epsilon \iota$ = בלבב שלם = wholeheartedly, etc., listed by Roth, *Rom und Hasmonäer,* 13 f.

The original is lost, and our text, as pointed out above, passed through several translations. There may, however, be a more important reason why the text of the treaty is defective. Eupolemus, who negotiated the treaty, may have been the one who upon his return from Rome translated the document into Hebrew; at least he must have reported to the leading rebels about the course of his mission. While Eupolemus was away the military situation had deteriorated. Eupolemus was sent to Rome some time after Judah's victory over the Syrian general Nicanor, which had occurred on the thirteenth of Adar of 161. Upon the return of the embassy from Rome, however, the situation changed as a result of the disastrous battle of Berea in Nisan of 160, in which Judah Maccabee was slain. In the gloom that must have followed, Eupolemus may have attempted to soften the bitter blow of general depression by inflating the contents of the document he brought back. At any rate, Eupolemus' accuracy or veracity, as attested in his own work, is *not* beyond reproach. If Eupolemus was responsible for the Hebrew version of the text of the treaty which underlies the Greek text in I Macc. 8, doubtful or ambiguous wording of the original may have been rephrased to bring hope and consolation to Jerusalem.

Eupolemus no doubt played an active role as Judah Maccabee's adviser. The mission to Rome marked the beginning of an adventurous Hasmonean foreign policy.[80] As a rule the Jews had a parochial view of the world. To play off Egypt against Syria and vice versa was for centuries basic Jewish policy. To bring in distant Rome indicates a fair acquaintance with contemporary power politics. In ancient times as well as in modern, a mission of such a nature is customarily led by the highest officers of the state, if not by the head himself. Judah could not go to Rome in 161 because without him the rebellion might have collapsed. The situation was perhaps precarious enough to have required the presence in Judaea also of the other brothers of the Hasmonean clan. It would seem that after the Hasmonean brothers, Eupolemus was Judah Maccabee's most influential adviser.

The explanation that Eupolemus achieved such a position because he was the son of a successful diplomat is not sufficient. Training and connections no doubt played an important role. But the fact that Eupolemus was interested in history must have been of some significance. It is conceivable that he not only executed the alliance, but had also conceived the plan to seek aid from the Romans. It should not be forgotten that the Nabataeans and Commagenians, as well as the Jews, rose against the Syrians. Having humiliated Antiochus Epiphanes, Rome was gaining the reputation as a friend of oppressed peoples of the Seleucid empire. The dispatching of historians to negotiate treaties was quite widespread. When Eupolemus was in Rome he may have met an Achaean deportee Polybius, the famous Greek historian, who helped to spread the myth of Roman magnanimity.

80 See Nahmanides, *Commentary,* Gen. 32:1 ff.: Grimm, *Handbuch,* on I Macc. 8:32, pp. 130 f.

Medieval and modern critics have censured Judah for inviting the Romans to intervene in Judaean affairs; they blame him for the disastrous relations between Rome and Jerusalem in later centuries.[81] This criticism, perhaps justified on moral grounds, ignores the fact that Pompey's conquest of Judaea in 63 B.C. was but part of the liquidation of the Syrian empire and had little to do with Judah's pro-Roman policy. Pompey reversed the traditional Roman policy of supporting the natives against Hellenistic cities. In the middle of the second century, however, restless segments of the Seleucid empire had found Rome an indispensable friend. The pro-Roman feelings of the Jews during the second century, expressed in I Macc. 8, stemmed from a realistic evaluation of the international interplay of power. The Hasmonean state had remained too insignificant throughout its existence to influence international power politics appreciably. Its fall resulted from internal disintegration and the incapacity of its rulers.

Very little is known of Jason the son of Eleazar, Eupolemus' fellow ambassador to Rome. He is probably not the one who wrote a history of Judah the Maccabee, now known in an abridged form as the Second Book of Maccabees. The latter Jason was from Jerusalem, the former from Cyrene. More significantly, a number of scholars have argued that Jason of Cyrene composed the biography as suggested by II Macc. 2:19, in the last two decades of the second century B.C. Another point of view maintains, however, that he was a contemporary of Judah Maccabee. If so, and assuming that he had come from Cyrene to settle in Jerusalem, the possibility should not be altogether excluded that Jason, the author of a five-book life of Judah, and Jason the son of Eleazar, Judah's ambassador to Rome, are the same person.

Like Eupolemus, Jason the son of Eleazar belonged to a priestly family, as suggested by his own and his father's name. A son of this Jason, Antipater, served as Jonathan's (in 144) and Simon's (in 140) ambassador to Sparta and Rome.[82] It is noteworthy that both Jason and his son Antipater are listed second to Eupolemus and Numenius, respectively, indicating that protocol was important in Jerusalem's priestly circles.

The tradition of diplomatic office in the Hakkos family was broken with Eupolemus. The head of the missions to Sparta and Rome in 144 and 140 was Numenius the son of Antiochus. By this time Eupolemus must have been either dead or too old to undertake the journey. Indeed, he was already an old man in 161. Chronologically, it is conceivable that Antiochus, the father

81   Cf. Herod's use of Nicolaus of Damascus (*A.J.,* XVI, 27 ff.; 90 TT 3-9) and Josephus' mission to Rome (*Vita,* 13-16).

82   I Macc. 12:1, 16-18.

of Numenius, was either the younger brother or the son of Eupolemus. But there is no evidence for such an assumption, except that the name Antiochus suggests strong pro-Seleucid sympathy, evident also in John and Eupolemus. The name Antiochus sounds rather strange for the father of a Jewish official in the 140's B.C. To be an ambassador in 140 this Antiochus must have been born prior to 168, before the persecution had started.

Meager as our sources are, it has been possible to show that Eupolemus' embassy to Rome stemmed from a close association with the priestly aristocracy of the Hasmoneans. He descended from a family which was at one time closely associated with the pro-Seleucid factions. The family was semi-Hellenized by the turn of the third century B.C., with recorded incidents of intermarriage as early as the return from the Babylonian exile in the sixth or fifth century. Both Eupolemus and his father, were no doubt members of the so-called Gerusia, the Council of Elders of Jerusalem, a priestly institution. Eupolemus' knowledge of the Temple and the daily sacrifices was firsthand since his family belonged to the privileged few who officiated in the week of the festival of Pentecost. But the family Hakkos also specialized in foreign affairs.

It is this association with the outside world that enabled Eupolemus to write in Greek and to become familiar with some of the Greek historical and geographical literature. In antiquity, diplomacy and the writing of history went hand in hand. Polybius, a contemporary of Eupolemus; Nicolaus of Damascus, a friend of Herod; and Josephus, a descendant of the Hasmoneans; all negotiated affairs of state in Rome and wrote memorable historical works.

WORKS

Carl Kuhlmey, writing in 1840, ascribed to Eupolemus three works:[83]

1. *On the Jews of Assyria* (περὶ τῶν τῆς Ἀσσυρίας Ἰουδαίων)
2. *On the Prophecy of Elijah* (περὶ τῆς Ἡλίου προφετείας)
3. *On the Kings of Judaea* (περὶ τῶν ἐν τῇ Ἰουδαίᾳ βασιλέων)

The first two titles were derived from Eusebius' citations of Eupolemus; the third, from the writings of Clement of Alexandria.[84] As will be shown below, however, both Clement and Eusebius knew Eupolemus only indirectly from the excerpts made by Alexander Polyhistor (*circa* 85-35 B.C.).

Freudenthal, whose study (written in 1875) has remained the authoritative text on Hellenistic Jewish historians, accepted only the third work on Kuhlmey's list. In a remarkable piece of detective work, Freudenthal showed

---

83 Kuhlmey, *Eupol. Fragm.,* 10.
84 Euseb., *P.E.,* IX, 17, p. 502, 19 = *FGrH* 724 F 1; IX, 30, p. 538, 14 = 723 F

that the first title in Kuhlmey's list was based on an erroneous interpretation of Eusebius.[85] Actually, the full sentence in Eusebius should have been translated: "Eupolemus in his *On the Jews* says: Babylon the city of Assyria. . . ." Furthermore, Freudenthal posited cogently that this fragment belonged to an unknown Samaritan author, but had been erroneously ascribed to Eupolemus.[86] This Samaritan fragment is now labeled Pseudo-Eupolemus.

Freudenthal also rejected the authenticity of *On the Prophecy of Elijah*.[87] Attested by Eusebius, this title heads the longest single remnants of Graeco-Jewish historical writing. It begins by mentioning some of the leading personalities after the death of Moses, and goes on to describe David quite differently from the biblical tradition. The pragmatic theme, however, is the Solomonic temple. Since the subject matter of the passage relates in no way to the Prophet Elijah, Freudenthal argued that the heading *On the Prophecy of Elijah* must be erroneous.[88] Eminent scholars, such as Schürer and Jacoby, have attempted to explain how such an error crept into Eusebius. Perhaps *On the Prophecy of Elijah* was not the name of a book, but rather the heading of a chapter.[89]

Even if *On the Prophecy of Elijah* is the title of a chapter rather than of the book, the problem is not solved. The text itself does not relate at all to the theme announced in the beginning of the quotation. The error, if such it was, must therefore be ascribed either to Alexander Polyhistor, who copied Eupolemus, or to Eusebius, who in turn transcribed Alexander Polyhistor, who copied Eupolemus, or to Eusebius, who in turn transcribed Alexander Polyhistor's work. But it is unlikely that either made such a slip: not Alexander Polyhistor, because he knew too little of Jewish history; and not Eusebius, because he knew too much to bind together a lengthy passage with an irrelevent title.

It is not inconceivable, however, that *On the Prophecy of Elijah* was quite a fitting title, at least for the beginning of the subject matter treated by Eupolemus. Possibly Eupolemus was referring not to Elijah the prophet but to the chief priest of Shiloh, Eli. The text, it is true, reads περί ᾽Ηλίου, the standard Greek transliteration of Elijah. But some manuscripts read ᾽Ηλεί, the Septuagint spelling of Eli.[90] A medieval scribe who was not aware that Eupolemus ascribed prophecy to the "judges" may have changed the ending into *On the Prophecy of Elijah*, instead of, *Eli*. Although Eli's name is missing at that point in Eupolemus' fragment where Joshua, Saul and Samuel are

2a. Clement, *Strom.*, I 153, 3, p. 95, 20 = 723 F 1b.
    85   Freudenthal, *Hell. Studien*, 82 ff. .
    86   See Wacholder, *HUCA*, 33 (1963), 83 ff.
    87   Freudenthal, *Hell. Studien*, 89-92; *FGrH*, 724 F 2.
    88   Freudenthal, *Hell. Studien*, 208 f.
    89   Schürer, III⁴, 475; Jacoby, *FGrH*, 723 F 2 b, p. 672, 30, app. crit.
    90   See Jacoby, *ibid.*, p. 672, 30, app. crit.

mentioned, Eli is recorded in the same fragment (anachronistically) as a participant in the coronation of Solomon.[91] Moreover, there are good reasons to believe that Eupolemus treated Shiloh and its chief priest Eli at length, but that the account was excised by Alexander Polyhistor. The sanctuary was Eupolemus' favorite topic and that of Shiloh was no exception. Eupolemus mentioned Shiloh twice: its foundation by Joshua and its liquidation by Solomon. He must have treated likewise its period of glory under Eli. If so, Eupolemus regarded Eli not only as Shiloh's priest but as its prophet as well.

Yet we shall not press the argument that Eupolemus had named a section of his work after the priest of Shiloh. The possibility, not to say the probability, remains that the full title of Eupolemus' work was *On the Prophecy of Elias,* and that it referred indeed to the Prophet Elijah. The title is not necessarily erroneous only because the extant fragment has nothing to say about the austere prophet. It should be recalled that the name of this prophet was frequently invoked by writers of the time.[92] During the Hasmonean rebellion the apocalyptic literature was entering a period of full bloom. This is attested in the Hebrew chapters of the Book of Daniel. According to I Macc. 14:41, King Demetrius II appointed Simon as high priest "until the true prophet would arise," meaning Elijah. According to the preamble of II Maccabees, the holy ark and the tablets of the law, hidden by Jeremiah after the destruction of the Temple, would once again be recovered at the time of the ingathering of the exiles. The allusion is clearly to Mal. 3:23-24, where Elijah's coming had been announced. As is indicated below,[93] there are good reasons to believe that the author of the preamble to the Second Book of Maccabees was indebted to Eupolemus' history. According to I Macc. 4:46, the Hasmoneans placed in *genizah* the defiled stones of the altar until the prophet (Elijah) decides what should be done with them. If so, Eupolemus may have in fact mentioned the coming of Elijah.

Of course, a mere allusion to Elijah does not justify the naming of the work *On the Prophecy of Elijah.* But it is not impossible that Eupolemus' interest in the chronology of the world was more than mere curiosity. It is known that, for didactic purposes, the church fathers as well as the rabbis labored hard to find the exact age of the world. The former used chronology in an attempt to determine the date of the second coming of Christ;[94] the latter, to find the day Elijah would announce the coming of the Davidic Messiah.[95] Hitherto, it has been thought that this chronological scheme is

---

91   Euseb., *P.E.,* IX, 30, p. 539, 12 = 723 F 2a, p. 673, 23.
92   Ecclus. 48:10; Ps. Sol., 17:28; cf. Enoch 89:52; 93:8; Mart.Isa. 2:11; II Baruch 7:24; Matt. 11:14, 16:14, etc.; Mark 6:15; Luke 1:17.
93   p. 40.
94   See H. Gelzer, *Sextus Julius Africanus* (Leipzig, 1880) I, 24 ff.
95   B. Avodah Zarah, 9a; Sanhedrin, 97a, Seder Eliyyahu Rabbah, edited by M. Friedmann (Vienna, 1904), 6 f; Seder Olam Rabbah (Wilno, 1897), 75a-76a.

post-Christian. It is, however, as old as the Maccabean period. The Hasidim had already utilized chronology for eschatological purposes. Daniel 7:25 reads:

> And they shall be given in his hand for a time, two times, and half a time.

The exact meaning of these mysterious numbers, written circa 164 B.C., is obscure. But the belief in divine action which would coincide with the rhythmical passage of time is quite evident. The influence of Zurvan (god of time) is also beyond doubt.[96] The Qumran texts once again testify to the popularity of the theme that time schemes play a significant role in determining the coming of the prophet or of the teacher of righteousness.[97] Jew and Christian had long believed that the redeemer would appear in the sixth millenium after Adam. A full exposition of this view is attested in the writings of Africanus and Eusebius, although the origin of this idea has not been known.[98] But in 158/7 Eupolemus did compute the age of the world to be 5149 years.[99] Was Eupolemus' interest in chronology motivated by the belief that the appearance of Prophet Elijah was soon at hand? If so, the title *On the Prophecy of Elijah* was quite appropriate.

Eupolemus was perhaps the first to exploit Elijah's name for a book not related to the prophet of Gilead. But if the first, he surely was not the last: The Apocalypse of Elijah is an intertestamental work;[100] the talmudic sources mention a work by Tanna debei Eliyyahu, with the reference perhaps to the predecessor of the Seder Eliyyahu (Major and Minor), written in the Talmudic and Geonic periods, respectively.[101] The medieval Jewish cabalists named him more often than any other biblical figure.[102]

Of the three titles which the ancients ascribed to Eupolemus, only the authenticity of *On the Kings of Judaea* has not been questioned by the critics. Here the heading conforms to the contents of the text. The choice of such a heading indicates once again that Eupolemus regarded himself a part of the Jewish, rather than of the common Hellenistic background. Demetrius,

---

96   See R. C. Zaehner, *Zurvan: A Zoroastrian Dilemna* (Oxford, Oxford University Press, 1955), 7 ff.

97   The opening section of the Damascus Documents and passim.

98   See above n. 94.

99   Clement, *Strom.,* I, 141 = 723 F 4 (Walter F 5).

100   See Th. Schermann, *Propheten- und Apostolenlegnden* (Leipzig, 1907), 109-111. See now Albert-Marie Denis, *Introduction aux Pseudépigraphes grecs d'Ancien Testament* (Leiden, Brill, 1971), 163-69, who, links Eupolemus (p. 160) with the Elijah apocryphal writers.

101   B. Sabbath, 13a; Pesahim, 94a; 112a; Megillah, 28b; Kiddushin, 80b; Avodah Zarah, 5b, 9a; Sanhedrin, 92a, 94a; Tamid, 32a. Cf. Friedmann, *Seder Eliyyahu Rabbah,* 44 ff.

102   See Zohar, Index.

the author of a biblical chronology, writing between 222 and 204 B.C., had given the same name to his own work. The identity of the titles of Demetrius and Eupolemus was certainly not coincidental. The name "On the Kings of . . ." was rather rare, if not unheard of, among heathen historians. There is reason to believe that *On the Kings of Judaea* (περὶ τῶν ἐν τῇ Ἰουδαίᾳ βασιλέων) was a rough rendition of ספר דברי הימים למלכי יהודה. Justus of Tiberias shows that he belonged to the Graeco-Jewish historians by entitling his book *Genealogies of the King of Judaea*.[103] His antagonist, Josephus, however, chose typical heathen nomenclature for his historical books: *The History of the War of the Jews Against the Romans and The History of the Ancient Lore of the Jews*.[104]

Eupolemus' history(ies) of the biblical period certainly dealt with Moses and continued to the destruction of the First Temple in 586 B.C.[105] But there are indications that Eupolemus actually began with Adam and concluded with an account of his own day. That Alexander Polyhistor erroneously attributed to him passages on the life of Abraham (in fact written by a Samaritan) can be explained if an account of Abraham by the real Eupolemus was then known. Eupolemus' chronological summary from Adam to 158/7 B.C. apparently concluded his chronicle.

Graeco-Jewish writers may be divided into two groups. Some, like Philo of Alexandria, although devotedly committed to their Judaic heritage, were primarily Hellenistic writers, and secondarily Jewish. Others, exemplified by Josephus, were first and foremost Jewish. The collation of the available facts about Eupolemus' life and works places him unequivocally among the latter. His Aaronite ancestry places him among the Zadokite priests who had regularly officiated in the Temple. His mission to Rome at Judah Maccabee's behest suggests that his politics in 161 B.C. coincided with the views of the anti-Seleucid rebels. The remnants of his works, as will be shown, recount minutiae of the Temple's past, confirming the tradition that their author was a priest. But his position on cultural, as distinguished from religious, Hellenization is not certain, not only because he wrote in Greek, but also because his treatment of Moses and the date of the Exodus suggests a man of considerable sophistication and cosmopolitan outlook. These factors must have influenced Judah Maccabee to choose him as his emissary to the most powerful state of his day.

---

103 Photius, Bibl., 33 = 734 T 2, p. 695, 15: ἡ ἐπιγραφὴ Ἰούστου τιβεριέως Ἰουδαίων βασιλέων τῶν ἐν τοῖς στέμμασιν.

104 For Josephus' title of the *Bellum* see app. crit. to the heading in Niese's edition IV, p. 3; for the *Antiquities*, I, p. 3. heading.

105 Euseb., *P.E.*, IX, 24 = 723 F 5 (Walter, F 4), describes Nebuchadnezzar's conquest of Jerusalem.

But before proceeding with our analysis of the Greek remnants of Jerusalem's priestly author, we pause to ascertain to what degree of probability the fragments attributed to Eupolemus substantially preserve the author's own words.

Chapter Two

THE TRADITION

What is the proof that the passages attributed to Eupolemus are genuine? Indeed, from time to time voices have been raised suggesting that the Graeco-Jewish fragments are nothing but Christian forgeries.[1] And even if they are not fabrications, how can we be confident that in the process of transmission they were not so much altered as to lose their original form?

The authentication of the remnants of the Graeco-Jewish literature before Philo and Josephus marks a glorious but largely unknown achievement of scholarly detective work.[2] But the main theme of this chapter is the importance and significance of Eupolemus' writings. Was he an obscure historian who left no traces, or did he substantially influence the Jewish or Christian tradition? Can it be shown that ancient or medieval writers quoted Eupolemus without acknowledging their source? And more importantly, is it possible to recover more of his lost writings?

FIRST AND SECOND MACCABEES

To answer the question, we must touch on the complex problem of the sources of the First and Second Books of Maccabees, which contain the oldest allusions to Eupolemus. These two Apocryphal books offer parallel accounts of the most interesting decade of the Second Temple, celebrating the victory of the few over the many, the martyred over the torturers. Yet,

---

1   The existence of Graeco-Jewish forgeries has been well established. One may only cite the verses of Pseudo-Homer, Pseudo-Hesiod, or Pseudo-Linus, quoted in Clement, *Strom.,* V, 107 and Eusebius, *P.E.,*XIII, 12; the Orphic poems, which have come down to us in various recensions, in Clement (*Strom.,* V, 78, 126 f.), Eusebius (*P.E.,* XIII, 12), Pseudo-Justin (*Against the Greeks,* 15). For attempts to group the writings of Alexander Polyhistor and Eusebius in the same pseudonymic tradition see J. Rauch, *De Alexandri Polyhistoris vita atque scriptis* (Heidelberg, 1843); J.G. Hulleman, *De Cornelii Alexandro Polyhistore: Miscellanea philologa et pegagoga* (Leiden, 1849); I, 153; P.M. Cruice, *De Flavii Iosephi fide* (Paris, 1844); L. C. Valckaner, *Diatribe de Aristobulo Judaeo, Philosopho Peripaetice Alexandrino* (Leiden, 1806); A. Elter, *De Gnomologiorum Graecarom historia atque origine commentatio* (Bonn, 1893-95); N. Walter, *Der Thoraausleger Aristobulos* (Berlin, Akademie-Verlag, 1964).

2   The credit belongs chiefly to Valckaner (see previous note) and J. Freudenthal, *Hellenistische Studien, I-II: Alexander Polyhistor and die von ihm erhaltenen Reste jüdaischer und samaritanischer Geschichtswerke* (Breslau, 1874-75).

the men and the accounts which they produced were quite different. Although his work now survives only in the Septuagint Greek, the author of First Maccabees wrote in Hebrew, using the style of the Chronicler, without the model's tendency to depart from factual data. Composed during or shortly after the reign of John Hyrcanus (135-04 B.C.), the austere language, chronological accuracy, sparse theologizing, and balance between reports of the local scene and the events outside Judaea have made First Maccabees an outstanding historical document. There is no doubt that the writer had access to reliable sources, which he used masterfully.[3]

In contrast to the First, the Second Book of Maccabees appears to be a Jewish version of late second century or early first century Greek rhetorical historiography.[4] Of the original five-book composition by a certain Jason of Cyrene, only the abridgement has survived. In both the prologue and epilogue, the epitomist reports of his concern for the proper style to produce a work in accordance with the contemporary tenets of dramatic histori-ography.[5] Excluding II Macc. 1:1-2:18, which was prefixed later, the book underwent stylistic changes and alterations in subject matter, so that it is often difficult to tell whether Jason of Cyrene or the epitomist is speaking.[6] Nevertheless, it is clear that the writer felt a greater need to verbalize his piety and was less meticulous in reporting facts than was their fellow Hebrew

3   See standard commentaries among others: Carl Grimm, *Kurzgefasstes exe-getisches Handbuch zu den Apokryphen des Alten Testamentes: Das erste Buch der Maccabäer* (Leipzig, 1855); *das zweite, dritte und vierte Buch den Maccabäer* (Leipzig, 1857); Hugo Bévenot, *Die beiden Makkabäerbücher, übersetzt und erklärt* (Bonn, Peter Hanstein, 1931); F.-M. Abel, *Les livres des Maccabées* (Paris, Librarie Lecoffre, 1949); 3rd ed. with notes by J. Starcky (Paris, 1961). *The First Book of Macabees,* English translation by Sidney Tedesche, Introduction and Commentary by S. Zeitlin (Dropsie College Edition of Jewish Apocryphal Literature; New York, Harper and Brothers, 1950).

As to the date of I Maccabees, see I Macc. 16:23 f., which seems to suggest that John Hyracanus (135-104 B.C.) was already dead, though this interpretation is not necessary. At any rate chapter 8, with its pro-Roman propaganda, precludes a date after 64 B.C. In addition to the discussion in the commentaries listed above, see Emil Schürer, *Gesch. des jüd. Volkes,* III[4], 194; E. Bickerman, "Makkabäerbücher," *R.E.,* XIV (1928), col. 792.

4   See previous note. Cf. B. Niese, *Kritik der Beiden Makkabäerbücher* (Berlin, 1900), 32-40, esp. 33 f., who likens Jason to Theopompus, Cleitarchus, and Phylarchus, noting Polybius' critique of Phylarchus (II, 56 ff.), as also applicable to parts of II Maccabees. Cf. now, Th. Africa, *Phylarchus of Athens* (University of California Press, Berkely and Los Angeles, 1961).

5   II Macc. 2:23-32; 15:37-39; Cf. 6:12-17; 10:10.

6   Scholars have often taken the Epitomist at his word: "All this that has been set forth by Jason of Cyrene in five volumes, we shall attempt to condense into a single book" (II Macc. 2:23). But there is no reason to take him literally any more than one does Josephus, who claimed that all he had done was merely to translate Scripture "neither adding nor omitting anything" (*A.J.* I, 17). Certainly, there is a self-consciousness in the prologue and epilogue of the book (see the previous note) that precludes the likelihood of a self-effacing abridger.

historian. The Second Book of Maccabees contains, moreover, a strong dose of apologetics, evident for example in the report that Antiochus IV Epiphanes, at the end of his life, expressed a wish to be converted to Judaism.[7]

Despite the linguistic and historiographic divergences, the parallelism of the two books is striking. Whether describing the pre-history of the Syrian persecution, Antiochus' journey from Egypt into Jerusalem, his death in Persia, or Judah's warfare, the sequence and background of the events are similarly reported in both Maccabean books.[8] Nevertheless, except for Schlatter, scholarly consensus has rightly abandoned the view that the two works were interdependent. Fundamental differences, such as the divergent chronology, and the differing roles of Antiochus and the Jewish Hellenizers, preclude the possibility that, as Schlatter argued, Jason was the model for the author of First Maccabees. But since the parallelism between the two books could be neither interdependent nor incidental, their shared features must be accounted for by supposing the existence of a common source or sources used by both Maccabean authors.[9]

As to the identity of the common source, there is good reason to assume, as has been suggested, that the authors of First and Second Maccabees utilized independently the so-called "Acts of Judah"   (λόγοι Ἰούδου).[10] This source is mentioned in I Macc. 9:22, which, after recounting at length Judah's exploits and recording his death, complains that "the rest of Judah's acts, his wars, and the brave deeds that he did, and his greatness, have not been written down, for they were many."[11] The implication seems to be that in contrast, for instance, to the written records of John Hyrcanus, described in I Macc. 16:23-24, the contents of "the Acts of Judah" were rather sparse.

---

7   II Macc. 9:17. Cf. however, I Macc. 6:12-13, where Antiochus is said to have repented his actions against the Jews.

8   See table below, p. 30.

9   See A. Schlatter, *Jason von Kyrene: Ein Beitrag zu seiner Wiederherstellung* (Festschrift ... Otto Zöckler, Munich, 1891), passim, esp. 1 ff.: A. Geiger, *Urschrift und Übersetzunger der Bibel in ihrer Abhängigkeit von der innern Entwicklung des Judentums*[2] (Frankfurt am Main, Madda, 1928), 219-23; Koster,   *Theologische Tijdschrift,* XII, (1878), 491 ff.; Kugler, *Beitrage,* 124-50; among others assumed that II. Macc. was dependent on I Macc. But this view is rightly rejected by Niese, *Kritik,* 25 f.: Schürer, *Gesch. d. jüd. Volkes,* III[3], 483; E. Meyer, *Ursprung und Anfänge des des Christentums* (Stuttgart, 1921), II, 357 f. For further literature, see Klaus-Dietrich Schunck, *Die Quellen des I. und II. Makkabäerbüches* (Halle, Max Niemeyer Verlag, 1954), 117 f.

10   I Macc. 9:22. This appears to be a reference to the slimness of this work, rather than to its non-existence. It certainly does not mean, as interpreted by Meyer, *Ursprung,* II, 458, n. 1, that the author relied on oral traditions exclusively. Cf. John 21:25.

11   The uniqueness of this negative mention reveals the author's amazement that his hero was not accorded what in his time every high priest had -- an official historian. He seems to forget that Judah was not a high priest and that as a guerilla chieftain he did not have court scribes, normal in the days of Jonathan or John Hyrcanus.

This original biography sparce as it may have been, seems also to have been the basic source of Jason-Epitomist's Second Book of Maccabees. As suggested by Schunck,[12] a synoptic presentation of I and II Maccabees might yield a rough outline of "the Acts of Judah" as follows:

I Maccabees		II Maccabees
	The Pre-history	
1:11-15		chapters 3-4
	Antiochus in Egypt and Jerusalem	
1:16-40		5:1-5; 17
	Judah's Early Actions	
3:1-9; cf. 2:42-48		8:1-7
	Nicanor and Gorgias	
3:38-4:25		8:8-29; 34-36
	Death of Antiochus IV	
(below)		chapter 9
	Purification of the Temple	
(below)		chapter 10
	Lysias' First Campaign	
4:26-35		chapter 11
	Purification of the Temple	
4:36-61		(above)
	Warfare with Neighboring Lands	
chapter 5		chapter 12
	Death of Antiochus IV	
6:1-17		(above)
	The Campaign of Antiochus V Eupator	
6:18-63		chapter 13
	Demetrius I and his General Nicanor	
chapter 7		chapters 14-15

In addition to the outline of "the Acts of Judah" recoverable from this synoptic presentation, there are a number of passages whose resemblance can be accounted for only as presumed remnants of "the Acts of Judah." One example follows:

I Macc. 7:47-49	II Macc. 15:28-36
Then they [the Jews] seized the spoils and the plunder, and they cut	When the action was over and they were returning with joy they recog-

---

12 Schunck, *Quellen*, 97, who however labels the work "Judasvita." This hypothetical Judas-Vita may have been also the source of the Maccabean dates recorded in the Scroll of Fasts. See Hans Lichtenstein, "Die Fastenrolle. Eine Untersuchung zur jüdisch- hellenistischen Geschichte," *HUCA* 8-9 (1931-32), 257-351.

off Nicanor's head and the right hand, which he so arrogantly stretched out, and brought them and displayed them just outside of Jerusalem. The people rejoiced greatly and celebrated that day as a day of great gladness. And they decreed that this day should be celebrated each year on the thirteenth of Adar.

nized Nicanor, lying dead, in full armor. And the man ... ordered them to cut off Nicanor's head and arm and carry them to Jerusalem ... And he hung Nicanor's head from the citadel ... And they all decreed by public vote never to let this day go unobserved, but to celebrate the thirteenth day of the twelfth month—which is called Adar in the Syrian language—the day before Mordecai's day.[13]

Aside from possibly preserving a fragment of the so-called "Acts of Judah," this text is significant for our discussion since it may shed light on the dependence on Eupolemus of our hypothetical work. In First Maccabees, Judah's victory over Nicanor serves as the prelude to Eupolemus' mission to Rome, described in Chapter Eight. The question then is whether Jason-Epitomist's failure to describe this mission suggests its absence in the original; or if the omission is due entirely to the fact that Second Maccabees happens to end with the previous episode of Nicanor's day?[14] There is no doubt that "the Acts of Judah" was the source of I Macc. 8, because the hero's biography, as is implied in I Macc. 9:22 concluded with his death and burial. Moreover, II Macc. 4:11 mentions the alliance between Judah and the Roman senate as resulting from Eupolemus' mission as if it were a summary of I Macc. 8:17 ff., even though, as shown above, the two books were not interdependent.

One of the sources of the so-called "Acts of Judah" was Eupolemus. It must have been his personal report that served as the basis for the account now preserved in I Macc. 8. This is so not only because of the unique nature of its contents but also because of its stylistic departures from the rest of First Maccabees.[15] The only problem before us is whether this chapter comes from an apparent collection of official documents or from Eupolemus' own

13   Cf. further I Macc. 1:41-53 with II Macc. 6:1-6, for another possible fragment. It should be noted that the Scroll of Fasts [see previous note] similarly records the "day of Nicanor" (*HUCA*, 8-9 (1931-32), 346.

14   See E. Meyer, *Ursprung*, II, 456, who presupposing a date of 125 B.C., brands as "undenkbar" the supposition that Jason's work ended as II Macc. does now, with Nicanor's death. The original, according to Meyer, included an account of Jonathan, at least up to his rise to the office of high priest. Although accepted by Bickerman (*R.E.*, XIX [1928], 793), this view ought to be rejected, because of the epilogue (II, Macc. 15:37), which suggests the contrary. Moreover, if it was inconceivable for Jason to conclude with Nicanor, why was it natural for the Epitomist to do so?

15   Cf., for example, Hugo Willrich, *Juden und Driechen vor der Makkabäischen Erhebung* (Göttingen, 1895), 73 f.

history of the Jewish people, assuming that his history concluded with the
events of his own day. On the basis of Fragment Five it was argued above that
the year 5149 anno Adami, 158/7 B.C., constituted the final date of his
biblical history.[16] If so, Eupolemus must have included the background of
the Judaeao-Roman alliance as well as the events of his own day as a fitting
climax to his concern for the Temple. It is suggested below, moreover, that
Eupolemus' account of David alluded to the Syrian pollution of the
Temple.[17] The possibility remains that he also recorded Judah's death, which
had occurred in 160 B.C., and perhaps a few episodes concerning Jonathan up
to 159/8 B.C. Is it sheer coincidence, then, that the author of First Maccabees
stops precisely at the year 159 B.C., having nothing to tell about the period
between 159 and 152? The hiatus between I Macc. 9:73 and 10:1 could
conceivably be explained in terms of the lapse from the end of Eupolemus'
history until the author found a new source in the account of Jonathan's life.
Speculation that Judah's historian and ambassador Eupolemus served as the
main source for the "Acts of Judah" or perhaps even was its author is
therefore not entirely unwarranted.

A rejection of this possibility on the basis that Eupolemus wrote in Greek,
while the First Maccabees was a Hebrew book would not be valid. A
considerable part of this book, such as the prehistory and the background for
the international policy, presumes the utilization of Greek sources anyway.
There is also a fair supposition that Eupolemus, like Josephus after him,
might have composed Hebrew or Aramaic books in addition to writing in
Greek. Assuming, as we must, that the "Acts of Judah," the main source of
First Maccabees, and an important source of Second Maccabees, was a
Hebrew document, still does not exclude the possibility that its author was
Eupolemus.

The matter is quite different when we move from the area of sheer
speculation to that of likelihood. Adolf Schlatter, followed by König,
Favaloro, and Schunck, has to a larger or lesser degree posited Eupolemus as
the author of First Maccabees. Schlatter supposes that Eupolemus was for the
First Book of Maccabees what Jason of Cyrene was for the Epitomist's Sacred
Book of Maccabees. In other words, First Maccabees was the Hebrew version
of Eupolemus' Greek account, which extended to Simon's accession in 142
B.C. (I Macc. 14) or even, conceivably, to the period of John Hyrcanus in 135
B.C. (I Macc. 16:22).[18] In fact, according to Schlatter, Jason of Cyrene's
five-book history was a marvelous example of a work that fused Greek
mastery of aesthetics and keen historical insight with Jewish legal and

---

16   See above, pp. 5-7. Cp. also I Macc. 8:19, words that seem to come from the
ambassador(s).

17   See Eus., *P.E.* IX, 30, 5 = 723 F 2; below, pp. 140 f.

18   Schlatter, *Jason of Cyrene,*, 43-50.

religious piety. The Epitomist's disregard for accuracy and concern for rhetoric, however, changed a masterpiece into a mediocrity.[19] But there is no doubt that the idealization of Jason into a kind of Jewish Thucydides bespoke Schlatter's rich imagination and was not based on fact. The same may be said of Schlatter's theory that Jason not only authored the Epitomist's Second Book of Maccabees but that he served as well as the model of Eupolemus and First Maccabees.[20]

Evidently, on the basis of Schlatter's wild theories, Favaloro asserted that chapters 1-15 of First Maccabees were probably a version of Eupolemus' work.[21] To give substance to this hypothesis, Schunck has listed nine points that relate Eupolemus to First Maccabees.[22] But most of these points merely refer to proofs that identify Eupolemus the historian with the Eupolemus who served as Judah's ambassador to Rome, The remainder may be summed up as follows:

1. The absence of Hasido-Pharisaic tendencies in both Eupolemus' fragments and First Maccabees;
2. The citation of official documents;
3. The tendency to exaggerate numbers;
4. Frequent use of chronological information, especially the use of the Seleucid dating by First Maccabees.

Thus, if we follow Schunck, Eupolemus may be regarded either as the author of the First Book of Maccabees or at least as its main source.[23]

But Schunck's arguments are not convincing. The loss of Eupolemus' history for the early Maccabean period, if in fact his work went that far, makes verification of point one impossible.[24] But even if we assume, as we should, that Eupolemus, like the author of First Maccabees, was not a member of the "Hasidic" or "Pharisaic" group, it still does not follow that

---

19 Schlatter, ibid. 51 f., evaluates Jason's attainments as a historian on the basis that First Maccabees was presumably dependent on him. But if so, why does I Maccabees lack any of the esthetic accomplishments Schlatter ascribed to Jason?

20 Schlatter, ibid., 1 ff.; see previous note. In fact, however, the general outlook of the author of I Macc. and that of Jason-Epitomist are quite divergent and cannot be reconciled. For example, the origin of the persecution, according to the former, was caused entirely by external forces (I Macc. 1:20-53); according to the latter, it was exclusively an internal struggle between rival priestly factions (II Macc. 3-4). The diverse chronology, the divergent date of Antiochus' death, and differing theological presuppositions are among the points that disprove Schlatter's hypothesis.

21 G. Favaloro, *Il Tramonto dell'imperialismo Nell'antica Siria* (Regio Calabria, 1925), 261 f.

22 Schunck, *Quellen,* 70-74, who in 74, n. 1, cites E. König, *Einleitung in das Alte Testament* (Bonn, 1893), 483, as agreeing with Schlatter.

23 Schunck, ibid., 70-74.

24 As Schunck himself (*ibid.,* 74 n. 1) admits.

one used the work of the other. The same may be said of the remaining contentions. The citing of official documents was a feature of Graeco-Jewish writers in general, including Josephus, who reproduced large chunks of archival collections pertaining to Jewish rights. All ancient historians tended to inflate numbers. As to the abundance of chronological data, it is true that First Maccabees contains some thirty dates and that Eupolemus apparently had a profound interest in chronography. But it is questionable whether this is sufficient proof to regard the two writers as interdependent in any way, much less identical. Beginning with Demetrius, Graeco-Jewish writers made chronology an important aspect of their work, as exemplified in the Book of Jubiliees, probably written about the end of the second century B.C., or in Daniel's schemes. What Schunck does prove, however, is that both the First Book of Maccabees and the fragments of Eupolemus were written in the style of their own day.

Although the evidence collected by Schlatter and Schunck does not suffice to prove that the First Book of Maccabees as a whole may be attributed to Eupolemus or that he had served as its main source, there are some intimations that their thesis is at least partly right. For although the author of First Maccabees depicted the Maccabean period, while Eupolemus allegedly described the Davidic monarchy, the geographical lore underlying both works appears to be quite similar. In both, as also done later in Josephus, the country was divided into Judaea, Samaria, Galilee, and Gilead. Among the neighboring countries listed are Ammon, Moab, Nabataea, Syria, and Phoenicia; and the two most important towns mentioned outside Jerusalem were Joppa and Scythopolis.[25] Remarkable as some of these similarities are, they show only that Eupolemus, in common with ancient historians in general, used the geography of his own day anachronistically to describe earlier periods.

In other words, the technical vocabulary is not decisive evidence that there are traces of Eupolemus in First Maccabees. And if there were, the Maccabean author, writing in Hebrew, might have recast the language of his source so completely as to eliminate any residue of the original. The author of First Maccabees avoided, for example, $\theta\epsilon\acute{o}\varsigma$ when referring to the deity, a term favored by Eupolemus. Schunck's suggestion that a Christian pen retouched the fragments of Eupolemus, adding "God," is absurd in view of the absolute absence of any Christological doctoring of our texts.[26] Another difference between Eupolemus and the First Book of Maccabees is that the latter usually used the term "Israel," as a rule avoiding "Jews," while the former employed "Judaea" and its related forms exclusively.[27]

25   However, there are also differences. Eupolemus assigns a significant role to Egypt, a country almost ignored in I Macc.
26   Schunck, *Quellen,* 73 n. 7.
27   Cf. Zeitlin, *The I Book of Macc.* 28 f. But see I Macc. 14:20, 22, 33, 34, 37, 40, 41, 47. Cf. the slight resemblance between Eupolemus' account of the Temple's furnishings (*P.E.,* IX, 34, 15, I, p. 544 = 723 F 2) and the report of Judah's purification

Biographical hints alone suffice, however, to reject the conjecture that Eupolemus was the author of the entire First Book of Maccabees. The mission to Rome in 161 B.C. by Eupolemus and Jason attained a remarkable success. But when Jonathan wished to renew the treaty in 144 B.C. he sent a certain Numenius the son of Antiochus and Antipater the son of Jason, possibly identical with Eupolemus' associate.[28] The fact that Eupolemus was not requested to go again to Rome suggests, as pointed out earlier, that he was either too old or already dead at that time. Eupolemus could, therefore, not have been the author of First Maccabees, who flourished during the reign of John Hyrcanus, if not later. Also, as suggested in Fragment 5 (4), Eupolemus' history did not go farther than 158/7 B.C., which would rule him out as the source of First Maccabees after the period.

Chapter Eight of First Maccabees, however, stands as proof that, despite what has been said, the author of the "Acts of Judah" did make use of Eupolemus. This chapter, as had often been noted, interrupts the flow and the unity of the book and may betray a different source from the other parts of Judah's life. Its authenticity is attested, however, not only in Josephus' paraphrase of First Maccabees, but also by the fact that a passage containing a eulogy of Roman imperialism would not have been written by a Jew after 64 B.C.[29] Furthermore, the fact that it is alluded to in Jason's account of II Macc. 4:11, there seems to be a basis for considering it an integral part of the hypothetical "Acts of Judah."[30]

The section of I Macc. 8:1-16 is remarkable in that though it is part of our book it has nothing to do with its theme. It purports to record Judah's opinion of Roman power and magnanimity, but it also tells of his acquaintance with the Republican form of government, sometimes quite erroneously. Nonetheless, it ascribes to the rebel leader a perceptive grasp of world history, recalling the Gallic invasions, Greek and Seleucid affairs, and exotic information about precious metals of Spain. All this suggests an author who was not preoccupied exclusively with events at home. The description of the Roman government gives away the writer's ignorance of some of the principles of the consular structure, but it seems to be the ignorance of an eye-

of the sanctuary (I Macc. 4:49).

28 I Macc. 12:16.

29 *A.J.*, XII, 414-19. It is generally agreed that chapter 8 of I Macc. dates the book as a pre-Pompeyan work (see Schürer, *Gesch. d. jüd. Volkes*, III⁴, 194). See A. Peretti, *La Sibilla Babilonese nella Propaganda Ellenistica* (Florence, 1942), 190; as cited in Valentin Nikiprowetzky, *La Troisiéme Sibylle* (Paris-La Haye, Mouton, 1970), 199 n.6, who argues that Or. Sibyll. III, 175-78, transmitted the pro-Roman sentiments of this chapter, thus dating the passage as having been written before 63 B.C. or even before 104 B.C., the date of composition of the I Maccabees. But Nikiprowetzky rightly rejects the view that the sibylline passage is necessarily pro-Roman.

30 The hypothetical preservation of "the Acts of Judah" in II Macc. could be used to trace the passages that were found in Jason's work, in contrast to the other material that might be Jason's or the Epitomist's.

witness. From what we know of his fragments, this combination of ignorance and sophistication better fits a writer like Eupolemus rather than the rebel Judah Maccabee. The first part of Chapter Eight may then be regarded as derived from Eupolemus' history, in which he probably enthusiastically endorsed the treaty he himself had negotiated in Rome.

The narrator did integrate this extraneous information about Roman history with the main theme in an interesting manner. I Macc. 8:1-16 reiterates again and again that Judah "heard" or "was told." The author makes it evident that the rebel leader was not really expected to have such geopolitical information at his finger tips, but that he had competent advisers.[31] I Macc. 8:1-16, relating the expectation of Roman intervention, adds one more reason for the revolt against the Seleucid Empire to those given in Chapter 1. Some of Judah Maccabee's advisers, if not Judah himself, were always hoping that Rome would somehow find it propitious to exploit the Judaean rebellion to advance her own interests. Apparently disappointed that Rome had failed to act thus far, Judah's advisers counseled him to take the initiative. We may conjecture that Eupolemus, whose father's serving in|a similar mission at the turn of the century had persuaded Antiochus III to intervene against the Ptolemaic rule, was one of these advisers. Eupolemus then, it would seem, has a threefold link with I Macc. 8: he persuaded Judah to send a mission; he himself headed the missions; and he reported.

The second half of Chapter Eight which contains the text of the Judaeo-Roman treaty (I Macc. 8:17-32) may, as noted above, preserve remnants of Eupolemus' style. The complaint that the journey was "long" suggests that we have before us the envoy's own report. Some of the technical vocabulary, such as ἔθνος Ἰουδαίων, the Judaean people, conforms to the usage found in Eupolemus' fragments. In fact, it is not impossible that Eupolemus himself was partially responsible for the inaccuracies found in the text. As suggested above, there is reason to believe that Eupolemus in his report of the treaty altered some of its clauses to create the impression of a more favorable treaty. Whether or not this is so, there are reasons to believe that the entire Chapter Eight of the First Book of Maccabees rested, to begin with, on Eupolemus' advice to Judah and his mission to Rome; and, ultimately, on his Jewish history which apparently ended with the year 158/7 B.C.

Whether or not the authorship of the "Acts of Judah," which supposedly lies behind much of Chapters 1-9 of First Maccabees and 3-15 of Second Maccabees, should also be attributed to Eupolemus is a moot question. The "Acts of Judah" was a Hebrew work, while Eupolemus wrote in Greek; but

---

31   Grimm, *Das Erste Buch der Maccabäer,* ad locum, p. 119, rightly suspects that "seine eigene Kenntniss von der Römern mit der dem Judas zu Theil gewordenen vermischte." See especially I Macc. 8:9b-10, where the writer boasts of his acquaintance with Roman intelligence.

there is good reason to conjecture that Eupolemus' native tongue was Hebrew. A main problem of such a presumed authorship is that the "Acts of Judah," as far as we can tell, presented as faithful an account of recent events as could be expected from a Jewish patriot, while the fragments of Eupolemus suggest a mendacious writer. Of course, Eupolemus' fragments deal with the period of the monarchy; but there is no reason to suppose that the same man would have become meticulous when recording events of his own day. Thus it is unreasonable to regard Eupolemus as the author of the "Acts of Judah."

The case is different, however, in regard to certain parts of the First Book of Maccabees. It is not impossible that, as is the case with I Macc. 8, references of the "Acts of Judah" to foreign affairs came from Eupolemus.[32] It is also conceivable that the document originally cited in the "Life of Jonathan the High Priest," proposing that the Spartans and the Jews had a common ancestry, went back ultimately to Eupolemus' history.[33] The alleged correspondence between Areius, a king of Sparta, and Onias, a high priest, claiming that the Jews and the Spartans share Abraham as their ancestor, appears to echo the fictional exchange of letters between Solomon and Vaphres, the king of Egypt, as found in the fragments of Eupolemus.[34] But

32　A considerable part of I Maccabees was no doubt ultimately based on Seleucid sources, such as royal chronicles; for example, the prehistory of Antiochus IV (I Macc. 1:1-28); the king's military and financial crises (3:27-41); or his stay in Persia (6:1-17). Bickerman (*R.E.*, XIV, 781-84) and Schunck (*Quellen*, 16-51) detect two divergent systems of chronology in I Maccabees - one based on native sources and the other on royal chronicles. Thus the official Seleucid era began in the fall of 312 B.C., while in Babylon and presumably in Jerusalem it began in Nisan 311. But Bickerman's hypothesis of two dating systems in I Maccabees is unlikely and has, moreover, been invalidated by the exact Babylonian dates now available from cuneiform tablets in R. Parker and W. Dubbenstein, *Babylonian Chronology* (Brown University Press, Providence, Rhode Island, 1952). See also the chronology proposed by Jean Starcky, in *Les livres Macc.*[3], (35-49) We are left with a chronological system for I Maccabees' whose era began in Nisan 312. It is still a matter of conjecture whether the author or I Maccabees used the Seleucid chronicles directly or whether he used the work of men, such as Eupolemus, who served the Maccabean princes.

33　I Macc. 12:5-23; cf. 14:16-23. Despite the considerable literature on this matter (see works cited by R. Marcus, in L.C.L. *Josephus,* VII [1943], 769), this strange link remains as puzzling as ever. Y. Gutman, *The Beginnings of Jewish-Hellenistic Literature* (Jerusalem, Bialik, 1958), I, 108-111; Martin Hengel, *Judentum und Hellenismus* (Wissenschaftliche) Untersuchungen zum Neuen Testament, 10 (Tübingen, 1969), 134, n. 121, place greater trust in the tradition of a Spartan-Jewish alliance than the account deserves, but even they wonder how the link came about. See next note.

34　Some indication that Eupolemus had reported a Spartan-Jewish alliance is suggested by Alexander Polyhistor (*FGrH* 273 F 121), who, in a badly preserved fragment, links Judah and Idumaea (?) with a Spartan Udaeus. Since Alexander Polyhistor quoted Eupolemus extensively, it is possible that the former had found the information in the latter's presumed account of the Hasmonean period.

whether or not this is so, there is no doubt that Eupolemus' history left a deep imprint on the First Book of Maccabees.

SECOND MACCABEES

That Eupolemus was regarded as an important personage by Jason-Epitomist, the authors of the Second Book of Maccabees, is attested, in II Macc. 4:11. Describing Antiochus IV's persecution of the Jews, II Macc. 4:11 adds: "He set aside the existing royal concessions to the Jews, secured through John the father of Eupolemus, who went on the mission to establish friendship and alliance with the Romans." The identification of a father by his son was, as Tcherikover pointed out, highly unusual. Tcherikover accounts for it by presuming that Jason and Eupolemus were contemporaries.[35] But is it not just as conceivable that for an author of a life of Judah Eupolemus was more important than his father because Jason had used Eupolemus' account for the writing of Judah's life? It is even possible that Jason had in fact acknowledged Eupolemus as one of his sources, hence the reverse identification, but that the name was eliminated by the epitomist.

The author of Judah's vita, according to I Macc. 9:22, complained of the paucity of sources. But somehow Jason, who may have written either in Jerusalem or, as is more likely, in the Diaspora,[36] from material not alluded to at all in First Maccabees, added much depth to our knowledge of the pre-Maccabean period. If the assumption argued in the preceding paragraph is cogent, it is conceivable that Jason made fuller use of Eupolemus' history of this period than did the author of the "Acts of Judah." This hypothesis could explain the origin of accounts in Second Maccabees of the fratricidal struggle between the members of the high priestly clan. Eupolemus, a member of the Hakkos clan, the son of John, who had served as the high priest's foreign representative, had ample opportunity to observe firsthand the intrigues in the Holy City leading to the Maccabean revolution. II Macc. 3-5, although

---

35   V. Tcherikover, *Hellenistic Civilization and the Jews,* (Philadelphia, The Jewish Publication Society, 1959), 384 f. Our conclusion does not necessarily invalidate Tcherikover's dating of Jason, a view accepted by Hengel, *Judentum und Hellenismus,* 180 f. But, judging from Jason-Epitomist's work, this is unlikely. II Macc. 9 may be correct after all, on the basis of the cuneiform texts, that Antiochus IV's death had occurred prior to Judah's rededication of the Temple. But the chapter must be regarded as largely fictional, written by a man far removed from the events. See Grimm, *Das II, III und IV Buch der Maccabäer,* 19; Meyer, *Ursprung,* II, 454-62; and Bickerman, *R.E.,* XIV, 793.

36   That Jason wrote in the Diaspora is a general assumption. But see Schlatter, *Jason von Kyrene,* 52, who makes him a long time resident of Jerusalem; and Hengel, *Judentum und Hellenismus,* 178-80, who finds his theology in greater consonance with the Palestinian Hasidim than with that of Alexandrian Hellenism. See also below, note 38.

careless with details, seems to have been based on a source that, in contrast to the parallel in First Maccabees, combined mendacity in reporting with a sophistication unparalleled in the rival account. His fragments as well as I Macc. 8, seem to suggest that Eupolemus was one of the most important of Jason's likely sources.[37]

In addition to the mention of his name in II Macc. 4:11 and the possibility, not to say probability, of Jason's dependence on Eupolemus, there is also a link between a tradition first preserved in Eupolemus' fragments and the main theme of the second epistle in II Macc. 1:10-2:18. Two epistles, the first dated in 124 B.C. and the second undated, from Jerusalem to the Jews of Egypt urged them to celebrate the feast of Hanukkah; it is well known that they were prefixed by a later hand to the Epitomist's work which began with II Macc. 2:18.[38] Although it purports to relate Judah's victory over the Greeks, two-thirds of the second epistle recounts Nehemiah's miraculous kindling of *naphtha* to light the restored altar. But this was no ordinary fire, since the use of such an element might have polluted the shrine. It was recalled by some priests, however, that Jeremiah, upon the burning of the First Temple, had hidden in a cave some of the sacred fuel which Nehemiah now hastened to recover. The source of this legend, according to II Macc.

---

37 This is especially evident in II Macc. 4:11, referring to John's concessions from Antiochus III, known also from *A.J.,* XII, 138-53. There is no reason to doubt that Eupolemus, assuming his history reached this period, had mentioned the Seleucid privileges granted to the Jews.

38 This section is usually divided into II Macc. 1:1-9, the first epistle, dated in 124 B.C., urging the celebration of the "feast of booths" in the month of Kislev, apparently Hanukkah; and 1:10-2:18, another letter of an uncertain date with a similar message. The prima facie time of the second epistle is between 164 and 160 B.C., as the name of Judah (Maccabee) heads the letter: "Those in Jerusalem and those in Judaea, and the Gerusia, and Judah. To Aristobulus, who is of the family of anointed priests, teacher of Ptolemy the king, and to the Jews of Egypt" (II Macc. 1:10). Indeed, Bévenot (p. 173), Abel, (289) and Starcky (27) date the letter in 164 B.C., soon after the rededication of the Temple. Niese (*Kritik,* 11 ff.), followed by Meyer (*Ursprung,* II, 454 f.), believes that Jason flourished in the year 125 B.C., the time given in II Macc. 1:9 (see note 14). If so, the epistle's heading is a forgery, unless, as has sometimes been proposed, Judah and Aristobulus refer to some obscure personalities, rather than to Judah Maccabee and Aristobulus, the founder of an allegorical school of Biblical hermeneutics. Bickerman (Ein Jüdischer Festbrief vom Jahre 124 v. Chr. [II Macc. 1:1-9], *ZNW.* 32 [1933], 233-58), on the basis of Exler's studies of the epistolary style of the papyri, concluded that II Macc. 1:10's salutation, Χαίρειν καὶ ὑγιαίνειν dates the second letter after 60 B.C. But as the first epistle's salutation found in II Macc. 1:1 also contains an uncommon formula, it suggests that Palestinian epistolary style was not necesarily identical with that of the Egyptian papyri. See now Jean Starcky (*Les livres des Macc.*[3], 27-30), who justly dates our epistle in 164 B.C. on the basis of these arguments: the author's misinformation on Antiochus' death (II Macc. 9:11-17); his mention of Judah (2:14); the use of the apocryphal Nehemiah (1:18-2:15).

2:4-5, reported further that the prophet had also sealed the Mosaic tent, ark, and the altar of incense in the unknown cave.[39] As it is pointed out below, the records (ἀναγραφαί) mentioned in II Macc. 2:1, 4, appear| to have been part of Eupolemus' description of the period of restoration, which continued the account of the extant fragments relating Jeremiah's hiding of the ark.[40] Indeed, the pattern of the listings of the sacred objects in II Macc. 2:5—the tent, the ark, and the altar of incense—bears a close resemblance to the formula repeatedly found in Eupolemus' writings.[41] It is likely, therefore, that II Macc. 1:18b-2:15, relating Nehemiah's dedication of the altar, has preserved a lost, if embellished, fragment of Eupolemus.[42]

PTOLEMY OF MENDES

A close reading of Fragment Five indicates that a historian writing in 40 B.C. made use of Eupolemus' chronology: "The total number of years from Adam to the fifth year of Demetrius' reign, the twelfth of Ptolemy's reign in Egypt, add up to 5149 years . . . . *From that time to the Roman consuls* Γαίου Δομετιανοῦ Κασιανοῦ *make a total of 120 years.*"[43] If the first part of this passage was written by Eupolemus, the italicized words are obviously not his. And if not Eupolemus' whose are they? Who can be the historian who flourished in the above-mentioned consulship, who concerned himself with biblical chronology and who made use of Eupolemus? Similarly, the question

---

39 Cf. Neh. 8:17-9:37. But the passage deals exclusively with the celebration of Sukkot; nothing is said of how the altar was lit. It should be noted that the first epistle (II Macc. 1:9) takes for granted the existence of a link between the feast of booths and of Hanukkah, a questionable proposition documented in the second epistle. This would seem to indicate that Bickerman's view (see previous note) of dating the first epistle in 124 and the second in 60 B.C. does not seem reasonable. Whatever the date -- whether 164, 124, or 60 B.C. -- of the second epistle, none precludes the possibility of its dependence on Eupolemus. But if the first date is correct, we have an interesting episode indicating that Eupolemus himself may have participated in the epistle's composition. See Jean Starcky, cited in note 38.

40 II Macc. 2:1, 4, 13, repeatedly stress the existence of written records. This could refer to some kind of Jeremiah apocryphon, as presumed by Ewald, cited below. Indeed, fragments of a Jeremiah Vita (in *Propheten- und Apostellegenden*) ed. by Th. Schermann, [Leipzig, 1907], 83 f.) parallels II Macc. 2:1 ff. But as pointed out by Schermann, p. 88, this Apocryphon could not have been the source of the Maccabean epistolographer. Eupolemus is the oldest authority for Jeremiah's hiding of the ark (Eusebius, *P.E.*, IX, 39, 5 = 723 F 4 [5]).

41 Eupolemus, in *P.E.*, IX, 34, 15 = 723 F 2b. Cf. I Macc. 4:49.

42 It may be of interest that II Macc. 2:13 f., reports concerning a collection of books allegedly gathered by Judah. It is quite possible that Eupolemus, Judah's friend, as well as his author, assisted him in the founding of a library which, according to some scholars, related to the canonization of some biblical books. See Grimm, *Handbuch,* ad locum, 56-59; O. Eissfeldt, *Einleitung*[5] (1964), 723; Starcky, cited in note 38.

43 Clement, *Strom.*, I, 141, 4 = 723 F 4 (Walter, F 5).

of the identity of the Demetrius whose fifth regnal year coincided with the twelfth of Ptolemy must be solved. Furthermore, the consuls' names in the manuscripts are corrupt and require emendation.[44]

Because it yields the date of the author, the synchronization of the two kings has been the most discussed problem relating to Eupolemus. As there were several Syrian kings by this name, the question arises which Demetrius was intended. "Demetrius" can be narrowed down to either Demetrius I Soter (162-50) or Demetrius II Nicator (145-139/8). Movers, Niebuhr, and Carl Mueller assumed that the latter was meant. But this has been ruled out because there was no Ptolemy whose twelfth regnal year synchronized with that of Demetrius II's fifth. Willrich, therefore, condemned the fragment as so corrupt as to be unusable. He then proceeded to date Eupolemus in the period of Alexander Jannaeus, king of Judaea (103-76).

Disregarding Willrich's rather untenable view, scholarly consensus now assumes that Eupolemus referred to Demetrius I, whose fifth year occurred in 158/7.[45] If so, the synchronism of "the twelfth year of the king of Egypt" must have referred to Ptolemy VII Euergetes II Physcon, who had become joint ruler of Egypt in 170 and whose twelfth year fell in 159/8. There is a year's discrepancy between the two dates. This may appear to be a rather slight error, but it is one that a contemporary such as Eupolemus would not have made. The main objection to the synchronism, however, is more serious. In 159/8 Ptolemy Physcon was not reigning in Egypt, having been exiled from 164 to 145 to Cyrene by the senior co-ruler Ptolemy VI Philometor (181-145). If so, Eupolemus, writing in 158/7, would not have called him king of Egypt. Incidentally, the custom of synchronizing the dates of the Seleucids with the Ptolemies became a common practice only in the first century B.C.

Briefly, there are three serious difficulties with the synchronism cited by Clement: 1) the corrupt names of the consuls; 2) the identity of the emendator writing 120 years after Eupolemus; and 3) Eupolemus' naming Ptolemy King of Egypt at a time when only the king of Cyrene.

Several generations of brilliant scholars have satisfactorily solved problems one and three. Alfred von Gutschmid suggested that the synchronism with Ptolemaic rulers was inserted by the same hand that brought Eupolemus' chronology up to 120 years after his own day. By the time the emendator lived (circa 40 B.C.), Ptolemy VII's reign was computed as beginning not, as in modern handbooks, from the year 145 B.C. when he became the undisputed ruler of Egypt, but from 170 when he was only a joint ruler. Nevertheless, the emendator erred by one year. The correct synchronism of

---

44 See above ch. I, n. 28.
45 See above ch. I, nn. 26-27.

Demetrius I's fifth year (158/7) was Ptolemy VII's thirteenth year, not his twelfth (159/8).[46]

The question about the identity of the Roman consuls was solved by Kulhmey's proposed emendation: Γναίου Δομετίου καὶ 'Ασινίου , i.e., Gnaeus Domitius (Calvinus) and (Gaius) Asinius (Pollio) who, according to Josephus were consuls in 40 B.C. The unknown writer, erring by three years, assumed that the fifth year of Demetrius was 160 B.C.[47]

Gutschmid accepted the names of the consuls proposed by Kuhlmey and Freudenthal, but wished also to identify the scribe who flourished in 40 B.C. In an unhappy suggestion of his own he proposed to read the corrupted text thus: Γναίου Δομετίου καὶ 'Ασινίου ὑπὸ Κασιανοῦ. The reader will notice that Gutschmid added two words to the previous emendation: "by Casianus." Gutschmid's reading had two virtues. It retained the manuscript reading and it yielded the identify of the emendator. "Cassianus," according to Gutschmid, refers here to Julius Cassianus, known only from an obscure reference in Clement as the author of a work by the title of *Exegetica*, the first book of which dealt with the antiquity of the Mosaic philosophy.[48] But Gutschmid believed him to have been a gnostic and a chronographer of the second century A.D., and a source of the chronological scheme of Julius Africanus. Such was Gutschmid's erudition that men like Susemihl, Wachsmuth, Schürer, and Jacoby accepted his emendation.[49]

In a recent study, Nikolaus Walter has successfully challenged Gutschmid's identification of the emendator.[50] Cassianus, according to Walter, was not a chronographer at all. In fact, Clement does not say that he was. It was only Eusebius' misreading of Clement which identified him as such. In support of this view Walter cites Jerome, who says that he had searched in the libraries for a copy of Cassianus' chronology but could not find one.

I am not sure that Jerome's failure to find a copy proves that none existed or that Eusebius misread Clement.[51] But I must yield to Walter's argument that, even conceding that Cassianus did compose a world chronology, it does

46   A. von Gutschmid, *Kl. Schr.*, II, 191. Cf. Schlatter in *Theologische Studien und Kritiken*, 4 (1891), 635; Jacoby, "Eupolemos No. 11, ," II *R.E.*, VI 1228. In his edition (723 F 3), Jacoby printed the presumably emended words in petite print.

47   Kuhlmey, *Eupolemi Fragmenta*, 34.

48   Clement, *Strom.*, I, 101, 2, repeated by Eus., *P.E.*, X, 12, 1 = Apion, 616 F 2 b. Gutschmid, *Kl. Schr.*, II, 192.

49   F. Susemihl, *Geschichte der griechischen Litteratur in der Alexandrinerzeit* (Leipzig, 1892), II, 649, n. 77; Wachsmuth, *Einleitung*, 155 f.; Schürer, *Gesch. d. jüd Volkes*, III[4], 476 f.; Jacoby, "Eupolemos," No. 11, *R.E.*, VI[1907], 1228.

50   N. Walter, "Der angeliche Chronograph Julius Cassianus," in *Studien zum Neuen Testament und zur Patristik; Erich Klostermann zum 90. Geburtstag Dargebracht* (Berlin, Akademie-Verlag, 1961), 177-92.

51   Referring to Cassian's "Chronography," Jerome says, "quod opusculum inverine non potui" (*De viris illustribus* in Migne, *P.L.*, XXIII, 687). Walter, ibid., 181 f., citing also (182 n. 1) P. Koetschau, *ThLZ*, 24 (1901), 420.

not explain why a second century gnostic would have added the names of Roman consuls of 40 B.C. Gutschmid's reasoning that for Cassianus the year 40 B.C. was a significant date because Herod became king in that year lacks cogency. Gutschmid's attempt to identify Eupolemus' interpolator with the gnostic Julius Cassianus must therefore be rejected. Thus the identity of the chronologist who added a passage to Fragment Five of Eupolemus remains unknown.

Suffice it to say that the interpolator lived in Egypt in 40 B.C. and that he used the chronological system of dating by the Roman consuls. He evidently was a professional synchronist, despite his error in correlating Ptolemaic with Seleucid royal years. But he seems to have also been interested in biblical chronology. Of the known historians, this could apply only to Ptolemy of Mendes. The only other author who might have been writing then about Jewish history was Nicolaus of Damascus. But Nicolaus, who had tutored the children of Antony and Cleopatra, and later became Herod's assistant and court historian, and biographer of Augustus, must be excluded, simply because in 40 B.C. Nicolaus, 24 years old, was probably not concerned with Jewish historiography. In fact, Nicolaus only became interested in Jewish history on account of his patron Herod, in 14 B.C., not in 40 B.C.[52]

Matters are different with Ptolemy of Mendes. He was an Egyptian priest who wrote a chronology of Egypt in three books.[53] He stated that the exodus of the Hebrews from Egypt occurred during the reign of Amosis, the king of Egypt, at which time Inachus reigned in Argos and Ogygus in Athens.[54] Very little has survived of Ptolemy's writings. But they were of great significance. Apion, the anti-Semitic historian; Justus of Tiberias, the rival of Josephus, and Julius Sextus Africanus, the "father" of Christian chronography, all apparently based their chronologies on that of Ptolemy of Mendes.[55] As has been suggested, he may also be the same Ptolemy who, attracted by Herod's gifts, wrote a flattering biography of the Jewish king, but this is unlikely.[56] Ptolemy of Mendes, who flourished in the middle of

52 Jacoby, *FGrH* 90 T 2 = Sophronius of Damascus, in Migne, *P.G.* LXXXII, 3, col. 3621d, mentions Nicolaus' stay in Alexandria; his interest in Jewish history is recorded in 90 F 134, dated in 14 B.C. Cf. Wacholder, *Nicolaus of Damascus* (University of California Press, Berkeley and Los Angeles, 1962), 14, 36.

53 Tatian, 38; Clement, *Strom.*, I, 101, 2 = 611 T la-b.

54 Tatian, 38; Clement, 101, 3-5; Africanus in Euseb., *P.E.*, X, 10, 15-22; Ps.-Justin, *Coh. ad Graec.*, 9 = 611 F la-c. On Ptolemy of Mendes, see H. Gelzer, *Sextus Julius Africanus* (Leipzig, 1880), I, 20, 203, 207; II, 28; W. Christ, *Philologische Studien zu Clemens Alexandrinus* (*Abh. d. bay. Ak. d. Wiss.*, 21, 3, Munich, 1901), 457-528; Dihle, "Ptolemaios," No. 74, *R.E.*, XXIII (1959), 1861.

55 Apion 616 F 2a-c; Justus of Tiberias, 734 FF 2-3; Africanus in Euseb., *P.E.*, X, 10. 15-22 (= Apion, 616 F 2c).

56 Ptolemy, *FGrH* 199 F 1, was identified as of Mendes (*FGrH* No. 611) by Meursius and Vossius, as cited, but the identification is denied by Jacoby *FGrH*, IID, 625, 22 f. Schürer's identification of Herod's biographer with Ptolemy of Askalon, the grammarian in Rome, is rightly rejected by Jacoby (625). Chronologically and

the first century B.C., was the first to synchronize ancient biblical history with the prevailing tables of the kings of Egypt, Argos, and Athens. As his source for Jewish history, Ptolemy evidently used, in addition to the Bible, the Hellenistic Jewish historians. Probably, as will be shown below, Ptolemy of Mendes reflected a tendency in first century B.C. Hellenistic histori-ography to utilize Graeco-Jewish chronicles in the dating of prehistory.[57]

Fragment Five attests, then, that an unidentified world historian—probably Ptolemy of Mendes—not only used Eupolemus' chronology to establish the age of the universe, but also brought it up to date in 40 B.C. Clement of Alexandria, attributing the entire passage to Eupolemus, was no longer aware of the presence of an interpolation. It would seem that through Ptolemy of Mendes, Eupolemus' chronology found its way to Apion (A.D. 20-50) and other anti-Judaean Alexandrian historians. The Church Fathers and the Byzantine chroniclers were directly dependent on Ptolemy of Mendes' synchronistic tables of world history, and so perhaps, indirectly, on Eupolemus.[58] But the survival and transmission of Eupolemus' work in the middle of the first century B.C. is not due only to the writings of Ptolemy of Mendes.

ALEXANDER POLYHISTOR

The credit for the preservation of Eupolemus' work belongs to Alexander Polyhistor of Miletes, the first truly intellectual historian, a writer whose purview encompassed many aspects of human affairs, whether political, religious, philosophical or anthropological. Although a contemporary of Diodorus of Sicily and Nicolaus of Damascus, Alexander Polyhistor shunned the artificial synthesis, which was the fashion and the curse of contemporary Hellenistic historical writing. Were it not for his collection of native lore our knowledge of Graeco-Jewish writing before Philo and Josephus would be almost nil. Unfortunately, all that is known about him can be stated in a few sentences. His full name was Alexander Cornelius Polyhistor of Miletes.[59] He

geographically, however, Ptolemy of Mendes was too far removed from Herod to have been the Jewish King's biographer. See also, Dihle, "Ptolemaios" No. 75 *R.E.,* XXIII (1959), 1861, who says that we lack evidence to identify Herod's biographer.

57   Whether or not the heathen writers used Hebrew Scriptures is still an open question (cf. I. Heinemann, "Moses," No. 1, *R.E., * XVI, 1933), 359-75.

58   Cf. below.

59   The fact that he is cited as an authority that Moses was a woman (273 F 70), quoting the anti-Semitic literature, suggests that he was not Jewish (Jacoby, *FGrH,* IIIa, 269, 25; 282, 2-284, 5; cf. Heinemann, *R.E.,* XVI, 360). Note also, quoting Cleodomus Malchus (*A.J.,* I, 240 = 727 F 1), Alexander Polyhistor says: "As Moses *their* lawgiver also reports" = καθὼς καὶ Μωυσῆς ἱστόρησεν ὁ νομοθέτης αὐτῶν. Nevertheless, since he had an interest in neo-Pythagoreanism as well as in philosophy in general, it is conceivable that his Jewish writings reflected more than sheer curiosity. If so, it is possible that he cited anti-Jewish writers only to ridicule them.

adopted the name from Gnaeus Cornelius Lentulus who had brought him to Rome as a slave during Sulla's Eastern campaign and who appointed him his pedagogue. Already an old man, Alexander perished when his house had burned down, whereupon his wife, Helene, committed suicide. Because of his remarkable productivity, the name Polyhistor was attached to him.[60] No less than twenty-five titles of his works have been preserved. His Latin pupil, Julius Hyginus (64 B.C.-A.D. 17), was in charge of the Palatine Library, founded by Augustus, and was almost as productive as his master. According to Jacoby, Alexander Polyhistor gained his freedom and Roman citizenship circa 82 B.C., when he was perhaps 20 or 30. The Oxford Classical Dictionary gives his date of birth as circa 105 B.C. Since Hyginus was brought by Caesar from Alexandria to Rome in 47 and studied under Alexander Polyhistor, the latter must have still been active in the 40's, and perhaps even the 30's B.C.[61]

The fragments of Alexander Polyhistor's writings are among the most significant that remain from the Hellenistic period. Our first and chief source for the neo-Pythagorean philosophical system, he served as an important source for the geographer Stephanus of Byzantium and for Diogenes Laertius' biographies of the Greek philosophers.[62] It is also through the writings of Alexander Polyhistor that we have remnants of men such as Berossus of Babylon (293/2 B.C.), who was the most important historian of Babylon to write in Greek.[63] Alexander Polyhistor was primarily interested in the East, although no section of the known world was outside his purview. Unfortunately, his writings suffer the same fate as that of the immense library he copied; none of it has survived. He is known to us chiefly through the specialized information preserved by Diogenes Laertius and Stephanus of Byzantium and through the writings of Clement of Alexandria and Eusebius of Caesarea.[64]

---

60   Alexander Polyhistor, *FGrH* 273 TT 1-3; Jacoby's commentary, IIIa 249 f.: Schwartz, "Alexander Polyhistor," in *R.E.*, I, 1449.

61   Seutonius, De *gramm.*, 20 = 273 T 3. Cf. Tolkiehn, "Iulius," No. 278, *R.E.*, X (1917), 628-51, esp. 628 f., for the biographical relationship with Alexander Polyhistor. See also von Gutschmid, *Kl. Schr.*, I, 160; Unger, "Wann schrieb Alexander Polyhistor?" *Philologus*, 43 (1884), 528-31; "Die Blüthezeit des Alexander Polyhistor," *Philologus*, 47 (1888), 177-83. The latest discussion, if not the most up-to-date, is in Albert-Marie Denis, *Introduction aux Pseudépigraphes grecs d'Ancien Testament* (Leiden, E. J. Brill, 1970), 244-46.

62   Steph. Byz. in Alexander Polyhistor, 273 FF 1-11, 13-16, 21-29, 31-63, 65-75, 78, 83-84, 95-96, 112-40; Diogenes Laertius in 273 FF 85-93; Diels-Krantz, *Die Fragmente der Vorsokratiker*[6] (1951), I, 43 (Pherecydes); I, 382, 30f. (Damon); I, 448, 33-451, 19 (Pythagoreans); I, 463, 30 f. (Pythagoreans); II, 236, 5-16.

63   Berossus, 680 FF la-b; 3a-b; 4a-b; 5; 8b; Abydenus, 685 FF 1-7; Alexander Polyhistor, 273 FF 79-81. See Eusebius, *Die Chronik* (Armenian), tr. by J. Karst (Die Griechischen christlichen Schriftsteller der ersten drei Jahrhunderte; König. Preuss. Akademie der Wissenschaften, Leipzig, 1911), 4-20, and passim; Paul Schanbel, *Berossos und die babylosnisch-hellenistische Literatur* (Berlin-Leipzig, Teubner, 1923).

64   See note 62. *FGrH* 273 F 19; Nos. 722-30; 732-33.

Eusebius has preserved a significant sample of Alexander Polyhistor's works in the *Praeparatio Evangelica*. Two-thirds of the ninth book of this work consists of extracts from Polyhistor's monograph *On the Jews*. In Mras' remarkable edition of the *Praeparatio*, the excerpt from Alexander Polyhistor's *On the Jews* fills more than forty-five pages of continuous Greek text.[65] Eusebius apparently kept intact the sequence of his original though he excerpted parts of it. More important, he by and large retained the names of the sources quoted in the original, and thus evidently has preserved the basic structure of Alexander Polyhistor's monograph, *On the Jews:*

1. [Eupolemus] (Pseudo-Eupolemus). On Abraham.[66]
2. Artapanus. On Abraham[67]
3. Anonymous (Pseudo-Eupolemus?). Abraham's descent from the giants.[68]
4. Appolonius Molon of Rhodes. On Abraham.[69]
5. Demetrius. On the sacrifice of Isaac.[70]
6. Philo (the Elder?). Abraham's circumcision.[71]
7. Cleodomus-Malchus. The African descendants of Abraham and Keturah.[72]
8. Demetrius. The chronology of Jacob's twelve sons and their descent into Egypt.[73]
9. Theodotus. The rape of Dinah.[74]
10. Artapanus. Joseph's rule of Egypt.[75]

65   Eusebius, *Die Praeparatio Evangelica,* ed. Karl Mras (Berlin, Akademie-Verlag, 1954), I, 502, 13-548, 20.

66   *P.E.,* IX, 17, I, 502, 17-504, 9. = 724 F 1. Cf. now Wacholder, *HUCA* 34 (1963), 83-113; Walter, *Klio,* 43-45 (1965), 282-90. See now Denis, *Introduction aux Pseudépigraphes Grecs,* 252-55, esp. 252.

67   *P.E.,* IX, 18, I, 504, 10-18 = 724 F 1. Denis, ibid., 255-57; A. Schalit, in *Encyclopaedia Judaica* (Jerusalem, 1971), 3, cols. 645-46.

68   *P.E.,* IX, 18, I, 504, 18-505, 3 = 724 F 2. Cf. note 66, and Wacholder, in *Encyclopaedia Judaica,* s. v. "Eupolemus," VI, cols. 964 f.

69   *P.E.,* IX, 19, I = 728 TT 1-5; FF 1-4; Cf. A. Schalit, in *Encyclopaedia Judaica,* 3, col. 188.

70   *P.E.,* IX, 19, I, 505, 19-23 = 722 F 1. Cf. now Wacholder, in *Encyclopaedia Judaica,* s. v. "Demetrius," 5, cols. 1490-91; Denis, Introduction aux *Pseudépigraphes grecs,* 248-51.

71   Philo, *P.E.,* 20, I, 506, 1-507, 4 = 729 F 1. Cf. now Wacholder, in *Encyclopaedia Judaica,* s. v. "Philo the Elder," 13, cols. 408-09; Denis, ibid., 270-73.

72   *P.E.,* IX, 20, 2, I, 507, 8-509, 4 = Jos., *A.J.,* I, 238-41 = 727 F 1. Cf. now Wacholder, in *Encyclopaedia Judaica s.v.* "Cleodomus-Malchus," 5, col. 603; Denis, ibid., 259-61.

73   *P.E.,* IX, 21, I, 508, 5-512, 10 = 722 F 2. See note 70.

74   *P.E.,* IX, 22, I, 512, 11-516, 10 = 732 F 1. Cf. now Wacholder, in *Encyclopaedia Judaica s.v.* "Theodotus," 15, cols. 1102-03; Denis, *Introduction aux Pseudépigraphes grecs,* 270-73.

75   *P.E.,* IX, 23, I, 516, 13-517, 14 = 726 F 2. See note 67.

11. Philo (the Elder?). Joṣeph's dream.[76]
12. Aristeas. Job and his three friends.[77]
13. Eupolemus. Moses the wisest of men.[78]
14. Artapanus. Moses repels an Ethiopian invasion of Egypt, founds the Egyptian religion, and liberates the Jews.[79]
15. Ezekielus. The epic of the exodus: Moses.[80]
16. Demetrius. The genealogy of Moses.[81]
17. Ezekielus. The epic of the exodus: Pharoah and the plagues.[82]
18. Demetrius. The bitter waters at Elim.[83]
19. Ezechielus. The epic of the exodus: The fiery pillar and the marvelous eagle.[84]
20. Demetrius. Whence did the Israelites receive their weapons in the desert?[85]
21. Eupolemus. From Moses to Solomon's construction of the Temple.[86]
22. Theophilus. The sculpture of the Tyrian princess made of the surplus gold of the temple.[87]
23. Eupolemus. The shields of the Temple and Solomon's death.[88]
24. Timochares. *On Antiochus*. The dimensions of the city.[89]
25. Anonymous (Xenophon of Lampascus?). *The Dimensions of Syria:* The location of Jerusalem and the dimensions of her walls.[90]

76 *P.E.*, IX, 24, I, 517, 15-518, 3 = 729 F 3. See note 71.
77 *P.E.*, IX, 25, I, 518, 5-22 + = 525 F 1. See now Wacholder, in *Encyclopaedia Judaica, s.v.* "Aristeas," 3, cols. 438-39; Denis, *Introduction aux Pseudégraphes grecs,* 258-59.
78 *P.E.*, IX, 26, I, 519, 5-7 = 723 F la. Cf. note 66.
79 *P.E.*, IX, 27, I, 519, 8-524, 12 = 725 F 3. See note 75.
80 *P.E.*, IX, 28, I, 524, 13-527, 26; J. Wieneke, *Ezechielis Exagoge fragmenta,* (Münster, Monasterii Westfalorum 1931), 2-8; Denis, *Introduction aux Pseudépigraphes grecs,* 270-77.
81 *P.E.*, IX, 29, I, 528, 1-18 = 722 F 2. See note 73.
82 *P.E.*, IX, 29, 4-14, I, 529, 1-536, 20 =Wieneke, *Ezechielis Exagoge,* 8-22. See note 80.
83 *P.E.*, IX, 29, 15, I, 536, 22-28 = 722 F 4. See note 81.
84 *P.E.*, IX, 29, 16, I, 537, 1-538, 6; = Wieneke, *Ezechielis Exagoge,* 22-26. See note 82.
85 *P.E.*,IX, 29, 16, I, 538 8-10 = 722 F 5. See note 83.
86 *P.E.*, IX, 30-34, 18, I, 538, 11-544, 16 = 523 F 2b. See note 78.
87 *P.E.*, IX, 34, 19, I, 544, 18-20=733 F 1. See *Encyclopaedia Judaica,* 7, col. 897.
88 *P.E.*, IX, 34, 20, I, 545, 1-4 = 723 F 3. See note 86.
89 *P.E.*, IX, 35, I, 545, 5-11 = 165 F 1.
90 *P.E.*, IX, 36, I, 545; 12-18 = 849 F 1. But contrary to Jacoby, as pointed out by Mras (App. Crit. on lines 14-18, p. 545), Timochares (see previous note) is probably also the author of this fragment, ascribed by Mueller to Xenophon of Lampascus (*FGH,* III, 228). As to the contradiction in the two fragments concerning circumference of Jerusalem it is likely that Timochares was citing here divergent authorities.

26. Philo (the Elder?). The water supply of Jerusalem.[91]

27. Aristeas (Letter of). The water supply of Jerusalem.[92]

28. Eupolemus. Jeremiah's prophecy and Nebuchadnezzar's destruction of the temple.[93]

All but one of Eusebius' twenty-eight quotations from Alexander Polyhistor were taken from the latter's *On the Jews*.[94] The exception (No. 7) was copied by Eusebius from Josephus' *Jewish Antiquities,* and evidently was derived from Alexander Polyhistor's account of Libya. In Eusebius' list, Alexander Polyhistor cited some fourteen different authors, six of them two to five times. The actual number of sources mentioned in Alexander Polyhistor's *On the Jews* must have been much larger, since Eusebius excerpted only a portion of the monograph.

Also of primary significance is the fact that both Alexander Polyhistor and his copyist Eusebius quoted their sources verbatim, paraphrasing very infrequently. An interesting example is No. 7, where Eusebius says that he is quoting Alexander Polyhistor indirectly from Josephus. As Josephus' text is extant, it is enlightening to compare the same passage in the critical editions of Eusebius and Josephus. Such a comparison shows that the literary remains of Eusebius have more faithfully preserved the original of Josephus than did the manuscripts of Josephus themselves.[95] Perhaps this was because Eusebius had here compared Josephus' quotation with the source in a copy of Alexander Polyhistor. It is more likely, however, that Eusebius simply had a copy of Josephus superior to the extant manuscripts of Josephus. At any rate, it is clear that Eusebius scrupulously noted the use of any source other than Alexander Polyhistor's own work. Eusebius' citations were more often than not full and verbatim rather than brief paraphrases. This was of course true not only in Eusebius' use of Alexander Polyhistor but in his use of other authors as well. Eusebius' quotations from Plato, according to Mras, are usually more reliable than the available manuscripts of the philosopher.[96]

91   *P.E.,* IX, 37, I, 546, 1-547, 5 = 729 F 2. See note 76.

92   *P.E.,* IX, 38, I, 547, 9-20 = Letter of Aristeas, 88-90, Denis, *Introduction aux Pseudépigraphes,* 105-106. Incidentally, of the proposed dates of the Letter of Aristeas, listed by Denis (109 f.), the ones that are after the last quarter of the first century B.C. must be erroneous if Eusebius is right that Alexander Polyhistor used this work.

93   *P.E.,* IX, 39, I, 548, 4-20 = 723 F 5 (Walter F 4). See note 88.

94   The quotation from the Letter of Aristeas (No. 27), evidently, is no exception, as Alexander Polyhistor cited it in his account of the dimensions of Jerusalem. See above, Ch. I, note 23.

95   Cf. Cleodomus-Malchus in *A.J.,* I, 238-41 with *P.E.,* IX, 20. A future editor of Josephus would do well to pay somewhat more attention to the testimony of Eusebius than did Niese, who has become the standard. However, as pointed out to me by John Strugnell, the fault here is not Josephus', but Niese's edition.

96   See Mras, introduction to *P.E.,* I, pp. LV-LVIII; "Ein Vorwort zur neuen Eusebausgabe," *Rh.M.,* XCII (N.F., 1944), 217-36.

The literary tradition of the excerpts from Alexander Polyhistor's *On the Jews* is, therefore, relatively well attested.

Granting that Eusebius as a rule quoted accurately—how do we know that Alexander Polyhistor did likewise? Hellenistic writers frequently transformed their sources, embellishing them or quoting out of context. It is impossible to prove that Alexander Polyhistor did not follow the same trend, but it is rather unlikely that he did so. The multiplicity of his works would indicate that they were formed by piecing together long quotations. Moreover, writers who radically transformed their sources were usually motivated by a desire to display their literary skills. Sometimes they set out to prove a certain point. In the extant fragments of Alexander Polyhistor there are no traces of such literary or ideological ambitions. Whenever a comparison can be made, such as when quoting meter, Alexander Polyhistor is no worse than any other ancient copyist. Josephus, for example, generally quotes ancient authors reliably, except that he tends to misinterpret or to quote out of context, but Alexander Polyhistor displays no such credal or nationalist bias. This is clear from the fact that, as long as the subject matter is the same, he strung together quotations from a passionate Jew, a Samaritan, and an Anti-Judaean. Anti-Jewish antiquarians could find in his works such gems as these: the name of an ancestor of the Jews was Gelos (Laughter = Isaac); Judah and Idumaea (Edom, Esau?) were the sons of Semiramis; and Moses was a woman.[97] The anti-Jewish literature thus antedates the first century B.C. Alexander Polyhistor did not hesitate to quote such passages side by side with lengthy excerpts which passionately extolled the virtues of the Jewish people. In other words, Alexander Polyhistor neither sided with the Jews nor with the anti-Semites and had no reason to doctor his sources one way or the other. He might be charged with a lack of discrimination, but never with writing tendentiously.

We can deduce from the table of contents that Alexander Polyhistor's monograph *On the Jews* probably began with an account of the giants, followed with a detailed and many-sided description of the days of the patriarchs and Moses, and continued through the destruction of the Temple in 586 B.C., abbreviating here and there, but generally reiterating the emphasis of the works that he was excerpting. It follows further that Alexander Polyhistor assembled his material on Jewish affairs according to the sequence of the historical books of the Bible, beginning with the early sections of Genesis and ending with the last chapter of II Kings or II Chronicles. The question has often been raised whether pagan writers were acquainted with the Greek version of the Hebrew Scriptures. Alexander Polyhistor not only displays a mastery of biblical history, but he also uses it

97   Alexander Polyhistor, 273 FF 70; 121. Cf. Appollonius Molon, 728 F 1. On the other hand, the fragments of Molon were distinctly anti-Jewish; this was not the case with the alleged descent of Juda from Semiramis, which was possibly intended to be flattering.

as the basis for his works on the Jews. And there is no reason to assume that he was the only heathen of the pre-Christian period with a knowledge of the Septuagint.

Whether or not Alexander brought down the history of the Jews to his own time is an open question. The fact that Eusebius' quotations cease with the destruction of the Solomonic Temple is no proof that the *On the Jews* likewise ended at this point. Because he regards Alexander Polyhistor as a present-centered historian rather than as a sheer antiquarian, Jacoby takes it for granted that the monograph concluded roughly with Pompey's annexation of Syria.[98]

Some support for this contention may be found in an abbreviated entry of the fifth century lexicographer Stephanus of Byzantium under the heading of *Judaea:* "Alexander Polyhistor: Semiramis' children Judah and Idumaea (as Claudius Jolaus reports), from Judaeus (Udaeus?) of Sparta, one who together with Dionysus beginning from Thebes led an expedition (to India). He was a national of the Judaeans but, according to some, of the Idumaeans."[99] Strange as it may seem, this bizarre genealogy was intended to be flattering to the Jews. But as pointed out by Momigliano, Alexander Polyhistor appears to be alluding to a tradition, preserved also in I Macc. 12:6-23, that concocted a common ancestry for the Spartans and the Jews. If so, perhaps Alexander Polyhistor dealt with this matter in his treatment of the Maccabean period. His indirect source was possibly Eupolemus, who may have noted the alleged kinship of two distinct and remote—yet in many respects remarkably alike—peoples.

Thus far our reasoning is based on the supposition that the fragment cited by Stephanus of Byzantium came from Alexander Polyhistor's monograph *On the Jews.* Although likely, this is not certain. For we know that Alexander Polyhistor wove Jewish themes into some of his other writings. He recorded the tower of Babel in his *Babylonica;* in his *Libyca,* the African descendants of Abraham and Keturah; in his account of Rome, the feminine sex of

---

98   Jacoby, *FGrH,* IIIa, 269, 12-17; cf. p. 255. Because of the extensive use by Steph. Byz. (see note 62), the geographical material in the fragments predominates, reflecting an emphasis on current affairs. But his interest in Neo-Pythagoreans (FF 93-94), Indians (F 18), and Jews (FF 19, 101), suggests a penchant for the bizarre.

99   Stephanus of Byzantiums, *s.v.* Ἰουδαία·Ἀλέξανδρος ὁ Πολυίστορ·ἀπὸ τῶν παίδων Σεμιράμιδος Ἰούδα καὶ Ἰδουμαία. . .ἀπὸ Οὐδαίου Σπάρτων <ἐν> ὃς ἐκ Θήβης μετὰ Διονύσου ἐστρατεύκοτος (Alexander Polyhistor, 273 F 121 = Claudius Iolaus, 788 F 4, but omitting the last sentence). The text was sharply abbreviated, almost to no comprehension. The manuscripts read Ἰουδαίος,but Schubart and Meineke emended this to Οὐδαίος. For a fuller treatment of the subject, see A. Momigliano, *Prime linee di storia della Tradizione maccabaica* (Turin, Casa Editrice Giovanni Chiantore, 1931; 2nd ed., Amsterdam, Hakkert, 1968), 144-51. Cf. H. von Geisau, "Udaios," No. 4, *R.E.,* Suppl. IX (1962), 1432.

Moses.[100] But it is still likely, though we cannot be sure, that Alexander Polyhistor's allusion to the common ancestry of the Jews and Spartans comes from his monograph on Jewish history. Furthermore, it is a fair assumption that Alexander Polyhistor was here dependent on the manufactured correspondence, recorded in I Macc. 12:6-23, between King Areius of Sparta and High Priest Onias. As has been noted above, Eupolemus was probably the mendacious authority used by the author of the First Book of Maccabees as well as by Alexander Polyhistor's source.

On the basis of Jacoby's reasoning that Alexander Polyhistor's specialized monographs on strange peoples were inspired by Pompey's conquest of the Seleucid empire, *On the Jews* would be dated about 60 B.C. But Jacoby's reasoning is not necessarily cogent. It might be argued with equal force that Alexander Polyhistor's works resulted from curiosity about the cultural and religious history of the East. The subject of many of the fragments is strictly religious, although many other remnants also deal with geography. However, Jacoby's assumption that Pompey had patronized Alexander Polyhistor would explain a puzzling problem.[101] From where did this pagan historian receive copies of rather obscure writers? If Alexander Polyhistor's other works were as detailed and as dependent on rare sources as was his monograph *On the Jews,* he must have had at his disposal the support of the state.[102] It would follow that his monographs were not merely antiquarian tracts, but handbooks that served as a background for the Roman occupation forces. As such they would have had to be as up-to-date as possible. Contrary to Jacoby, however, there remains a possibility that the Rome of Cicero and Caesar was a sophisticated place where books were readily available. But even if Jacoby's reasoning is rejected, it is unlikely that Alexander would have concluded his Jewish history with the Babylonian captivity; this would be quite an unnatural ending point for a pagan author. Rome's conquest of Syria probably would have made a wonderful finale.

In the fragments of *On the Jews,* Alexander Polyhistor quotes Eupolemus more often than any other historian. Specifically, we know that the pagan historian cited Eupolemus' accounts of Abraham, Moses, the span of centuries from Joshua to the construction of the temple by Solomon;

---

100   Alexander Polyhistor, 273 F 102 = *A.J.* I, 238-40; 273 F 79 = Abydenus 685 F 4. Alexander Polyhistor's citation of Or. Sibyll. III, 97 ff. = 273 F 79 = *A.J.,* I, 118 = Syncellus, *Chronographia* (Paris, 1652), 44. Concerning Alexander Polyhistor's part in the transmission of the Sibylline tradition, see Nikiprowetzky, *La Troisiéme Sibylle,* 11-36.

101   Jacoby, *FGrH,* IIIa, 256, 22-30.

102   It is conceivable, though, that the wide interest in Judaism in Roman circles accounts for the rather rare material found in Rome. See Varro's interest in Judaism. (Cf. Norden, "Varro über den Gott der Juden," in *Festgabe Harnack* [Tübingen, 1921], 298 f.).

Jeremiah; and the chronological summaries. An error in Alexander Polyhistor would seem to show that Eupolemus was indeed his most important source for the history of the Jews. The account of Abraham attributed by Alexander Polyhistor to Eupolemus was proven conclusively by Freudenthal to have been penned by a Samaritan.[103] Such an error would be reasonable if it were assumed that Alexander Polyhistor habitually quoted Eupolemus.

JOSEPHUS

Although the pagan historian Alexander Polyhistor made extensive use of the writings of the Graeco-Jewish historians, the Jews Philo of Alexandria and Josephus studiously ignored their predecessors. Philo's failure to cite the allegorical exegete Aristobulus was due perhaps to his custom of not acknowledging his predecessors, of whom there must have been many.[104] Josephus, however, mentioned Eupolemus twice. He paraphrased I Maccabee's account of Eupolemus' diplomatic mission to Rome. Again, as has already been pointed out, Josephus listed Eupolemus along with Demetrius (confused there with the one of Phaleron) and Philo the Elder as Gentile historians dealing with Jewish history who, although they did their best, knew little, since the Hebrew sources were locked to them.[105] This inaccurate statement of Josephus should have led to the conclusion that Josephus' knowledge of Graeco-Jewish historians was rather minimal. Nevertheless, men such as Bloch, Schlatter, Gaster, and Thackeray have maintained that Josephus quoted Eupolemus as well as the other Graeco-Jewish historians without acknowledging his indebtedness.[106] This is a view based primarily on intuition, not a single passage having been adduced to substantiate their position.[107]

103   See Wacholder, *HUCA*, XXXIV (1963), 83-85; Walter, *Klio*, 43-45 (1965), 282-90.

104   For Philo's debt to his predecessors, see E. Stein, *Die allegorische Exegese des Philo aus Alexandreia* (Giessen, 1921); "Alttestamentliche Bibelkritik in der apäthellenistischen Literatur," *Collectanea Theologica*, XVI (1935), 38-83.

105   *A.J.*, XII, 415-19; *C. Apionem*, I, 218.

106   H. Bloch, *Die Quellen des Flavius Josephus in seiner Archäologie* (Leipzig, 1879), 58 ff.; A. Schlatter, "Eupolemus als Chronolog und seine Beziehungen zu Josephus und Manetho," in *Theologische Studien und Kritiken* (1891), 633-703; *The Asatir: The Samaritan Book of the "Secrets of Moses,"* edited and translated by M. Gaster (London, the Royal Asiatic Society, [1927], 63-65, 69-71). Of all the writers who assume Josephus' dependence on Eupolemus, Schlatter is the most extreme. Josephus' chronology, scattered throughout the works, novella of Moses (*A.J.*, II, 232-253), of Tobiads (*A.J.*, XII, 154-236), and similar material, when not dependent on Nicolaus of Damascus, was borrowed from Eupolemus. However, Josephus knew Eupolemus only through Alexander Polyhistor, according to Schlatter.

107   Schlatter (see previous note), maintained that Josephus' biblical chronology (*A.J.*, XX, 224-240) was taken from Eupolemus' (723 F 4). In fact Eupolemus and Josephus diverge more often than they agree. For a different treatment of Josephus'

Other scholars (Freudenthal, Staehlin, Schwartz, Hölscher, Reinach) maintain that Josephus did made use of Hellenistic Jewish writers, but that he knew them only indirectly through Alexander Polyhistor's collection.[108] Two passages are cited in support of this theory. In *Antiquities*, I, 240-241, Josephus quotes an otherwise unknown historian Cleodomus-Malchus that the progeny of Abraham and Keturah populated Africa.[109] Here Josephus expressly says that he knew Cleodomus-Malchus only from Alexander Polyhistor's work. It is the only passage in which Josephus names Alexander Polyhistor.

Unhappily, Josephus was not always as scrupulous in reproducing both his direct authority and the authority's source. This becomes evident from a passage, also found in *Antiquities*, where Josephus supports the historicity of the biblical tower of Babel with a quotation from the Sibylline Oracles.[110] As this work is extant, it is possible to check on the historian. The substance of the statement that mankind had originally been monolingual is indeed found in the third book of this work, but the quotation in *Jewish Antiquities* is a prose paraphrase of the original. That Josephus himself was not responsible for the paraphrase becomes clear from the fragments of Abydenus (flourished during the second century of the Christian era). Abydenus made extensive excerpts from Alexander Polyhistor's monograph on Babylonia, including his paraphrase of our passage in the Sibylline Oracles.[111] Since Abydenus was not aware of Josephus, the identical wording of the quotation from the Sibyll in both can only be accounted for by the assumption that

chronology, though dealing primarily with the later period, see G. Hölscher, *Die Hohenpriesterliste bei Josephus* (Heildelberg, 1940). Of the preserved Graeco-Jewish historians, the only account possibly used by Josephus is Artapanus' tale of Moses' Ethiopian campaign (*A.J.*, II, 238-57); Artapanus, (*P.E.* IX, 27 = 726 F 3). But as has been often pointed out (cf. Thackeray, ad locum), there is no reason to suppose that Josephus' version was based either on Artapanus or on Alexander Polyhistor's paraphrase thereof, though the two accounts were obviously related.

108   Niebuhr, *Gesch. Assur's*, 13; Freudenthal, *Hell. Studien.*, 26-31, 46, 49, n. 1, 61, n. 1, 161, 169-71; Stählin, in *Gesch. d. Griech. Lit.*, II[6], 1, p.594, n. 4; Hölscher *Die Quellen d. Josephus f. die Zeit von Exil bis* zum jüdischen Kriege (Lepizig, 1905), 50-52; Th. Reinach, in the French edition of Josephus (Paris, 1902), VII (*C. Apionem*, I, 218), p. 40, nn. 2, 4. According to Hölscher, Josephus copied I Macc. (*A.J.*, XII, 240-XIII, 214) from Alexander Polyhistor's version (Hölscher, p. 52).

109   Alexander Polyhistor, 273 F 102 = Cleodomus-Malchus, 727 F 1.

110   *A.J.*, I, 118 = Orac. Sibyll., III, 97-104. It is likely, as Alexandre pointed out (Charles Alexandre, *Oracula Sibyllina curante S.A.* II [Paris, 1856], 409-15), III, 1-96, had originally been part of Or. Sibyll. Book II, which is of Christian origin. If so, Alexander Polyhistor quoted the very beginning of the Book III. Nikiprowetzky (*La Troisiéme Sibylle*, 60-66), however, unconvincingly, I believe, defends the integrity of the entire Book III.

111   Berossus, 680 F 4a-b, p. 382, 19-383, 8 = Abydenus, 685 F 4.

both were relying on Alexander Polyhistor's rewording.[112]   Thus at least on
one occasion Josephus cited a Jewish work, even if it was one possibly
otherwise known to him, via the words of Alexander Polyhistor. And if he
knew Alexander Polyhistor, does it not follow that Josephus must have been
aware of the Graeco-Jewish writers cited prominently in Alexander Polyhistor's work?

Thus far the evidence is contradictory, *Contra Apionem* I, 218, indicates
Josephus assumed that Demetrius, Philo the Elder, and Eupolemus were
non-Jews. If so, it follows that he did not know the Graeco-Jewish historians
first-hand. However, it has been shown that Josephus did quote Cleodomus-
Malchus from Alexander Polyhistor and that he had also made reference to
the Sibylline Oracles, which he knew only through Alexander Polyhistor's
monograph. And having read Polyhistor, would Josephus not have recognized
that Eupolemus was a Jew?

The solution to this problem lies in a cogent suggestion made by Alfred
von Gutschmid and supported by Schwartz and Jacoby.[113]   Gutschmid
argued that Josephus' quotation of Cleodomus-Malchus was not taken from
Alexander Polyhistor's book *On the Jews*, but from that on Libya,[114]   and
that although Josephus knew Alexander Polyhistor's other monographs, he
did not, in fact, use the pagan's work on Jewish history.[115]   By itself this
would seem rather unreasonable. However, the other passage cited above—

112   Abydenus' date is not attested. Gutschmid, *Kl. Schr.,* I., 287, placed him
during Antiochus IV Ephiphanus' reign. Marcus von Niebuhr, *Geschichte Assur's und
Babel's seit Phul* (Berlin, 1857), 15, however argued that Abydenus was younger than
Josephus; otherwise the Jewish historians would have cited him. Since silence proves
little, this argument is rejected by Gelzer, *Sextus Julius Africanus,* II, 28, who showed
that Abydenus adopted Castor's chronology. Castor flourished in the middle of the first
century B.C. But Müller, *FGH,* IV, 279, dated Abydenus two centuries later, a view
accepted by Gelzer and Jacoby. There is no reason to assume, therefore, that he was
aware of Josephus' works. Both he and Josephus used Alexander Polyhistor independently (Wachsmuth, *Einleitung in das Studium der alten Geschichte,* 374 f.).

113   Gutschmid, *Kl. Schr.,* II, 182; E. Schwartz, in *R.E.,* I (1884), 1451: 43 Jacoby,
FGrH, IIIa, 287, 20 f.: 301, 10-17: "Kleodomos," in *R.E.* (1921), 675; Walter, *Der
Thoraausleger,* 55 n. 1.

114   Gutschmid, ibid. II, 182. For the fragments of his *Libyca* see 273 FF 32-47;
115; 120; 124. In "Cleodomus-Malchus," in *Encyclopaedia Judaica,* 5 col. 603, I argue
that a) the fact that Josephus called him a prophet; b) the reference to Moses as *their*
lawgiver (*A.J.* IX, 240); c) the attribution of the Book of Genesis to Moses; and d) the
synchretistic genealogy make it more likely than not that Cleodomus-Malchus was not a
Jew. See below, note 119, for the view that regard him either as a Jew or a Samaritan.

115   In Josephus' list of the heathen historians who wrote about Jews (*C. Apionem,*
I, 213-18), Alexander Polyhistor's name is missing. Did then Josephus regard him as a
Jewish writer: cf. above, notes 97-102.

from the Sibylline Oracles—tends to support Gutschmid's theory.[116] Alexander Polyhistor's paraphrase of the Sibylline Oracles, as attested by Abydenus, comes from his monograph on Babylonia rather than from his Jewish history.

It should be noted that Josephus knew the quotation only from Alexander Polyhistor's paraphrase instead of from the original text of the Sibylline Oracles. This indicates that the pseudograph was probably not available to him and that, like many of his coreligionists, he regarded it as a pagan work. Had he been aware of the Jewish contaminations, it is hardly likely that he would have cited it as a heathen testimony for the veracity of a biblical tradition. In the case of the Sibylline quotation, however, Josephus may be excused for failing to recognize its Jewish origin. He happened to be interested in Berossus' account of the Babylonian Xisuthros (Noah), which he knew only through Alexander Polyhistor.[117] There he found the Sibylline reference, which Alexander Polyhistor had inserted to complement Berossus' version of the period of the giants.[118] It was rather difficult for Josephus to show a clear link between Berossus and the Bible, but a connection between the Sibyll and the story of Babel was easy to prove.

As has been pointed out above, Alexander Polyhistor made use of works dealing with Jewish history not only in his specialized monograph on this subject but in other works as well. Josephus knew Alexander Polyhistor's *Libyca* in which he cited Cleodomus-Malchus' claim that linked the African tribes with Abraham. Incidentally, it is possible that this Cleodomus-Malchus was a heathen—not a Jew, as is generally believed; nor a Samaritan, as maintained by Freudenthal.[119] Josephus also knew Alexander Polyhistor's

---

116   *A.J.*, I, 118 = Or. Sibyll., III 97-104; cf. Berossus, 680 F 4a-b; Abydenus, 685 F 4. Cf. Paul Schnabel, *Berossos und die babylonisch-hellenistische Literatur* (Leipzig-Berlin, Teubner, 1923), 79-93. For the tradition that Sabbe or Sibylle, the daughter of Berossus and his wife Erymanthe, was the author of the Babylonian-Jewish Sibylline Oracles, see Pausanias, X, 12, 9; Ps.-Justin, *Exh. to the Greeks*, 37; *Suda*, s. v. "Sibylla Delphis" = Berossus, 680 T 7a-c.

117   See Gutschmid, *Kl. Schr.* IV, 491 f.

118   Alexander Polyhistor, *Chaldaeca*, but the title is not certain, *Assyriaca* and/or *Babyloniaca* is just as possible. See 273 T 7a-c. This work is primarily preserved in Eusebius' *Chronique* (in Armenian) and Abydenus' *Chronography*, as quoted by Syncellus. For a collection see 273 FF 79-81; 680 F 1a-b; Abydenus, 685 FF 1-6.

119   Freudenthal (*Hellenistische Studien*, 130-36) postulated that Cleodomus-Malchus was a Samaritan on the basis of the syncretistic coloring of his fragment as well as on his non-Jewish name, whom Alexander Polyhistor had labeled him "the prophet." Schürer (*Gesch. d jüd. Volkes*, III⁴, 481) and Jacoby (*R.E.* XI [1921], 675) reject Freudenthal's reasoning, regarding Malchus as a Jew. Cf. however, Herzfeld (*Gesch. d. Volkes Yisrael*, III, 489, 577); Ewald (*Gesch. d. Volkes Israel*, VII, 92); and above note 114, for a contrary view.

Babyloniaca which quoted the Sibyll. Of Alexander Polyhistor's collection of Jewish historians, however, Josephus knew very little, if anything.[120]

Contra Apionem, I, 218, does show that Josephus was aware of Demetrius, Philo the Elder, and Eupolemus. Whether he knew their works directly or only through Alexander Polyhistor's collection is the question. It is hardly believable that, as in the case of the Sibylline passage, Josephus assumed they were pagans, because he knew their writings only through a pagan source. The consideration of such a supposition, however, depends on one's opinion of Josephus' critical acumen. Another possibility is that Josephus' mention of these three historians was a response to criticism directed against him. For many years Josephus had enjoyed the imperial patronage as court historian of the Jews. But during the last decade of the first century he was challenged by Justus of Tiberias, a protégé of King Agrippa II, who was a great-grandson of Herod the First. Like Josephus, Justus wrote two histories. In the first he not only gave a different version of the Jewish-Roman war, but claimed to unmask Josephus' anti-Roman role. In the second, he wrote a detailed but concise history of the Jews from their early beginnings, including chronological tables.[121] It was apparently a highly learned piece of work, based on pagan and Jewish synchronistic tables. There is evidence that Justus made use of the Graeco-Jewish historians.[122] By stressing chronology, Justus revealed a glaring weakness in Josephus' works. In Justus' work one could find such information as who the rulers of Egypt, Argos, or Athens were in the time of Moses, and similar synchronisms for other leading personalities.[123] In other words, Justus interwove Jewish with general history. But

120   Cf. Gutschmid, *Kl. Schr.,* IV, 491 f., who shows that Josephus' quotation of Berossus (*A.J.,* I, 93-95 = 680 F 4c) was based on his reading of Alexander Polyhistor, rather than of the original.

121   Justus is known mostly through strictures in Josephus' *Vita.* But Photius, the ninth century Byzantine patriarch of Constantinople, reviewed a copy of Justus' chronicle (Photius, *Bibl.* 31 = 734 T 2). Photius castigated Justus for his failure to allude to Jesus or Christianity. Cf. H. Luther, *Josephus und Justus von Tiberias* (Halle, 1910), 49-54; Schürer (*Gesch. d. jüd. Volkes,* I[4], 58-63, esp. 59) questions, without good reason, the tradition (734 T 1 = Jer., *Der vir. ill.,* 14) that Justus had written biblical commentaries. In a poorly preserved author, due to the fact that nothing has survived, it is insufficient proof that it had not existed, The commentarial tradition was already several centuries old among the Jews, dating to since Aristobulus and Philo, as well as the Dead Sea scrolls; among the Greeks since 500 B.C., as Homeric allegory was first utilized by Theagenes of Rhegium; but compendious line-by-line commentaries (*Hypomnemata*) were written by Aristarchus of Samothrace (c. 215-145 B.C.) and Didymus of Alexandria (80-10 B.C.).

122   Cf. his title (Photius, *Bibl.* 31 = 734 T 2, 695, 15; heading of FF 1-3) with that of Demetrius (722 F 1), and of Eupolemus (723 F 1b).

123   Justus, 734 FF 2-3. The use of, among others, Castor, Ptolemy of Mendes, and perhaps Alexander Polyhistor is implied (cf. Gelzer, *Sextus Julius Africanus,* 207; Jacoby, "Iustus'. No. 9, *R.E.,* X [1919], 1344 f.).

Justus apparently considered himself part of the Graeco-Jewish literary tradition. Josephus, however, presented himself not as part of a chain, but as the first Graeco-Jewish historian.[124] *Contra Apionem,* I, 218, makes it clear that, as far as he knew, Josephus never utilized the writings of Demetrius, Philo the Elder, or Eupolemus. And this no doubt was also true of other Graeco-Jewish writers, including Aristeas the historian; Artapanus, Theodotus, Theophilus, Timochares, and a host of others whose names have been forgotten. The only Graeco-Jewish historian Josephus ever admits knowing was his antagonist Justus of Tiberias, and this only in his *Autobiography.*[125]

This is not to say that the case was as clear-cut as Josephus wishes us to believe. The fact is that he did use Jewish works, such as the Sibylline Oracles on the tower of Babel, Cleodomus-Malchus' list of Abraham's African progeny, the several versions of Pseudo-Hecataeus, or for that matter the Letter of Aristeas.[126] But although the Jewish authorship of most, if not all, of these works is certain, as far as Josephus was concerned they were pagan writings attesting to the glory of the Jewish people. Although it is possible to argue otherwise, Josephus' books display a naivité which suggests that his belief in the non-Jewish origin of these works was quite sincere.

THE CHURCH FATHERS

The fate of the Graeco-Jewish historians during the second century of our era is obscure. Gaster argued that since the Seder Olam, attributed to Rabbi Jose ben Halafta (*circa* 150), gave the same date for Solomon's age at his coronation as did Eupolemus, it follows that the former derived this bit of information from the latter.[127] On the other hand, Nestle, Kittel, Stade, Rahlfs, and Montgomery have maintained that III Kingdoms 2:12, which reports the same date, was also dependent on Eupolemus.[128] It seems,

---

124   Josephus (*A.J.,* XVI, 174-78) says that his history was addressed to the Greeks. The point he seems to be making is that, in contrast to the Graeco-Jewish writers, who had written for the Hellenized Jews, he thought exclusively of the pagan audience. (f 737 F 3.)

125   See below. It should be noted that although Josephus mentions Philo (*A.J.,* XVIII, 259 f.), he does it only in connection with the Alexandrian's embassy to Rome, not his writings.

126   Josephus, *A.J.* XII, 17, goes beyond the original when he makes Aristeas an influential official, denying his Jewishness to the king (XII, 23).

127   IMoses Gaster, "Demetrius und der Seder Olam," in *Festskrift Simonsen* (Copenhagen, 1923), 243-52.

128   R. Kittel, *Die Bücher der Könige* (Leipzig, 1904), 68; P. Nestle, "Wie alt war Salomo als er zur Regierung kam?" *ZAW,* II (1882), 321-14; A. Rahlfs, *Septuaginta Studien,* III (1911), 112 f.; J.A. Montgomery, *The Books of Kings* (The International Critical Commentary: New York, Charles Scribner's Sons, 1951), 91.

however, that a tradition found in such diverse sources was evidently based on a lost Hebrew work, perhaps a divergent Hebrew text of the Book of Kings.[129] We cannot, therefore, assume that the author of Seder Olam depended on Eupolemus.

The preservation of bits of Hellenistic Graeco-Jewish writings was due entirely to the Church Fathers. The rabbinic authorities felt no need to prove that the Jews were more ancient than the Greeks. The tannaitic ban on "Greek wisdom" supposedly included the writings of the Graeco-Jewish historians and philosophers.[130] This is not to say that these writings were fully suppressed. The paintings on the walls of the synagogue at Dura-Europos show that the artists were inspired by the Hellenistic versions of biblical history. Curiously, the themes preserved in Eupolemus' fragments are also among those painted on the walls of the synagogue, such as the site of the ark at Shiloh, the bringing of the ark to Jerusalem, Solomon's temple in a Hellenistic style, and the prophet Elijah.[131] The fresco of the exodus in Dura-

---

129   LXX III Kingdoms 2:12; Eupolemus, in Eus. IX, 30, 8 = 723 F 2b, p. 673, 23; cf. Seder Olam, 14, p. 31a-b (B. Ratner edition, Wilno, 1897). See also Sifre, Deut. 34:7, No. 357 (Finkelstein ed.), 429; Gen. Rabbah, 10 (Albeck ed.), p. 1295; B. Nazir, 5a; Sanhedrin, 69b; Temurah 15b; *Sefer Hasidim* (Berlin, 1891), 21; Rabbi Eliezer ben Nathan, *Even Ha'ezer,* No. 118. The rabbinic sources seem to be dependent on the Seder Olam. But Seder Olam's wording implies that the author had no access to a Hebrew version of LXX III Kingdoms 2:12; otherwise there would have been no need to employ farfetched midrashic proofs.

A similar example is the identification of Job wth the Edomite king Jobab (Gen. 36:33), asserted by Aristeas (Euseb., *P.E.* IX, 25 = 725 F 1), by the Graeco-Jewish historians, and the Additions to the LXX Job (the latter on the authority of an Aramaic text) as well. Likewise, Pseudo-Philo (8:8; 11), Targum (*Igrot Shdl* [Przemysl, 1884], IV, 741 f.), Test. of Job (title; 1:5), among others, identify Jobab with Job. Freudenthal (*Hell. Studien,* 140 f.) posited that the LXX followed here Aristeas; Wendland ("Aristeas," in *J.E.,* 92a-b) argued that Aristeas was dependent on the LXX Additions to Job. Since the Greek claims seem to be a rendition of the Aramaic, it is conceivable that Aristeas' account was also based on the Syriac text. The spelling, however, suggests that Aristeas is dependent on the LXX Job, as pointed out by Wendland. But Ibn Ezra on Gen 36:32, rejects the identification of Job-Jobab. The problem of LXX-Eupolemus-Seder Olam is even more complex than that of Aristeas-LXX-Job-Targum.

130   Mishnah Sotah, IX, 13; B. Sotah, 49b; Baba Kamma, 82b, Menahot, 74b. Cf. Saul Lieberman, *Hellenism in Jewish Palestine* (New York, 1950), 99-114, who argues that only the teaching of "Greek wisdom," *to children,* not study per se, was forbidden. Forbidden or not, the rabbis in fact show an almost total ignorance of Greek literary or philosophical texts, whether written by Jews or heathens. The science, cosmology, and philology of the rabbis is similar to pre-Greek thought. An occasional phrase of Homer (see Lieberman, 113 f.) found in late midrashic texts confirms the effective isolation of the talmudists from Greek culture. The points of contact seem to have been in government, architecture, and perhaps manufacturing. Literarily, the separation seems to have been total. In other words, the rabbis depended heavily upon vulgar Hellenism, but not on intellectual Hellenism.

131   See especially, Kurt Weitzmann, "Die Illustration des Septuaginta," *Münchener Jahrbuch der bildenden Kunst,* III-IV (1952-53), 96-120, who argues that early Byzantine art presupposes the existence of an illustrated version of the Septuagint

Europos offers a graphic illustration of the popularity of the Graeco-Jewish writings among the semi-Hellenized Jewish circles of the Diaspora.[132] This may explain why the Church Fathers had no difficulty in locating copies of the allegorical commentary on the Pentateuch by Aristobulus or Alexander Polyhistor's collection of Jewish historians.[133] The Christian apologists of the second or the third century—Pseudo-Justin (3rd century), Tatian the Syrian (c. A.D. 175), Theophilus of Antioch (c. 180)—found in the Graeco-Jewish writings ready ammunition with which to attack pagan Greek culture. The Graeco-Jewish writers had invented the formula, which became so dear to the Apologists of utilizing pagan criticism of Greek texts to denounce Greek literature. Likewise, occasional praise from the Greeks for the Jews was grossly inflated, but was cited as proof that even the Greeks had recognized the superiority of Judaism. Many of the pagan tributes to the Sabbath and monotheism were nothing but Jewish fabrications.[134] But the Christian apologists adopted them in good faith, and employed them for their own needs.

The crude formula of using forged texts to discredit pagan Greek culture was developed into an art by three men: Clement of Alexandria (died before 215), Julius Africanus (died after 240) and Eusebius of Caeserea (died in 339). Clement, born probably in Athens, educated in Alexandria, had acquired a full grasp of the Christian texts, but made a profound study of profane literature as well. He was able to quote no less than 360 authors, although admittedly many of them he knew only through anthologies and collections.[135] Confronted with the conflict between Homer and Plato, on the one hand, and the Gospels, on the other, Clement found the solution in the Graeco-Jewish writings; not in the extravagant allegorisms of Philo of

stories. Cf. also C. H. Kraeling (*The Synagogue: The Excavation of Dura Europos.* Final Report, VIII, 1 [New Haven, Yale University Press, 1956], 66-239, esp. 176 f.); J. Gutmann ("The 'Second Commandment' and the Image in Judaism," *HUCA,* 32 [1961], 161-74), and A. D. Nock ("The Synagogue Murals of Dura Europos," in *H. A. Wolfson Jubilee Volume,* Jerusalem, American Academy for Jewish Research, 1965, II, 631-39)

132   Cf. Demetrius, 722 F 5 = Eus., *P.E.,* IX, 29, 16, with the fresco of the exodus. in Dura-Europos. Sukenik (*The Synagogue of Dura-Europos and Its Paintings* [Jerusalem, 1947], 179-81 [in Hebrew]) argues that the fresco' interpretation of חמושים ın Exod. 13:18 as meaning "armed" ıwas based on the Targum, Aquila, and Symmachus, echoed also by Jerome in the Vulgata; differing with the LXX. But Demetrius, writing at the end of the third century B.C. and Ezekielus already take the interpretatıon of "armed" for granted.

133   If we may judge from Eusebius of Caesarea's collection of books, the libraries of Palestine were stocked with some of the most technical books. Mras' praise of the diocesean library of Caesarea (in his introduction to *P.E.,* p. LVIII) is perhaps applicable to many other places as well.

134   Cf. the Pseudo-Orphic poems as it has come down in several recensions (Ps.-Justin, *Mon.* 2; *Coh.* 15; Clement, *Strom.* V, 78; Eusebius, *P.E.* XIII, 12; the Theosophy of Tübingen); the Sabbath poems attributed to Homer (*Strom.,* V, 107) and Eusebius (*P.E.,* XIII, 12 f.). See now Denis, *Introduction aux Pseudépigraphes,* 221-38.

135   Cf. Berthold Altaner, *Patrology* (Freiburg, Herder, 1960), 215-22.

Alexandria, whom he quotes frequently, but in the more moderate biblical exegesis of Aristobulus.[136] Thus the Christian apologists began a search for the writings of the then half-forgotten Graeco-Jewish philosophers, poets and historians. Those writers had, long before, denounced Greek literature as obscene and Greek rhetoric as repugnant. Did not Plato receive his wisdom from Moses? And did not Plato denounce the immoralities of the deities in Homer and Hesiod? Greek philosophy, especially as formulated by Plato, seemed the only significant part of pagan culture. Even it, however, was but an introduction to the gnosis or true knowledge of God.

The famous library of Alexandria must have contained copies of the collected works of Alexander Polyhistor, and among them Clement probably found the anthology of Jewish historians. But he also found there a host of Jewish works, such as the writings of Aristobulus, Josephus, and Justus of Tiberias.[137] Other papyrus rolls purportedly written by famous pagan authors—Pseudo-Democritus, Pseudo-Hecataeus, Pseudo-Heraclitus, Pseudo-Homer, Pseudo-Phocylides—upheld the veracity of the Jewish traditions.[138] Clement never realized that almost all of these pagan works were nothing but pious forgeries. This is perhaps fortunate. Otherwise, he would not have filled most of the first book of the *Stromata* with citations from these writings; and without them our knowledge of Hellenistic Jewish literature would certainly have been grievously impaired.

Whether Clement knew of Eupolemus only through the medium of Alexander Polyhistor's collection or whether he actually possessed a copy of Eupolemus' works is difficult to say. Clement's paraphrases of Eupolemus are preserved in a more complete form in Eusebius and must have been based on Alexander Polyhistor's monograph.[139] Fragment Five, however, not known from any other source, was probably not taken from Alexander, although Unger argued that it was.[140] Clement took this passage, as is shown above,

136   See now Walter, *Der Thoraausleger Aristobulos,* 150-202.

137   Clement cited Aristobulus about a dozen times (see Walter, *Thoraausleger,* 264-66); Josephus (*B.J.,* VI, 439), once in *Strom.* I, 147, 2 f. There is no reference to Justus in Stählin's exhaustive index, but see Euseb., *Chron.* (ed. Helm), p. 7B, where Clement and Justus are grouped together; Eusebius probably believed that Clement had derived much of his chronology from Justus. Cf. also works cited above, note 123.

138   Clement cites Ps.-Democritus in *Strom.,* I, 69, 4-6 = *Vorsokratiker* III[6], 208-10 = *FGrH* 263 F 1; Ps. Hecataeus in *Strom.,* V, 113, 1 = 264 F 24; Clement lists Ps.-Demetrius as one of the LXX translators (*Strom.,* I; 150, 1, quoting Aristeas, 8 f. and Aristobulus, respectively).

139   723 FF 1b; 2a. Alexander Polyhistor's lengthy quotations made Clement forget that Eupolemus was their author.

140   In Jacoby, *FGrH* 723 F 4 = *Strom.,* I, 141, 4. Clement's discussion of the tendentiousness of the chronological systems of Demetrius (722 F 6), Philo (729 T 2), and Eupolemus might suggest that he still possessed substantial parts, perhaps most, of the writings by these authors. But again, the entire passage might have been taken from his source, most likely Ptolemy of Mendes. That it comes from Alexander Polyhistor, see Unger, *Philologus,* XLIII (1884), 528-531; XLVII (1888), 177-188; cf. Christ, *Philologische St.* (Munich, 1900), 500 f.

from an Alexandrian source written in 40 B.C., probably Ptolemy of Mendes, an Egyptian priest and chronographer.

Fragment Five actually belongs to a larger unit in Clement consisting of fragments of Demetrius (722 F 6), Philo the Elder (729 T 2), and Eupolemus, in which the biblical chronological systems of the Jewish historians before Josephus are compared. Gutman and Walter argue that Clement's sequence implies also the descending time sequence: first Demetrius, then Philo the Elder, then Eupolemus.[141]   Alexander Polyhistor based his list of the historians strictly on subject matter: Eupolemus (actually Pseudo-Eupolemus), Artapanus, Apollonius Molon, etc. (see above, pp. 40-44); it follows that Clement's source here was someone other than Alexander Polyhistor.[142] In other words, as far as can be determined, Clement knew concerning Eupolemus, Philo the Elder, and Demetrius from at least two sources, but there is no evidence that he had access to Eupolemus' original writing.

Clement cites Eupolemus twice by name and once through Alexander Polyhistor without mentioning the latter's source.[143]   Are there any indications that Clement quoted Eupolemus without acknowledging his authority at all?

There is no doubt that the Church Fathers in general and Clement in particular preserved large chunks of the Graeco-Jewish writings, but failed to spell out the sources. For example, Aristobulus, a contemporary of Eupolemus, was cited by Clement directly six times; but Valckaner and Walter have shown conclusively that in several passages Clement quoted Aristobulus without attribution.[144]   In a few instances at least this may have also been the case in regard to Eupolemus.

In Clement, *Stromata,* I, 113 we read: "After this (the death of his father) Solomon, his son of David reigned 40 years. Nathan continued to prophesy during his time. Achias of Selom was also a prophet, even though both David and Solomon were prophets themselves." As far as we can tell, Nathan's paramount role in Solomon's temple is asserted only in Eupolemus: "So [the

---

141   Gutman, *The Beginnings of Jewish-Hellenistic Literature,* I, 221, n. 1; Walter, "Der angebliche Chronograph Julius Cassianus: ein Beitrag zu der Frage den Quellen des Clemens Alexandrinus," *Studien zum Neuen Testament* . . . Erich Klostermann . . . dargebracht (Berlin, 1961), 181, n. 2.

142   Provided, of course, that the view of Gutman and Walter is accepted. See, however, note 140.

143   Eupolemus 723 F 1b and 5 (Walter, 4) are cited by Clement as from Eupolemus; but he does not specify that 2a also comes from him (cf. Euseb. 2b).

144   Clement mentioned Aristobulus in *Strom.,* I, 72, 4 (Walter, T 1); 150, 1 (T 2); and V, 97, 7 (T 3), quoting him by name in *Strom.* I, 150, 1-3 (Walter F 3a); and VI, 32, 3-33, 1 (F 2a). Valckaner, *Diatribe de Aristobulo Judaeo,* has shown that *Strom.* I, 148; 1 (F 3b); V, 99, 3 (F 4a); VI, 137, 4-138, 4 (F 5a); VI, 141, 7b-142, 1 (F 5b); VI, 142, 4b (F 5c); V, 107, 1-4 (F 5d) come from Aristobulus; Walter, *Der Thoraausleger Aristobulos,* 8, 101 f. found quotations in *Protr.,* 73, 2 (F 4b) and *Strom.,* V, 104 (F 4c). This list of Clement's quotations from Aristobulus is probably not exhaustive.

precise dimensions of the temple] Nathan, the prophet of God, commanded him (Solomon)."[145]   As already noted by Stählin, Clement was here dependent on Eupolemus.[146]

According to Clement, Achias of Selom, in addition to Nathan, who retained the office he had held during David's reign, also served as Solomon's prophet.[147] But the kings David and Solomon were themselves prophets.[148] Although there is no direct indication that this statement comes from Eupolemus, the fact that this sentence concludes a passage that relates Nathan's role found only in Eupolemus, indicates that the paragraph as a whole came from the same source.[149]   Certainly, Clement's attribution of a prophetic role to David and Solomon harmonizes with Eupolemus' report that Moses and Joshua were prophets.[150]   Finally, Clement counts Zadok, Solomon's priest, as the eighth in line after Aaron. Stählin labels this as a lie. It is clear, however, that Clement would not have invented such details on his own. But as in the report of Nathan's paramount role in the building of the Temple, the Alexandrian Church Father here followed Eupolemus, whose independence from the biblical account will be noted in the following chapters.

Furthermore, there is some evidence that significant sections of chapter XXI of Clement's first book of the *Stromata* (101-150) were derived to a large extent from Graeco-Jewish historians such as Demetrius, Philo the Elder, and Eupolemus. This chapter consists of an amalgam of Greek, Roman and Jewish chronicles. Clement makes it clear that he was merely summarizing what the older sages had joined, while adding here and there bits of his own learning to prove the relative antiquity of the Jews vis-à-vis the

145 Eupolemus in *P.E.*, XI, 34, 4 = 723 F 2b, p. 675, 13 f.

146 Stählin, *Clemens Alexandrinus*[3] II (Berlin, Akademie-Verlag, 1960), II, 522. "Diese Angabe [concerning Nathan's role in the construction of the Temple] steht nicht in A. T., aber bei Eupolemos bei Euseb. Praep. ev. IX, 34, 4, 15." Professor John Strugnell comments that this is not conclusive, as Clement might have found it in some aggadic text rather than in Eupolemus. But since no aggadic tradition, as far as we know, attributes to Nathan an important role in Solomon's Temple, except Clement and Eupolemus, the former's dependence on the latter appears quite likely.

147 Σηλώμ = שלה = Shiloh. See I Kings 11:29 ff., on Ahiah the prophet of Shiloh, who flourished during Jeroboam I's reign. Of some interest is the fact that Clement's spelling Selom is unusual in LXX, but is identical to that used in Eupolemus 723 F 2, p. 676, 25 = *P.E.*, IX, 34, 15. But the spelling is not consistent as, in IX, 30, 1, the shrine is named Silo (Σιλω).

148 Clement, *Strom.*, I, 113, 1.

149 See note 145.

150 *Strom.*, I, 113, 1; Eupolemus, in Euseb., *P.E.*, IX, 30, 1 = 723 F 2b. In the Bible, the term "prophet" is applied in Gen. 20:7 to Abraham, Exod. 7:1 to Aaron, to Moses, and to Moses his counselors in Num. 11:25-29; cf. Hos. 12:14. But only Eupolemus called Joshua a prophet, and David and Solomon are labeled so only by Clement. Clement likewise names Moses' successors as prophets (*Strom.* I, 109, 1). But Josephus (*B.J.*, I, 68) ascribed the gift of prophecy to John Hyrcanus.

Greeks.[151]   The Christian predecessors who made the same point, according to Clement, were Tatian and Cassian. But as Clement himself says, and as is confirmed in Tatian's treatise *Against the Greeks,* the older treatment of the subject was quite brief and superficial. Clement, however, believed that he could exhaust the subject by summarizing all that had been known on this theme. He begins by citing the synchronism found in Ptolemy of Mendes and mentioned also by Apion; Moses-Amosis (Egypt)-Inachus (Argos). To prove the accuracy of the synchronism Clement named some of the most famous Greek and Roman chronographers—Timaeus, Erastosthenes, Apollodorus, Castor, Dionysius of Halicarnassus. It was of course impossible to compute a detailed time table of the Hellenic gods and mythical heroes, but Clement rested his case on the reputedly authoritative accounts of the professional chronographers.[152]

Although Clement cites his sources for the Graeco-Roman chronology, this is not the case with Jewish history. Aside from the Greek Bible, he seems to have some entries that presuppose the use of the masoretic text, which he could have used only indirectly. It becomes clear, moreover, that although he read the biblical texts to get totals for the period from Moses to Cyrus, Clement based his account primarily on older reworkings of biblical computations. For the length of the period of the judges,(*Stromata* I, 113) Clement cites divergent opinions; he attributes to "some" 595 years from the death of Moses to King Solomon, but according to "others" the total is 576 years, although Clement's own favorite computation was 523 years and 7 months. Who then were the chronographers whom Clement cites several times without naming them?[153]

We can show that none of these referred to Josephus, and probably not to his rival Justus of Tiberias either. For *Stromata* I, 147, 2, mentions the

151   For a treatment of Eupolemus' chronology, see below, 103-112. On Cassian, see above, 40-44.

152   The number of pagan chronographers used in this chapter of Strom. is remarkable: Agias (I, 104 = 305 F 2); Acusilaus (103 = 2 F 23); Alexander Polyhistor (130 = 273 F 19b); Apion (101 = 616 F 2b); Apollodorus (117 = 244 F 63b); Apollonius (105); Aristeas of Argos (106 = Mueller *FGH,* IV, 327); Aristippus of Argos (106 = 317 F 1); Arctinus (131, 5), to list only those whose names begin with the letter *A*. On the general subject, see Jacoby, "Zeittaffeln," Nos. 239-61, IIB, 992-1229; *Atthis: The Local Chronicles of Ancient Athens* (Oxford, Clarendon Press, 1949). In *Atthis,* p. IV, he criticizes the theory, propounded by Mommsen and Wilamowitz, that annals represented the earliest form of writing; which according to Jacoby were a later development.

153   ὡς μὲν τινές φασιν (some say), ὡς δὲ ἕτεροι (according to others) ἀκριβέστερον δὲ ἡ καθ' ἡμᾶς χρονογραφία (but according to my accurate computation), *Strom.* I, 113, 3-114, 1. I suspect that perhaps Clement was somewhat embarrassed to be able to list only a few men who dealt with biblical chronography compared with the large number of Hellenic writers who dealt with Greek chronography.

chronology of the "Jew Josephus" in a concluding note as if it were an afterthought. And the computation ascribed to Josephus differs with any of the totals listed in his main discussion. Clement, moreover, seems to be using a corrupt text of the *Bellum* (VI, 435-42), apparently totally unaware of the existence of Josephus' *Jewish Antiquities*.[154]   As to Justus, there is no evidence that Clement ever used him. Certainly, Africanus' chronology which did roughly follow Justus' tables, approached the subject differently than did the sources cited by Clement. And Justus is never mentioned in Clement's works.[155]

The matter is different with the Graeco-Jewish historians Demetrius, Philo the Elder, and Eupolemus. Citing their summaries, *Stromata* I, 141, states that the biblical chronology of Demetrius was different from those of Philo the Elder and Eupolemus. What Clement appears to be saying here is that, aside from his own research, which he identifies (I, 114, 1), the chronological tables for the bibilical period were those of Demetrius, on the one hand, and of Philo the Elder and Eupolemus, on the other.[156]

A number of anonymous statements quoted by Clement seem to correlate with Eupolemus' fragments. *Stromata* I, 109, 2, says: "After the death of Moses the leadership passed to Joshua, who made war for five years and rested for twenty-five more years; but according to the Book of Joshua, the above-mentioned man was Moses' successor for twenty-seven years." Our biblical texts do not contain the last number at all. But Eupolemus, and no other

154   Clement (I, 147, 2, II, p. 91, 21, cites the book as *Jewish Histories* ὁ τὰς Ἰουδαϊκὰς συντάξας ἱστορίας, a title not elsewhere attested in Josephus. Stàhlin, ad locum, refers the quotation to *B.J.* VI, 435-42. But his text gives only part of Clement's citation—the period of 1179 years from David to Vespasian (Titus in Josephus)—but not the first part—585 years from Moses to David, a number not found in our copies of Josephus. In *A.J.*, VII, 68, Josephus gives 515 years from Joshua to David's conquest of Jerusalem; in VIII, 61, from the exodus to Solomon's building of the Temple, 592 years. These two numbers, as pointed out by Justus von Destinon (*Die Chronologie von Josephus* [Kiel, 1882], 11-15), are internally inconsistent perhaps the only consistent aspect of Josephus' confused chronology. But Clement's citation apparently cannot be reconciled with any of these numbers. It follows either that Clement did use *B.J.* VI, 440, but that his text contained a number for the period of judges not found in the manuscripts used by Niese; or that Clement saw only a secondary citation of the *Bellum*. At any rate the number 585 years for the period of the judges remains puzzling. On *Strom.*, VI, 132, II, 498, 21-27, Stàhlin refers to *A.J.*, IV, 320-26. But there is no reason to assume that Josephus was Clement's source. See also below note 169.

155   Cf. H. Gelzer, *Sextus Julius Africanus*, I, 23, who shows that Africanus did not use Clement's chronology. Cf. above, note 137; for Africanus' dependence on Justus, see below.

156   *Strom.* I, 141, 1-2=Demetrius 722 F 6; 141, 3 Philo 729 T 2; 141, 4 = 723 F 4 (Walter 5). It should be noted that Clement used Menander and Laetus independently of Josephus, but was dependent on Tatian, dating for example Solomon in the days of the Trojan war (Menelaus). See Tatian, *Ad. Graec.*, 37; Clement, *Strom.*, I, 114, 2 = Menander 783 F 2 = Laetus, 784 F 1.

authority, does say that Joshua prophesied for thirty years. The fact, however, that biblical proof may be adduced for such a conclusion robs us of conclusive evidence that Clement was here dependent on Eupolemus.[157]   The length of Saul's reign, corrupt in the biblical   texts, Eupolemus gives as twenty-one years, but Clement as only twenty.[158]   But the fact, as has been mentioned above, that only Eupolemus and Clement affirmed Nathan's paramount role in the construction of the Solomonic Temple tends to confirm the general impression that throughout his chronological discourse Clement was heavily dependent on Eupolemus.[159]

Clement seems to allude to Eupolemus also in subject matter that is not chronological. *Stromata,* I, 72 says: "But by far the oldest philosophy of all men is that of the Jewish people. And the fact that their philosophy was written before that of the Greeks was shown with telling proofs by Philo the Pythagorean, without naming Aristobulus the Peripatetic, and *many* others, whose names I have no time to mention." That Eupolemus was one of the "many others" follows from Fragment 1b, where Clement quotes from the Graeco-Jewish writer that Moses was the first wise man.[160]

Incidentally, it is likely that, because of the analogy with Fragment 1a (in *P.E.* IX, 15, 4), scholars have incorrectly assumed that Clement's citation of Eupolemus (F 1b = Strom. I, 153, 4), ends with the statement that the Greeks received the elements of culture from the Phoenicians.[161]   A close reading of the text suggests that the next paragraph (153, 5) also quotes Eupolemus: "Growing up to manhood, he [Moses] increased in wisdom, becoming so ardent in the paideia of his people, till he killed with a stroke an Egyptian who had maliciously attacked a Jew."[162]   There is no reason to believe that this passage is Clement's own, and it should certainly be differentiated. from what follows (154, 1), which Clement attributes to the allegorical interpreters of the Bible (μύστοι).Since in Philo there is no such text which claims Moses slew the Egyptian with a word, it is likely that Clement was alluding to Aristobulus, quoted often in the *Stromata,* and most immediately in I, 150. After this brief hiatus, *Stromata,* I, 154, 2, resumes the lengthy citations of Artapanus and Ezekielus, using Alexander Polyhistor's monograph. Thus it is reasonable to assume that Clement has preserved more of Eupolemus' account of Moses than has generally been supposed.

On the basis of the foregoing, it can be concluded that significant segments of the first book of Clement's *Stromata* were directly or indirectly derived

---

157   See Numb. 14:33 f.; Josh. 14:7; 24:29.

158   See I Sam. 13:1. The LXX's text is similar to the Hebrew, but Lucan has 30 years for Saul's reign. *A.J.,* VI, 378, has 18 years during Samuel's lifetime plus 22 years thereafter.

159   See Stählin's comment cited above, note 146.

160   See below, pp. 72-77.

161   Eus. *P.E.* IX, 26 = Clement, *Strom.* I, 154, 4 = 723 F 1a-b.

162   Clement parenthetically cites Acts 5:1-10, comparing Peter with Moses.

from the Graeco-Jewish writings in general and from Eupolemus in particular. The fact is that early Patristic literature as a whole was to a large extent nothing but a continuation of the Graeco-Jewish literary tradition. Wolfson has shown the indebtedness of the Church Fathers to Philo's allegorical exegesis.[163]   But Wolfson seems to have erred in overstating the Philonic legacy while hardly mentioning the rich literary heritage bestowed upon the Christian apologists by the Graeco-Jewish predecessors. Even the Christian use of the Greek classical literature had been molded by Hellenistic Jewish writers. Despite the likelihood that Clement and other Church Fathers quoted certain passages from Graeco-Jewish writers, only formally attested citations of Eupolemus in Clement are treated in this book.

Fortunately, except for Fragment Five, Clement's citation of Eupolemus serves only as corroborative evidence. The chief witness is Eusebius. Although copied more than a century later, the quotations in Eusebius, as noted above, surpass those of Clement both in quality and quantity. Eusebius' citations are not only more generous but also more carefully drawn. The source as well as the source's source is given.[164]   From Clement we learn the importance of the Hellenistic Jewish literature for the Church Fathers. From Eusebius we are able to reconstruct much of its structure.

This is not to say that Eusebius unfailingly presented the original Eupolemus. Errors, chiefly those of Alexander Polyhistor, have crept in either through ignorance or through scribal transmission. As a model transmitter, Eusebius scrupulously copied even the most grotesque mistakes, such as that David was Saul's son.[165]   But such gross errors are exceptional, and no ancient text is completely free of them. The degree of reliability of the Graeco-Jewish Hellenistic fragments attested by Eusebius is rather high.

Fragment Five of Eupolemus is an exception.[166]   Its quality is low. It is found only in Clement and has no parallel in Eusebius. This may have been due to the accident of selection. But Eusebius' omission of Eupolemus' chronological scheme as well as that of Demetrius and Philo the Elder was probably deliberate. It illustrates the difference between the two Church Fathers in their attitude to and use of the Graeco-Jewish writers. In the second century the Christian apologists drew their ammunition against paganism almost entirely from Jewish sources. The Hellenistic Jewish writers had acknowledged the immense contribution of Greek philosophy, but had argued that it was derived exclusively from Mosaic and prophetic teachings. This fiction remained as the cornerstone of the Christian apologists. But

---

163   H. A. Wolfson, *The Philosophy of the Church Fathers: Faith, Trinity, Incarnation* (Cambridge, Mass., Harvard University Press, 1956).

164   See Mras' Introduction to *P.E.*, pp. LV-LVIII.

165   Eupolemus, 723 F 2b, p. 673, 4 f. = *P.E.*, IX, 30, 3.

166   In Jacoby, 723 F 4 = *Strom.*, I, 141, 4.

Clement and other second century Christian writers also copied the chronology of the world from the Graeco-Jewish writers, even when those dates differed from the biblical tradition.[167] In fact ancient chronology as transmitted by Tatian and Clement rested entirely on that of Demetrius, Philo the Elder, and Eupolemus.[168]

Independent of Clement, his younger contemporary Julius Sextus Africanus of Jerusalem developed a biblical chronology that was in part derived from a branch of Graeco-Palestinian writers, such as Justus of Tiberias, and in part from a return to a thorough analysis of Scripture. Eusebius used both Clement and Africanus, but should be regarded as the disciple only of the former. Returning to biblical texts, Eusebius reconstructed a new ancient Jewish chronology. Thus Eusebius' omission of Eupolemus' chronological scheme is significant because it illustrates a diminution of the Graeco-Jewish influence on Christian chronography.

For the medieval tradition, Eusebius' influence was pervasive. Aside from the crude and unsophisticated Graeco-Jewish fabrications which were used to counter pagan influence, there existed also pamphlets such as the *Contra Apionem* of Josephus. This book illustrates the fact that a careful selection of heathen Greek writers, faithfully quoted, could be used to attack paganism. In the middle of the second century, Josephus was still ignored in favor of the older Graeco-Jewish historians. Clement, who cited Eupolemus three times, but names Josephus only twice, once confusing him with Philo of Byblos, the translator of Sanchuniathon into Greek.[169] The second century apologists, Justin Martyr and Tatian, hardly mentioned Josephus, although they frequently referred to the Graeco-Jewish historians.[170] It would seem that it was Eusebius' good sense which dethroned the Hellenistic Jewish writers and which crowned Josephus as *the* historian of the Jews.

But it is also Eusebius to whom we are indebted for the remains of the writings of the Graeco-Jewish writers before Philo and Josephus. From Tatian and Clement, but primarily from Eusebius, a host of medieval churchmen held it as a dogma that Greek philosophy had been nothing but a derivative from Hebrew teachings. The names of Eupolemus, Artapanus, Alexander Polyhistor and others were frequently copied from Eusebius or Clement by

---

167   See Gelzer, *Sextus Julius Africanus,* I, 19-24 and passim. See below Chapter IX.

168   See Gutschmid, *Kl. Schriften,* II, 194; Gelzer, *Sextus Julius Africanus,* II, 364.

169   See above note 154. Clement is quoted by Cyrill of Alexandria that Josephus had translated Sanchuniathon from the Phoenician into the Greek (Cyrill, *Contra Iulianos,* VI, 2, cited in Stählin, *Clement Alexandrinus,* III, 225, 6-14).

170   The reference to Josephus in *Coh. ad Graec.* 9; 13, are not Justin's, as this work is a post-Eusebian product. Note Tatian's citations from Phoenician and Egyptian writers dealing with Jewish history (Orat. adv. Graec. 37 f.), where texts *not* cited by Josephus are mentioned. Justin (*Dial.* 52) makes Herod a native of Ascalon, suggesting that he used Justus of Tiberias (cf. Africanus, in Eusebius, *Ecc. Hist.,* I, 6, 2).

writers such as Jerome, Pseudo-Justin, Gegorius Cedrenus, Georgius Hamartolus, Michael the Syrian, and Bar Hebraeus.[171] But the Hellenistic Jewish historians might just as well have been ghosts. Their significance and contribution was lost.

What was their import? The claim that Greek philosophy and culture were derived from the Bible tended to encourage medieval monks to save and preserve many ancient Greek texts. One thinks of the Moslem conqueror of Alexandria who said (according to some) that if the books of the famous Alexandrian library contained the same learning as the Koran, then they were superfluous; but if their teaching was contrary to the Koran, then they should be burned.[172] The Moslems subsequently recanted and employed translators to render many Greek words into Arabic. Happily, the learned monks were never faced with the dilemma which confronted the Arabs during their conquest of the centers of culture. "Who was Plato except Moses speaking in Greek?"[173]

The names of Eupolemus and Artapanus never disappeared from the medieval chronicles. But the period and circumstances which these men represented were lost. Of the Graeco-Jewish literature only Philo and Josephus retained and even expanded their influence during the Middle Ages. Rabbi Azariah dei Rossi (1513?-1578) of Mantua strove valiantly to arouse among the Jews an interest in the Greek-Jewish texts, notably the writings of Josephus, Philo, and the peripatetic philosopher, Aristobulus.[174] But the times were not propitious. Joseph Caro, the famous codifier, attempted to ban Azariah's works,[175] which challenged elements of talmudic historiography. Joseph Justus Scaliger (1540-1609) was more successful. Although he slandered Eusebius as a fool, Scaliger was the first to suggest the identification of Eupolemus, Judah Maccabee's envoy, with the historian quoted by Clement and Eusebius.[176] During the ensuing two centuries,

---

171 Cyrill Alexandrinus, *Contral Iulianos,* VII; Jerome (*De vir. ill.,* 38) lists Aristobulus, Demetrius, and Eupolemus, in addition to Josephus, who attacked paganism; Ps. - Justin (see previous note, *Coh. ad Graec.,* 9) mentions Alexander Polyhistor; *Chronicon Paschale* (Migne, *P.G.* 92, col. 253); Georgius Cedrenus (I, 87, 8-11); Georgius Hamortolus, *Chronicon* [Petersburg, 18], I, 26; in I.N. Cramer (*Anecdota Graeca Oxon,* [Oxford, 1837], 245, 23-34); Bar Hebraeus (*Chronography* [Oxford Univ. Press, 1932], I, 20, 26); Micheal the Syrian (*Chronique* ed. J. B. Chabot [Paris, 1899], I, 62; Cf. pp. 15 f.). All allude to Eupolemus. Cf. the "Greek tradition" found in Syriac authors, recently reviewed by R. M. Tonneau, in *Moïse, l'homme de l'alliance* (Tournai, Declée et Cie., 1955), 156-65, esp. 261.

172 E. A. Parsons, *The Alexandrian Library, Glory of the Ancient World* (London, Cleaver-Hume Press, 1952), 392.

173 Clement, *Strom.,* I, 150, 4, citing Numenius; Euseb., *P.E.,* IX, 6, 9; XI, 10, 14.

174 Azariah dei Rossi, *Me'or Einayyim,* (Wilno, 1866), 146, 154, citing Aristobulus, whom he knew via Eusebius (and Clement?).

175 H. Y. D. Azulai, *Mahazik Berakhah* (Livorno, 1785), 133.

176 J. J. Scaliger, *Thesaurus Temporum* (Leiden, 1606); Isaac Vossius, *Chronologia Sacra ad Josephi mentem* (Hague Comitum), 119; *De LXX interpretibus,* 1661), ch. 2.

scholars were engaged in bitter debates as to whether Artapanus, Demetrius, Philo the Elder, and Eupolemus were Jews or Gentiles;[177] whether the fragments attributed to Alexander Polyhistor were genuine or forgeries; and whether Eusebius should be regarded as a reliable witness to their ancient texts. (The reader who wishes to pursue the learned through often not too penetrating discussions may consult the literature cited in Schürer's still indispensable work.[178])

But several writers must be cited both because of their notable contributions to Hellenistic Jewish studies and because they are indispensable for an understanding of the state of present knowledge. Kuhlmey defined the view that Eupolemus was a heathen. Though published in 1874-75, Jacob Freudenthal's *Alexander Polyhistor* has deservedly remained the main guide to the Graeco-Jewish historians.[179] Because of his profound knowledge of Greek literature, his common sense, and his acquaintence with the rabbinic traditions, Freudenthal's study of the complicated problem of Jewish Hellenism has remained unsurpassed. He proved conclusively the reliability of both Alexander Polyhistor and Eusebius; and he solved perplexing questions, such as the Samaritan provenance of Pseudo-Eupolemus' fragment on Abraham. Alfred von Gutschmid, who himself illuminated many dark passages in the Graeco-Jewish lore, called attention in a review of Freudenthal's book to the great significance of Alexander Polyhistor's fragments: "Few remnants of the old literature can be compared to these fragments in their many-sided significance—for the understanding of the Hellenistic spirit, for the dating of the Septuaginta, even for the text of the Bible . . . ."[180] It should not be forgotten, however, that Freudenthal's study was made possible by the publication of the monumental collection of Greek historical fragments by Carl Mueller.[181]

In the twentieth century, Felix Jacoby's new edition of the fragments of the Greek historians constitutes one of the most notable contributions to the recovery of a lost literature. For the first time the remnants of the Greek historical texts pertaining to the Jews had been assemblied.[182] In reediting the Graeco-Jewish texts Jacoby was also assisted by luck. When Jacoby had published Alexander Polyhistor's fragments (273) in Volume IIIA (1940), he relegated his quotations from the Jewish historians to a subsequent volume,

---

177 See Kuhlmey, *Eupolemi Fragmenta,* 12-41.

178 Schürer, *Gesch. d. jüd. Volkes,* III⁴, 468-482.

179 *Hellenistische Studien, 1-2: Alexander Polyhistor und die von ihm erhaltenen Reste judäischer und samritanischer Geschichtswerke* (Breslau, 1874-75).

180 A. von Gutschmid, "Zeit und Zeitrechnung der jüdischen Historiker Demetrios und Eupolemos," *Jahrbücher f. protestantische Theologie,* I (1875), 744-53; *Kl. Schriften,* II (1890), 180..

181 C. Mueller, *Fragmenta Historicorum Graecarum,* III (Paris, 1849), 211-230.

182 Jacoby's list (*FGrH,* IIIC, 2, pp. 666-713, Nos. 722-737) is the most complete collection of Graeco-Jewish historians now available.

which appeared only in 1958. Meanwhile, Karl Mras' edition of Eusebius' *Praeparatio Evangelica,* surpassing the earlier versions by far in accuracy and collation, was published in 1954; Jacoby was then able to utilize it for his text of the Jewish historians. Unhappily, Jacoby's death has deprived us of a prodigious commentary on these writers, whom he considered to be of unusual significance.[183]

Despite the notable contributions of Valckaner, Mueller, Freudenthal, von Gutschmid, and Jacoby, many problems remain unsolved. The basic questions, those of the provenance, dating, and identity of Eupolemus, have been solved. In this chapter, the indebtedness to Eupolemus of the Christian historians from the second century onward has been documented. But much more evidence than is presented here is needed before it can be posited that Christian historiography—that of Pseudo-Justin, Tatian, Clement of Alexandria, Julius Africanus—was a mere continuation of the Hellenistic Jewish historical outlook. Nonetheless, as will be shown in the next chapter, the Christian intellectual response to the pagan challenge was identical to that of the Hellenistic Jewish writers such as Eupolemus. As our commentary on Eupolemus' fragments develops, other problems will be raised, though not always solved. What was Eupolemus' cultural baggage? Was his training primarily that of a biblical student who had gained a smattering of Greek, or had he acquired the *paideia* of an enlightened Hellenistic author as well? Was our author writing a missionary tract for the Gentiles, as suggested by Dalbert,[184] or was he addressing himself primarily to Jews? And if the latter, which of the many Judaic factions did he have in mind?

These and similar questions will be considered, but the focus of our commentary lies elsewhere. It attempts to study Eupolemus' attitude to the literary heritage of his people, which he must have known well. It will also analyze the methods that he used to present this rich heritage in a language which was foreign to the subject matter and which he himself knew only rudimentarily. In other words, this commentary is a line-by-line study of cultural fusion between Hellenism and Judaism.

183   Cf. Jacoby, *FGrH,* IIIa, 268, 33 ff.; IIIb (Suppl.), I, 383, 3 ff.; IIIC, 2, 678, app. 13; 680, app. 1-2; 692, app. 10-11; 695, app. 20.

184   Dalbert, *Die Theologie der hellenistisch-jüdischen Missions-Literatur,* 35-42, esp. 35 f. Cf. also J. Giblet, "Eupoléme et l'histographie du Judaïsme hellénistique," *Ephemerides theologicae lovanienses,* 63 (1963), 539-54, who sees Eupolemus' aim was to harmonize various accounts of Scripture; repeated in Albert-Marie Denis, *Introduction aux Pseudépigraphes Grecs,* 254. In fact Eupolemus' reports frequently contradict the tradition, creating more discord than do any differences found in the Bible.

Chapter Three

THE HELLENIZED MOSES – JEWISH AND PAGAN

Fragment One differs basically from the other remnants of Eupolemus' writings. The latter deal with chronological summaries or with the building and destruction of Solomon's Temple, thus forming a kind of Greek language version of the Book of Chronicles. Their author, the spirit of the writings leaves no doubt, was a Jerusalem priest. Fragment One, however, appears to reflect a different Eupolemus. The writing is polemical and addresses itself to the outside world. Moses was important not, as in the Scriptural tradition, as the transmitter of God's Law to his chosen people Israel, but in his role as the father of Oriental and Greek civilizations.

The contrast between Fragment One and Eupolemus' other writings is so sharp that a question may be raised as to whether or not the same author wrote both. As has been pointed out elsewhere, although Alexander Polyhistor attributed an account of Abraham to Eupolemus, it is generally accepted that Fragment One belongs instead to a Samaritan now called Pseudo-Eupolemus. Certainly, Eupolemus' description of Moses' role as the father of writing and law would be a worthy sequel to Pseudo-Eupolemus' presentation of Enoch and Abraham as the discoverers of the sciences and astrology. Pseudo-Eupolemus' assertion that Enoch discovered astronomy, which he instructed first to the Babylonians, who, rather than the Egyptians, were the earliest practitioners of this science, harmonizes with the challenging wording of our fragment. Apparently, even more closely connected with Fragment One is a passage assigned to an Anonymous author identified by Freudenthal as Pseudo-Eupolemus, which claims that Abraham taught astronomy first to the Phoenicians, and only subsequently to the Egyptians.[1] Should then Fragment One, putatively attributed to Eupolemus, be ascribed also to Pseudo-Eupolemus?

In all probability, the answer is no. It is unlikely that the Pseudo-Eupolemus who made Enoch the discoverer of astrology and Abraham the disseminator of the sciences among the Phoenicians and Egyptians would have inconsistently labeled Moses as the first wise man. In fact the pseudepigraphic tradition, discussed below, makes Enoch a "divine scribe,"

---

1   J. Freudenthal, *Hellenistische Studien* (Breslau, 1874-75), 82-103; Wacholder, *HUCA,* 34 (1963), 83-113; N. Walter, *Klio,* 43-45 (1965), 282-90; see my article on Eupolemus and Pseudo-Eupolemus in *Encyclopaedia Judaica,* 6 (1971), 964-65.

suggesting that he was a kind of first wise man.[2] Our passage making similar
claims for Moses appears to be a refutation of, or at least a counterpoint to,
the Enochite partisans. It follows that the fragments on Abraham and on
Moses, reflecting as they do diverse schools, were not written by the same
man.

From our discussion an interesting fact emerges, nevertheless. Although
the fragments of Eupolemus show him to have been a priest of Jerusalem, a
part of his writings may also be labeled cosmopolitan, perhaps even
universalistic. Although he imitated the biblical style of history writing,
Eupolemus also belongs to the Graeco-Jewish tradition of a less intense
ethnic-centered Judaism. It cannot be denied, however, that the synchretistic
Samaritan writer Pseudo-Eupolemus and the Judaean Eupolemus were part of
a school that presented the biblical partiarchs as if they were wise men
famous for their contributions to the welfare of man. Of these, if such a
school indeed existed, Eupolemus apparently was the younger member,
reflecting perhaps the Maccabean reaction against the synchretistic views of
the Hellenizers. It follows that even the anti-Hellenizers, whose views
Eupolemus supposedly shared, were not without some adherents to a kind of
humanistic Weltanschauung which regarded Moses' teachings as a legacy to
mankind as a whole as well as to Israel.

So appealing was this theme to the Church Fathers that Clement of
Alexandria and Eusebius of Caesarea made the universalized Moses the major
topic of their own works.[3] But their wording of Eupolemus' Fragment One,
telling of Moses' gifts, is slightly different:

<table>
<tr><td>Clement, Strom. I, 153, 4</td><td>Eusebius, P.E. IX, 26</td></tr>
<tr><td>But Eupolemus says in his On the Kings of Judaea: "Moses was the first wise man. And he was the first who taught the Jews 'grammar' (letters?); the Phoenicians received it from the Jews; the Greeks from the Phoenicians."[4]</td><td>But Eupolemus says: "Moses was the first wise man. And he taught the alphabet to the Jews first; the Phoenicians received it from the Jews; the Greeks from the Phoenicians.
Also, laws were first written by Moses for the Jews."[5]</td></tr>
</table>

2   Enoch 12:3; Jub. 4:17-19; 23-24; see below, pp. 75-76.
3   For the design of Clement's Stromata, see Eusebius, Hist. Eccl., VI, 13,
quoting Strom., I, 153, 4 (Eupolemus 723 F 1). As to Eusebius, his P.E., as outlined in
XV, by the author himself, was designed to prove the thesis that Moses' contribution to
human knowledge antedated that of the Greeks and was superior to it.
4   Εὐπόλεμος δὲ ἐν τῷ Περὶ τῶν ἐν τῇ Ἰουδαίᾳ Βασιλέων τὸν Μωυσῆ φησι
πρῶτον σοφὸν γενέσθαι καὶ γραμματικὴν πρῶτον τοῖς Ἰουδαίοις παραδοῦναι
καὶ παρὰ Ἰουδαίων Φοίνικας παραλαβεῖν, Ἕλληνας δὲ παρὰ Φοινίκων. Used by
Cyrillus of Alexandria, Contra Julianus, VII (Aubert, 231 D-E = Migne, P.G., LXXVI,
853 B-C).
5   Εὐπόλεμος δὲ φησι τὸν Μωσῆν πρῶτον σοφὸν γενέσθαι καὶ γράμματα παραδοῦναι τοῖς Ἰουδαίοις πρῶτον παρὰ δὲ Ἰουδαίων Φοίνικας παρα-

Although both Clement and Eusebius quoted Eupolemus, neither in fact cited Eupolemus' history directly. Eusebius, as mentioned in the preceding chapter, says that he found our passage in Alexander Polyhistor's monograph on the Jews.[6] But whether or not the same was true of Clement is subject to question. For although Clement also used Alexander Polyhistor, as is suggested in the sequence Eupolemus-Artapanus-Ezekielus, we know that Clement had on occasion also quoted Eupolemus from another source, perhaps from Ptolemy of Mendes.[7] But Alexander Polyhistor-Eusebius undoubtedly have transmitted here a more authentic version of Eupolemus' words than did Ptolemy of Mendes(?)-Clement. This may account for the latter's, or perhaps only the copyist's, confusion of *grammatike* ("grammar") for *grammata* (alphabet).[8] It may also explain Clement's failure to mention Eupolemus' third boast that Moses invented written law.

In some respects, however, Clement's citation seems to be superior to that of Eusebius. He gives the title of Eupolemus' work, omitted by Alexander Polyhistor; and he places the second "first" in the same place as the other two "firsts" rather than, as in Eusebius, at the end of the sentence. Clement, moreover, seems to reproduce not Alexander Polyhistor's context, as does Eusebius, but Eupolemus' own. For Alexander Polyhistor cited our passage as a link in the string of excerpts that made up his history of the Jews from Abraham to his day. Clement, however, used Eupolemus' passage as one of the chief weapons in his frontal attack on Greek philosophy. Thus Fragment One of Eupolemus, Eusebius says, became part of the central theme of *Stromata* ("Pathwork"), Clement's major work.[9] Eusebius' own *Praeparatio Evangelica* is a more sophisticated presentation of the same thesis which by

---

λαβεῖν Ἕλληνας δὲ παρὰ Φοινίκων. νόμους τε Μωσῆν πρῶτον γράψαι τοῖς Ἰουδαίοις. This passage of Eusebius is cited frequently in the Byzantine chronicles: *Chronicon Paschale,* Migne, *P.G.,* XCII, 201; Georgius Cedrenus, *Histor. Comp.* (ed. I. Bekker, Bonn, 1838-39), I, 87 - Migne, *P.G.,* CXXI, 116; Georgius Hamartolus, *Chronicon* (Petrograd, 1859), Prolegomena, pp. xxiv; 29 = Migne, *P.G.,* CX, 27 f.; Cramer, *Anecd. graeca* (Oxford, 1837), 238, 245.

In modern texts: C. Mueller, *FHG* (Paris, 1883), III, 220; Freudenthal, *Hell. St.,* 225; Jacoby, *FGrH,* 723 F 1a, IIIC, p. 672; N. Walter, in his forthcoming collection of Greco-Jewish fragments. Also, with significant omissions, and notes, in Wallace Nelson Stearns' *Fragments from Graeco-Jewish Writers* (Chicago, The University of Chicago Press, 1908), 29-41.

6   *P.E.,,* IX, 25, 4-26, 1 = Alexander Polyhistor, 273 F 19a.

7   See above. pp. 60-66.

8   Professor John Strugnell, commenting on a draft of this chapter, notes that Clement's "gramatike" was more likely to have been Eupolemus' word, but because the term may also misleadingly mean "grammar," Eusebius changed it to "grammata."

9   See Eusebius, *Ecclestistical History,* VI, 13, 7, quoting *Strom.* I, 72, 4, though omitting Eupolemus' name.

then assumed the standard formulation in the Byzantine chronicles.[10]

There is a possibility that the Byzantine chronicles of Georgius Nomachus Hamartolus, who flourished in 850, and Georgius Cedrenus, who flourished in the eleventh century, after quoting Eupolemus on Moses, continue to cite the lost author's detailed account of Moses' education: "But Moses left behind the life of Egypt and lived in the desert pursuing knowledge, where he was instructed by the Archangel Gabriel, concerning the creation of the world, the first man and those who followed him, the flood, the confusion of the tongues, even from the first man to his own day; and concerning the code of law which he wished to give to the Jewish people, concerning the location of the stars and the planets, arithmetic and geometry, and concerning all of the sciences, as it is mentioned in Little Genesis."[11]

But this passage is not found in, and its contents is contrary to the spirit of, the Book of Jubilees, a work often called by Hamartolus and Cedrenus "Little Genesis." Jub. 1:1 does record an extensive revelation to Moses, but it was the Lord's message on Sinai. In fact, the Archangel Gabriel is not mentioned in Jubilees, though Jub. 1:27-29 reports that God ordained the Angel of Presence to write down the Law for Moses. Generally, however, except for the account of creation, Jubilees does not report on, and is foreign to the author's interest in the discovery of scientific matters. It is likely that Hamartolus, having mentioned Eupolemus' account of Moses, followed it up with a contamination of Jubilees' version of creation. Alternately, Hamartolus might have been indebted to some unknown source which had fused the two accounts. There is also an intriguing possibility that Hamartolus' citation of "Little Genesis" here was in fact only a continuation of what is now Fragment One of Eupolemus. The difficulty with this hypothesis is that Eusebius, Hamartolus' authority as far as Eupolemus was concerned, has no reference to Gabriel's training of Moses.[12] Should one assume that Cedrenus, who flourished in the ninth century, had access to the Graeco-Jewish writings independently of the Church Fathers such as Clement and Eusebius?

I

Eupolemus' presentation of Moses reflected a Euhemeristic view of the position of ancient man. Biblical lore does not lend support at all for the

---

10   For Eusebius, see his outline of this work in *P.E.*, XV, 1; for the others, see notes 4-5. Cf. also the Syriac tradition found in Theodore bar Koni, as cited by R. M. Tonneau, in *Moïse, l'homme de l'alliance* (Tournai, Desclée & Cie., 1955), 261.

11   Georgius Cedrenus, I, 87 (cited in part by Charles, *Jubilees,* p. LXXIX); Georgius Hamartolus, p. 26; Cramer, *Anecdota Graeca,* IV, 245, 24-33.

12   Cf. Cedrenus, I, 48, citing "the Little Genesis": "But the Lord's angel taught him (viz., Moses) the Hebrew tongue." The passage is not found in our Jubilees, though Jub. 3:28, does imply that Hebrew was Adam's language. It should be noted, however, that this may be due to a lacuna before Jub. 2:23 (mentioned in Epiphanius, *De mens.*

classification of the patriarchs—Enoch, Abraham, or Moses—as "wise men," much less as inventors of astronomy or the alphabet. Nonetheless, as has been suggested, the pseudographical literature presents Enoch as a kind of first wise man.[13] "The Book on the Courses of Heavenly Luminaries," bearing Enoch's name as its author, was probably composed in 150 B.C., in 200 B.C. according to Charles, a century earlier according to others.[14] Ben Sira celebrates the fame of the wise man, mentioning Enoch first.[15] Enoch's reputation as an astronomer certainly goes back to the third century B.C., as his precedence is also attested in such diverse works as Pseudo-Eupolemus[16] and the Genesis Apocryphon,[17] as well as in the Book of Jubilees and the "Wisdom of Enoch." Jub. 4:17-20 reads: "And he [Enoch] was the first among men born on earth who learned writing and knowledge and wisdom and who wrote down the signs of heaven according to their months in a book ... And he was the first to write a testimony ... And what was and what will be he saw in a vision of his sleep, as it will happen to the children of men throughout their generations until the day of judgment, he saw and understood everything, and wrote his testimony, and he placed the testimony on earth for all the children of men and for all their generations."[18]

XXII; Syncellus, I, 5; cf. Midrash Tadshe, VI) which mentions 22 generations from Adam to Jacob, the same as the number of Hebrew letters and, according also to Josephus (C. Apionem, I, 38), of the books of the Bible. This passage is also quoted by Cedrenus, I, 9.

13   Enoch 12:3-4, 15:1; Jub. 4:17; 23-24. Commenting on Enoch 12:3, Charles (The Book of Enoch [Oxford, 1921], 28), maintains that the epithet "heavenly scribe" was of Babylonian origin, being identical to Nabu, also Ezekiel's figure with a scribal inkhorn (Ezek. 9:2-3, 11). However, Enoch 69:9, ascribes the invention of writing to the Fallen Angel Penemue, an achievement of which the author seems to disapprove, "for men were not created for such a purpose." Is the difference that the angel invented writing, but that Enoch invented the alphabetic script?

14   For the dating of the various sections of Enoch, see R. H. Charles, Introduction to The Book of Enoch[2] (London, 1912), pp. LII-LVII, who dates the chapters 83-90 before 161 B.C. The astronomical section (chapters 72-82) is cited in Jub., written circa 110 B.C.; Schürer, Gesch. d. jüd. Volkes, III[4], 274-283; Pfeiffer, History of N. T. Times, 76 f.; D. Flusser in Encyclopedia Biblica, III (Jerusalem, 1958), 203-210. See also M. Rist, in the Interpreter's Dictionary of the Bible, II (1962), 103b, who dates the Book of Enoch during the Herodian period, regarding the Dead Sea evidence as unevaluated.

15   Ecclus. 44:16; 49:14. Cf. Ecclus. 49:14 (Segal ed.) with II Enoch 18:2.

16   P.E., IX, 17, 9 = Pseudo-Eupolemus, 724 F 1. Cf. Wacholder, HUCA, 34 (1963), 97-99.

17   Gen. Apocryphon (Jerusalem, Magnes Press of the Hebrew University, 1956); Col. II, 22-26; XIX, 25(?); see J. A. Fitzmyer, The Genesis Apocryphon of Qumran Cave I (Rome Pontifical Biblical Institute, 1966), p. 46 (Col. V), 52.

18   See above note 13. See also Test. of XII Patriarchs: Simeon 5:4; Levi 10:5; 14:1 (b); 16:1 (b).

The ascription of knowledge to Enoch was based upon Gen. 5:24: "Enoch walked with God, and he was no more, for God had taken him." Unless an oral tradition is assumed, there is nothing in this verse to posit Enoch was the first wise man.[19] As the claim of the patriarch Abraham to have been considered the father of civilization must have appealed to the surging nationalistic feelings among some Jewish writers, Gen. 15:5 relates that the Lord told Abraham to count the stars, a passage that was sometimes taken by midrashists as proof of the patriarch's astrological education.[20] Pseudo-Eupolemus, a Samaritan writing about 200 B.C., ascribed the discovery of the sciences to the biblical patriarchs, but hesitated between Enoch and Abraham. Unfortunately, Pseudo-Eupolemus' account of Moses, if any ever existed, has not survived. But Josephus and Philo, who do stress Abraham's contributions to the sciences and especially to astrology, fail to credit the Jewish lawgiver with any significant scientific achievement. It is nonetheless true that Philo repeatedly attaches to Moses the epithet "all-wise" (*pansophos*), although his favorite title, like the pagan allusions to Moses, is "lawgiver." Philo likewise credits the young Moses with the ability to solve problems which baffled the capacity of his instructors.[21] But only Eupolemus makes Moses the originator of civilization, supposedly reflecting the surge of national feeling in the aftermath of the Maccabean uprising. [22]

Fragment One reveals that Eupolemus wrote for men who were exposed to a fair amount of Hellenistic education. There is little doubt that in calling

---

19   The Book of Enoch is among the oldest witnesses to what later became a widespread custom to compose works bearing the name of a famous biblical patriarch. The fact that "wisdom" was ascribed to pre-Abrahamic figures was perhaps an attempt to explain how civilization had spread among many peoples and was not exclusively a Jewish monopoly.

20   On the figure of Abraham in Graeco-Jewish literature, see S. Sandmel, *Philo's Place in Judaism* (Cincinnati, Hebrew Union College Press, 1956); in Josephus, L. H. Feldman, "Abraham the Greek Philosopher in Josephus," *Transactions and Proceedings of the American Philological Association,* 99 (1968), 143-56; Wacholder, *HUCA,* 34 (1963), 83-113.

21   Cf. *A.J.,* II, 228-37 and previous note. For Philo's treatment of Moses, see his *De Vita Mosis*; for Moses as the "pansophos" see *Leg. All.,* II, 87; *Det.,* 169, 173; *Gig.,* 56; *Abr.,* 13; as a prodigious child, *Vit. Mos.,* 21 f. For other passages see Colson's index in LCL, X, 387 f., note. But Philo's favorite epithet for Abraham is also "sophos," though "pansophos" appears once (*Cher.,* 18) in Colson's index (X, p. 278). In contrast to Abraham, about whose alleged inventions Graeco-Jewish writers were almost unanimous, Philo and Josephus appear to have been unaware of Eupolemus' claims that Moses invented the alphabet.

22   For modern reconstructions of the Hellenistic Moses, see Isaac Heinemann, "Moses," *R.E.,* 31 (1933), 359-75; G. Vermès, in *Moïse, l'Homme de l'alliances,* 63-92; German translation (Patmos-Verlag, Düsseldorf, 1963), 61-93; John Gager, *"The Figure of Moses in Greek and Roman Pagan Literature"* (Harvard University Ph.D. Thesis, 1968); *Moses in Graeco-Roman Paganism* (Society of Biblical Literature, Monograph Series, 1972).

Moses the first wise man Eupolemus expected his readers to have been acquainted with the Hellenistic lore relating the famous Seven Wise Men of Greece. The Seven Wise Men, according to popular accounts, antedated the philosophers; the term *philosophia,* supposedly invented by Pythagoras,[23] was intended to contrast with wisdom, since "No one is wise save God." In the Oriental tradition the wise man evoked an image of a royal adviser, a magician, a prophet, or even an artisan.[24] But the Seven Wise Men of Greece—Thales of Miletus, Solon of Athens, Chilon of Sparta, Bias of Priene, Pittacus of Mytilene, Cleobulus of Lindos, and Periander of Corinth—were regarded as the pillars of civilization.[25] They were the "philosophers" before philosophy was discovered. Their gnomic sayings were on everybody's lips, the most famous of which, "Know thyself," by Chilon, was inscribed in the Delphic temple of Apollo.[26] Eupolemus' claim that Moses was "the first wise man"($πρῶτος σόφος$) must then be understood in the Greek sense, making him older than the Seven Wise Men who flourished in the seventh and sixth centuries B.C. In our fragment the text refers only to the priority of Moses, but what we know of Graeco-Jewish writings leaves little doubt that Eupolemus meant by *protos* also the foremost and originator of wisdom. Certainly, Eupolemus could claim that Moses' Pentateuch exhibited more wisdom that the slight collections of the laconic proverbs of the Seven Wise Men.[27] Moses was the father of culture and civilization.

II

The next two sentences, claiming that Moses invented the alphabet and the written law, remove any doubt as to what Eupolemus meant by the Mosaic wisdom. As to the former, the term attributed to Eupolemus in Eusebius is $γράμματα$ (letters); in Clement $γραμματική$, a term which is normally the equivalent of "grammar," but may also mean script or alphabet.[28]

23   On the Seven Wise Men, see Diels-Kranz, *Fragmente der Vorsokratiker,* I[6] (Zurich, Weidmann, 1968), 61-66, (10) with supplemental bibliography on p. 584. On Pythagoras, ibid., pp. 466-480 (58); Diog. Laertius, I, 12 (quoting Heraclides); cf. W. Guthrie, *A History of Greek Philosophy* (Cambridge, Cambridge University Press, 1962), I, 164 f.

24   Cf. the texts edited by J. B. Pritchard, *Ancient Near Eastern Texts Relating to the Old Testament*[2] (Princeton, N.J., Princeton University Press, 1955), 402-52; H. Zimmarn, "Die sieben Weisen Babyloniens," *Zeitschrift für Assyrologie*, NF. 1 (1924), 151-54. See also S. H. Blank, "Wisdom," in *The Interpreter's Dictionary of the Bible* (New York, Abingdon Press, 1962), IV, 852-61.

25   Diels-Kranz, *Vorsokratiker,* I[6] (1951), 61-66; note the comment by Dicaearchus (300 B.C.), "The Wise Men were neither 'wise' nor philosophers, but intelligent men and lawgivers" (Diogenes Laertius, I, 40).

26   Plato, *Prot.* 343A = *Vorsokratiker*, I, 62 (10, 2).

27   Possibly, Eupolemus understood under "Moses" not only the Pentateuch, but also the Prophets and the Wisdom Books of the Hagiographa.

28   See note 8.

Whatever the wording, Eupolemus leaves some ambiguity as to which letters Moses invented. In his day the Greek and Phoenician alphabets were standard, but among the Jews two scripts were used—the so-called square script (כתב אשורי) still in use in our own day, and the "Hebrew" script that was apparently already becoming archaic in the middle of the second century B.C.[29] The older style of writing was retained for coinage, and, in some instances, for the copying of the Lord's name, it is still used by the Samaritans. Unless we assume that Eupolemus was merely repeating a common view, he must have meant the archaic script. For it alone resembled the North-Semitic alphabet employed by the Phoenicians, from which the Greek letters had been derived.[30] But in Eupolemus' view, as in the opinion of some modern partisans, the Phoenicians merely served as middle men between the Jews and the Greeks.

It is significant perhaps that the verb employed by Eupolemus to describe the first use of the alphabet is $\pi\alpha\rho\alpha\delta\iota\delta\omega\mu\iota$, denoting "to impart," "to transmit." If the use of this term was deliberate, Eupolemus seems to have intended to convey the impression that Moses himself had not discovered the alphabet, but merely handed it over to the Jews. The alphabet was a divine gift to Moses who imparted it to the Jews. The proof text from Scripture may have been Exod. 32:16: "And the tablets were the tablets of God and the script was the script of God." Conceivably, Eupolemus meant to say that the ancient Hebrew script was a part of God's gift when he gave the Jews the Decalogue. In another passage, Eupolemus wrote that when Nebuchadnezzar destroyed the Solomonic Temple and carried its spoils to Babylonia, Jeremiah retained the tablets of the law handed down by Moses.[31] Is there a connection between the two passages?

Eupolemus' main topic, however, was the pedigree of the Greek alphabet—the father of all alphabetic scripts used in the West. This was a hotly debated theme throughout antiquity. It is rather doubtful that Eupolemus was aware of the full scope of the dispute, but it is possible that we are underestimating his intellectual baggage. At any rate, it is clear that some of the arguments had penetrated into the holy walls of Jerusalem.

Two issues were involved here: first, the origin of the script; and second, the meaning of the names of the letters. Hecataeus of Miletus (500 B.C.), the master of the Father of History, noted that the origin of the alphabet was to

29   M. Megillah, III, 11; Yer. ibid., I, 11, p. 71b; B. Sanhedrin, 21b. Professor N. T. Tur-Sinai (Encyclopaedia Biblica, IV (Jerusalem, Mosad Bialik, 1962, 378) unconvincingly denies that these and similar talmudic references allude to the Samaritan script, but rather to two divergent copies of the Samaritan and Ezra's Pentateuchs.

30   S. Yeivin, The History of the Jewish Script (Jerusalem, 1938) [in Hebrew]; D. Diringer, Le iscrizioni antico-ebraiche palestinesi (Florence, 1934); F. M. Cross and N. D. Freedman, Early Hebrew Orthography (Baltimore, 1952); Cf. also A. Spiro, Proceedings of the American Academy for Jewish Research 20 (1950), 284, n. 22.

31   P.E. IX, 39, 5 = Eupolemus, 723 F 5 (Walter 4).

be found in Egypt from whence before the time of Cadmus, Danaüs brought it to Hellas.[32] Others ascribed its invention to the aboriginal Pelasgians, Cretans, Assyrians, to Heracles, or even to Linus, the mythical son of Apollo and Amathe.[33] The fact that "phoenicia" was another Greek term for the letters of the alphabet caused many antiquarians, beginning with Herodotus himself, to trace the transmission of the alphabet by Cadmus, the reputed son of Tyre, to Ionia.[34] Modern scholarship by demonstrating that the Greek letters were an adaptation of the North-Semitic script of the ninth or eighth century confirms Herodotus' view.[35] But whether this script was strictly autochthonous in Phoenicia or was a modification of the Egyptian hiero-glyphics is still a matter of dispute. In Greek antiquity, as in modern times, the main contention was between the Egyptian and the Phoenician origin of the alphabet.

In Hellenistic times the Egyptian theory, as mentioned above, had its most able defender in Hecataeus of Abdera, who postulated the Egyptian origin of civilization. Though he granted Herodotus' contention that Cadmus brought the alphabet to Ionia, Hecataeus maintained that Cadmus was a native of Egyptian Thebes. In fact, he said, Cadmus and Danaüs left Egypt when a wave of xenophobia swept the country. The first two colonized Hellas, the last settled Judaea.[36] In another passage, apparently also belonging to Hecataeus, he illustrates further this pan-Egyptian origin of civilization. It is said that Egypt peopled the world: Bellus founded Bablyon, Danaüs colonized Argos, and the Colchis of the Pontus and the Jews, who live between Arabia and Syria, two people who practiced the rite of circumcision, borrowed the custom from the Egyptians. Many Athenian words and customs make sense only

32   Hecataeus of Miletus, 1 F 20. See also Anaximander, 9 F 3; Dionysius of Miletus, 687 F 1; Apollodorus of Athens, 244 F 165; Anticildus of Athens, 140 F 11a-b, who also maintained that the Greek alphabet had its source in Egypt. See Jacoby, on 1 F 20 (*FGrH* Ia, p. 324), who notes that before the Miletian school introduced Cadmus, Danaüs was believed to have brought the alphabet from Phoenicia, originally invented by the Egyptians, whose civilization impressed the Greeks as the oldest in existence.

33   See Hecataeus, 1 F 20; Dosiades, 458 F 6; Diod., V, 74, 1; Pliny, N.H., VII, 193 = ((Pseudo)-Berossus, 680 F 16a-b. For the polemic see also Photius-Suida, s.v. φοινικήια γράμματα.

34   Herod., V. 58; Ephorus of Cyme, 70 F 105; Aristotle, F 501 (Rose). See Jacoby, cited in note 32.

35   Based upon the resemblance of Greek and Phoenician letters of the period. David Diringer, *The Alphabet: A Key to the History of Mankind* (London, Hutchinson of London, 1968), 145-83; 356-66. But see Alan Gardner, *Egypt of the Pharaohs* (Oxford, Clarendon Press, 1962), 15 f.

36   Hecataeus of Abdera, 264 F 6 = Diod., XL, 3 = Th. Reinach, *Textes d'auteurs grecs et romains*, 14 f.

if assumed that they were derived from Egypt.[37]

In the Graeco-Jewish fragments, Artapanus seems to embellish Hecataeus' hypothesis, that made Egypt the origin of civilization, with the modification that the apparent Egyptian discoveries were in fact taught to them by Abraham, Joseph, and especially Moses.[38] Abraham introduced astrology to Egypt, Joseph brought agriculture, Moses—supposedly identical with Musaeus and the teach'er of Orpheus—was responsible for a large number of inventions. Artapanus catalogues them haphazardly: shipbuilding, weaponry, machines to move stone, engines for irrigation, philosophy, and the peculiar Egyptian religion. Moses is also credited by Artapanus with the invention of the hieroglyphics, for which the priests honored him as a God, calling him Hermes, "because he interpreted the sacred letters" διὰ τὴν τῶν ἱερῶν γραμμάτων ἑρμηνείαν[39]. Artapanus' words must be understood in light of Diodorus' account of Egypt, taken as is generally agreed from Hecataeus' words: "It was by Hermes, for instance, according to them (the Egyptians), that the common language of mankind was first further articulated, and many objects which were still nameless received an appellation, that the alphabet was invented (τήν τε εὕρεσιν τῶν γραμμάτων), and that ordinances regarding the honors and offerings due to the gods were duly established; he was the first to observe the orderly arrangement of the stars and the harmony of the musical sounds and their nature . . . The Greeks were also taught by him the exposition (ἑρμηνεία) of their thoughts, and it was for this reason that he was given the name Hermes. In a word, Osiris taking him (Hermes) for his priestly scribe, communicated with him on every matter and used his counsel above all the others. The olive tree also, they say, was his discovery, not Athena's, as the Greeks say."[40] By identifying Moses with the Egyptian Hermes, Artapanus betrays that his authority was not a native Egyptian source, but a Greek account of Egypt, namely that of Hecataeus.[41] As far as we know, only Hecataeus and the writers dependent on him made Egypt the

---

37   Diod. I, 28, 1-4 = Hecataeus 264 F 25. That Diodorus was here paraphrasing Hecataeus, see Jacoby, *FGrH*, IIIa, p. 49, 12-21, who also notes (lines 21 ff.) differences between F 6, where it is said that the foreigners were expelled, and F 25 (I, 28-29), asserting that settlements resulted from colonization. For the Egyptian origin of the practice of circumcision, see Herod. II, 104, who probably was Hecataeus' source that the Colchians and the "Syrians of Palaestine" had a common practice.

38   *P.E.*, IX, 18, 1; 23; 27 = Artapanus, 726 FF 1-3.

39   *P.E.*, IX, 27 = 726 F 3.

40   Diod. I, 16 = 264 F 25; cf. Diod. I, 12.

41   See Hugo Willrich, *Juden und Griechen vor der Makkabäischen Erhebung* (Göttingen, 1895), 168-71; *Judaica* (Göttingen, 1900), 111-16; Schürer, *Gesch. d. jüd. Volkes*, III[4], 479, notes that Artapanus' Egyptian nationality, "bedarf bei dem starken Hervortreten der ägyptischen Beziehungen nicht erst des Beweises." But Schürer fails to mention that the Egyptian lore may have been taken secondhand via Hecataeus. See also Y, Gutman, *The Beginnings of Jewish-Hellenistic Literature* II, 109-35, who rightly stresses Artapanus' dependence on Hecataeus (pp. 121 ff.).

mother of all culture and civilization, emphasizing Hermes as a versatile deity who discovered both the alphabet and hermeneutics. In the older tradition, Hermes had many functions, but they were of a rather subordinate role. Linked with "sacred stones," he was a messenger of Zeus and other gods, or as god of the flocks, merchants and thieves. Hecataeus elevated him to Osiris' companion, bestowing literary tastes upon him. It was Hecataeus' Hermes, refined further by Artapanus and others, who ultimately became "Thoth the Very Great" or Hermes Trismegistus, the author of works on magic, alchemy and astrology.[42] For our discussion, however, the significant point is Hecataeus' argument that the traditions of Egyptian civilization were more reliable than those of the Greeks. The Greek writers beginning with Hecataeus of Miletus and Herodotus were quite impressed with Egyptian antiquities and admired the uniqueness of the Egyptian civilization, but it remained for Hecataeus of Abdera to view the country on the Nile as the source of the Hellenic and Barbarian achievements.

Excepting the ardent phil-Egyptians, the fact that in Greek "Phoenikeia" was another name for the letters of the alphabet made the legend ascribing the Greek script to Cadmus of Tyre appear plausible.[43] But many Greek patriots could not resist the temptation to claim this marvelous invention for some favorite Hellenic locality. Writing in Alexandria in the middle of the second century B.C., Dionysius Skytobrachion of Mitylene, as preserved by Diodorus, reiterated the story of Cadmus and the Phoenician antecedent of the Greek alphabet, but added that Linus adopted the foreign alphabet for Hellenic speech.[44] Zeno of Rhodes denied, however, the Phoenician origin of the Greek alphabet. The alphabet, like astrology and other sciences, says Zeno, was discovered by the Heliadae, the early settlers of Rhodes and Athens. But since these natives perished, the Egyptians unfairly appropriated the invention of astrology, and the Greeks, ignorant of their original contribution, ascribed the origin of the Greek letters to the foreigner Cadmus.[45]

Not to be outdone, an anonymous Cretan author—perhaps, as Jacoby says, Laosthenidas—says that the alphabet was discovered on his island. For Zeus saw to it that the Muses should discover the letters of the alphabet, to combine words in such a way as to make poetry. The Phoenicians, according to Laosthenidas, merely reshaped the letters used by other peoples, hence the

---

42   See R. Reitzenstein, *Poimandros: Studien zur grichisch-ägyptischen und frühchristlichen Literatur* (Leipzig, 1904), 123, 365, and passim; A.J. Festugière, *La Révélation d'Hermès Trismégiste* (Paris, 1950-54).

43   Cf. Herod. V, 58; Ephorus of Cyme, *FGrH* 70 F 105.

44   Diod. III, 67, 1 = Dionysius Scytobrachion, 32 F 8; cf. Tacitus, *Annales* XI, 14; *Suda* s. v. "Linos." According to this theory, the Pelasgians discovered single letters for different sounds, but as a group the alphabet was brought from Phoenicia to Greece by Cadmus, and Linus adopted it for Hellenic use.

45   Diod. V, 57, 1-5 = Zeno of Rhodes, 533 F 1.

story of Cadmus and the name "Phoenikeia" meaning the letters of the alphabet.[46]

It should be noted, however, that Laosthenidas takes it for granted that the putative inventors of the alphabet were the Syrians, but that the Phoenicians, having learned it from the Syrians, passed it on to the Greeks.[47] This ascription of the alphabet to the Syrians, as distinct from the Phoenicians, appears to be mentioned nowhere else by the Hellenistic writers. Unfortunately, it is not clear exactly who was meant by the Syrians. Schwartz says that the reference was to the Aramaeans; Jacoby, to the Assyrians.[48] Jacoby's contention has support in the Jewish tradition, since the talmudists refer to the square Hebrew script as "Assyrian."[49] But Greek geographers, from Herodotus onwards, often said Syria when they meant Palestine or Judaea; and since only the Hebrews of the region developed a script quite distinct from the North-Phoenician, it is likely that Laosthenidas—if he was the author—referred to the Hebrews as the alleged discoverers of the alphabet.[50] What is remarkable is the parallel between the traditions cited by this Cretan author and by Eupolemus:

Eupolemus	*Laosthenidas' rejected tradition*
He [Moses] taught the letters first to the Jews; the Phoenicians received them from the Jews, the Greeks from the Phoenicians.	The Syrians were the discoverers of the letters; the Phoenicians having learned them from the Syrians, passed them on to the Greeks.[51]

The name of the man who invented the North-Semitic alphabet—from which all alphabetic writing is derived—is as much a mystery today as it was in antiquity. David Diringer, in a recent study of the history of writing, sums up the subject neatly: "Since classical times the problem has been a matter of serious study. The Greeks and Romans held five conflicting opinions as to who were the inventors of the alphabet: the Phoenician, the Egyptian, the Assyrian, the Cretan, and the Hebrew, and in modern times, various theories, some not very different in part from those of ancient days, have been

---

46   Diod. V, 74, 1-2 = Crete (Anhang), 468 F 1. Concerning the identification of the author of this polemic as Laosthenidas, see Jacoby, IIIb, 341-64.

47   Diod. V, 74, 1 = 468 F 1. Jacoby (IIIb, I, 357, 40-58, 3, notes that the polemic is directed against writers who saw the origin of the alphabet, not in Egypt, as was maintained in the older Greek tradition, but in Assyria. See next note.

48   E. Schwartz, *R.E.*, V, 1598, 11 ff.; Jacoby, *FGrH*, IIIb, II, 213, note 118.

49   See above note 29.

50   See Herod. VII, 63; cf. II, 105; V, 89, "The Syrians of Palestine." Herod. IV, 87, records Darius' monument, inscribed with "Assyrian writing" (γράμματα), referring to cuneiform writing, as is attested in Darius' inscription. For Syrian script used by the Nabataeans, see Diod. XIX, 96, 1.

51   Diod. V, 74, 1 = 468 F 1: πρὸς δὲ τοὺς λέγοντας ὅτι Σύροι μὲν εὑρεταὶ τῶν γραμμάτων εἰσί, παρὰ δὲ τούτων Φοίνικες, μαθόντες τοῖς Ἕλλησι παραδεδώκασιν.

current."[52] Diringer himself places the inventor of the alphabet "among the greatest benefactors of mankind"[53] —in Syria and Palestine possibly during the reign of the Hyksos. Echoing Eupolemus, Professor H. Tur-Sinai argues that the twenty-two letter alphabet "was created in Israel, for the purpose of Israel's religious law," expressed in the origin of the Torah.[54]

III

"Also, laws were first written by Moses for the Jews."[55] It is possible to regard this independently from Moses' invention of the alphabet. But since traditionally the "wise man" became almost equivalent to the great lawgiver,[56] it makes more sense to treat it as a part of a unitary thought: Moses was the first "wise man"—hence he was the father of "wisdom," the antecedent of (a) Greek philosophy; (b) the alphabet; and (c) written laws. Only in regard to the letters of the alphabet is it clearly stated by Eupolemus that Moses established a universal legacy. There is no reason to assume, however, that he wished to restrict the universality to Moses' invention of the alphabet alone. It was singled out because only here could a reasonable case he made that even pagan records credit the Jews with the invention of the alphabet. But Eupolemus may have argued that Mosaic Law was the oldest book that utilized a twenty-two letter script. Thus the invention of written law, according to Eupolemus, was the climax of Moses' other benefits bestowed on mankind. All three inventions—"wisdom," the alphabet, and written legislation—were indispensable for the development of a civilized society, and therefore were of neither Greek nor Barbarian origin.

Eupolemus' gnomic wording leaves doubt as to whether he meant that the Mosaic contribution consisted of the idea of written law, or whether the pagan legal systems were ultimately derived from Jewish jurisprudence. The latter was intended surely if alphabetic writing and written legislation are taken to be parallel. Dealing with the same subject more than two centuries after the Maccabean period, Josephus perhaps offers a fair commentary on what Graeco-Jewish writers—although not necessarily Eupolemus—meant by the priority of the Jewish law. After pointing out the necessity of law for an orderly society and the attempts by various nations to present their own legal system as the oldest, *Contra Apionem,* II, 154-56 asserts:

> Now, I maintain that our legislator is the most ancient of all legislators in the records of the whole world. Compared with him, your Lycurguses, and Solons, and Zaleucus, who gave the Locrians their

---

52   David Diringer, *The Alphabet,* I, 146.
53   Ibid. I, 163 f; see also 145-72.
54   Ibid. 163, quoting Tur-Sinai.
55   *P.E.,* IX, 26, I, p. 519, 6 = 723 F 1a.
56   Diogenes Laertius, I, 40, quoting Dicaearchus *Fragm. d. Vorsokratiker,* 10, 1 (I, p. 61, 5-7).

laws, and all who were held in such high esteem by the Greeks appear to have been born but yesterday.[57] Why, the very word "law" (νόμος) was unknown in ancient Greece. Witness Homer, who never employs it in his poems. In fact, there was no such thing in his day; the masses were governed by maxims (γνῶμαι) not clearly defined and by orders of royalty, and continued long afterwards the use of unwritten laws (ἔθεσιν ἀγράφοις)   many of which were from time to time altered to suit particular circumstances. On the other hand, our legislator Moses, who lived in the remotest past (that, I presume, is admitted even by our most unscrupulous detractors), proved himself the people's best guide and counsellor; and after framing a code (νόμος)to embrace the whole conduct of their life, induced them to accept it, and secured on the firmest footing its observance for all time.

Here we have the Jewish understanding of the Law. But Josephus' denigration of the "unwritten ethos," in contrast to the Mosaic written Law, appears somewhat more Sadducean than what we believe to have been the Pharisaic understanding of the Torah.[58]   Conceivably, the Pharisee Josephus borrowed this account from a Sadducean author. We know nothing of Eupolemus' party allegiance, if any, but as a priest and friend of Judah Maccabee, he subscribed, it may be presumed, to the Sadducean doctrine which may have regarded as Mosaic only the written law.

By Mosaic laws (νόμοι) Eupolemus meant, despite his use of the   plural, the Torah as a whole.[59]   It would be unreasonable to limit his words to the Decalogue. Whatever it meant, the significance of the statement should not be overlooked. It did, however, escape the attention of Peter Dalbert, who reasons that Eupolemus did not attach much significance to the law, having mentioned it only once in connection with Moses.[60]   Although this was the only formal allusion to the law, Dalbert has disregarded the influence of the Pentateuch on other parts of Eupolemus' work. For Eupolemus does refer, directly and indirectly, to the Mosaic tabernacle. He says of the Temple's

57   Lycurgus was the mythical founder of the Spartan state (Herod. I, 65 f; vita in Plutarch). Solon (c. 640/35-561/60) reformed the Athenian constitution (Aristotle, *Ath. Pol.*, 1-13; Plutarch, *Solon*). The ancients debated whether or not the reputed founder of the Italian Locrian laws was historical (Timaeus, 566 F 130 a; cf. T. S. Brown, *Timaeus of Tauromenium* [Berkeley and Los Angeles, University of California Press, 1958], 49 f.).

58   It is possible though, that for Josephus the concept of "unwritten laws" was not identical to "ancestral traditions" (cf. Josephus, *Vita*, 191; *A.J.*, XIII, 297; Philo, *De sp. leg.* IV, 149 f.). Josephus' term for the rules of prenomistic civilization is ἔθη ἄγραφα; for the halakhic customs νόμιμα ἄγραφα. Cf. A. Schlatter, *Die Theologie des Judentums nach dem Bericht des Josefus* (Gütersloh, 1932), 62.

59   For the meaning of νόμος see Liddell and Scott, s.v., and W. Gutbrod, *ThWBNT,* IV, 1016-50.

60   P. Dalbert, *Die Theologie der hellenistisch-jüdischen Missions-literatur unter Ausschlus von Philo und Josephus* (Hamburg, 1954), 42.

lampstands, that Solomon modelled them after the one "made by Moses in the tent of testimony."[61]   The biblical authors of I Kings and II Chronicles make it clear that in fact Solomon's temple owed little to the desert tabernacle, except for the Mosaic tablets.[62]   Eupolemus, however, went out of his way to stress that the desert tabernacle served as a blueprint for Solomon. He frequently departs from the accounts of I Kings and II Chronicles to make it appear as if the Solomonic structure harmonized with that of the Pentateuch.[63]   The fact that Eupolemus makes Jeremiah preserve the holy tablets of the Law, when the Babylonians destroyed the Temple, shows how dedicated the Hellenistic historian was to the Mosaic Books.[64]

IV

Thus far we have attempted to reconstruct the image of Eupolemus' Moses—the "wise man," the inventor of the alphabet, the legislator. There remains, however, the puzzle as to why Eupolemus presented Moses as he did. The possible generalization that he glorified the Jewish lawgiver because some Hellenizers had disparaged the ancestral traditions does not explain why Moses was presented by Eupolemus and other Graeco-Jewish writers as the benefactor of mankind. Whether the presentation was intended for the Jewish readers or for the pagans, there appears a standardized Mosaic figure. Interestingly, the pagan Greek and Roman accounts of Moses often conform to a large extent to this glorified standard.

The reason seems to be that most pagan and Jewish descriptions of Moses were directly or indirectly based on the same model. The source was found in the work of Hecataeus of Abdera, a philosopher-historian who flourished in the last quarter of the fourth century B.C.[65] His history of Egypt, inadequately summarized in Diodorus' first book, reflects a love of Egypt's people and religion.[66] Tucked away in this work was the first and most

---

61   723 F 2b = *P.E.*, IX, 34 (5), 7; see also IX, 34 (2), 4: 13 (15). Note the fear of ritual pollution, 34 (15), 13.

62   The accounts of the construction of the Temple in I Kings 6-9 and II Chr. 1-7 are given without reference to the Mosaic tabernacle, except I Kings 8:9 = II Ch. 5:10, which records the presence of the stone tablets in the holy of holies. Some scholars, moreover, antedate the description of the Solomonic Temple in Kings to that of Moses' tabernacle in Exodus.

63   See below pp. 184-86.

64   *P.E.*, IX, 39, 5 = 723 F 5 (Walter, F 4).

65   On Hecataeus of Abdera, see E. Schwartz, *Rheinisches Museum* 40 (1885), 223-62; *R.E.*, V (1905), 670-72; Jacoby, "Hekataios" No. 4, *R.E.*, 7 (1912), 2750-69; *FGrH* No. 264, esp. the commentary in IIIa, pp. 29-87.

66   Hecataeus' *Aegyptiaca,* is preserved in Diogenes Laertius, I, 9-11 (264 FF 1;3; Plutarch, *De Isis* 6; 9 (264 FF 4-5: Photius *Bibl.* 244 (264 F 6 = Diod. XL, 3); Diod. I, 10-98 (264 F 25). A number of recent studies have attempted unsuccessfully, I believe,

sympathetic, and certainly most influential, description of the Jewish lawgiver.[67]

All that is left of Hecataeus' Mosaic accounts are two mentions in the remains of Diodorus' historical library. Diodorus, I, 94-95, lists, no doubt paraphrasing Hecataeus, the names of the most distinguished lawgivers ever known, from Mneves (Menes), the founder of the Egyptian state, to the Persian King Darius. The foremost of these, according to Hecataeus, was Mneves, "the first to persuade the masses of Egypt to adopt written laws" (ἐγγράπτοι νομοί).[68] Although it is difficult to prove conclusively, it is reasonable to assume that Eupolemus' attribution of the invention of written laws to Moses was a conscious imitation of Hecataeus' account of Mneves.

The fact that Hecataeus had linked Moses with Mneves (Menes) makes Eupolemus' indebtedness to the pagan historian-philosopher even more probable. Describing Mneves as "not only of a great soul but also the most public spirit of all lawgivers ever recorded,"[69] Hecataeus, as paraphrased by Diodorus, goes on to compare him with Greek and barbarian lawgivers of parallel if inferior rank. First listed are Minos of Crete, who received the laws from Zeus; and Lycurgus of Sparta, who received the laws from Apollo, just as Mneves attributed the laws he had invented to Hermes. Diodorus, using the words of Hecataeus, lists three barbarian legislators who used similar devices: the Persian Zarathustra claimed that the "Good Daemon" gave him the laws; Zalmoxis attributed the laws which he gave the Getae to Hestia, the goddess of the hearth; and "among the Jews Moyses who invoked the name of Iao (Ἰαώ)."[70]

---

to rehabilitate Diodorus' literary independence. See Richard Laqueur, "Diodorea," *Hermes,* 86 (1958), 257-90; W. Spoerri, *Sp’äthellenistische Berichte über Welt, Kultur und Götter: Untersuchungen zu Diodor von Sizilien* (Schweitzarische Beiträge zur Altertumswissenschaft, 9, Basel, 1959). Despite Spoerri, there is no reason to doubt that Diodorus' account of Egypt follows essentially Hecataeus' *Aegyptiaca.* As to Reinhardt's claim (*Posidonios* [note 73], 56-60) that Diodorus followed here Posidonius, see John Gager, *Moses,* 30.

67   Photius, *Bibl.* 244 = Diod. XL, 3 = 264 F 6. See also Diod. I, 27, 2; 94, 2 = 264 F 25.

68   Diod. I, 94, 1 = 264 F 25. Hecataeus (Diod. I, 43, 5) ascribes to Menas [Μηνᾶς] (apparently identical to Manetho's Menes [Μήνης] in 609 F 2, p. 16, 6) the introduction of luxury, for which he was later criticized.

69   Diod. I, 94, 1 = 264 F 25.

70   Diod. I, 94, 1. Cf. Varro, in Lydus, *De Mensibus,* IV, 53, who attributes the name Ἰαώ to mystical incantations of the Chaldaeans. The name יהו , of which Ἰαώ is apparently derived, is a lengthened form of יה and shortened of יהוה .See Ps. 104:35 – "hallelu-Yah"; Cowley, *Aramaic Papyri,* p. xviii. As to the actual pronunciation of the ineffable name, Hecataeus and Varro are the only pre-Christian witnesses. It is a fair question whether the letters reproduced here were based on the pronunciation of the Alexandrian Jews or of Jerusalemites. For the early Christian testimony regarding the pronunciation of this name, see B. N. Anderson, in *The Interpreter's Dictionary of the Bible,* II, 409b, who does not cite Hecataeus or Varro. Cf. also Gager, *Moses,* 30 f.

This strictly rationalistic, multinational presentation of the origins of law, was, however, unacceptable to Eupolemus. But by ignoring other names mentioned in the source and by paraphrasing the passage in a way that places Moses far above Mneves, Eupolemus altered the Euhemeristic spirit of the original. Surely, pagan gods were but human inventions, unlike Moses' ineffable Yahweh. But by avoiding the mention of the deity altogether, Eupolemus bypassed the problem of attribution found in his model. But Eupolemus used Hecataeus differently than did Artapanus. The latter simply identified Moses with Hermes, the deity to whom Mneves, according to Hecataeus, attributed the laws.[71] It was as an Egyptian, Artapanus implies, rather than as a Jew, as in Eupolemus, that Moses made the wonderful inventions.[72] Unlike Artapanus, Eupolemus, as far as we know, ignored the view that the alphabet originated in Egypt. But the diverse adaptations of Hecataeus' accounts of Egypt by Artapanus and Eupolemus make contrasting histories of how two Jewish Hellenists transformed the same pagan passages on Moses. Artapanus retained the Euhemeristic elements found in the original; Eupolemus purged them.

Hecataeus of Abdera's influence on Graeco-Jewish writing was not limited to Eupolemus and Artapanus. Euhemerism, as first formulated by Hecataeus and Leon of Pella,[73] permeates the fragment of Pseudo-Eupolemus, in which the Samaritan author identifies Enoch with the Hellenic Atlas.[74] The name of the heathen Hecataeus of Abdera, moreover, became a popular pseudonym among Jews who used his name for their forgeries.[75] It is also possible that Hecataeus' account of ancient Judaism contained the first transliteration of Jerusalem as "Hierosolyma."[76]

---

71   Diod. I, 1-3; 17, 1; 43, 6 = Hecataeus, 264 F 25; Artapanus, *P.E.*, IX, 27, 6 = 726 F 3.

72   Artapanus, *P.E.*, IX, 27, 1-10 = 726 F 3.

73   Euhemerus (*FGrH* No. 63), Hecataeus (264), and Leon of Pella (659) were contemporaries. All flourished at the end of the fourth and the beginning of the third centuries B.C.; Hecataeus was perhaps the oldest of the three and Leon the youngest. Euhemerus wrote tales in which he presented the gods as humans; Hecataeus and Leon dealt with mythical history, especially Egyptian religion, as a state of human evolution, a kind of primitive version of "Darwinism." Philosophically, the three men belonged to the school of Democritus. The fullest formulation of this theory is reproduced in Diod. I, 7-9. Cf. I. Reinhardt, "Posidonios über Ursprung und Entartung," *Orient und Antike*, 8 (1928); Jacoby, *R.E.*, VII (1912), 2750-69; *FGrH*, IIIa, 29-87, esp. pp. 31, 85.

74   *P.E.* IX, 17x, 1-8; 18, 2 = Pseudo-Eupolemus, 724 FF 1-2; cf. Wacholder, *HUCA* 34 (1963), 83-113; N. Walter, *Klio*, 43-45 (1965), 282-89.

75   See Hecataeus, 264 TT 7-8 = *C. Apionem*, I, 183-85; 213; *A.J.* I, 158-59; FF 21-24 = Jos. *C. Apionem*, I, 186-205; II, 42-47; Letter of Aristeas, 31; Clement, *Strom.*, V, 131, 1. Cf. Walter, *Der Thoraausleger Aristobulos*, 7-13; Speyer (below note 79), 156, 160 f.

76   The Greek form Hierosolyma (Ἱεροσόλυμα) appears for the first time in Hecataeus (Photius-Diod. XL, 3, 3 = 264 F 6), a transliteration based on a Greek exegesis of the name; the older Greek form of Jerusalem (Ἱηρουσαλημ) is preserved in the LXX.

Important as Hecataeus was for the Jewish Hellenistic historians, he was even of greater significance for the formulation of the image of Moses in pagan Graeco-Roman historiography.[77] Although Herodotus alluded to the Palestinian rite of circumcision and Aristotle related some lore concerning Judaea,[78] there is no attested mention of Moses in Greek literature prior to the Macedonian conquest of the Persian empire. After that of Hecataeus, discussed below, the oldest mention of Moses, if we can believe here the tradition recorded in Clement of Alexandria, was found in Leon of Pella's *Alexander's Letter to His Mother,* a work written in 300 B.C. describing the gods of Egypt. According to Leon, "Isis whom the Greeks called Demeter lived in the days of Lynceus, the eleventh generation after Moses."[79] Unfortunately, the context of this allusion is not clear, and its authenticity in Clement is questionable.[80] What should not be forgotten is that ancient Jewish history penetrated the Greek literary world via the interest in things Egyptian, and under the banner of Euhemerism.[81] These two factors remained paramount until the advent of Christianity, even as Judeophobia, born in the aftermath of the Maccabean rebellion, began to be a significant literary motive. Moses, and Moses alone, remained the only biblical Jew—with the exception of Apollonius Molon's and Trogus Pompeius' allusions   to Abraham and Joseph—ever mentioned by pagan writers.[82]

Thus Hecataeus' account of Moses, partly reported by Diodorus and preserved in Photius, was of epochal significance. Central in this account was the figure of Moses as the founder of a new religion. For background it must be remembered that Hecataeus, as has been mentioned, listed Moses as one of the barbarian legislators who found it convenient to claim that he received

77   See Reinach, *Textes d'auteurs grecs et romains*, passim; I. Heinemann, "Moses," *R.E.*, 31 (1933), 359-75; "Antisemitismus," *R.E.*, Suppl. V (1932), 3-43. For a full discussion of the general subject see Gager, "The Figure of Moses in Greek and Roman Pagan Literature"; and recently published as *Moses in Graeco-Roman Paganism* (1972).

78   Herod. II, 104; Aristotle (cited in *C. Apionem,* I, 176-83), quoted by Clearchus (Mueller, *FHG*, fr. 69, II, 323 f.).

79   Leon of Pella, in Clement, *Strom.*, I, 106, 3 = 659 F 7. He is known chiefly from the early Christian writers, including Augustine (659 TT 1-2; FF 1-9); cf. now Wolfgang Speyer, *Die literarische Fälschung im heidnischen und christlichen Altertum* (Munich, C. H. Beck'sche Verlagsbuchhandlung, 1971), 146.

80   Jacoby (659 F 7) suspects that the date of Moses, attributed to Leon, may have been a post-Hecataean interpolation, if not made by Clement himself.

81   When Celsus, writing at the end of the second century, after the Christian era, attacks Moses, he sounds as if he were disputing Hecataeus' version of the Jewish lawgiver. *C. Cels.*, I, 23, 26; V, 41, argues that Moses was a rebel, using the list of sages found in Hecataeus (264 FF 6; 25); *C. Cels.* I, 16b, maintains that because of their strange customs, Moses should be excluded from the list of "wise men," naming Linus, Musaeus, or Zoroaster among others.

82   Apollonius Molon, in *P.E.*, IX, 19, 1-3 = 728 F 1; Justin, XXXVI, 2, 11-16.

the laws from a deity.[83] But Moses and the Jews were of interest to him as an example of the spread of the Egyptian religion throughout the earth. Belus who appointed the priestly cast of Chaldeans to supervise the Babylonian religion; Danaüs who settled Argos, the first Greek city; the Jews—the name of Moses is absent in Diodorus' paraphrase here—and Erechtheus the son of Athena, the builder of Athens, were all Egyptians who founded foreign colonies.[84] Hecataeus attempted to emphasize the paramount role that religion and ritual played in the formation of human societies. Characteristically, Belus was not just another Babylonian or Assyrian king, as in Herodotus, but was the founder of Chaldean priesthood. What interested Hecataeus most about Athens was Erechtheus' importation of the Eleusian mysteries from Egypt.[85]

With such a belief in the origin of civilization, it is understandable why Hecataeus devoted a lengthy description to Moses, preserved in Photius' highly abridged version.[86] According to this version, a plague passed through Egypt and the mob blamed the foreigners for causing it. Danaüs left for Argos, Cadmus for Hellas, and a large group headed by Moses, a brave and wise man, settled in the region called Judaea, then a desert. He built many cities there, the foremost of which was Jerusalem, where he constructed the most holy temple.[87] He devised a constitution and a cult that were unlike any other known human institution. He divided the people into twelve tribes in relation to the twelve months of the year. Idolatry was abolished because Moses believed it wrong to ascribe anthropomorphic features to God. The manner of living and the sacrificial cults of the Jews thus differed from those of any other people. Having been expelled as aliens, they themselves adopted a hatred of foreigners. Moses chose the most capable men as priests and guardians of the cult and the laws. The Jews never had a king; instead, Moses appointed a high priest, who was regarded by the people to be God's messenger.[88] The people prostrated themselves while the high priest interpreted the divine law to them, a law which concluded with the (written)

83.   Cf. above notes 69 f.

84   Diod. I, 28, 1-29, 6 - 264 F 25. See note 37.

85   Diod. I, 29, 1-5; cf. I, 11-27 = 264 F 25, devoted to a description of Egyptian cult.

86   Cf. W. Jaeger,   *Diokles* 151; "Die hekataische Erzählung ist wesentlich farbiger und reicher zu Detail gewesen, als ihr bei Diodor konserviertes Gerippe sie erscheinen lasst," a view seconded by Jacoby, *FGrH*, IIIa, 48, citing Diod. XL, 3, 8, as an example of only headings, without Hecataeus' "facten."

87   Diod. XL, 3, 3. See note 76.

88   Cf. *C. Apionem*, II, 184-87. Did Josephus use Hecataeus' glorification of the theocratic form of government?

words: "Moses, having heard God, imparted these words to the Jews."[89]

Social legislation, according to Hecataeus, was of paramount concern to Moses: "The lawgiver revealed great foresight in military matters; and he required the young men to acquire courage through exercise, perseverance, and especially the ability to withstand all kinds of suffering.

"He led an expedition against the neighboring peoples, conquering much territory, which he divided into portions, the common people receiving equal lots; the priests larger ones, so that enjoying large incomes they could, without distraction, devote themselves to God's cult.[90] It was forbidden for the common people to sell their lots so that avaricious men would not acquire the land to the detriment of the poor and causing thereby a diminution in the citizenry."[91]

"He obligated the inhabitants to bring up their children; and since the feeding of infants incurs only minor expenses, the Jewish people was always growing in numbers."[92]

"The customs of marriage and burial of the dead he made quite different from those of other men."[93] Though Hecataeus may have given some examples, the differences are not spelled out in our fragment.

The account concludes with a statement which, as pointed out by Jacoby, was added by Diodorus: "Under the jurisdictions that were established later,

89   Diod. XL, 3, 6 = 264 F 6. For the identification of this presumed biblical verse, see Reinach (*Textes grecs et romains,* 18, n. 3) suggests LXX Lev. 26:46; Jaeger (*Diokles,* 146); Gutman (*Beginnings of Jewish-Hellenistic Literature,* I, 66), Deut. 28:69 (29:1); Gager ("The Figure of Moses," 36, Harvard University Thesis, 1968), adds as an equally possible text, LXX Deut. 32:44, but concludes that "all of these verses are forms of a common formula and each bears an almost equal resemblance to Hecataeus' quotation." Perhaps, as noted to me by Professor Strugnell, this was not a quotation but appeared as a colophon of the Law (τοῖς νόμοις ἐπὶ τελευτῆς), recited at the conclusion of the public reading of Scripture. See below note 118.

90   Priestly ownership of land was forbidden by Mosaic legislation (Numb. 18:23 f.) and priests were presumably excluded from the actual division of the land (Josh. 12:14). Gager ("The Figure of Moses," 18 f.) maintains that Hecataeus reflects Ezekiel's ideal division of the land (Ezek. 45:1-8; 48:1-29), in which the priests received a large share, mirroring the wealth of the priests in the postexilic period. The connection with Ezekiel is doubtful, however; the Greek author seems to be imagining things in light of Egyptian conditions and appears to have no relationship to the historical reality of the Holy Land. See below note 93.

91   Cf. Lev. 25:23, where the reason given, however, is that the land belongs to God.

92   Cf. *C. Apionem,* II, 202. Gager ("The Figure of Moses," 40 f.) cites Aristotle's interest in the problem of child exposure (*Politics,* 1335b).

93   Diod. XL, 3, 8. See Jaeger, "Greeks and Jews: The First Greek Records of Jewish Religion and Civilization," *Journal of Religion,* 18 (1938), 127-43; *Diokles,* 134-53; and supported in detail by Gutman, *The Beginnings of Jewish-Hellenistic Literature,* I, 39-73; and Gager, ibid. 41-44, maintains that Hecataeus' account was consistently an idealization of the Mosaic constitution. Jacoby (IIIa, 48 f.) argues, however, that Hecataeus recorded the Jewish customs "nicht als vorbildlich, sondern nur als fremdartig empfunden hat." The two views—Judaism as a model as well as a strange

the Persian hegemony and subsequently under the Macedonians who conquered the Persians, the Jews changed many of their ancestral customs because of the intervention of the foreigners." Writing about 300 B.C., Hecataeus could not have implied that Judaea had been under Macedonian rule for a long time, certainly not long enough to change the traditions of the land. Hecataeus, moreover, believed that the ancient Mosaic constitution was still in full force in his own day.[94]

As to Hecataeus' source(s) for the treatment of Moses, it is difficult to arrive at a definite conjecture. Certainly, he could not have consulted the Septuagint version, presumably produced during the reign of Ptolemy I. Was there then a Greek translation of parts of the Pentateuch that had antedated the Septuagint? Although such claims have been made by Aristobulus in the middle of the second century B.C.,[95] and by Kahle in recent time,[96] no plausible case can be made for such assertions. In fact, after surveying the entire literary remnants of pagan writing dealing with the Jews up to the Christian period, Heinemann concluded that although there existed great interest in things Jewish, there is no evidence that any of the heathen writers—beginning with Hecataeus and ending with Cicero, Posidonius, Strabo, or Tacitus—ever had direct access to the Bible.[97] Referring specifically to Hecataeus, scholars have often pointed to his misrepresentations of ancient Jewish history as proof that the information he received was secondhand. Thus Hecataeus says that the Jews never had a king, and that Moses had founded Jerusalem and built its Temple. Heinemann concludes therefore that Hecataeus knew of the Bible only indirectly, from his discourses with Egyptian Jews.[98] However, Jaeger, stressing the positive, cites Hecataeus' quote of a Pentateuchal verse—somewhat mangled, to be sure—as evidence of his knowledge of the Bible.[99]

---

religion—need not have been foreign to Hecataeus. Thus though he idealized Egypt, Hecataeus (Diod. I, 94, 1) goes on to describe Egyptian custom as "unusual and strange" (ἐξηλλαγμένα καὶ παράδοξα), or "contrary to the common customs of mankind" (παρὰ τὸ κοινὸν ἔθος τῶν ἀνθρώπων, Diod. I, 27, 1). It is difficult to imagine that his reference to the Egyptian law which permits men marrying their sisters, as intended to serve as a model for the Greeks; or, as maintained by Gager, as merely neutral. In regard to Egypt, Hecataeus seems to have said that despite some uncivilized behavior of the Barbarians, they served as the source of Greek philosophy (264 F 1) and that many of the barbarian customs deserved emulation. This ambivalent attitude also seems to be reflected in his chapter on Mosaic legislation.

94   Cf. Jacoby, app. crit. to 294 F 6, p. 15, lines 13-16; IIIa, 52; cf. Posidonius,/87 F 70.

95   Aristobulus, in *P.E.*, XIII, 12, 1-16.

96   Paul Kahle, *The Cairo Geniza*[2] (New York, F. A. Praeger, 1959), 213, citing the Letter of Aristeas, 314-16.

97   Heinemann, "Moses," *R.E.*, 31 (1933), 361; "Antisemitimus," *R.E.*, Suppl. V, 23 f.

98   Heinemann, *ibid.*; Gager, "The Figure of Moses," 46.

99   Jaeger, *Diokles,* 146.

The question remains as to whether or not Hecataeus ever visited Jerusalem. The consensus is that whatever he says about Moses, he heard from Alexandrian Jews.[100] The fragment never alludes to the Jews of the Diaspora, however. The description of the people prostrating themselves before the high priest, moreover, suggests that we are dealing here with personal impressions. Certainly, the mention of the hostile attitude of the Judaeans toward foreigners apparently reflects an eyewitness' testimony.[101] From Herodotus we learn that personal contact with Egypt's priests does not save one from misrepresentations. The same is evidently true of Hecataeus' visit to Jerusalem which, if it occurred at all, took place about the second or third decade after Alexander's conquest of Coele-Syria. For aside from the inherent difficulty of communication between a travelling foreigner and the natives, a tourist's basic cause of misrepresentation arises from the wish to please the visitor by telling him whatever he wants to hear. Judaea was an integral part of the Egyptian state, and a Greek going from Athens to Alexandria would have normally stopped in Tyre. With the Palestinian coast nearby, Hecataeus may have taken a detour to the city whose exotic temple was beginning to gain fame. There is nothing implausible, then, in the assumption that Hecataeus' account was partly based on what he himself saw.

The influence of Hecataeus' works was such that his account of Moses became the basis of many repetitions, corrections, polemics, and pseudographs. The strange description of the Jewish sacrificial code in Theophrastus' *On Piety,* first proposed by Jaeger and accepted by Jacoby, was taken from Hecataeus.[102] Certainly, most of Posidonius' account of the Jewish lawgiver, as preserved in Strabo, is but another précis—in some respects fairer than Diodorus' presentation—of Hecataeus' Moses.[103] And in a more restricted way Manetho's report of the Exodus was but an expansion of a theme begun by Hecataeus. Via these writers, elements of the oldest Greek presentation of the Jewish lawgiver, always embellished, often with anti-Jewish remarks,

---

100   Jaeger, *Diokles,* 143 n., 156; *Journal of Religion,* 18 (1938) 146; Jacoby, *FGrH,* IIIa, 51; Gager, "The Figure of Moses," 46. See next note.

101   Jaeger, *Diokles,* 146, says that Hecataeus must have had contact with Alexandrian Jews, as a journey to Palestine is hardly believable. Jacoby, *FGrH,* IIIa, 51, 19-30, repeating Jaeger's inconclusive argument, adds that Hecataeus does not betray any expertise about the country. Ignorant as the Egyptian Jews might have been, it does not follow, as maintained by Jaeger and Jacoby, that they are the authority behind Hecataeus' misrepresentations of Mosaic history.

102   Theophrastus, in Porphyry, *De abst.* II, 26. Jaeger, *Diokles,* 125-53, esp. 142-44; Jacoby, IIIa, 38, 3-8; 38, 16 ff.

103   Strabo, XVI, 2, 34-45 = 87 F 69. E. Norden, "Jahve und Moses in hellenistischer Theologie," *Festgabe . . . Harnack* (Tübingen, 1921), 293-301; Jacoby, *FGrH,* IIC, 196-99; I. Heinemann, *R.E.,* Suppl. V, 34 f.; Gager, "The Figure of Moses," 47-78.

surface again and again in Lysimachus, Apollonius Molon, Apion, Varro, Tacitus, Plutarch, and Porphyry.[104]

Theophrastus, cited in Porphyry's *On the Abstinence of Animal Food,* maintained that man was originally a vegetarian, offering sacrifices to the god only in fruits, alluding perhaps to the story of Cain and Abel. According to Theophrastus, the Jews do not eat the meat of animal offerings, but after having poured over it honey and wine at night, which consumes the flesh before the sun could see such an unseemly spectacle, they throw the entire sacrifice into fire. During the night, Theophrastus goes on to say, the Jews being a people of philosophers, discussed the nature of divinity, watching the stars and invoking God with their prayers.[105] As pointed out by Bernays, this account is full of errors. It may be presumed, however, that Theophrastus had no independent knowledge of Judaism, except for what he had originally found in Hecataeus' idealized formulation of the Mosaic constitution.[106]

There is more solid evidence for Posidonius' utilization of Hecataeus' account of the Jews than for Theophrastus'. The extant fragments of Theophrastus never mention Moses by name, and it is not even certain that Hecataeus treated the Jewish sacrificial code. The matter is different with Posidonius of Apamea (c. 135-51 B.C.), a friend of Pompey and Cicero. From him we hear for the first time that when Antiochus IV entered Jerusalem's Temple he found an ass's head, which he thought represented the figure of Moses, the founder of Jerusalem. Another version, also cited in Posidonius, reports that Antiochus IV found in Jerusalem's sanctuary a man, who had been kidnapped for the annual ritual of consuming a Greek.[107] With such tales of contemporary Jewish practices, one would have expected Posidonius' treatment of Moses to have been written in a similar vein. But Strabo's protrait of the Jewish lawgiver, certainly dependent on Posidonius, echoes Hecataeus' enthusiasm about the Mosaic accomplishment.[108] There are also differences, however. In contrast to the Jewish tradition that makes Moses and the Jews only temporary sojourners in Egypt, or Diodorus' report that the Jews were expelled from Egypt because they were foreigners, Strabo (who follows here Posidonius) makes Moses an Egyptian priest who left the country because he was dissatisfied with the Egyptian religion. But Strabo,

---

104   See below note 116. Pompeius Trogus, preserved in Justin (XXXVI, 2, 1-16) seems to be an exception, as his account of Moses apparently is free from Hecataeus' version of the Mosaic state.

105   Porphyry, *De abst.* II, 26.

106   Jacob Bernays, *Theophrasts Schrift über die Frommigkeit* (Berlin, 1866); Jaeger, *Diokles,* 123-153.

107   *C. Apionem,* II, 79-96 = Posidonius, 87 F 69; Diod. XXXIV, 1-4 = F 109. For the rise of the anti-Semitic literature, and Posidonius' share in it, see Heinemann, "Antisemitismus," *R.E.,* Suppl. V, 3-43; Jacoby, *FGrH,* IIC, 196, 4-199, 27.

108   Strabo, XVI, 2, 34-45 = 87 F 70.

paraphrasing Posidonius, attributes to the Jewish lawgiver the same dissatisfactions that Hecataeus does as quoted in Diodorus. Moses, according to Posidonius, rejected the Egyptian presentation of the deity in the form of animals or in the Greek anthropomorphic images, and led his followers to settle in Jerusalem. There he instituted in imageless religion "which would not oppress the people who adopted it either with expenses or with divine obsessions or with other absurd troubles."[109]   Finally, like Hecataeus, Posidonius compares Moses with, among others, Zamolxis, founder of an allegedly Pythagorean worship among the Getae, and the Spartan Lycurgus.[110] Thus Posidonius essentially retained Hecataeus' enthusiastic account of Moses, but combined it with the anti-Jewish version fashionable in the aftermath of the Maccabean revolt, which stressed the Mosaic *misoxenia* or hatred of the foreigners, merely alluded to by Hecataeus.

Scholarly consensus has agreed that Manetho's history of Egypt was an attempt to formalize Hecataeus' hypothesis making Egypt the mother country of all ancient civilizations.[111] What needs to be pointed out is that Manetho's description of the expulsion of Hyksos from Egypt, based in part on native sources, also aimed to correct Hecataeus' account of Moses. Hecataeus had said that the expulsion of Moses from Egypt had resulted from a general wave of xenophobia following a plague.[112] Manetho indirectly defended the expulsion since he said Moses and his followers were lepers.[113] Moreover, the expelled foreigners were none other than the hated Hyksos invaders of Egypt.[114]   But wishing to credit Egypt with everything noteworthy, he added that the Jewish lawgiver had been an Egyptian priest

---

109   Strabo, XVI, 2, 35-36 = 87 F 70. Unlike Diod. XL, 3, 2-3 (Hecataeus) who asserts that Moses was expelled from Egypt in a wave of xenophobia; Strabo XVI, 34 (Posidonius) makes Moses "one of the Egyptian priests." But see above note 37; Diod. I, 28, 1-5 (Hecataeus 264 F 25), which suggests that Hecataeus was inconsistent as to whether Moses was expelled from Egypt or whether the Jews, like the other settlers of Argos, Babylon, left of their own volition.

110   Cf. Strabo, XVI, 2, 38 = Posidonius 87 F 70 with Diod. I, 94, 1-5 = 264 F 25.

111   For the link of Manetho with Hecataeus see Plut. *De Isid.* 9, p. 354 CD = Manetho, 619 F 19 = Hecataeus, 264 F 4; cf. also Diod. I, 13, 2 = 264 F 25. See G. L. Barber, in *Oxford Classical Dictionary* (Oxford, Clarendon Press, 1961), 533b: Manetho's "claim to have consulted the lists of kings (ἱερὰ γράμματα) implies that his version was more official than that of Hecataeus of Teos (Abdera)."

112   Hecataeus, 264 F 6 = Diod. XL, 2-3.

113   *C. Apionem,* I, 227-32 = Manetho, 609 T 7b; F 10. Jacoby is inconsistent in questioning the authenticity of F 10, and not the same material in T 7b.

114   *C. Apionem,* I, 90; 94 = 609 FF 8-9. Note also Manetho's mention of Danaüs (*C. Apionem,* I, 102 f.; 231 (Manetho, 609 F 10), said by Hecataeus to have been a contemporary of Moses (see note 112).

before changing his native name of Osarsiph to Moses as he migrated to Jerusalem.[115]

Hellenistic historiography was extremely stereotyped, as exemplified by the Greek treatment of Moses and the Jewish religion. Given the grossly distorted Greek image of the Jewish lawgiver—either as an idealized forerunner of Plato or as the inventor of a monstrous ritual—pagan historians merely copied what they had found in a few creative works, adding a few embellishments here and there.[116] Scholars such as Bickerman, Eduard Meyer, and Isaac Heinemann have debated the question as to whether or not any of the pre-Christian pagan writers were acquainted with the Greek version of the Bible.[117] As far as our evidence goes, contrary to Heinemann and Meyer, knowledge of some parts of the Pentateuch is indicated in the fragments of Hecataeus of Abdera, Apollonius Molon, Alexander Polyhistor, Apion, Nicolaus of Damascus, and perhaps also, if he was not a Jew, Cleodomus Malchus.[118] As far as the other Greek and Roman pagan writers, such as Manetho, Posidonius, and Pompeius Trogus, conclusive proof is lacking. The fact that these writers do not allude to the Bible is, however, no proof of the negative. Whatever did not fit into the accepted Hellenistic literary tradition—whether the Bible, Berossus, or Manetho—was as a rule

---

115   *C. Apionem*, I, 238, 250, 261, 265, 279 = Manetho, 609 F 10. It should be noted that Josephus' point that Manetho was inconsistent as to making Moses a native priest of Heliopolis or a foreigner (see I, 279 f.), in which some scholars see that Josephus had access, in addition to the genuine Manetho, also to a pseudo-Manetho (Laqueur, *R.E.*, 14 [1928], 1064-80) was probably due to Hecataeus, where a similar inconsistency is evident; see note 109. Manetho's treatment of Moses should not, however, be branded as anti-Semitic. He was merely interested in his hypothesis that Egypt's culture was the most ancient, fleshing out Hecataeus' glorification of Egypt with authentic hieroglyphic records.

116   What was sheer intellectual speculation in Hecataeus and Manetho, assumed an anti-Semitic character in Lysimachus (*C. Apionem*, I, 304-11; II, 16-20, 145, 236 = Lysimachus, 621 T 1a-b; FF 1-4); and Apollonius Molon (728 FF 1-3); Apion (616 TT 4; 15 FF 1; 4 = *C. Apionem*, passim); Varro, as cited by Augustine (*City of God*, IV, 31, 2); Tacitus (Histories, V, 2-10).

117,   E. Bickerman(n), *MGWJ*, 71 (1927), 177, maintains that the Bible was known to the pre-Christian pagan writers. This is denied by E. Meyer, *Ursprung und Anfänge des Christentums*, III, 313 f.; Heinemann, "Antisemitismus," *R.E.*, Suppl. V, 23-25; "Moses," 31, col. 361. Hecataeus' knowledge of the Bible, is apparently attested by citing a Mosaic text (Diod. XL, 3, 6); cf. Gager, *Moses in Graeco-Roman Paganism*, 162-64, and passim.

118   For Hecataeus, see above note 89; Apollonius Molon (*P.E.*, IX, 19, 3 = 728 F 1) calling Isaac Gelon, alluding to LXX Gen. 21:6; Alexander Polyhistor, quoting Demetrius, quoting Exod. 15:22-27, preserves the oldest mention of the Holy Bible (273 F 19 = *P.E.*, IX, 29, 15); Nicolaus of Damascus' record of Moses *A.J.*, I, 94 = 90 F 72); Apion (*C. Apionem*, II, 21; 25 = 616 F 4) knows of Moses' ascent to Mount Sinai. For Cleodomus Malchus, see above, pp. 53-55.

ignored, but this does not mean, however, that the Greek Pentateuch was not accessible to some pagans.[119]

Hecataeus of Abdera's account of Moses was of paramount significance since it formed the archetype of both Graeco-Jewish and heathen versions of the Jewish religion. All of Jewish history—the conquest of Palestine, the building of the Temple and its cult—became popularly telescoped in the figure of Moses. Hecataeus' treatment of the Jewish lawgiver, like his treatment of Egypt, presented a typically Greek mixture of hasty generalizations, keen perception, and profound ignorance. As has been said, the Hebrew Bible was accessible to him in the same manner that the Egyptian Hieroglyphic texts were—via priestly interpreters, possibly in Jerusalem. Unwittingly, the Mosaic institutions came to resemble more and more Plato's ideal polis. In addition to Plato, as pointed out by Bidez and Jacoby, elements of Democritus' free-thinking Weltanschauung superimposed on Euhemerus' historical romances appear to be the basis of Hecataeus' Moses.[120] Such was Hecataeus' influence that Moses became a well-known lawgiver in pagan historiography and popular as an "ingredient" in magical incantations.

Hecataeus' Moses became even more significant for the Graeco-Jewish biblical histories. Almost every nonbiblical characterization found in Eupolemus and Artapanus is traceable to this heathen historian-philosopher. There is therefore more than a grain of truth in the tradition, claimed in the fictive Letter of Aristeas, that Hecataeus played a key role in the Greek translation of the Pentateuch.[121] Paradoxically, Jewish apologetics, as the Graeco-biblical accounts are often branded, were a strictly pagan invention. Alexander's conquest of the East opened the eyes of some Greeks to the tremendous accomplishments of Egypt and Babylon. Did not Greek philosophy and Greek science—Hecataeus asserted—really originate in Egypt? But Pseudo-Eupolemus, following the Enochite tradition, ascribed the origin of civilization to Enoch and Abraham. Eupolemus, however, holding onto Hecataeus' *Aegyptiaca*, postulated Moses as the first wise man, the inventor of the alphabet, the author of the first lawbook—the greatest benefactor man has ever known.

---

119   Cf. Philo who says that he wrote the *Life of Moses* to make the name of his hero better known, "for while the fame of the laws which he has left behind him has travelled throughout the civilized world and reached the ends of earth, the man himself as he really was is known to few. Greek men of letters have refused to treat him as worthy of memory . . . " (*Vita Mosis,* I, 2, F. H. Colson's translation in the L.C.L.). Heinemann (*R.E.*, Suppl. V, 24) takes Philo's claim that Moses was ignored by Greek writers seriously, but disregards Philo's other contention that the Mosaic Laws were well known among the pagans.

120   K. Reinhardt, "Posidonios," *Orient und Antike,* 6 (1928), 9-11; "Hekataios von Abdera und Demokrit," *Hermes* 45 (1912, 492-513; Bidez-Cumont, *Les Mages Hellénisés,* I, 21, 240-42; Jacoby, *FGrH*, IIIa, 52.

121   Aristeas, 31. Cf. Jacoby, *FGrH*, IIIa 65, 35-66, 20.

Chapter Four

HELLENISTIC BIBILICAL CHRONOLOGIES[1]

Qualitatively, Fragment Five is the most inferior remnant of Eupolemus'
writings. Preserved only by Clement of Alexandria, it lacks the relatively
reliable tradition of the other fragments found in Eusebius' *Praeparatio
Evangelica*. Moreover, Fragment Five has suffered from scribal corruptions.
Nonetheless, because it deals with biblical chronology it is of unusual
significance. This is not to suggest that Eupolemus can clear up for us some of
the muddled problems of biblical datings. Rather, because of its technical
nature, chronology affords us glimpses into the state of biblical studies among
Greek-writing Jews. As is attested in the Book of Daniel, chronology was
utilized by apocalyptic writers to foretell the fall of the Macedonian empires.
Furthermore, Graeco-Jewish chronography is important because of its
profound influence upon early Christian and Byzantine historiography, which
viewed the world from the biblical perspective. Fragment Five preserves one
of the earliest attempts to date creation and the exodus.

This chapter treats Graeco-biblical chronography in some detail because
the field has never before been investigated and because only through an
overall analysis can Eupolemus' datings be viewed in their proper perspective.
The immense strides made by Alexandrian Hellenistic chronography have
been brilliantly illuminated by Eduard Schwartz and Felix Jacoby.[2] This
discussion extends these inquiries into Graeco-biblical studies from about 250
B.C. to A.D. 150. The diverse chronological systems found in Josephus,
however, are excluded from our study because they have been extensively
treated elsewhere[3] and because Josephus ought not to be considered as part
of the Hellenistic biblical schools. Sectarian chronology such as the Samaritan

---

1 Portions of this chapter have appeared in the *Harvard Theological Review*, 61,
3 (1968), 451-81. I am indebted to its editors, especially to Professor Krister Stendahl,
for their suggestions which have improved this rather difficult study.

2 E. Schwartz, *Königlisten des Eratosthenes und Kastor* (Göttingen, 1884);
Jacoby, *Das Marmor Parium* (Berlin, 1904); *Apollodors Chronik. Philologische Unter-
suchungen*, XVI (Berlin, 1902); *FGrH*, IIB, "Zeittafeln," Nos. 239-260; IIIB, 323a-334;
IIIb (Supplement); *Atthis, the Local Chronicles of Ancient Athens* (Oxford, 1949).

3 See J. von Destinon, *Die Chronologie des Josephus* (Kiel, 1880); A. Bosse, *Die
chronologischen Systeme im Alten Testament und bei Josephus. Mitteilungen der
Voderasiatischen Gesellschaft* (Berlin, 1908); Olof Linton, "Synopsis Historiae Universalis," in *Festkrift udgivet af københavns Universitet* (1957), 73-86.

and Qumran (Jubilees?) systems of datings can be touched only lightly as far as they directly shed light upon the Graeco-biblical traditions.[4]

FIRST STAGE – RECONCILING BIBLICAL DATES

Traces of a biblical chronological school are perhaps evident already in the Septuagint version of the Pentateuch, i.e., in the first half of the third century B.C. The Hebrew text of Exod. 12:40 records the tradition that the Israelites stayed in Egypt 430 years. The Greek translation, however, apparently because only four generations are accounted for, emended the passage to read "in the land of Egypt *and* in the land of Canaan," halving the Israelites' stay in Egypt to 215 years.[5] The Hebrew and the Greek versions diverge also in regard to the number of years which had elapsed from Adam to Abraham.[6] When the years given in the Hebrew text are added up, the flood occurred 1,656 years after Adam, and Abraham was born 292 years after the flood, making a total of 1,948 years from Adam to Abraham. According to the Septuagint, however, the antediluvian period adds up to 2,264 years, while that of the pre-Abrahamic epoch totals 3334 years.

The significant divergence of 1,396 years between the Hebrew and Greek texts did not escape the notice of the ancients. Josephus shows awareness of the differing chronological schemes, and the Church Fathers commented upon the question at length.[7] In fact, for the latter the problem of the differing texts was of immediate and vital concern. The Christians had believed firmly that Jesus Christ would rise again soon after the world entered the sabbatical millennium. The greater the age of the world the sooner the New Age would appear. Christian chronographers, therefore, beginning with Clement of Alexandria, Judas, Julius Africanus, Hippolytus, and Eusebius,

---

4   See below note 7, on Josephus' chronology. For the sectarian views, see Wacholder, "How Long did Abram Stay in Egypt? A Study in Hellenistic, Qumran, and Rabbinic Chronography," *HUCA*, 35 (1964), 41-56; cf. S. Hahn, "Zur Chronologie der Qumran-Schriften," *Acta Orientalia,* 9 (Budapest, 1960), 181-89.

5   The Samaritan version and Codex Alexandrinus, Exod. 12:40, emends further [the Israelites] "and their ancestors," to make sense out of the corrected text which, anachronistically, alludes to the patriarchs as "Israelites." Like the LXX and the Samaritan versions, talmudic exegesis interprets the 430 years to be referring to their stay in both Canaan and Egypt. However, the rabbis counted 220 years for Canaan and 210 for Egypt (Seder Olam 2-3).

6   Gen. 5:3-31; 11:10-25; LXX duplicating the generation of Cainan of Gen. 5:9 f. See commentaries ad locum, e.g., Skinner, (*ICC,* New York, 1925).

7   Josephus' chronology for the antediluvian period conforms with LXX (*A.J.*, I, 82-88), but for the Noachites he used the Hebrew (*A.J.* I, 148-150). All witnesses, except RO, which represent here a compromised emendation, attest that Josephus used the Hebrew. Unhappily, Niese chose to print RO in the body. Thackeray (Loeb Classical Library) was quite wrong in defending Niese. See Destinon, *Die Chronologie des Josephus,* 5-9.

accepted the Septuagint version as authentic.[8] The problem of explaining the lower numbers of the Hebrew version moved the Syrian classical author Ephraem of Nisibis (c. 306-373) and the Monophysite Bishop of Edessa Jacob (died in 708) to charge that the Jews had altered the Hebrew text to discredit the Christian belief in the imminent second coming of Jesus.[9] Heinrich Graetz, equally perplexed, reversed the charges, accusing the Church Fathers of intentionally lengthening the number of years by falsifying the texts of the Septuagint.[10] However, since Josephus was already aware of the diverging Hebrew and Greek numbers here, they must have antedated the Christian period.[11]

We are, then, confronted with the often debated problem of whether the Greek rendition reflects a Hebrew proto-text or if the differing numbers in the Septuagint resulted from an alteration made in the Greek version. It should be noted that the presumption of diverging Hebrew proto-texts merely rephrases the difficulty into how they had come into being.

In this case the argument between a proto-Hebrew copy and a Greek alteration of the original text can be resolved on the basis of external evidence. The existence of a biblical chronographical school during the third century B.C. is first indicated in the remnants of the Hellenistic Jewish writer named Demetrius. Demetrius flourished during the reign of Ptolemy IV Philopator (221-204 B.C.) and wrote a work called *On the Kings of Judaea* dealing partly with biblical exegesis, but mainly with biblical chronology. The advanced stage of the hermeneutic art in the fragments as well as expressions such as "some ask" suggest that Demetrius ought to be considered as representative of an exegetical and chronographical school rather than an isolated writer. Clement of Alexandria (died before 215), the first Christian scholar who delved deeply into Hellenistic biblical chronology, regarded Demetrius, Philo (perhaps identical with the one Josephus labelled "Philo the

---

8   For Clement, see *Stromata,* I, 125; Judas, in Euseb. *H.E.* VI, 7 = Jacoby, *FGrH* 261 F 1, writing in 202; on Africanus, see Gelzer, *Sextus Julius Africanus und die byzantinische Chronographie* (Leipzig, 1880), I, 24-26; Hippolytus' Commentary on Daniel, *passim*; cf. note 3. The statement in Seder Eliyyahu (Friedmann ed.), 6 f; Bab. Avodah Zarah 9a; Sanhedrin 97a, announcing the messianic age in the sabbatical millenium, makes sense only if it is supposed that it was taken from a text which had followed the readings of LXX. For the rabbinic texts assume a 3 X 2000 division before the sabbatical year. This was apparently an attempt to fit talmudic biblical chronology into a scheme which believed that the sixth millenium had already passed.

9   See Ephraem Syrus, in Assemani, *Bibliotheca Orientalis* (Rome, 1719), I, 65 f.; cf. Eusebius, *Chronik* (ed. Karst, Leipzig, 1911), 27 ff. Cf. Albiruni, *The Chronology of Ancient Nations* (ed. E. Sachau, London, 1879), 18.

10   H. Graetz, "Fälschungen in dem Texts der Septuaginta von christilicher hand sur dogmatischen Zwecken" *MGWJ*, 2 (1853), 432-436.

11   See note 7. Confronted with two chronological systems, Josephus resolved the problem by using the LXX for the Adamite generations but the Hebrew for the Noachites. See also below note 140.

Elder"), and Eupolemus as part of divergent schools of Graeco-Jewish chronography.

We gain an insight into this exegetical school from questions such as why Joseph neglected to report to Jacob his rise in Egypt. Demetrius says it was because he was afraid his family's occupation of shepherding would disgrace him in Egypt. From where did the departing Israelites receive weapons (Exod. 16:18) after having left Egypt unarmed? From the drowned men (Egyptians?).[12] But the subtlety of this school becomes discernible mostly in its chronological schemes. Some calculations appear at first glance to have been based merely on simple additions of biblical numbers. A close reading of the fragments, however, indicates that each computation was but part of general explanations intended to make the Scriptural events appear "rational" and part of a preconceived plan.

Thus Demetrius formulates the chronology of Abraham to show that Zipporah and the Kushite woman (Numb. 12:1) were but different designations for the Midianite wife of the monogamous Moses, the sixth generation after Abraham and Keturah:

1. Abraham + Sarah	1. Abraham + Keturah (Chettura)
2. Isaac	2. Jokshan (Iezan)
3. Jacob	3. Dedan (Dadan)
4. Levi	4. Reuel (Rhaguel)
5. Kohath	5. Jethro (Iothor)
6. Amram	6. Zipporah
7. Moses	

Demetrius accounts for the gap of a generation because Abraham was a hundred years old when Isaac was born (Gen. 21:5), 140 when he married Keturah, and 142 when his second son by Keturah (Jokshan, Iezan), the ancestor of Zipporah, was born.[13] The interval of forty years for a generation was standard ancient practice. But the biblical texts suggest that Abraham was 137 years old when Sarah died (Gen. 17:17; 23:1), indicating that the patriarch remained a widower after the matriarch's death. Proof for this is apparently taken from a combination of Gen. 25:1-6, where Abraham's marriage to Keturah is reported, and Gen. 25:20, which suggests that

---

12   The fragments are collected by Mueller, *FHG,* III (Paris, 1888), 208 ff.; Freudenthal, *Hellenistische Studien* (Breslau, 1874-75), 219-223; Jacoby, *FGrH,* IIIC 2 (Leiden, 1958), No. 722 FF 1-7, 666-671. See specifically, 722 F 1 = *P.E.*, IX, 21, 13; F 7 = *P.E.*, IX, 19, 4.

13   Euseb. *P.E.*, IX, 21, 13 = 722 F 1; *P.E.* IX, 29, 3 = 722 F 2. That the "Kushite woman" was identical with Zipporah, see Ezechielus, *Exagoge* (ed. Wieneke, 1931), 8, probably dependent on Demetrius; and Sifre on Num. 12:1 (Friedman, 99). It does not necessarily follow, though, that Demetrius was the midrash's direct source.

51865

Abraham was 140 years old when Isaac married Rebekah. Demetrius concluded that the patriarch would not have remarried while his favorite son remained a bachelor. Still bothered by the lack of proof for this identification of Zipporah with the Ethiopian woman, Demetrius alludes to Gen. 25:6 where "it says that Abraham sent the children to settle in the East." The land of the East (Gen. 25:6) equaled for Demetrius both Midian (Exod. 2:15) and Ethiopia (Num. 12:1).

Significantly, there is a link between Demetrius' genealogy of Zipporah and the Greek text of Gen. 25:3, detailing the descendants of Jokshan:[14]

Hebrew	LXX	Demetrius
Jokshan	Iexan	Iezan
Dedan	Daedan	Dadan
Asshurim, etc.	Rhaguel	Rhaguel

The variants of the Septuagint make sense only if they are based on the presumption that Zipporah's genealogy was developed by Demetrius.[15]

Not all of Demetrius' concoctions can be as rationalized as his attempt to save the Jewish lawgiver from the charge of polygamy. According to Demetrius, Jacob begat twelve children within seven years,[16] apparently because seven was a sacred number. Contrary to II Kings 17:2; 18:9, Demetrius ascribed the destruction of the Northern Kingdom of Samaria, which had occurred in 722/1, to Sennacherib (705-681)[17]—to contrast the deliverance of Judah with the sad fate of her neighboring state.

Demetrius set out to demonstrate the exact date of the exodus. He showed that 215 years elapsed from Abraham's entry into the land of Canaan to Jacob's descent into Egypt. For this he had biblical proof.[18] His detailed presentation, however, that 215 years had also elapsed between Jacob's coming to Egypt and the exodus was fanciful: Levi was forty-three years old when brought to Egypt and he was sixty years old when he begat Kohat;

---

14   722 F 2 = *P.E.* IX, 29, 3. Cf. also LXX I Chr. 1:32 (A). Demetrius is the oldest commentator who attempted to reconcile among the divergent traditions concerning the name of Zipporah's father: Reuel (Exod. 2:18), Jethro (3:1), Hobab the son of Reuel (Numb. 10:29). Demetrius solves the problem, like Pseudo-Jonathan and Ibn Ezra (Exod. 2:18), by proposing that Jethro was the son of Reuel and the father of Zipporah. Unique is Demetrius' view that Hobab was Reuel's son and Jethro's brother.

15   See LXX Exod. 2:16-21, esp. v. 18.

16   722 FF 1, but specially *P.E.*, IX, 21, 1-5.

17   Clem. Al., I, 141 = 722 F 6. Mishnah Yadayyim IV, 4; Tos. Qiddushin, V, 4 (Zuckermandel), p. 342, 9-11; This does not necessarily imply that rabbinic chronology followed Demetrius' scheme, though the coincidence is hard to explain. Cf. M. Gaster, "Demetrius und Seder Olam. Ein Problem der Hellenistischen Literatur," in *Festkrift Simonsen* (Copenhagen, 1932), 243-52.

18   Abraham settled in Canaan when he was 75 years old (Gen. 12:4), begat Isaac at 100 (21:5), who begat Jacob at 60 (25:26), who in turn came to Egypt at the age of 130 (47:9): 25 + 60 + 130 = 215.

Kohat was forty years old when he begat Amram; Amram was seventy-eight when Moses was born, in whose eightieth year occurred the Exodus (60-43) + (40+78+80) = 215.[19] The scheme to give the year and month of the birth of each of Jacob's sons appears to have been intended to present proof that the Israelites' sojourn in Egypt equaled exactly the length of the patriarchs' stay in the land of Canaan.[20] Demetrius' detailed and repetitive concoction of evidence makes sense only if it is assumed that the Septuagint reading of Exod. 12:40, crediting a part of the 430 years in Egypt to Canaan, was of recent origin, if not an invention of Demetrius himself.[21]

Demetrius computed the date of the flood as 2,264 years and the birth of Abraham as 3,334 years after Adam, exactly as in the Septuagint text.[22] There is no direct proof that Demetrius had tampered with the biblical texts to lengthen the antediluvian and pre-Abrahamic periods. But the chances are, as in the dates of the Israelites' stay in Egypt, that Demetrius (or chronographers of a similar school) emended the text to make it conform to a preconceived chronological scheme.[23] The Septuagint readings of Gen. 25:3 have already been shown to be derived from Demetrius' notion of Zipporah's pedigree.

This interpretation differs from that of Freudenthal, who regarded Demetrius as a precursor of the midrashic literature. Demetrius, says Freudenthal, was a close reader of the Bible, occasionally presenting bits of information which differed with the Hebrew text, but almost never departing from the Greek version, which must have been already fixed in the form we have it during the last decades of the third century B.C.[24] However, it was

19   Euseb. *P.E.*, IX, 21, 19 = 722 F 1.

20   See Wacholder, *HUCA* 35 (1964), 43 - 56.

21   The Book of Jubilees, written in Palestine nearly a century after Demetrius, suggests the permissive attitude in regard to changing biblical datings. The identity of the datings in Demetrius and LXX surely shows dependence. Since the former offers their "rationality", it follows that he, or his school, was the originator of this scheme, rather than mere commentator. See below note 25.

22   Demetrius counted from Adam to the coming of Jacob into Egypt 3,624 years; from the flood to the same time, 1,360; from then to the exodus 215 years (*P.E.*, IX, 21, 18 = 722 F 1), 3,624 - 1,360 = 2,264. It becomes clear that he was concerned almost as much with the date of Jacob's arrival into Egypt, possibly his native country, as with the Israelites' departure.

23   See also LXX I Kings 6:1, where the Greek gives 440 years from the exodus to the commencing of the temple's construction, instead of 480 in the Hebrew text. It is generally agreed that the Greek chronological departures from the Hebrew were deliberate corrections (see, for example, J. Montgomery, *Critical Commentary on Books of Kings* [New York, 1951], 143; S. J. DeVries, "Chronology," in *Interpreter's Dictionary of the Bible* [1962], I, 581.

24   Freudenthal, *Hellenistische Studien,* 35-82; H. B. Swete, *An Introduction to the Old Testament in Greek* (Cambridge, 1902), 17 f.; 369 f.; Schürer, Geschichte d. jüdischen Volkes (Leipzig, 1909), III[4], 426, 473; Stählin, in Christ's *Griechische Literaturgeschichte* (Munich, 1920), II[6], 488 f.

shown above that Demetrius, contrary to Gen. 46:11, gave Egypt as Kohat's place of birth. The dates of Jacob's sons, Kohat and Amram, are Demetrius' inventions. It may be assumed, then, that although Demetrius frequently followed Scripture closely, he was not a literalist. He did not hesitate to modify the text when some passages contradicted his chronological schemes.[25]

What was Demetrius' (or some other Hellenistic Jewish chronographer's) possible motivation in lengthening the pre-Abrahamic period from the 1,948 years found in the Hebrew to the Greek 3,234? Perhaps—through unlikely—the explanation lies in the state of contemporary Alexandrian historial scholarship. Some of the techniques used by Eratosthenes of Cyrene (275-194 B.C.) are also evident in Demetrius, such as a consistent chronological scheme and minute textual analysis.[26] But Eratosthenes had spurned attempts to assign dates to the mythical period of Greece, thus founding scientific chronography. Demetrius, however, dated creation and the flood. For the ancients, it should be noted, the longevity of the Adamite and Noachite generations as recorded in Genesis was consistent with their outlook that early man was something of a demigod or a superman. The credibility of the biblical tradition was the inverse of what confronts the modern reader. Babylonian and Egyptian writers, such as Berossus and Manetho,[27] ascribed to these semi-divinites reigns of myriads of years. The relatively short duration of this period in the Pentateuch appeared rather incredible. Influenced by this view, it would seem, Demetrius lengthened the reign of the giants by consistently adding a century to the age of the patriarchs when their first sons were born. By making the world somewhat older, he had Scripture appear more realistic.

The writings of Demetrius marked the first stage of Hellenistic bibilical chronology. He established the so-called *annus Adami* and divided biblical

---

25 Conceivably, but unverifiably, Demetrius, whose chronology was written during the last two decades of III century B.C., was himself one of the so-called "Seventy" translators. That the name Demetrius is not found in the Letter of Aristeas among the seventy-two names is no proof one way or the other, as the list is pure fiction, seemingly appended to the text by another hand. I am now inclined to doubt any direct nexus (see sources cited in the previous note) between Demetrius and the midrashic methods, except that both showed an amazingly close knowledge of the Scriptural text. The Book of Jubilees, written perhaps nearly a century after Demetrius, and the recently discovered Genesis Apocryphon (Jerusalem, 1956), follow a schematic chronology that often overrides the Pentateuchal traditions. The idea that nonlegal texts (even the Pentateuch) of Scripture were authoratative and unalterable is evidently post-Maccabean.

26 On Eratosthenes, see Jacoby, *Apollodor's Chronik,* 10 ff.; fragments in *FGrH* 241 FF 1-48.

27 E. Schwartz, "Berossos," *RE,* III (1897), 309-316; *FGrH* 680 FF 1-22. Manetho, ed. Waddell (LCL, 1940); *FGrH* 609 FF 1-28. See also, J. Pritchard, *Ancient Near Eastern Texts Relating to the Old Testament* (Princeton, 1955), 165 f.

history into epochs, assigning absolute dates to the flood, the patriarchs, the exodus, and the destruction of the Northern and Southern kingdoms. It is possible, even likely, that the chronological alterations adopted in the Septuagint version of the Pentateuch were a product of Demetrius' chronographic schemes. Although we speculated above that Demetrius was influenced by the contemporary Alexandrian chronographic schools, it should be noted that the evidence for such a claim is precarious. Possibly Demetrius lived in Alexandria as did Eratosthenes; both were professional chronographers. But there is no direct proof, however, of non-Jewish influence in Demetrius' chronology.

SECOND STATE – FUSION OF BIBLICAL AND GREEK MYTH

The essential characteristic of the second stage of bibilical chronography is the fusion of Hebrew traditions with Oriental and Greek mythology. As far as is known, Pseudo-Eupolemus, a Samaritan who lived possibly about 200 B.C., marks the first attempt to identify the Noachite generations of Genesis with what seemed to him to be their Babylonian and Hellenic equivalents.[28] The progenitors of Abraham, according to Pseudo-Eupolemus, were the giants, the "Sons of God" who had escaped the flood and built the tower of Babel. Babylon, the first city in history, which they had originally named Belus, after their leader, was also constructed by them. Belus' father was also named Belus.[29] The elder Belus, it is evident, equalled Noah; and the younger, Nimrod. The Greek equivalent of the Babylonian Belus (Nimrod) was Kronos. The Hellenic Atlas was identical with Enoch of Genesis, the discoverer of the astral sciences.[30] Pseudo-Eupolemus' set of equivalents were syncretistic rather than synchronistic. It should not be forgotten, however, that Belus was regarded as a datable figure and that Enoch, Noah, Nimrod, and Abraham were usually assigned absolute time scales. Even so sober a historian as Eusebius followed the mendacious Ctesias in making Ninus the son of Belus the first Assyrian king (in whose forty-third year, says Eusebius, Abraham was born).[31] The set of equivalents of biblical and Hellenic mythical figures,

---

28   On Pseudo-Eupolemus, see Freudenthal, *Hellenistische Studien,* 35-82; Gut-schmid, *Kleine Schirften,* II, 180-185; Wacholder, *HUCA,* XXXIV (1963), 83-113; N. Walter, "Zu Pseudo-Eupolemos," *Klio* (1965), 282-90.

29   Euseb. *P.E.*, IX 17; 18, 2 (Anonymous) = *FGrH* 724 FF 1-2.

30   Euseb. *P.E.*, IX, 17, 9 = 724 F 1.

31   Ctesias is preserved primarily in Diodorus II, 1-28, Nicolaus of Damascus, 90 FF 1 ff., and Photius. The fragments are collected in Jacoby, *FGrH* 688 FF 1-74. It is doubtful that Ctesias had assigned an absolute date for Ninus, though the presumed 52-year reign usually creidted to Ninus was made up by Ctesias. For a recent attempt to exonerate Ctesias, see R. Drews, "Assyria in Classical Universal Histories," *Historia* 14 (1965), 129-142. Eusebius' chronology of Assyria follows Ctesias', as did that of Castor (Euseb. *Chronik,* 26 ff.; *FGrH* 688 F 1a).

in addition to the synchronism, prompted the Jewish author of the Third Book of the Sibylline Oracles (140 B.C.?) to fuse Hesiod's *Theogony* with Genesis. This resulted in a scene which depicts the battle between Yahweh and the Titans. In a sense, this was a fusion of chronography and Euhemerism.[32]

Artapanus, writing probably in the second century B.C., named the pharaohs who, he said, lived in the days of Abraham, Joseph, and Moses. When the patriarch came to Egypt, the name of the king was Pharethothes;[33] an obvious concoction of Pharaoh and Thoth. The name of another pharaoh, who evidently ruled during Jacob's arrival into Egypt, was Mempsasthenoth. His son Palmanothes initiated the enslavement of the Jews, forcing them to build Heliopolis and Tanis.[34] Palmanothes' daughter Merrhis, who rescued Moses, was married to Chenephres, the king of Memphis and the pharaoh of the Exodus.[35] It is otiose to speculate on what basis Artapanus had made up these names. Joshua Gutman suggests that Artapanus had sound historical reasons for identifying the contemporary of Moses as Chenephres, whom Gutman designates as of the Thirteenth Dynasty in the eighteenth century.[36] This assumption has no basis, however. Mueller, slightly emending Manetho, finds Chenephres to have been the ninth king of the Second Dynasty (2800-2700 B.C.).[37] But this is rather unlikely, if for no other reason than that Artapanus would not have chosen the name of someone of whom Manetho had remarked that nothing worth saying occurred during his reign.[38] Because the name of this pharaoh reads Nechephreus, Jacoby cites as a possible identification the first king of the Third Dynasty, Necherophes (2700 B.C.).[39] (Compare Eupolemus' date of the exodus in the manuscripts in 2738 B.C.) Of greater significance than these speculations, however, is the fact that to make credible his fantastic attribution of the Egyptian religion to Moses, Artapanus supplied Egyptian sounding names for the pharaohs

---

32   Or. Sibyll., III, 106-160. See Wacholder, *HUCA*, 34 (1963), 92 f.

33   Euseb. *P.E.*, IX, 18, 1 = 726 F 1.

34   *P.E.*, IX, 27, 1 = 726 F 3.

35   P.E., IX, 27 = 726 F 3a. In Clement (*Strom.*, I, 154, 2 = 726 F 3b), the name is spelled Νεχεφρῆς, but emended on the basis of Eusebius.

36   Y. Gutman, *The Beginnings of Jewish-Hellenistic Literature* (Jerusalem, 1963), 135 [in Hebrew]. Gutman dates Chenephres on the basis of Artapanus' statement that there then were many pharaohs in Egypt, a rather weak proof.

37   C. Mueller, *FHG*, III, 221; Manetho, in *FGrH*, FF 2-3a-b, IIIC, p. 20, where the text reads Χενερῆς see app. crit., line 19.

38   See previous note. Euseb. *Chronik* (Armenian), p. 65.

39   Manetho, in *FGrH* 609 F 2, IIIC, p. 22; Artapanus, 726 F 3b, p. 684, app. crit.

recorded in the Pentateuch.[40] Artapanus synchronized biblical and Egyptian figures, but there is no evidence that he was interested in assigning absolute dates to either.

In the aftermath of the Maccabean revolt, it would seem, the trend toward assimilation among Hellenized Jews declined. Artapanus' synchronization was not taken seriously by subsequent writers. In Palestine at the end of the second century B.C., we see that the anonymous authors of Genesis Apocryphon and the Book of Jubilees constructed a biblical chronology independent of, but along the lines of, Demetrius. There is nothing in these texts, however, to indicate an interest in the synchronization of biblical events with those of the outside world. But for Greek-reading Jews such a synchronization was of paramount significance.

Eupolemus, a Palestinian Jew and a friend of Judah Maccabee, writing in 158 B.C., had laid down the principle, discussed in chapter three, upon which all subsequent synchronization was based: "Moses was the first wise man; and he was the first who had imparted the alphabet to the Jews, the Phoenicians received it from the Jews, the Greeks from the Phoenicians. Moses was also the first to have written laws for the Jews."[41] Boasts such as these about one's own people were quite common in antiquity. What was remarkable about Eupolemus' claim was that with the passage of time even some pagan and atheistic chronographers accepted its premise. The Church Fathers phrased this view by quoting Numenius, the second century A.D. heathen precursor of Neo-Platonism: "Who was Plato except Moses speaking in an Attic dialect?"[42]

THIRD STAGE – FUSION OF BIBLE WITH WORLD CHRONICLE

The Mosaic origin of civilization is the principle which underlies the third stage of Hellenistic biblical chronology. Its basic premise is that none of the mythical Hellenic kings could have antedated the Jewish lawgiver. What to do

---

40   Except that he lived before Alexander Polyhistor (85-35 B.C.), no attempt has been made to date Artapanus. O. Linton, *Synopsis Historiae Universalis,* 74, dates him in 30 B.C., which must be a misprint. His extreme syncretism coupled with the knowledge of the Book of Exodus seems to place him during the first half of the second century B.C.; before the Maccabean rebellion reaffirmed the monotheistic belief. A somewhat stronger indication of Artapanus' date is his statement that the pharaoh of the exodus was the first person to have been afflicted with elephantiasis (Euseb. *P.E.* IX, 27, 20 = 726 F 3, p. 684, 10 f.). This disease was apparently first named circa 200 B.C. by Bolos Democritus. Artapanus, whose writings show a kinship with those of Bolos, attributed the malady to the Egyptian king in line with the traditional interpretation of Exod. 1:3 (Diels-Kranz, *Die Fragmente der Vorsokratiker,* II[6], 1952, p. 216, 9 ff.).

41   Clement Al., *Strom.,* I, 153, 4; Euseb. P.E., IX, 25, 4 = 723 F la-b. Freudenthal, *Hell. St.* 105-130.

42   Clement Al., *Strom.,* I, 150.

with the long lists of Babylonian and Egyptian kings in Berossus and Manetho presented a problem, but not a serious one. These Oriental authors could be ignored, reinterpreted, or somehow made to fit into a world chronicle which placed Moses at a time when man was just emerging from barbarism or semidivinity, depending on one's view of early man.[43] Increasingly, as in Alexandria and in Rome, interest in matters Babylonian or Egyptian declined as the past of the Jews assumed greater significance.[44]

Although there is no doubt that Eupolemus made use of Herodotus, Ctesias, Manetho, and Graeco-Phoenician historians, there is little in Eupolemus' fragments to show how he synchronized Jewish with universal history. Indeed, it is sometimes difficult to guess the basis for his assigning of dates for the biblical figures. It is worth comparing the Scriptural chronological data with that of the fragments:

	Scripture		Eupolemus	
	lifespan	active	lifespan	active
Moses	120	40	?	40
Joshua	110	– –	110	30
Saul	– –	uncertain text	?	21
David	– –	40	?	40
Solomon	– – (Mas.)	40	52	40
	–52 (LXX)			

Only in regard to Moses and David does Eupolemus follow the biblical tradition, though the data here are not complete. Eupolemus also depended on Josh. 24:29 (30), which records Joshua's death at the age of 110. But Eupolemus is the only ancient authority who assigned Joshua a rule of thirty years. Josephus apportions to Moses' successor a duration of twenty-five years; Clement and the Christian tradition as well as a medieval masoretic note (quoted by Baer), twenty-seven years; the talmudic Seder Olam, twenty-eight; Pseudo-Philo, forty.[45] It has been argued that Eupolemus based

43 Manetho, according to Eusebius, counted 13,900 years for the period of the gods' rule, 24,900 years for the semi-gods; followed by the 30 dynasties lasting (according to Africanus) 1,050 years; totaling 39,850 years (Euseb. *Chronik,* 63 ff.; *FGrH* 609 FF 2-32; Anlage I, pp. 56-63). These numbers of years were in part reduced by the Jewish chronographters to months (see Gelzer, *Sextus Julius Africanus,* II, 59 ff.).

44 Ctesias in Diodorus (Book II; 688 F 1b); Plutarch (688 FF15a; 17-23; 26; 28-29) became the authority of Babylonian history, while Berossus of Babylon (290 B.C.) was ignored. Menatho (609 FF 1-28) had been preserved only by Jewish and Christian writers. The interest in Egypt, however, never ceased in the Greco-Roman world, but declined sharply from its high point in the 4th and 3rd centuries. See "Aegypten" in Jacoby, *FGrH,* IIIC, pp. 1-277.

45 Jos., *A.J.,* V, 117; found also in the Samaritan chronicle. Clement, *Strom.,* I, 109, 3; Eusebius, *Chronik,* 163; S. Baer (ed.), *Libri Josuae et Judicum* (Leipzig, 1891), p. 129. Seder Olam, 12. Ps.-Philo, *Biblical Antiquities,* XXIV, 6.

his statement on a close analysis of Scripture: Josh. 14:7 asserts that he was forty years old when sent as a spy by Moses; Num. 14:32-33 reports that, after the return of the spies, the Israelites spent forty years in the desert; Joshua died at the age of 110. Hence, 110 - (40 + 40) = 30.[46] Cogent as this proof seems, I am not convinced that Eupolemus arrived at the number 30 in this manner. Such exegesis would conform to the methods used by Demetrius, but not Eupolemus. The agreement here between Eupolemus and Scripture is, I suppose, merely coincidental.

That Saul reigned twenty-one years is recorded only in Eupolemus. The relevant verse in the Hebrew version of I Sam. 13:1 that reads: "Saul was one year old when he became king and he reigned two years," is obviously corrupt. This passage is missing in some Septuagint manuscripts, but mentioned in others. Josephus gives Saul a rule of twenty years. In another passage, however, the Jewish historian divides Saul's forty-year reign into eighteen years during Samuel's lifetime and twenty-two thereafter.[47] Because Acts 13:21 adopted a forty-year reign for the first Hebrew king, the Christian chronographers have necessarily reiterated this view, though they usually followed the early Graeco-Jewish historians. Eupolemus' unique dating of Saul is perhaps explainable by assuming he used a now lost source. It is more likely, however, that Eupolemus here again showed that his dating of Saul was superior to that reported in Scripture, the text of which was already corrupt in his time.

Of great chronographic interest is Eupolemus' claim that Solomon ascended to the throne at the age of twelve and that the king commenced the building of the Temple at the age of thirteen.[48] Since Eupolemus assigned the customary forty-year reign to Solomon, the age at the coronation hardly affects the overall chronology. The date of the building of the Temple, however, was significant for computing the exodus as well as the length of the existence of the First Temple.[49] No ancient authority repeats Eupolemus' date of the construction of the Temple. But some Septuagint manuscripts of I Kings 2:12a, as well as the talmudic chronological treatise Seder Olam, supports Eupolemus' date of Solomon's coronation.[50] Freudenthal has

---

46   Walter, notes ad locum.

47   *A.J.*, X, 143, assigns Saul a 20-year reign, differing with VI, 378, which gives 40. Marcus, approvingly, quotes S. Rappaport, *Halaka und Exegese bei Flavius Josephus* (Vienna,1930), that the latter number resulted from a Christian emendation, which attempted to correct Josephus in light of Acts 13:21; this is unlikely, since chronological inconsistencies in Josephus abound.

48   *P.E.*, IX, 30, 8 = 723 F 2b; *P.E.*, IX, 34, 20 = 723 F 3.

49   Cf. I Kings 6:1.

50   Seder Olam Rabbah, 14; Seder Olam Zuta (Cracow, 1581), 166b; Sifre, Deut., 357. Perhaps the inspiration of the dating is I Chr. 22:5; 29:1, where David refers to Solomon as young.

maintained that Eupolemus depended here upon the Septuagint reading.[51] As has been shown elsewhere, however, there is no evidence that Eupolemus had made use of the Greek text of the Book of Kings. It is more reasonable to assume that LXX I Kings 2:12a is dependent here upon Eupolemus.[52]

Also problematical is whether Seder Olam Chapter XIV depended here on the Graeco-Jewish tradition of Solomon's chronology. In fact, that this talmudic treatise considers Solomon's age at his coronation of great importance is indicated by the elaborate proof provided. The underlying principle of Seder Olam's evidence is that the sequence of events recorded in Second Book of Samuel and the final chapters of I Chronicles reveal Solomon's age.[53] His birth is recorded in II Sam. 12:24-25. About this time occurred the rape of Tamar (13:1 ff.), a crime avenged by Absalom when the young Solomon was two years old (13:23). After Absalom's exile of three years (13:38) and the passage of two more years before David's reconciliation with Absalom (14:28), Solomon reached the age of seven. Then the famine ravished for three years (21:1) and the misfortune of the census lasted nine months and twenty days (24:8), at which point the future king was ten years nine months and twenty days old, which the Seder Olam rounds out to eleven years. At this point Seder Olam arbitrarily draws from I Chr. 23-27, relating David's reorganization of the priestly offices, which presumably lasted one year, after the completion of which the king died. This proves, according to Seder Olam, that Solomon was crowned at the age of twelve. The concoction of the evidence shows that the author of Seder Olam did *not* rely upon the Greek text of I Kings 2:12a; if he had, the complicated proofs would have been unnecessary. The Seder Olam, however, knew of a tradition in which Solomon's lifespan equalled that of Samuel, who, it was said, died at the age of fifty-two after judging Israel for forty years.[54] The remaining question is whether Seder Olam's source was dependent upon Eupolemus or whether both derived the date from some older Hebrew text.

The balance of the evidence suggests that Eupolemus originated the date of Solomon's coronation, which a number of Septuagint texts and the talmudists have somehow copied. The possibility that Eupolemus based his date upon an older tradition must be rejected just as his claim that Solomon began the construction of the Temple at the age of thirteen, in the first year

51   Freudenthal, *Hell. St.,* 118.

52   See below, pp. 251-52.

53   The underlying verse is II Sam. 15:7, where the Hebrew and the LXX (but not L and *A.J.,* VII, 196) read that Absalom's rebellion occured at the end of the 40th year of David's reign, which is inconsistent with the rest of the book. Seder Olam attempts to prove that this was in fact in the 37th year of David, but 40th of Saul's accession. Seder Olam's source may in fact be Sanhedrim 69b; Temurah 14b-15a; Nazir 5a, rather than, as assumed by Ratner, Seder Olam, *ad locum,* that Bab. Talmud borrowed from Seder Olam. This treatise, as we have it now, is a posttalmudic publication.

54   See Yer. Berakhoth, IV, p. 7b; Bikkurim, II, p. 64c; Ta'aniyot, IV, p. 67c; Bab. Mo'ed Katan, 28a; Ta'anit, 5b; Seder Olam, 13; Semahot, III, 8; Sifre 357; Gen. Rabbah, C, p. 1295, 1.

of his reign, has no historical validity. Also to be rejected is the possibility that Eupolemus had utilized the Seder Olam's proofs to date Solomon. The question, however, remains what motivated Eupolemus, on this source, to invent a lifespan for Solomon of fifty-two years?

Conceivably, the answer lies in Eupolemus' acquaintance with Graeco-Phoenician texts dealing with Solomon's contemporary, Ḥiram. That Eupolemus was indeed familiar with such accounts is shown in our discussion of Eupolemus' report that Solomon shipped to Tyre the Temple's surplus gold, which was dedicated to the local Zeus.[55] Menander, the Phoenician historian who told about Hiram's construction of Zeus' golden pillars, also reported Hiram's chronology. Menander said that Hiram lived fifty-three years.[56] It is not impossible that Eupolemus, borrowing from Menander, assigned a similar length to Solomon's reign. The cipher fifty-two, moreover, was popular with Ctesias, another of Eupolemus' sources.[57] Also, if Josephus is trustworthy here, the Phoenician tradition maintained that Jerusalem's Temple was built in the twelfth year of Hiram's reign,[58] which may explain why Solomon's age at his coronation was given as twelve.

Since we now have a possibility that Eupolemus synchronized Solomon with Hiram (called in the fragments Suron), it is perhaps worthwhile to fuse Menander's date of Hiram with Eupolemus' of Solomon, accepting the premise that Hiram's first year of reign occurred 155 years before the foundation of Carthage (814/3 B.C.):[59]

| | *Hiram* (Menander) | | *Solomon* (Eup.) | | *Solomon* (LXX) | |
	age	B.C.	age	B.C.	age	B.C.
born	----	988/7	----	971/0	----	974/3
crowned	19	969/8	12	959/8	12	962/1
built temple	30	958/7	13	958/7	16	958/7
died	53	935/4	52	919/8	52	922/1

The synchronism with Menander perhaps removes some of the puzzle as to why Eupolemus challenged the tradition that Solomon began building the Temple in the fourth year of his reign (I Kings 6:1). Evidently, Eupolemus

55   See Theophilus, 733 F 1 = *P.E.,* IX, 34, 19-20; 723 F 3; and supra, p. 16.

56   See Josephus, *C. Ap.,* I, 112-126 (A.J., VIII, 144-149) = Menander, 783 F 1; Dius, 785 F 1; but particularly, *C. Ap.,* I, 117.

57   See Castor, 250 F la, who here follows Ctesias, and F 2 (p. 1135, 20) Euseb. = *Chronik,* pp. 26, 23; 30, 30 f.; 81, 25; 82, 1.

58   *C. Ap.,* I, 126 = Menander (?) 783 F 1.

59   See previous note. See also F. Kugler, *Von Moses bis Paulos* (Münster, 1922), 172-176; W. F. Albright, in *Mélanges Isidore Lévy* (Brussel, 1955), 1-9; *Yahweh and the Gods of Canaan* (Garden City, New York, Anchor Books, 1969), 218, note 29. Cf. also H. J. Katzenstein, "Is there a Synchronism between the Reigns of Hiram and Solomon?" *Jounal of Near Eastern Studies,* 24 (1965), 116 f.

calculated that the construction of Jerusalem's sanctuary began in the same year as that of Tyre, hence his adjustment in the dating of the Temple.

Returning now to the more general question, whether or not Eupolemus synchronized Jewish history with that of the neighboring countries, the answer is not conclusive. The allusion to Hiram's building of the temple of Zeus would indicate that he did. The same is also suggested by Eupolemus' mention of Astibares, the supposed king of Media, as the contemporary of Nebuchadnezzar and the last king of Judah.[60] On the other hand, the synchronization of the tenth century B.C. Solomon with Vaphres, the pharaoh during the destruction of the first Temple, is convincing evidence that Eupolemus did not take chronology seriously.

Nevertheless, Clement regarded both Philo (perhaps identical with Philo the Elder) and Eupolemus to be expert chronographers. The two, according to Clement, challenged the chronographer Demetrius' dates. To illustrate the differences between the two chronological schools, Clement cites first Demetrius' computation of the time that elapsed from the Assyrian conquest of Samaria to the destruction of the first Temple and from the latter to the reign of Ptolemy IV (221-204).[61] This is contrasted with Eupolemus' dating of creation and the exodus.[62] Unfortunately, Demetrius' computations have come down to us in such a corrupt form that they are now meaningless. Moreover, it is no longer possible to compare the two schools since Demetrius and Eupolemus refer to different events in the passages cited. It is to be assumed that Demetrius dated the fall of the Hebrew kingdoms both from Adam to the fall of Samaria and Judah and from the fall of these kingdoms to Demetrius' own time. The first dating, however, is missing in Clement's summary.

We can deal here only with Eupolemus' dates: "Also Eupolemus says in subject matter similar (to that of Demetrius and Philo) that the total number of years from Adam to the fifth year of Demetrius' reign (158/7) ... make up altogether 5149 years; from the time Moses brought the Jews out from Egypt to the afore-mentioned day a total of [two?] thousand five hundred and eighty ..."[63] It follows that Eupolemus dated Adam 5307/6 B.C. As to the exodus, if the manuscript reading is preserved, it occurred 2569 anno Adami, i.e. 2738 B.C. Here a difference between the chronological systems of Demetrius and Eupolemus becomes clear. The latter dated the Exodus in 2569 anno Adami while the former used 3839.

---

60   723 F 5 (Walter F 4) = *P.E.,* IX, 39, 4.
61   Demetrius, 722 F 6 = *Strom.* I, 141, 1-2; Philo, 729 T 2 = *Strom.* I, 141, 3.
62   See next note.
63   723 F 4 (Walter, F 5), = *Strom.,* I, 141, 4: ἔτι δὲ καὶ Εὐπόλεμος ἐν τῇ ὁμοίᾳ πραγματείᾳ τὰ πάντα ἔτη φησὶν ἀπὸ Ἀδὰμ ἄρχι τοῦ πέμπτου ἔτους Δημητρίου βασιλείας ... συνάγεσθαι ἔτη ερμθ. ἀφ οὗ δὲ χρόνου ἐξήγαγε Μωυσῆς τοὺς Ἰουδαίους ἐξ Αἰγύπτου ἐπὶ τὴν προειρημένην προθεσμίαν, συνάγεσθαι ἔτη [διο]χίλια πεντακόσια ὀγδοήκοντα.

BIBLICAL CHRONOLOGIES DURING THE GRAECO-ROMAN PERIOD

Annus Adami

	Pentateuch						Seder	Jos.	Jos.		
	Hebrew	LXX	Samar.	Demetrius	Eupolemus	Jubilees	Olam	I	II	Clement	Africanus
Flood	1656	2242	1307	2264	– –	1308	1656	1662	2262	2148	2262
Birth of Abraham	1948	3314	2249	3334	– –	1876	1948	2082	3255	3398	3202
Exodus	2668	3319	2754	3839	2569 or 3569	2410	2448	2510	3760		3707

Since Demetrius' chronology of Genesis and Exodus is interdependent with that of the Septuagint, does it follow that Eupolemus' was based upon the Hebrew version? If we add the data of the latter version, the exodus occurred in 2668 anno Adami, exceeding Eupolemus' date by exactly a hundred but one. Despite the discrepancy, which may be accounted for by a different dating of the pre-Abrahamic patriarchs, Eupolemus' use of the Hebrew text of the Bible may explain his departures from Demetrius' chronology.[64] If so, Clement's mention of the two schools is the first allusion to the controversy between the followers of Greek and Hebrew versions of Genesis.

Modern editions, however, have emended the manuscript reading of two thousand five hundred and eight to one thousand five hundred and eighty,[65] thus increasing Eupolemus' date of the exodus from 2569 to 3569 and bringing it within 280 years of the Septuagint date of 3849 anno Adami. The rationale of the emendation is not necessarily to reconcile Eupolemus with the Septuagint, but to establish that Eupolemus could not have computed 2580 years from the exodus to 158 B.C. This is sound reasoning if Eupolemus were following otherwise normal chronographic methods. For a writer such as Eupolemus, however, it may have seemed that it was more important to preserve the integrity of the Hebrew Pentateuch than to consider exactly the postexodus period.[66] Moreover, an early date of the exodus, such as 2738 B.C., would confirm the thesis advanced by Eupolemus that Moses was the father of civilization.[67] The latter would, however, imply that Eupolemus was concerned with the problem of integrating biblical with universal history.

Nevertheless, a century after Eupolemus, world chronicles which synchronized Jewish and Greek history gained currency. That the synchronization

64   For Eupolemus' use of the Hebrew text, see below, pp. 250-54.
65   Bracketing [διο]χίλια· (Clinton, Freudenthal, Stählin, Jacoby, Walter).
66   See also below, p. 184, where it is argued that Eupolemus attempted to reconcile the accounts of the Mosaic tabernacle with the Temple.
67   723 F la-b = P.E., IX, 26, 1; Strom., I, 153, 4.

was based on Jewish calculations is presumed because it favored the antiquity of Moses and because it is attested by authors who are known to have used Jewish sources. But only the names of pagan writers have been preserved: Alexander Polyhistor, Varro (116-27 B.C.), Ptolemy of Mendes, Apion (first century A.D.), Thrasyllus (before A.D. 36), and Thallus (Hadrianic period). They all cited chronicles which had incorporated the dates of the Noachite flood and the exodus. Since Alexander Polyhistor, writing in the sixties B.C., already takes such a chronicle for granted, referring to it by a Jewish nomenclature, its existence during the second century B.C. is indicated.

A few words must be said about the state of Greek chronography before its fusion with Oriental history. The Oriental peoples possessed relatively authoritative lists of kings assembled through the centuries by their priesthoods; the Greeks had none. But eager to prove their own antiquity, Greek mythographers from the fifth century B.C. on, hastily constructed genealogical tables going back to divine progeny. Antiquarians, in turn, collected these tables, remnants of which have been preserved. These lists counted by generations and made no attempt to assign absolute dates.[68] Timaeus of Tauromenion (c. 357-260 B.C.) invented the Olympic era, dating it in 776 B.C., which became popular among historians.[69] Eratosthenes preferred the Trojan era, beginning with the fall of Troy, in 1184 B.C., reputedly the first datable event in Hellenic history.[70] Anything before 1184 was regarded as mythical. From the point of view of Greek history, Eratosthenes' method was brilliant, but the Babylonian (Berossus), Egyptian (Manetho), Phoenician (Menander, Dius), and Jewish (Demetrius, Philo, Eupolemus) historians correctly disregarded the fall of Troy as the beginning of recorded history.

The existence of a world chronicle during the second century B.C. is attested also in the so-called Pseudo-Apollodorus. Apollodorus of Athens (150 B.C.), following the footsteps of Eratosthenes, wrote a chronicle which was limited to Hellenic history beginning with the Trojan date of 1184 B.C.[71] But soon thereafter there appeared a history which fused Berossus' history of Babylonia and Manetho's annals of Egypt and a royal papyrus of ancient Egypt with Apollodorus' chronographic account of Hellas.[72] Thus a world chronicle was spread which boasted of the great antiquity of the

68   Jacoby, *FGrH,* IIIb (Suppl.), I, 380-383; cf. Atthis, 1 ff.

69   Polybius, XII, 11, 1 = Timaeus, 566 T 10. This was the first use of an era for historical purposes. Cf. T. S. Brown, *Timaeus of Tauromentium* (Berkeley and Los Angeles, University of California Press, 1958), 10-13.

70   Jacoby, *Apollodors Chronik,* 75-77.

71   Jacoby, *Apollodors Chronik,* 1 ff.; *FgrH* 244 FF 1-87.

72   244 FF 83-87. E. Schwartz, *Königlisten,* dated Pseudo-Apollodorus in 100 B.C.; Gutschmid, *Kleine Schriften,* I, 164, in 63 B.C. But as noted above, the use of the chronicle by Alexander Polyhistor makes a second century B.C. date probable. Conceivably, this world chronicle had been a Jewish fabrication, as is indeed suggested by *FGrH* 244 FF 83-86.

Oriental states as compared with the late appearance of the Greeks in the history of civilization.

To refute such boasts, it would seem, Castor of Rhodes, circa 60 B.C., concocted a world chronicle which attempted to restore Greek parity with, if not superiority over, the Orient.[73] Castor ignored Manetho and Egyptian history altogether and replaced the rather reliable Berossus with the mendacious Ctesias as the authority on Babylonian antiquities. He introduced dates for the mythical period of Greek history, manufacturing a long list of kings of Sicyon, the oldest of whom (Egialeus) ascended the throne in 2123 B.C., the same year as Ninus, the first king of Assyria.[74]

Castor's chronicle made no mention of the Jews. As suggested by Gelzer, this was perhaps because of the rampant Judaeophobia in Rhodes.[75] But since Castor's annals ignored Egypt as well, and since they viewed Babylonia through the Greek eyes of Ctesias, it seems that Jewish history was ignored not because of Judaeophobia, but because of pro-Hellenism.[76] At any rate, Castor's chronicle cannot be cited as evidence that it was customary to disregard biblical history in the current world histories.[77]

Ordinarily, there would be no reason to posit that the above-mentioned universal chronicle of Pseudo-Apollodorus had incorporated Jewish history. But Alexander Polyhistor (flourished 85-35 B.C.), the first historian who cited Pseudo-Apollodorus, quoted a world chronicle which had synchronized the biblical flood with the one recorded in Berossus. Berossus, said Alexander Polyhistor, had reported that a flood occurred during the reign of Xisuthrus, the tenth mortal king of Babylonia, who ruled for 64,000 years.[78] Alexander Polyhistor added that this was "the first and great flood" about which Moses had written.[79] Chances are that Alexander Polyhistor copied the admixture

73   E. Schwartz, *Königlisten des Eratosthenes und Kastor;* Kubitschek "Kastor," *R.E.,* X (1919), 2347-56; Jacoby *FGrH* 250 FF 1-20.

74   Eusebius, *Chronik,* 26 ff.; 81 ff.; *FGrH* 250 FF 1-4; see also Jacoby's comment in IIIb (Suppl.) I, 380-390. The invention of the Sicyonic kingdom's supposed antiquity indicates that Castor revised the traditional Greek chronology to make it at least as ancient as Assyria.

75   Gelzer, *Sextus Julius Africanus,* II, 89; cf. Posidonius, 87 FF 69-70; Apollonius Molon, 723 FF 1-3.

76   A disliked people was usually not ignored, but rather, vilified. There is nothing to indicate that Castor attacked the Jews in his writings.

77   The treatment of Jewish history by pagan historians during the second and certainly the first century was quite extensive, considering the political insignificance of th Jewish state. Posidonius (87 FF 69-70), Teucrus of Cyzicus (274 T 1), Timagenes (88 FF 4-6), Diodorus, XL, 3, to mention a few, either wrote monographs on Jewish history or summed up their history. See *FGrH* 737 FF 1-23; and below note 126.

78   Berossus in Eusebius, *Chronik,* 4 ff.; 680 F 32, pp. 374-377. Cf. also Abydenus, in Euseb. *Chronik,* 15 f.; Ctesias, 688 F 2.

79   Euseb. *Chronik,* p. 4, 26 ff. (680 F 3, p. 375a), in Karst's tanslation, quotes: "von Alores [scil. Assyria's], dem ersten König, bis zu Xisuthron, unter welchem, sagt er die grosse und erste Sintflut gewesen sei, deren auch Moses erwähnung tut." *Sagt er* can here refer to either Berossus or to Alexander Polyhistor, from whose work Eusebius

of Genesis and Berossus from the universal chronicle of Pseudo-Apollo-dorus.[80] The credit for equating Noah-Xisuthrus-Utnapishtim belongs not to the modern decipherers of cuneiform texts, but to the second or first century B.C. chronographers.

Alexander Polyhistor may also have preserved the name of the Jewish Chronicle as it was known to the heathen world. He parallels the *Atthides* with the *Syria*.[81] The former were annalistic histories of Athens, written by natives or sympathizers, the most renowned of which were by Hellanicus of Lesbos (fifth century B.C.) and Philochorus (c. 340-263). Despite their questionable origin, brilliantly illuminated by Jacoby, these works were reputed to have been authoritative in matters of custom and genealogy. The *Syria* apparently were for Jewish history what the *Atthis* were for Athenian. Here we have evidence that in the first half of the first century B.C. Greek and Oriental chronicles had already been fused.

In his *History of Chaldea,* citing as authority the third book of the Jewish Sibylline Oracles, Alexander Polyhistor also mentioned the tower of Babel.[82] He synchronized the builders of the biblical tower with Titan and Prometheus. Here, too, Alexander Polyhistor apparently was quoting a Jewish writer who in an Euhemeristic vein had fused Genesis with Berossus and Hesiod.[83] The Babylonian contemporary of the tower has unfortunately not been preserved. Conceivably, though, Alexander Polyhistor was alluding here to his own citation from Pseudo-Eupolemus in the monograph *On the Jews,* naming Belus II as the builder of the tower and founder of Babylon.[84] That Ninus, the son of Belus, was a contemporary of Abraham became a common synchronism since antiquity.[85]

Alexander Polyhistor set Moses' date during the reign of Ogygus, the first autochthonous Attic king, in whose day the flood of Deucalion occurred,

---

was quoting Berossus. Jacoby, *FGrH* IIIb (Suppl.), II, 282, n. 50, differentiates between *die grosse und erste* flood (p. 4, 27), which he attributes to Alexander Polyhistor, and *die grosse* flood (pp. 5, 22; 10, 24), which Jacoby ascribes to Berossus. But it is more reasonable to assume that the epithet "the first" antedates Alexander, and was found in a world chronicle, where it was quite fitting. See also next note.

80   Pseudo-Apollodorus is cited by Eusebius (*Chronik,* 4, 18; 244 F 83a-b) as having identified the Xisuthros flood with that recorded by Moses. Conceivably, Pseudo-Apollodorus, composed during the end of the second century B.C., was a work written by a Jewish author. See note 72.

81   Alexander Polyhistor, 273 F 101 = *P.E.,* X, 10, 8: paralleling οἵ τε τὰ Συρία with οἱ τὰς Ἀτθίδας. For the vulgar form, see Mras. *Rh. M.,* XCII (1944), 26 f. See below note 105.

82   Eusebius, *Chronik,* 12 f.; Alexander Polyhistor, 273 F 79, IIIA, p. 110; Berossus, 680 F 4, IIIC 382 f.; Abydenus, 682 F 4; Orac. Sibyll. 3:97 ff.; cf. Josephus, *A.J.,* I, 118.

83   See previous note. Hesiod, *Theogony,* 421 ff.

84   See *FGrH* 724 FF 1-2; Wacholder, *HUCA,* 34 (1963), 90-94.

85   Diodorus, II, 1, 4 ff.; Euseb., *Chronik,* 28 = 688 F 1a-b; Euseb.-Jerome (ed. Helm, Berlin, 1956) 20a-b, 6.

1020 years before the first Olympiad (776 B.C.), i.e., 1796 B.C.[86] Since, as mentioned above, Eupolemus dated the exodus about 1738 B.C.,[87] the question arises whether Alexander Polyhistor followed here the Hellenistic Jewish historian, or whether he arrived at this date independently. And if the latter, what was his basis for dating Moses in 1796 B.C.?

The answer, conceivably, lies in the divergent genealogical treatments of the mythical period. Herodotus and Thucydides named Cecrops as the first human king of Attica.[88] For them, as for Castor and Strabo, Ogygus was a term used for the primeval period of immortal kings.[89] It had never occurred to Herodotus or Thucydides to assign absolute dates for the mythical period. During the Hellenistic period, however, "scientific" chronography demanded precise time tables for the genesis of Hellenic history. Thus Cecrops, the first mortal king of Attica, according to the *Marmor Parium,* ascended the throne in 1581 B.C., but according to Castor, in 1556 B.C.[90]

Although Philochorus (340-263 B.C.) disputed their dating, another school of chronographers pushed the autochthonous rule of Attica back to Ogygus. Ogygus, it was said, had died 189 years before Cecrops, the next known monarch, gained dominion over Attica.[91] Alexander Polyhistor evidently followed this tradition.[92] If so, he must have dated Ogygus' death either in 1770 (Marmor Parium) or in 1745 (Castor). The date of Ogygus' ascent to kingship, however, is nowhere directly recorded. But, as shown above, Alexander Polyhistor maintained that in 1796 B.C. Ogygus was the contemporary Attic king when the Israelites departed from Egypt. It follows that the reputed first king of Attica must have ruled, according to Marmor Parium's computation, at least twenty-six years; but according to Castor's, fifty-one years.[93] Theoretically, either number is acceptable, but the larger one is more likely. Autochthonous kings were habitually assigned long reigns,

---

86   Euseb., *P.E.,* X, 10 (see Mras, I, 592, on lines 9-18) =Alexander Polyhistor, 273 F 101a-b. In this passage Africanus cites quite an array of authorities: Acusilaus (2 F 23), Diodorus (?), Thallus (256 F 7), Castor (250 F 6), Polybius (254 F 3), Hellanicus (323a F 10), in addition to Alexander Polyhistor. (See also Ps. Justin, *Coh. ad Graec.,* 9.) Jacoby (*FGrH* IIIb [Suppl.] I, 385-387, on Philochorus, 328 F 92), regards Alexander Polyhistor as the author who had dated Moses 1020 years before the Olympic games. Instead, Alexander Polyhistor must be viewed as the first transmitter of this tradition.

87   See, however, above , where the Ms. reading of Eupolemus would seem to date the exodus in 2738 B.C.

88   Herod. VII, 141; Thuc. II, 15, 1.

89   Strabo, IX, 1, 18; Castor, *FGrH,* 250 F 4.

90   *Marmor Parium, FGrH* 239, IIB, p. 993, 3 f.; Castor, 250 F 4, IIB, p. 1140, 11 ff.

91   Philochorus, *FGrH,* 328 F 92 (IIIb [Suppl.], I, 383-85).

92   According to *Marmor Parium,* FGrH 239 A 1, Cecrops died in 1770 B.C.; Castor, 250 F 4, apparently dated his death in 1745 B.C.

93   See previous note.

and the cipher fifty-two or so for the first monarch appears to have been customary.[94]

BIBLICAL DATES IN HEATHEN CHRONICLES

It follows that Ogygus, the first mortal Attic king, ascended to the throne in 1797 B.C. It follows further that Alexander Polyhistor's dating of the Hebrew exodus from Egypt a year later in 1796 is explainable in terms of Hellenic dating.[95] There is no need, then, to posit a link between Eupolemus and Alexander Polyhistor. Such a link, moreover, would have to account for the discrepancy between Eupolemus' date of 1738 B.C. for the exodus and Alexander Polyhistor's of 1796. The basis of the latter's date appears to have been the premise, introduced by Eupolemus, that the Jewish civilization was at least as old as the Hellenic one. Hence Moses was a contemporary of Ogygus.

Nevertheless, it would be erroneous to conclude that Alexander Polyhistor had a consistent chronology of biblical events. The opposite is true. Part of the confusion stemmed from his attempt to synchronize Hebrew, Babylonian, and Attic mythologies. A popular record of Athenian chronology is preserved in the *Marmor Parium,* inscribed in 264 B.C.[96] It begins, as mentioned above, in 1581 B.C., with Cecrops, during whose reign King Deucalion of Mount Parnassus survived a flood.[97] In the Greek tradition the flood of Deucalion did not have the paramount significance of the one recorded in the Babylonian and Hebrew texts. But, consistent with the style of paralleling the Oriental and Greek mythology, Pseudo-Apollodorus and Alexander Polyhistor identified the flood of Deucalion, said to have occurred in the days of Ogygus instead of Cecrops, with that of the Oriental Noah and Xisuthrus (Utnapishtim).[98] It is difficult to see how Alexander Polyhistor could have reconciled the dating of Noah as well as that of Moses in the day of Ogygus. Possibly, though, he was merely quoting Pseudo-Apollodorus' chronicle when he made Noah a contemporary of Ogygus, while his own view was that the

94   Thus Castor, following partially Ctesias, ascribed a reign of 52 years to Ninus (250 F 1d) as well as to the first king of Sicyon, the oldest Greek monarch (Euseb. *Chronik,* 30; 81). Inachus, the first king of Argos, is assigned but 50 years (p.83).

95   Is there a relationship between Josephus' dating of the bondage of the Jews during the Hyksos period of the XVII Dynasty (1800-1550 B.C.) and Alexander Polyhistor's date of the exodus in 1796? Unfortunately, nothing remains of his mongraph on Egypt where Alexander Polyhistor may have treated the issue again. For a recent review of the evidence in Josephus, see O. Eissfeldt, in *Cambridge Ancient History,* rev. ed., II, Ch. XXVI(a) [Cambridge, 1965], who dates the exodus in the XIII century.

96   Jacoby, *Das Marmor Parium* (Berlin, 1904); *Rh. M.* LIX (1904), 63-107; *FGrH* 239, IIB, 992-1005; IID, 665-709.

97   *Marmor Parium, FGrH* A1-2, IIB, 993.

98   Alexander Polyhistor, 273 F 101.

latter lived in the days of Moses. Moreover, as a compiler there was no need for Alexander Polyhistor to be consistent. The main point, however, is unquestionable. Both Pseudo-Apollodorus (circa 100 B.C.) and Alexander Polyhistor, who flourished a generation later, had incorporated biblical history into the world chronicles.

The synchronization of biblical with general history is also attested in the writings of Varro (116-27 B.C.). Varro was sympathetically inclined to Judaism, remarking once that he had found the true god of philosophy only in the Roman Jupiter and in the imageless One honored by the Jews.[99] Varro's interest in ancient chronography, like that of some Jews, stemmed from his desire to synchronize Roman history with that of the Greeks. In a work written in 43 B.C., *De gente populi Romani,* fragments of which have been preserved in Censorinus, Varro divided the past into three periods: a) the unknown (ἄδηλον); b) the mythical; and c) the historical.[100] The first period began with the first man, whose time could not be determined, and ended with the "first flood" of Ogygus. The second period began with Ogygus and ended in the first Olympiad, a total of 1,600 years—400 years from Ogygus (2376 B.C.) to Inachus (1976), 800 years from the latter to the fall of Troy (1176 B.C., in round numbers, actually 1184), and from the fall of Troy to the Olympic era 400 years (776 B.C.). Accurate information was available only for events after 776 B.C.[101]

In marking the flood as the dividing point between the first and second epoch of human history, Varro shows that he was influenced by the biblical tradition.[102] But the apparent equivalent Noah-Ogygus indicates, as suggested by Jacoby, that he may have received the account of the flood from the writing of Alexander Polyhistor.[103] Both Varro and Alexander Poly-

---

99   Varro, in Augustine's *City of God,* IV, 31, 2. Cf. Norden, "Varro über den Gott der Juden," in *Fesgabe für Harnack* (Tübingen, 1921), 298 f.; Dahlmann, "Varro," *R.E., Suppl.* VI (1935), 1235.

100   Censorinus, *De die natali,* 21, quoting Varro: "Hic enim tria discrimina temporum esse tradit. Primum, ab hominum principio ad cataclysmem priorem, quod proter ignorantiam vocetur ἄδηλον; secundum, a cataclysmo priore ad Olympiadem primam, quod quia in eo multa fabulos referentur, μυθικόν nominatur; tertium, a prima Olympiade ad nos, quod dictur ἱστορικόν . . . "There is no reason to assume (so Jacoby, *FGrH,* IID, 709, 20 ff.; Linton, *Synopsis Historiae,* 72 f.) that Censorinus was quoting here Eratosthenes, because the latter and Varro differ here.

101   Censorinus, *De die natali,* 21.

102   See note 99. Whether or not the Graeco-Roman writers were acquainted with the Greek translations of Hebrew Scripture or received their information from pro- or anti-Jewish propagandists is still an open question (cf. Heinemann, "Antisemitismus," *R.E.,* Suppl. V, 3 ff.). There is no doubt, however, that Varro's chronological scheme was based on some earlier chronographer, rather than on a reading of Genesis.

103   Dahlmann (*R.E.* Suppl. VI, 1240) assumed that Varro's source was Castor, whom Varro cited once. This limiting of Varro to a single source is rightly challenged by Jacoby (*FGrH,* IIIb, Suppl., I, 387, 12-18), who suggests Alexander Polyhistor as an additional antecedent, because of the mention of Ogygus. This divergence between Varro

histor speak of the "first flood," hinting that there was another one. The basic divergence is that the Deucalion flood occurred according to Alexander Polyhistor during the days of Ogygus and Moses, while Varro dated Ogygus during the days of the first flood, referring apparently to Noah.

It is not known whether Varro dated Moses in his detailed description of the mythical period of history. It is likely that he did. The fact that the Church Fathers do not cite Varro is no evidence to the contrary, since they rarely quoted Latin works. Augustine apparently was the first Christian author to perceive that Varro's scheme of history was somehow related to Scripture. If Varro did mention Moses, he must have synchronized him with the Argive king Inachus (1976 B.C.), who in his view marked a new epoch in the mythical period of history.

Varro's dating of Moses remains uncertain. But the synchronization of Moses-Inachus is attested in the writings of Ptolemy of Mendes (40 B.C.), Apion of Alexandria (A.D. 40), Justus of Tiberias (flourished 60-100), and perhaps by Thrasyllus of Rhodes (before A.D. 36), Polybius (before A.D. 46), Thallus (before A.D. 150), and Phlegon of Thralles (150 A.D.), as well as in Christian chronography.[104] Unhappily little is known of Ptolemy, the oldest authority that Moses lived in the days of Inachus, the first king of Argos. Ptolemy was the priest in an Egyptian temple of Mendes and wrote a chronicle of Egyptian history in three books.[105] That Ptolemy flourished during the last pre-Christian century is deduced from the fact that Apion of Alexandria, whose activity stretched throughout the first century A.D., was quoting Ptolemy.[106] Conceivably, Ptolemy of Mendes is the anonymous

and Alexander Polyhistor, however, is sufficient to presume that both made use of a world chronicle.

Strabo (XII, 8, 13) records that the city of Apamea was also called $\kappa\iota\beta\omega\tau\acute{o}\varsigma$, a name given in Jewish texts to Noah's ark. Gutschmid (*Kl. Schr.* II, 392), Babelon (*Revue de l'histoire des Religions,* XXIII, 1891, 176), and Schürer (III, 29) presume that this suggests that knowledge of Noah's flood had spread to Phrygia in the pre-Christian period. The biblical lore about Enoch, according to Babelon and Schürer, was also known in Phrygia in the Hellenistic period. For Hermogenes (*FGrH* 795 F 2), cited by Zenobius (*Prov.* VI, 10), records that Nannacus, a king of Phrygia during the time of Deucalion, foresaw the impending flood, which he tried to prevent by gathering the people into the temples for crying session. Nannacus is here identified with Enoch, an identification supported by Stephanus of Byzantium, *s.v.* Ἰκόνιον (*FGrH* 800 F 3). Knowledge of Noah and Enoch may have spread to Phrygia via the universal world chronicle. The evidence, however, for the identification of Nannacus with Enoch is problematical. The proverbial use of Nannacus tears is found were used already in Herodas, the third century B.C. dramatist.

104 Ptolemy of Mendes, preserved in the writings of Tatian (38), Clement of Alexandria (*Strom.* I, 101, 3), Eusebius (*P.E.,* X, 10, 15-20), and Pseudo-Justin (*Cohortatio ad Graec.* 9 = *FGrH* 611 F 1).

105 611 TT 1-2b.

106 Apion of Alexandria and Oasis wrote his work circa 39 A.D., before he headed the Alexandrian delegation against the Jews (Josephus, *A.J.,* XVIII, 257-59 = 616 T 6).

historian who in 40 B.C., according to Clement of Alexandria, adjusted Eupolemus' annus Adami to the equivalent of 5269.[107]

Ptolemy synchronized Moses not only with Inachus, the king of Argos, but also with Amosis, the king of Egypt.[108] An old chronicle, quoted by Clement and attributed by Jacoby to Ptolemy, gives the date of the exodus: "The exodus took place during the reign of Inachus, for Moses left Egypt more than 345 [Pessl emends, 445][109] years before the Sothic cycle [i.e. 1676 or 1666 B.C.]. From the time of Moses' leadership and Inachus to the flood of Deucalion—I understand it to mean the second flood—and the conflagration of Phaethon, which had occurred in the time of Crotopus forty [?] generations are counted, a century being three generations."[110] The account, citing Thrasyllus, goes on to detail events of 310 years to the fall of Troy (dated here in 1194) and continued with 417 years to the first Olympiad in 776 B.C.[111]

The use of the Sothic cycle suggests an Egyptian provenance, justifying Jacoby's speculation that the author of this passage was Ptolemy of Mendes, known for his synchronistic Egyptian history, rather than Thrasyllus, who is cited at the end of the quotation, and about whom nothing is known. Whoever he was, the author was a heathen specializing in synchronistic history.

In dating the exodus in 1676 or 1666, there is a striking similarity between this author and Varro. Thrasyllus (?) counted 900 years from Inachus to the Olympic era (776 B.C.), while Varro computed roughly 800 years to the fall of Troy. Ptolemy (?) also diverges from Alexander Polyhistor, who calculated 1,020 years from Ogygus to 776, i.e., 1796 B.C. This difference would almost vanish, however, if Unger's emendation of Clement's text is accepted, making the date of the exodus a neat millennium before the Olympic era.[112] Nevertheless, one must beware of the temptation to tamper with manuscripts in order to manufacture remarkable coincidences.

---

107   See Eupolemus in Clement, 141, 4 = 723 F 4; Gutschmid, *Kleine Schriften*, II, 192, emends the text to refer to a certain Cassian (*Strom.*, I, 101), whom Clement was supposedly citing. This view is reightly rejected by N. Walter, "Der agnebliche Chronograph Julius Cassianus," in *Studien . . . Erich Klostermann* (Berlin, 1961), 177-192.

108   611 F 1a-c.

109   G. Unger, *Chronologie des Manetho* (Berlin, 1867), 54, 167, emends 435; Pessl, *Das chronologische System Manethos* (Berlin, 1878), reads 445.

110   Clement, *Strom.* I, 136, 3-4 = Thrasyllus, *FGrH*, 253 F 1; Th. Reinach, *Textes d'auteurs grecs et romains relatifs au Judaïsme* (Paris, 1895), 113 f. See next note.

111   Jacoby, *FGrH* IID, 830, 2 f., 5, citing Gutschmid (*Kl. Schr.*, I, 154 f.) believes that the passage quoted in the previous note may have emanated from Ptolemy of Mendes, rather than from Thrasyllus. Only *Strom.* I, 135, 5, is ascribed to Thrasyllus. Unfortunately, too little is known of either to be certain; though in this paper the hypothesis is tentatively accepted.

112   See note 83.

Fortunately, we have independent testimony for Ptolemy of Mendes' dating of the exodus. As was already said, he had synchronized Moses-Inachus-Amosis. In Manetho's Egyptian history, Amosis is listed as the first pharaoh of the XVIII dynasty dated by Eusebius, in 294-319 anno Abrahami, 1723 - 1698 B.C.[113] This is somewhat, but not seriously, out of joint with the Sothic date, attributed by Jacoby to Ptolemy of Mendes, of 1676 or 1666 B.C. Although Eusebius' most remarkable book on the chronology of the ancient world was based on the Hellenistic chronicles, it must be considered largely an independent work. This cannot be said of Africanus, for example, who, through quoting Ptolemy, dated the exodus, as did Alexander Polyhistor, in 1797/6 B.C.

The somewhat divergent dates of the exodus, deduced from composite quotations in the writings of the Church Fathers, need not becloud the bits that are known of biblical chronography during the first century B.C. Alexander Polyhistor, no doubt quoting Jewish and Samaritan historians, identified Enoch with Atlas, Noah with Belus I and Xisuthrus, and Nimrod with Belus II. He synchronized Moses with the Athenian king Ogygus, in whose time the flood of Deucalion took place. The date of the exodus in Alexander Polyhistor seems to have been 1797/6. A tradition attributed to Eupolemus, however, gave (as emended by modern editors) 1738 B.C. as the year of the Israelites' departure from Egypt. Perhaps 1676 or 1666 B.C. and 1723 - 1698 were among the other proposed datings of Moses. The different solutions suggested indicate an intense interest in the subject matter despite the lack of means to solve the problem.

In contrast to Alexander Polyhistor's synchronization of Moses with Ogygus, Ptolemy of Mendes (and perhaps Varro) placed the Jewish legislator in the days of Inachus, the first king of Argos. The artificial feature of both synchronisms is that Ogygus and Inachus appeared rather late in the respective Athenian and Argive genealogies of mortal kings. The older Greek tradition had listed Ogygus and Inachus as Titans. When and by whom these worthies were transformed into humans is still an open question. Jacoby attributes the change to Castor, who flourished in the middle of the first century.[114] The fact is, however, that in the first century the name of Moses was already linked with Ogygus *or* Inachus. The synchronization of Moses with Ogygus is even attested in the first half of the first century, in the fragments of Alexander Polyhistor and Pseudo-Apollodorus. Conceivably, the same chronographer who classified Ogygus as the first mortal king also dated him in the days of Moses. It is more likely, however, that the shift of Ogygus from the immortals to the mortals and his synchronization with the exodus

113   Manetho (in *FGrH*), 609 FF 2-3c, IIIC, pp. 36 f.
114   See Jacoby, *FGrH*, IIIB (Suppl.), I, 386 f.

were consecutive developments in Hellenistic chronography.[115] Circumstantial evidence suggests, then, that during the second century B.C. an unknown author composed a universal world chronicle.

From the writings of Tatian, Clement, and Africanus, it would seem that Alexander Polyhistor's dating of Moses in the days of Ogygus and Ptolemy's dating in the period of Inachus were identical.[116] There is no doubt, however, that the learned Church Fathers were in error. For Inachus and Ogygus represented two rival schools of Hellenic antecedence. Some genealogists, like Castor, who named Inachus, regarded Athens (Ogygus) as a late comer on the Hellenic scene.[117] The invention of Ogygus as the first autochthonous king, on the other hand, was intended to antedate Attica before Argos. The synchronism Moses-Ogygus-Inachus was, therefore, a contamination of two mutually exclusive chronographic approaches. Dionysius of Halicarnassus asserts flatly that Inachus of Argos was the first mortal king.

Ptolemy of Mendes' addition of the pharaoh of the exodus created a triangular synchronism Moses-Inachus-Amosis.[118] The link became almost universal when an unknown chronicler supplied the Babylonian (Assyrian) contemporary of Moses: Belochus, the eighth king after Ninus in Ctesias' manufactured list of Assyrian kings, who supposedly reigned thirty-five years, and in whose thirty-second year the exodus occurred, 402 years after the founding of the Assyrian empire.[119] This suggests that a bibilical chronographer had synchronized the patriarchal period of the Jews with the widely

115   Jacoby, *FGrH,* IIIb (Suppl.), I, p. 387, 18 ff.: "The question may remain open whether it was he Alexander Polyhistor who created the syncretistic combination of Greek and Oriental tradition which counts the floods and puts the first under the name of Ogygus, or whether the Jewish chronographers preceded him, the knowledge of whom in Christian chronography may entirely derive from Alexander Polyhistor." The first alternative, that Alexander Polyhistor had fused Jewish and Greek mythology, must be rejected. For, as far as we can judge from the fragments, his works consisted of compiling diverse quotation, rather than of concocting the material himself. Moreover, there is nothing to suggest that a heathen on his own would have put Moses in such favorable light. The synthesis of Greek and Jewish chronology probably antedates Alexander Polyhistor. See note 81.

116   Tatian, *Oratio adversus Graecos,* 38; Clement Al., *Strom.,* I, 101 (Euseb., *P.E.,* X, 12, 2-4); Africanus in *P.E.,* X, 10 (Ps.-Justin, *Coh. ad Graec.,* 9) = Alexander Polyhistor, 273 F 79; Ptolemy of Mendes, 611 F 1; Apion 616 F 2a-c.

117   Castor in Euseb., *Chronik* (Karst), p. 86 (*FGrH* 250 F 4, p. 1140) makes Cecrops the first Athenian king as the Marmor Parium (Jacoby, *FGrH* 139 A 1-2). Castor, however, antedated Sicyon before Argos.

118   Ptolemy of Mendes in Eusebius, quoting Africanus, *P.E.,* X, 10, 16 ff. = 611 F 1.

119   Clement Al., *Strom.,* I, 102, 4; Euseb., *P.E.,* X, 12, 8; *Chronik,* 31, 3; 85, 14.

read Assyrian history of Ctesias.[120] To do so, the ancient Jewish historian was forced to juggle Ctesias' figures, at least as they are attested in Castor. The basic assumption of the biblical chronicler was the synchronism of Abraham-Ninus, a view which remained the starting point of the entire Byzantine chronography.[121] Since Moses was the seventh generation after Abraham, the parallel Assyrian king in Ctesias' list might have been Amramithes, the seventh after Ninus. But since the exodus occurred in the eightieth year of Moses and 430 years after Abraham's arrival into Canaan, the eighth generation after Ninus, Belochus, seemed preferable. In Castor, according to Eusebius, Belochus ascended the throne 271 years after the birth of Assyria. The Jewish chronicler changed this number to 402, so that in Belochus' thirty-second year the bibilical 430 years (Exod. 12:40 LXX) would have been completed. Thus the contamination of Argive and Athenian claims plus the additions from Manetho and Ctesias resulted in a neat universal synchronism; Moses-Ogygus-Inachus-Amosis-Belochus. This list represented, respectively, the Jews, Attica, Argos, Egypt, and Babylonia (Assyria).

Since Gelzer and Gutschmid, the unified synchronism of the exodus has been ascribed to Justus of Tiberias, the renowned rival of Josephus.[122] Justus was the author of a chronicle which began with Moses and ended with the reign of Justus' patron Agrippa II in the year 94,[123] a work still available to Photius in the middle of the ninth century. Unfortunately, the two fragments of Justus dealing with the date of the exodus are of inferior quality, which makes it impossible to verify the attribution to him of the universal synchronism.

Furthermore, the two passages of Justus are divergent. According to Eusebius, Justus repeated the synchronism Moses-Inachus.[124] Africanus,

---

120   Ctesias, as preserved in Castor (see previous note) 250 F 1c-d; Cephalion 93 F 1. None of these sources mention Ctesias by name. But there is no question he was the ultimate authority for both Castor and Cephalion, as indicated by Diodorus (II, 23, 1 = Ctesias 688 F 1) and Nicolaus of Damacus (90 F 2).

121   Eusebius-Jerome, *Chronik* (Helm) pp. 14, 20a; Eusebius, *P.E.*, IX, 10, 11; X, 9, 10; Malalas, V, 7c; Epiphanius, *Pan. Haer.*, III, 12.

122   Gelzer, *Sextus Julius Africanus*, I, 4, 20, 118, 265; Gutschmid, *Kl. Schr.* II, 203; Wachsmuth, *Einl. der alten Geschichte* (Leipzig, 1896), 439; Cf. Schürer, *Gesch. d. jud. Volkes*, I, 61 f.

123   On Justus, see the now inadequate study of H. Luther, *Josephus und Justus vom Tiberias* (Halle, 1910). Known mainly from Josephus' *Vita*, he is cited also (aside from passages quoted below) in Photius, Bibl. 31. Since Valesius, it is assumed that the *Suda*, *s.v.* "Phlegon," contains a reference to Justus' work (Gutschmid, *Kl. Schr.* IV, 349; Schürer, I, 61). But, if the text of the *Suda* needs emendation, the reading of Josephus perhaps makes more sense than Justus (see Jacoby, *FGrH* 737 F 3, app. crit. to lines 19-20).

124   Eusebius-Jerome, *Chronik* (Helm), 7b (Syncellus) 734 F 2.

preserved in Syncellus, said that Justus made Moses the contemporary of Phoroneus and his successor Apis, the two first kings of Argos, and of Amosis of Egypt.[125] Now Justus may have dated Moses either in the days of Phoroneus, the first king of Argos in the old tradition; or in the time of Inachus, a name added by second or first century chronographers. But Justus would not have synchronized Moses with *both* Phoroneus and Inachus. All that can be said of Justus' chronology is that, unlike Josephus, Justus seems to have made full use of the Hellenistic universal chronicles.

The assumption, maintained by Gelzer, that whatever the Church Fathers report of Hellenistic bibilical chronology had filtered through Justus is also untenable on general grounds. Africanus' biblical chronology was derived from Justus. But there is enough evidence to suggest that biblical chronology was not a subject limited to Jews. By the first century B.C., treatments of Jewish antiquities had already become standard in universal histories.[126] The pagan chronographers Polybius (A.D. 47) and Thallus (under Hadrian?), synchronized Moses with Assyrian, Athenian, Argive, and Egyptian history.[127] The third century Porphyry, whose chronographic technique enabled him to date the Book of Daniel accurately, said that the Assyrian Semiramis had lived after Moses but 150 years before Inachus, and that Moses flourished about 1984 B.C.[128] Porphyry no doubt merely echoed the dates given in the Hellenistic world chronicles. By and large, pagan chronologists before the spread of Christianity placed Moses in an honored place, implicitly accepting for Judaism the most extreme antiquity they could imagine.[129]

125   Syncellus, p. 116 = 734 F 3. Both fragments (see previous note) are marked by Jacoby as defective.

126   The treatment of Jews in Greek heathen texts had begun with Hecataeus of Abdera, in the end of the fourth century B.C. (Diod. XL, 3 = *FGrH* 264 F 6). Megasthenes, writing in the period of the Diodochi, likewise glorified the Jews (Josephus, *A.J.,* X, 227 = 715 F; Clement Al., *Strom.* I, 72, 4 f. = 715 F 2). Theophrastus discussed the priestly code (W. Potscher, *Theophrastos* [Leiden, 1964], Fragment 13, pp. 72-76). Aside from Alexander Polyhistor, Teucrus of Cyzicus also wrote a monograph on the Jews in the first century B.C. (274 F 1); and Conon (26 F 4). For other treatment, see the now inadequate work of Reinach, *Textes d'auteurs grecs et romains relatifs au Judaïsme;* and Jacoby's *FGrH, passim.* Cf. above n. 52.

127   Polybius, *FGrH* 254 FF 1-4; Thallus, 256 FF 1-8.

128   Porphyry in *Adversus Christianos,* Harnack ed. (Berlin, 1916), fragment 40; Jacoby, *FGrH* 260 F 33; Eusebius-Jerome (Helm ed.), p. 8: "Porphyrius . . post Moysem Semiramin fuisse adfirmat, quae aput Assyrios CL ante Inachum regnavit annis. Itaque iuxta eum DCCC paene et quinquaginta annis Troiano bello Moyses senior inuenitur." Jacoby, *FGrH,* IID, p. 878 on F 33, points out that Porphyry merely repeated the older tradition, since his own chronicle began with the Trojan wars.

129   The view gained from Josephus' *Contra Apionem* and repeated by Reinach (*Textes D'auteurs grecs et romains,* pp. VIII-XX) that, with a few exceptions in the early period, the Greek heathen writers were anti-Jewish, is decidedly misstated and overstated. The dominant treatment was decisively pro-Jewish.

ANTI–JUDAEAN BIBLICAL CHRONOLOGY

Anti-Jewish authors, therefore, had to contend not only with Jewish propagandists, but also with the rather favorable attitude to Jews reflected in heathen chronography. The synchronism Moses-Inachus-Ogygus-Belochus must have been rather displeasing to Alexandrian Jew baiters, who were struggling to deny Jews the rights of citizenship. It is not paradoxical, then, that Apion, the author of a diatribe against the Jews, himself acknowledged the antiquity of the Jewish people when he reiterated Ptolemy of Mendes' synchronism of Moses-Inachus-Amosis.[130]

There was, however, another side to Apion's dating of Moses. The development of Alexandrian heathen treatment of ancient Jewish history is still obscure. Manetho, as claimed by Josephus, had given the first Egyptian account of the Hebrews' stay in the land of the pharaohs. But despite Josephus, it appears that Manetho merely described the Hyksos, whom the Jewish historian identified with the Jews. Manetho may not have alluded to the Jews at all.[131] Conceivably, though, Manetho did mention the exodus of the Israelites, which he dated in the reign of Tuthmosis, the seventh king of the XVIII dynasty (1626 - 1618).[132] If so, Ptolemy of Mendes' (or Thrasyllus') synchronization of Moses with Amosis (1766 B.C.) was by the nature of the material only a slight correction.[133] This is not true of the chronology of Lysimachus (who flourished before Apion), who dated Moses in the reign of Bocchoris.[134] Wittingly or unwittingly, Josephus' remark that Bocchoris lived nearly "1700 years ago" has falsified Lysimachus' intent to show that the appearance of the Jews on the historical scene occurred at a late date.[135] For we know that Bocchoris, mentioned in Manetho's tables and also in Diodorus, was in fact the pharaoh of the XXIV dynasty, in 770-635 B.C.,[136] nearly a millennium later than the time assigned to him by Josephus. It follows that Lysimachus as well as Apion dated the exodus in the

---

130　Apion, 616 F 4a-c.

131　Gutschmid, *Kl. Schr.,* IV, 402, 439 f.; R. Laqueur, "Manetho," *R.E.,* XIV, (1928), 1064 ff., proposes that Josephus (*C. Apionem,* I, 74-92, utilized a Pseudo-Manetho written by a polytheistic author, whom Josephus believed to have been real. See Jacoby, *FGrH,* IIIC, 84, app. crit. Cf. also, E. Meyer, *Aegyptische Chronologie* (Berlin, 1904), 71; R. Weill, *La fin du moyen âge Egyptien* (Paris, 1918), 68 ff.

132　*Contra Apionem,* 86-90 = *FGrH,* 609 F 8, pp. 87 f. See the authorities cited in the previous note, especially, Meyer, "Nachträge" (1907), p. 34, n. 5.

133　Ptolemy of Mendes, 611 F la-c.

134　Lysimachus is known only through Josephus, *C. Apionem,* I, 304-11; II, 16 f.; 20, 145, 236 = 621 FF 1-4. He antedates Apion, but is later than Ptolemy of Mendes.

135　*C. Apionem,* II, 16 = 621 F 2.

136　Manetho in Eusebius, *Chronik,* p. 68, "under whom the lamb spoke" (609 FF 2-3c, pp. 46 f.); Diod. I, 45. 2; 65, 1; 79, 1; 94, 5, makes him the greatest lawgiver of Egypt or even of the world.

eighth century B.C. Apion further refined Lysimachus' dating of the exodus, making it occur in the eighteenth year of Bocchoris' reign, i.e., in 753 B.C.[137]

Josephus' testimony, as shown above, is contradicted by the Church Fathers' attribution to Apion of the synchronism Moses-Inachus-Amosis.[138] Gutschmid reconciles the contradictory evidence by assuming that Apion had merely synchronized Inachus with Amosis, referring to the period of the Hyksos, to which Justus and the Church Fathers had appended the name of Moses.[139] This explanation is not satisfactory, as Apion was clearly quoting Ptolemy of Mendes, who certainly had synchronized the Jewish lawgiver with Amosis and Inachus.

A possible solution seems to be that Josephus and the Church Fathers were quoting different parts of Apion's work. Apion, indeed, had mentioned the synchronism Moses-Inachus-Amosis, but only to refute it, a point the Christian chronologists evidently did not bother to cite. Apion's own date of the exodus, however, is undoubtedly 753 B.C., that ascribed to him by Josephus. It is not known why Josephus failed to allude to the synchronism Moses-Inachus-Amosis, mentioned not only by Apion, but also in the current universal chronicles.[140] Of course, chronology per se was of little interest to the Jewish historian. He was more interested in refuting the charges that the Jews had been expelled from Egypt because of leprosy, than in establishing the date of the exodus. Conceivably, though, Josephus' failure to allude to the Moses-Inachus-Amosis synchronism was due to the fact that it had been the cornerstone of Hellenistic chronicles, works he refused to acknowledge even indirectly.[141] At any rate, after A.D. 70 the anti-Jewish synchronism Moses-Bocchoris gained wide currency in Rome, as attested in Tacitus.[142]

137   Apion in C. Apionem, I, 17 = 616 F 4.
138   Tatian, 38; Clement, Strom., I, 101; Eusebius, P.E., X, 10 = Jacoby, Apion 616 F 2a-c.
139   Gutschmid, Kl. Schr. IV, 362. Mueller, FGH, II, p. 509, F 3, suggested that the dating of the exodus in 753/2 was mistakenly attributed to Apion's fourth book of Aegyptiaca. Jacoby (616 F 4) also questioned the title of the book in which Apion dated the exodus.
140   Because Josephus' biblical chronology has been subjected to several studies, its treatment has been excluded from this essay. M. Bueddinger, "Die Exodus nach Manetho," Sitzungsber. d. k. Akad. d. Wissensch., LXXV (Vienna); Bosse, Die chronologischen System in Alten Testament und bei Josephus, as well as in discussions of Josephus and the Bible relating to chronology. Moreover, as evidently felt by the Church Fathers, Josephus' chronology was frequently contradictory and unrelated to the main stream of biblical historiography antecedent to him.
141   See C. Apionem, I, 218, where Josephus groups several Graeco-Jewish historians with those heathen writings. At any rate, it is clear that Josephus made no use of his Graeco-Jewish predecessors, including Philo of Alexandria, whom he mentioned once (A.J., XVIII, 259 f.).
142   Tacitus, Hist., V, 3, 1.

Apion's dating of the exodus in 753 B.C. is noteworthy. According to Josephus, it was constructed to synchronize with the foundation of Carthage which Apion placed in the same year as the exodus. The traditional year of the foundation of Carthage was 814 B.C., a view stated by Timaeus and repeated by Dionysius of Halicarnassus, the Roman historian.[143] Apion apparently had wished to correct Dionysius, whose reputation he coveted,[144] pointing out the remarkable coincidence that Rome and Carthage had been built within one year. Ironically, by dating the exodus at the same time as the founding of Carthage and Rome, Apion unwittingly assigned greater world significance to this event than he had intended.

It has been taken for granted that in antiquity interest in biblical chronology was restricted to the Jews and Christians. This study has demonstrated that heathen historians—Alexander Polyhistor, Varro, Ptolemy of Mendes and others—were likewise eager to date the main events recorded in the Bible. Interest in biblical chronology during the first century B.C. went hand in hand with the incorporation of ancient Jewish history as part of universal history. The writings of Posidonius, Diodorus, Nicolaus of Damascus, and Strabo contained lengthy accounts about Moses, far exceeding the political or geographical significance of Judaea. In part, the widening of the horizons of the universal historians resulted from the ecumenical nature of the Roman state. But monothesim and the majestic description of creation and the flood in the Book of Genesis were beginning to attract the attention of the heathen learned community. It is doubtful, although not impossible, that the heathen writers read the Book of Genesis itself. It is more likely that they received their knowledge of the Bible through Hellenistic Jewish reworkings of biblical events, of which there were many. The incorporation of biblical chronology into the world chronicles explains the honored position given Moses by heathen historians centuries before Christian chronography made its appearance. In fact, philo-Jewish chronography antedated the anti-Jewish variety.

It is not surprising that the Jewish and heathen attempts to date the flood or the exodus ended in complete failure despite these immense efforts. Modern scholars with all the advantages of scientific tools have not been more successful. The significance of the synchronistic world chronicle is twofold. Biblical traditions had penetrated heathen historiography through the world

---

143 C. Apionem, II, 17 = 616 F 2a; Timaeus, 566 F 60 = Dionysius of Halicarnassus, A.R., I, 74, 1. Timaeus had placed the foundation of Carthage and Rome in the same year (814 B.C.), a view which rightly mystified Dionysius. Apion followed Timaeus in the synchronism of the foundation of Carthage and Rome, but modified the date.

144 Cf. the Suda, s.v. Apion, 616 T 1.

of Graeco-Jewish writers. And when Christian scholars subsequently attempted to prove the greater antiquity of the Jews in relation to the Greeks, they invoked the testimony of heathen authors who had echoed the Graeco-Jewish writers: "Who was Plato, except Moses speaking in Attic?"

The study of biblical chronology began in the third century, not much later than the translation of the Pentateuch into Greek. At first this study was only an Alexandrian extension of Palestinian hermeneutics. Chronological hermeneutics soon developed an impetus of its own, creating rationale and order for meaningless Scriptural dates and numbers. Eupolemus has preserved one of the oldest attempts to date creation and the exodus precisely. He also formulated the principle which brought biblical chronology into the service of the apologists.

Chapter Five

FROM MOSES TO DAVID

1

JOSHUA-SAMUEL-SAUL

Before introducing David, Fragment Two begins with Moses: "Eupolemus says in his *On the Prophecy of Elijah:* 'Moses prophesied for forty years; then Jesus the son of Naue, thirty years. He lived one hundred and ten years and pitched the holy tabernacle in Shiloh. Afterwards, Samuel became prophet; then, by God's will, Saulus was chosen king by Samuel, who [Saul] died after a reign of twenty-one years. Then his son David succeeded him to the reign.' "[1]

In the previous extract from Eupolemus, Moses' contributions to civilization were reported; now we come to his death. Nothing in between is preserved. This is probably because Alexander Polyhistor, to whom we are indebted for these extracts from Eupolemus, preferred the even more fanciful version of Moses given by another Graeco-Jewish writer named Artapanus. The latter's account of the Jewish lawgiver, as we can see in the long excerpt given by Eusebius, was very colorful. Artapanus reported that Moses had invented the Egyptian religion in order to assist the Pharaoh in keeping law and order in the country.[2] Beginning with Moses' death, Alexander Polyhistor returned to copying from Eupolemus' writings.

That Joshua is given only a sentence and that the judges of Israel are ignored altogether is surprising. So is the meager treatment of the foundation of the monarchy, including the gross error that David was Saul's son. Did Eupolemus write the summary, or was his full treatment of this period abridged by his excerptors—notably Alexander Polyhistor?

Histories written during the Hellenistic period display a freedom to expand or contract, presumably sometimes to please their readers, but more often to

---

1 Eupolemus, 723 F 2b = *P.E.*, IX, 30, 1: Εὐπόλεμος δέ φησιν ἔν τινι Περὶ τῆς Ἠλίου ποοφητείας Μωσῆν προφητεῦσαι ἔτη μ´ εἶτα Ἰησοῦν, τὸν τοῦ Ναυῆ υἱόν, ἔτη λ´ βιῶσαι δ᾿ αὐτὸν ἔτη ρι´ πῆξαί τε τὴν ἱερὰν σκηνὴν ἐν Σιλοῖ. μετὰ δὲ ταῦτα προφήτην γενέσθαι Σαμουήλ. εἶτα τῇ τοῦ θεοῦ βουλήσει ὑπὸ Σαμουὴλ Σαοῦλον βασιλέα αἱρεθῆναι, ἄρξαντα δὲ ἔτη κα´ τελευτῆσαι. εἶτα Δαβὶδ τὸν τούτου υἱὸν δυναστεῦσαι.
2 Artapanus, 726 F 3a-b = *P.E.*, IX, 27, 1-38; Clement, *Strom.*, I, 154, 2-3.

129

present the past from a particular point of view. Pseudo-Philo, edited perhaps after 70 A.D., though typical of the old school of writing, retold the ancient history of the Jews from Adam at least to King David. This pseudonymous but interesting author sums up quickly or omits entirely most of the biblical stories, dwelling at length on invented tales or genealogies.[3] Such a method can also be found in parts of the Books of Enoch, Jubilees, and the Genesis Apocryphon. Conceivably, this could explain Eupolemus' outlook. He says nothing about the judges while Pseudo-Philo devotes more than half of his book on that period. It is conceivable that our section quotes from Eupolemus' chronological survey rather than from his presumably more detailed narrative.[4] This explanation, nevertheless, does not account for the failure to mention the judges.

The hypothesis that Alexander Polyhistor is responsible for the condensation of the account found in Eupolemus is, however, more attractive. Several technical indications, though not conclusive, support this view. Freudenthal noted that the phrase "afterwards" ($\mu\epsilon\tau\grave{\alpha}$ $\delta\grave{\epsilon}$ $\tau\alpha\hat{\upsilon}\tau\alpha$) which introduces Samuel, is not found elsewhere in the fragments and was intended to indicate a lacuna.[5] Evidence that the excerptor merely scanned through the text is perhaps suggested by the error which labeled David as Saul's son. Interestingly, Manuscript B reads $\gamma\alpha\mu\beta\rho\acute{o}\varsigma$, making David the son-in-law of Saul; but this is clearly a correction of Longinus, the thirteenth century scribe.[6] It is not inconceivable, however, that Alexander Polyhistor is innocent of the charge of having misquoted Eupolemus. Not wishing to enter into a complicated and seemingly discreditable story of how David became king, Eupolemus may have deliberately misstated the facts about the succession.[7]

---

3   See for example *The Biblical Antiquities of Philo,* edited by M. R. James (London, 1917); by Guido Kisch (University of Notre Dame, Indiana, 1949).

4   Freudenthal, *Hell. St.,* 121: "Abweichungen von der Bibel finden sich bei Eupolemos häufig genug, aber undenkbar ist, dass er von der Heldenzeit der Richter Nichts gewusst und Nichts berichtet habe." A. Spiro, *Proceedings of the American Academy for Jewish Research,* 20 (1952), 298, note 37, however, remarks that the reading of the Book of Judges was discouraged during the Second Temple; and that the book was not known to Eupolemus.

5   Assuming this passage is a chronological summary, we have the following scheme: Moses   40
           Joshua   30
           (Tabernacle   ?)
           Samuel   (?)
           Saul   31

6   See App. Crit. on *P.E.* (Mras), I, 538, 17. On Longinus, see Mras, pp. XIX-XXIII.

7   A. Spiro, *Manners of Rewriting Biblical History from Chronicles to Pseudo-Philo* (unpublished diss., Columbia Univ., 1953), 135 f., may be right here in assuming that the falsification was deliberate. But I doubt that this was for the strictly propagandistic reason, as maintained by Spiro, to impress upon the pagan world the continuity of the early Jewish monarchy. The monarchical form of government had long disappeared and besides needed no defense.

A similar simplification appears in the passage below, where Eupolemus reports that Solomon was crowned in the presence of the high priest Eli.[8] To begin with, Eli was priest of Shiloh four generations before Solomon. Furthermore, as is ,recorded in the biblical texts, the descendants of Eli supported the wrong party and lost their lives, while the rival priest Zadok sided with Solomon.[9] Eupolemus' addition of Eli into Solomon's coronation ceremony cannot be charged to the abridger, and it indicates that perhaps in order to avoid alluding to Solomon's bloodletting Eupolemus actually falsified the name of the high priest. And if this is the case, it is not impossible that it was Eupolemus himself who also made David a son of Saul.

Nonetheless, the mention of Eli below is the strongest indication so far that our summary for the period from Moses to David differs at least in one detail from that reported by Eupolemus. For if Eupolemus mentioned Eli during Solomon's coronation, he must have alluded to him, or rather to his ancestors, in a previous account.[10] In fact, Eupolemus tends to repeat names, especially false ones, such as Suron for the King of Tyre, and Vaphres for the King of Egypt. Freudenthal may be correct after all in assuming that our report is a mere skeleton of Eupolemus' account of the period of Joshua and Judges. But as has been suggested, it is not impossible that Alexander Polyhistor was quoting here from a chronological summary, which would explain the source of confusion of making David the son of Saul.

Although much contracted, the few sentences dealing with the period from Moses to David contain points of interest. Moses is designated as a prophet. The chronology is rather strange, certainly nonbiblical.[11]   Of Joshua, only his construction of the shrine in Shiloh is recorded. These loose ends will be considered after an examination of Eupolemus' treatment of King David.

2

DAVID'S CAMPAIGNS

"Then his [Saul's] son David became the ruler; who subdued the Syrians living on the River Euphrates and in the region of Commagene and the Assyrians of Galadene and the Phoenicians. But he also campaigned against the Idumaeahs and the Ammonites and the Moabites and the Ituraeans and

---

8   723 F 2b = *P.E.*, IX, 30, 8.

9   I Kings 1:7-2:27. Cf. *A.J.*, VIII, 10-12, suggesting (see *A.J.* Montgomery, *The Books of Kings* [International Critical Commentary, 1951], 93), that the controversy between the priests who had claimed descent from Eli (Ithamar) and those from Zadok (Eleazar) continued during the second Temple. See also below, pp. 151-55.

10   Eupolemus appears to be defending the traditional priesthood rather than the monarchy. See below the lengthy description of the Temple. See above note 4.

11   See below, p. 154.

the Nabataeans and the Nabdaeans. Again he campaigned against Suron, the king of Tyre and Phoenicia, whom [all these] 'he compelled to pay tribute to the Jews. But with Vaphres, the king of Egypt, he made an alliance of friendship."[12]

Although there are some puzzling geographic names in Eupolemus' account of David's wars, the general direction is clear enough. David first marched against the peoples of the north and northeast, then followed a campaign against those of the east and southeast. Finally, the king subdued the Phoenicians of the northwest. With his distant southern neighbor—Egypt—David made an alliance. Thus David's empire, according to Eupolemus, stretched from Mount Taurus to the borders of Egypt and from the Mediterranean to the Arabian desert.

It is worthwhile to recall here the Davidic conquests listed in II Samuel. The singular achievement of David was his confinement and subjugation of the Philistine city-states which had controlled most of southern Palestine during Saul's days (II Sam. 5:17-25).[13] Then David made tributaries of the kingdoms of Edom, Ammon, and Moab. To the north, David conquered the kingdom of Aram (Damascus) and Aram Zobah, the realm of Hadadezer, located between Mount Lebanon and Anti-Lebanon and bordering in the north with the kingdom of Hamath.[14] Reflecting perhaps roughly the northern limits of the Davidic state, Num. 34:10-12 lists Hazar-Enon, Shefam, Riblah, and Kadesh; the last two named on the Orontes and the location of which are certain. However, II Sam. 8:3 (keri = I Chr. 18:3) says that the king's empire bordered on the Euphrates.

In contrast to the scriptural accounts of David's martial exploits, Eupolemus makes no reference to the king's singular achievement in subjugating Philistia, evidently because it had disappeared from the scene and had no meaning during the middle of the second century B.C.[15] In II Samuel, David's lands in the north reach roughly halfway between the 34th and 35th parallels. In Eupolemus, the king's armies govern "the Syrians living on the river Euphrates and in the region of Commagene." What exactly was meant

---

12   723 F 2b = P.E., IX, 30, 3: εἶτα Δαβὶδ τὸν τούτου υἱὸν δυναστεῦσαι, ὃν κα-ταστρέψασθαι Σύρους τοὺς παρὰ τὸν Εὐφράτην οἰκοῦντας ποταμὸν καὶ τὴν Κομ-μαγηνὴν καὶ τοὺς ἐν Γαλαδηνῇ Ἀσσυρίους καὶ Φοίνικας. στρατεῦσαι δ᾽ αὐτὸν καὶ ἐπὶ Ἰδουμαίους καὶ Ἀμμανίτας καὶ Μωαβίτας καὶ Ἰτουραίους καὶ Ναβδα-ίους, αὖθις δὲ ἐπιστρατεῦσαι ἐπὶ Σούρωνα βασιλέα Τύρου καὶ Φοινίκης· οὓς καὶ ἀναγκάσαι φόρους Ἰουδαίοις ὑποτελεῖν· πρός τε Οὐαφρῆν τὸν Αἰγύπτιον βασιλέα φιλίαν συνθέσθαι.

13   II Sam. 5: 17-25; 8:1.

14   II Sam. 8:2-14. The conquest of Jerusalem by David is not recorded, either because it was excised by the abridger or because Eupolemus attempted to give the impression that the Holy City had been a Jewish possession long before David.

15   Cf. now J. C. Greenfield, "Philistines," in the Interpreter's Dictionary of the Bible, III, 791-95.

by the Syrians living at the Euphrates is not clear, but the borders of Commagene are known. This region, which seceded from Seleucia in 163 B.C., bordered on the Taurus Mountains in the north, Mount Amanus on the west, the river Beroea to the south, and the upper Euphrates, as it begins its southwest course until it turns again southeast. The Hellenistic state of Commagene had as its capital Samosata. It is clear that Eupolemus pushed rather generously the northern border of David's empire from the biblical limit at about the 35th parallel as far north as the 37th or 38th parallel. In fact, as is attested by Dionysius Periegetes (877), the Hellenistic geographers considered Commagene an integral part of Syria.

Exactly what Eupolemus meant by the "Assyrians and Phoenicians in the region of Galadene," is not clear. Normally, one would assume that Galadene equals Gilead, which Eupolemus twice elsewhere calls "Galaaditis."[16] But it does not make sense to assume that Eupolemus joined together Commagene with Gilead, a region of Transjordan bordering on the south with Ammon. Walter suggests possibly Gaulanitis, also in Transjordan, east of the Sea of Galilee. But this emendation, too, must be excluded, for there were no "Assyrians" in Gaulanitis; and besides, the context requires a more northerly region.

Professor John Strugnell, in a note on our typescript, has suggested that instead of ΓΑΛΑΔΗΝΗ, found in the manuscripts, we should read: ΓΕΒΕΛΗΝΗ, a reference to the ancient Phoenician city of Gebal (Byblos). Alternately, and more simply, without emending the text, the passage could be translated: "the (As)Syrians who live in Gilead, and the Phoenicians." Either suggestion posits two campaigns against Phoenicia, a view reflected by "again" (αὖθις), when Eupolemus speaks of David's final military exploit.

The peoples recorded in David's second campaign are, on the whole, more easily identifiable. The fact that Eupolemus mentions the Idumaeans, Ammonites, and Moabities, does not necessarily mean that he was acting strictly as a historian, recording geographic or political units that might have become obsolete by that time. Idumaea preserved its ancient name until the Roman period. The name Ammon was still recognized in the Zenon papyri (260-240 B.C.) and is recorded in I Macc. 5:13.[17] In fact, Eupolemus' list (Idumaeans, Ammonites, Moabites, Ituraeans, Nabataeans, and Nabdaeans) no doubt reflects the names of various Arab tribes or states which inhabited the eastern and southern parts of Palestine in his own day. The Nabdaeans, however, are not attested elsewhere, but perhaps are identifiable with

---

16   723 F 2b = *P.E.,* IX, 33, 1; F 4 (5) = IX, 39, 5. Walter suggests that   by Assyrians is meant Ashuri, in the neighborhood of Gilead, recorded in II Sam. 2:9. The most plausible view is that it means Syrians.

17   *Corpus Papyrorum Iudaicarum,* I (Cambridge, Harvard University Press, 1957), No. 1, p. 119. lines 3, 13: Ammanitis.

Nadabath (mentioned in I Macc. 9:37), or, as is more likely, with "the Arabs who are called Zabadaens" (I Macc. 12:31).[18] The inclusion of the Ituraeans and Nabataeans, although not geographically continguous, is noteworthy. The former were a predatory Arab tribe, which occupied the Lebanon and Hermon mountains, whose capital Heliopolis (modern Baalbek) was in Chalcis. The Nabataeans, whose capital was Petra (Reqem), controlled in Eupolemus' time most of Transjordan. Eupolemus' listing of the Nabataeans, Ituraeans, and Commagians may be significant because those peoples, like the Jews, were then attempting to gain independence from the weakened Syrian empire.[19]

Evidence of an anti-Phoenician bias is displayed in Eupolemus' remarks that David campaigned against Suron (Hiram), the king of Tyre and Phoenicia, who was "compelled to pay tribute to the Jews." Here Eupolemus clashes with I Kings 5:15, where it is said that relations between the Tyrian and Hebrew kings were always cordial. To solve the problem of how Eupolemus had dared to contradict the Bible, Freudenthal cited Ps. 83 (82):7-9, listing the enemies of Israel:

> The tents of Edom and the Ishmaelites,
>   Moab and Hagrites,
> Gebal and Ammon and Amelek,
>   Philistia with the inhabitants of Tyre;
> Assyria also has joined them;
>   They are the strong arm of the
>   children of Lot. Selah.[20]

Eupolemus, says Freudenthal, followed here the Psalmist instead of I Kings 5:15, holding the former more reliable since he believed in the Davidic authorship of the Book of Psalms.

But Freudenthal here presupposes that Eupolemus was acting not unlike a modern scholar who weighs the relative merit of each statement in the light of the authority behind it. What we know of Eupolemus suggests no such meticulous scholarship. Moreover, despite some similarity between the list of Eupolemus and that of Ps. 83(82):7-9, the two are quite different. The fact that the fragments of Eupolemus do not mention the Philistines and several other peoples of the Psalms, while the Psalmist fails to include the Syrians is not all that argues against Freudenthal's hypothesis. Eupolemus, it should be noted, recorded three campaigns of David, whereas the Psalmist speaks of only one. The absence of drama in the accounts of the Hellenistic historian,

---

18   See Freudenthal, *Hell. St.,* 209, citing Ναβδεήλ and Ναβαιώθ in LXX Gen. 25:13 (Hebrew: נביות and ארבאל). Kuhlmey, *Eupolemi Fragmenta,* 70.   See also Walter, *ad loc.; ANT* (ed. Pritchard), 298b-300.

19   Diod., XXXI, 19, see *Cambridge Ancient History, IX* (1932), 602 f.; Honigmann, "Kommagene," *R.E.,* Suppl. IV (1924), 978-90.

20   Cf. Freudenthal, *Hell. St.,* 115; Walter, *ad locum.*

while the poet reports that all the nations were assembled to fight Israel, suggests that the Psalmist was *not* Eupolemus' source.

But even granting that Eupolemus did follow Ps. 83(82):7-9 here, the main question remains unsolved. The problem is not that Eupolemus differs with a biblical passage; most of what he reports does so. The puzzling question about David's Tyrian campaign is why, of all the neighbors of Judaea, the Phoenicians were singled out to be mentioned twice? And why did Eupolemus contrast the Egyptians, who are said to have been David's allies, with the Phoenicians, who are said to have been the king's enemies?

In the absence of any record in the biblical texts of an alliance between David and the king of Egypt or of any enmity towards Tyre (despite Ps. 83:8), it is reasonable to suggest that Eupolemus' account reflects the contemporary political scene rather than the situation depicted by the ancient Hebrew sources. The Samaritan Pseudo-Eupolemus, writing perhaps a few decades earlier than his namesake, in an account of the patriarch Abraham, expressed his sympathies with Phoenicia while apparently attacking Egypt. The Phoenician civilization, said Pseudo-Eupolemus, was older than the Egyptian.[21] In Eupolemus, however, the sympathies seem to be reversed; Egypt is favored and Phoenicia is despised. Eupolemus' sentiments make sense if, as was shown independently above, he was writing in the 160's or 150's B.C. There seems to have been an identification of the ancient Phoenicians and Syrians with the Seleucid empire during the Maccabean revolt. Tyre had desperately resisted the Macedonian conquest of the Persian Empire, but she and her sister port of Sidon, as is attested in Phoenician coinage, became favored cities of Antiochus IV.

These anti-Syrian sentiments may shed some light on a hitherto unsolved puzzle in the fragments. Eupolemus says that Suron (Σούρων) was the name of the Tyrian king and Vaphres (Οὐαφρῆς) was king of Egypt while David and Solomon reigned in Jerusalem.[22] In the Bible, the name of the King of Tyre is Hiram (variants: Hirom, Huram).[23] Scripture records the name of the pharaoh who was a contemporary of Solomon and his successor as Shishak (Σουσακείμ), the founder of the Twenty-Second Dynasty (940-915), who invaded Palestine circa 920.[24] Vaphres, however, who

21   724 F 1-2 = *P.E.*, IX, 17, 4; IX, 18, 2. Cf. Wacholder, *HUCA* XXXIV (1963), 103 f. Orac. Sibyll. III, 168, knows of a war of Solomon against Phoenicia, as well as against other Asiatic nations. Cf. now 1 QM 1:1 ff.; depicting the war against the forces of darkness.

22   723, F 2a = *Strom.*, I, 130, 3; F 2b = *P.E.*, IX, 30, 4, 8; 31, heading; 32, heading; 33, heading.

23   As a rule II Sam. and I Kings have חירם (but see I Kings 5:24; 32), but Chronicles has the vowel חורם (but *qeri* I Chr. 14:1 etc.).

24   Sheshak invaded Jerusalem in the V year of Rehoboam (I Kings 14:25 f.). According to Manetho, Smendis reigned during 1004-978; Psusennes, 978-937, Nephercheres 937-933, Amenophthis ruled Egypt 933-924; Osochor, 924-918 B.C. (Eusebius, *Chron.* Arm. Karst, p. 62; *FGrH* 609 F 2-3a-c pp. 44 f.).

according to Eupolemus was the contemporary of David and Solomon, was in fact the seventh or eighth king of the Twenty-Sixth Dynasty (588-566).[25] In Jer. 44:30, he is called Hophra, transliterated in the Septuagint as Vaphres.[26] Why, they, did Eupolemus identify the sixth century Vaphres as the king of Egypt in the days of David and Solomon? It must be noted, however, that since the Bible does not identify the pharaoh who reigned during David's or the early Solomon's days, Eupolemus may have chosen Vaphres for no other reason other than that, among the names of the rulers of Egypt, he found an assonance between Vaphres and the scriptural pharaoh. But why did he change the bibilical form of Hiram into Suron?

Philological attempts have failed to solve the last question. The Greek translators of the Bible transcribed Hiram into $X\epsilon\iota\rho\acute{\alpha}\mu$; and Josephus, on the authority of Menander and Dius, Phoenician historians, wrote $E\ddot{\iota}\rho o\mu o\varsigma$.[27] Since Scaliger, this name has given rise to various conjectures. It is customary to explain $\Sigma o\acute{\nu}\rho\omega\nu$ from the Hebrew צורי (Zori), meaning a Tyrian.[28] Freudenthal, citing Gesenius, noted that the Greek letter Σ was occasionally used by the Septuagint for the Hebrew ח (Ḥ); the change from M to N was also frequent. Thus Hiram or Hirom was transformed into Suron, Freudenthal suggests, because of certain linguistic rules, and because Herodotus, VII, 98, recorded a certain Tyrian by the name of $\Sigma\acute{\iota}\rho o\mu o\varsigma$.[29] All this is unacceptable. These explanations show how under certain conditions Hebrew letters were transformed into Greek forms, but offer no good reason why Hiram was transliterated into Suron.

There are, however, two partial parallels to Suron in intertestamental texts. Judith 2:28 lists Sur ($\Sigma o\acute{\nu}\rho$) among the coastal Phoenician cities overrun by Nebuchadnezzar's armies. But the reference could not be to Tyre (Hebrew: Zor), since this city is already listed in the verse. Parenthetically, it should be noted that independent of the Sur-Suron relationship, there appears to be some kinship between the geography employed in the Book of Judith and that of Eupolemus.[30] Another instance of Sur, here uncontro-

---

25   The traditions of Manetho differ as to the length of Vaphres' reigh, 609 FF 2-3a-c (*FGrH* IIIC, 50 f.), from 19, to 25, to 30 years.

26   Herod. II, 161, ff., spelled $\mathrm{A}\pi\rho\acute{\iota}\eta\varsigma$ (Diod. I, 68).

27   *C. Apionem*, I, 120 = Menader of Ephesus, 783 F 1; *C. Apionem*, I, 112 = Dius 785 F 1.

28   Scaliger, *Fragmenta*, 5, as cited by Kuhlmey, *Fragmenta Eupolemi*, 70. This is another witness for the change from *M* to *N*, a frequent occurence. See now E. J. Kutscher, *Studies in Galilean Aramaic* (Jerusalem, 1952), 38-43 [in Hebrew].

29   Freudenthal, *Hell. St.*, 108 f., 209. Cf. LXX $\Sigma o\nu\rho\acute{\iota}$ for Hebrew חורי (Numb. 13:5).

30   Cf. Judith 2:15 and 7:2 with Eupolemus F 4 (5), for the list of the armies. See also below . But see Y. M. Grintz, *Sefer Yehudith* (Bialik Institute, Jerusalem 1957), ad locum, who cites the parallel Greek martial tradition. Nevertheless, the number of the soldiers is found only in Eupolemus.

verted, is the legend that the Prophet Jonah after the repentance of Nineveh, settled among the foreigners (ἀλλόφυλοι) of Sur.[31]

The citation of parallels, however, does not solve the problem. The point to be settled is why a writer, living in Jerusalem and certainly capable of reading Hebrew, would have transliterated Hiram into Suron. Moreover, the use of Suron cannot be divorced from the question of naming the sixth century Vaphres the contemporary of David and Solomon.

Any attempt to penetrate into the mind of a fabricator is necessarily speculative. But it would seem that a solution might lie in Eupolemus' set of equivalents. As has been suggested above, Eupolemus equated the Syria and Phoenicia of David's time with the Seleucid realm of his own day, the enemy of the Jews and Judaism. Egypt, however, served as a place of refuge from the hated Syrians. King David made an alliance with Egypt, Eupolemus states, but subdued the Syrians. Eupolemus, it would seem, abandoned the form Hiram because this name was closely associated in Scripture with the building of the Temple. Suron, however, evidently resembled the form of *Suryah* and *Suri,* the Aramaic or Hebrew equivalents of Syria and Syrian, respectively. And during the Maccabean revolt, the term "Syrian" certainly assumed pejorative connotations. Incidentally, Eupolemus used a similar mixture of Semitic and Greek forms to "explain" the etymology of Jerusalem-Hierosolyma as derived from ἱερόν (holy temple) and Solomon.[32]

Other pieces of the puzzle now begin to fall into place. Eupolemus may have made Vaphres a contemporary of David because it was this pharaoh who had offered a haven to many Jews who were fleeing from their Babylonian enemies in the last years of the First Temple.[33] Conceivably, the Ptolemaic kingdom secretly abetted the Hasmonean rebels.[34] So Vaphres (Hophra, Jer. 44:30) became David's only ally. The biblical tradition has no record of Egypt's role in the construction of the temple, but Eupolemus assigned to Vaphres a significant share in the Solomonic sanctuary, perhaps even exceeding that of the Phoenician king. Eupolemus' father, it should be remembered, represented the priestly class which, in about 200 B.C., had welcomed Antiochus III's conquest of Coele-Syria.[35] Now that political winds were changing, Eupolemus doctored biblical history accordingly.[36]

---

31   His mother was said to have been from Sur. See Jonah's vita in *Propeten- und Apostollenlegenden,* ed. by Th. Schermann (*Texte und Untersuchungen,* XXXI, 3, Leipzig, 1907), pp. 56-59.

32   *P.E.,* IX, 34, 12 = 723 F 2b.

33   Cf. Jer. 43:8-44:30.

34   Cf. Daniel 11:1-45.

35   II Macc. 4:11.

36   See Leviticus Rabbah, alluding to Ezek. 28:2, XXVII, 2 (Margulies ed. p. 402); Tanhuma *Va'era,* 16 (Buber, 9): Yalkut, Jer. 330, where Hiram is likewise linked with a pharaoh (Hophra ?) in connection with the construction of the Temple. Cf. Movers, Die *Phönizier,* II, 1 (Berlin, 1849), 338 n. 40.

As has been noted, David's empire in Eupolemus' description stretched from the Taurus Mountains and the upper Euphrates to the Gulf of Aqabah, including even the Red Sea islands. These boundaries sound fantastic even for the Davidic empire. But they are not unique to Eupolemus. When Abraham inspected the land promised to his seed, according to the Genesis Apocryphon, an Aramaic scroll found among the Qumran texts, the patriarch reported: "And I Abram went forth to journey about the land and to look upon it. And I began to wander from the River Gihon and I came to the shore of the sea until I reached the mount of the Ox (Taurus). And I journeyed from the shore of this Great Salt Sea and I went along the mount of the Ox (Taurus) eastward in the breadth of the land, till I reached the River Euphrates and I wandered near the Euphrates eastward till I reached the Red Sea and I went on along the Red Sea till I reached the tongue of the Sea of Reeds that goes out from the Red Sea and I turned southward till I came to the River Gihon."[37] In other words, Abraham's vision roughly reflected the utopian borders of the Davidic empire as reported by Eupolemus. This does not mean, however, that there is necessarily a direct dependence of one source upon the other. For in the rabbinic texts, too, Greater Syria is considered part of the Holy Land, making the Amanus chain, which bordered on Commagene, the northmost part of the country.[38] A tradition that is found in Hellenistic, Qumran, and Rabbinic sources must have been of deep antiquity as well as of wide currency.

Eupolemus' reconstruction of the Davidic campaigns, contrary to claims made from time to time, adds nothing to our knowledge of the early monarchy.[39] Nevertheless, it is of unusual significance for the student of Judaea during the Hasmonean period. Here can be seen not only an anachronistic utilization of geographic names, such as Nabataea and Commagene, which appeared on the historical scene centuries after King David, but also an account of Israelite history which has little basis in the biblical texts of II Samuel and I Chronicles. Since the sources for this period are among the fairest found in Scripture, the fact that Eupolemus disregarded them must not be ascribed to his possession of more reliable traditions. The conclusion is inescapable that Eupolemus' description of the Davidic empire

37   Genesis Apocryphon, col. XXI, 15-18. See now J. A. Fitzmyer, *The Genesis Apocryphon of Qumran Cave I* (Biblia et Orientalia, 18; Rome, Pontifical Biblical Institute, 1966), 135-39.

38   See Tosefta Terumoth, II, 12; Hallah, II, 11; Yerush. Shevi'it, VI, 1, 36d; Hallah, IV, 8, 60a; B. Gittin, 8a.

39   See however, Movers, *Die Phönizier,* II, 1, pp. 326 ff.; Gutman, *The Beginnings of Jewish-Hellenistic Literature,* II, 85, ff., who insist that Eupolemus has preserved some historical information not found elsewhere. For contrast see now Th. A. Busink, *Der Tempel von Jerusalem von Salomo bis Herodes* (Nederlands Instituut voor het Nabije Gosten, Studia Francisci Scholten Memoriae Dicata, Leiden, E. J. Brill, 1970), I, 28.

reflected a midrash-like version of ancient history in the light of the political scene of the middle of the second century B.C.

3

DAVID CHOOSES THE SITE FOR THE TEMPLE

The Solomonic temple forms the central theme of the surviving fragments of Eupolemus' writings. Four-fifths of the extracts describe some aspect of the Jerusalem shrine. Conceivably, this could have reflected the interest of the extractor rather than the emphasis of the author. But here this is not the case. Alexander Polyhistor, the excerptor, had no sympathy for the priestly view of Judaism. The devotion and enthusiasm for the temple evident in the fragments must be credited to Eupolemus and to no one else. From Ezra to Bar Kochba and Rabbi Judah Hanasi, it was the sanctuary of Jerusalem which dominated all other aspects of Jewish life. But even viewed in this light, Eupolemus' fragments stand out as written from a sectional perspective. This is perhaps to be expected of a writer who represented the highest echelons of priestly aristocracy, and who wrote at a time when the temple constituted the rallying point of the rebels.

"When David wanted to build a temple for God he prayed to God to show him the place for the altar. Thereupon an angel appeared to him above the place, where the altar (abomination?) was standing in Jerusalem. And he commanded him not to build the temple himself, for he was defiled with human blood and with many years of warfare. His name was 'Dianathan.' "[40]

The biblical account of how the site of the Solomonic temple was chosen differs substantially from Eupolemus' version. According to the Bible, it all began with David's incredible bungling. The king had unpropitiously ordered a census, evidently for the purpose of raising a levy, whereupon the angel of death—Satan, according to the Chronicler—spread a mortal plague, killing thousands. Having confessed his sin, David saw the angel of death stop at Araunah's threshold, which, upon Prophet Gad's advice, he hastened to acquire for an altar. This stopped the plague and determined the site of the Solomonic Temple.[41] In Eupolemus, most of the elements of the Samuel-Chronicles account are present, yet the story is quite different. The angel is no longer Satan, but a divine messenger come to answer David's prayer to be shown where to build the Temple. In II Sam. 24:16 (I Chr. 21:15) the angel

---

40   723 F 2b = *P.E.*, IX, 30, 5-6: βουλόμενον τε τὸν Δαβὶδ οἰκοδομῆσαι ἱερὸν τῷ θεῷ ἀξιοῦν τὸν θεὸν τόπον αὐτῷ δεῖξαι τοῦ θυσιαστηρίου. ἔνθα δὴ ἄγγελον αὐτῷ ὀφθῆναι ἑστῶτα ἐπάνω τοῦ τόπου, οὗ τὸν βωμὸν ἱδρῦσθαι ἐν Ἱεροσολύμοις, καὶ κελεύειν αὐτὸν μὴ ἱδρύ<ε>σθαι τὸ ἱερόν, διὰ τὸ αἵματι ἀνθρωπίνῳ πεφύρθαι καὶ πολλὰ ἔτη πεπολεμηκέναι· εἶναι δ᾽ αὐτῷ ὄνομα Διαναθάν·

41   II Sam. 24; I Chron. 21:1-22:1.

was standing *with ('im)* Araunah; in Eupolemus, God's messenger appears *above* (ἐπάνω) the site. The Chronicler repeats essentially the story of Second Samuel, even if the selection of the site is more purposeful. Eupolemus' main departure from the biblical tradition, however, is in the claim that the revelation came to David as a response to his prayers. Eupolemus abandoned both accounts to construct one that appears less anthropomorphic and more exalting.[42]

A phrase apparently betrays Eupolemus' purpose in changing the biblical account: "Where the altar (was? is?) standing in Jerusalem."[43] Perhaps Eupolemus did not alter the scriptural story of the selection of the site because he wished to whitewash King David. This may be merely incidental. Eupolemus' main point is that in his own day the temple was still standing on the same site which the angel had shown to David. The full significance of these words becomes clear when it is recalled that the altar symbolized Antiochus IV's persecution. The main grievances listed in the Books of Daniel and I Maccabees were the erection of the *shikkuz meshomem,* "the abomination that makes desolate" and the abolition of the continual sacrifices.[44] It is not known whether Eupolemus' description of the selection of the site was written during the persecution or after the altar had already been purified. The persecution began on the fifteenth of Kislev 167 B.C. and the rededication of the temple occurred on the twenty-fifth of Kislev 164 B.C.

It is possible, however, Eupolemus was writing while the Syrian idol Zeus Olympius still profaned the sanctuary. I Macc. 1:54 reads: "And on the fifteenth day of Kislev of the 165th year (167 B.C.) they built a desolate abomination upon the altar; and in the surrounding cities of Judaea they also built altars."[45] Though the English translation uses "altar" twice, the Greek does not, employing instead θυσιαστηριόν for the former and βωμός the latter. According to many commentators, the first term refers to the altar of the burnt offering; the second form is used pejoratively for the Syrian stone altars of the idols known as Ba'alshamaim or Zeus Olympus.[46] Combining I Macc. 1:54 with verse 59 where βωμός is used once again to refer to the "abominable desolation," Bickerman argues that the worship of idolatry during the Hasmonean period consisted of bomolatry.[47] Without

42   This is the only instance in Eupolemus in which it seems that he changed a tradition to make it less anthropomorphic.

43   οὐ τὸν βωμὸν ἱδρῦσθαι ἐν Ἰεροσολύμοις: F 2 = *P.E.,* IX, 30, 5.

44   See Daniel 11:30 ff.; 12:11; I Macc. 1:54 f.;II Macc. 6:1 ff.

45   Cf. I Macc. 1:47, 59.

46   C.L. Grimm, *Kurzgefastes exegetisches Handbuch zu den Apokryphen des Alten Testamentes* (Leipzig, 1855), 30f.; Bickerman, *Gott der Makkabäer,* (Schocken-jüdischer Buchvelag, Berlin, 1936), 105-16; *Les Livres des Maccabées,* 32, 25, 27 3rd ed. pp. 66, 92; Dancy, *A Commentary on I Macc.,* 78-91.

47   Bickerman, *Gott der Makkabäer,* 109-11. See also I Macc. 1:47; II Macc. 10:2; *A.J.,* XII, 253, all texts using *bomos* to describe the idolatrous sacrifices.

going quite as far, it is nevertheless clear that the Greek version of I Maccabees differentiates between θυσιαστηρίον and βωμός, as if between the holy and the profane.[48]

The question is, then, whether or not the differentiation found in First Maccabees between *thysiasterion* and *bomos* exists also in Eupolemus' passage. To choose a site, according to our fragment, David prayed to God to indicate to him the propitious place for an altar (θυσιαστηρίον). "Whereupon the angel appeared standing above the place, οὗ τὸν βωμὸν ἱδρῦσθαι ἐν Ἱεροσολύμοις; and he commanded him not to build the Temple . . ." The Greek clause seems to mean "where the altar (βωμός) was erected in Jerusalem." Now this *bomos* might conceivably refer to the altar built by David. But the entire clause, since it is followed by the angel's command not to build (μὴ ἱδρῦσθαι) the Temple, and since "in Jerusalem," as used by Eupolemus, implies a post-Davidic name, it is likely that our passage could not refer to the Davidic altar.[49] Neither could it in our context allude to that of Solomon. The most plausible construction, it would seem, is that Eupolemus points to "the *bomos* that was erected (recently) in Jerusalem."

Eupolemus' account of the selection of the site may also be seen from a different perspective. The plague of Israel, reported in the concluding chapter of II Samuel and its parallel in I Chronicles, must have appeared as a rather crude way to choose a place to build the Temple, II Chr. 3:1 had already suggested that Araunah's threshold, acquired by David, was identical with Mount Moriah where Abraham had bound his son Isaac. This legend added new significance to the temple site. Traditions of an uncertain date, but recorded in biblical, intertestamental and rabbinic texts, attributed cosmic significance to the site of the Temple. Not only was it chosen before the creation of the world; but the location of the Holy of Holies marked the center of the earth.[50] Although there are no other indications that Eupolemus shared the belief in these myths, his account of the selection of the site appears to reflect a popular piety.

Eupolemus' version of David's warfare, as we have seen, related as much to his own days as it did to the times of King David. This tends to support the

---

48   I Macc. 1:47, 54, 59. See also I Macc. 2:23-25; 45; 5:68., where *bomos* is used in the sense of an idolatrous altar. Contrast the use of *thysiasterion* in I Macc. 1:24, 54, 59; 4:38, 44-59; 5:1; 6:7; 7:36, referring to the purified altar of the Temple. John Strugnell has kindly alerted me to the study by Suzanne Daniel, *Recherches sur le vocabulaire du culte dans la Septante* (Études et Commentaires LXI; Paris, Librairie C.Klincksieck, 1966), 15-32, which treats the subject with admirable detail.

49   The presumption being that Eupolemus was writing in Jerusalem; otherwise no such deduction can be made, for it is possible to place the comma before "in Jerusalem."

50   Cf. Exod. 25:8, 22; 29:46; I Kings 8:22f.; Ezek. 40:1 ff.; Ps. 78:69 ff.; Jub. 1:27; 25:21; Mishnah Kelim, I, 6-9; B. T. Pesahim, 54a; Genesis Rabbah I, 4 p. 6; LXIX, 17 pp. 796 f.

view that Eupolemus indeed referred to the Antiochan persecution. The selection\of the location of the Temple runs parallel to but independent of the biblical account. Therefore, when Eupolemus follows literally a passage of Chronicles it is worthy of notice. This is the case in Eupolemus' account of why Solomon, rather than David, had the distinction of erecting the Temple. I Kings 5:17 answers, quoting Solomon, that David was too preoccupied with wars to have time for building the house of the Lord. A variant answer to this question is given indirectly by the prophetic historian in II Sam. 7 (= I Chr. 17). There David was bothered by the fact that the Lord was dwelling in a tent while the king resided in a palace. The Lord retorted through Nathan that He rather enjoyed the rustic life which recalled the simplicity of the desert. However, David's son would be vouchsafed to erect a permanent house for the Lord. The Chronicler uses blunter language to explain David's failure: "The Lord said to David: You have shed much blood and waged great wars; you shall not build a house unto my name because you have shed much blood before me upon the earth!" That these wars were waged on Yahweh's behalf is forgotten in Chr. 22:8. But Eupolemus, writing evidently in the midst of persecution and revolution, repeats almost verbatim the account of the Chronicler, no doubt a fellow priest.

The seer associated, in II Sam. 24 and in I Chr. 21, with David's acquisition of the Temple site was the prophet Gad. Eupolemus' fragments make no mention of a prophet by such a name. But according to the Greek text, the name of the angel was Dianathan; because "Dianathan" does not make sense, it is customary to emend the text. Kuhlmey proposes to see in Dianathan a monstrous contraction of Θεός and נתן ("God" and "Nathan").[51] Freudenthal changed the Greek from "His name was Diana-than" to read instead, "He [God] sent him [David] a message through Nathan (διὰ Νάθαν)."[52]   That Dianathan is somehow derived from the name of the prophet Nathan makes sense, because Nathan is cited twice more in the fragments, once by name and once indirectly. It is generally agreed, therefore, that either Alexander Polyhistor or a scribe's error changed Nathan into Dianathan.

John Strugnell, going beyong Freudenthal's identification, points out that, for syntactical reasons, our passage relates, not to Nathan's interpretation of the angel's appearance, but to the prophet's role in the planning of the

51   Kuhlmey, *Fragmenta Eupolemi*, 71.
52   Freudenthal, *Hell. St.*, 121.

Temple, which is the subject of the following paragraph.[53] The emendations changing "Dianathan" into Nathan are eminently sensible. Some lingering doubts remain, however. A writer who transformed Hiram into Suron, made Vaphres the pharaoh in Solomon's time, and found the etymology of Hierosolyma (Jerusalem)—*hieros* plus Solomon—was capable of making concoctions, including perhaps Dianathan.

Eupolemus' formulation of the angel's role is of interest. In II Sam. 24:1, Yahweh's anger at Israel provokes the census, causing a pestilence by a smiting angel (24:15-16). The Chronicler, however, replaces Yahweh with Satan (21:1). Although Yahweh remains supreme in the Chronicler's account the supreme role he had in Second Samuel, the improved status of the angel is striking: "And David lifted up his eyes and saw the angel of the Lord standing between earth and heaven [i.e., suspended in the air], and in his hand a drawn sword stretched out over Jerusalem. Then David and the elders, clothed in sackcloth, fell upon their faces" (I Chr. 21:16).[54] Eupolemus' account of the hovering angel retains the improved position of the angel found in the Book of Chronicles, but transforms the angel from a smiting spirit, known to us from Num. 22:22 and Josh. 5:13, into one who has come in response to prayers.

We can only conjecture as to Eupolemus' motive for changing a hostile angel into a benevolent one. Certainly, David's piety is less blemished in the Greek fragments than in the older traditions, and the choice of God's dwelling place more exalted. But there is also a possibility that Eupolemus rejected the dual angelology quite popular in his day, as suggested in the Enochite and Dead Sea Scrolls.[55] Moreover, it should be noted that, according to Acts 23:8, "the Sadducees say 'that there is no resurrection, nor angel, nor spirit, but the Pharisees acknowledge them all." If the absolute denial attributed to the priestly faction was a fact in the middle of the second century B.C., Eupolemus could not have been a Sadducee. It is doubtful, however, that Sadducean doctrine was quite so emphatic in this matter, at least in the days of Judah Maccabee. Yet, Eupolemus' account of the angel's role in the selection of the Temple's site, when compared to the biblical tradition, may reflect a more moderate view of the existence and role of

---

53   724 F 2 = *P.E.* IX, 34, 4 (2), mentions Nathan, the prophet of God; IX, 34, 15 (13), alludes to a prophet, evidently Nathan. Professor John Strugnell proposes to read: $\epsilon\tilde{\iota}\nu\alpha\iota$ δ' $\alpha\grave{\upsilon}\tau\tilde{\omega}$ $<\pi\rho o\phi\eta\pi\acute{\eta}\nu>$ $\grave{o}\nu o\mu\acute{\alpha}\tau\iota$ Nαθαν:"The name of his prophet was Nathan." "Such a new subject," says Strugnell, "is supported by the δ' $\alpha\grave{\upsilon}\tau\tilde{\omega}$,which would not be necessary if we were still dealing with the account of the angel."

54   See now Wilhelm Rudolph, *Chronikbücher* (Handbuch zum Alten Testament, 21; Tübingen, Mohr, 1955), 141-49, for a detailed account of the Chronicler's view of the angelic tradition.

55   Cf. Enoch 40:7; 53:3; 56:1; 62:11; 63:1; 1QH 4:6; 45:3; Zadokite Fragments 2:6; B. Shabbat, 55a, for a sample of the numerous references to hostile angels. See also T. H. Gaster, *The Interpreter's Dictionary of the Bible,* (1962) 128-34.

celestial beings, a position Eupolemus' fellow priests—supposedly Sadducees—possibly shared.[56]

Our passage is less ambiguous, however, on the subject of Eupolemus' concept of the role of the prophet. In the Greek fragments Nathan plays a prominent position in the construction of the Solomonic Temple. Assuming that our emendation of "Dianathan" is valid, it was Nathan, not Gad, as Second Samuel reports, who interpreted the angel's message to the king. Clement of Alexandria, perhaps repeating Eupolemus, says Nathan was Solomon's prophet.[57] In Eupolemus' fragments the term "prophet" occurs nine times,[58] suggesting the author's veneration of the seer's role. "Surely the Lord God does nothing without revealing his secret to his servants the prophets" (Amos 3:7). There is no doubt that Eupolemus could have associated himself with this view.

56   Whether or not the factional names "Pharisee" and "Sadducee" are quite applicable for the 160's or 150's B.C. is an open question. Certainly, the Sadducees claimed the Sons of Zadok as their ancestors (Ezek. 40:45 f.; 43:19). Eupolemus, the son of John of Hakkos, belonged to the group of priests who served in the Temple (I Chron. 24:10), and he must be regarded as a priest of the "Sons of Zadok." Josephus, however, alludes to the Saducean sect for the first time in the days of Jonathan (A.J., XIII, 171-73), suggesting that they originated in the aftermath of the Maccabean victory. For the vast literature on this subject, see R. Marcus, in *American Academy for Jewish Research; Proceedings,* 16 (1946-47), 135-37; cf. also A.C. Sundberg, "Sadducees," in the *IDB,* 4 (1962), 159-63; A. Guttmann, *Rabbinic Judaism in the Making* (Detroit, Wayne University Press, 1970), 124-176.

57   Clement, *Strom.,* I, 113, 1. Zohar (II, 108 ?) reports that Nathan was Solomon's teacher. In II Sam. 7 (I Chron. 17), Nathan promises David that his son would build God's house; in II Sam. 12:1-25 (no parallel in Chron.) the prophet castigates the king on the murder of Uriah. Nathan also plays a decisive role in Solomon's succession of his father, according to I Kings 1 (no parallel in Chron.). The author of Chronicles knows of Nathan's memoirs (I Chron. 29:29, II Chron. 9:29), as well as of his participation in organizing the sacrificial cult during David's reign (II Chron. 29:25). It is coneivable, although unlikely, that Eupolemus was familiar with a Nathan apocryphon, if any indeed existed. See *Propheten- und Apostollgenden* (Schermann), 99-101.

58   The technical term is applied to Elias (title), Moses (Joshua), Samuel (723 F 2b = P.E., IX 30, 1); Nathan ("Dianathan," IX, 30, 6; 34, 4 2; 34, 15, 13); Jeremiah (F 4 = *P.E.,* IX, 39, 2).

4

DAVID PROVIDES FOR THE TEMPLE

Nathan prescribed to David the specific role of making preliminary preparations for the erection of the Temple: "And he [the angel] commanded him not to build the temple himself, for he was defiled with human blood and many years of warfare . . . And he [Nathan] commanded him to entrust the construction to his son, but that he himself should provide all the pertinent building stock: gold, silver, copper, [precious?] stones, cypress and cedar wood. When David heard this he built a fleet in Elana, an Arabian city; and he sent miners to the island of Urphe, which lies in the Red Sea and which contains gold mines. From there the miners transported the gold into Judaea."[59]

This passage is of unusual interest because it may shed light on Eupolemus' position when the biblical tradition itself was in conflict. There is no doubt that in regard to the Solomonic succession Eupolemus' account was closer to that of the First Book of Chronicles than to the older, less biased tradition of II Samuel and I Kings.[60] The spilling of blood by David as a cause for the divine refusal to vouchsafe the king's erection of the Temple is recorded in I Chr. 22:8 as well as in Eupolemus. The Chronicler adds here a play on Solomon's name. Verse 9 reads: "Behold a son shall be born to you; he shall be a man of peace; and I shall grant him rest from his surrounding enemies, for Solomon [Shelomoh] shall be his name and I will grant peace [shalom] and quiet to Israel in his day." Our passage does not mention this pun, but it is evident that it was known to Eupolemus, because he alludes to it below when mentioning Solomon's death.[61] Of course, both the Chronicler and Eupolemus fail to make any reference to the bloodbath instituted by Solomon to secure the succession, as recorded in I Kings 1-2. That David had made extensive efforts to assemble the materials for the erection of the Temple is reported in Scripture only by the Chronicler.[62] Here also Eupolemus follows him.

Citing these correlations, Freudenthal rightly concluded that Eupolemus had followed the Book of Chronicles in preference to the traditions found in

---

59   723 F 2b = *P.E.*, IX, 30, 6-7 (7·8): προστάξαι τε αὐτῷ τοῦτον ὅπως τῷ υἱῷ ἐπιτρέψῃ τὴν οἰκοδομίαν, αὐτὸν δὲ εὐτρεπίζειν τὰ πρὸς τὴν   κατασκευὴν ἀνήκοντα, χρυσίον, ἀργύριον, χαλκόν, λίθους, ξύλα κυπαρίσσινα καὶ κέδρινα. ἀκούσαντα δὲ τὸν Δαβὶδ   πλοῖα ναυπηγήσασθαι ἐν Ἐλάνοις πόλει τῆς Ἀραβίας καὶ πέμψαι μεταλλευτὰς εἰς τὴν Οὐρφη νῆσον, κειμένην ἐν τῇ   Ἐρυθρᾷ Θαλάσσῃ, μέταλλα χρυσικὰ ἔχουσαν· καὶ τὸ χρυσίον ἐκεῖθεν,   μετακομίσαι τοὺς μεταλλευτὰς εἰς τὴν Ἰουδαίαν.

60   See below, pp. 151-55.

61   723 F 3 = *P.E.*, IX, 34, 20.

62   I Chron. 22; 28-29. Cf. II Sam. 8:11 f., where Hiram, it is said, supplied David with building material for his own house.

II Samuel and I Kings.[63] Nevertheless, of equal importance is Eupolemus' independence of the biblical tradition as a whole, whether the Books of Samuel and Kings or Chronicles. His accounts of David and Nathan, as we have seen, suggest that he felt freer to alter the old traditions than did the author of Chronicles.[64] The differences as well as the similarities between the Chronicler and Eupolemus must be taken into consideration. According to the Chronicler, David assembled the provisions for the Temple on his own initiative; for Eupolemus, David did so at the command of Nathan.[65] Another minor, but perhaps significant divergence is in Eupolemus' list of the building materials collected by the king. I Chr. 22:2-4 stresses the bringing of cedar wood shipped from Lebanon by the Phoenicians as well as materials from the king's quarries and the copper and iron mines. Because of its importance, special emphasis is given to iron, mentioned again in I Chr. 29:2. In Eupolemus, however, iron is entirely missing. The omission could not have been an accident, since the identical list is repeated again and again, always without iron.[66] The idea is clear. The Chronicler no doubt exaggerates the weight of the precious metals that were consumed in the building of the Temple. But his was still a realistic description of the kind of material needed for construction.[67] Eupolemus, however, maintained that nothing but precious metals were used in the building of the Temple. Iron was certainly taboo.

The omission of iron from Eupolemus' lists was probably related to Exod. 20:22: "But if you make for me an altar of stones, do not build it of hewn stones; for by wielding your iron ("sword") upon them you have profaned them." This passage is elucidated in Deut. 27:6 and Josh. 8:31 to refer to the altar exclusively. But I Kings 6:7 broadens the prohibition to apply to the use of any iron tool for the sanctuary as a whole.[68] However, since the stones

---

63   Freudenthal, *Hell. St.,* 106-08. See Schürer, *Gesch. d. jüd. Volkes*, III, 474-77; Stählin in *Gesch. Griech. Lit.*, II, I, 589 f.; Dalbert, *Theologie,* 35 ff. Spiro, *Proceedings of the American Academy for Jewish Research*, 20 (1952), 303 n. 65, building on Freudenthal, argues that the Books of Kings were read (in Eupolemus' time) only by antiquarians. This is now contradicted by the Dead Sea Scrolls (Zadokite Documents, V, 2-6; Pesher Samuel; cf. 4 Q 160, in *Discoveries*, V; and note also the several copies of Samuel and Kings found at Qumran).

64   Cf. however, J. Giblet, *Ephemerides Theologicae Lovanienses*, 39 (1963), 539-54; Albert-Marie Denis, *Introduction aux Pseudépigraphes grecs d'Ancien Testament*, 254 f.

65   I Chron. 22; 28-29; Eupolemus 723 F 2b = *P.E.*, IX, 30, 6.

66   723 F 2b = P.E., IX, 30, 6; 30, 8; 34, 17.

67   See I Chron. 23: 2f.; 29:1-9.

68   "When the house was built it was with unhewn stone, prepared at the quarry; neither hammer, nor ax nor any tool of iron was heard in the house while it was being built" (I Kings 6:7). Mekhilta, *Bahodesh*, XI, explains that the Pentateuchal command to use unhewn stone referred strictly to the altar, that I Kings 6:7 only meant to say that the stone was not dressed at the building site, although it was hewn at the quarry. A differing interpretation is cited in B. T. Sotah 48b, that no iron at all was used to dress stones of the entire temple, not just those of the altar. Cf. I. Macc. 4:47.

used by Solomon were somehow dressed, a rabbinic legend explains the discrepancy by maintaining that Moses and Solomon made use of a kind of a fabulous worm—called *shamir,* a word that must have originally meant diamond—for the hewing and dressing of stones, thus dispensing altogether with the need for the base metal.[69] It should be noted that although there was some difference of opinion as to whether or not iron had been used for the chiseling of stones for the sanctuary, there is nothing to support Eupolemus' exclusion of iron from the Temple's precincts altogether. This view runs contrary to the Chronicler's claim that Solomon consumed huge amounts of iron (I Chr. 22:3[2]).

Conceivably, however, Eupolemus' list—gold, silver, copper, stone, cypress and cedar wood—was inspired by the prescription of the Mosaic tabernacle (Exod. 25:3-7). Iron is significantly missing from the items listed there. But even assuming that Eupolemus followed here the catalogue of the tabernacle, his independence from Exod. 25:3-7 is striking. It is not Eupolemus' omission of minor items found in the Mosaic tradition that is noteworthy, but his shift from precious stones to plain stone and from acacia wood to that of cedar and cypress used in the Mosaic tabernacle. Of course, *lithoi* in Eupolemus may mean precious stones, which would correspond more closely to the Pentateuchal list.

Nevertheless, the differences between the Chronicler and Eupolemus may possibly be regarded as trivial. This cannot be said of the latter's account of David's gold mines. I Kings 9:26-28 and its parallel II Chron. 8:17 f. report that King Solomon had built a fleet in Elath on the Gulf of Aqabah, where with Phoenician guidance his ships brought gold from Ophir. Although the proverbial Ophir gold is mentioned in connection with David in I Chr. 29:4, there is nothing in Scripture to support Eupolemus' account which ascribed the building of the Red Sea fleet to King David.

The biblical tradition stresses the crucial assistance rendered by Hiram, the Phoenician king; this point is ignored in the fragments. This silence seems consistent with the Hellenistic historian's bias, which—contrary to I Kings-I Chronicles—asserted that there was enmity between Jerusalem and Tyre during David's reign. Indeed, Eupolemus' version of the foundation of the Davidic empire, as pointed out above, diverges rather basically from that recorded in the Hebrew texts. Serious deviations from the bibilical tradition are not limited to Eupolemus' treatment of David, but occur throughout the fragments. Unlike Josephus' departures from the traditions, which are usually mere embellishments or rhetorical devices, Eupolemus' deviations frequently clash with the biblical texts.

Freudenthal suggested that Eupolemus had consistently favored the accounts of the Books of Chronicles, which he regarded as more authoritative

---

69   B. T. Sotah, 48b; Gittin, 68a.

than the traditions of Samuel-Kings.[70] A close analysis of the fragments, however, indicates a more complex literary relationship between the Chronicler and Eupolemus than that described by Freudenthal. Unhappily, Eupolemus' account of Moses is lost, making it impossible to say whether or not the Hellenistic Jewish historian regarded the Pentateuchal history as unalterable. But he certainly felt free to embellish old traditions, sometimes radically, whether they had been recorded in the prophetic works of Samuel-Kings or in the priestly Chronicles. He frequently echoed the version of the latter not, as Freudenthal proposed, because he regarded that tradition as more authoritative. Eupolemus' own account frequently differs substantially even from the version of events presented by the priestly Chronicler.

Eupolemus, more often than not, tended to agree with the Chronicler, because both belonged to the same priestly school of biblical historiography. In contrast to the prophetic historians, the priestly school tended to whitewash David's misdeeds, instead building up an image of him as the ideal king and as Yahweh's representative on earth. This tendency, evident already in Chronicles, is even more pronounced in Eupolemus' fragments. David's empire, according to Eupolemus, extended over territories not even mentioned either in the Book of Samuel or Chronicles. God's dwelling place among man was not chosen, as recorded in the Hebrew tradition, by the failure of Satan to penetrate into Araunah's threshold, but by a clear heavenly signal. In Eupolemus, the process of idealization of David into a perfect king was already in an advanced stage.[71]

Although Eupolemus frequently followed the Chronicler's lead, the Hellenistic historian's roots were firmly grounded in his own soil. Eupolemus was supposedly depicting the world of the tenth century B.C., but the Davidic empire is crowded with second century B.C. peoples—Commageneans, Ituraeans, and Nabataeans. The biblical name for the port on the Gulf of Aquabah is Eloth, with a variant Elath, and the Septuagint reads usually Aelath ($A\iota\lambda\acute{a}\theta$).[72] But Eupolemus' spelling is "Elana," almost identical with that found in late Greek writers—Aelana, who give the same name to its gulf.[73] The Red Sea route was known to the Hellenistic writers through Eratosthenes, who had recorded the circumnavigation of the Red Sea from the Gulf of Aqabah to the Persian Gulf in line with the reports of Alexander the Great's admirals, Hieron and Anaxicrates.[74] The identification of Aelana (Elana) as "an Arabian city" indicates either that Eupolemus

70   See above notes 63-64.
71   Here we have another link which explains why the title of Eupolemus' work was called *On the Prophecy of Elias*.
72   I Kings 9:26; II Chron. 8:17; cf. LXX text of II Chr. 8:17, where BA read $A\iota\lambda\alpha\mu$. The Mss. of Josephus (*A.J.*, VIII, 163) differ: $\mathring{I}\lambda\alpha\nu\mathring{\eta}\varsigma$, $\mathring{E}\lambda\acute{\alpha}\nu\eta\varsigma$; Lat.: Hilana.
73   Strabo, XVI, 4,4 (cf. XVI, 2, 30—Aela); Glaucus, *Arabiae Archaeologia, FGrH* 674 F 7 = Steph. Byz., *s.v.* $A\mathring{\iota}\lambda\alpha\nu o\nu$; also mentions Aela. Cf. also Dionysius Periegetes, in Mueller, *GGM*, I, 160, 910; Philo of Byblos, 790 F 38.
74   See Aelian, *Varia Historiae*, IX, 26.

believed that the locality was unfamiliar to his readers, or that the name plus its identification was taken from a Hellenistic geographical guidebook. The port of Aelana gained fame as the starting point of a trading route which ultimately carried goods between the Near East and India and China.[75]

Of some curiosity also is Eupolemus' description of Ophir (which he calls Urphe (Οὑρφη), as a Red Sea island. Because of its legendary gold mines, the mystery of the location of Ophir has excited ancient and modern antiquarians, as well as fortune hunters. Speculation about its location has ranged from South Arabia, Africa, India, and after Columbus, to Peru in South America.[76] The interest of the Septuagint translators is indicated by their transliteration of Ophir into Sopher (Σοφείρ), the form found also in Josephus, who added that it was located in India.[77] Freudenthal proposes to emend Urphe, the form found in the fragments, to Uphre; perhaps related to Afra, the spelling in Jub. 8:15, meaning apparently, Africa.[78] But Africa could not have been the name of an Arabian island. It is more likely that the name Urphe as a Red Sea island was taken from then-current geographic texts.

We venture to guess that, directly or indirectly, the source may have been the *Sacred Scripture* by Euhemerus of Messene (300 B.C.), a fictional travelogue which related how the ancient heroes and kings Uranus, Kronos, and Zeus became gods. The scene of the romance was located in Panchaia, a mythical island adjoining Arabia Felix. Euhemerus described the island's fabulous wealth as follows (according to Diodorus): "The land possesses rich mines of gold, silver, copper, tin, and iron, but none of these metals is allowed to be taken from the island . . . There are great many dedications of gold and of silver which have been made to the gods, since time has amassed a multitude of such offerings. The doorways of the temple are objects of wonder in their construction, being worked in silver and gold and ivory and citrus-wood. And there is a couch of the god, which is six cubits long and four wide and is entirely of gold and skillfully constructed in every detail of its workmanship. Similar to it both in size and in costliness in general is the table of the god which stands near the couch."[79] If the hypothesis that the Arabian island Urphe (Ophir) was modeled after Panchaia is valid, Eupolemus appears to have corrected Euhemerus' remark that the mineral wealth never left the Arabian island, since David's miners had allegedly transported

---

75   On the Nabataean routes to the Far East and India, see Margaret Murray, *Petra, the Rock City of Edom* (London, Balckie & Son, 1939), 122, quoting Hirth, *Rome and the Roman Orient*; N. Glueck, *The Other Side of Jordan* (New York, 1940), 89-113.

76   See G. Ryckmans, "Ophir," *Supplement au Dictionnaire de la Bible* (1959), 744-51.

77   *A.J.*, VIII, 164. Cf. I, 147. Perhaps Josephus, like Eupolemus, located Ophir in Euhemerus' Panchaia, hence near the Indian Ocean. See note 79.

78   Freudenthal, *Hell. St.*, 210.

79   Diod. I, 46, 4-7 = Euhemerus, 63 F 3. Cf. Pliny, *N.H*, VII, 197 = 63 F 23.

precious metals to Judaea. Eupolemus' wording is therefore quite precise: "the island Urphe, which lies in the Red Sea and which contains gold mines." By identifying Urphe (Ophir) with Panchaia, Eupolemus attempted to make believable his claim that after expending 1,600,000 gold talents on Yahweh's Temple, Solomon still had enough left to present some of the surplus to construct golden pillars for Zeus' temple in Tyre.[80] In fact, Eupolemus' constant reiterations of the role of gold in Solomon's temple appears to echo Euhemerus.

---

80   *P.E.*, IX, 34, 16-18 = 723 F 2b.

Chapter Six

KING SOLOMON

1

THE CORONATION

The two biblical texts tell the story of Solomon's coronation quite differently. According to I Kings 1-2, Solomon won the crown only after a bitter struggle with his older brother Adonijah, a struggle resulting in the death of David's intimate advisers. The two concluding chapters of First Chronicles, however, suggest that Solomon not only had no rivals, but that his coronation was inevitable as the inflexible will of Yahweh. Eupolemus' account clearly sides with the Chronicler: "David ruled forty years, he handed over the administration to Solomon, who was then twelve years old, in the presence of Eli, the high priest, and the twelve heads of the tribes. And he also handed over to him the gold, silver, copper, stone, cypress and cedar wood. Then he died; and Solomon became king."[1] Eupolemus apparently chose his words carefully. David himself presented the realm $(\grave{\alpha}\rho\chi\acute{\eta})$ to Solomon, but the latter became king $(\beta\alpha\sigma\iota\lambda\epsilon\acute{\upsilon}\epsilon\iota\nu)$ only after David's death. Like the Chronicler, Eupolemus avoids any mention of civil strife in connection with the succession. And like the Chronicler, Eupolemus says that David designated Solomon his heir in the presence of Israel's twelve tribal leaders. Finally, in both Chronicles and Eupolemus, the old king bestows on his successor the most cherished plans for the construction of the Temple.

Nevertheless, Eupolemus' account must not be regarded as a mere summary of I Chronicles 28-29. A major difference is in the identity of the priest who presided over the coronation ceremonies. According to

---

1   723 F 2b = *P.E.*, IX, 30, 8: βασιλεύσαντα δὲ τὸν Δαβὶδ ἔτη μ′ Σολομῶνι τῷ υἱῷ τὴν ἀρχὴν παραδοῦναι, ὄντι ἐτῶν ιβ′, ἐνώπιον Ἡλεὶ τοῦ   ἀρχιερέως καὶ τῶν δώδεκα φυλάρχων καὶ παραδοῦναι αὐτῷ τόν τε χρυσὸν καὶ ἄργυρον καὶ χαλκὸν καὶ λίθον καὶ ξύλα κυπαρίσσινα καὶ κέδρινα. καὶ αὐτὸν μὲν τελευτῆσαι, Σολομῶνα δὲ βασιλεύειν.

Eupolemus, his name was Eli. The reference could only be to the priest of Shiloh and judge of Israel, the predecessor of Samuel (I Sam. 1-4). Inclusion of the priest of Shiloh is an anachronism, but Eupolemus also fails to mention Zadok, the priest who did play a leading role in Solomon's victory. According to I Kings 1-2, the only ancient historical source, David's chief priest Abiathar had sided with the faction which was supporting the succession of David's older son Adonijah. When Solomon won, he exiled Abiathar and appointed Zadok in his place. (Thus from the tenth century to the middle of the second century B.C., the descendants of Zadok allegedly were the foremost priestly family of Jerusalem.) Zadok is given even greater prominence in the account of the Chronicler, who asserts that while Solomon was installed as king, Zadok was anointed high priest (I Chr. 28:22).

The divergence between Eupolemus and the Hebrew sources is explicit. I Kings 2:27 remarks: "So Solomon expelled Abiathar from being priest to the Lord, thus fulfilling the word of the Lord which He had spoken concerning the house of Eli in Shiloh." Eupolemus' version, which has Eli presiding over Solomon's coronation, clashes directly with this assertion. Freudenthal, who posited a consistency between the Chronicler and Eupolemus, ascribes the error to Alexander Polyhistor, Eupolemus' pagan excerptor.[2] This view must be rejected; although Alexander Polyhistor might not have been aware of the import of the nomenclature, it is unlikely that he would have known enough to substitute Eli for Zadok. Also, it would be a rather otiose undertaking to emend the text of a writer like Eupolemus whenever his account is anachronistic. It must be assumed, then, that just as the Chronicler was "correcting" the version of Solomon's succession as reported in I Kings, so Eupolemus by substituting Eli for Zadok was "correcting" both Hebrew texts.

We can only conjecture that Eupolemus' substitution of Eli for Zadok was related to the old struggle between the two priestly factions—the Eleazarites and Ithamarites. A string of biblical passages tell that of Aaron's four sons, the two oldest were eliminated from the Aaronite succession at a relatively early stage, while the remaining two sons—Eleazar and Ithamar—were either equals or the former was paramount.[3] Of the twenty-four priestly divisions

---

2   Freudenthal, *Hellenistische Studien*, 121; Walter, *ad locum*.

3   Exod. 28:1 lists the four sons of Aaron. Lev. 10:1-20; Num. 3:2-4; 26:61, etc., explain that Nadab and Abihu eliminated themselves, with the result that they either left no progeny (Num. 3:4) or that their progeny was eliminated from the census (26:61). The lists of the high priests of the first Temple, in I Chr. 5:27-41, etc., are of Eleazarite descent—Aaron, Eleazar . . . Zadok . . . Jehozadak. But I Chr. 24 presents the extent of the split between the two priestly clans. See now Rudolph, *Chronikbücher*, 159-161.

officiating in the Temple, according to I Chr. 24:3, two-thirds were descended from the house of Eleazar and one-third from that of Ithamar. Certainly, it is clear that in the Chronicler's time—during the second Temple—the two priestly clans were not reconciled. Even in Josephus' day, it would seem, the factional struggle had not been settled. Otherwise it is difficult to understand why Josephus embellished the biblical account three times adding that Solomon's removal of Abiathar, and his replacement with Zadok, the Eleazarite, reflected the divine will.[4] But Eupolemus, by making Eli the high priest who crowned Solomon, would seem to side with the Ithamarite clan. Was then Eupolemus' ancestor, Hakkos one of the eight priestly divisions believed to have descended from the Ithamarites?

If Eli was Eupolemus' favorite priest, Shiloh was his favorite shrine. Of Joshua's accomplishments nothing is recorded in our chronological summary other than his pitching the tabernacle at Shiloh.[5] This place is named once again in Eupolemus' account of the dedication of the Solomonic temple.[6] There is no doubt, as was already alluded to above, that he had given a long description of Eli's office at Shiloh. By mentioning Eli here again as presiding over Solomon's coronation, Eupolemus simplified matters and at the same time pointed out the continuity linking Shiloh with Jerusalem. Joshua, Moses' disciple, had founded the shrine at Shiloh; now Eli (or rather a descendent of his), the priest of Shiloh, crowned Solomon, the builder of the Temple.[7]

Conceivably, though, Eupolemus' omission of Zadok's name was intended to slight the Jewish Hellenizers. It is worth recalling that the two last Zadokite high priests, Jason and Menelaus, were regarded as having become polluted because of their collaboration with the Syrian kings.[8] The final repudiation of the Zadokite dynasty, it is true, did not occur until 152 B.C., when the Hasmonean Jonathan was appointed high priest—allegedly the first non-Zadokite since Solomon to hold this office.[9] But the Hasmonean rebels

---

4   See *A.J.*, V, 361: "Eli was the first to bear rule of the house of Ithamar, the second of Aaron's sons" (Thackeray's translation in LCL). See also *A.J.*, VII, 110; VIII, 11 f.: "And so the house of Ithamar was deprived of the priestly privilege . . . just as God had foretold to Eli the grandfather of Abiather."

5   723 F 2b = *P.E.*, IX, 30, 1.

6   723 F 2b = *P.E.* IX, 34, 14. The spelling of Shiloh, though, is different there.

7   If so, Eupolemus intended to dispute the historicity of I Kings 1-2, a view for which there are other indications in the fragments.

8   II Macc. 4:7-5:17; 11:27-34; 13:7 f. See also Zadokite Documents V, 5, where Zadok is labeled as the cleanser of idolatry from Israel. C. Rabin, *Zadokite Documents* (Oxford, Oxford University Press, 1958), ad locum, suggests that the reference is to Hilkiah (II Kings 22:8). But the Manual of Discipline suggests (I, 2:24; II, 3; V, 2, 9; IX, 14) that the Qumran sect identified itself with Zadok, the Solomonic high priest. The ancestry of Ezra (7:1-5) is also traced back to Zadok.

9   I Macc. 10:20 f.; *A.J.*, XIII, 45; XX, 238. Cf. Ez. 44:15, quoted and interpreted in the Zadokite Documents, III, 21-IV, 5.

must have denounced the Zadokite clan some years before the foundation of the new high priestly dynasty.[10] If so, Eupolemus' failure to mention Zadok's participation in the coronation of Solomon was just another attempt to rewrite history to suit the political situation.

There are other differences between Eupolemus' account of the coronation and that of the Book of Chronicles. In the latter, the list of the participants is quite extensive: the officials of Israel, the tribes, the king's commanders in charge of the divisions, the officers of the hundreds and the thousands; the administrators of the royal estates, in addition to the eunuchs and the mighty men.[11] Of this long catalogue, Eupolemus retained only the high priest and the twelve phylarchs in whose presence Solomon was crowned. That Eupolemus attached greater significance to the traditional tribal division than did either the author of Kings or Chronicles is also evident below, where it is said that foreign laborers were sustained by the tribes. At any rate, it is clear, Eupolemus intended to give the impression that after the king and the high priest, the twelve tribal heads were the highest officials of the state, evidently playing the same role as the Gerusia (Council of Elders) during the pre-Hasmonean period. But the direct reference to the tribal divisions was conceivably inspired by Ezra 6:17, the Greek version (I Esdras 7:8) which records an offering of twelve he-goats for the twelve phylarchs at the dedication of the Second Temple.[12]

In I Chr. 22:5 and 29:1, King David is quoted as having asserted that he was offering the kingdom and the building of the Temple to one of "young and tender age." Josephus agrees with the Chronicler, maintaining that Solomon was fourteen years old when he was crowned king.[13] Eupolemus, however, says that Solomon became king at the age of twelve, a view also recorded in LXX I Kings 2:12, and in the talmudic chronographic treatise Seder Olam.[14] The relationship of the sources has been discussed above. Here

---

10   According to Josephus (A.J. XX, 237), the high priestly office was vacant for seven years (159-152 B.C.). Josephus repeatedly says (ibid.; XII, 387) that Alcimus was the first Aaronite priest of a non-Zadokite clan, an implication not necessarily present in I Macc. 7:13 f., since the Hasidim, it is said, were deserting Judah Maccabee because Alcimus was "a priest of the house of Aaron." II Macc. 14:7 seems to affirm that Alcimus was of Zadokite descent, and there is nothing, except Josephus, to contradict it. It follows that Jonathan's ascent to the highest priestly office was made possible when the entire house of Zadok became discredited. See also above note 3.

11   I Chr. 28:1; cf. 29:6; 24.

12   The γερουσία of Jerusalem in Eupolemus' time is recorded in II Macc. 1:10; 4:44; 11:27; during Jonathan's rule - I Macc. 12:6; cf. Judith 4:8; 11:14; 15:8. See also Schürer, Gesch. d. jüd. Volkes II[4], 241 f. See also below, notes 37-43, for Eupolemus' possible use of I Esdras.

13   A.J., VIII, 211. Cf. also ibid., VIII, 2, where the king is described as a mere youth upon his accession to the throne.

14   Seder Olam, 14. See Ratner's comment in Seder Olam, 31b n. 22; cf. also, Sifre, Deut., 357; Gen. Rabbah, C p. 1294 f.

it is worth mentioning only that Eupolemus connected Solomon's age at the coronation with the commencement of the building the Temple in the following year—contrary to Scripture—making a total of thirteen; this is supposedly the first allusion to the *bar mitzvah* tradition found anywhere.[15]

2

SOLOMON'S CORRESPONDENCE

King David, according to Eupolemus, had allied himself with Egypt and subdued Phoenicia. Upon assuming the crown, Solomon's first act was to write letters to their rulers: "But Solomon became king; and he wrote to Vaphres, the king of Egypt, the letter copied below:[16]

SOLOMON'S LETTERS[17]

KING SOLOMON TO VAPHRES, KING OF EGYPT, HIS FATHER'S FRIEND, GREETINGS!	KING SOLOMON TO SURON, KING OF TYRE, SIDON, AND PHO-ENICIA, HIS FATHER'S FRIEND, GREETINGS!
Know that, with the help of God the Most High, I have received the kingdom from my father David. He commanded me to build the Temple to God, who created the heavens and earth; but also at once to write to you that you send me men from the peoples who are subjected to you, who will be assisting me till every requirement [of God] will be completed, as I have been commanded.[18]	Know that, with the help of God the Most High, I have received the kingdom from my father David. He commanded me to build the Temple to God, who created the heavens and earth; but also at once to write to you that you send me men from the peoples who are subjected to you, who will be assisting me till every requirement of God will be completed, as I have been commanded.
	I have also written the same to Galilaea, Samaritis, Moabitis, Ammonitis, and Galaaditis that they

15   Cf. Luke 12:42; Mishnah Niddah, V, 6; Abot, V. 21; B. Yoma, 82a; Ketuvoth, 50a, whether the obligation to observe the commandments begins at the age of 12 or 13.

16   In the fragments, Vaphres' answer precedes the text of Solomon's letter to Suron. However, for the sake of clarity, they are presented here in parallel columns.

17   The headings, as cited by Mras, are found in Mss. BION. Jacoby omits them. Eusebius, rather than Alexander Polyhistor, presumably introduced them.

18   723 F 2b = *P.E.*, IX, 31: Βασιλεὺς Σολομῶν Οὐαφρῇ βασιλεῖ Αἰγύπτου φίλῳ πατρικῷ χαίρειν

Γίνωσκέ με παρειληφότα τὴν βασιλείαν παρὰ Δαβὶδ τοῦ πατρὸς διὰ τοῦ μεγίστου, [καὶ] ἐπιτεταχότος μοι οἰκοδομῆσαι ἱερὸν τῷ θεῷ, ὅς τὸν οὐρανὸν καὶ τὴν γῆν ἔκτισεν, ἅμα δέ σοι γράψαι ἀποστεῖλαί μοι τῶν παρὰ σοῦ λαῶν, οἳ παραστήσονταί μοι μέχρι τοῦ ἐπιτελέσαι πάντα|κατὰ τὴν χρείαν, καθότι ἐπιτέτακται.

provide them with their needs from the fruit of the land: 10,000 *coroi* of grain monthly; (a *coros* is six *artabae*) and 10,000 *coroi* of wine (a liquid *coros* is ten meters); oil and other needs should be supplied from Judaea; slaughter animals for the supply of meat from Arabia.[19]

A COPY OF[20] VAPHRES' LETTER

KING VAPHRES TO THE GREAT KING SOLOMON, GREETINGS!

When I read your letter I rejoiced greatly. I and my entire administration set aside a feast day upon the occasion of your succeeding to the kingdom of such a kind man and one approved of by so mighty a God.

As to the matter that you have written to me—concerning the peoples who are my subjects—I am sending you 80,000 men. And I am informing you as to their number and their place of origin: 10,000 men from the (Sebrithitic)[21] Sethroitic nome; from the Mendesian and Sebennitic nomes—each 20,000; but from the Busiritic, Leontopolitan, and Athribitic provinces–10,000 from each.

Give due consideration to their

SURON'S LETTER

SURON TO THE GREAT KING SOLOMON, GREETINGS!

Praised be God who created the heavens and earth, who chose a kind man and the son of a kind man. When I read your letter I rejoiced greatly. I praised God that you have succeeded to the kingdom.

As to the matter that you have written to me—the peoples who are my subjects—I am sending you 80,000 Tyrians and Phoenicians; and I am also sending you an architect, a man of Tyre, the son of a Jewish mother of the tribe of (David) [Dan]. Whatever problem under the heavens that you will ask him relating to architecture he will guide you and carry out the tasks.

As to the needed food supplies for the slaves, you will do well to order

---

19   723 F 2b = *P.E.*, IX, 33: Βασιλεὺς Σολομῶν Σούρωνι τῷ βασιλεῖ Τύρου καὶ Σιδῶνος καὶ Φοινίκης φίλῳ πατρικῷ χαίρειν

Γίνωσκέ με παρειληφότα τὴν βασιλείαν παρὰ Δαβὶδ τοῦ πατρὸς διὰ τοῦ θεοῦ τοῦ μεγίστου, ἐπιτεταχότος μοι οἰκοδομῆσαι ἱερὸν τῷ θεῷ, ὅς τὸν οὐρανὸν καὶ τὴν γῆν ἔκτισεν, ἅμα δὲ καὶ σοὶ γράψαι ἀποστειλαί μοι τῶν παρὰ σοῦ λαῶν, οἳ συμπαραστήσονται ἡμῖν μέχρι τοῦ ἐπιτελέσαι τὴν τοῦ θεοῦ χρείαν, καθότι μοι ἐπιτέτακται. γέγραφα δὲ καὶ εἰς τὴν Γαλιλαίαν καὶ Σαμαρεῖτιν καὶ Μωαβῖτιν καὶ Ἀμμανῖτιν καὶ Γαλαδῖτιν χορηγεῖσθαι αὐτοῖς τὰ δέοντα ἐκ τῆς κώρας, κατὰ μῆνα κόρους σίτου μυρίους· ὁ δὲ κόρος ἐστὶν ἀρταβῶν ἕξ· καὶ οἴνου κόρους μυρίους· ὁ δὲ κόρος τοῦ οἴνου ἐστὶ μέτρα δέκα. τὸ δὲ ἔλαιον καὶ τὰ ἄλλα χορηγηθήσεται αὐτοῖς ἐκ τῆς Ἰουδαίας, ἱερεῖα δὲ εἰς κρεωφαγίαν ἐκ τῆς Ἀραβίας.

20   In Ms. I: ἀντίγραφος.

21   Emendation suggested by Kuhlmey (*Eupolemi fragmenta*, 75), Freudenthal (*Hell. St.*, 110), and Walter (ad locum).

food supply and other needs, punc-
tual pay, and that they return home
as soon as they will have completed
their tasks.[22]

the local governors to provide the
needed foods.[23]

We have Eupolemus' own word that these messages represent a letter by
letter copy of the Solomonic correspondence, including the headings.[24]
Strangely, Franz Movers, the author of a nineteenth century valuable history
of Phoenicia, considered the text reproduced by Eupolemus as essentially
genuine.[25] Although somewhat more skeptical, Yehoshua Gutman says that
Eupolemus, albeit writing in a fictional vein, had possessed valid traditions
which he incorporated into the narrative.[26] The Hellenistic writer himself,
according to Gutman, indicated the fictional aspects of the letters by the
omission of a closing salutation.[27] But more than a third of the actual
diplomatic letters in the papyri during the Hellenistic period have no
salutations.[28] Certainly, Eupolemus alleges that he was copying authentic

22   723 F 2b = *P.E.*, IX, 32: Βασιλεὺς Οὐαφρῆς Σολομῶνι βασιλεῖ μεγάλῳ
χαίρειν
    "Ἅμα τῷ ἀναγνῶναι τὴν παρὰ σοῦ ἐπιστολὴν σφόδρα ἐχάρην καὶ
λαμπρὰν ἡμέραν ἤγαγον ἐγώ τε καὶ ἡ δύναμίς μου πᾶσα ἐπὶ τῷ παρειληφέναι
σε τὴν βασιλείαν παρὰ χρηστοῦ ἀνδρὸς καὶ δεδοχιμασμένου ὑπὸ τηλικούτου
θεοῦ. περὶ δὲ ὧν γράφεις μοι, περὶ τῶν κατὰ τοὺς λαοὺς τοὺς παρ, ἡμῖν,
ἀπέσταλκά σοι μυριάδας ὀκτώ, ὧν καὶ τὰ πλήθη ἐξ ὧν εἰσι διασεσάφηκά σοι·
ἐκ μὲν τοῦ Σεβριθίτου νομοῦ μυρίους, ἐκ δὲ τοῦ Μενδησίου καὶ Σεβεννύτου
δισμυρίους· Βουσιρίτου, Λεοντοπολίτου καὶ Ἀθριβίτου ἀνὰ μυρίους· φρόντισον
δὲ καὶ τὰ δέοντα αὐτοῖς καὶ τὰ ἄλλα, ὅπως εὐτακτῇ, καὶ ἵνα
ἀποκατασταθῶσιν εἰς τὴν ἰδίαν, ὡς ἄν ἀπὸ τῆς χρείας γενόμενοι."
    23   723 F 2b = *P.E.*, IX, 34, 1-3: Σούρων Σολομῶνι βασιλεῖ μεγάλῳ χαίρειν.
    Εὐλογητὸς ὁ θεός, ὃς τὸν οὐρανὸν καὶ τὴν γῆν ἔκτισεν, ὃς εἵλετο
ἄνθρωπον χρηστὸν ἐκ χρηστοῦ ἀνδρός· ἅμα τῷ ἀναγνῶναι τὴν παρὰ σοῦ
ἐπιστολὴν σφόδρα ἐχάρην καὶ εὐλόγησα τὸν θεὸν ἐπὶ τῷ παρειληφέναι σε τὴν
βασιλείαν.
    περὶ δὲ ὧν γράφεις μοι, περὶ τῶν κατὰ τοὺς λαοὺς τοὺς παρ' ἡμῶν,
ἀπέσταλκά σοι Τυρίων καὶ Φοινίκων ὀκτακισμυρίους καὶ ἀρχιτέκτονά σοι
ἀπέσταλχα ἄνθρωπον Τύριον, ἐκ μητρὸς Ἰουδαίας, ἐκ τῆς φυλῆς τῆς Δαβίδ.
ὑπὲρ ὧν ἄν αὐτὸν ἐρωτήσῃς τῶν ὑπὸ τὸν οὐρανὸν πάντων κατ' ἀρχιτεκτονίαν,
ὑφηγήσεταί σοι καὶ ποιήσει. περὶ δὲ τῶν δεόντων καὶ ἀποστελλομένων σοι
παίδων καλῶς ποιήσεις ἐπιστείλας τοῖς κατὰ τόπον ἐπάρκοις, ὅπως
χορηγῆται τὰ δέοντα.
    24   καὶ γράψαι πρὸς Οὐαφρῆν . . . τὴν ὑπογεγραμμένην ἐπιστολήν   (723
F 2b = *P.E.*, IX, 30, 8). See also the ms. readings, cited by Mras, to I, 540, line 1.
    25   F. Movers (*Die Phönizier*, II, 1, 334) and Kuhlmey (*Eupolemi Fragmenta*,
77-81) dealing with "De veritate ac fide epistolarum," defend the historicity of the
letters against Alexander Natalis, who labeled the letters as fiction.
    26   *The Beginnings of Jewish-Hellenistic Literature*, II, 84.
    27   Gutman, Ibid., 84.
    28   Cf. F. X. J. Exler, *The Form of the Ancient Greek Letter. A Study in Greek
Epistolography* (Catholic University of America, Washington, 1923), 69.

ancient documents. Moreover, since Solomon's letter to Suron was identical (at least in its first part) to the one sent to Vaphres, there was no reason to reproduce it again if both were to be considered fictional. This needless repetition makes sense only if the author was attempting to create an impression that he was presenting priceless documents from King Solomon's archives. Obviously, Eupolemus' claims are false.[29]

Although the composition of the allegedly Solomonic letters must be credited to Eupolemus himself, they were not a complete invention. I Kings 5:16-23 reports that Solomon requested assistance from Hiram in the building of the Temple, as Jerusalem had no qualified craftsmen to perform such tasks.[30] The Chronicler, however, rewrote the message in accordance with his own view of the Temple's significance. In II Chr. 2:2-9, Solomon's frank admission that the Jews were inferior craftsmen is missing. Instead of the modest "house" of I Kings, the Chronicler makes Solomon depict the cultic details of the Temple and boast to be the future builder of its architectural wonders.[31] Josephus, however, ignored here the version of II Chronicles, paraphrasing rather faithfully the report of I Kings.[32]

But Eupolemus' major innovation consisted in claiming that parallel to the exchange of letters between Jerusalem and Tyre there was an exchange between Jerusalem and Egypt. Apparently, to emphasize the point, Eupolemus placed the Solomon-Vaphres letters before the Solomon-Suron correspondence. Since there is no allusion whatsoever in Scripture to Egyptian notes, and since there is no reason to assume that he possessed independent traditions, it would seem that Eupolemus wanted his account to supplant the biblical versions. If so, he was directing himself primarily against the Chronicler's reports with whom the Hellenistic historian apparently attempted to supplant rather than against the author of I Kings whose description bears little relationship to that of Eupolemus.

The text of the Solomonic correspondence as reported by Eupolemus may have its roots in Hebrew historiography, but its form follows the stereotype of Hellenistic epistolography. The caption consisted of the formula "A to B

29   See Freudenthal, *Hell. St.*, 109-112, who argues that Eupolemus, though he borrowed some phrases from the Letter of Aristeas (42), himself authored the Solomonic correspondence.

30   Cf. also II Sam. 5:11 f.; I Kings 5:24-32; 7:13 ff.

31   Cf., however, II Chr. 8:17 f.; 9:21, where the Chronicler seems to preserve the earlier source.

32   *A.J.*, VIII, 50-54, adding that the Solomon-Hiram correspondence was still in the Tyrian archives in his own day (VIII, 55). Although there is always a possibility that Josephus was referring to the alleged letters, reported in Eupolemus, it is likely that he means to allude to *A.J.*, VIII, 104-49; cf. *C. Apionem*, I, 106-27, the writings of Graeco-Phoenician authors.

(sends) greetings ($\chi\alpha\acute{\iota}\rho\epsilon\iota\nu$)."[33]   The analogous Hebrew or Aramaic term is שלום . The heading also defined the relationship between the correspondents. Solomon called his colleagues "King," though they addressed him "Great King," thus no doubt indicating his superior status. That Suron's position was inferior to that of Vaphres is suggested perhaps by the omission of any title before his name when Suron addressed Solomon. The headings indirectly define Egypt and Phoenicia as Jewish client kingdoms. Solomon's position clearly placed him in the class of the Persian kings or Alexander the Great, that of world emperor.[34]

The differences between patron and client are also reflected in the body of the letters. The former's style is severe and terse; the latter's laudatory and submissive. Solomon's message to Suron (the one to Vaphres seems to have a part missing) consists of two sections—the nature of the command and the provisions to carry it out. The replies are made up of three parts—an encomium of the king, the fulfillment of the command, and a request of their own. The obsequiousness and obedience of the first two paragraphs fade in the third, where the client kings insist upon their rights. The structure of these notes indicates that Eupolemus had studied closely the prevailing diplomatic formularies.[35] (No wonder Judah sent him to Rome on a diplomatic mission!)

The introductory lines of the letters are obviously designed to impress the reader with Solomon's piety. In I Kings (5:17-20) the author ascribes to Solomon the initiative to build the Temple. In the version of the Chronicler (I Chr. 2:2-9) the young king credits David with making the preparations; but the text regards the building of the sanctuary as primarily Solomonic. Only Eupolemus' passage gives the impression that Solomon was merely bringing to fruition his father's plans. Even more impressive is the obeisance to God found in the letters. Solomon received the kingdom "with the help of God, the Most High"[36] ; he was going to build a temple for "God who created the heavens and earth"; Suron said, "Praised be God, who created the heavens and earth." The last cited phrase is already quoted in I Chr. 2:11, but there is

33   Exler, *The Form of the Ancient Greek Letter*, 24-68. But cf. the letter by Rabban Gamaliel to the provinces announcing an intercalation (Tosefta Sanhedrin, II, 6, p. 416).

34   For the lore dealing with Solomon as one of the emperors, including Alexander, see Pirke d'Rabbi Eliezer, 11; Midrash Aseret Melakhim; Targum Sheni Esther 1:1. These texts, however, assume their present form during the Byzantine period.

35   See, however, L. Ewald, *Geschichte des Volkes Israel* (Göttingen, 1864-68), III[3], 305, who ascribes the text of the letters to an apocryphon, Eupolemus' source.

36   $\theta\epsilon\grave{o}\varsigma\ \mu\epsilon\gamma\acute{\iota}\sigma\tau\sigma\varsigma$ = $\theta\epsilon\grave{o}\varsigma\ \acute{\upsilon}\psi\acute{\iota}\sigma\tau\sigma\varsigma$ See LXX Esther 8:12q; II Macc. 3:36;   cf. Dalbert, *Die Theologie,* 38. But this phrase has been taken here from I (III) Esdras,   a work that Eupolemus used for composing the letters.

no doubt that in the intensity of phrasing of Solomon's prayer, Eupolemus projects a stronger reverence than does the Chronicler.

Thus far our discussion has compared the biblical accounts of the Solomonic Temple to that of Eupolemus. But Eupolemus' version of Solomon's temple was influenced by Zerubabel's structure, of which he was a contemporary. It may be claimed that though describing the Solomonic building, the Hellenistic historian sometimes followed closely the Book of Ezra, especially the Greek version of this book known as I Esdras.[37] The following parallels exemplify the relationship:

Eupolemus	*I Esdras*
1. τὴν ὑπογεγραμμένην ἐπιστὸλήν[38] (the letter copied below)	1. τὴν ὑπογεγραμμένην ἐπιστόλην (2:12)
2. Βασιλεὺς Σολομῶν Οὐαφρῇ Βασιλεῖ . . . . Χαίρεω.[39] Γνοσκέ . . . (King Solomon to King Vaphres: Greetings: Know)	2. Βασιλεῖ Δαρίῳ Χαίρειν. Πάντα γνωστὰ ἔστω (6:8).
3. εὐλογητὸς ὁ Θεός, ὃς τὸν οὐρανὸν καὶ τὴν γῆν ἔκτισεν[40] (Blessed be God who created the heavens and earth)	3. εὐλογητὸς (8:25) . . . παῖδες τοῦ κυρίου τοῦ κτίσαντος τὸν οὐρανὸν καὶ τὴν γῆν (6:13)
4. μέχρι τοῦ ἐπιτελέσαι τὴν τοῦ Θεοῦ χρείαν καθότι ἐπιτέτακται[41] (Until every requirement of God will be completed)	4. καὶ πάντα . . . ἐπιτέλει 8:16... εἰς τὴν χρείαν τοῦ ἱεροῦ τοῦ Θεοῦ σου (8:17)

These and similar verbal links apparently show a clear interdependence.[42] But since I Esdras is a translation of the Aramaic parts of the Book of Ezra, we must assume that Eupolemus, in composing the Solomonic correspondence, recalled passages from the Greek version. And it is interesting to note that the measures (*kor, artabe,* measure) that Eupolemus used for the First Temple correspond to those given in the apocryphal book for the Second. In fact the generous contribution of the Persian and Macedonian kings to Jerusalem's sanctuary seems to have primarily inspired Eupolemus' wording of the Solomonic letters. But the influence goes beyond the sheer wording.

---

37   On I (III) Esdras see Charles Torrey, *Ezra Studies* (Chicago, 1910), 1-61; 115-39; *The Apocryphal Literature* (Yale University Press, 1945); R. H. Pfeifer, *History of the New Testament Times* (New York, Harper & Brothers, 1949), 233-57; O. Eissfeldt, *Einleitung in das Alte Testament*[3] (Tübingen, J. C. B. Mohr, 1964), 677-81.

38   *P.E.*, IX, 30, 8; I, 539 = 723 F 2b. This is a rather infrequent phrase.

39   *P.E.*, IX, 31, 1; 33, 1. Here a most familiar formula is combined with "know."

40   *P.E.*, IX, 34, 1.

41   *P.E.*, IX, 33, 1 = 723 F 2b.

42   See above, note 12.

For in Eupolemus, as in the Book of Ezra (but not in I Kings or II Chronicles), the royal correspondence presumes to tell a vital chapter in the construction of Jerusalem's Temple.[43]

Peter Dalbert, in his study of the Hellenistic Jewish writers, extracts the theological implications of the passages under discussion. Dalbert notes that Eupolemus referred to the deity as "God" ($\Theta\epsilon\acute{o}\varsigma$) rather than "the Divinity ($\acute{o}$ $\Theta\epsilon\acute{\iota}o\nu$)" in the more abstract form.[44] This, Dalbert rightly points out, indicates that Eupolemus was one of those Hellenistic Jews who were as yet not unaffected by philosophical thought. Dalbert says that Eupolemus' direct use of the name of the deity, rather than of circumlocutions like those employed by the rabbis makes him a "Hellenistic Jew," not unlike the Greek translators of the Bible, Philo, and Josephus. Eupolemus may have been a typical Hellenistic Jew, but the use of $\Theta\epsilon\acute{o}\varsigma$ is no proof one way or the other. For the rabbis employed redundant speech only when referring to the deity in sacred tongues—Hebrew and Aramaic. Reference to God in any other language would by rabbinic definition be regarded as a circumlocution. Moreover, since Eupolemus claimed to paraphrase Scripture, any use of redundancies would have sounded a false note. Certainly, the rabbis never avoided the use of God's name (except the tetragrammanon) in either Scriptural or prayer passages.[45]

Dalbert has also called attention to the phrase used three times, "God, who created heavens and earth." Eupolemus, Dalbert notes, used $\kappa\tau\acute{\iota}\zeta\epsilon\iota\nu$, for the Hebrew br^c ('create'), an "unmistakable" assertion of the Jewish concept of creation ex nihilo.[46] It does not follow, however, that Eupolemus made Solomon assert a theological concept found only in the literature of a later period.[47] Dalbert has neglected to point out that the phrase "God who had created the heavens and earth," was taken by Eupolemus not from II Chr. 2:11, but from Gen. 14:19. Hiram is quoted in II Chr. 2:11 as having written to Solomon: "Blessed be the Lord, God of Israel, who made the heavens and earth." The Chronicler used "made" (עָשָׂה = LXX $\acute{\epsilon}\pi o\acute{\iota}\eta\sigma\epsilon\nu$). Why then did Eupolemus ascribe the phrase not only to Hiram, as did the

43 If this reasoning is cogent, Eupolemus' fragments would seem to confirm the hypothesis that I Esdras dates at least from the middle of the second century B.C., a view often voiced (see the works cited above in note 37) only on the basis of internal evidence. Conceivably, Eupolemus, or someone else who was closely linked with Judah Maccabee, was in fact responsible for the present make-up of I Esdras. See below that a number of the Greek translations of the Bible were in fact produced in Palestine.

44 Dalbert, *Theologie*, 38.

45 Cf. Mishnah Berakhot, IX, 5 end; Sanhedrin, X, 1; Yerush. Berakhot IX, 14c; BT Makkot 23 b, where the use of the tetragrammanon is permitted in greetings, according to an ordinance ascribed to Boaz.

46 Dalbert, *Theologie*, 38; cited also by Walter, ad locum.

47 The LXX renders the Hebrew br^c of Gen. 1:1; 2:4 as $\pi o\acute{\iota}\epsilon\iota\nu$, in contrast to Josephus and Aquila, who employ $\kappa\tau\acute{\iota}\zeta\epsilon\iota\nu$. According to Dalbert and Walter, Eupolemus followed the later versions.

Chronicler, but also to Solomon? And why did he use κτίζειν (create) where
"make" (עשׂה = LXX ποιεῖν), was expected? It is safe to assume that the
Chronicler and Eupolemus both knew the Pentateuch well. The Chronicler
evidently attributed such blessing to Hiram, because he recalled a similarly
worded blessing by Melchizedek. The Chronicler may have assumed that
Hiram was familiar with the wording of Melchizedek, who was said after all,
to be his Phoenician ancestor.[48] The Chronicler, however, slightly changed
the wording–קנה (create) into עשׂה (make). Disapproving of the changed
wording in Chr. 2:11, Eupolemus restored the text of Gen. 14:19, where the
Hebrew term is rendered in LXX as κτίζειν.[49] Moreover, he evidently also
recalled that the phrase "who created the heavens and earth" was not only
used by the heathen (Gen. 14:19), but also by Abram (v. 22). It seemed to
Eupolemus to be proper that their respective descendants–Solomon and
Suron–should compose letters using the same key phrase. And since Gen.
14:19, 22, whether in the Hebrew text or in LXX, does not necessarily mean
creation ex nihilo, neither does it in Eupolemus.

A phrase ascribed to Solomon's letters confirms the impression that
Eupolemus utilized the exchange between Abram and Melchizedek (Gen.
14:18-22). The Hebrew king invoked the aid of the "Most High" (Θεός
ὑψίστος). Eupolemus gave here a translation of El Elyon, the divine epithet
used in Gen. 14:18, 19, and 22; in the last two verses immediately preceeding
the phrase "who created the heavens and earth." Since the Chronicler in his
presentation of Hiram's letter has no reference to the El Elyon found in Gen.
14, the fragments could not have been directly dependent on his paraphrase,
as claimed by Dalbert. There is, moreover, a generalization which applies to
all ancient Jewish authors; when in doubt about the choice of alternate
sources of a citation, the presumption is that the reference is to the
Pentateuch.

Dalbert errs also in assuming that Eupolemus was necessarily using the
Septuagint. The LXX Gen. 14:18, 19, 22, renders El Elyon as Θεός
ὑψίστος[50] In fact, only in late texts such as the Greek Additions to Esther
8:12q and III Macc. 1:16 is the epithet "Theos Megistos" found. Dalbert
wonders, then, why Eupolemus, writing in the first half of the second
century, made use of it. The answer is that, unlike Pseudo-Eupolemus, who
rendered El Elyon exactly as found in the Septuagint,[51] Eupolemus made his
own translation. In fact, some technical terms merely transliterated LXX

---

48   Canaan (Gen. 10:5, 15-19) including the king of Salem, Melchizedek, was
regarded as identical with Phoenicia. Cf. Pseudo-Eupolemus, 724 F 1 = *P.E.*, IX, 17, 4 f.;
Wacholder, *HUCA*, 34 (1963), 94.
   49   κτίζειν and its cognates are used as the equivalent of *knh;* but see Tob. 8:5.
   50   Dalbert, *Theologie*, 38.
   51   Gen. 14:19, 22; Pseudo-Eupolemus 724 F 1 = *P.E.*, IX, 17, 5.

are rendered into Greek by Eupolemus.[52] The conclusion is clear that Eupolemus not only made use of Gen. 14:18-22 for his composition of Solomon's correspondence, but he also used the original Hebrew instead of the Greek translation.

The body of the letter, however, deals with more mundane matters. Solomon demanded that his client kings send laborers to construct the Temple. Curiously, though, the request says nothing about the number needed. Vaphres and Suron each sent exactly 80,000 men, for a total of 160,000. From what did Eupolemus derive this number of foreign laborers? Evidently Eupolemus rounded the number given in I Kings 5:28-29 for the total levy of 153,000 or in II Chr. 2:16-17 of 153,600. I Kings asserts, however, that the Solomonic levy was made up of Israelites; II Chronicles says that they were foreigners (*gerim*) residing in the land. Only Eupolemus claimed that they were sent as tribute by client kings. That this was a conscious attempt to dispute the biblical tradition can be seen in Eupolemus' report as to the nationality of the laborers. The 80,000 Phoenicians are divided into Tyrians and Sidonians. The names of six provinces are listed as the homes of the Egyptian contingent. By supplying details, Eupolemus put forth the claim that his traditions were more accurate than those of I Kings or II Chronicles.

Since the nomes recorded in Eupolemus all lie in the Nile Delta, Gutman concluded that Eupolemus must have been in possession of reliable information, because during the tenth century B.C. the pharaoh's power was limited to the Delta.[53] It may be doubted, however, that he had available to him this bit of information researched by modern scholars. The fact that he named the sixth century Vaphres as the correspondent of Solomon indicates that Eupolemus was rather careless or else ignorant of the political situation of Egypt during the tenth century B.C.

Eupolemus' list of nomes has puzzling aspects which have not been solved. There are textual corruptions of the first and sixth provinces; Sethoritic and Athribitic are emended readings.[54] A more difficult problem is why Eupolemus chose the six particular nomes out of the thirty-six provinces? And why did he divide them into two groups, one group of nomes contributing 10,000 each, and another group of nomes giving 20,000 men each?[55]

---

52   See Freudenthal, *Hell. St.*, 119 f.

53   Gutman, *The Jewish-Hellenistic Literature*, II, 87.

54   The emendations are based on the assumption that the listed provinces were all located in the Delta. See note 21.

55   Actually, in three groups: 1) the Sethroitic nome (?), 10,000 men; 2) the Mendesian, and the Sebennitic, 20,000 men from each; and 3) Busiritic, Leontopolitan, and Athribitic nomes, 10,000 from each. Does the separation of 1) from 3) indicate merely sloppy writing?

An analysis of Herodotus' account of Egypt's provinces may offer some explanation. It is suggested above that Eupolemus borrowed from Manetho the sixth century Vaphres, and made him the contemporary of the tenth century David and Solomon because Herodotus attributed to Vaphres (called in Herodotus Apries) the conquest of Tyre and Sidon. According to Eupolemus, David evidently joined by his ally Vaphres, marched against these Phoenician cities. It should be recalled that Herodotus interrupted his long account of Apries (Vaphres) to give a sketch of Egypt's administrative divisions. Thus, it may not be mere coincidence that four of the six provinces listed by Eupolemus are also found in Herodotus' description.[56] This suggests that Eupolemus' list was taken from Herodotus. As to the names of the two nomes mentioned by Eupolemus but not by Herodotus—Sethoritic and Leontopolitan—the first is a modern emendation and need not be considered.[57] Conceivably, the addition of Leontopolis may be explained as a taunt against the place where Onias IV, the son of the high priest, Onias III, had built a temple to Yahweh about 162 B.C.[58] Eupolemus may have attempted to create the impression that Leontopolis, which was then as a possible threat to the uniqueness of Jerusalem, had ironically sent 10,000 men to help construct the Solomonic Temple.[59] The Mendesian and Sebennytic nomes are singled out in Herod. II, 17, as being of special economic and political significance because of their location at the mouths of the Nile. In Eupolemus, these two provinces contributed twice as many workers as the others. In other words, Eupolemus was showing off his knowledge of Egyptian geography as reported by Herodotus or other geographic handbooks.

As is the case with David's empire, Eupolemus also "corrected" the tradition about the extent of Solomon's realm. I Kings 4 names the twelve officials who administered the districts of the country, which included the entire west side of the Jordan River plus most of Transjordan. Ammon and Moab, however, were tributary states ruled by their own kings, and not under Solomon's direct control. In Eupolemus' scheme, however, Ammon and Moab were integral parts of the Hebrew state proper, just as Galilee and Gilead (Galaaditis) were. Elsewhere the fragments suggest, like I Kings 4, a

---

56   See above, notes 23-25. Herod. I, 161-171 describes Amasis' revolt against Apries, of which 164-167 digress to list the classes and provinces of Egypt.

57   See above notes 21 and 54.

58   Cf. Josephus, *A.J.*, XII, 387 f.; XIII, 62-73, 285; XX, 236 f.; B.J., I, 33; VII, 422-32; Mishnah Menahot, XIII, 10. Since the temple of Leontopolis was built during the reign of Antiochus V Eupator (163-162), Eupolemus was a contemporary of the event. Leontopolis is listed as a nome in Strabo, XVII, 1, 20; 1, 40, who otherwise mentions Mendes (XVII, 1, 18), Sebennytis (19), Busiris (19), Athribitis (20).

59   Willrich, *Juden und Griechen*, 158 f., deduces from Eupolemus' mention of Leontopolitan workers at the Solomonic temple that the Hellenistic historian sympathized with the schismatic shrine built there. Is not the converse as, if not more, logical?

duodecimal division of the country.[60] But in Solomon's letter, Eupolemus implies that it was split into seven provinces: Galilee, Samaritis, Moabitis, Ammonitis, Galaaditis, Judaea, and Arabia. This provincial division obviously reflects the political situation of the pre-Maccabean period. Samaria was founded two centuries after Solomon. Arabia, by which Nabataea is probably meant, is first heard of in post-exilic times.[61] Incidentally, the talmudic tradition also maintained that Ammon and Moab were to be regarded cultically as integral parts of the Holy Land.[62]

Eupolemus' scheme of how Solomon proposed to provide for the massive influx of foreign labor is also of interest. The provinces, except Judaea and Arabia, contributed grain and wine. Judaea supplied oil and Arabia meat. George Adam Smith cites Eupolemus as evidence that Palestine as a whole suffered a shortage of meat, which had to be imported from Arabia, meaning the Arabian Peninsula.[63] But by Arabia Eupolemus evidently meant a province located between the Dead Sea and the Gulf of Aqabah, as is perhaps indicated by his calling Elath (Elana) an Arabian city.[64] This, too, apparently reflected the economic situation of the second century B.C. when the Nabataeans became the suppliers of meat for Palestine. I Kings 5:3-4 (4:23-24) implies, however, that the meat for the king's table was imported from outside Palestine. But Smith may after all be right that by Arabia Eupolemus meant here the Arabian Peninsula.

Exaggeration of numbers was common in antiquity, and Eupolemus was no exception. This can be illustrated in his report of Solomon's provisions.

	I Kings 5:2 5	II Chr. 2:9	Eupolemus	Josephus [65]
Cors or baths		(annually)[66]	(monthly)	(yearly)
wheat	20,000	20,000	10,000	20,000
barley	--	20,000	--	--
wine	--	20,000	10,000	20,000
oil	20 (20,000:LXX)	20,000	indefinite	20,000
meat	--	--	indefinite	--

Eupolemus gave half of the biblical numbers, but made the contributions monthly instead of annually, as reported in Scripture, thus increasing them

---

60 723 F 2 *P.E.*, IX, 30, 8.

61 The same is true of Judaea, Galilee, and Samaria, which in Eupolemus assumes their post-exilic, perhaps even Hellenistic, administrative divisions.

62 Cf. Mishnah, Yadayyim IV, 3; Tosephta, Yadayyim, II, 16.

63 G. A. Smith, *Jerusalem* (London, 1907), I, 315.

64 723 F 2 = *P.E.*, IX, 30, 7.

65 *A.J.*, VIII, 57.

66 II Chr. 2:9 does not say whether the supplies were contributed monthly or annually. Presumably, the meaning there is the same as in I Kings 5:25.

sixfold. Conceivably, though, the amounts listed in Solomon's letter to Suron were also given in the message to Vaphres. So the total monthly provision consisted of 20,000 cors, a number suggested in scripture.

Freudenthal notes Eupolemus' use of Hebrew measures, instead of their common equivalents, which Eupolemus supplies.[67] The dry *cor*, says Eupolemus, equalled six *artabae* and the wet, ten meters.[68] As the *artabae* were a measure introduced by the Persians, Freudenthal notes the anachronism in Solomon's letter.[69] In defense of Eupolemus here, it may be said that the common equivalents for the *cor* were perhaps intended to be read not as Solomon's but as the author's glosses.

The retaining of original measures, evident also in the Septuagint, was meant to preserve some of the foreign flavor.[70] However, where Eupolemus lists Solomon's gifts to his client kings below, he uses the Greek names of the measures.[71] The difference may perhaps be accounted for by the use of the sources. For his account of the provisioning of the workers Eupolemus was dependent on the biblical tradition; hence the use of Hebrew measures. The report of Solomon's gifts, however, was Eupolemus' own concoction; hence Greek measures. But, as has been shown above, Eupolemus' inspiration for the list of supplies, as for the entire diplomatic era, appears to have been Artaxerxes' letter as reported in I Esdras 8:20.

Freudenthal noted that Eupolemus was here using the Hebrew text of II Chr. 2:9 rather than the Septuagint, as the latter renders the name of the wine measure into Greek.[72] It can be shown, however, that if Eupolemus indeed followed any text, Hebrew or Greek—it was only I Kings; for only I Kings, like Eupolemus, employs *cor* as the name of both the dry and wet measures.[73] Eupolemus, it should be noted, was aware of this anomaly when he interpreted the different equivalents of the dry and wet *cor* into Greek.

The dry *cor*, according to Eupolemus, equaled six *artabae* and the wet *cor* ten meters. The Greek translation of Is. 5:10 gives the same relationship for the dry measure, though the Hebrew term used there is *homer*.[74] Josephus, less accurately perhaps, says that the *cor* equaled ten Attic medimnoi, about

---

67   Freudenthal, *Hell. St.*, 107.

68   Note that Eupolemus was using here the Hebrew of I Kings 5:25, which also gives *cor* for both the dry and wet measures, unlike LXX III Kingdoms 5:25 and the Hebrew and LXX of Chr. 2:9, which use *cor* as the dry measure and *bath* for the wet. Josephus (*A.J.*, VIII, 57) defines the *bath* as 72 sextari.

69   Freudenthal, *Hell. St.*, 107.

70   Note LXX Is. 5:10; Bel 3.

71   723 F 2b = *P.E.*, IX, 34, 17.

72   Freudenthal, *Hell. St.*, 107.

73   I Kings 5:25. See note 68.

74   *Homer* = *bath* (Ez. 45:14). See LXX Is. 5:10, where the Hebrew *homer* is rendered as six *artabae*.

eighteen bushels.[75] Basically, the question is whether Eupolemus referred to the Persian *artabae* (roughly sixty-one pounds) or to the Ptolemaic (about forty-three pounds). The former is more accurate if Eupolemus referred to the Assyrian *cor,* which equaled about eleven and one-third bushels.[76] If so, according to Eupolemus, 10,000 *cors* of wheat measured approximately 113,000 bushels monthly; when divided by 160,000 workers yields about twenty-six pounds of wheat per man every thirty days.[77] This plus an equivalent ration of wine, some oil and meat, looks like a remarkably close subsistence diet. It is likely, however, that the ration should be doubled, since Eupolemus, in the letter to Suron, gave the measures only for the 80,000 Phoenicians. This accounts for the fact that he used a myriad while the biblical texts always record two myriads of produce.

There is no doubt that Eupolemus' basic purpose here was to show that even the laborers were treated luxuriously by Solomon. The king's generosity was the import of the exaggerated weights and measures given by Eupolemus. This impression is also confirmed in the text below where Eupolemus says that when returning home each worker received a golden shekel—the equivalent of a gold talent.[78] The use of large round numbers indicates,[79] however, that they were not arrived at by some kind of computation, but were fabricated to prepare the reader for the fabulous nature of the Solomonic temple.

In this discussion of Eupolemus' version of the Solomonic correspondence, the exchange between the Hebrew king and the king of Phoenicia is given particular emphasis. Here we are able to evaluate Eupolemus' version in the light of biblical tradition. But Vaphres' letter deserves close scrutiny as it is a pure concoction. Indeed, Ewald suggests that Eupolemus depended on an apocryphon for the version of epistles.[80] But, as noted by Freudenthal, this is unverifiable in the absence of any traces of a similar piece of writing.[81]

Contrary to Fruedenthal, however, there are some indications of the possible existence of an apocryphon relating to the correspondence between Solomon and Vaphres. The Pesiqta d'Rab Kahana, one of the older midrashic

---

75   *A.J.*, XV, 314; but in III, 321, he equaled 70 cors with 41 Attic medimnoi, the latter perhaps a corrupt text.

76   See Stern, in *Encycl. Biblica*, IV (Jerusalem, 1962), 853 f.

77   See *R.E.*, II (1895), 3001; Suppl. I, 142-144; cf. Walter, *ad locum*.

78   273 F 2b = *P.E.*, IX, 34, 17.

79   Sellers in *Interpreter's Dictionary of the Bible*, IV (1962), estimates the weight of a shekel as ranging from 8.33 to 16.76 grams, depending on whether common or royal, light or heavy; that of a talent from 30 to 61.2 kgs.

80   Ewald, *Geschichte d. jüd. Volkes*, III, 305.

81   Freudenthal, *Hell. St.*, 110.

texts edited in the fifth or sixth century,[82] reports that Pharaoh Neco (609-594 B.C.) had received orders from Solomon (tenth century B.C.) to send craftsmen for the building of the Temple. The Egyptian king was in a quandry. Upon the advice of his astrologers, Neco dispatched men about whom it was foretold that they would die within the year. Solomon, himself an expert astrologer, sent them immediately back home with gifts of burial garments.[83] The common features of Eupolemus and the rabbinic story are the participation of the Egyptian work force in the building of the Temple,[84] the mention of wages, the correspondence between Solomon and Pharaoh, and perhaps the deliberate anachronizing of Pharaoh Neco in the Pesiqta and of Vaphres in Eupolemus. The rabbinic version was possibly meant to satirize Eupolemus, but more likely it referred to some lost apocryphon. There is no evidence, however, that such an apocryphon had existed before the days of Eupolemus.

Freudenthal, however, built a strong case for the argument that in composing the Solomonic correspondence Eupolemus used the Letter of Aristeas as his model. Freudenthal listed several terms found in both of these texts.[85] But seemingly conclusive evidence of interdependence was Vaphres' letter to Solomon and the Letter of Aristeas by the High Priest Eliezer of Jerusalem to King Ptolemy Philadelphus (185-47):

Eupolemus (*P.E.*, IX, 32)	Letter of Aristeas
When I read your letter I rejoiced greatly. I and my entire administration set aside a feast day, etc.	42. When we received your letter we rejoiced greatly because of your resolution and your goodly plan, we assembled our entire people and read it out to them, etc.
Give due consideration . . . that they return home as soon as they will have completed their tasks.	46. We shall be obliged to you, righteous king, if you enjoin that when the transcription of the books is completed the men may be restored to us again in safety.

With a few exceptions, scholars have generally accepted Freudenthal's position of an interdependence between Eleazar's and Vaphres' opening and

---

82   For the date of the Pesiqta d'Rab Kahana, see Albeck, in Jubilee Volume (Hebrew section) of Louis Ginzburg (New York, 1946), 25 ff.; M. Margulies, *Midrash Wayyikra Rabbah*, V (Jerusalem, American Academy for Jewish Research, 1960), pp. XXVII-XXXIII; B. Mandelbaum, ed., *Pesiqta de Rab Kahana* (New York, The Jewish Theological Seminary, 1962), I (Hebrew section), 13 f.

83   Pesiqta d'Rav Kahana (New York, 1962), I, 60; Num. Rabbah, XIX, 3; Eccl. Rabbah, on 7:23; Pesiqta Rabbati (ed. Friedmann, Vienna, 1880), 59b.

84   In the midrashic texts, though, the Egyptians were sent home immediately, perhaps before actually participating in the construction of the Temple.

85   Freudenthal, *Hell. St.*, 110 n.

closing paragraphs.[86] And if so, Eupolemus must have used the Letter of Aristeas. The inverse would not have been true because the author of Pseudo-Aristeas was a quite proficient Greek stylist, something which cannot be said of Eupolemus. It was only the Hellenically half-educated priest of Jerusalem who had found a form in the Letter of Aristeas. Freudenthal, of course, presupposed that Pseudo-Aristeas had antedated Eupolemus.[87]

The thesis that Eupolemus depended upon the Letter of Aristeas must be rejected. Schürer questioned the conclusiveness of the evidence in 1875, when Freudenthal's book appeared.[88] But the computer-like analysis of Henry Meecham, who had followed Freudenthal in an earlier study,[89] has shown that the similarities between Pseudo-Aristeas and Eupolemus may safely be ascribed to the common style of Hellenistic epistolography.[90] Moreover, as Freudenthal himself said, except in the respective letters, there seems to be no kinship between Eupolemus and Pseudo-Aristeas.[91] Finally, there is no reason to date Pseudo-Aristeas before Eupolemus in the early years of the second century B.C.; and it would be absurd, as already noted, to assume that Pseudo-Aristeas copied Eupolemus.

But if Eupolemus employed a Greek diplomatic formulary to compose the introductory lines of Vaphres' letter, he chose for Suron's letter a Hebrew formula. A correlation of Suron's first pharagraph with the biblical sources offers an example of the development of Hebrew liturgy from the pre-exilic times to that of the Maccabean period:

---

86   *Ibid.*, 110-112; Susemihl, *Die Griechische Litteratur in der Alexandrinerzeit*, II, 648-51; Stählin in *Griechische Literaturgeschichte*, II[6], 589 n. 5; Jacoby, "Eupolemos," No. 11, *R.E.*, VI (1907), 1229; Walter, *ad locum*.

87   Catholic scholars tend to date Aristeas circa 200 B.C. (Tramontano, *La lettera di Aristea*, Naples, 1931; Vincent, *Revue Biblique*, V (1908), 555 f.; Pelletier, *Lettre d'Aristée* (Paris, 1962), 57 f. Otherwise scholars differ widely. Bickerman's dating (*ZNTW*, XXIX, 1930)), 280-298, esp. 293, as between 145 and 127 B.C., is accepted by Hadas (Aristeas to Philocrates, p. 18). Walter, who dates Aristeas in 100 B.C. *(Thoraausleger,* 49 n. 1) is inconsistent in accepting Eupolemus' dependence on Aristeas (see above n. 86).

88   Schürer, *Zeitschritt für wissensch. Theologie*, XVIII (1975), 441 f.

89   H. G. Meecham, *The Oldest Version of the Bible* (London, 1932), 236.

90   H. G. Meecham, *The Letter of Aristeas* (Manchester, 1935), 327 f. Cf. also Wendland, *Die Hellenstisch-römische Kultur*, 198 n. 2.

91   Freudenthal, *Hell. St.*, 112.

I Kings 5:21(7.)	*II Chr. 2:10-11*	*Eupolemus*
Blessed be the Lord this day who has given David a wise son to rule over this great people.	Because the Lord loves his people he has made you king over them . . . Blessed be the Lord, God of Israel, who has given King David a wise son endowed with discernment and understanding, who will build a house for the Lord and a house for his kingdom.	Praised be God who created heaven and earth, who chose a kind man, the son of a kind man. When I read your letter I rejoiced greatly. And I have praised God that you have succeeded to the kingdom.

The prophetic historian in I Kings recalls the concise form of ancient blessings. As given by the Chronicler, however, Hiram's words echo the introductory words of the "Eighteen Blessings," the most ancient nonbiblical prayer of Jewish liturgy. Eupolemus' version essentially conforms with the rules laid down in the Mishnah Berakhot and recorded in the Palestinian Talmud: A "long prayer" begins and concludes with the formula *praised be . . .*[92]

3

KING SOLOMON'S FIRST YEAR

After completing the Solomonic correspondence, the fragments of Eupolemus report on the young king's final preparations to build the Temple: "But Solomon, accompanied by his father's friends, traversed Mount Libanus, and together with the Sidonians and Tyrians carried the wood, which his father David had cut, by sea to Joppe and from there by land to Hierosolyma. And he began to build the Temple of God when he was thirteen years old. The work was done by the above-mentioned people; and the twelve Jewish tribes provided the 160,000 men with all their needs, each month a tribe."[93]

This passage raises several problems, apart from textual ambiguities. The phrase "accompanied by his father's friends" may be translated instead, as

---

92   See Mishnah Berakhot, I, 4; Yerush. ibid., I, 8, p. 3d.

93   723 F 2b = *P.E.*, IX, 34, 4: Διελθὼν δὲ Σολομών, ἔχων τοὺς πατρικοὺς φίλους, ἐπὶ τὸ ὄρος τὸ τοῦ Λιβάνου μετὰ τῶν Σιδωνίων καὶ Τυρίων, μετήνεγκε τὰ ξύλα τὰ προκεκομμένα ὑπὸ τοῦ πατρὸς αὐτοῦ διὰ τῆς θαλάσσης εἰς Ἰόππην, ἐκεῖθεν δὲ πεζῇ εἰς Ἱεροσόλυμα. καὶ ἄρξασθαι οἰκοδομεῖν τὸ ἱερὸν τοῦ θεοῦ, ὄντα ἐτῶν τρισκαίδεκα, ἐργάζεσθαι δὲ τὰ ἔθνη τὰ προειρημένα καὶ φυλὰς δώδεκα τῶν Ἰουδαίων καὶ παρέχειν ταῖς ἐκκαίδεκα μυριάσι τὰ δέοντα πάντα, κατὰ μῆνα φυλὴν μίαν.

"having received the replies of his father's friends," referring to the letters of Vaphres and Suron.[94] The reiterated assertion that Solomon's preparations to build the Temple lasted only one year is utterly inconsistent with the unanimous tradition that the foundations of the Temple were laid in the fourth year of Solomon's reign.[95] Once again Eupolemus stresses Solomon's youth when ascending the throne. There is evidently some inconsistency between the statement above where the responsibility to feed the foreign workers is assigned to the provinces, including the Ammonite and Moabite versions, and the account here making the provisioning of the workers the exclusive duty of the twelve Jewish tribes. Finally, nowhere except in Eupolemus is it said that King Solomon himself had climbed Mount Lebanon to supervise the transportation of the cedar to Jerusalem.[96]

Freudenthal asks why Eupolemus stressed that the wood transported by Solomon had been cut by his father. His answer is that Eupolemus, as a fair exegete, attempted to reconcile the two divergent scriptural passages. I Kings 5:17-32 ascribed to Solomon the cutting of cedar for the Temple; I Chr. 22:1-5 attributed to David the gathering of all supplies. Eupolemus' explanation, according to Freudenthal, is that the former had cut the wood, but the latter shipped it to Jerusalem.[97] This view that Eupolemus built his account on exegetical methods must be rejected, because the Hellenistic historian frequently disregards Scripture altogether, something a fair exegete never would do.

Rather than treating him as a historian using midrashic methods, as Freudenthal suggested, Eupolemus must be viewed as a revisionist. In Eupolemus' day, midrashic hermeneutics indicated a novel approach to Scripture, while the rewriting of old texts to conform to a somewhat more contemporary point of view represented a venerable practice.[98] The story of King David's reign as told in the Second Book of Samuel plus the first two chapters of First Kings exhibits the most mature piece of historical writing of biblical texts. Its author was well informed and could see David's greatness without overlooking his many weaknesses. The account of Solomon's reign, as told in I Kings 3-11, however, was reconstructed by a prophetic historian.[99] Though Solomon was credited with the building of the Temple,

---

94   See Walter, *ad locum.*

95   I Kings 6:1; II Chr. 3:2.

96   In fact Kings 5:15-32 implies the contrary.

97   Freudenthal, *Hell. St.,* 114.

98   Chronicles, Ben Sira, Jubilees, Pseudo-Philo's Biblical Antiquities, the Dead Sea scrolls, for example, indicate that during the second Temple the prevalent style was to rewrite the past in conformity with the present rather than to employ the midrashic hermeneutics evident in the post-70 rabbinic texts.

99   Cf. Eissfeldt, *Einleitung*[3], 374 f., 402.

his passion for foreign women and the housing of foreign gods were considered grievous sins. The Chronicler frequently further revised the image of David and Solomon in the light of the religious climate during the post-exilic period. David emerges in the account of the Chronicler as a priestly king· who was mainly concerned with cultic affairs. The Book of Second Chronicles had little to add to the model of Solomon, found in First Kings, as a man of peace who had devoted his life to the building of Yahweh's Temple; except, significantly, to omit any reference to the king's harem and his idolatrous tendencies.[100]

Eupolemus apparently was convinced that the Chronicler's revision had not gone far enough. The dimensions of David's borders had been drawn far too stringently by the Chronicler. The plans and provisions for the forthcoming Temple had been in a much greater state of readiness during David's lifetime than in the older tradition recorded. What could a twelve-year-old king have accomplished anyhow? Eupolemus admitted, however, that minor contributions were made by Solomon. He wrote letters to the client kings to remind them of their obligations to his father. Solomon himself climbed the Lebanon to supervise the shipping of the lumber which had been cut by David. The Hebrew tradition maintained that construction of the Temple had begun in the fourth year of Solomon's reign. Eupolemus cut the time from the fourth to the second year to indicate that there was no reason for tarrying when everything was in such a state of readiness. In the First Book of Kings, the Temple of Jerusalem was wholly Solomonic. The Chronicler assigned a significant share in the planning of the Temple to King David. Eupolemus made David's share paramount. The apotheosis of David seems to have begun.

---

100   Rudolph, *Chronikbücher*, pp. III-XXV; Eissfeldt, *Einleitung*[3], 728-734.

Chapter Seven

THE TEMPLE OF SOLOMON

The veneration of gods constituted the core of religious life in the ancient Near East. It was taken for granted that homage to the gods could be paid only in properly built altars and sanctuaries. Paradoxically, despite the vast allusions to the shrines in the Near Eastern literary or epigraphical texts, there apparently was no need to record the designs of the immense temples built to appease and honor the gods. Even the Greeks, the most literate people of antiquity, have left it to modern archaeologists to detail some of their most famous shrines at the Delphi and Parthenon. Only the worshippers of the invisible and unutterable Yahweh engaged in detailing the measurements of his dwelling place. The repetitive accounts of the Mosaic Tabernacle may not satisfy the modern architect, but more than a third of the Book of Exodus, most of Leviticus, and much of Numbers is devoted to it. The glorious construction of the Temple holds a pivotal position in the Book of Kings. The dimensions of the soon-to-be-rebuilt sanctuary takes up eight chapters in Ezekiel's vision. The recounting of weights and measures of Yahweh's house aroused a fervor and devotion among the ancient Hebrews which the modern reader often fails to appreciate.

Graeco-Jewish writers inherited this literary piety. The pagan ambassadors of Ptolemy Philadelphus who had come to Jerusalem in search of men able to render the Hebrew Scriptures into Greek, according to the fictive Letter of Aristeas, were so dazzled by the wonders of the shrine that they brought back to Ptolemy a minute (and characteristically Jewish) report of it.[1] Even Josephus, who reputedly wrote for Greeks and Romans, did not leave out the accounts of the Tabernalce and Solomon's Temple. He has preserved the only reliable report of the construction of the Herodian sanctuary.[2] Other descriptions of Jewish sanctuaries were once numerous, but have since been lost.[3]

---

1 Letter of Aristeas, 83-120, an account absent in Josephus' paraphrase of this treatise (*A.J.*, XII, 12-118).

2 *A.J.*, III, 102-183; VIII, 63-98, passim.

3 Cf. Ps.-Hecataeus, in *C. Apionem*, I, 198-199 = 264 F 21; Philo the Elder (?), *On Jerusalem* 729 FF 1-4; Timochares, 165 F 1; 849 F 1 = *P.E.*, IX, 35-36.

The fragments of Eupolemus offer a glimpse into the early Greek accounts of Jerusalem's Temple. More than one-fourth of these remnants deals with the designs of the Temple and its furnishings, and if one adds the description of the preparations and dedication, the proportion increases to three fourths. Granting the haphazard manner by which these texts have been preserved, there is nevertheless no doubt that the shrine of Jerusalem constituted one of the focal themes of Eupolemus' history.

In a series of sentences almost each of which, as in the Bible, begins with "he built" or "he made," Eupolemus depicts, on the one hand, the familiar structure and its cultic objects, and on the other hand, either by wild exaggeration of the precious metals, by changing the recorded dimensions, or by omitting well-known features and inventing others, a new Temple. The sequence is natural. He begins, as does I Kings 6:2, with the naos (*heikhal*), its walls, adornments and roof, but he fails to mention the porch ('ulam, αἰλαμ LXX). Neither do the fragments allude to the Holy of Holies (*debir*, adyton, LXX). After describing the roof, the account offers the dimensions of the two pillars, giving their location but not their names, Jachin and Boaz. Here follows a unique description of the seventy lamps, the doors, a portico (stoa) supported by forty-eight pillars in the north of the Temple, the lave and its twelve stands, the king's platform, the altar, and finally the latticework with its contrivances which, suspended over the entire Temple, held the scarecrow.

Excepting the Holy of Holies mentioned above, Eupolemus' abbreviated blueprint omits nothing of significance. The description is orderly, beginning with the foundations and ending with a shield that protected against ritual pollution. Eupolemus appears to be a master of the technical subject matter. This is true both in his account of the Temple's construction and in his use of the specialized nomenclature. Thus he uses naos to describe the main building, but *hieron* for the Temple as a whole.[4] Unlike the Septuagint,

---

4   Naos is used in the fragments for the first time in connection with the building: *P.E.* I, 542, 2 (here with "of God"); 542, 8; 542, 14; 543, 17; 544, 8 = 723 F 2. Th. A. Busink, *Der Tempel von Jerusalem* (Leiden, E. J. Brill, 1970), I, 27, n. 109, says: "Eupolemos gebraucht den Terminus naos sowohl für das Tempelgebäude (cites *P.E.,* I, 542, 14-15), that the pillars were of the same height as the naos), als für den Tempelraum (cites ibid, 542, 8, "he gilded the naos on the inside"). In unserer Stelle is naos erst in Sinne des Tempelraums, dann in Sinne des Tempelgebäudes gebraucht. Eine Angabe über die Höhe fehlt, und dies hatte sinen Grund wohl darin, dass der Verfasser von den zwei Säulen sagte, sie seien ebenso hoch wie der Tempel (naos) gewesen. Esra 6:3 nennt als Höhe des (zweiten) Tempels 60 Ellen. Säulen solcher Höhe hatte auch Eupolemos wohl nicht für möglich gehalten." But no distinction between the first use of naos and second is justified. Eupolemus' term for the building as a whole is *hieron* (e.g. 543, 22; 26), not naos. The latter term is reserved exclusively for the main room. As pointed out below, there is no doubt that Eupolemus' height for the Temple was not 60 cubits, as in Ezra 6:3, but 20 cubits, the height he ascribes to the scarecrow network. Certainly, the writers of the New Testament draw a similar distinction between naos and *hieron* (I Cor. 9:13; Matt. 26:16f. and passim).

however, which often transliterates the Hebrew technical terms, every word of the fragments is standard Greek. This does not necessarily mean that his words are always clear. Precisely because Eupolemus often departs from the Septuagint, the intent of some of his phrases remains obscure. Nonetheless, it would seem that Eupolemus was quite familiar with the subject matter. As a priest and as a historian, he knew both the Hebrew and Greek versions of King(dom)s, and the Hebrew of Chronicles, though not necessarily as these texts have come down to us. Everything else being equal, the supposition is valid that he was aware of the profound divergence between the bulk of the biblical tradition of the Solomonic Temple and his own description. Our commentary, in addition to striving to simplify the technical nature of the material, compares Eupolemus' version of the Solomonic Temple with Yahweh's house as reported in the Books of Kings and Chronicles. It should be remembered, however, that Eupolemus knew two Temples, the first from the lore depicting the Solomonic sanctuary, and the second, the Temple built by Zerubabel, which was, though in the ravaged conditions, still standing in his day. Unfortunately, except for scholarly surmises, very little is known of Zerubabel's Temple. Eupolemus' fragments shed some light on the structure of that sanctuary.

FOUNDATION AND THE WALLS

"He [Solomon] laid the foundations of the walls of the Temple of God, sixty cubits long and sixty cubits wide, but the thickness of the masonry and the foundations was ten cubits. For thus had commanded him Nathan the prophet of God. But he built alternately a course of stone and a layer of cypress wood, bonding the two courses together with bronze clamps of a talent weight."[5] According to Freudenthal and Busink, οἰκοδομή rendered here as "masonry," referred instead to the Solomonic porch (vestibule, RSV) or ulam, in Hebrew; in Greek αἰλαμ.[6] If so, Eupolemus follows here the Hebrew version of I Kings 6:3, missing in the Greek and altogether in Chronicles, which gives the porch's width as ten cubits.[7] With Mras and Walter, however, it is reasonable to assume that the disputed term means

---

5   *P.E.*, IX, 34, 4-5 = Eupolemus, 723 F 2b:‖θεμελιῶσαί τε τὸν ναὸν τοῦ θεοῦ, μῆκος πηχῶν ξ', πλάτος πηχῶν ξ', τὸ δὲ πλάτος τῆς οἰκοδομῆς καὶ τῶν θεμελίων πηχῶν ι': οὕτω γὰρ αὐτῷ προστάξαι Νάθαν τὸν προφήτην τοῦ θεοῦ. 5. οἰκοδομεῖν δὲ ἐναλλὰξ δόμον λίθινον καὶ ἔνδεσμον κυπαρίσσινον, πελεκίνοις χαλκοῖς ταλανιτιαίοις καταλαμβάνοντα[ς] τοὺς δύο δόμους.

6   Freudenthal, *Hellenistische Studien*, 211; Busink, *Tempel*, I, 27 f., who criticizes Giblet (*Ephemerides Theologicae Lovanienses*, 39 [1963], 543) for rendering this term as *palais*.

7   II Chr. 3:4 describes the ulam as 20 cubits wide and 120 cubits high; LXX III Kingdoms 6:3, makes it a square of 20 cubits.

something like wall masonry.[8] This is so not only because οἰκοδομή has this meaning in the Septuagint, but primarily because it is required by the context of our text.[9] Moreover, the passage would probably have given the dimensions of the length of the porch, as does the biblical tradition, if the porch were meant. It follows that Eupolemus, unlike First Kings and Second Chronicles, as well as Josephus, fails to allude to any of the two other parts of the Temple's rooms—the porch and the holy of holies (adyton). Neither does Eupolemus mention to the side-structure, given in I Kings 6:5, but omitted by the Chronicler.

Eupolemus' dimensions of the Solomonic naos agree only partly with the biblical tradition:

	I Kings and II Chron.	Eupolemus	Josephus[10]
length	60 (LXX Kings 40)	60	60
width	20	60	20
height	30 (LXX Kings 25)	——	60

To bring Eupolemus in line with the ancient traditions, Freudenthal proposed to emend the fragments from the manuscript reading of sixty cubits to twenty cubits.[11] Walter changes "width" into "height," in consonance with Josephus' measurements of the First Temple and the Book of Ezra's (6:3) for the second.[12] But Freudenthal's emendation makes Eupolemus agree with the Masoretic version of the Bible, which raised the question of instead making the fragments conform to a width of twenty cubits, as reported in the Septuagint. The other suggestion finds fault with one of Eupolemus' fragments only to emend it with what is apparently another defective passage of Ezra 6:3. For as has often been pointed out, the wording of Ezra 6:3, giving the height and breadth of the Second Temple, implies that originally the verse contained the length as well. One should therefore as a rule follow

---

8   Mras, *P.E.* I, 542, App. Crit. to line 1; Walter, ad locum.

9   Cf. LXX I Chron. 26:27; LXX Ez. 40:2; Liddell and Scott, *s.v.* οἰκοδομή.

10   *A.J.*, VIII, 64, who adds on the basis of II Chr. 3:4 another story of 120 cubits in height.

11   Freudenthal, *Hell. St.*, 111; 227, 27; regarded as possibly by Busink, *Tempel*, I, 27, note 109.

12   Mras, *P.E.*, I, 542, App. Crit. to line 1; Walter, *ad locum;* Busink, ibid., I, 27, note 109.

the manuscript tradition, as emendations are risky, especially with a writer such as Eupolemus.[13] Moreover, it would seem that Eupolemus, by invoking at this point Nathan's authority apparently implies that his own dimensions of the Temple were more authoritative than those found in the biblical traditions.

A remark by Mras that Eupolemus' account was inspired by the postexilic sanctuary, standing in his day, seems to offer the key to several peculiarities which the Greek fragments ascribe to the Solomonic Temple. Solomon's Temple, according to Eupolemus, as has been mentioned, consisted of one structure, without the porch and holy of holies. The reason for this seems to be that the Hellenistic historian attached little significance to the porch of the post-exilic sanctuary. Its holy of holies, instead of being a separate room, as in Solomon's time, was like that of Herod, merely screened off by a veil.[14]

Eupolemus' account of the dimensions of the Solomonic Temple apparently relates more to those recorded in Cyrus' memorandum than to the tenth century B.C. structure. The problem, as mentioned, is that the passage relating to the Temple's measurements in Ezra 6:3 is defective. The text must, as pointed out by Rudolph, have read either "its height (... cubits, its length) sixty cubits, its width sixty cubits," or alternately, "its height sixty cubits, its width (...cubits, its length) sixty cubits." The Greek fragments suggest that the first alternative is more likely. On the other hand, if Cyrus' measurements are combined with those of Eupolemus, we receive a cube of sixty cubits. But this runs against scholarly consensus, based on Solomon's measurements, that Zerubabel's Temple was sixty cubits long, twenty wide, and thirty high. There is no doubt, however, that, according to Eupolemus, the Temple's height was twenty cubits. This is so not because, as Freudenthal says, he followed the Scriptural tradition, but because this is the height of the network which Eupolemus says covered the naos. Incidentally, of some interest to our subject is a Temple Scroll in the Qumran texts recently discovered by Yigael Yadin, envisioning an eschatological Temple with "three courts, each an exact square, one inside the other."[15] Was Eupolemus, like the Qumran author, drawing a messianic Temple which he proceeded to retroject to the tenth century Hebrew king?

---

13   See however, below, that Fruedenthal's emendation appears to be justified after all on the basis of internal evidence.

14   The porch (vestibule) of Zerubabel's temple is mentioned nowhere else, but there is little doubt that it existed, as it remained a feature of the Herodian structure (*B.J.,* V, 207); as to the Herodian holy of holies, see Josephus (*B.J.,* V, 219).

15   Y. Yadin, "The Temple Scroll," *Biblical Archaeologist,* 30, 4 (1967), 135-39, esp. 139. See now Busink's comments (*Tempel,* I, 21 f.), but the scroll's text has so far not been published, as far as I know.

That there is indeed a close relationship between Cyrus' edict and Eupolemus' account may be shown by the following juxtaposition, referring to construction of the Temple's walls:

I Esdras 6:24 (2 5)=Ezra 6:4	*Eupolemus*
Three courses of hewn stone and one course of native timber.	He Solomon built alternately a course of stone and a layer of wood, holding the two courses together with bronze clamps, of a talent weight.

Neither Kings nor Chronicles contains any allusion to courses in regard to the Temple's walls; only the inner court, according to I Kings 6:36; 7:12, was built of "three courses of hewn stone and a course of cedar beams." But I Kings 6:7 clearly states that the Temple's walls consisted of quarried stone. Zerubabel's Temple, however, as reported officially in Ezra 5:8 to King Darius, was built of "huge stones with timber lain in the walls."

Dependent as Eupolemus was here on Zerubabel's Temple, his account is not a duplicate. Cyrus' decree speaks of four courses, one of wood and three of stone. Eupolemus' account of Solomonic walls with alternate courses of stone and wood, mentions only two courses. With regard to the beautification of the walls, moreover, Eupolemus follows the Solomonic tradition: "After having thusly constructed them, he [Solomon] boarded the inside walls with cedar and cypress wood so that the stone walls were not visible."[16] Evidently, Eupolemus meant that the cedar course faced the outside, and that the stone course was in the middle, and was covered with paneling from the inside. Here I Kings 6:15a was clearly Eupolemus' source: "He lined the walls of the house on the inside with boards of cedar, from the floor of the house to the rafters." However, that the stone of the Temple's walls was not visible even from the outside is original with Eupolemus and has no supporting evidence in the other sources. I Kings 6:18c, "no stone was seen," refers apparently to the inside only.

Concerning the relationship between Eupolemus and the Greek biblical tradition, the evidence is rather complex. On the one hand, there is no doubt that much of Eupolemus' nomenclature and phrasing was dependent on the Septuagint. Certainly, as shown in the previous chapter, when influenced by the post-exilic sources, his account is closer to I Esdras than to the masoretic Hebrew of Ezra or its Septuagint version. Thus, to describe the stone and wooden courses of the walls, Eupolemus uses the technical vocabulary of I

---

16   *P.E.,* IX, 34, 5 = 723 F 2b: οὕτω δ' αὐτὸν οἰκοδομήσαντα ξυλῶσαι ἔσωθεν κεδρίνοις ξύλοις καὶ κυπαρισσίνοις, ὥστε τῆς λιθίνην οἰκοδομὴν μὴ φαίνεσθαι.

Esdras 6:24 (δόμοι λίθινοι), rather than that of III Kingdoms.[17] But Freudenthal exaggerates Eupolemus' links to the Septuagint by arguing that the Hellenistic historian combined III Kingdoms 6:15, where the paneling is said to have been cedar, with LXX Chron 3:5, which mentions instead cypress paneling, by saying that both kinds of wood were used.[18] In our fragments, however, "cedar and cypress" is an often-repeated formula rather than a learned observation.[19]

After mentioning the Temple's paneling, Eupolemus depicts its gilding. "Then he [Solomon] overlaid the naos with gold on the inside by casting golden bricks row by row, of five cubits long, and he fastened them to the paneled wood with silver nails, each weighing a talent, shaped like a breast, four in number."[20] At first glance this passage seems to say the walls of the entire naos—not only the holy of holies, as in the biblical tradition—were gilded. Walter points out that because of II Chron. 3:8-9, the subordinate clauses must be regarded here as misplaced, meaning rather that the phrase "five cubits long" refers to the silver nails and the "talent weight" to the golden bricks.

But it is worth citing the cognate passages not only to refute Walter's conjecture, but also to show the complex relationship between Eupolemus and the biblical sources:

LXX I Kings 6	*II Chron. 3*
20. The length (of the debir was) twenty cubits and the breadth (was) twenty cubits, and he covered it with pure gold.	8. And he made the holy of holies; its length, corresponding to the breadth of the house, was twenty cubits; he gilded it with pure gold for fine cherubs, to (the weight of) six hundred talents. 9. And the weight of the nails, of each one was fifty shekels of gold. And he gilded the upper chamber with gold.

Both the author of Kings and the Chronicler speak of the gilding of the *debir* or, as called by the latter, the holy of holies. But Eupolemus, as has been mentioned above, did not envisage such a structure, evidently because none existed in Zerubael's Temple; there only a veil separated the ark from the rest of the building. But whether Eupolemus indeed meant to extend the gilding to the entire naos remains doubtful, because he says that each golden brick,

---

17   Cf. III Kingdoms 7:12, where similar rows are named στίχοι(A).

18   Freudenthal, *Hell St.,* 119, note; Walter ad locum.

19   See *P.E.,* IX, 30, 6, I, 539, 7 = 723 F 2b, 673, 18; 34, 8, I 543 = 676 2.

20   *P.E.,* IX, 34, 5 = 723 F 2b: χρυσῶσαί τε τὸν ναὸν ἔσῶθεν χωννύντα πλινθία χρυσᾶ πενταπήχη καὶ προστιθέναι προσηλοῦντα ἥλοις ἀργυροῖς, ταλαντιαίοις τὴν ὁλκήν, μαστοειδέσι τὸν ῥυθμόν, τέσσαροι δὲ τὸν ἀριθμόν.

of which there were four, was five cubits long and apparently five cubits wide. If so, the total would be twenty square cubits—the measurements of the Holy of Holies.

What is certain, however, is that there was a linear development from the accounts of First Kings to Second Chronicles to Eupolemus. I Kings 6:19-20 describes the *debir* (adyton) as gilded throughout, but without any mention of nails and without giving the weights of the precious metal. To this the Chronicler added that the gold which covered the walls weighed 600 talents and each of the nails fifty shekels. In Eupolemus, however, the nails are of silver, each weighing a talent, and each golden brick five cubits long. The trend seems to have been from the royal historian, who knew almost nothing of the Mosaic account of the tabernacle; to the Chronicler, who apparently gave some recognition to Exod. 26:32, 37, which mentions golden nails; to Eupolemus, who took a great deal from the Pentateuchal source. The wording of LXX Exod. 26:37d: "And you shall cast them five brazen sockets" seems to be echoed in Eupolemus' fragments, except that the latter changes the bronze to gold, as was befitting a Solomonic structure. The mention of silver, original with Eupolemus, may also be derived from Exod. 26:32, which records the silver sockets of the tabernacle.

The fragments' account of the gilding of the naos further illustrates Eupolemus' method of summarizing the Scriptural tradition: "Thus he covered it [the naos] with gold from the floor to the ceiling; and the ceiling he made of golden tiles; but the roof he made bronze, of bronze tiles, having poured the bronze and cast it into molds."[21] As to the gilding of the walls and ceiling, Eupolemus here modified considerably the Scriptural tradition. I Kings 6:15 reports that the walls of the "house" (*hekhal*) were covered with panels (boards) "from the floor to the inner walls and to the beams" (so LXX); but the Hebrew text adds "from the floor to the walls and to the ceiling with cedar." The Chronicler (II Chron. 3:57), in addition to mentioning the wood paneling, here said to be cypress, adds a generalized description: "So he lined the house with gold—its beams, its thresholds, its walls, and its doors." Eupolemus reproduces essentially the version of I Kings, but in line with II Chron. 3:5, changes the wood paneling to gold. This is another example of the historiographic continuum from Kings to Chronicles to Eupolemus.[22]

---

21   *P.E.*, IX, 34, 6 = 723 F 2b: οὕτω δ' αὐτὸν χρυσῶσαι ἀπὸ ἐδάφους ἕως τῆς ὀροφῆς τό τε ὀρόφωμα ποιῆσαι ἐκ φατνωμάτων χρυσῶν, τὸ δὲ δῶμα ποιῆσαι χαλκοῦν ἀπὸ κεραμίδων χαλκῶν, χαλκὸν χωνεύσαντα καὶ τοῦτον καταχέαντα.

22   In I Kings the basic metal used in the Temple was bronze, with gold serving as an ornamentation. I Kings 7:51 (II Chron. 5:2), however, records David's hoarding of "silver and gold and utensils, which (Solomon) brought to the storehouses of the house of the Lord." See also I Chron. 22:14-16.

The Temple's bronze roof (δῶμα) is original with Eupolemus. Our biblical traditions do not describe the housetop. This would explain why, as often occurs in the fragments, Eupolemus reiterates the action, stressing the manner of manufacturing and mentioning the metal three times. Conceivably, though, as in the case of the Temple's dimensions, Eupolemus ascribed a bronze roof to the Solomonic sanctuary because it was one of the features of Zerubabel's Temple. Eupolemus returns to this subject again when he records the bronze scarecrow.[23]

Eupolemus' depiction of Solomon's Temple frequently borrowed aspects of Zerubabel's sanctuary, but there is little evidence that he followed Hellenistic architectural designs. There are, however, exceptions. Certainly, the claim that Solomon's golden nails were shaped like breasts appears to be of pagan origin. Also perhaps Hellenistic is the mention of the building technology, an aspect altogether ignored in the Hebrew tradition. Eupolemus goes into some detail as to how the golden and bronze tiles were manufactured and then molded into the walls of the sanctuary. This, however, is quite doubtful. It is more likely that the allusion to building techniques reflects the Pentateuchal tradition of the tabernacle rather than an alien tradition.[24]   Thus despite Eupolemus' constant divergence with the biblical accounts, his version of the Solomonic Temple reflects a continuous priestly literary tradition that was devoted to the sacrificial code. The accounts that follow of the pillars, lamps, laver, and scarecrow illustrate further the form this Hebrew tradition assumed in Graeco-Jewish historiography.

THE PILLARS

No other feature of the Temple is as frequently and as minutely described in Scripture as the pillars.[25] Yet their basic design and function have been hotly debated. Because of their technical nature, the verses of I Kings 7:15-22 seem to have undergone corruption and are difficult to reconstruct. Nevertheless, it would be fair to summarize the passage as follows: Each of the two bronze pillars was eighteen cubits high with a circumference of twelve (LXX: fourteen) cubits. The capitals of the pillars were formed as a bowl-shaped top, five cubits high each, and covered with a checker-work pattern, along with an adornment of narrow leaves of lily, reaching the height of four cubits. Two hundred pomegranates were suspended on a string and hung on each capital. The pillars were set at the porch of the main hall (hekhal). The one on the right was named Jachin and the one on the left Boaz. The height of the

---

23   P.E., IX, 34, 11 = 723 F 2b.
24   Exod. 25:9, 40.
25   I Kings 7:15-22; II Kings 25:16-17; Jer. 52:20-23; II Chr. 4:12-13; cf. A.J., VII, 77 f.

capitals in II Kings 25:17 is three cubits, instead of five, as reported in the other texts. Again, the height of the pillars according to II Chron. 3:15, as well as in the Greek version of Jer. 52:21, was 35 cubits excluding the capitals. Aside from scribal corruptions, these differing dimensions suggest 'corrections' by later authors, who attempted to make sense out of difficult passages by making them conform with their own images of the pillars.

To these confusing traditions, that of Eupolemus should be added: "He also made two pillars of bronze and covered them with pure gold, a finger thick. The pillars were of the same height as the naos, the circumference of each pillar was ten cubits; and he set one pillar on the right and the other pillar on the left of the house."[26]

The height of the pillars, according to Eupolemus, was the same as that of the naos. But though the fragments give its length and breadth, the height is missing. If Eupolemus meant by naos the main hall, I Kings 6:2 says its height was 30 cubits; the Greek version of this text says it was only 25 cubits. If Eupolemus meant the porch, as claimed by Freudenthal, II Chr. 3:4 gives its height as 120 cubits. None of these numbers conforms with any of the recorded Scriptural texts as to the height of the pillars, with or without their capitals and adornments. It was suggested above, however, that in his description of the gilding of the naos Eupolemus referred to the *devir* or, as it is called in some late sources, the holy of holies. The height of the holy of holies in the biblical sources, and it would seem also in Eupolemus, was 20 cubits. If so, the height of the pillars for Eupolemus was also 20 cubits.[27]

For their circumference, Eupolemus gives ten cubits, apparently a half of the pillar's height. The circumference in I Kings 7:15 and Jer. 52:21 is twelve cubits; in the Greek version of I Kings, 14 cubits. Only Eupolemus maintains that the pillars were gilded, though the biblical texts impress on the reader that the pillars were one of the most notable features of the Temple's architecture. Eupolemus stresses his disagreement with the older sources by reporting that the gold which covered the bronze pillars was pure and a finger thick. These divergences from the tradition appear to contradict Freudenthal's evidence that Eupolemus' account of the pillars depends upon the wording of the Greek text of II Chr. 3:15.[28] The common phrases found

---

26   *P.E.*, IX, 34, 6-7 = 723 F 2b: ποιῆσαι δὲ δύο στύλους χαλκοῦς καὶ καταχρυσῶσαι αὐτοὺς χρυσίῳ ἀδόλῳ, δακτύλου τὸ πάχος. εἶναι δὲ τοὺς στύλους τῷ ναῷ ἰσομεγέθεις, τὸ δὲ πλάτος κύκλῳ ἕκαστον κίονα πηχῶν δέκα· στῆσαι δὲ αὐτοὺς τοῦ οἴκου ὃν μὲν ἐκ δεξιῶν, ὃν δὲ ἐξ εὐωνύμων.

27   Cf. also the height of the network as given by Eupolemus (P.E. IX, 34, 11 = 723 F 2b).

28   Freudenthal, *Hell. St.*, 119 note, compares Eupolemus (in *P.E.*, IX, 34, 7, p. 542, 15 f.), above note 26, with II Chr. 3:17: καὶ ἔστησεν τοὺς στύλους κατὰ πρόσωπον τοῦ ναοῦ, ἕνα ἐκ δεξιῶν καὶ τὸν ἕνα ἐξ εὐωνύμων. Certainly, the Chronicler's midrash as to the meaning of Jachin and Boaz—representing perhaps the names of builders or of Solomon's sons—but which LXX renders *katorthosis* (Stability?) and Ischys (Strength) was not known to Eupolemus.

in both the Hellenistic historian and in the Greek version of Chronicles are too pedestrian to conclude that either translation was dependent on the other. It is, moreover, unlikely that Eupolemus would have borrowed certain phrases from a source while departing from it in all other respects.

Modern scholarship is divided as to the function of the pillars. One school of thought maintains that the roof of a thirty cubit-high hall would be in danger of collapsing unless supported by something more than the walls. This, some scholars say, as suggested by the Byzantine churches, was the function of the two pillars. Other authorities maintain that the bronze pillars were of a strictly decorative, symbolic, or cultic nature, and that they were free-standing. The evidence from excavated temples in neighboring localities is divided.[29] Eupolemus' wording, implying that the height of the pillars equalled that of the naos, whatever its historical worth, supports the latter point of view.

It is conceivable, though, as will be shown below, that Eupolemus assigned a function to the pillars undreamt of by modern scholarship. According to Eupolemus, it would seem that suspended upon the pillars were two networks of ring-like chains with bells attached to them, which served as a gigantic scarecrow.[30] Eupolemus shows the significance that he attached to the pillars once again when he mentions them in his summary of the weights of the Temple's metals. This significance becomes even greater when one is aware that the pillars Jachin and Boaz were unique to Solomon's sanctuary, which the subsequent drawers Ezekiel, Zerubabel, and Mishnah Middot ignored. In this instance Eupolemus writes then as an antiquarian; he was not merely retrojecting the present Temple and gilding it fantastically to make it appear Solomonic. Nevertheless, his fantastic claim that a finger-thick layer of pure gold weighing millions of talents covered the pillars reveals the most characteristic feature of Eupolemus' fragments.

THE LAMPS

Following the pillars, our fragments describe the lampstands and lamps, a sequence that gives us an inkling of Eupolemus' cultic hierarchy. The author's invocation of the Mosaic authority suggests once again that his departures from the biblical traditions were conscious: "But he [Solomon] also made ten golden lampstands, each weighing [ten][31] talents, having taken as his model the one set up by Moses in the tent of testimony. He placed them on

29   For the literature see "Nabonidus and the Clergy of Babylon, " L. Oppenheim, in *Ancient Near Eastern Texts Relating to the Old Testament,* edited by J. B. Pritchard (Princeton University Press); Busink, *Tempel,* I, 299-321.

30   Freudenthal, *Hell. St.,* 114, 119. Busink, *Tempel,* I, 27, remarks that this "ist fraglich," because Eupolemus does not mention the network when describing the pillars.

31   The addition of this word follows Seguier and Mras; see below note 33.

both sides of the sacred enclosure, some on the right, some on the left. But he also made seventy golden lamps so that each lampstand had seven lamps."[32] As to the number of the lampstands, Eupolemus repeats I Kings 7:49 and II Chron. 4:7. Eupolemus' statement that each lampstand weighed ten talents, however, is not found in the biblical texts. But it should be stressed that the reading "ten" (talents) is conjectural, though, I believe, sound. Freudenthal and Walter, because of Exod. 25:39, 37:24, change the plural to one "talent."[33] If so, this would be one more instance of the historian's fusing of the tabernacle with the Solomonic Temple. But, as pointed out by Mras, Eupolemus must have felt that the traditional weight of the tabernacle's lampstand was too modest for Solomon's lampstand.

Eupolemus' claim that each of the ten Solomonic lampstands contained seven lamps may have been influenced by either the desert model or by the one used in his own time. It was to bolster his linking of the seven-branch menorah with Solomon's ten lampstands that Eupolemus invoked the Mosaic authority; not as Freudenthal and Walter argue, to show the weight of the lampstands. The Chronicler (II Chron. 4:7), in reproducing the mention of the ten lampstands of I Kings 7:49, added that they were made "as prescribed" (*kemishpatam*); Eupolemus, on the basis of Exod. 25:40, evidently interpreted this as referring to the Pentateuchal menorah.[34]

Another factor that may have influenced Eupolemus' account was the lampstand of Zerubabel's Temple. His invocation of the Mosaic authority appears to attest to the paramount significance that the seven-branched menorah was beginning to assume. For the author of First Kings the candle sticks are still primarily functional.[35] The Prophet Zechariah describes his dream: "I see, and behold, a lampstand all of gold with a bowl on the top of it, and seven lamps on it, with seven lips on each of the lamps that are on top of it."[36] In Eupolemus' time, among the abominable misdeeds ascribed to Antiochus IV, the taking of the lampstand was listed next to the confiscation

---

32 *P.E.*, IX, 34, 7-8 = 723 F 2b: ποιῆσαι δὲ καὶ λυχνίας χρυσᾶς ⟨δέκα⟩, δέκα τάλαντα ἑκάστην ὁλχὴν ἀγούσας, ὑπόδειγμα λαβόντα τὴν ὑπὸ Μωσέως ἐν τῇ σχηνῇ τοῦ μαρτυρίου τεθεῖσαν· 8. στῆσαι δ᾽ ἐξ ἑκατέρου μέρους τοῦ σηκοῦ τὰς μὲν ἐκ δεξιῶν, τὰς δὲ ἐξ εὐωνύμων. ποιῆσαι δ᾽ αὐτὸν καὶ λύχνους κρυσοῦς ο᾽, ὥστε καίεσθαι ἐφ᾽ ἑκάστης λυχνίας ἑπτά.

33 Freudenthal, *Hell. St.*, 211; Walter, ad locum.

34 The same fusion is found in the Melekhet-Hamishkan, 10; B. T. Menahot 29a; see also Kimhi on I Kings 7:49.

35 See now Busink, *Tempel*, I, 293-99.

36 Zech. 4:1-14. Cf. also the menorah as painted in the synagogue of Dura-Europos (*The Synagogue* by C. H. Kraeling [New Haven, Yale University Press], 119).

of the altar.[37] The Hasmoneans, if the talmudic tradition is trustworthy, replaced the golden menorah with a wooden one.[38] But a magnificent golden version was carried to Rome in 70 A.D., a facsimile of which is depicted on Titus' Arch and in the synagogue of Dura Europos. Writing when the golden menorah had been desecrated by the Syrians, Eupolemus perhaps had a special reason to invoke its Solomonic prototypes.

It is perhaps possible, though unlikely, that the Mosaic model of the menorah invoked by Eupolemus referred particularly to the divine source of its workmanship. According to the rabbinic exegesis, based on Exod. 25:40 and Num.8:4, God showed to Moses a model of the menorah to enlighten him on its technical and artistic features.[39] According to Freudenthal, the rabbis, like Eupolemus, also give the weight of each of the ten lampstands as one talent, adding that Solomon had poured the gold into the smelting pot a thousand times before he succeeded in making it exactly a talent.[40] The multiple of seven times ten lamps with which Solomon was said to have lit up the Temple is also mentioned in Midrash Tadshe. This medieval text whose roots seem to go back to the Hellenistic period, says that the seventy lamps symbolized the seventy nations allegedly under Solomon's domain.[41]

In the account of the dedication of the sanctuary. Eupolemus lists the Mosaic menorah among the items which Solomon transferred from Shiloh to Jerusalem; he emphasizes this point, by asserting it in the name of the prophet.[42] Unless there is a contradiction, we must assume that the ten lampstands made by the king were in addition to the one of the desert.[43] If so, Eupolemus meant to say that Solomon's lampstands were exact reproductions of the Mosaic blueprint. This might explain why Eupolemus says that the royal lampstands were set up in the *sekos,* the holy precinct, whereas the tabernacle's menorah was placed in the "house." Here is another example of Eupolemus' attempt to reconcile the Pentateuchal menorah with those of the Solomonic period, something which the earlier sources failed to do. The talmudists, like Eupolemus strove to interpret the tradition of the Solomonic lampstands to be in accord with the accounts of the tabernacle's menorah. But for them, unlike for Eupolemus, the issue was strictly exegetical, as can be seen by the utterly irreconcilable opinions expressed.

---

37   Cf. I Macc. 1:21, recording Antiochus' despoiling of the Temple; I Macc. 4:50 describes the Maccabean rededication: "Then they burned incense on the altar and lighted the lamps on the lampstand, and these gave light in the temple." Here once again the lampstand is linked with the altar.

38   Menahot 28b.

39   T. B. Menahot, 29a; Mekhilta d'Rabbi Ishmael, *Pasha* 2; Sifre Num. 61; Pesikta d'Rab Kahana, *Hahodesh* (ed. Mandelbaum), I, 104, and parallels.

40   Yer. Shekalim, VI, 3, ; B. Menahot, 29a. Freudenthal, *Hell. St.,* 116.

41   Midrash Tadshe (ed. A. Epstein, Vienna, 1887), p. XXVI.

42   *P.E.,* IX, 34, 15 = 723 F 2b.

43   Melekhet Hamishkan, 10; B. Menahot, 29a, give a similar interpretation.

Eupolemus, as we have seen, was concerned with harmonizing historical traditions with the divergent practices of his own day.[44]

THE GATES

A meager and stilted sentence is all that Eupolemus offers concerning the openings to the sanctuary: "He [Solomon] also built the gates of the Temple and adorned them with gold and silver and covered them with panels of cypress and cedar wood."[45] It is worth comparing this with the technical but fascinating version given in I Kings 6:31-35: "For the entrance of inner sanctuary (adyton) he made doors of olivewood; the lentel and the doorposts he formed a pentagon (?). He covered the two doors of olivewood with carvings of cherubim, palm trees and open flowers; he overlaid them with gold, upon the cherubim and upon the palm trees. So also he made for the entrance to the nave doorposts of olivewood, in the form of a square, and two doors of cypress wood; the two doors of cypress wood; the two leaves of the one door were folding and the two doors of the other door were folding. On them he carved cherubim and palm trees and open flowers; and he overlaid them with gold evenly applied upon the carved work." Verses 31-32 depict the adyton's doors, 33-35 those of the *hekhal* (nave). The Greek fragments, however, refer to the "doors of the Temple" (πύλαι τοῦ ἱεροῦ), presumably meaning all the doors of the Temple. Certainly, II Chron. 4:22b and Ezek. 41:23-25 combine the descriptions of the entrances of both the Holy of Holies and the Hekhal. Nonetheless, as pointed out above, since our fragments make no mention of the Holy of Holies, apparently because the temples of Zerubabel and Herod did not have such a room, it is unlikely that Eupolemus would have referred to its doors.

As to the adornments of the doors, I Kings and Ezekiel offer elaborate descriptions of the woodwork, but this is ignored by the Chronicler, who merely mentions the gilding. Eupolemus, however, although his account in its brevity resembles the Chronicler's gives equal treatment to the the gilding and the wood paneling. But neither may his description be regarded as a copy of I Kings. The latter says that the doors of the adyton were of olive wood, covered with carvings of cherubim and palm trees; and that the hekhal's doors were of cypress wood covered with palm. Eupolemus' summary does not mention the material of the doors, but describes them as engraved with gold

---

44   Pseudo-Hecataeus (*C. Apionem*, I, 198 = 264 F 21), who was no doubt an eye witness: "Beside the Temple stands a great edifice, containing an altar and a lampstand, both made of gold and weighing two talents. upon these there is a light that is never extinguished." Cf. Also *B.J.*, VII, 148 f.

45   *P.E.*, IX, 34, 8 = 723 F 2b: οἰκοδομῆσαι δὲ καὶ τὰς πύλας τοῦ ἱεροῦ καὶ κατακοσμῆσαι χρυσίῳ καὶ ἀργυρίῳ· καὶ καταστεγάσαι φατνώμασι κεδρίνοις καὶ κυπαρισσίνοις.

and silver, and covered with cypress and palm wood. Thus far we have seen that Eupolemus' version of the Solomonic Temple was eclectic. But in one detail he is original. None of the biblical sources allude to silver, which Eupolemus claims adorned the Temple's doors. Josephus (*A.J.* VIII, 98) is no exception, since his silver doors refer only to the porches of the court. Silver is also mentioned in the fragments as the material of the talent-weight nails used to fasten the gold panelings to the walls. The recording of silver here, though not found in the biblical sources, may therefore not be regarded as a mere slip, but rather as part of a deliberate rewriting of the ancient tradition.

Eupolemus' wording of the adornment of the gates lacks coherence. It is probable that under *pylai* he meant to include the doors. But the phrases "he adorned them" ($\kappa\alpha\tau\alpha\kappa\omega\sigma\mu\acute{\epsilon}\omega$) and "he covered them" ($\kappa\alpha\tau\alpha\sigma\tau\acute{\epsilon}\gamma\omega$) leaves the reader wondering whether the doors were made of precious metal and then covered with wooden panels or that he really meant to say that the wooden doors were adorned with gold and silver. And there is also the possibility that by *pylai* Eupolemus referred to only the stone entrances.

But in describing the *pylai* Eupolemus follows the biblical tradition of hierography. Not only does Scripture offer a detailed workmanship of the gates and doors of the Temple, but it appears to regard them among the most remarkable features of the sanctuary. It is recorded, for example, that King Hezekiah shipped the doors of the Temple as a bribe to Sennacherib to forestall an Assyrian invasion. In Ezekiel's visions the gates play a greater role than any other feature of the Temple, devoting a fair portion of chapters 40-46 to them. According to the Maccabean historian, one of the first tasks performed by Judah and his brothers consisted in renewing the gates of the desecrated Temple. The accounts of the Herodian sanctuary in the Mishnah and Josephus describe the gates at length.[46] In describing the gates and their gilding of the Solomonic Temple, Eupolemus follows a tradition that attached immense importance to that part of the sanctuary.

THE PORTICO

After describing the main structure, Eupolemus deals with the cultic adjuncts that stood in the Temple's precinct. Curiously, the first item is not recorded in the Hebrew accounts of the Temple, but the Septuagint appears to have alluded to something similar. Eupolemus says: "He Solomon also made a portico at the northern part of the Temple and suspended it upon forty-eight

---

46   See Ezek. 41:23-25; Cf. 41:2 ff.; I Macc. 4:57; Josephus, *A.J.*, VIII, 74, who, perhaps on the basis of Ex. 41:2, gives the doors' dimensions as twenty cubits; cf. *B.J.*, V, 201-06; Mishnah Middot, IV, 1-2. For the secondary literature, see now works cited by Busink, *Tempel,* I, 186-93.

pillars of bronze."[47] The Greek text of I Kings 7:31 (Hebrew: 45), however, after listing the Temple's pots, incoherently inserts the passage: "And the forty-eight pillars of the house of the king and of the house of the Lord"; completing with words found in the Hebrew text: "all the works of the king which Hiram made were entirely of brass."[48] From the apparent relationship of the two texts Freudenthal concluded that Eupolemus was here dependent upon the Septuagint's version of the pillars.[49] Freudenthal proceeds to link these accounts with "Solomon's portico" mentioned in the New Testament in connection with Jesus.[50] Josephus, likewise describing the Herodian Temple, supplies the details of an eastern portico, although he says the other sides of the Temple were exposed: "It was part of the outer sanctuary, located in a deep ravine, 400 cubits long made of square stones, completely white, each stone was twenty cubits long and six cubits high."[51] Lest one might think that this portico was of late construction, Josephus asserts its Solomonic origin.[52] Although Eupolemus located the portico in the north and Josephus in the east, Freudenthal concludes that both were ultimately dependent upon the Greek version of I Kings 7:31.[53]

Freudenthal's conclusions here must be rejected. There is no reason to assume that Josephus' references to "Solomon's portico" are dependent upon or even related to LXX III Kingdoms 7:31. The Jewish historian records the details of the portico in his *Bellum,* V, 185, and again in the *Jewish Antiquities,* XX, 220-221, both in connection with his description of the Herodian Temple. There is no allusion to it in his detailed description of the Solomonic sanctuary in his *Jewish Antiquities,* VIII, 63-90, though this work was written a decade after the *Bellum* had already been completed.[54] In fact, Josephus' version of the Solomonic Temple would seem to preclude the possibility of an eastern portico during the pre-exilic period. Textually, it should be noted that the Septuagint's reference to the forty-eight pillars makes no mention of the portico and Josephus' account of the portico says nothing about the pillars. Moreover, as shown in Rahlfs' detailed study, there

---

47   *P.E.,* IX, 34, 9 = 723 F 2b: ποιῆσαι δὲ καὶ κατὰ τὸ πρὸς βορρᾶν μέρος τοῦ ἱεροῦ στοὰν καὶ στύλους αυτῇ ὑποστῆσαι χαλκοῦς μη'.

48   See also I Kings 7:6-7; (LXX) 7:43-44.

49   Freudenthal, *Hell. St.,* 118; Walter, ad locum.

50   John 10:23; Acts 3:11; 5:12.

51   *A.J.,* XX, 221.

52   *B.J.,* V, 185; *A.J.,* XX, 220-221.

53   Freudenthal, *Hell. St.,* 118; Walter, ad locum.

54   *A.J.,* VIII, 91-98, describing Solomon's Temple courts, however, were based on some non-biblical source, perhaps on an apocrypha, though Thackeray ascribes it to the Herodian Temple. See also, Busink, *Tempel,* I, 151-53. Josephus (98), speaks of double porticoes that surrounded the Temple's (Herod's?) precincts.

is no reason to believe that Josephus had ever made use of the Greek translation of I Kings.[55]

But does not Josephus himself say that the eastern portico had been constructed by Solomon? It would appear that Josephus basically followed his sources. His model for the Herodian Temple, and perhaps his own memory as well, recorded the magnificent eastern portico. The popular name of Solomon's portico, as is also attested in the New Testament, gave rise to the legend that it was constructed by that famous king. This bit of lore must have already been mentioned in Josephus' source for his account of the Herodian Temple. However, when describing the Solomonic sanctuary, except for some embellishments and minor errors, Josephus essentially followed the Hebrew texts of I Kings and II Chronicles. Justifiably, he did not contaminate his description with anachronistic allusions to the Solomonic Temple to be found in accounts of the Herodian Temple. In other words, the eastern Solomonic portico constituted a significant part of the Herodian architectural design of the holy precinct. Whatever the origin of its nomenclature, "Solomon's portico" did not go back to the times of the famous king.[56]

As pointed out by Freudenthal, there is no doubt, however, of the interdependence between LXX Kings 7:31 and Eupolemus. But this is assured not, as Freudenthal suggests, because these two sources both record the existence of forty eight pillars in the Solomonic temple, a fact not otherwise known. It is precisely because the reliable texts as well as the architectural experts contradict the existence of such pillars that the interdependence between our fragments and the Septuagint becomes certain. The problem is, who invented this feature—Eupolemus or the Greek translator of I Kings?

An analysis of the Septuagint verse precludes the likelihood, affirmed by Freudenthal, that the Greek translator must be regarded as the original and Eupolemus as the copyist. The full text of the Septuagint passage, whose context records the furnishings and decorations, reads: "And the kettles and the tongs and the bowls and all of the furniture, which Hiram made for King Solomon for the house of the Lord. *And the forty eight pillars of the house of the king and of the house of the Lord;* all the works of the king which Hiram made were entirely of bronze" (III Kingdoms 7:31). The italicized words have no contextual relation whatsoever to the text, and must be regarded as an extraneous insertion. The mention of Hiram twice, which also does not occur in the Hebrew, supports the view that this was an unnecessary interpolation. Moreover, the insertion fails to make clear the function of the forty eight bronze pillars.

---

55   See A. Rhalfs, *Septuaginta Studien,* I (1904).

56   Busink, *Tempel,* I, 152, comments: "Josephus' Berichte über den salomische 'Tempelberg,' es braucht kaum noch betont zu werden, sind für die Rekonstruktion der Salomoburg ohne Wert."

Eupolemus' statement may, therefore, be regarded not as an expansion of the Septuagint, but as the original. The fragments of Eupolemus state clearly the function and location of the pillars. Eupolemus invented the northern portico in Solomon's sanctuary, perhaps because he was inspired by the description of Prophet Ezekiel's visionary Temple, which was based on Solomon's structure destroyed by the Babylonians. That both Ezekiel and Eupolemus mention the northern portico immediately after the description of the Temple's doors would seem to support this hypothesis. But it is just as likely that Eupolemus reported a northern portico because Zerubabel's Temple did in fact contain such a structure. Contrary to Freudenthal and Walter, the evidence seems to point to an assumption that the italicized passage was inserted into the Septuagint from Eupolemus, perhaps first as a marginal note.

THE LAVER

Of all the furnishings of the Temple, the author of First Kings devotes the most space to the description of the Temple's 'molten sea' and the ten lavers. The "molten sea," according to I Kings 7:23-26, was round, ten cubits in diameter and five cubits high, and held a total of 2,000 baths. It stood on twelve sculptured oxen; its brim was lily wrought flower, with two rows of gourds. I Kings 7:27-39 depicts the workmanship of the ten stands upon which the lavers rested, though their precise shape remains obscure. The Chronicler repeats verbatim First Kings' version of the "molten sea" (II Chron. 4:2-5), but devotes only a few words to the ten lavers. Each laver stood on a wagon, whose square of four cubits and three cubits high had a capacity of forty baths (I Kings 7:38).

Eupolemus' account, however, offers a new version of the Temple's wash basins: "He [Solomon] also constructed a bronze laver, twenty cubits long, twenty cubits wide, and five cubits high. But he made around it a brim, a cubit long, projecting it to the outside, so that the priests may stand upon it when they sprinkle their feet and dip their hands. He also made the twelve legs of the laver of cast metal (or: oxen)[57] the height of a man, and he attached them to the lower parts of the laver's rear, to the right of the altar."[58]

---

57   So Mss. Mras, Jacoby, Freudenthal and Walter read 'cast oxen'   (τούρους χωνευτους).

58   P.E., IX, 34,9 = 723 F 2b: κατασκευάσαι δὲ καὶ λουτῆρα χαλκοῦν, μῆκος πηχῶν κ' καὶ πλάτος πηχῶν κ', τὸ δὲ ὕψος πηχῶν ε· ποιῆσαι δὲ ἐπ' αὐτῷ στεφάνην πρὸς τὴν βάσιν ἔξω ὑπερέχουσαν πῆχυν ἕνα πρὸς τὸ τοὺς ἱερεῖς τούς τε πόδας προσκλύζεσθαι καὶ τὰς χεῖρας νίπτεσθαι ἐπιβαίνοντας· ποιῆσαι δὲ καὶ τὰς βάσεις τοῦ λουτῆρος τορευτὰς χωνευτὰς δώδεκα καὶ τῷ ὕψει ἀνδρομήκεις καὶ στῆσαι ἐξ ὑστέρου μέρους ὑπὸ τὸν λουτῆρα, ἐκ δεξιῶν τοῦ θυσιαστηρίου.

Eupolemus' laver at first appears to consist of a fusion of the Solomonic "molten sea" and the ten lavers. Scripture does not say that the "molten sea" was made of bronze, but Eupolemus follows tradition, as II Kings 16:17 assures us that this was indeed the sea's metal. But surprisingly, Eupolemus, unlike the Chronicler and Josephus,[59] avoids the term "sea," perhaps because he regarded it as too pretentious. More enigmatic are the dimensions Eupolemus ascribes to the laver. A rectangular prism of 20 x 20 x 5, Eupolemus' laver differs from the biblical "sea," which was either cylindrical or hemispheric. On the other hand, while the biblical tradition ascribes to Solomon ten lavers, Eupolemus knows of only one. The former, each had a capacity of forty baths; the latter, of 2,000 cubic cubits. It would seem then that Eupolemus borrowed the laver's capacity from that of the "molten sea," which according to I Kings had a volume of 2,000 baths.

Eupolemus' dependence on the Hebrew version of First Kings seems here assured. The Septuagint text (except Codex Alexandrinus) omits altogether the capacity of the "sea," and II Chron. 4:5 says that its capacity was 3,000 baths.[60] It should be made clear, however, that by changing the Hebrew bath into a cubic cubit, Eupolemus, by modern measurements, probably supposed a laver that was roughly six times larger than the biblical "sea." The ancient bath equaled, according to Busink's estimate, twenty-three liters (24.24 quarts),[61] which multiplied by 2,000 makes the capacity of the Solomonic "sea" in the account of I Kings 7:26, 46,000 liters (48,622 quarts). Eupolemus' dimensions of a 2,000 cubit bath, however, making the cubit about 50 centimeters (20 inches) or six baths per cubic cubit, adds up to a total of 12,000 baths or 276,000 liters (291,732 quarts). The cubic dimensions of the bath in the fragments clash strongly with the tradition exegesis of the Septuagint, which renders *bath* either as *chus,* equaling perhaps 3.44 liters; or metretes, twelve *choes,* or about 38.88 liters. This type of exaggeration is perhaps typical of Eupolemus. As has already been noted above, Eupolemus preserves the biblical amounts of Solomon's supplies, but by making them into monthly rather than annual provisions, as reported in the tradition, increased them twelvefold.

But Eupolemus' account here, and throughout this description of the Temple, was influenced by the Mosaic description of the tabernacle's laver. By making the base's brim a prominent feature of the Solomonic laver, Eupolemus recalls the brim (στεφάνη) of the altar recorded in Exod. 30:3,

---

59   Josephus (*A.J.,* VIII, 79) explains the peculiar name in terms of the laver's size.

60   So also Josephus (*A.J.,* VIII, 80), who assumes that the 'sea' had the shape of a hemisphere.

61   See Busink, *Tempel,* I, 326-28, esp. note 611,   which cites the relevant literature.

but which he seems to have ascribed also to the bronze base of the Mosaic laver (Exod. 30:18). Certainly, the biblical tradition relating to Solomon's "sea" and lavers does not know of such a brim.

According to Eupolemus, the laver's brim extended a cubit in order to perform its prescribed function. This brim (*zer;* στεφάνη) should not be confused with the rim (*safah;* LXX: χεῖλος) of the molten sea, in I Kings 7:26: "Its thickness was a handbreath, and its brim was made like the brim of a cup, like the flower of a lily." These technical details tell exclusively of the "sea's" artistic makeup. Eupolemus' claim that the laver's stand was the height of a man seems to be based on the stands of the ten Solomonic lavers, which, according to I Kings 7:27, were three cubits high, about 1.50 meter, or five feet tall. Add to this the height of five cubits of the laver itself, mentioned in the fragments, and Eupolemus' brim was necessary for the laver to be of any practical use.[62]

Like the brim, the lower part of the "molten sea" is described artistically in the biblical texts. Its twelve ornamental gourds below the brim, as well as the twelve oxen, facing at right angles in four directions, are missing in Eupolemus' austere summary. He does mention twleve legs of "cast metal," no doubt a pedestrian equivalent of the twelve oxen. If Freudenthal and Walter are right, however, by a slight emendation of the Greek, Eupolemus could be made to repeat the biblical "twelve cast oxen."[63] It is reasonable, nonetheless, with Mras and Jacoby, to retain the manuscript reading because a) it is dangerous to make a writer such as Eupolemus conform with the traditional versions; and b) in contrast to the Bible, Eupolemus may have deliberately avoided the mention of animal figures. For one who participated in the Maccabean revolt, the representation of animal figures may have come too close to violation of the second commandment of the Decalogue.

Instead of the lavish decorations of First Kings, Eupolemus stresses the laver's function: "So that the priests may stand on it (i.e. the laver's brim) when they sprinkle their feet and dip their hands."[64] Because II Chron. 4:6b says that the lavers served "to rinse off what was used for the burnt offering, and the sea was for the priests to wash in," Walter points out that Eupolemus followed here the Chronicler. This is rather unlikely, since Eupolemus ignores the Chronicler's account of the "sea" altogether. Moreover, Eupolemus and

---

62   Some scholars maintain that the Solomonic "sea" served no practical function, except as a symbol, of the sky or ocean, thus denying the view of II Chron. 4:6 (Kittel, *Studien,* 236; Rudolph, *Chronikbücher,* 207). But Busink, *Tempel,* I, 336, rightly upholds the functional purpose of the sea.

63   See note 57.

64   Eupolemus' use of different verbs to describe the washing of the hands (νίπτω) and feet (προσκλύζω) suggests that he was an expert in the priestly exegesis; cf. B.T. Hullin, 106a; Torat Kohanim, *Mezora* (Weiss), 77a .

Chron. 6:4b refer to diverse functions. The latter tries to define the various uses of the lavers and the "sea"; the former is concerned here only with the laver's brim unmentioned in the Solomonic sources.

Eupolemus' source here was not the Chronicler, but Exod. 30:17-21, the account of the tabernacle's laver. Verses 18 and 20 stress that Aaron and his sons under the penalty of death "shall wash their hands and feet when they come near the altar." Eupolemus places the Solomonic laver to the right of the altar, resembling Exod. 30:18, which ordains the setting up of the Mosaic laver "between the tent of meeting and the altar." It is likely, moreover, that Eupolemus' account, as has been noted, reflected some of the basic features of the contemporary laver of the Temple, which our historian in a magnified form attributed to Solomon. Mishnah Middot, similarly inspired by Exod. 30:18, also locates the Herodian equivalent: "The laver was located between the porch and the altar, turning southward."[65] The biblical accounts of the Solomonic Temple were by and large free from the Pentateuchal influences, though this is less true of the author of Chronicles than of Kings. For Eupolemus, however, the Law was an authoritative work even in such matters as depicting Solomon's sanctuary. And for a priest, the laver was surpassed in cultic significance only by the altar.

THE KING'S PLATFORM

Following the mention of the priestly use of the laver, Eupolemus describes the adjoining platform of the king, again stressing the cultic function of the Temple's furnishings: "He [Solomon] also made a bronze platform, two cubits high, near the laver. So that the king may stand upon it when praying, that he would be seen by the Jewish people."[66] The existence of the king's platform is attested directly only in II Chr. 6:13: "For Solomon had made a bronze platform, five cubits long, five cubits wide, three cubits high, which he placed inside the court and upon which he stood." This verse is missing in the parallel passage of I Kings 8:22. It would be misleading, however, to assume automatically that Eupolemus borrowed the passage from the Chronicler.[67] The differences between the two sources are rather significant. Eupolemus says the platform's height was two cubits; the Chronicler, three. The former places it behind the laver, the latter in the court. Moreover, the Chronicler records the platform only as a gloss on I Kings 8:22, to explain upon what the king was standing. Eupolemus lists the platform as standard furniture.

---

65   Mishnah Tamid, III, 6; B. T. Zevahim, 58b-59a, citing as its authority Exod. 30:19.

66   *P.E.*, IX, 34, 10 = 723 F 2b: ποιῆσαι δὲ καὶ βάσιν χαλκῆν τῷ ὕψει πηχῶν δυοῖν κατὰ τὸν λουτῆρα· ἵν᾽ ἐφεστήκῃ ἐπ᾽ αὐτῆς ὁ βασιλεύς, ὅταν προσεύχηται ὅπως ὀπτάνηται τῷ λαῷ τῶν Ἰουλαίων.

67   See Freudenthal, *Hell. St.*, 115 f.; Walter, ad locum.

Despite these objections, Eupolemus' source would have to be the Book of Chronicles if Wellhausen's view that II Chr. 6:13 was an anachronistic embellishment of I Kings 8:22 is accepted. Rudolph, however, has rightly pointed out that II Chr. 6:13, instead of being an addition, was rather a copy of a more faithful recension of I Kings.[68] The existence of the king's platform during the pre-exilic Temple cannot be doubted. Archaeologists have found it in the palaces of the Near Eastern kings. King Josiah from a similar stand exhorted the mob to murder the hated princess Athaliah, and to restore the Yahwistic cult. King Josiah proclaimed the famous Deuteron-omistic reform while standing upon such a platform.[69]   Because of the alterations, it is difficult to extrapolate Eupolemus' source. But it is not inconceivable that he modeled Solomon's platform after the one used by the high priest in Eupolemus' own time.

Of interest is Eupolemus' nuance that the platform's function was to make the king visible to the people when praying. The Hellenistic historian implies that the king led public worship. We know that the platform had other purposes as well. During postexilic times, it is recorded that Ezra expounded Scripture while standing upon a platform, albeit the text stresses that, unlike in former times, the platform was of wood.[70] The platform was a wooden one, according to the Mishnah, when King Aggripa II recited from the Book of Deuteronomy during the pilgrim festival of Tabernacles.[71] In its Greek equivalent βῆμα, the wooden platform retains a central function in the synagogue.

THE ALTAR

The sacrificial altar was no doubt the central structure of the ancient cult. The fragment alludes to it at the very beginning, as David prays for a propicious spot to build the altar. Eupolemus also tells us that Solomon's laver was located at the right of the altar. In the list of the holy objects of the Tabernacle, which Solomon transferred to his Temple, the Mosaic altar heads the items named. But Eupolemus devotes only a line to its makeup: "He [Solomon] also built an altar, twenty-five cubits by twenty cubits, and twelve cubits high."[72] Some editors (Kuhlmey, Freudenthal, Jacoby, Walter;

68   J. Wellhausen, *Prologemena to the History of Ancient Israel* (New York, Meridian Library 1952), 186; E. L. Curtis, *Chronicles* (ICC, 1910), ad locum. But see Rudolph, *Chronikbücher,* 213.

69   II Kings 11:14 = II Chr. 23: 13; II Kings 23:3; cf. Deut. 17:18, comparable to the *pnyx,* or *bema.*

70   Neh. 8:4; Cf. 9:4.

71   Mishnah Sotah, VII, 8; cf. Anan the Karaite's code (ed. Harkavy, Petersburg, 1903) 19 f.

72   *P.E.,* IX, 34, 10 = 723 F 2b: οἰκοδομῆσαι δὲ καὶ τὸ θυσιαστήριον πηχῶν κε ἐπὶ πήχεις κ΄, τὸ δὲ ὕψος πηχῶν δώδεκα.

but not Mras) emend the cipher 25 to 20, in order to make the altar square and to bring Eupolemus in greater consonance with ancient testimony:

Source	altar	length	width	height
II Chron. 4:1	Solomon's	20	20	10
Jos. *A.J.*, VIII, 88	Solomon's	20	20	10
Eupolemus	Solomon's	25 (20?)	20 (25?)	12
Pseudo-Hecataeus (264 F 21)	Zerubabel's	20	20	10
Jos. *B.J.*, V, 25	Herod's	50	50	15
Middot, III, 1	Halakhic			
	(foundation)	32	32	8
	(top)	24	24	—

Of course, the mere fact that the fragments are out of step with the unanimous tradition is in itself insufficient reason to emend a mendacious writer such as Eupolemus. But the emendation seems perhaps reasonable here as the passage appears corrupt and a dittography would explain the corruption. As to the change of the altar's height from the traditional ten cubits to twelve, Freudenthal apparently solved the problem by correlating Eupolemus with Exod. 27:1. The dimensions of the desert altar were 5 x 5 x 3, which Eupolemus multiplied by four.[73] Otherwise, it is just as conceivable to make Eupolemus' altar a square of twenty-five cubits.

The material from which the altar was constructed is not mentioned in the fragments. The nature of the altar becomes complicated because of the Pentateuchal prescription to build it of stone (though no doubt with a metal covering).[74] The post-exilic altars were likewise of unhewn stone.[75] When Judah Maccabee liberated Jerusalem, the altar of burnt offerings was declared to be defiled. After some hesitation the old stones were carefully stored away until the days when the Prophet will come, and rule on their ritual status.[76] Pseudo-Hecataeus likewise reports an altar of unhewn stone for Zerubabel's Temple, and Josephus and the Mishnah delineate the same for Herod's.[77] It must be assumed that Eupolemus, despite II Kings 16:14-15 and II Chron. 4:1, likewise referred to a stone altar. The fragments mention the metal of each cultic item; so its omission here must be significant. Moreover, there is no doubt that Zerubabel's altar, which seems to have been the basis of Eupolemus' account, was of stone, one of the materials David had prepared.

Though he informs us that the laver was located at its right, Eupolemus is silent as to the altar's location. An analogous problem is the height of the pillars, said to have been the same as the naos, but neither altitude is

---

73   Freudenthal, *Hell. St.*, 211.
74   Exod. 20:25; Deut. 27:5-6; Josh. 8:31.
75   I Macc. 4:56.
76   I Macc. 4:42–47; M. Middot, IV, 6.
77   264 F 21 = C. Apion. I, 198; Mishnah Middot, III, 4; *B.J.*, V, 225.

recorded. This may suggest that our fragments are defective here. But it is also conceivable that the altar's location was so well known that there would have been no reason to mention it. But if so, it follows that Eupolemus was writing for fellow Jews, rather than for pagan readers.

THE SCARECROW

The scarecrow for keeping the sanctuary free of pollution is the concluding feature of Eupolemus' account of Solomon's Temple. No other item listed in the fragments is given more space nor described in greater detail. Certainly, the sacrificial altar that was central to the cult must have been more important than the alleged scarecrow. Yet, the fragments devote a line and a half to the former, and seven lines to the latter. Of course, this is partly in consonance with the biblical literary tradition; the account of Solomon's Temple in First Kings fails to mention the altar but devotes thirteen verses (I Kings 7:27-39) to the lavers' stands. There seems to have been no point in dwelling at length on a commonplace, but a new feature deserved the author's closest attention. Solomon's altar was just like any other altar, but his scarecrow, not attested elsewhere, and apparently invented by Eupolemus, received his scrutiny: "And he [Solomon] made also two bronze ringlike lattices and he set them upon contrivances, which rose above the naos twenty cubits; and they cast a shadow over the entire sanctuary. And he suspended upon each network 400 bronze bells of a talent weight. And he made the entire latticed network so that the bells would toll to frighten away the birds, that none would settle upon the Temple neither to nest in the panels of the gates and the porches nor to pollute the Temple with their dung."[78]

The translation "two bronze rings of latticework" is only a conjecture since the Greek ($\delta\alpha\kappa\tau\upsilon\lambda\acute{\iota}o\upsilon\varsigma$ $\delta\acute{\upsilon}o$ $\chi\alpha\lambda\kappa o\tilde{\upsilon}\varsigma$ $\mathring{\alpha}\lambda\upsilon\sigma\iota\delta\omega\tau o\acute{\upsilon}\varsigma$) is not quite certain. Freudenthal labeled the phrase "ganz klar: Zwei an Ketten befestigte Ringe tragen ein Netzwerk..." Busink likewise says that Eupolemus attributed a network to Solomon's Temple.[79] As noted by Mras, however, our phrase means: "chain-lace, a network made of rings, for which Eupolemus uses below $\delta\iota\kappa\tau\acute{\upsilon}\alpha$ "network." It seems that Eupolemus presumed two networks, not one.

---

78 P.E., IX, 34, 11 = 723 F 2a:$\pi o\iota\tilde{\eta}\sigma\alpha\iota$ $\delta\grave{\epsilon}$ $\kappa\alpha\grave{\iota}$ $\delta\alpha\kappa\tau\upsilon\lambda\acute{\iota}o\upsilon\varsigma$ $\delta\acute{\upsilon}o$ $\kappa\alpha\lambda\kappa o\tilde{\upsilon}\varsigma$ $\mathring{\alpha}\lambda\upsilon\sigma\iota\delta$-$\omega\tau o\grave{\upsilon}\varsigma$ $\kappa\alpha\grave{\iota}$ $\sigma\tau\tilde{\eta}\sigma\alpha\iota$ $\alpha\mathring{\upsilon}\tau o\grave{\upsilon}\varsigma$ $\mathring{\epsilon}\pi\grave{\iota}$ $\mu\eta\chi\alpha\nu\eta\mu\acute{\alpha}\tau\omega\nu$ $\mathring{\upsilon}\pi\epsilon\rho\epsilon\chi\acute{o}\nu\tau\omega\nu$ $\tau\tilde{\omega}$ $\mathring{\upsilon}\psi\epsilon\iota$ $\tau\grave{o}\nu$ $\nu\alpha\grave{o}\nu$ $\pi\acute{\eta}\chi\epsilon\iota\varsigma$ κ' $\kappa\alpha\grave{\iota}$ $\sigma\kappa\iota\acute{\alpha}\zeta\epsilon\iota\nu$ $\mathring{\epsilon}\pi\acute{\alpha}\nu\omega$ $\pi\alpha\nu\tau\grave{o}\varsigma$ $\tau o\tilde{\upsilon}$ $\mathring{\iota}\epsilon\rho o\tilde{\upsilon}\cdot$ $\kappa\alpha\grave{\iota}$ $\pi\rho o\sigma\kappa\rho\epsilon\mu\acute{\alpha}\sigma\alpha\iota$ $\mathring{\epsilon}\kappa\acute{\alpha}\sigma\tau\eta$ $\delta\acute{\iota}\kappa\tau\upsilon\iota$ $\kappa\acute{\omega}\delta\omega\nu\alpha\varsigma$ $\chi\alpha\lambda\kappa o\grave{\upsilon}\varsigma$ $\tau\alpha\lambda\alpha\nu\tau\iota\alpha\acute{\iota}o\upsilon\varsigma$ $\tau\epsilon\tau\rho\alpha\kappa o\sigma\acute{\iota}o\upsilon\varsigma\cdot$ $\kappa\alpha\grave{\iota}$ $\pi o\iota\tilde{\eta}\sigma\alpha\iota$ $\acute{o}\lambda\alpha\varsigma$ $\tau\grave{\alpha}\varsigma$ $\delta\acute{\iota}\kappa\tau\upsilon\alpha\varsigma$ $\pi\rho\grave{o}\varsigma$ $\tau\grave{o}$ $\psi o\varphi\epsilon\tilde{\iota}\nu$ $\tau o\grave{\upsilon}\varsigma$ $\kappa\acute{\omega}\delta\omega\nu\alpha\varsigma$ $\kappa\alpha\grave{\iota}$ $\mathring{\alpha}\pi o\sigma o\beta\epsilon\tilde{\iota}\nu$ $\tau\grave{\alpha}$ $\acute{o}\rho\nu\epsilon\alpha$, $\acute{o}\pi\omega\varsigma$ $\mu\grave{\eta}$ $\kappa\alpha\vartheta\acute{\iota}\zeta\eta$ $\mathring{\epsilon}\pi\grave{\iota}$ $\tau o\tilde{\upsilon}$ $\mathring{\iota}\epsilon\rho o\tilde{\upsilon}$ $\mu\eta\delta\grave{\epsilon}$ $\nu o\sigma\sigma\epsilon\acute{\upsilon}\eta$ $\mathring{\epsilon}\pi\grave{\iota}$ $\tau o\tilde{\iota}\varsigma$ $\varphi\alpha\tau\nu\acute{\omega}\mu\alpha\sigma\iota$ $\tau\tilde{\omega}\nu$ $\pi\upsilon\lambda\tilde{\omega}\nu$ $\kappa\alpha\grave{\iota}$ $\sigma\tau o\tilde{\omega}\nu$ $\kappa\alpha\grave{\iota}$ $\mu o\lambda\acute{\upsilon}\nu\eta$ $\tau o\tilde{\iota}\varsigma$ $\mathring{\alpha}\pi o\pi\alpha\tau\acute{\eta}\mu\alpha\sigma\iota$ $\tau\grave{o}$ $\mathring{\iota}\epsilon\rho\acute{o}\nu$.

79 Freudenthal, *Hell. St.*, 211; see also 114, 119.

As to the source for this account, it has already been said that our biblical tradition does not know of such a scarecrow. But Eupolemus' description of the scarecrow was certainly heavily indebted to the Septuagint's version of the pillars and their capitals. The Hebrew of I Kings 7:17 mentions "nets of checker-works, and wreaths of chain-work" (JPS) that adorned the capitals. Jer. 52:22, however, says "a network and pomegranates" (RSV); II Chron. 4:12, "And the two networks to cover the two bowls of the capitals that were on the top of the pillars; (13) and the four hundred pomegranates for the two networks" (RSV). Of the three Hebrew passages, only the Chronicler's speaks of two networks, a text preserved also in the Greek version of I Kings 7:17. Eupolemus seems first to define the nature of the two networks as a latticework, which he calls *dictyi,* the feminine gender of the Septuagint masculine term for the Hebrew *sebakhah.*[80] Scholars agree that the word *sebakhah*—net—was derived from the Akkadian *sabiku,* a headgear. But the exact shape of the lattice is not known, since no specimen of such chain-like metal work has survived. Nonetheless, the biblical tradition and modern scholarship almost unanimously agree that the purpose of the lattices was strictly decorative, to adorn the capitals of the two pillars of Jachin and Boaz, whose meaning remains a mystery.

In Eupolemus' description of the two pillars, discussed above, nothing is said of their purpose. But even there the fragments hint of the forthcoming account suggesting apparently that this height was necessary for the scarecrow's networks. Relying on his previous account of the pillars, Eupolemus now describes the networks that rested on contrivances or machines (μηχανημάτα), without feeling the need to mention that the machines rested on the two pillars. We are told here, however, that the networks rose twenty cubits above the naos. Since the pillars were of the same height as the naos, it follows that the machines plus the networks must have extended vertically twenty cubits in order to reach the altitude given by Eupolemus. This is quite absurd even for a writer such as Eupolemus. The only reasonable explanation would seem to be that the twenty cubits refers not to distance above the naos, but to the height of the naos itself. This meaning may be achieved without emending the text simply by inserting a comma between *naos* and *cubits* (πήχεις). The passages may be translated: "And he placed them [the lattices] upon the contrivances that rose above the height of the naos, [which was] twenty cubits [high]." If so, Eupolemus fills in here a detail that was omitted in the descriptions of the Temple's walls and their pillars.

What did Eupolemus mean by his claim that the bronze networks cast a shadow over the entire sanctuary (*hieron*)? To perform such a task, the metal chain-forming rings must have been thickly woven so that they almost formed

80   I Kings 7:17-18, 20, 42; II Kings 1:2; 25:17; Jer. 52:22; Job 18:8.

a roof. The use of *hieron* here, instead of naos, which in the fragments and elsewhere refers to the main structure, suggests that Eupolemus wants us to believe that the scarecrow extended over the entire Temple, not only over the most sacred area. This in turn presumes the existence of other pillars, in addition to the two called Jachin and Boaz, to hold the contrivances upon which the networks rested. Conceivably, the forty-eight pillars of the portico, mentioned earlier by Eupolemus, were used for this purpose. Possibly, however, Eupolemus meant merely that latticed networks created an illusion of a shadow, and this only at sunset.

Using the same technical terminology as the Septuagint in its description of the pillars, Eupolemus records the bronze bells ($κώδωνοι$), but he differs with the biblical tradition as to their number, their weight, and their purpose. I Kings 7:20 knows of 200 pomegranates (*rimmonim*), arranged in two rows of each capital, but this verse is missing in the Greek version; Jer. 52:22 and II Chron. 3:16 each report only a hundred. II Chron. 4:13, however, in asserting that there were 400 bells was the source of Eupolemus' number. But by attributing this number to each of the two networks, Eupolemus doubled them to a total of 800 bells. Each of these bronze bells, according to Eupolemus, weighed a talent. Indirectly, Eupolemus scorns the tradition that made the bells merely a decorative feature. By increasing their number and by attributing to them a weight of 800 talents, Eupolemus stresses their ritual significance. Their unbearable noise kept the birds from flying over the Temple's precinct. What or who propelled the contrivances to make the bells toll, Eupolemus does not say.

Freudenthal believed that Solomon's Temple had a contrivance which protected it from the birds' dung. Eupolemus, says Freudenthal, preserved here an ancient tradition.[81] But there is no doubt that Busink is right in branding Eupolemus' reconstruction of the use of the pillars as sheer fantasy.[82] Busink's assumption, however, that Eupolemus could only have built his account on the Greek version is not necessary. The Septuagint passage that comes under consideration is II Chron. 4:12-13, and here the differences between Eupolemus and the Greek text are considerable.

If Eupolemus' account of a scarecrow in the Solomonic Temple is fanciful, the existence of such a contrivance in the Herodian one is historical. Josephus reports that sharp golden spikes protruded from the Temple's top "to prevent the birds from settling upon and polluting the roof."[83] It is remarkable that Josephus' wording in describing the purpose of the scarecrow is rather similar to that of Eupolemus. As there is no other evidence for a hypothesis that Josephus ever copied from his Hellenistic predecessor, the use of similar

---

81   Freudenthal, *Hell. St.*, 118.
82   Busink, *Tempel*, I, 27.
83   *B.J.*, V, 224:   κατὰ κορυφὴν δὲ χρυσέους ὀβελοὺς ἀνεῖχεν τεθηγμένους, ὡς μή τινι προσκαθεζομένῳ μολύνοιτο τῶν ὀρνέων.

Greek terms is probably coincidental, especially since both writers reflect the same priestly background. The technique used to frighten the birds away, however, is completely different in the two versions. And the practicability of Josephus' device is even more questionable than of Eupolemus'.

A contrivance to keep the birds off the Temple's roof is mentioned also in the Mishnah Middot, edited around A.D. 200, whose topic is presumably the dimensions of the Herodian sanctuary. According to Middot IV, 6, the walls were covered, in sequence, first with a cubit-high paneling, followed by a two-cubit-high drip-receptacle, then a cubit-deep ceiling, upon which a roof railing three cubits was attached, and finally "a cubit-high raven-scarer."[84] A raven-scarer specifically to protect the altar of the tabernacle is also recorded in *Melekhet Hamishkan,*[85] a rabbinic text of uncertain date which appears to be an early medieval collection of second century A.D. tannaitic statements. How this device kept the birds away is not recorded in the old rabbinic texts. Medieval commentators differed as to its description. Some rabbis, similarly too, but independently of Josephus, suggested iron nails protruding from the roofs. Others said discs of human or animal images were used (rather offensive in view of the Second Commandment).[86] Because of Josephus' testimony, there is no doubt that the Mishnah referred to protruding nails.

The medieval rabbinic scholars also differed as to whether Solomon's Temple possessed a raven-scare. The Franco-German tosaphists agreed with Eupolemus.[87] But an old text, perhaps derived from a lost midrash, cited in the tenth century, affirms heatedly that the pre-exilic Temple was without any device to prevent the birds from nesting in the Temple. None was needed, because the birds themselves instinctively sensed the sanctity of the holy precinct and did not dare to fly over it.[88] No such bar existed, however, during the post-exilic Temple, with its supposedly lesser degree of sanctity. Note also that the Psalmist, depicting his longing to return to the holy place, was somewhat envious of the birds:

---

84   See also B.T. Shabbath, 90a; Mo'ed Katan, 9a; Menahot 107a; Arakhin, 6a. Middot was dated by L. Ginzberg, "The Mishnah Tamid," *Journal of Jewish Lore and Philosophy,* I (1919), 33-44, 197-209, 265-95. But there is no reason to place the composition of this tractate before A.D. 70.

85   See Melkhet Hamishkan (ed. Friedmann, Vienna, 1908), XI, p. 71, and note p. 73. (The reference to the scarecrow is attested in the mss. Cf. S. Lieberman, *Hellenism in Jewish Palestine* (New York, The Jewish Theological Seminary of America, 172-75). Rashi, Menahot, 107a. See Maimonides, Commentary on M. Middot IV, 6; Obadiah of Bartenoro, and *Melekhet Shelomoh* to same passage.

86   Nathan of Rome, *Arukh, s.v. khl* (Kohut ed., II, 226a).

87   Tosafot, Shabbath, 90a; Menahot, 107a; Arakhim 6a.

88   *Arukh,* s.v. *khl* (II, 226).

Even the sparrow finds a home,
And the swallow a nest for herself,
Where she may lay her young, O Lord of Hosts (Ps. 84:4 [3]).

Since the scarecrow was not a feature of the Solomonic Temple, what prompted Eupolemus to invent it? Lieberman's suggestion that Eupolemus took it from the Septuagint version of II Chr. 4:13, is not acceptable. There is no basis for Lieberman's view that the Greek translators of the Second Book of Chronicles "ascribed to the Temple of Solomon the existence of a mechanism used in the Egyptian temples of their time."[89] Lieberman here makes the translators responsible for something they never said. There is no hint in the Greek translation that there existed a scarecrow in Solomon's Temple. At the worst they are guilty only of rendering the Hebrew term *rimmon* as bell rather than the usual equivalent of pomegranate. It is also unlikely that Eupolemus' account of the scarecrow in Solomon's Temple was inspired by Egyptian or Hellenistic parallels. For the devices that are attested in ancient texts refer to discs or spikes; tolling bells to chase away birds appears to be recorded only in Eupolemus.[90]

It is conceivable, however, that the post-exilic Temple in Eupolemus' day did possess a device to drive or distract birds from the Holy Temple, and that the one used in Herod's structure was an adaptation of one from Zerubabel's. The odds, however, are that Eupolemus himself invented the contrivance of tolling bells, although he ascribed it to Solomon. Perhaps he was suggesting that it be adopted in the contemporary sanctuary?

The scarecrow is the last item in Eupolemus' account of the construction of the Temple. Many significant features of the sanctuary, such as the details of the holy of holies and the cherubim, are missing. Conceivably, these details were omitted by the excerptors. Possibly, though, Eupolemus never intended to duplicate the fullness of First Kings or Second Chronicles. He evidently mentioned only those features which, in his view, had been misdescribed or overlooked altogether in the ancient tradition. Eupolemus' corrections were not based on better texts of either First Kings or Second Chronicles, or some other ancient text, as claimed by Freudenthal; they were either anachronistic additions or visionary fabrications. In this sense, Eupolemus' account of Solomon's Temple is more related to those of Ezekiel and of the Mishnah Middot than to the fairly historical traditions of the Bible.

If Ezekiel's eschatological Temple was modeled after the pre-exilic structure, and if the Mishnah's futuristic account reflected the Herodian sanctuary, Eupolemus' version of the Solomonic Temple apparently served as

---

89   S. Lieberman, *Hellenism in Jewish Palestine,* 173 f. In fact the attribution of the scarecrow to the tabernacle was simply copied from Mishnah Middot, IV, 6; not from Egyptian temples, as maintained by Lieberman.

90   See Lieberman, *ibid.,* 176, n. 111.

a contrast with that of Zerubabel's. Recently, Yigal Yadin has announced the finding of a "Temple Scroll" in the Judaean desert, describing the dimensions of the "ready-made," "God-built" sanctuary. All these accounts have in common a dissatisfaction with Yahweh's contemporary or recently destroyed dwelling places. For the exilic prophet as for the tannaim of the Mishnah, it would seem, the fact that God allowed the destruction of his holy of holies sufficed to convince them of the need to make major revisions in the design of any future rebuilding of the Temple. The sinfulness of the priests who controlled Jerusalem persuaded the authors of the Qumran scrolls that the polluted temple of their day would one day be replaced by a truly divine temple. Eupolemus' account of the Solomonic structure may reflect the feeling of humiliation prevalent among certain members of Jerusalem's aristocratic priests when the Temple was ravaged by years of bitter wár. Although ostensibly describing the Solomonic structure, Eupolemus may have in fact depicted a futuristic Temple, built of the precious metals garnered from the entire world, protected from even accidental uncleanliness. The description of the past was intended to serve as a vision of the future. In addition to his role as a historian, Eupolemus possibly suggests that he was also a prophet.

Chapter Eight

JERUSALEM

A basic difference between the priestly author of the Book of Chronicles and the royal historian of I Kings is in their attitudes toward secular life. The former depicts the splendor of Solomon's own palace no differently than he does Yahweh's "house." The latter seems categorically oblivious to Solomon's luxury and extravagance, except when it concerns the Temple. The Chronicler had avoided the criticism later voiced by some talmudists that Solomon showed greater diligence in advancing his private glory than he did on behalf of the Lord's.[1] This priestly attitude is also reflected in Eupolemus. After detailing at length Solomon's construction of the Temple, he devotes a bare sentence to the other royal buildings: "He [Solomon] also surrounded the City of Jerusalem with walls, towers, and trenches; and he built for himself a royal palace."[2] Unlike the biblical texts (I Kings 9:15-19) which mention Solomon's fortifications in the country (Hazor, Megiddo, Gezer) and outside (Tadmor), Eupolemus notes only those of the Holy City. Pseudo-Hecataeus, a second century B.C. Jewish historian, asserts that though Palestine had many towns, it had only one fortress.[3] A native of the holy city, Eupolemus, too, it appears could imagine no place other than Jerusalem that the king would have found worth fortifying.

It is nonetheless paradoxical that Eupolemus, who reports that Solomon's empire extended from Phoenicia and Syria in the North to Egypt in the South, makes the same king build walls, trenches and towers. To be sure, I Kings 3:1 and 9:15 mention Solomon's ill-understood Millo, plus a wall that filled "the breach of his father's City of David." Without real evidence,

---

1   See I Kings 6:35-7:1, where it is said that Solomon built the Temple in seven years and his own palace in thirteen; Songs Rabbah, I, 5; Exod. Rabbah, XI, 1; Num. Rabbah, XIV, 1. It should be noted that the rabbinic criticism of Solomon is, citing I Kings 6:35-7:1, turned into praise. The rabbis allude to Prov. 22:29 as an indication that Solomon was more diligent in the construction of the Temple, completing it in seven years, while he tarried thirteen years on the building of the palace. Cf. Pesikta Rabbati, VI (ed. Friedmann, Vienna, 1860), p.23b. See also Josephus, *A.J.*, VIII, 130: the building of the palace lasted 13 years for it was not built with the same industry as the Temple.

2   723 F 2b = *P.E.*, IX, 34, 12: περιβαλεῖν δὲ καὶ τὰ Ἱεροσόλυμα τὴν πόλιν τείχεσι καὶ πύργοις καὶ τάφροις· οἰκοδομῆσαι δὲ καὶ βασίλεια ἑαυτῷ.

3   *C. Apionem* I, 197 = *FGrH*, 164 F 21.

Josephus (*B.J.*, V, 143) claims that David and Solomon had built the most ancient and nearly impregnable walls that were still standing during the days of Vespasian. Nevertheless, Eupolemus' description of Solomon's fortifications seems not only to be contrary to the biblical tradition, but to reflect Hellenistic siege warfare rather than that of the tenth century B.C.[4]

Even more misleading is Eupolemus' explanation of the name Jerusalem: "The shrine was first called the 'Temple of Solomon' (Ἱερὸν Σολομῶνος), but subsequently, on account of the Temple, was falsely named Jerusalem (Ἱερουσαλήμ); by the Greeks however it is correspondingly called (Ἱερο-σόλυμα) Hierosolyma."[5] If we understand him correctly, Eupolemus says that the first syllable of the Hebrew or Aramaic name of Jerusalem—Yeru-, Jeru-, or Jero—was related to the Greek *hiero* meaning Temple; and that -salem equaled S(a)lomon, but that originally this name was restricted to the shrine, i.e. the precinct of the Temple. The name Jerusalem erroneously came to embrace the entire city, hence the equally corrupt Greek form Hierosolyma.

The significance of this passage is not in what Eupolemus has to say about the etymology of Jerusalem, but in its polemical stance. This passage makes it clear, contrary to Freudenthal and Giblet, who claimed that the fragments reflected an attempt to reconcile conflicting biblical traditions, that Eupolemus branded as corrupt accounts which differed from his own. Equally interesting is the fact that Eupolemus faults the Greek version of Jerusalem indirectly. Hierosolyma, according to Eupolemus, is an inexact version of Jerusalem, which was itself corrupt because the nam had originally been restricted to the area of the Temple.

That Eupolemus chose to voice disapproval of older traditions in connection with the derivation of Jerusalem does not appear judicious. But it should be remembered that the ancients—whether the Babylonians, Greeks or Jews—lacked any grasp of historical or scientific etymology. Derivation of words, however, was in antiquity a favorite pasttime, not only for popular enlightenment but also for philosophers and writers of history. And it is not surprising that the peculiar name of the Holy City aroused the curiosity of Jew and pagan alike.[6]

---

4   For a summary of the current archaeological evidence regarding Solomon's fortification of Jerusalem, see Busink, *Tempel*, I, 98-101; B. Mazar, "The Excavations of the Old City of Jerusalem," *Eretz-Israel* IX (1969), 161-74 (Hebrew Section); X (1971), 1-33.

5   723 F 2b = *P.E.*, IX, 34, 13: προσαγορευθῆναι δὲ τὸ ἀνάκτορον πρῶτον μὲν ἱερὸν Σολομῶνος, ὕστερον δὲ παρεφθαρμένως τὴν πόλιν ἀπὸ τοῦ ἱεροῦ Ἱερουσαλὴμ ὀνομασθῆναι, ὑπὸ δὲ τῶν Ἑλλήνων φερωνύμως Ἱεροσόλυμα λέγεσθαι.

6   For examples see Claudius Iolaus' etymology of Gedara (Γάδειρα) as derived from γῆ and δειρά (Claudius, *FGrH* 788 F 3) or his claim that Juda and Idummaea were sons of the Assyrian queen Semiramis (788 F 4; Alexander Polyhistor, *FGrH* 273 F 121).

Men of diverse backgrounds, such as Hecataeus of Abdera, Clearchus of Soli (in Cyprus), Polybius, Ben Sira, Josephus, as well as the Apostolic Fathers and Talmudists, attempted to "explain" the meaning of Jerusalem.[7] Hecataeus, writing about 300 B.C., seems to have been the first to comment on Hierosolyma, finding especially remarkable its first part. It was Moses, according to Hecataeus, who founded the city and built therein the most famous temple (hieron).[8] The polymath Clearchus (250 B.C.) likewise noted the odd name of Hierusaleme ('Ιερουσαλήμη).[9] Polybius, who mentions the city in connection with his report on its occupation by Antiochus III, notes the pun in these words: "And after a short time came over to him [Antiochus] the Jews who live near the Temple (*hieron*) that is called *Hiero*solyma." Cautious lest the play on words would be missed, Polybius adds: "Concerning which we have more to say, especially about the fame of the Temple (hieron)."[10] It is curious, and perhaps not accidental, that both Polybius and Eupolemus use the same verb (προσαγορεύω) to designate Hierosolyma as the name of the Temple, rather than of the city.[11] Unfortunately, Polybius' promised account of the Temple is lost. This makes it impossible to verify a suspicion that the Megapolitan historian of Rome utilized the writings of his contemporary Eupolemus.[12]

But there was also an argument over the second half of the name Hierosolyma. Pseudo-Eupolemus, who apparently antedated Eupolemus, reports that Melchizedek entertained Abraham at "Argarizin, which may be rendered as the Mountain of the Most High."[13] Pseudo-Eupolemus attempts to show that Melchizedek, whom Scripture identified as the priest and the king of Salem (Gen. 14:18), was a native of Salem near Shechem in Samaria,

---

7   The city is recorded in the Egyptian "Execration texts" of the early centuries of the second millenium as Urushalim, and in the Tell el-Amarna letter as Urusalim. It meant, perhaps. the foundation of Shalem. At any rate it is obvious that the ancients preserve no recollection of the history or meaning of the city (cf. M. Burrows, "Jerusalem," in the *Interpreter's Dictionary of the Bible,* II 843 f.).

8   Hecataeus of Abdera, as cited in Diodorus, XL, 3, 3 = *FGrH* 264 F 6 (preserved in Photius, *Bibl.* 244).

9   *C. Apionem*, I, 179 = *FGrH* 737 F 1.

10   *A.J.*, XII, 136, citing Polybius' XVI book, now lost. See next note.

11   Cf. Eupolemus, 723 F 2b = *P.E.*, IX, 34, 13 (see note 5) with Polybius, in *A.J.*, XII, 136: καὶ τῶν Ἰουδαίων οἱ περὶ τὸ ἱερὸν προσαγορευόμενον Ἱεροσόλυμα κατοικοῦντες, came over to Antiochus III (see next note).

12   Incidentally, it is quite likely that Eupolemus' father John (II Macc. 4:11) was one of the Jews who, Polybius says (ibid.), sided with Antiochus III against the Ptolemaic rule of Palestine.

13   Pseudo-Eupolemus, *FGrH*, 724 F 1 = P.E. IX, 17, 5; Freudenthal, *Hellenistische Studien*, 224, 14f. For the spelling of Ἀργαρίζιν see Ἀρμαγέδων (Rev. 16:16).

rather than of Jewish Jerusalem.[14] Pseudo-Eupolemus' departure from the biblical text to interpret "Argarizin" as the Mountain of the Most High makes sense if as a Samaritan he was trying to counter the claim that the name Hierosolyma gave that city a special position as the site of a famous Temple. For the Samaritan shrine at Mount Gerizim was not inferior since its name denotes in Greek the Most High.[15]

Of primary significance for the ancients, however, were the alleged allusions to Hierosolyma in Homer. The *Iliad* records a certain people named Solymi who were said to have been the enemies of the Lycians.[16] Speculation as to the identity of the Solymians gave rise to many intriguing answers, which may be found in the *Odyssey*, Herodotus, and Strabo, among others.[17] Choerilus of Samos, a friend of Herodotus, who wrote a poetic account of the Persian-Greek wars, listed, among the armies of Xerxes that marched against Greece, the inhabitants of the Solymian hills, who he said spoke a language related to Phoenician.[18] Choerilus borrowed the phrase Solymian hills from the *Odyssey*, which couples the inhabitants with the Ethiopians, whom the poet seems to identify with a people of Asia Minor.[19] Josephus, following no doubt a Hellenistic Jewish tradition, takes it for granted that Choerilus was alluding to the fact that Homer referred to the Jews of Hierosolyma.[20] This belief was not restricted to Jewish syncretistic apologists. Lysimachus, an anti-Semitic writer of Alexandria who flourished at the end of the first century B.C., was bothered by the supposed link between Homer's Solyma and Hierosolyma. He suggested that the original name of Jerusalem was not Hierosolyma, but Hierosyla (a temple of robbers).[21] Nonetheless, the link between Homer's Solyma and Hierosolyma was widely accepted in antiquity, as is attested in Tacitus, a writer not specifically friendly to Jews.[22]

14   See Wacholder, "Pseudo-Eupolemus' Two Greek Fragments on the Life of Abraham," *HUCA*, 34 (1963), 83-113, esp. 107 f.

15   For the literary rivalry between Shechem and Jerusalem compare the epic of Theodotus, dealing with the rape of Dinah (*P.E.*, IX, 22 = 732 F 1) and Philo's poems "On Jerusalem" (*P.E.*, IX, 20, 23, 24 = 729 FF 1-3).

16   *Iliad* VI, 184, 204; Pindar, XIII, 90.

17   Od. V, 283, lists the hills of Solyma after mentioning the Ethiopians. Herodotus (I, 173) says that the Solymi were the old Mylyans of Lycia. Strabo repeats here Herodotus (XIV, 3, 10), but misinterpreting Herodotus, he disputes the view that the Solymi were the old Lycians; Strabo adds several other possible solutions to the identity of the Solymi (XII, 3, 27; 8, 5; XIV, 3, 10). Cf. A. von Gutschmid, *Kleine Schriften* (Leipzig, 1893), IV, 471-475.

18   Cited in *C. Apionem*, I, 172-74 = *FGrH* 696 F 34e.

19   See note 17. Choerilus seems to follow the view of his friend Herodotus.

20   It has been frequently noted that, though the quotation is genuine, when he claims that the poet referred to Jerusalem, Josephus misinterprets Choerilus. See Gutschmid, *Kleine Schriften*, IV, 577 f.

21   *C. Apionem*, I, 311, 317 f = Lysimachus, *FGrH*, 621 F 1.

22   Tacitus, *Histories*, V, 2, 5; Stephanus of Byzantium, s.v. "Hierosolyma." See also Martialis, VII, 55; XI, 94; Pausanias, VIII, 16, 1.

In his polemics with the Alexandrian anti-Jewish writers, Josephus scoffs at Lysimachus' suggestion that the Jews changed the original name of *"hierosyla"* because they no longer wished to be known as temple-robbers. Furthemore, Josephus argues, *hierosyla* does not mean the same in the Jewish tongue as it does in Greek.[23] This irrefutable argument loses its acuteness, however, by the fact that in his earlier works Josephus used similar etymologies to glorify the name of the holy city. In his first allusion to this issue, the *Jewish War,* V, 438, records that after Melchizedek, because he "was the first who officiated as priest of God and the first to build a temple *(hieron)*, the city previously called Solyma became Hierosolyma." In this passage Josephus does not explain the etymology of Solyma, presumably because he took it for granted that the knowledgeable reader would link it with the Homeric Solyma.

In the *Jewish Antiquities* (VII, 67), however, Josephus apparently became aware that he had ascribed a Greek meaning to a Canaanite or Hebrew word, but the attempt to clarify only resulted in more confusion: "Thus David, who was the first to drive the Jebusites out of Jerusalem, named the city after himself [City of David]. For at the time of our ancestor Abraham it was called Solyma; but afterwards—some say that Homer also called it Solyma—Hierosolyma. For *hieron* (temple) in the Hebrew tongue means the same as Solyma, designating in Greek security *(aspahlia)*."[24] In this text, as attested in the manuscripts, Josephus appears to argue that *hieron* means in Hebrew *security,* the same as the Greek *asphalia,* which is allegedly the equivalent of *Solyma* or the Hebrew Shalem.

Conta Apionem, I, 174 makes another jump. There Josephus ignores the connection between temple *(hieron)* and *Hiero*solyma. Having defined Solyma as ἀσφαλία (security), Josephus links it with the bituminous lake of the Dead Sea(Ἀσφαλῖτιν λεγομένην λίμνην).

Of the three discussions on this subject, the passage in the *Jewish Antiquities* bears some resemblance to our fragment of Eupolemus. Like Eupolemus, Josephus says that the city was at one time named after a Jewish king.[25]   But the view that Josephus was here dependent on Eupolemus ought to be rejected.[26] Josephus never quite abandons the link between Hierosolyma and the Homeric Solyma, tracing the name of Jerusalem to the

---

23   See note 21; cf. *A.J.* I, 180; VII, 67; *B.J.,* VI, 438.

24   *A.J.,* VII, 67. See Niese's remarks ad locum and in Preface to Vol. I, p. xxxii, as well as Marcus' note ad locum in the edition of Loeb Classical Library. But the Ms. tradition is undoubtedly correct, for the Homeric reference to Jerusalem remains a constant in Josephus (*B.J.* V, 438; *C. Apionem,* I, 174).

25   *A.J.* VII, 67. Cf. Hebrews 7:1-2, for a similar interpretation. The Or. Sibyll. (IV, 115-27), describing the destruction of Jerusalem in the year 70, appears to be the latest ancient source using Solyma as the equivalent of Hierosolyma. Was the omission of the first two syllables, now that the Temple no longer existed, intentional?

26   Cf. Freudenthal, *Hell. St.,* 120, note.

time of Abraham. Eupolemus, however, clearly finds no antecedents earlier than Solomon, and even then only in reference to the Temple's precinct. Moreover, Josephus' report was based in part on II Sam. 5:9: "And David dwelt in the fortress; and he called it the City of David. And David built the city round about from the Millo inward."[27] What Eupolemus says of the history of Jerusalem's name was more applicable to David than to Solomon. There is therfore no reason to assume that Josephus here used Eupolemus. In fact, Josephus' account is pedestrian, while that of Eupolemus is completely original and denies a commonly-held opinion.

Possibly, moreover, Eupolemus' contentious remarks were directed against Hellenizers who had linked Hierosolyma with the Poet. This view is rejected by Eupolemus, who invokes the native form (H)ierusalem to refute the Hellenizers' contention that the old name was Solyma. To invalidate the opponents' view, apparently, it was necessary to find a substitute derivation; hence the invention that Hierosolyma really meant the Temple of Solomon and that the name had originally referred to the precinct of the Temple only.[28]

Another possibility is that Eupolemus' etymology of Hierosolyma was politically inspired. Although Judah Maccabee succeeded to wrest the Temple from the control of the Hellenizers, the fortified part of the city called Acra remained in Syrian hands until 142 B.C.[29] The explanation that Hierosolyma referred only to the Temple may have been intended to neutralize the claims of the Hellenizers that they occupied parts of the Holy City.[30] Eupolemus' fanciful etymology may have been technical and legal rather than practical. This may partially explain Eupolemus' own inconsistency in using the name Hierosolyma in his account of David, despite the fact that he says the name had originated only after Solomon.[31]

THE DEDICATION OF THE TEMPLE

Eupolemus' fragments sum up the fortifications of Jerusalem and the building of the royal palace in a sentence, but contain a paragraph concerning the

27   The City of David (II Sam. 5:7, 9; 9:15, 24; 11:27) is recorded even in Neh. 3:15. See Busink, *Tempel*, I, 89-96.

28   For another explanation of Jerusalem, see Genesis Rabbah, LVI, p. 608 (ed. Theodor-Albeck): God had named it Shalem (Gen. 14:18), but Abraham added the prefix *yir'eh*, "He will see" (Gen. 22:14). Here again it is conceivable that the rabbis intended to counter the derivation based on *hieron*.

29   I Macc. 13:49-52; *A.J.*, XIII, 208; cf. Megillat Ta'anit, V.

30   See E. Bickermann, *Der Gott der Makkabäer* (Berlin, Schocken, 1937), 73-80: "Für die Verfasser der Makkabäerbücher waren die 'Söne der Akra' natürlich abtrünnige. Für die königliche Regierung vertrat aber diese priestliche Aristokratie, die der griechische Sitte verfallen war, nicht ohne grund das Judentum" (p. 80).

31   *P.E.*, IX, 30, 5 = 723 F 2b, p. 673, 14; *P.E.*, IX, 34, 12 = 723 F 2b, p. 676, 20. Perhaps no consistency should be expected from a writer such as Eupolemus, since the name was used loosely.

dedication of the sanctuary: "After having completed the Temple and after having walled the City, he [Solomon] went to Selom (Shiloh) and offered a sacrifice to God, a whole burnt-offering of 1,000 oxen. Then he took the tent and the altar and the vessels, which Moses had made, to Jerusalem and placed them in the house. And the ark and the golden altar and the lampstand and the table and the other vessels he also placed there, as the prophet had ordered him. But he brought a myriad sacrifice to God, 2,000 sheep and 3,500 oxen."[32]

On the surface, this passage appears to illustrate Freudenthal's and Giblet's opinions that, with minor embellishments, Eupolemus essentially paraphrased the Scriptural account.[33] Like Eupolemus, I Kings and II Chronicles report that Solomon brought two sacrifices. The first consisted of 1000 burnt offerings, the same number given by Eupolemus. The second was a peace sacrifice of sheep and oxen offered during the transfer of the holy vessels from the Tabernacle to the Temple, described in I Kings 8:5 as innumerable, but listed in verse 63 as 22,000 oxen and 120,000 sheep. The discrepancies between Eupolemus and the Scriptural tradition were that the latter placed the first sacrifice in Gideon, while the former placed it in Shiloh and that Eupolemus ascribed a considerably smaller number of victims to Solomon's second sacrifice.

A more basic difference between Eupolemus and the Scriptural tradition should not be overlooked. I Kings 3:3-4 and II Chr. 1:2-6 report that the purpose of the first sacrifice was to celebrate the ascent of Solomon to the throne. To emphasize this point, the biblical historians excuse the king for sacrificing on high places (bamot), explaining that Gibeon was the contemporary central shrine since Jerusalem's Temple had not been built yet. The Chronicler adds that the Mosaic tabernacle was located in Gibeon. Neither of these apologies, however, would sanction Solomon's act if Eupolemus' version were correct that the celebration took place during the removal of the tabernacle from the old shrine to the new. Since the Temple was then already built, Solomon committed a sacrilege by sacrificing in Shiloh. This is another example where the Hellenistic author appears to challenge the accuracy of the biblical tradition.

---

32   *P.E.*, IX, 34, 14-16 = 723 F 2b: 14. συντελέσαντα δὲ τὸ ἱερὸν καὶ τὴν πόλιν τειχίσαντα ἐλθεῖν εἰς Σηλὼμ καὶ θυσίαν τῷ θεῷ εἰς ὁλοκάρπωσιν προσαγαγεῖν βοῦς χιλίους. λαβόντα δὲ τὴν σκηνὴν καὶ τὸ θυσιαστήριον καὶ τὰ σκεύη, ἃ ἐποίησε Μωσῆς, εἰς Ἱεροσόλυμα ἐνεγκεῖν καὶ ἐν τῷ οἴκῳ θεῖναι. 15. καὶ τὴν κιβωτὸν δὲ καὶ τὸν βωμὸν τὸν χρυσοῦν καὶ τὴν λυχνίαν καὶ τὴν τράπεζαν καὶ τὰ ἄλλα σκεύη ἐκεῖ καταθέσθαι, καθὼς προστάξαι αὐτῷ τὸν προφήτην. 16. προσαγαγεῖν δὲ τῷ θεῷ θυσίαν μυρίαν, πρόβατα δισχίλια, μόσχους τρισχιλίους πεντακοσίους.

33   Freudenthal, *Hell. St.,* 119-121 and passim; J. Giblet, "Eupolème et l'historiographie du *Judaïsme* hellénistique," *Ephemerides Theologicae Lovanienses,* XXXIX (1963), 539-554, esp. 549 f.

In fact, Eupolemus seems to have prepared a case against the Scriptural tradition at the very beginning of his account of the post-Mosaic period. He reports nothing about Joshua other than that the successor of Moses consecrated a shrine at Shiloh. Here he reiterates the significance of Shiloh.[34] That Eupolemus erred was pointed out by Kuhlmey,[35] citing the Scriptural tradition that the tent was in Solomon's time in Gibeon. Freudenthal countered that since there is no direct biblical statement recording the move of the cultic vessels from Shiloh to Gibeon, Eupolemus must have deduced correctly, that Solomon had brought the tabernacle's furniture from Shiloh.[36] Both I Kings and II Chronicles make clear, however, that the shrine where the Mosaic tabernacle and its furniture were located was Gibeon, not Shiloh.[37] Walter, therefore, posits that Eupolemus identified Gibeon and Shiloh as the same place. This, again, is difficult to accept, since Eupolemus was a native of Judaea.[38] The basic presumption ought to be that Eupolemus was aware that his version differed with the reports in the biblical books.

Why, then, did Eupolemus replace Gibeon with Shiloh? It is stated in the Deuteronomistic texts that before Jerusalem's Temple had been built, the offering of sacrifices outside of the shrines was permitted.[39] Sanctuaries had existed in many high places, including the more important ones in Gilgal, Shiloh, and Gibeon.[40] Such a doctrine may have been exploited by two

34   Josh. 18:1 ff. In *P.E.*, IX, 30, 1 = 723 F 2b, p. 673, 2 it reads $\grave{\varepsilon}\nu\ \Sigma\iota\lambda\omega\hat{\iota}$ IX, 34, 14, $\Sigma\eta\lambda\omega\mu$. The latter spelling is the usual form found in the LXX, e.g., Gen.38:5; Josh. 18:1; I Sam. 1:24.

35   C. Kuhlmey, *Eupolemi Fragmenta* (Berlin, 1840), 94 f., note 19.

36   Freudenthal (*Hell. St.,* 112) notes that the author of Chronicles was the champion of the sanctuary of Gibeon (I Chr. 16:39 f.: 21:29; II Chr. 1:3) in contrast to the historical tradition which located the shrine at Shiloh (I Sam. 1:3; 3:3; 4:3; 14:3; Jer. 7:12; 26:6, 9; Ps. 78:60). Support for the view that Shiloh was the shrine, according to Freudenthal, is also found in Mishnah Megillah, I, 11.

37   I Kings 3-4 faults Solomon for sacrificing on the high places, but asserts that the most important high place was located in Gibeon. Verse 5 reports that the king's dream occurred in Gibeon (I Kings 9:2). The Chronicler (II 1:3-4) defends Solomon against the Deuteronomist's charges, asserting that the Mosaic tabernacle had its abode in Gibeon. Freudenthal's citations (see previous note) refer to the period before David. M. Megillah, I, 11, cites Shiloh as a contrast to Jerusalem, rather than as an indication of exclusiveness. See M. Zebahim, XIV, 4-8, where Gibeon is listed as the tabernacle's shrine prior to its move to Jerusalem, though its gradation in the scale of sanctity was lower than that of Shiloh.

38   Watler, ad locum. Gibeon remained a settled town at least as late as the period of Alexander Jannaeus (J. B. Pritchard, *Hebrew Inscriptions and Stamps from Gibeon*, [University Museum Monographs, University of Pennsylvania Press, 1959]).

39   Deut. 12: 4 ff.; cf. Lev. 26:30; Ps. 78:58.

40   Gilgal—Deut. 11:30; Josh. 9:6; Judg. 3:19; Shiloh—Gen. 49:10; Josh. 18:1 I Sam. 1:3; Gibeon—I Kings 3:3 f. See Pseudo-Philo, *Biblical Antiquities* tr., by M. R. James (Society for Promoting Christian Science, London, 1917), XXII, 8, p. 140: "For until the house of the Lord was built in Jerusalem . . . . the people were not forbidden to

factions in Eupolemus' day. The Hellenizers may have defended the offering of sacrifices throughout the land as an ancient practice sanctioned by such men as Joshua, Samuel and Solomon. It is also conceivable that some Hasidim, members of the pious group, found it desirable, now that the impious had polluted the Temple, that the upbringing of sacrifices outside Jerusalem be sanctioned as it had been in ancient days. Notice also should be taken of Yahweh's temple at Heliopolis in Egypt, built by Onias IV, the former High Priest of Jerusalem's sanctuary.[41]

Eupolemus' emphasis throughout the fragments appears to be upon the centrality and the sanctity of Jerusalem's temple. Furthermore, contrary to the tradition of I Kings and II Chronicles, he seems to deny that there was ever a period in Jewish history when local high places and sanctuaries were sanctioned. Consistent with this view, Eupolemus mentions Joshua's supposed thirty-year long leadership only in connection with his construction of the sanctuary at Shiloh.[42] He seems to maintain that Shiloh remained the only shrine of Yahweh until, by God's command and the angel's guidance, the site of Solomon's temple was chosen.[43]   Just as Joshua, Moses' assistant in the desert, formed a link between the sanctuary of the desert and that of Shiloh, so Eli, the chief priest of Shiloh, according to Eupolemus, was present at Solomon's coronation.[44] It was the alleged historical continuity, rather than historical accuracy, that concerned Eupolemus.[45]

Freudenthal has perceptively noted that Eupolemus splits into two operations his report of the transfer of the holy vessels into the Temple.[46] First, he mentions the tent, the altar, and the vessels; he then lists the ark, the golden altar, the lampstand, and the other vessels, apparently transferred in another move.[47] According to Freudenthal, Eupolemus here displays his

---

offer therein (Galgala) because the Truth and the Demonstration revealed all things in Shilo. And until the ark was set by Solomon in the sanctuary of the Lord they went on sacrificing there unto that day. But Eleazar the son of Aaron the priest of the Lord ministered in Shilo." Cf. Spiro, *Proceedings of the American Academy of Jewish Research*, XX (1952), 349 n. 143.

41   *A.J.* XII, 38 f.; XIII, 62-73, 285; XX, 236; *B.J.,* VII, 421-425; Mishnah Menahot, XIII, 10. Cf. also the temple of Yeb recorded in the Elephantine Aramaic papyri (A.E. Cowley, *Aramaic Papyri of the Fifth Century B.C.* [Oxford, Clarendon Press, 1923]).

42   *P.E.,* IX, 30, 1 = 723 F 2b, p. 673, 2.

43   *P.E.,* IX, 30, 5 = 723 F 2b, p. 673, 11-13.

44   *P.E.,* IX, 30 8 = 723 F 2b, p. 673, 23.

45   Cf. the statement that David was Saul's son (*P.E.,* IX, 30, 2 = 723 F 2b). Gutman, *The Beginnings of Jewish-Hellenistic Literature,* II, 92, maintains that Eupolemus had access to reliable historical traditions that Solomon visited Shiloh after the completion of the Temple, which is rather unlikely.

46   Freudenthal, *Hell. St.,* 112; now followed by Walter, ad locum.

47   *P.E., IX, 34, 14-15* = 723 F 2a, note especially, p. 676, line 27:   καὶ τὰ σκεύη and line 29: καὶ τὰ ἄλλα σκεύη. I Macc. 4:49 lists the items that Judah restored to the Temple in a manner similar to Eupolemus: the lampstand, the altar of incense and the table.

grasp of the relevant Scriptural texts. For I Kings 8:3-4 reports the shipping of the ark, the tent, and the holy vessels from the City of David (Zion) to the Temple; II Chr. 1:3 f. notes that though Yahweh's ark was located in Gibeon, the tent of meeting had been brought into Jerusalem by David. From this Eupolemus deduced that the ark and tent were in two different locations. Furthermore, Eupolemus must have been aware of II Sam. 6:2, which tells that the ark was already located in Jerusalem in the days of David.[48]

Despite its seeming cogency, there is no reason to accept Freudenthal's explanation as to why Eupolemus differentiated between the two types of furniture brought into the Temple. It cannot be assumed that II Chr. 1:3f. (I Kings 3:4) was the basis of Eupolemus' account, since these biblical verses refer to the period of coronation rather than to the bringing of the cultic vessels to the Temple. Moreover, these texts speak, as noted above, of Gibeon rather than of Shiloh, as reported by Eupolemus. The biblical passages which do relate the moving of the holy vessels, such as I Kings 8:1-9 and II Chr. 5:2-9, report that the ark and the tent of meeting were brought from the City of David to the Temple; but Eupolemus says that the tent came among the vessels brought from Gibeon and that the ark was among the sacred objects whose source is not specifically stated. Furthermore, there is no biblical evidence whatsoever for Eupolemus' claim, as interpreted by Freudenthal, that the altars used in the pre-Temple shrines such as Shiloh or Gibeon, were reused in Solomon's sanctuary. It must also be noted that the passages of II Chr. 1:3-4 and I Kings 3:4 indulge in absolving Solomon of the charge of sacrificing in the prohibited high places, a point which, if one follows Freudenthal and Walter, Eupolemus completely missed.

The solution to these problems seems to lie in Eupolemus' own words. Speaking of the tent and altar, Eupolemus concludes with their Mosaic origin; but referring to the ark and the lampstand and the table, he says they were manufactured "as the prophet commanded him."[49] Although the phrase employed here was modeled after the Pentateuchal formula "as the Lord commanded Moses," the prophet, as explained elsewhere in the fragments, was Nathan.[50] In other words, Eupolemus seems to have differentiated between the sacred furnishings which had dated back to the desert and the objects manufactured by Solomon. Except for the secondary passage relating to two tablets of the law, which are the only objects ascribed to Moses, the authors of I Kings and II Chronicles seem to be completely oblivious of the

---

48   Freudenthal, *Hell. St.,* 112.

49   *P.E.,* IX, 34, 14-15 = 723 F 2b, p. 676, lines 27, 29.

50   See *P.E.,* IX, 34 5 = *FGrH* 723 F 2b p. 675, 13; ibid., IX, 30, 6 = ibid. p. 673, 15. The formula "as the Lord commanded Moses," appears more than a dozen times in the account of the tabernacle (Exod. 35:29-40:21).

Mosaic tabernacle.[51] In fact some scholars have questioned whether the account of the desert sanctuary, reported in the Book of Exodus, was available to the royal historian when he recorded Solomon's construction of the Temple.[52] Nevertheless, Eupolemus was fully conscious of the discrepancy between the sanctuaries said to have been built by Moses and by Solomon. Hence Eupolemus informs us that Solomon did not discard the remnants of the less gilded but more ancient abode of Yahweh. He appeased the Mosaic vessels with a thousand whole-burnt offerings, of which no mortal men could partake. But Solomon consecrated his new furnishings with even more lavish offerings. When the victorious Maccabees took possession of the Temple, they dismantled the old altar and placed its stones in Genizah.[53] Solomon must have done the same some eight centuries earlier.[54]

THE EXPENDITURES ON THE TEMPLE

It is characteristic of Eupolemus to invent precise weights and measures to add an impression of authority and verisimilitude. The tendency to exaggerate numbers is present in many ancient writers, but Eupolemus employed it even more than was customary. Occasionally, however, he copied the numbers recorded in a more ancient text, and sometimes even reduced the swollen biblical figures. Eupolemus repeats the account of Solomon's sacrifice of a thousand victims, as is reported in I Kings 3:4; and he reduces the dedicatory sacrifice from 120,000 sheep and 22,000 oxen, as counted in I Kings 8:63 (II Chron. 7:5) to 2,000 and 3,500, respectively.

In contrast with Exod. 38:24-31, which sums up the weights of the metals used in Moses' tabernacle, Scripture does not preserve a summary of Solomon's expenses for the construction of the Temple. As noted elsewhere,[55] Eupolemus modeled his account after the priestly historian, and which the following provides another example: "The total weight of gold

---

51   The only old rabbinic text that deals with this problem seems to be the Beraitha Melekhet Hamishkan. Citing I Kings 8:3, which reports that the elders of Israel carried the ark, and verses 6-9, which relate the placement of the ark in the holy of holies, the Melekhet Hamishkan says: "Although Solomon made the likeness of all the furnishings (of the tabernacle), he did not make the likeness of the ark" (ed. Friedmann, Vienna, 1908), 48; L. Ginzberg, *Genizah Studies in Memory of Doctor Solomon Schechter* (Jewish Theological Seminary, New York, 1928), I, 278 f.

52   P to whom the accounts of the tabernacle are usually ascribed, is dated by some scholars as of the early Persian period. Cf. O. Eissfeldt, *Einleitung in das Alten Testament*[3] (Tübingen, J.C.B. Mohr, 1964), 271-275.

53   I Macc. 4:44-46.

54   See the opinion of Judah ben Lakish (Tosefta, Shekalim, III, 18, p. 212 (ed. Leiberman); Sotah, XIII, 1; Yer. Shekalim, VI, 1, p. 49c; B. Yoma, 53b; Melekhet Hamishkan, VII, p. 49, (ed. Friedmann), who says that Solomon hid the ark in the grounds of the holy of holies.

55   See for example notes 1-3 to Chapter VI, pp. 151-52.

expended on the two pillars and the Temple amounted to 4,600,000 talents; silver for the nails and the other furnishings, 1,232 talénts; bronze for the columns, the laver, and the porch, 18,500 talents."[56] The resemblance to Exod. 38:24-31 consists not only in the fact that a summary of the expenses is reported, but also in the manner of incorporating the more important furnishings with the weights of either gold, silver or bronze.[57] The Chronicler frequently embellished the account of the Temple found in the Book of Kings, but as a rule he repeated mechanically the older and more reliable source.[58] Eupolemus, however, disregarded the Deuteronomistic historian more flagrantly, feeling free to adopt more fully the priestly historiographic tradition.

Although the Chronicler does not detail Solomon's expenses, he does report King David's inventory of metals for the construction of the Temple, which can be compared with Eupolemus' summary of Solomon's expenses:

Talents	I Chr. 22:14	I Chr. 29:4 (7)	Eupolemus	Tabernacle (Exod. 38:2)
gold	100,000	3,700 (5,000 + 10,000 darics)	4,600,000	29 + 730 shekels'
silver	1,000,000	7,000 (10,000)	1,232	100 + 1,775 shekels
bronze	countless	—— (18,000)	18,500	70 + 2,400 shekels
iron	countless	—— (100,000)	——	———

Eupolemus' partial dependence on the Chronicler is suggested in the weight of bronze. Eupolemus' amounts are otherwise independent of any comparable biblical authority, although the fact that iron is missing in the fragments underlines again suggests that Eupolemus was inspired by the Pentateuchal account of the Tabernacle.

The immense total of 4,600,000 gold talents used in the construction of Solomon's temple puzzled Freudenthal, especially because it did not conform to his hypothesis that Eupolemus faithfully followed·theChronicler. Both the amounts and the proportion of gold and silver in Eupolemus are completely out of harmony with his presumed source. Finding also a slight syntactic problem, Freudenthal erased the word *myriads,* thus reducing the weight of the gold from the 4,600,000 talents, as attested in the fragments, to the quite

---

56   *P.E.,* IX, 34, 16 = *FGrH* 723 F 2b, p. 677, 1-4: τὸ δὲ σύμπαν χρυσίον τὸ εἰς τοὺς δύο στύλους καὶ τὸν ναὸν καταχρησθὲν εἶναι τάλαντα μυριάδων νξ´· εἰς δὲ τοὺς ἥλους καὶ τὴν ἄλλην κατασχευὴν ἀργυρίου τάλαντα χίλια διακόσια τριάκοντα δύο· χαλκοῦ δὲ εἰς τοὺς κίονας καὶ τὸν λουτῆρα καὶ τὴν στοὰν τάλαντα μύρια ὀκτακισχίλια πεντήκοντα.

57   The summary of Exod. 38:24-31 does not detail how the gold was expended as it does in regard to the silver and bronze; cf. ibn Ezra's Commentary, ad locum, which explains that it would have required a very long accounting of the gold since it was used to adorn many objects.

58   See W. Rudolph, *Chronikbücher*, pp. X f., 195, 225.

reasonable sum of 460.[59] But, as noted by Mras,[60] the smaller amount runs counter to the main point made by Eupolemus, which was that the wealth of Solomon's Temple was fabulous. It is primarily to emphasize his differences with the Chronicler that Eupolemus seems to have reduced the weight of silver to relative insignificance, thus making gold the basic metal of Solomon's Temple. It may be worth recalling that, in Eupolemus' days, Antiochus IV stripped the Temple's precious adornments and golden vessels, shipping them to the royal treasury in Antioch.[61] Accounts of the ancient days, such as those by Eupolemus, seem to have served as psychological props, recalling a more glorious chapter of the Jewish past. A parallel report is the recently discovered "Copper Scroll," apparently written after the Temple's destruction in the year 70, which catalogues a treasure of some 4,630 talents of gold and silver, primarily the latter.[62] Josephus likewise records that John Hyrcanus (135-104 B.C.) paid 3,000 talents of silver as ransom to Antiochus Sidetes, money he had allegedly dug up in David's tomb where it had been hidden for 1,300 years. In his search for revenue, Herod did not overlook the legendary wealth hidden in the Temple grounds, but it was said that being a wicked man, he could find nothing.[63] Eupolemus' account is part of this legendary tradition of King Solomon's fabulous wealth.[64]

SOLOMON'S GIFTS FOR THE EGYPTIANS AND PHOENICIANS

The expense of 4,600,000 talents of gold on the Temple, according to Eupolemus, left a huge surplus. It was distributed to the 160,000 Egyptian and Phoenician slaves who, as will be recalled, had been sent by Solomon's client kings to construct the Temple. A fictional letter from Vaphres, the king of Egypt, says Eupolemus requested that the men's wages be paid punctually and that they be sent home promptly upon the completion of their task.[65] Now Eupolemus reports that the king indeed magnanimously honored this plea: "Then Solomon sent back the Egyptians and the Phoenicians to their respective homes, and he gave each ten golden shekels (a

---

59   That $\tau\acute{\alpha}\lambda\alpha\nu\tau\alpha$ is followed by $\mu\nu\rho\iota\acute{\alpha}\delta\omega\nu$ in the genitive (Freudenthal, *Hell. St.,* 112).

60   See Mras, in *P.E.,* I, p. 542, 15, app. crit., commenting upon Freudenthal, ibid., 211.

61   I Macc. 1:21-23; cf. II Macc. 3:6 ff.

62   Cf. now the so-called Copper Scroll, found among the Dead Sea texts: J. T. Milik, "Le rouleau de cuivre provenant de la grotte 3Q (3Q15)," in *Discoveries in the Judaean Desert of Jordan III* (Oxford, Clarendon Press, 1962), 199-317, esp. 280 ff. Whether the author of 3Q15 knew of Eupolemus' account of Solomon's Temple is an interesting question. Cf. also the description of New Jerusalem, *Discoveries,* III, 184-93.

63   *B.J.,* I, 61; *A.J.,* VII, 393; XIII, 249; XVI, 179. Josephus, it should be noted, was a firm believer in the existence of these treasurers.

64   Was he also their originator?

65   *P.E.,* IX, 32, 1 = 723 F 2b.

shekel equals a talent). And to Vaphres, the king of Egypt, he sent 10,000 *metretes* of oil, 1,000 *artabae* of dates, 100 barrels of honey, and spices. But to Suron, he sent to Tyre the golden pillar, which was set up in Tyre to the temple of Zeus."[66]

The gold distributed to the foreign laborers weighed 160,000 shekels or talents. But it is unlikely that Eupolemus actually meant that a golden shekel equaled a talent of the same metal. A talent was, in fact, the equivalent of 3,600 or, later, 3,000 shekels. Even granting his extravagance, it is inconceivable that Eupolemus would have been so inaccurate. Eupolemus may have meant to say drachma or some similar coin, instead of talent, as handed down in the manuscripts.[67] Elsewhere, Eupolemus seems to set realistic equivalents for weights and measures. Possibly, he should be given the benefit of the doubt here. If, however, Eupolemus did equate the talent with the shekel, he may have interpreted the "holy shekel," recorded in the Pentateuch, as more valuable than the common one.[68] But there is no reason to assume that the "holy shekel" approximated a talent in value.

There is no biblical source whatsoever for Eupolemus' claim that Egypt dispatched workers for the construction of the Temple. But as has been noted, a midrashic tale indeed relates that the workers sent by Pharoah were on the verge of death when King Solomon returned them immediately with burial garments as presents.[69] There is not even a hint in the rabbinic texts of gifts from the Hebrew king to the king of Egypt. I Kings 5:25-26, however, reports that, in exchange for the cedar wood, Solomon supplied the Tyrian king with 20,000 cors of wheat and 20 (LXX: 20,000) cors of beaten oil annually. Of this nothing is said in the fragments. But Eupolemus claims that Solomon presented Vaphres of Egypt with 10,000 measures of oil, 1,000 artabae of dates, and 100 barrels of honey, in addition to spices. Incidentally, it is notable that in his account of the provisioning of the Temple's workers, Hebrew measures are stressed. But the weights and measures of the gifts sent to Egypt are strictly Hellenistic. The reason may be that the former were inspired by Hebrew texts, while the latter were Eupolemus' own invention.

---

66   *P.E.*, IX, 34, 17=723 F 2b: ἀποπέμψαι δὲ τὸν Σολομῶνα καὶ τοὺς Αἰγυπτίους καὶ τοὺς Φοίνικας, ἑκάστους εἰς τὴν ἑαυτῶν, ἑκάστῳ χρυσοῦ σίκλους δόντα δέκα· τὸ δὲ τάλαντον εἶναι σίκλον. καὶ τῷ μὲν Αἰγύπτου βασιλεῖ Οὐαφρῇ ἐλαίου μετρητὰς μυρίους, φοινικοβαλάνων ἀρτάβας χιλίας, μέλιτος δὲ ἀγγεῖνα ἑκατὸν καὶ ἀρώματα πέμψαι·. See below note 70.

67   LXX Exod. 39:3 gives 1 drachma = 1/2 of a holy shekel; cf. *A.J.*, III, 195, where a shekel = 4 drachmae; *A.J.*, XVIII, 312.

68   See Exod. 30:13; Lev. 5:15; Num. 3:47.

69   Pesikta d'Rab Kahana, *Parah*, p. 60 (ed. B. Mandelbaum).

YAHWEH'S GOLD IN ZEUS' TEMPLE

THEOPHILUS

Eupolemus' approach to history bears greater resemblance to the style of the priestly authors of the Old Testament than to that of Hellenistic historiography. Indeed, many passages of the fragments may be cited as products of a pietistic tendency. As has been shown, Eupolemus cleansed his history from any allusion to Solomon's importation of foreign gods for the king's harem. The final sentence of Fragment Two is therefore most surprising: "But to Suron he [Solomon] sent a pillar of gold which was set up in Tyre in the temple of Zeus."[70]

Eupolemus' words relating to the fate of the Temple's surplus gold may be understood to mean either that Solomon himself in presenting the gift to Hiram knew that it would be dedicated to Zeus, or that the Israelite king could not be held accountable for the use of the gold in Tyre. The second alternative is somewhat more plausible in the Greek text. But the fact that Eupolemus found it worth mentioning suggests that he approved Solomon's action—or at least felt no disapproval. In either case, the story of Yahweh's gold in Zeus' temple is a syncretistic passage in the remnants of Eupolemus. Because the fragments are otherwise free of pagan tendencies, the possibility that the last sentence of Fragment Two was an addition by another hand should not be excluded altogether.

The ambiguity in Eupolemus' reference to Zeus is also found in Theophilus, cited by Alexander Polyhistor to amplify Eupolemus' ambiguous words: "Theophilus says that Solomon sent the superfluous gold to the king of Tyre, but he constructed a life-size likeness of his daughter, and he adorned the golden pillar of the statue with a covering."[71] It is not inconceivable that the last words "which was set up at Tyre in the temple of Zeus," attributed by Alexander Polyhistor to Eupolemus, in fact merely anticipate the excerptor's quotation from Theophilus. It is safer, however, to proceed with the assumption that the attested text correctly transmitted Eupolemus' views. According to Alexander Polyhistor, Eupolemus and Theophilus say that Solomon's gift was used to adorn a Tyrian monument. The difference between the two is that Eupolemus makes no allusion to the statue of Hiram's daughter mentioned by Theophilus. There is no doubt that some Judaeans would have been offended by these accounts which reported that offerings made to Yahweh were destined for idolatrous purposes.

---

70   *P.E.*, IX, 34,18 = 723 F 2b: τῷ δὲ Σούρωνι εἰς Τύρον πέμψαι τὸν χρυσοῦν κίονα, τὸν ἐν Τύρῳ ἀνακείμενον ἐν τῷ ἱερῷ τοῦ Διός.

71   Theophilus, cited in *P.E.*, IX, 34, 19 = *FGrH* 733 F 1: Θεόφιλος δέ φησι τὸν περισσεύσαντα χρυσὸν τὸν Σολομῶνα τῷ Τυρίων βασιλεῖ πέμψαι·τὸν δὲ εἰκόνα τῆς θυγατρὸς ζῷον ὁλοσώματον κατασκευάσαι, καὶ ἔλυτρον τῷ ἀνδριάντι τὸν χρυσοῦν κίονα περιθεῖναι.

Little is known of Theophilus,[72] but nothing in Eupolemus has prepared the reader for such a flagrant contradiction of Scripture. According to I Kings 9:11-13, Solomon presented Hiram with twenty Galilean towns, which the Tyrian king haughtily declined. Verse 14 adds that Hiram presented King Solomon with a gift of 120 talents of gold. To the author of Chronicles, however, it seemed unbelievable that Solomon would have offered portions of the Holy Land to an uncircumcized. II Chr. 8:2 reports instead (it would seem illogically) that the Galilean towns were Hiram's gift to Solomon, wherein the Israelites settled.[73] Talmudic writers were somewhat fairer to the king of Tyre. They relate that Hiram was one of the handful of mortals who was permitted to enter paradise alive as a reward for his share in the construction of the Temple, but was driven out because of his artistic pride and overbearing character.[74] There is nothing in the Jewish tradition about Solomon's strange gift to Hiram mentioned in Eupolemus.

---

72   See *Contra Apionem,* I, 216, where Josephus lists heathen historians who mention Jews; Theophilus heads the list, followed by Theodotus, Mnaseas, Aristophanes, Hermogenes, Euhemerus, Conon, and Zopyrion. Th. Reinach, *Oeuvres complétes de Flavius Josèphe,* VII (Paris, 1902), p. 40 n. 2, identifies Theophilus, mentioned in Josephus, with our author. Jacoby, *FGrH* 733 T 1, is not certain whether the two should be considered the same man. This doubt is justified because of the combination of authors listed by Josephus: Theodotus, who is sometimes identified with the author of an epic on Shechem *(FGrH* 732 F 1; see below, chapter XI); Mnaseas of Patara (?), the third and second century mythographer (cf. *C. Apionem,* II, 112-14); Aristophanes is probably not the famous librarian of Alexandria, as Thackeray notes (in L.C.L. editions of Josephus); but Euhemerus is the famous rationalizer of Greek myths; Conon is a first century mythographer, in the court of Archelaus of Cappadocia, whose daughter (Glaphyra) married Herod's son (Alexander) in 14 B.C.; Zopyrion was a lexicographer. whose extensive dictionary of the Greek language was completed by his pupil Pamphilus of Alexandria (50 B.C.). As to Hermogenes, Jacoby suggests Hermogenes of Tarsus   *(FGrH* 851 T 1; IIIC, p. 936, 10, 19), the author of a book on Coile-Syria; but it is impossible that Josephus would have quoted a writer who flourished in A.D. 161-80. Th. Reinach's suggestion that Josephus referred to Hermogenes, the author of a book on Phrygia *(FGrH* 795), who had alluded to Noah's ark (795 F 2), is still the most reasonable guess.

Since Josephus lists Theophilus among the Greek mythographers and lexicographers *(C. Apionem,* I, 216), instead of among the Jewish writers (I, 218), it would seem to follow that he was regarded as a heathen. But the fragment found in Alexander Polyhistor suggests that Theophilus was a Jew, since it credits Tyre's glory to Solomon. Incidentally, it is not correct to say, as claimed by Reinach and repeated by Thackeray, that Josephus' list in *Contra Apionem,* I, 216, was taken from Alexander Polyhistor, since most of these writers were apparently not quoted by Alexander Polyhistor *(FGrH* 273). Neither is the style of citing, found in Josephus, that of his pagan predecessor.

73   Josephus' summary of I Kings 9:11-15, though somewhat exaggerated, seems to be fair *(A.J.,* VIII, 141-143). The alterations of the Chronicler (cf. however W. Rudolph, *Chronikbücher,* p. 219) and those of Eupolemus appear to reflect an anti-Phoenician tendency, evident also elsewhere in Eupolemus' fragments (see above).

74   Gen. Rabbah, XCVI, 4 (p. 1197); Tanhuma, Va'era, 8 (Buber); Exod. Rabbah, VIII, 2. Cf. L. Ginzberg, *The Legends of the Jews* (Philadelphia, The Jewish Publication Society, 1928), IV, 155.

Heathen sources, however, may explain the basis for Eupolemus' and Theophilus' reported link between the temple of Yahweh in Jerusalem and that of Zeus in Tyre. Dius, a Graeco-Phoenician historian known only through Josephus, described Hiram as the great builder of Tyre, noting particularly his enlargement of the city by uniting it through a causeway with the temple of the Olympian Zeus, "which he adorned with offerings of gold."[75] A parallel account by Menander of Ephesus, apparently a pupil of Eratosthenes (275-194 B.C.) is even more specific. Hiram "dedicated the golden pillar to the temple of Zeus."[76] To this Eupolemus seems to add that Hiram's gold for Zeus came from Solomon's inexhaustible wealth.[77]

Eupolemus' use of the Graeco-Phoenician historians is significant. This is the first instance where it can be shown that Jewish Hellenistic writers supplemented their paraphrasing of the Bible with heathen sources. Even more notable is the fact that Eupolemus stumbled upon reliable texts. For there is no doubt, as shown by Movers,[78] that Dius and Menander here independently followed genuine Phoenician traditions.[79] The quality of these traditions is comparable to that of the Book of Kings, which was based on royal records. The historiographic methods of the fragments of Dius and Menander, it would seem, reflect the common cultural heritage of Phoenicia and the Hebrew monarchy. Both the Phoenician and Hebrew records stress the architectural innovations, the construction of temples, the hauling of cedar from Mount Libanus, and the wealth and wisdom of the respective kings. Does it follow that Eupolemus and Theophilus have preserved historical traditions from Phoenician sources?

Here the evidence is not clear-cut. Contrary to Josephus' claims,[80] his own verbatim citations do not justify the inference that Menander and Dius alluded to Solomon's temple. The Phoenician historians, however, do report that the "tyrant" of Jerusalem excelled in composing riddles for which Hiram

---

75   Dius in *C. Apionem*, I, 113 = *A.J.*, VIII, 147 = *FGrH* 785 F 1. Cf. Herodotus (II, 44) who reports that he saw in Tyre two pillers in front of Heracles' temple.

76   Menader in *Contra Apionem*, I, 118 = *A.J.*, VIII, 145 = *FGrH* 783 F 1. According to *Suda* (783 T 1), Menander was the pupil of Eratosthenes, which would mean that Menander flourished about 200 B.C.

77   723 F 2b = *P.E.*, IX, 34, 18.

78   Movers, *Die Phönizier*. II, 1 (Berlin, 1849), 138 ff.; Gutschmid, *Kleine Schriften*, IV, 471, citing J. J. Scaliger, *De emendations temporum* (Paris, 1583), Proleg. 38. Cf. W. F. Albright, "The New Assyro-Tyriand Synchronisms and the Chronology of Tyre," in *Melanges Isidore Lévy* (Annuaire de l'Institute de Philologie et d'Histoire Orientales et Slaves. Université Libre de Bruxelles, 1955), 1-9.

79   Josephus says that Menander translated ancient Phoenician texts into Greek (*A.J.*, VIII, 144; IX, 283; *C. Apionem*, I, 116 = *FGrH* 783 T 3).

80   See *C. Apionem*, I, 109, in Thackeray's translation: "There was good reason why the erection of our temple should be mentioned in their (Phoenicians') records for Hirom, king of Tyre, was a friend of our king Solomon."

at first was fined for failing to solve; but the situation was reversed when a certain Abdemon exceeded Solomon's wit. The stress is on the rivalry rather than on the cooperation between the two kings.[81] These fragments make unlikely Josephus' assertion that the erection of the temple in Jerusalem was recorded in Phoenician texts. Eupolemus' contention that Hiram (Suron) erected a golden pillar to Zeus is attested in Menander.[82] Not attested, however, remains Eupolemus' statement that the gold came from the surplus of Jerusalem's temple.

On balance it would seem rather unlikely that either Menander or Dius alluded to the supposed foreign origin of the pillars of Zeus. For in describing Hiram's architectural genius, the Phoenician historians appear to have intended to correct Herodotus. The Father of History relates that he visited the ancient shrines of Tyre to determine whether Heracles' ancestry was human or divine. There he marvelled at the two pillars, one of emerald and one of gold, standing beside the Temple of Heracles (Melqart), which the native priests boasted was 2,300 years old, contemporaneous with the supposed foundation of Tyre.[83] This eyewitness report appears to be disputed by Dius and Menander. Zeus (Baal), not Heracles (Melqart), was the senior Tyrian deity. In fact, according to Menander, Hiram (969-935) erected Heracles' temple and also built the marvelous pillars in front of Zeus' sanctuary. It is rather unlikely that after having gone out of his way to depict the antiquity of Zeus, Menader would have admitted that the pillars in front of his temple were but a foreign gift. Eupolemus, one may suspect, in turn "corrects" Menander, stating that the golden pillars were of Solomonic origin.

References by the Church Fathers, however, appear to contradict the conclusion that Menander made no mention of the Temple and that his allusions to Solomon were rather condescending. The second century Christian apologist Tatian the Syrian cites Laetus, who supposedly translated the Phoenician works of Theodotus, Hypsicrates, and Mochus into Greek, and who wrote the lives of the ancient Phoenician philosophers.[84] Says Tatian: "In histories of the above mentioned authors it is shown that the abduction

81   Menander, *FGrH* 783 F 1 = *C. Apionem,* I, 119; *A.J.,* VIII, 148 f.; Dius, 785 F 1 = *C. Apionem,* I, 114; *A.J.,* VIII, 146.

82   783 F 1 (see previous note).

83   Herod, II, 44. Menander dated the foundation of Tyre 155 years before the accession of Hiram (*C. Apionem,* I, 126 = 783 F 1); cf. Albright, cited in note 78.

84   On Laetus, see Tatian, *Ad Graec.,* 37. = *FGrH* 784 T 1; R. Laqueur, "Laitos," *R.E.,* XIII (1924), 517 f., who accepts the tradition that Mochus, Theodotus, and Hypsicrates were indeed ancient Phoenician historians. Jacoby, "Hypsikrates," *R.E.,* IX (1914), follows the conventional view, no doubt rightly, that these authors are pseudonymous, like Sanchuniathon, whose existence was invented by Philo of Byblos (*FGrH* 790). On Mochus, see Diels-Kranz, *Die Fragmente der Vorsokratiker*[6] II, 98, 18-26.

of Europa occurred under one of these kings; that Menelaus came to Phoenicia when Chiramus was king, who gave his daughter into marriage to Solomon the king of the Jews, and who supplied wood and all kinds of trees for the building of (Solomon's) Temple. Menander of Pergamus made mention about the same matter."[85] Tatian's last sentence might be interpreted to mean that Menander's account of Solomon virtually repeated that of Laetus. In fact, Clement of Alexandria, whose knowledge of the Phoenician historians was here derived from Tatian, understood this to be the case: "Hiram gave his daughter to Solomon at the time when Menelaus came to Phoenicia after the fall of Troy, as Menander of Pergamum and Laetus report in their Phoenician histories."[86] Certainly, in Tatian's summary, Laetus was rather proud of Hiram's participation in the construction of Jerusalem's Temple and of Solomon's marriage to the Phoenician princess.

There are several differences between Josephus' quotation from Menander dealing with Solomon and that of Tatian: a) according to the former Hiram became king of Tyre in 970/69 B.C., whereas the latter dates him soon after the fall of Troy, evidently in 1184 B.C.; b) Menander mentioned Hiram's bringing of the cedar for the temple of Zeus, according to Josephus, not for Yahweh's temple, as reported by Laetus; and c) Josephus knew of no report by Menander of Solomon's marriage to Hiram's daughter.[87] A rereading of Tatian, however, shows that Clement appears to have misinterpreted the Syrian churchman. The latter attributed a) and b) to Laetus, adding, no doubt on the basis of Josephus, that Menander likewise alluded to Hiram and Solomon. Clement mistakenly makes Tatian say that Menander's account was identical to that of Laetus. In reality, Tatian was merely summing up in order to bolster his argument that the Phoenician historians Laetus and Menander linked Solomon with the Tyrian king Hiram.

There remains the question as to which of the two diverging reports is reliable—that of Menander or that of Laetus? Menander's passage as found in Josephus is a verbatim quotation, while that of Laetus is Tatian's brief summary. That Josephus cited here more or less accurately is also made clear by the fact that his citation does not support his own basic contention that Menander had alluded to the Temple.[88] Moreover, Laetus apparently was one of those Phoenician writers under whose name Phoenician records were fabricated. He claimed that men with such Hellenistic names as Theodotus and Hypsicrates, in addition to Mochus, wrote Phoenician history before the

85   Tatian, *Ad. Graec.*, 37 = 784 F 1a.
86   Clement, *Strom.*, I, 114, 2 = 784 F 1b.
87   Cf. Gutschmid, *Kleine Schriften*, IV, 488 f.
88   See previous note and note 84.

fall of Troy.[89] This seems to diverge with Menander's report which, as has
been noted, dated Solomon in the tenth century B.C. Thus the conclusion is
inescapable that there is no reason to doubt the veracity of Menander as
reported in Josephus. Laetus' account of Hiram and Solomon, as reported in
Tatian, however, appears to be a product of Graeco-Phoenician writers who
embellished histories with Jewish lore in order to make their tales believable.
Laetus (Mochus) wrote at the latest in the beginning of the second century
B.C., but he belongs to a long tradition of Phoenician writers who dressed the
native lore with a Hellenistic garb, attributing it to the Trojan period. It is
remarkable that the relationship between Menander and Laetus parallels that
between the First Book of Kings and the Graeco-Jewish writers, such as
Eupolemus and Theophilus. Laetus' assertion that Solomon had married
Hiram's daughter seems to have been the basis for Theophilus' claim that
Yahweh's gold was used to make a statue of this Phoenician princess. There is
no reason, however, to assume that I Kings 11:1, which reports that Solomon
imported foreign women for his harem, including some from Sidon, served as
the basis for our story.

Conceivably, this Theophilus, about whom nothing is known, is identical
with Theodotus, whose name has been corruptly handed down, and who
according to Tatian, was one of the three Phoenician sources of Laetus. If so,
Theophilus (or Theodotus) antedates Laetus, whose work was cited by
Posidonius (c. 135-50 B.C). The presumption that Theophilus (or Theodotus)
was a Jew would also explain why Laetus' account was flattering to Solomon.
Chronological considerations, however, make the sequence Menander,
Eupolemus, Theophilus, Laetus unlikely. A more reasonable conjecture
would seem to be that, building upon Menander's report of Hiram's pillars of
Zeus Olympius' (Baal) temple, Eupolemus invented their Solomonic origin,
which Theophilus fused with Laetus' account of Solomon. As to the
historicity of the story, some scholars give it credence, citing I Kings 11:1 as
proof.[90] There is no doubt, however, that other than those of Menander and
Dius, whose accounts were based on native royal records, the Hellenistic
accounts of Hiram and Solomon are pure fiction. Incidentally, medieval
legends claim that Solomon's duaghter married a bastard, and to the chagrin
of her father this was announced to him by the eagles in the presence of

---

89   Posidonius (in Strabo, XVI, 2, 24 = *FGrH* 87 F 67) identifies Mochus as a
Sidonian from before the Trojan perios (Mochus, 784 F 6). Tatian (*Ad Graec.* 37 = 784
F 1) says that Solomon married Hiram's daughter at about the Trojan times; Clement
(*Strom.* I, 114, 2), after the fall of Troy. Cf. Philo of Byblos on Sanchuniathon: "a most
ancient man, of the Trojan times" (*P.E.* I, 9, 19 = 790 F 1).

90   See Movers, *Die Phönizier,* II, 1, pp. 336 f.; Gutman, *The Beginnings of
Jewish-Hellenistic Literature* [in Hebrew] , II, 94.

Hiram.[91] Eupolemus, however, uses the detail of Solomon's disposition of the gold, whatever the source, to support his contention that Solomon's wealth was inexhaustible.

Eupolemus and Theophilus fused Hellenistic accounts of Tyrian history with biblical traditions. But instead of reproducing these sources more or less accurately, they embellished them, with details such as Solomon's marriage to Hiram's daughter, or the assistance that the supposed Median king Astibares offered to Nebuchadnezzar's conquest of Jerusalem.

It should be noted, moreover, that there appears to have been a parallel development of Hellenistic Jewish and Hellenistic Phoenician historiography. Tyre and Gaza were among the few Eastern cities which bitterly defended the Persian empire against Alexander. In the ensuing centuries the victory of Hellas seemed to presage the death of the native Eastern cultures. But the scribes and priests of Babylon, Jerusalem, and Egypt resisted the Greek encroachments. In Babylon, during the reign of the early Seleucids, there seems to have been a revival of cuneiform scientific and literary productivity, with a similar thriving of Aramaic and Hebrew writings in Phoenicia and Judaea. The Macedonian rulers, however, were unlike any others who had conquered the East. To meet the challenge of this dynamic civilization, native priests, such as Manetho of Sebennystos and Berossus of Babylon, attempted to interpret the native lore in the Greek tongue. In Phoenicia and in Judaea, two trends seem to have developed: a) the more or less faithful reproduction of native records and texts in Greek translation; and b) the manufacturing of native records which claimed that the barbarians had antedated or invented Greek science and philosophy. This claim was justified in some disciplines, such as astronomy and mathematics. Among the Jews the first trend is represented by the Septuagint and the second by the fragments of Seven Verses, Eupolemus, and Artapanus. In Phoenicia, Menander and Dius preserve some of what seems to have belonged to the first tendency, as Laetus (Mochus), Theodotus, Hypsicrates, and Sanchuniathon do of the second.

SHIELDS

SOLOMON'S DEATH

The mention of Solomon's gift to Suron formally ends Fragment Two. In fact, however, after a brief interruption to quote from Theophilus, Eupolemus' account continues with what is now labeled Fragment Three: "Eupolemus says that Solomon made also 1,000 golden shields, each of which weighed 500 (shekels?) gold. But he lived fifty-two years, forty of

91   See Ginzberg, *Legends of the Jews,* VI, 303 n. 100; Tanhuma (ed. Buber, Introduction; Wilno, 1885), p. 136. For other rabbinic legends dealing with Hiram, see note 74; *Ozar Midrashim,* ed. Eisenstein (New York, 1915), I, 179a-180b.

which he reigned in peace."[92] In Scripture, the making of the shields is merely one item in the glowing description of the Solomonic palace, inserted between the story of the Queen of Sheba's visit and the account of Solomon's ivory throne.[93] It is curious that in the fabulous depiction of Solomon's splendor, Eupolemus chose to record only the decorative shields. Perhaps, though, the responsibility for this banal selection lies with the excerptor— Alexander Polyhistor. Eupolemus' account of the Temple remains to a large extent, but of his account of Solomon's reign little has survived.

The contents of Fragment Three conform to the pattern demonstrated in Fragment Two. It can be defined, on the one hand, as a close kinship with Scripture and, on the other hand, as a challenge to the accuracy of the biblical tradition. The Hebrew texts list 500 (LXX: 600) shields of two vintages—200 (Kingdoms LXX: 300) shields (צנה , δόρατα, θυρεοί) each of which weighed 600 (LXX: 300) gold shekels and 300 shields (מגן , ὅπλα, ἀσπιδα), each weighing 300 shekels. Eupolemus, however, counted 1,000 shields, each of 500 pieces of gold, presumably shekels. His departure from the biblical version seems pointless here, primarily because the context is missing. Freudenthal suggested that the number of shields was based upon a work Eupolemus regarded as Solomonic, the Song of Songs 4:4:[94]

> Your neck is like the tower of David,
> built upon courses of stone
> whereupon hang a thousand bucklers,
> all of them shields of warriors.

Freudenthal's explanation, although attractive, does not explain why Eupolemus altered the weights from the biblical tradition.[95] Moreover, his departures from Scriptural texts reflect design rather than a gleaning of obscure references. Eupolemus' statement that Solomon died at the age of fifty-two is part of this design.[96]

The concluding remark, that Solomon's forty-year reign was peaceful, is consistent with the biblical tradition, although it is stated explicitly only in Eupolemus.[97] It is also consistent with Eupolemus' own insistence that the Temple could not have been built by David because of the blood he had spilled in his many years of warfare. This remark also sums up the spirit in

---

92 *P.E.*, IX, 34, 20= 723 F 3:Ποιῆσαι δέ φησιν ὁ Εὐπόλεμος τὸν Σολομῶνα καὶ ἀσπίδας χρυσᾶς χιλίας, ὧν ἑκάστην πεντακοσίων εἶναι χρυσῶν. βιῶσαι δὲ αὐτὸν ἔτη πεντήκοντα δύο, ὧν ἐν εἰρήνῃ βασιλεῦσαι ἔτη μ΄.

93 I Kings 10:16 f. = II Chr. 9:15 f.

94 Freudenthal, *Hell. St.*, 114.

95 Eupolemus' wording makes it clear that he was dependent here on the historical books of Scripture, for there seems to be no echo from the Song of Songs in Eupolemus' fragments.

96 For the chronological problems, see above, pp. 106-11.

97 Cf. I Kings 5:4f.; III Kingdoms 2:46g.

which Eupolemus viewed the reign of Solomon. For Eupolemus the Temple, with its site chosen by an angel, its fabulous wealth, and its Mosaic furnishings, represented the focus of Jewish history—the special relationship between Yahweh and Israel—where the deity dwells among man. Although never mentioned, it is nevertheless clear to Eupolemus that a people whose political, economic, and religious center was the Temple must have priests as its ruling class. And if the ideals implied in our fragments mirror those shared by the priests as a whole, it would seem to be a class which placed high values on the immense material wealth of the Temple rather than upon its spiritual riches.

Chapter Nine

THE FALL OF JERUSALEM

Paradoxically, Eupolemus' description of the fabulously gilded Temple is followed by a fragment recording its destruction.[1] The opening sentence of this fragment answers the question as to why Yahweh allowed, indeed ordered, the heathens to destroy his House: "Then Jonachim (Ἰωναχείμ) became king, during whose reign the Prophet Jeremiah prophesied. Sent by God, he caught the Jews sacrificing to the golden idol named Baal."[2] The peculiar spelling of the king's name, repeated three times, adds to the problem of identification.[3] Eupolemus may have referred either to Jehoiakim, the king of Judah from 609 to 598, or to Jehoiachin (also known as Jeconiah), his successor from December 598 to March 597.[4] Some indications suggest that Eupolemus meant the former; others, the latter; still others suggest that he was referring to Zedekiah. Certainly, the collision between king and prophet, according to the Book of Jeremiah, historically alludes to Jehoiakim: "Therefore thus the Lord said concerning Jehoiakim the son of Josiah, king of Judah:

They shall not lament for him, saying
'Ah my brother' or 'Ah my sister' ...
With the burial of an ass he shall be buried,
dragged and cast forth beyond the gates of Jerusalem (Jer. 22:18 f.)[5]

---

1 Eusebius (*P.E.*, IX, 39, 1 = *FGrH* 723 F 5) introduces this excerpt: "In addition to this (the description of Jerusalem), Alexander Polyhistor makes mention of Jeremiah's prophecy, and it would be most illogical for us to leave it unnoticed, let this also be put down." The fact that Eupolemus is not mentioned has prompted some editors to place a question mark in regard to Eupolemus' authorship of this fragment. But all the Manuscripts (BION) contain the heading: "Eupolemus' On the Prophecy of Jeremiah, Same" (ὁμοίως, not in B), which in addition to the stylistic resemblance (Freudenthal, *Hell. St.*, 208 f.; Walter, ad locum), prove conclusively Eupolemus' origin.

2 *P.E.*, IX, 39, 2 = *FGrH*, 723 F 5 = Walter, F 4 (see previous note):   ΕΥΠΟ-ΛΕΜΟΥ ΠΕΡΙ ΙΕΡΕΜΙΟΥ ΤΟΥ ΠΡΟΦΗΤΟΥ ΟΜΟΙΩΣ

Εἶτα Ἰωναχείμ· ἐπὶ τούτου προφητεῦσαι Ἰερεμίαν τὸν προφήτην. τοῦτον ὑπὸ τοῦ θεοῦ ἀποσταλέντα καταλαβεῖν τοὺς Ἰουδαίους θυσιάζοντας εἰδώλῳ χρυσῷ, ᾧ εἶναι ὄνομα Βάαλ.

3 In the LXX the two kings—Jehoiakim and Jehoiachin—usually have an identical transliteration: Ἰωακείμ; as they do in Josephus: Ἰωάκειμος.

4 II Kings 24:1-17 = II Chr. 36:5-10.

5 See also Jer. 1:3; 26:1.

The second mention of Jonachim in this fragment, discussed below, which records that the king threatened to burn Jeremiah alive, again suggests Jehoiakim.[6] But the concluding section of our text, which recounts the destruction of Jerusalem and the Babylonian captivity, cannot refer to Jehoiakim, who died in Jerusalem. It was Jehoiachin (Jeconiah) who was taken to Babylon as a prinsoner.[7] Yet Eupolemus' final reference seems to allude to the last king of Judah, Zedekiah, and the destruction of the Temple in the year 587/6 B.C.[8] It is clear then that Eupolemus here telescopes events of the reigns of the last three kings of Judah and that he uses Jonachim as a collective name. The spelling of Jonachim, if not a scribal corruption, is typical of the peculiar transliterations found in Eupolemus' fragments, such as Suron (Hiram) and Urphe (Ophir).

The collision between Yahweh and Baal as the cause for the destruction of the Temple is a motive original with Eupolemus. According to II Kings, the shedding of human blood was the gravest sin committed by the last rulers of Judah.[9] The Deuteronomistic historian, however, appears to have been aware of the sinister role of the alliances, made necessary by the kingdom's geopolitical position as the buffer state between Babylonia and Egypt.[10] The Chronicler, however, finds the cause of Jerusalem's fall in the people's imitation of abominable heathen customs and in their refusal to listen to the repeated warnings of the prophets, including the prophet Jeremiah.[11] Contrary to Eupolemus, who seems to stress the stealthy nature of idol worship, Jeremiah says that images of Baal were a common sight in the streets of Jerusalem and Judah.[12]

Closer to Eupolemus is the view of Ben Sira:

> They [the foreigners] burned the Holy City
> And made its streets desolate
> On account of Jeremiah whom they afflicted;
> Yet he had been consecrated as a prophet from the womb.[13]

---

6   Cf. Jer. 26:11; 36:23.

7   Cf. *P.E.,* IX, 39, 5 = *FGrH* 723 F 5 = Walter, Eupolemus, F 4; II Kings 24:12 ff.; II Chr. 36:10; D. J. Wiseman, *Chronicles of Chaldean Kings* (Oxford, Oxford University Press, 1956), 20-32; 65-75.

8   II Kings 25:1-19 = Jer. 52: 1:25 = II Chr. 36:11-21.

9   II Kings 24:4; 24:3 recall the abominations of Menasseh, which the Lord had not forgiven.

10   II Kings 24, esp. verse 7.

11   II Chr. 36:12-17.

12   Jer. 2:8; 7:9; 11:11-14; 17; 12:16; 19:5; 32:29, 35. These and similar passages suggest that the worship of Baal remained a public feature; cf. though Jer. 2:23, which does mention, if only as a denial, the worship of Baal.

13   Ecclus. 49:6-7. Cf. Tosefta Menahot, XIII, 22-23; Yer. Yoma, I, 1, 38c; L. Ginzberg, *The legends of the Jews,* VI, 388 f.

Here too Judah suffers because of the outrage to Jeremiah. But only Eupolemus pinpoints the cause of the enmity between Jeremiah and the king. Eupolemus seems to suggest that Jeremiah's encounter was not unlike that of Moses, when he descended Mount Sinai, and witnessed the Israelites dancing around the golden calf.

In a famous scene, Moses burns the golden calf, grinds it into powder, mixes it with water and makes the Israelites swallow it.[14] According to Eupolemus, the situation was similar when Jeremiah found the Israelites worshipping the golden Baal.: "He warned them of the forthcoming disaster, but Jonachim attempted to burn him alive. But he said that with this wood they [the Israelites] shall cook dishes for the Babylonians and as captives they shall dig channels in the Tigris and Euphrates."[15] Why the threat to Jeremiah's life was not carried out is not explained. Perhaps Nebuchadnezzar's sudden reaction saved the prophet.[16] Although Jer. 26 tells how the prophet was jailed and Jer. 36 tells of the burning of the prophet's scroll, Eupolemus' version must be regarded as his own invention.

Eupolemus' account is perhaps explainable in the light of his time. During the Syrian persecution, as recorded in the contemporary literature, fire was the chief instrument of execution. It is said that when the seven brothers refused to obey the royal decree to eat pig's meat, according to II Macc., Antiochus prescribed burning as the punishment of the eldest.[17] The minutiae of execution by fire are even more gruesome in the Fourth Book of Maccabees.[18] It is tempting to speculate that Eupolemus is suggesting here a parallel between Jeremiah's encounter with the golden Baal and the readiness of the Hasidim of his own day to die rather than sacrifice to the Syrian deity Baal Shamin (Lord of Heavens). Jeremiah, like some of the Hasidim, was willing to be martyred for Yahweh's sake.

More difficult to follow is Eupolemus' attributions to Jeremiah the admonition that the captives would cook dishes and dig trenches in Babylonia. Eupolemus' words make sense if it is assumed that the prophet caught the Jews partaking of the meat of idolatrous sacrifices. The partaking

---

14   Exod. 32:1-20.

15   *P.E.*, IX, 39, 3 = 723 F 5; Walter, Eupolemus F 4: τοῦτον δὲ αὐτοῖς τὴν μέλλουσαν ἀτυχίαν δηλῶσαι. τὸν δὲ Ἰωναχεὶμ ζῶντα αὐτὸν ἐπιβαλέσθαι κατακαῦσαι· τὸν δὲ φάναι τοῖς ξύλοις τούτοις Βαβυλωνίοις ὀψοποιήσειν καὶ σκάψειν τὰς τοῦ Τίγριδος καὶ Εὐφράτου διώρυχας αἰχμαλωτισθέντας.

16   Jer. 36:26 reports that the king ordered the seizure of Baruch the scribe and of Jeremiah, but that "the Lord hid them." Josephus (*A.J.*, X, 95) relates the arrest and escape of Jeremiah, but mention of the means used for the escape appears to be missing.

17   II Macc. 7:3.

18   IV Macc. 9:19-21. Cf. Babli Abodah Zarah 18a; parallels in the Midrash of the Ten Martyrs (has come down in many versions, see Jellinek, ed., *Bet ha-Midrasch* [Leipzig, 1853], II, 68), which also describes a scene of execution by burning.

of a heathen dish was regarded as abominable. Daniel and his friend, we are told, endangered their lives to avoid violating such a commandment. Especially obnoxious was the eating of swine's meat, symbol of fealty to the pagan cult. Eupolemus seems to be retrojecting the symbols to the pre-exilic period. Instead of burning the Baal, as Moses had done in his time, the Israelites threatened to burn God's messenger. As retribution for the eating of idolatrous sacrifices, they would have to cook dishes for their captors. However, this interpretation remains conjectural, and the symbolism of the digging of trenches is still unexplained.

NEBUCHADNEZZAR'S CAMPAIGN

Consistent with his view that the encounter between Jeremiah and Baal caused the destruction of Jerusalem, Eupolemus extends the prophet's influence beyond the borders of the kingdom: "But when Nebuchodonosor (Ναβουχοδονόσορ), the king of the Babylonians, heard of Jeremiah's prediction, he summoned Astibares, the king of the Medes, to join him in a campaign."[19] Here it is claimed that a casual relationship existed between the prophet and the Neo-Babylonian king. Eupolemus, it would seem, was comparing the political situation during the last years of the monarchy with that of his own time, when there was a close link between the Seleucid overlords and the Jewish Hellenizers. In both instances a great power is said to have intervened on behalf of those who wished to perform the religious structure of the state. Babylon, like Assyria in former times, was the rod of Yahweh's anger.[20]

It appears, moreover, that Eupolemus was contrasting the contemporary impotence of the Jewish state with its supposedly former status of great power. In preparation for war with Jonachim, Nebuchadnezzar made certain that his Median allies would join him in the campaign: "After having collected both Medians and Babylonians, he [Nebuchadnezzar] collected 180,000 foot soldiers, 120,000 horsemen, and 10,000 chariots for the infantry."[21] There is nothing in our biblical sources to suggest that the Medians participated in the destruction of Jerusalem.[22] Neither does Scripture record the tribal or numerical composition of the Babylonian forces.

---

19 *P.E.,* IX, 39, 4 = 723 F 5 = Walter, Eupolemus, F 4: τὸν δὲ τῶν Βαβυλωνίων βασιλέα ἀκούσαντα Ναβουχοδονόσορ τὰ ὑπὸ τοῦ Ἱερεμίου προμαρτευθέντα παρακαλέσαι Ἀστιβάρην τὸν Μήδων βασιλέα συστρατεύειν αὐτῷ.

20 Cf. Isa. 10:5-18; Deut. 28:25; a rather common prophetic view.

21 *P.E.,* IX, 30, 5 = 723 F 5:   παραλαβόντα δὲ Βαβυλωνίους καὶ Μήδους καὶ συναγαγόντα πεζῶν μὲν ὀκτωκαίδεκα, ἱππέων δὲ μυριάδας δώδεκα καὶ πεζῶν ἅρματα μυρία.

22 Jer. 51:11, 28 makes Media the enemy of Babylonia.

It was shown above that Eupolemus utilized Graeco-Phoenician sources to supplement the lore about King Solomon. Here too the Jewish author wove divergent accounts from the Greek classical historians into the biblical tradition. Herodotus does not mention Nebuchadnezzar (605-562), but he records the deeds of his famous Median contemporaries—Cyaxares (625-585), the conqueror of Nineveh (Ninos), and his successor Astyages (585-550), the last two kings of the Median empire.[23] Although cuneiform tablets have now substantially confirmed Herodotus' account, in antiquity it found little credence.[24] The favored history of Babylonia was that of Ctesias of Cnidos, the physician of Artaxerxes Mnemon (404-359/8), who wrote a fanciful reconstruction of the fall of Assyria and Media and the rise of Persia.[25] To discredit the Father of History, Ctesias manufactured a list of names of Median kings, the eighth or ninth of whom was Astibares.[26] Since Astibares is an invented name,[27] Eupolemus' claim that this Median king joined Nebuchadnezzar's campaign against Judah certainly shows his dependence on Ctesias.

Ctesias' histories of Persia and India were written in a sensational style, and his dramatic romances were widely copied.[28] The question arises, therefore, whether Eupolemus used Ctesias directly or whether he knew of Ctesias' history only through its many abridgements and paraphrases. As far as can be judged from the writings of Diodorus and Nicolaus of Damascus, Ctesias related little about this penultimate king of Media. Astibares' forty-year reign was uneventful, according to Ctesias, except for the revolt of

---

23   Herod. I, 16, 46, 73-75, 103, 106, 107 f., 119, 123, 127-130, 139.

24   Diodorus, Nicolaus of Damascus, and Eusebius, for example, fail to use Herodotus' account of the fall of Assyria, relying entirely on Ctesias. For the whole issue of the reading of Herodotus in antiquity, however, see F. Jacoby, "Herodotos," in *R.E.*, Suppl. II (1913), cols. 504-13, who documents Herodotus' wide influence. But Jacoby (509 f.) admits that the historian's failure to visit Persia, in contrast to Ctesias, weakened in the eyes of the ancients the reliability of his histories via-à-vis his competitor. (See next note.)

25   See F. Jacoby, "Ktesias," *R.E.*, XI, 2032 ff.; *FGrH* 688 TT 1-19; FF 1-45. Large sections of Ctesias are preserved in the fragments of Nicolaus of Damascus (see my *Nicolaus of Damascus,* 68 f.), Diodorus, Plutarch, Eusebius, Photius, among others.

26   See Diod. II, 32, 5-34, 6 = *FGrH* 688 F 5. Cf. Jacoby, "Ktesias," *R.E.*, XI, 2032 ff.

27   Most of Ctesias' names of the Median kings follow a pattern: seven out of nine have as their initial letters an *a*; four, (including Astibares) *ar*; two *as*; the name Astibares was clearly intended to replace Herodotus' Cyaxares (cf. Eusebius, *Die Chronik,* tr. from the Armenian by J. Karst, Königl. Preussischen Akademie der Wissenschaften, Leipzig, 1911, p. 32, 27).

28   *FGrH* 688 TT 1-19; Nicolaus of Damascus 90 FF 1-6; "Ktesias," R.E., XI, 2032 ff.; Wacholder, *Nicolaus of Damascus,* 67-69; 122.

the fun-loving queen of Sacae, Zarinaea.[29] Since even Nicolaus, Herod's historian, detailed Zarinaea's love affairs as reported by Ctesias without mentioning the king's campaigns against Jerusalem,[30] it seems probable that Ctesias did not allude to those campaigns either. In fact, one may suppose, Ctesias never mentioned even Nebuchadnezzar.[31] If our reasoning is correct, it follows that although the name Astibares goes back to Ctesias, Eupolemus here depended on another source. This source, found in our fragment of Eupolemus, identified Astibares with Cyaxares, known to the ancients from Herodotus as the one who had crushed the Assyrian empire.[32]

We have other indications that Eupolemus had before him a book that had fused the accounts of Herodotus and Ctesias with some native Babylonian and Jewish traditions. In Ctesias, the fictional Median general, Arbaces, and the Babylonian Belesys joined forces to overthrow their master Sardanapallus, the effeminate king of Assyria. None of Ctesias' names is historical and there is no reason to assume that he mentioned Nebuchadnezzar.[33] Herodotus, as has been noted, correctly credits the fall of Assyria to the Median king Cyazares, but he fails to allude to the significant role played by Nabopolassar (625-605), the founder of the Chaldean dynasty and the father of Nebuchadnezzar, whom he never mentions.[34] Although none of these sources suggest a Medo-Babylonian alliance, the historicity of this alliance is now attested in the cuneiform clay tablets.[35] Some scholars have conjectured, independently of Eupolemus, that Median forces indeed assisted Nebuchadnezzar, who was Cyaxares' son-in-law.[36] Such reliable information could have become available to Eupolemus only from a native source, which

---

29   Diod. II, 34, 1, 6 (where the name is spelled Astibaras) = Ctesias, 688 F 5; cf. C. H. Roberts, in *Oxyrhynchus Papyri,* XXII (London, 1954), 81 ff. = 688 F 8b. Nicolaus of Damascus, 90 F 5, as indicated by the papyrological evidence, seems to have copied Ctesias here verbatim.

30   See preceding note; my *Nicolaus of Damascus,* 64-70.

31   Ctesias, of course, dealt only incidentally with Babylonian history and had no reason to mention Nebuchadnezzar.

32   See note 23. Eusebius, whose accounts of Median history follow Cteasias (*Eusebius, Chronik,* ed. Karst, pp. 28, 30-33, 9), contaminating Ctesias with Herodotus: the names of the first five kings of Media were taken from the former, the last three from the latter.

33   Diod. II, 23-32 = Ctesias, *FGrH* 688 FF 1a; 5; Nicolaus of Damascus 90 FF 2-5.

34   Herodotus records the capture of Ninos (Nineveh) by the Medians only incidentally (I, 185 f.), suggesting that he was not aware of the Medo-Babylonian campaign against Assyria.

35   Wiseman, *The Chronicles of the Chaldaean Kings,* 14, 20 ff., and passim.

36   For the marriage, see Euseb., *Chronik,* p. 18 = Abydenus, 685 F 5, p. 405, whose source was Berossus, 680 F 7, p. 587, 21 ff.; A. L. Oppenheim, "Nebuchadrezzer," in the *Interpreter's Dictionary of the Bible,* 328b. See also M. Niebuhr, *Geschichte Assur's und Babel's seit Phul* (Berlin, 1857), 112 f. However, unlike Pseudo-Eupolemus, there is no evidence that Eupolemus ever used Berossus' works.

may have already fused Herodotus and Ctesias with accounts based on old Babylonian records. Curiously, Eupolemus tends to be utterly mendacious when paraphrasing the Bible; the few instances where his fragments seem to make a contribution to historical facts deal with foreign affairs and seem to have been based on non-Jewish sources. The Medo-Babylonian alliance, if not a lucky guess, is one of them.[37] It is nevertheless characteristic of Eupolemus to pick Ctesias' fictional name of Astibares instead of the historical Cyaxares. The main question, however, remains whether or not there existed a source which specifically reported the presence of Median forces in the destruction of the Temple, or even in one of the Babylonian campaigns against the trans-Euphrates countries.

Little can be said about the identity of this source, except that Babylonia and Media frequently serve as the background for accounts in biblical and apocryphal works.[38] The concluding passage of the Book of Tobit reports that its hero Tobias died in Ecbatana of Media at the age of 127 years, but that before his death Tobias heard of the fall of Nineveh to Nebuchadnezzar and Ahasuerus.[39] If one substitutes the names of Nabopolassar (Nebuchadnezzar's father) and Cyaxares, respectively, for Nebuchadnezzar and Ahasuerus, the author of Tobit appears to have been rather well informed about the events leading to Nineveh's fall. In fact it is conceivable that the author was transliterating here Astibares, whom Eupolemus evidently identified with Cyaxares, the conqueror of Nineveh and Nebuchadnezzar's associate in the context of Jerusalem, for Ahasuerus, the king of Media. If so, the Ahasuerus of the Book of Esther, puzzlingly identified as Artexerxes, may conceivably refer to Astibares, Ctesias' fictional king of Media.[40] This would explain the most baffling passage of Esther 2:6, where Mordecai is said to have been a contemporary of both Nebuchadnezzar and Ahasuerus.[41] It should be noted that Dan. 9:1 identifies Ahasuerus as the king of Media,

---

37   For another example see above, relating to Solomon's gift to the Phoenician King Suron (Hiram).

38   Jephet the son of Noah settled in Media (Jub. 10:35 f.). Cf. Dan. 6:1; 9:1; I Esdr. 3:1.

39   Tob. 14:14; cf. 1:14.

40   For the literature on this subject see, H. H. Rowley, *Darius the Mede*[2] (Cardiff, University of Wales Press, 1959).

41   There appears to be a remarkable resemblance between the Book of Esther and the writings of Ctesias. In both, romance serves as the background for the political state of Persia, in which the queens play leading roles in removing unfaithful ministers. Some of this similarity may be ascribed to the conditions in Persia with which the biblical author, like Ctesias, may have had a firsthand acquaintance. But the literary frame of Esther contains elements such as the sustained dramatic movement, and the constant shifts of fortune seems to be modeled after a secular author, the closest parallels of which seem to be the fictionalized histories of Assyria and Media of Ctesias. All this is, however, strictly speculative. A positive assurance of Esther's dependence upon Ctesias requires more detailed study.

whose son Darius (perhaps identical with Aspandas, the son of Astibares, in Ctesias),[42] ruled over the Chaldean kingdom as well. Thus when Eupolemus linked Nebuchadnezzar with the Median king Astibares, perhaps he was following not only Ctesias but Jewish traditions as well. All this, however, is highly conjectural. For it is reasonable to assume that the Ahasuerus of Tobit is to be identified with Cyaxares of Media.

The numbers of the Medo-Babylonian armies as given by Eupolemus are of course highly exaggerated. Nevertheless, it appears that Eupolemus here followed a knowledgeable source. Both ciphers, the 180,000 infantry and the 120,000 cavalry, are divisible by 60,000, the basic unit of the Babylonian and Persian armies. Curiously, the enemy's armies before Jerusalem as given by Eupolemus totaled 300,000 men, the same number recorded by Herodotus of the Persian camp before Salamis in 479 B.C.[43] Perhaps these numbers reflect typical ancient exaggerations of very powerful armies. But it is more likely that Eupolemus borrowed the numbers from Herodotus, suggesting that just as Zerxes did at Salamis, so Nebuchadnezzar mobilized all the resources of the state to conquer Jerusalem.

That Eupolemus' account was modeled after Herodotus is further evidenced by the next passage: "At first he Nebuchadnezzar subdued Samaritis, Galilaea, Scythopolis, and the Jews who dwelled in Galaaditis. Then, finally, he conquered Hierosolyma and took captive the king of the Jews, Jonachim."[44] It will be recalled that before attempting to take Athens, Darius and Xerxes conquered the weaker and less indomitable cities and islands of Hellas.[45] Apparently, according to Eupolemus, this was also Nebuchadnezzar's strategy.

Cataloguing the three lists of geographical names found in the fragments shows that the details of Eupolemus' account of the Babylonian-Median campaign are fictional:

42   Diod. II, 34, 6 = Ctesias, 688 F 5, "whom the Greeks call Astyages," evidently a reference to Herodotus (I, 73-75).

43   Herod. VIII, 113; IX, 32. In Herodotus (VIII, 113) the Medians play a role only slightly less important than the main actors, the Persians. Eupolemus assigns a similar role to the Medians as allies of Nebuchadnezzar. Cf. also Judith 2:5, where King Nebuchadnezzar orders Holofernes to lead 120,000 foot soldiers and 12,000 cavalry.

44   *P.E.,* IX, 39, 5 = *FGrH* 723 F 5; Walter, Eupolemos, F 4:   πρῶτον μὲν τὴν Σαμαρεῖτιν καταστρέψασθαι καὶ Γαλιλαίαν καὶ Σκυϑόπολιν καὶ τοὺς ἐν τῇ Γαλααδίτιδι οἰκοῦντας Ἰουδαίους· αὖϑις δὲ τὰ Ἱεροσόλυμα παραλαβεῖν καὶ τὸν Ἰουδαίων βασιλέα Ἰωναχεὶμ ζωγρῆσαι.

45   Herod. VI, 94-101, and passim.

David's conquests[46]	Solomon's provinces[47]	Nebuchadnezzar's conquests
Syrians of Euphrates		
Commagene		
Galaaditis	Galaaditis	Galaaditis
Assyria		
Phoenicia		
Idumaea		
Ammonitis	Ammonitis	
Moabitis	Moabitis	
Ituraea		
Nabataea	(Arabia)	
Nabdaea		
	Galilee	Galilee
	Samaritis	Samaritis
	Judaea	Judaea (Hierosolyma)
		Sythopolis

These lists show that Eupolemus tended to follow a standard formula, is noticeable also in the thoughtless listing of the conquest of Samaria before Galilee by Nebuchadnezzar's armies marching southward from Babylonia. Possibly, though, Eupolemus chose his words carefully when he says, "He first subdued Samaritis," to suggest perhaps that, because of Jonachim's resistance, the invading forces bypassed the Northern province to take Samaria first, thus surrounding the Jewish armies of Galilee. Nevertheless, the conclusion remains that we are dealing here with a basically fictional reconstruction of biblical history. An official report of the movements of the Babylonian armies during Nebuchadnezzar's reign is now available in the recovered cuneiform tablets.[48] According to these texts, the conquered locations, in addition to Jerusalem, were Tyre and Ascalon, not the places listed in Eupolemus.

Incidentally, Eupolemus' account of a Medo-Babylonian alliance that conquered Jerusalem in the first decades of the sixth century B.C. may serve to explain a puzzling passage in *Contra Apionem*. Josephus quotes Pseudo-Hecataeus, that "myriads of Jews were deported to Babylon by the Persians."[49] Since the reference is clearly to Nebuchadnezzar's deportations, scholars have debated why Hecataeus attributed them to the Persians rather than to the Babylonians. This error, according to Lewy and others,[50] who

---

46   *P.E.*, IX, 30, 18 = 723 F 2a.

47   IX, 33, 1 = 723 F 2a.

48   D.J. Wiseman, *Chronicles of the Chaldean Kings, (626-556 B.C.) in the British Museum* (London, the British Museum, 1956).

49   *C. Apionem*, I, 194.

50   The most detailed defense of the authenticity of Jsephus' citation (*C. Apionem*, I, 183-204) is found in H. Lewy, "Hekataios von Abdera *Peri Iudaeon*," *ZNW*, XXXI (1932), 117-132. Th. Reinach, in his 1902 edition of *C. Apionem*, quoted approvingly I. G. Müller's *Des Flavius Josephus Schrift gegen Apion* (Basel, 1877), p.

defend the authenticity of Josephus' source, shows that the passage quoted by Josephus indeed emanates from Hecataeus of Abdera, who flourished at the end of the fourth century B.C. The prevailing opinion, and, I think, the correct one, however, remains that Josephus was quoting a Jewish author who wrote under the name of the heathen Hecataeus.[51] II Macc. 1:19, a passage surely of Jewish provenance, also speaks of a Persian captivity.[52] Why, then, would a Jewish writer have attributed Nebuchadnezzar's deportations of the Jews to the Persians? The answer, possibly, is that Pseudo-Hecataeus, whose account of the Temple otherwise resembles that of Eupolemus,[53] followed Eupolemus also when he relates that Jerusalem was conquered by a combination of Babylonian and Median forces. Pseudo-Hecataeus seems, therefore, to be saying that the Persians, or the Medians, whom the Jewish tradition frequently considers identical with, or twins of, the Persians,[54] participated in the destruction of Jerusalem. This is not to say that Pseudo-Hecataeus was unaware of the fact that the Babylonians played the leading role in the destruction of the Temple. But he mentions only their allies here because Pseudo-Hecataeus seems to have wished to link the fall of Jerusalem with the fall of the Persian empire, suggesting perhaps a cause and effect, as Alexander is mentioned in the next sentence of the fragment.[55] If so, Eupolemus and Pseudo-Hecataeus shed light on each other and may be regarded as part of the same historiographical development.[56] But, as noted elsewhere in this study, the writings of Josephus are independent of the Hellenistic Jewish historical tradition. In this instance, too, the Jewish hirtorian follows the biblical texts of the Books of Kings, Chronicles, and Jeremiah, which perhaps correctly, do not know of a Medo-Babylonian alliance.[57]

175, that this error proves the authenticity of the Hecataean origin of Josephus' quotation, but in the 1930 edition reversed his opinion on account of II Macc. 1:19. Thackeray's note on *C. Apionem*, I, 119, is based on Reinach's first edition.

51   See now Walter, *Der Thoraausleger Aristobulos* (Berlin, Deutsche Akademie der Wissenschaften zu Berlin, 1964), 86-88, 173-178, 187-201; Wacholder, "Hecataeus and Pseudo-Hecataeus," *Encyclopaedia Judaica* (Jerusalem, 1971), VIII, 236 f.

52   However, C. L. Grimm, *Kurzgefastes exegetische Handbuch zu den* Apocryphen. Vierte Lieferung (Leipzig, 1854), 43, ad locum, explains "Persia" to refer, in the later period, to the trans-Euphrates region.

53   See below, p. 270.

54   Cf. LXX II Chr. 36:20, where the Hebrew equivalent of Persia is rendered as Media; Dan. 6:1; 9:1.

55   *C. Apionem*, I, 194 = Ps.-Hecataeus, 264 F 21.

56   See below, pp. 266-74.

57   See *A.J.*, X, 84, (II Kings 24:1), 96-98 (Jer. 52:28), 99 (II Kings 24:10), is clearly dependent on Scripture. But in *C. Apionem*, I, 133-137, Josephus, quoting Berossus (680 F 8), seems to be well informed when he reports that Nebuchadnezzar defeated, along with the Hebrews, the Phoenicians and the Arabians.

JEREMIAH SAVES THE ARK

The fragments of Eupolemus contain a long description of the Temple, but its destruction is treated in one sentence. Nebuchadnezzar conquered Jerusalem and took her king into captivity, and Eupolemus says: "But the gold, silver, and bronze of the Temple he sent to Babylon as tribute. Except the ark and the tablets therein; these Jeremiah retained."[58] It is symbolic that Eupolemus did not alter the formula he used in his account of the Temple's construction—the identical grouping of precious metals are now shipped to Babylon. The fragment, however, does conclude with a somewhat hopeful note. All of the fabulous wealth may have been lost, but the prophet guarded over what was the most significant: the Decalogue. Here we see once again that Dalbert's suggestion, mentioned above, that Eupolemus tended to disregard nomistic Judaism, is misleading.[59] The biblical texts, which detail painstakingly the wealth carried away from Jerusalem, knew nothing about Jeremiah's retention of the ark. According to Jer. 3:16, the ark would soon be forgotten; and according to Jer. 39:14, 40:4, the prophet, in chains, was in no position to save the ark. In the light of the tendencious nature of the fragments as a whole, Eupolemus' statement here must be viewed as one more 'correction' of the Scriptural tradition.

Nevertheless, the theme that some of the most sacred furnishings of the Temple somehow escaped Nebuchadnezzar's pillage recurs in Hellenistic, Christian, and Rabbinic sources. One of the oldest of these is the long epistle of the Judaean elders to Egypt, prefixed to the Second Book of Maccabees (1:10-2:18). The avowed purpose of the letter is to urge the Alexandrian Jews to celebrate the feast of Hannukah, that is to say, Nehemiah's "feast of fire." When Nehemiah rebuilt God's altar, he ordered a search for the fire hidden by the exiled priests prior to their departure to 'Persian' captivity. The recovery of the "nephtha" (naphtha) gave rise to the feast of fire.

To substantiate the story of the hidden fire, the author(s) of the epistle digressed to quote at length from authorities unknown to us: "One finds in the records" ($\dot{\epsilon}\nu$ $\tau\alpha\hat{\imath}\varsigma$ $\dot{\alpha}\pi\sigma\gamma\rho\alpha\phi\alpha\hat{\imath}\varsigma$)[60] that Jeremiah ordered the exiles who were being deported to hide some of the fire of the Solomonic Temple. "It was also in the writing" ($\dot{\epsilon}\nu$ $\tau\alpha\hat{\imath}\varsigma$ $\dot{\alpha}\nu\alpha\gamma\rho\alpha\phi\alpha\hat{\imath}\varsigma$)[61] that this prophet received an oracle to order the tent and the ark to follow him—leading to the cave in the

---

58   *P.E.*, IX, 39, 5 = 723 F 5; Walter, Eupolemos F 4: $\tau\grave{o}\nu$ $\delta\grave{\epsilon}$ $\chi\rho\upsilon\sigma\grave{o}\nu$ $\tau\grave{o}\nu$ $\dot{\epsilon}\nu$ $\tau\hat{\omega}$ $\dot{\iota}\epsilon\rho\hat{\omega}$ $\kappa\alpha\grave{\iota}$ $\ddot{\alpha}\rho\gamma\upsilon\rho\sigma\nu$ $\kappa\alpha\grave{\iota}$ $\chi\alpha\lambda\kappa\grave{o}\nu$ $\dot{\epsilon}\kappa\lambda\dot{\epsilon}\xi\alpha\nu\tau\alpha$ $\epsilon\dot{\iota}\varsigma$ $B\alpha\beta\upsilon\lambda\hat{\omega}\nu\alpha$ $\dot{\alpha}\pi\sigma\sigma\tau\epsilon\hat{\iota}\lambda\alpha\iota,\chi\omega\rho\grave{\iota}\varsigma$ $\tau\hat{\eta}\varsigma$ $\kappa\iota\beta\omega\tau\sigma\hat{\upsilon}$ $\kappa\alpha\grave{\iota}$ $\tau\hat{\omega}\nu$ $\dot{\epsilon}\nu$ $\alpha\dot{\upsilon}\tau\hat{\eta}$ $\pi\lambda\alpha\kappa\hat{\omega}\nu\cdot$ $\tau\alpha\dot{\upsilon}\tau\eta\nu$ $\delta\grave{\epsilon}$ $\tau\grave{o}\nu$ $\dot{I}\epsilon\rho\epsilon\mu\dot{\iota}\alpha\nu$ $\kappa\alpha\tau\alpha\sigma\chi\epsilon\hat{\iota}\nu$.

59   P. Dalbert, *Die Theologie der hellenistisch-judischen Missionsliteratur unter Ausschluss von Philo und Josephus;* 42.

60   II Macc. 2:1. For the meaning of $\dot{\alpha}\pi\sigma\gamma\rho\alpha\phi\alpha\hat{\iota}$ see 2:13. It is the word now used for apocrypha, but its usage in antiquity is not attested. See LXX Dan. 1021; cf. Abel, *Les livres des Maccabées,* 303, ad locum.

61   II Macc. 2:4, 13.

mountain where Moses had been buried. There he hid the tent and the ark and the altar of incense. The spot where these furnishings were left was unknown even to the men who followed the prophet to the cave—and shall remain secret to the end of days. Nonetheless, just as in the days of Moses fire came down and just as Solomon in his days had received some of the fire to kindle the altar of the Temple, so had Nehemiah."[62] Here the storyteller paused as if to ask where it is recorded that Moses used divine fire. He answers by quoting a non-extant verse: "And Moses said: 'And they were consumed because the sin offering had not been eaten.' "[63] The epistle's digression concludes with a list of works, which had been lost and which Judah now recovered and offered to the Jews of Alexandria; but which unfortunately has been lost again.

Both Eupolemus and the author(s) of the epistle maintained that Jeremiah saved the ark from the Babylonian looters. The question is whether these two sources were interdependent or whether both were derived from a text no longer accessible to us. Freudenthal took it for granted that a common source underlay Eupolemus and the epistle.[64] This hypothesis, however, merely adds another unknown to a field full of questions, especially since II Macc. 2:1,4,13 reiterates the existence of a written source. But the alternative—that these two texts were interdependent—is not without problems either. The fragment mentions the saving of the ark only, whereas the Maccabean text reports the hiding of the tabernacle and some of the holy fire as well. Furthermore, many of the details in the latter source are absent in the former. It would seem, then, that Eupolemus could not have been the source of II Macc. 2:1-8. These arguments, however, lose their potency when it is recalled that they could be used against Freudenthal's view and that Eupolemus' remark about the ark appears in the fragment at the very end. Since it may be assumed that Eupolemus continued his description of the exile, it is conceivable that he also recorded the hiding of some fire in Moses' burial place.

The hypothesis that Eupolemus and the epistle may have been interdependent raises the question as to which of these two was the original source. The chronological evidence seems decisive. It has been shown above that some passages of the fragments date from the time of the Syrian persecution, i.e., 167-164 B.C. Judah dispatched Eupolemus to Rome in 161 B.C. Finally, we have Eupolemus' chronology of the world which ended with 158/7 B.C., yielding a combined date of Eupolemus' fragments as written in 167-158/7 B.C. The time of II Macc. 1:10-2:18 (known as the second epistle) has been one of the most argued questions of this hotly debated book. The dating of the epistle in 124 B.C., as favored by scholars at the turn of the century,

62   II Macc. 2:1-10.
63   II Macc. 2:11.
64   Freudenthal, *Hell. St.,* 118.

because of the year given in II Macc. 1:9, is now correctly rejected.[65] On the basis of internal evidence, however, the date of the epistle is between the death of Antiochus IV in the summer of 163 B.C. and that of Judah in the Spring of 160 B.C.[66]   If so, Judah's epistle and Eupolemus' history may have been written within three years of one another.

Although chronology does not definitely determine which source was the original one and which the secondary, it does suggest a surprising possibility—that the author of the fragments was identical with the author of the epistle. The subscript of the epistle reads: "Those in Jerusalem and those in Judaea and the Senate and Judah. To Aristobulus, who is of the family of annointed priests, teacher of Ptolemy the king, and to the Jews in Egypt: Greetings and good health!"[67] In theory, this was a letter from Judah, the Gerusia and all the Jews of Judaea to all the Jews of Egypt. In practice, it was written by a Greek scribe on Judah Maccabee's authority to Aristobulus, the author of a philosophical commentary on the Pentateuch. The Palestinian scribe(s) knew well his (their) counterpart in Alexandria—flattering him with his distinguished ancestry and crediting him as a royal mentor. Walter, however, argues that the last boast was invented by Aristobulus himself, who at the most had on his own dedicated a work to Ptolemy.[68] It is reasonable to assume that the Greek-writing scribe of Jerusalem and the Alexandrian recipient of the letter were personally acquainted. Since Judah chose Eupolemus as his ambassador to Rome and since the latter, like Aristobulus, specialized in works on biblical subjects—one ancient testimonium links Aristobulus and Eupolemus—it is conceivable that Eupolemus was ultimately responsible for the epistle in II Macc. 1:10-2:18.

---

65   See for example B. Niese, *Kritik der beiden Makkabäerbücher* (Berlin, 1900), 2 f.; who dates the Second Maccabees in 124 B.C. the arguments for attributing this date to 1:1-9, see W. Laqueur, *Kritische Untersuchungen zum zweiten Makkabäerbuch* (Strassburg, 1904), 52-71; W. Kolbe, *Beiträge zur syrischen und jüdischen Geschichte* (Berlin, 1926), 121 f.

66   E. Bickerman(n), *ZNW*, 32 (1933), 234 f., dates Ii Macc. 1:10-2:18 in about 60 B.C., on the basis of the formulary greeting of 1:10, branding the epistle a forgery. This has been accepted by N. Walter, *Der Thoraausleger Aristobolos*, 17. But Bickerman's dating on the basis of a single formula, allegedly attested only in the papyri of this time, is questionable. It certainly cannot withstand Abel's criticism (*Les Livres des Maccabées*, 289 f.). See also M. Hengel, *Judentum und Hellenismus* (Tübingen, Mohr, 1969), 186, n. 332. A forger, moreover, would not have used the name of Aristobulus, as the leader of Egypt's Jewry, who must have been an obscure figure a century after the supposedly alleged date of the epistle. See also Jean Starcky, *Les livres des Maccabées*,[3] 27-30.

67   II Macc. 1:10.

68   The likelihood of a Jew as the *didaskolos* of Ptolemy VI Philometor (180-145), the only king, who comes under consideration, has been long questioned. Grimm, in his commentary, on 1:10 (p. 37), regarded him as a *Berather* or, still better, possibly a *Günstling*, believing that the king favored the Jews. Willrich, *Juden und Griechen*, 163,

Several features common to both the fragments of Eupolemus and the epistle tend to show interdependence between these texts. It is true that stylistically, the two texts are quite different. The letter in II Maccabees 1:10-2:18 was written by someone with a rich Greek vocabulary whereas the fragments show an author with a limited vocabulary. It is conceivable, though, that in writing the letter Eupolemus had the help of a staff. Both Eupolemus and the epistle ascribe to Jeremiah a paramount role in the fate of the Jews during the Temple's destruction. Both also make a conscious attempt to link the furnishings of the Temple with those of the desert tabernacle, that is, with Moses and possibly with the Messiah as well.

Solomon Zeitlin perceptively wonders why II Macc. 2:11 makes Jeremiah conceal the tabernacle, which in the author's day had become obsolete long ago.[69] Eupolemus' fragments, however, suggest that the desert tabernacle was not obsolete when the Temple was constructed. Eupolemus claimed that by the Prophet Nathan's orders the tabernacle and its furnishings were stored in the Solomonic Temple. The blatant misquotation of Scripture in II Macc. 2:11 is not dissimilar to Eupolemus' methods. The long digression to events in the days of Jeremiah and Nehemiah in a letter dealing with the recent purification of the altar suggests a historian at work. Finally, the allusion to records and writings, when dealing with famous historical personalities, may have been a reference to his own works—particularly since the Jerusalem scribe complimented the Alexandrian on his authorship. If so, Eupolemus had written his history, or at least portions thereof, before the epistle in II Macc. 1:10-218 was written.

Another Hellenistic reference to Jeremiah's "theft" of the ark exists in Christian remnants of the pre-Christian prophetic lives. How the legend of the retention of the ark turned into theft still needs explanation. But, as pointed out by Schermann, there is no doubt that the Vitae's story of Jeremiah's retention of the ark essentially goes back to Eupolemus.[70]

argued that Aristobulus' alleged career as mentor of Ptolemy VI is fiction, as no Jew could have held such a high position with a king who was reputedly a phil-Hellenist. Walter, *Der Thoraausleger Aristobulos,* 17-33, and passim, accepts this argument, but on the basis of Eusebius (*P.E.,* VIII, 9, 37), who speaks of Aristobulus' dedication of his book to the king, interpreted *didaskolos* (II Macc. 1:10). But Ptolemy died at the age of 35 and the Aristobulus at the alleged date of the letter of about 164 B.C. could have tutored him before Ptolemy had reached the age of sixteen. And there seems to have been an Egyptian tradition to hire a foreigner as one of his princely tutors. Cf. Nicolaus of Damascus as a tutor of Anthony's and Cleopatra's children (*Patralogia Graeca,* ed. Migne, LXXXVII, 3, col. 3621d = *FGrH* 90 T 2). The issue of Aristobulus' Jewishness is probably not relevant to the discussion of something that had occurred prior to the clash between Judaism and Hellenism in the 160's B.C.

69   S. Zeitlin, in *The Second Book of Maccabees* (New York, Harper and Brothers, 1954), 11, on 1:4.

70   D. Th. Schermann, *Propheten- und Apostellegenden* (Leipzig, 1907), 88. Jean Starcky (*Les Livres des Maccabee*[3], 228, note *a*) after citing the ancient allusions to Jeremiah's hiding of the ark, also speculates that "le responsable de la légende pourrait être l'historien juif Epolème."

Despite these arguments, it should be noted that Eupolemus' authorship of the epistle remains only a possibility. Chances are that as in the Lives of the Prophets, the author of the preamble to the II Maccabees was merely embellishing on Eupolemus' invention that Jeremiah had hidden the ark.

Dependent upon Eupolemus, indirectly if not directly, are the Samaritan, apocryphal, and rabbinic texts which also deal with the fate of the Temple's furnishings. Josephus scoffs at the Samaritan story that the sacred vessels of the tabernacle were deposited by Moses on Mount Gerizim, evidently a variant of the tradition that they were buried in Mount Nebo, Moses' burial place.[71] It is related in the Apocalypse of Baruch, written at the end of the first Christian century, that when the four angels with torches in their hands were about to set the Solomonic Temple on fire, a fellow angel warned them to wait until the holy furniture was removed. Thus "the curtains, holy ephod, ark and tablets, and the forty-eight precious stones of the high priest's garments were preserved as the earth opened its mouth and swallowed the holy vessels. There they remain hidden until the advent of the messiah."[72]

The fate of the sacred furnishings as recorded in the rabbinic and medieval literature was based on two independent, perhaps cognate, traditions. Yosephon and the Chronicles of Jerahmeel derived their accounts, directly or indirectly, from II Maccabees.[73] Like Eupolemus, the talmudic writers wondered what happened to the tabernacle upon the completion of the Temple. Their answer, however, like that of the Syriac Baruch, applied to the furnishings of the Temple: the vessels were placed in *genizah* by Solomon or, according to some, and contrary to II Chron. 35:3, by King Josiah. A dissenting opinion of Rabbi Eleazer maintained that all furnishings, including

---

71   *A.J.*, XVIII, 85-86: An unnamed messianic pretender during the procuratorship of Pontius Pilatus asked the mob to come to Mt. Gerizim, where Moses had put in safekeeping the tabernacle's sacred vessels, which the people regarded as plausible. Unfortunately, Josephus fails to explain why this was regarded as plausible. The simplest construction is that the pretender exploited a common belief current among the people, claiming to have found the spot of Moses' burial place (Deut. 32:49; 34:6), though the Jewish lawgiver never crossed the Jordan.

72   Apocalypse of Baruch, 6:7-10, dependent clearly on II Macc. 2:4-8, especially, the lists of items. See also Paralipomena Jeremiae 3:7-8, which is more related to the rabbinic tradition, cited in note 72.

73   See The Hebrew Yosephon, I, 3; Chronicle of Jerahmeel (ed. Gaster, London, 1899), LXXVII, 9, pp. 333 f. Jerahmeel is no doubt a word-by-word copy of his Josephon text. According to S. Zeitlin, (n. 69), 40, following A. A. Neumann, *Landmarks and Goals* (Philadelphia, Dropsie College, 1953), 35-57, esp. 57, argues that Yosephon had before him documents older than our present editions of the Apocryphal works, including II Maccabees; "The two versions, that of *Josippon* and that of the Second Maccabees, are clearly independent of each other." It should be noted that aside from the usual links, Yosephon adheres strictly to the Second Maccabees, apparently his only source.

the ark and the decalogue, were shipped by Nebuchadnezzar to Babylon.[74] The absence in the talmudic tradition of any allusion to Jeremiah's role in concealing the ark in the talmudic lore suggests that the Graeco-Hellenistic story was either ignored or forgotten in the time of the Mishnah. But the rabbis, like Eupolemus, were deeply concerned primarily with the fate of the ark rather than with that of any other vessels.

Eupolemus' main point, however, need not be obscured. The immense amounts of gold and silver that made up the Temple proved of no avail; only the ark and its tablets containing the Law remained indestructible.

[74] Mishnah Shekalim, VI, 1, speaks of an "ancestral tradition" (מסורת בידם מאבותיהם), that the ark was hidden on a certain spot of the Temple. Yer. Shekalim, VI, 1, identifies the spot as the place where the wood was stored. Cf. Tosefta Shekalim, II, 18 (Lieberman, p. 212); Sotah, XIII. 1; B. Yoma, 52b, 53b; and Melekhet Hamishkan, ed. Friedmann (Ish-Shalom), VII, pp. 48 f., which is a collection of talmudic texts related to the hiding of the ark.

Chapter Ten

THE SOURCES

Source analysis is still an infant science. Because of the absence of comparative material, the task of analyzing Eupolemus' antecedents is even more problematical than is typical with fragmentary ancient texts. Graeco-Jewish writings before Josephus dealt almost exclusively with Pentateuchal themes. Thus it is possible to deduce that the dramatist Ezekielus was dependent on Demetrius the chronographer; or that Philo of Alexandria extended the boundaries of biblical allegorical exegesis founded by Aristobulus nearly two centuries earlier. In the case of the fragments of Eupolemus, however, no other Graeco-Jewish account for the period of the monarchy is known.[1] We have only the Scriptural traditions.

The following outline shows a rough relationship between the biblical tradition and Fragments 1-5:

Fragment 1

Moses

	first wise man	original;
	invented writing for the Jews	original;
	Jews taught writing to the Phoenicians	original;
	invented written law for the Jews	original;

Fragment 2

	prophet 40 years	Exod. 7:7; Deut. 34:7.
Joshua		
	(prophet) 30 years	original?; cf. Josh. 14:7; Num. 14:34; Josh. 24:29;
	lived 110 years	Josh. 24:29;
	pitched the holy tent at Shiloh	Josh. 18:1 LXX.
Samuel		
	prophet	I Sam. 1:1;
	chooses Saul as king	I Sam. 9:1 ff.
Saul		
	ruled 21 years	original; cf. I Sam. 13:1 ?

---

1 This is not to say that none existed. Pseudo-Philo's Biblical Antiquities must have treated the monarchical period, though our copies end abruptly with King Saul at Endor. Philo the epicist, Theophilus and, no doubt, Justus of Tiberias, to mention a few, included this period in their histories.

David

war against Syrians, Assyrians, etc.	original; cf. I Sam 8:1-14;
campaign against Suron of Phoenicia	Ps. 83:7; I Chr. 18:1-11;
treaty of friendship with Vaphres of Egypt	original;
Temple: Preparations: angel shows spot of altar	original; cf. II Sam. 24:25;
Commands him not to build Temple his son would build Temple	II Sam. 7; I Chr. 22:8;
commanded by Nathan to collect metals and wood	I Chr. 22 ;
sends fleet to Elana (Aelath), Urphe (Ophir)	original; cf. I Kings 9:26-28;
collected metals and woods	I Chr. 22; 29;
after a rule of 40 years	I Kings 2:11;
hands over kingdom to Solomon	I Chr. 28:1 ff.

Solomon

12 years old when crowned	III Kingdoms 2:12;
before Eli the high priest	original;
and 12 tribal heads	original;
sends letter to Vaphres of Egypt	original;
text of letter to Vaphres	original;
Vaphres' response to Solomon	original;
text of letter to Suron of Tyre	original; cf. I Kings 5:15-25;
Suron's response to Solomon	original; cf. I Kings 5:15-25;
journey to Mt. Lebanon	original
transportation of wood from Lebanon via Jaffa	II Chr. 2:15; cf. Ezra 3:7;
began building Temple at the age of 13	original;
work done by the foreigners (Egyptians, Phoenicians)	original; cf. II Chr. 2:16 f.
and 12 tribes, each tribe provided supplies a month	original; cf. I Kings 5:6 ff.

Solomon's Temple

foundation walls	cf. I Kings 6:3; Ezra 6:3-4; original;
walls and paneling	original; I Kings 6:15-19; II Chr. 3:4-7;
ceiling	cf. II Chr. 3:7;
brass roof	original; cf. Exod. 30:3;
2 gold-plated pillars	I Kings 7: 15-21;
10 lampstands, modeled after the tabernacle	I Kings 7:49;
70 lamps, 10 per lampstand	original; cf. Exod. 25:31-40;
adorned gates	I Kings 7:50; II Chr. 4:22;
porch and 48 pillars	original; cf. III Kingdoms 7:31;
laver bathtub	cf. I Kings 7:23;
laver's brim	original; cf. Exod. 30:17-21;

12 molten stands of the laver	cf. I Kings 7:27-39; II Chr. 4:2-6;
brass platform for the King	original; II Chr. 6:12-13;
altar	cf. II Chr. 4:1; original;
chain network with bells as scarecrow	original.

Solomon's Jerusalem

walls, towers and trenches	original;
Royal palace	I Kings 7:1-12;
"Temple of Solomon" former name	original;
false name given to city, Hierosolyma	original.

Celebrations

sacrifice at Selom (Shiloh)	original;
transfer of the holy vessels of Tabernacle	original ?; cf. II Chr. 6:2-10;
sacrifice at the Temple	cf. II Chr. 7:5.

Conclusion

summary of expenses	original;
homegoing for foreign workers	original;
present for Vaphres	original;
present for Suron	original; cf. I Kings 9:11-13.

Fragment 3

1,000 shields	number original; cf. I Kings 10:16 f.;
length of reign lived 52 years	original; cf. I Kings 2:12 LXX
reigned 40 years in peace	I Kings 11:42.

Fragment 4 (Jacoby, F 5)

King Jonachim	II Kings 24:1 or 8;

Prophet Jeremiah

found Jews worshipping Baal prophesied calamity	original; cf. Jer. 11:13;
King threatened to burn Jeremiah alive	original;
Jeremiah predicted the digging of channels in the Tigris	original.

Nebuchadnezzar's campaign

result of Jeremiah's prophecy	original;
Nebuchadnezzar summoned Astibares of Media	original;
size of hostile army	original;
conquest of Samaria, Galilee, Scythopolis	original;
seizure of Jerusalem	II Kings 24:12;
Joachim taken captive	II Kings 24:12;
shipment of Temple's vessels to Babylon	II Kings 24:13; 25:13-17;

| ark and the tablets of the law retained | original; cf. II Macc. 2:4-8. |

Fragment 5 (Jacoby, F 4)

Chronological summary

| from Adam to the fifth year of King Demetrius | original; |
| from the Exodus to the fifth year of King Demetrius | original. |

This synopsis suggests that although Eupolemus followed the outline of the historical books of the Bible, his work was essentially a new history. New were the accounts of David's campaigns, Solomon's correspondence, Jerusalem's Temple, and Jeremiah's role. Nothing found in the fragments appears to be sheer copy of the traditional texts. Most original, however, were Eupolemus' chronological summaries of the period between Moses and David, and his chronicle listing the time that elapsed between Adam and the Macedonian King Demetrius. The additions to the Jewish historical traditions served to fuse biblical with Hellenistic historiography. But Eupolemus also fused the Pentateucal lore of the desert tabernacle with that of Solomon's Temple, suggesting rather a single sanctuary of Yahweh. Thus Eupolemus used the Mosaic Books, Kings and Chronicles, and the works of Herodotus and Ctesias to create a new history responsive to the needs of a generation that witnessed the war between the Hasideans and the Hellenizers.

THE PENTATEUCH

Although Eupolemus' account of Moses is lost, leaving us with only the mention of the length of his prophecy, a discussion of the historian's sources properly begins with the Pentateuch. (Fragment One, affirming the originality of Moses' inventions, belongs to extrabiblical traditions and has been treated in Chapter Three.) But the single allusion to Moses, as has been said above, should not suggest to the reader that Eupolemus ignored the period of the Israelite wanderings in the desert.[2] But Alexander Polyhistor, our ultimate source, preferred Ezechielus' dramatic renditions of the Exodus and Artapanus' synchretistic fantasies of Moses to the dry and uninspiring history by Eupolemus.[3] For the periods of Joshua and the monarchy, however, because of the dearth of available Greek summaries, Alexander Polyhistor depended entirely upon Eupolemus. Without Eupolemus' treatment of the Mosaic Law, it is impossible to define his relationship to the Mosaic traditions.

---

2   See above, pp. 129-31.
3   Cf. Alexander Polyhistor's abridgement of Ezekielus' epic when the poet followed the Holy Scriptures (ἡ ἱερὰ βίβλος), in P.E., IX, 29, 4-16 = FGrH 273 F 19 = 722 F 4 = Ezekielis Iudaei poetae Alexandrini. Edited by J. Wieneke (1931), 22.

But Eupolemus leaves no doubt as to the authoritativeness of the Law. He goes out of his way to cite Moses when the authors of Kings and Chronicles felt no such need. After describing the lampstands of Solomon's Temple, he adds: "Having taken as a model the tent of testimony made by Moses."[4] This citation seems to have had two purposes. Eupolemus apparently affirms the traditional exegesis of the passages, in Exod. 25:40 and Num. 8:4, that the tabernacle's lampstand was manufactured according to God's own specifications. The Hellenistic historian, moreover, invokes the Law supposedly to stress his dissent from the accounts found in First Kings 7:48 and Second Chronicles 4:7, in which the lampstands differ basically from that of Exod. 25:31-40. Eupolemus' own version of the Temple's lights—ten lampstands with seven lamps each—reconciles the divergent Mosaic and Solomonic lampstands.

Eupolemus refers to Moses again in his report of the placing of the tabernacle's vessels into the new Temple. According to Eupolemus, the tent, altar, and vessels were placed in the new Sanctuary; as told in the Kings-Chronicle tradition, only the ark and the Mosaic tablets were brought into the Solomonic Temple.[5] And as if retorting to a possible challenge to the veracity of his account, he adds that this transfer was ordained by the prophet, evidently meaning Nathan.[6] These references, as well as the indirect allusions to the Law, noted elsewhere in this study, show that Eupolemus regarded the Mosaic accounts of the Tabernacle as quite basic for the making of the Solomonic sanctuary.

Like the other Graeco-Jewish writers, from Demetrius to Philo and Josephus, Eupolemus shows frequent dependence upon the Greek version of the Pentateuch. For again and again in describing the furnishings of the Temple—the ark ($\kappa\iota\beta\omega\tau\acute{o}\varsigma$)[7] the tent [of meeting] ($\sigma\kappa\eta\nu\acute{\eta}$),[8] the burnt offering ($\acute{o}\lambda o\kappa\acute{a}\rho\pi\omega\sigma\iota\varsigma$)[9] —the technical vocabulary was that of the Septuagint. That Eupolemus used a text similar to our Greek translation of the Book of Joshua becomes obvious from the reference to Josh. 18:1:

Eupolemus	*LXX*
πῆξαι τε τὴν ἱερὰν σκηνὴν ἐν Σιλωῖ	εἰς Σηλώ καὶ ἔπηξαν ἐκεῖ τὴν σκη-
	νὴν τοῦ μαρτυρίου[10]

---

4   *P.E.*, IX, 34, 7 = 723 F 2b, p. 675, 26f.

5   I Kings 8:1; II Chr. 5:2, 5; Eupolemus, in *P.E.*, IX, 34, 15 = 723 F 2a.

6   *P.E.*, IX, 34, 15 = 723 F 2a, p. 676, 30.

7   *P.E.*, IX, 34, 15, I, 544, 4 = 723 F 2a, p. 676, 28.

8   *P.E.*, IX, 30, 1, I, 538, 15; = 723 F 2a, 673, 2, uses ἱερὰ σκηνὴ, "holy tent," instead of "tent of testimony," σκηνὴ τοῦ μαρτυρίου, found in Josh. 18:1, but which Eupolemus used to refer to the Mosaic structure (ibid. 8, I, 543, 1 = 675, 29).

9   *P.E.*, IX, 34, 14, I, 544, 1 = 723 F 2a, 676, 25.

10   Cf. Freudenthal, *Hell. St.*, 119, note.

The evidence is less decisive, however, in regard to the other biblical books. Certainly, the form of Jesus the son of Nun (Ἰεσοῦς τὸν ͇τοῦ Ναυῆ)[11] is typically Judaeo-Greek. The spellings of Samuel (Σαμουήλ),[12]   Eli (Ἠλεί),[13]   and Elijah (Ἠλίου)[14] conform to the Greek equivalents of the Septuagint. But, Saul (Σαῦλος),[15] Solomon (Σολομῶν),[16] and more importantly, Hiram (Σούρων),[17] Ophir (Οὐρφῆ),[18] Joachim (Ἰωναχείμ),[19]   and Elana (Ἐλάνα),[20] do not. More weight must be given to the exceptions than to the mean. For scribes generally tended to alter the divergent orthographic forms of famous names to conform with the more familiar biblical spellings. This tendency explains perhaps the form of Hierosolyma instead of Jerusalem in the fragments, although Eupolemus branded the former as incorrect. Eupolemus' departures from the Graeco-biblical traditional spellings, surely more radical than those of Josephus, raise questions as to his dependence on the Greek versions of the Books of Kings and Chronicles.

Certainly only a fraction of Eupolemus' description of David's military campaigns—the Ituraeans, Nabataeans, or the Syrians of Commagene[21] —was tenuously related to either the Greek or Hebrew version of the Book of Samuel. Especially noteworthy is his failure to mention the Philistines. Was Eupolemus correcting the biblical tradition in light of the contemporary political situation of the Maccabean world?[23]

KINGS AND CHRONICLES

We catch some glimpses of Eupolemus' methodology in the exceedingly sketchy allusions to Saul and David, but the technique can only be gauged from his Hellenistic version of the Solomonic Temple. Freudenthal shed considerable light on this matter when he noted that Eupolemus generally followed the Book of Chronicles rather than Kings whenever the two biblical

---

11   *P.E.,* IX, 30, 1, I 538, 14 = 723 F 2a, 673, 1.

12   Ibid. line 15 = ibid., line 3.

13   Ibid., I, p. 539, 12 = ibid. p. 673, 23.

14   Ibid. I, p. 538, 13 = ibid. 672, 30. Mss. ON read: Ἠλιου·

15   Ibid. line 16 = ibid. p. 673, 4; so also Lucian; LXX has no ending.

16   Ibid., p. 539, 11 = ibid. line 22; LXX always Σωφιρ(ά).

17   Ibid. p. 538, 22 = ibid., line 9; cf. above pp. 136-37.

18   Ibid. p. 539, 9 = ibid. 20; cf. above pp. 145-50.

19   Ibid. IX, 40, 1, I, p. 548, 6 = 723 F 5 (4).

20   Ibid., IX, 30, 7, I, 539, 9 = 723 F 2a, p. 673, 19.

21   Ibid. 538, 20f.; 18-21; = ibid. lines 4-8.

22   Cf. Rudolph, *Chronikbücher,* 225, who notes the influence of the second Temple on the Chronicler's report of II Chr. 1-9.

books diverge.[23] This is evident, as noted above, in Eupolemus' failure to mention the bloody events that preceded Solomon's succession, dramatically described in I Kings 1-2, but ignored by the author of Chronicles. Eupolemus alludes to David's collection of metals for the Temple, expands upon the correspondence between the king of Tyre and Solomon, mentions the king's stand for prayer—all more closely related to the events as described in Chronicles rather than in Kings.

More significant than direct dependence, however, is Eupolemus' intellectual debt to the histographic school as illustrated in the Books of Chronicles, Ezra and Nehemiah. The Greek title of Chronicles is Paralipomenon, implying that it records events omitted from the Books of Kings. Presumably, according to the Chronicler, the description of the Temple in I Kings needed correction in order to bring it into greater harmony with the Mosaic Books. Thus II Chr. reports that Solomon built the Temple on the same spot where, according to Gen. 22:2, Abraham bound Isaac. Solomon is said in II Chr. 3:14 to have made a "veil of blue and purple and crimson fabrics," based no doubt on Exod. 26:31.[24] Eupolemus, as has been shown above, felt the same way about the Chronicler as the latter did about the author of Kings. Eupolemus felt a need for even greater harmonization between the Tabernacle and the Temple. Hence, it probably was inconceivable to the Hellenistic historian that Solomon would have constructed lampstands that differed in shape from those of the Tabernacle.

In his description of the golden lampstands Eupolemus was perhaps influenced by another characteristic of postexilic historiography—the ascription of features of the Second Temple to the Solomonic structure. Eupolemus' dimensions of the Temple and altar, and especially the presence of an elaborate scarecrow to guard against pollution of the Temple, reflect a tendency to retroject to Solomon's time features of Zerubabel's sanctuary.[25] In the same vein, from the second century viewpoint, it was inconceivable that the biblical tradition would report a correspondence between the king of Tyre and Solomon without mentioning the king of Egypt; hence Solomon's letter to Vaphres. But whether the Temple built by Onias, a contemporary and fellow priest in Heliopolis, as has been suggested, had influenced Eupolemus' report of the importation of the mass of Egyptian laborers for the construction of the Temple, remains an open question.[26]

This analysis of the biblical sources suggests that Eupolemus may not be explained in terms of the materials he used. His proclivity to change and

---

23   Freudenthal, *Hell. St.,* 119 f. Cf. H.B. Swete, *An Introduction to the Old Testament in Greek*[3] (New York, Ktav, 1968), 370; J. Giblet, "Eupolème et l'histographie du Judaïsme hellénistique," *Ephemerides Theologicae Lovanienses,* 39 (1963), 539-54, esp. 548.

24   Rudolph, *Chronikbücher,* 225 f.

25   See now Th. A. Busink, *Der Tempel von Jerusalem* (Leiden Brill, 1970), I, 27.

26   For an outline of Graeco-Palestinian literature, see below, pp. 259-306.

"correct" the older traditions indicates that he treated the biblical texts as a mere starting point rather than as an authoritative history. In this sense Eupolemus must be regarded as a follower of the Chronicler's school. His duty was, it would seem, to fill the gaps which he believed, or better, he wished others to believe, had been left unfilled by the earlier sources. The priestly historiography was as yet uncanonized; furthermore it was still alive and it could be continued, not only in Hebrew or Aramaic, but also in Greek.[27]

The presumed classification of Eupolemus within a Graeco-biblical historiographic tradition raises the question as to his relative use of Greek and Hebrew sources. Eupolemus touches indirectly on this problem. He says that he preferred the simple transliteration of Jerusalem to the current Greek form of Hierosolyma.[28] He naively makes Solomon explain to the Tyrian king the common Greek equivalent of the Hebrew measure *coros*.[29] As has been pointed out above, his use of the Septuagint Hexateuch to supplement the history of the monarchical period is certain. The question before us now is whether the same is true of the Greek versions of Kings and Chronicles.

Two passages from the III Kingdoms assure interdependence between the Septuagint and Eupolemus. Eupolemus says that Solomon was twelve years old when crowned,[30] this opinion is handed down in some manuscripts of III Kingdoms 2:12. He also says that Solomon built a porch and forty-eight pillars,[31] information that is attested only in the Greek version of Kings 7:31. Freudenthal and Walter take it for granted that the Greek was here Eupolemus' source.[32] Generally, considering the Hellenistic historians' consistent use of the Septuagint, such a presumption is valid. But in these two instances, since it is questionable whether or not in the middle of the second century a Greek translation of Kings existed, and since we have no other trace of the Greek version in Eupolemus, it is just as reasonable to assume that here both Eupolemus and the Greek version depended on a pre-masoretic version. Alternately, as has been suggested above, the possibility that the Greek version was interpolated from Eupolemus should not be excluded.[33] This is especially valid in regard to III Kingdoms 7:31, which mentions the porch disjointedly in a verse that otherwise catalogues the Temple's silverware,

---

27   The author of the Book of Jubilees' version of the Pentateuchal traditions is another example of the freedom to alter or reinterpret.

28   *P.E.*, IX, 34, 13, I, 543, 23-26 = 723 F 2a, 676, 21-24.

29   Ibid., 33, I, 541, 2f. = ibid. 676 21-23.

30   Ibid., 30, I, 539, 13 = ibid. 673, 23.

31   Ibid., 34, 9, I, 543, 6 f. = ibid. 676, 3 f.

32   Freudenthal, *Hell. St.,* 118; Walter, ad locum.

33   See above, pp. 108-10; 189-90.

suggesting that 7:31b was inserted by a careless scribe.[34] As to Solomon's age, the fact that the rabbinic tradition, in addition to Eupolemus and the Septuagint, maintains that the king was crowned at the age of twelve, tends to show that we are dealing here with an ancient tradition. On the other hand, Eupolemus' work devoted considerable space to chronology, especially to that of Solomon.[35] And, as is argued below, there is reason to assume that some of the Hellenistic chronological tables were incorporated into our Greek biblical tradition. Certainly, these two references alone do not suffice to prove Eupolemus' use of the Greek version of I Kings.

It is remarkable that although Eupolemus and III Kingdoms 6-7 treat the same topic, the dimensions and the technical vocabulary of the Solomonic Temple diverge widely within the two. There are, of course, a number of identical terms, such as altar ($\theta \upsilon \sigma \iota \alpha \tau \acute{\eta} \rho \iota o \nu$),[36] temple ($o \mathring{\iota} \kappa o \varsigma$),[37] tent or tabernacle ($\sigma \kappa \eta \nu \grave{\eta} \ \tau o \mathring{\upsilon} \ \mu \alpha \rho \tau \acute{\upsilon} \rho \iota o \upsilon$),[38] but they may reflect the fact that both Eupolemus and the Greek·translator of I Kings were familiar with the Greek Pentateuch. So sure was Freudenthal of Eupolemus' dependence on the Septuagint that he failed to notice that in the two the same words may sometimes have different meanings: a) because he interpreted the Hebrew word יציע of I Kings 6:10 to mean *Anbau*, he says that the Septuagint's and Eupolemus' equivalent $\mathring{\epsilon} \nu \delta \epsilon \sigma \mu o \varsigma$ means the same,[39] but as pointed out by Mras, the Greek term in Eupolemus means a partition of stone; b) $o \mathring{\iota} \kappa o \delta o \mu \acute{\eta}$ and $\delta \acute{o} \mu o \varsigma$ Freudenthal translates as *Vorbau*, on the basis of III Kingdoms 6:3, instead of *a course of stone*, as required by fragment's context.[40] The use of the same terms for different meanings suggests the opposite of Freudenthal's claims that Eupolemus utilized the Greek version of Kings 6-7. But even if we grant all of the parallel words which, according to Freudenthal, prove Eupolemus' dependence on the Septuagint, the negative parallels ought to be given some consideration. And these by far outnumber

---

34   Cf. Josephus, *B.J.*, V, 184 f. and *A.J.*, XX, 184-89, for the tradition that the portico went back to Solomon. But it is clear that Josephus' reference was to III Kingdoms 7:31b, a feature constructed during the Second Temple, but ascribed to Solomon.

35   *P.E.*, IX, 34, 4, I, 541, 20 f. = 723 F 2a, 675, 8 f. See also, ibid. 34, 20, I, 545, 3 f. = 723 F 3, 677, 14, where Solomon's age at his death is given as 52 = 12 (coronation) + 40 (reign).

36   Ibid., IX, 30, 5, I, 539, 2; 34, I, 543, 12, 15, 544, 2 = 723 F 2a, 676, 9, 12, 27.

37   Ibid., 34, 7, I, 542, 16; 644, 3 = ibid. 675, 25; 676, 28.

38   Ibid., 30, 1, I, 538, 15; 34, 14, I, 544, 2 = ibid. 673, 2; 676, 27.

39   Ibid., 34, 5, I, 542, 5 = ibid. 675, 14. Freudenthal, *Hell. St.*, 119; 211.

40   See Mras, App. Crit. to P.E., IX, 34, 5, I, 542, 3, 5; Walter, ad locum.

the positive.[41] Certainly, Eupolemus seems to contradict more of the Temple's details as depicted in III Kingdoms than he affirms. From the contradictions it is quite likely that Eupolemus never saw a copy of our Greek version of I Kings.

The question that confronts us now is whether or not Eupolemus may have ignored the Septuagint version of I Kings because his primary source for the period was the Book of Chronicles. Indeed, Freudenthal's case for Eupolemus' dependence on the Greek version of Chronicles certainly seems more impressive than the case for III Kingdoms. But this does not extend to its Greek translations. More often than not the technical vocabularies of the Greek of II Chr. 3-4 and Eupolemus diverge widely. Certainly, the divergence between the author of Chronicles and Eupolemus exceeds by far that between the two anonymous translators of I Kings 6-7 and II Chron. 3-4.[42] Following the Hebrew text, for example, the most common phrase for the Temple in II Chronicles is "the house of the Lord," a term used only twice in the fragments. Eupolemus employs instead "the Temple of God" (ἱερὸν τῷ θεῷ) thirteen times and ναός 'five times though the latter may also be used as the equivalent of אולם , a term left untranslated by the Chronicler.[43]

The following is a list of words transliterated from the Hebrew by the Chronicler for which Eupolemus used common Greek renditions:

Hebrew	RSV	II Chr.		Eupolemus
אולם	vestibule	αἰλαμ	(3:4)	στόα[44]
גולות	capitals	γωλωθ	(4:12)	δακτύλαι[45]
מכונות	stands	μεχωνοθ	(4:14)	μηχανήματα[46]
שרשרות	chains	σερσερωθ	(3:16)	ἁλυσιδοτοί[47]

As was already pointed out by Freudenthal, there is no question that Eupolemus utilized the Hebrew text of II Chr. 2-3.[48] With the exception of

---

41   Thus the term for the Temple, the LXX like the Hebrew uses "the house of the Lord." But Eupolmus uses the shortened form twice (see Note 37), ναός five times, and ἱερόν 13 times. ἀνάκτορον used once by Eupolemus (P.E., 34, 13, I, 543, 24 = 723 F 2a, 676, 22) is never recorded in the LXX. Similarly, σηκος , used once in the fragments (ibid. 34, 8, I, 543, 2 = ibid. 675, 28) is found only in II Macc. 14:33. See also below for other terms used by Eupolemus but not found in the Greek Bible.

42   On the Greek version of Chronicles, see G. Gerleman, *Studies in the Septuagint II: Chronicles* (Lund, Lunds Universitets Årsskrift, N.F. Adv. 1, 1946, Bd. 43, Nr. 3).

43   See note 41.

44   *P.E.,* IX, 34, 9, I, 543, 6 = 723 F 2a, 676, 3. Cf. Freudenthal, *Hell. St.,* 119, who believes that Eupolemus' term is οἰκοδομή. But see Mras, ad locum.

45   Ibid., IX, 34, 9, 10, I, 543, 16 = ibid. 676, 13.

46   Ibid., line 16 = ibid. line 14. Cf. Josephus, *A.J.,* VIII, 85, who does use the LXX's transcription.

47   Note 45.

48   Freudenthal, *Hell. St.,* 119 f.

Josephus, who sometimes used the Hebrew text although he normally depended on the Greek translation, Eupolemus is the only Graeco-Jewish writer whose knowledge of Hebrew seems attested.[49]

It should be stressed that although Eupolemus' use of our Greek Hexateuch is certain, this was not the case with the Greek biblical accounts of the Solomonic Temple. Eupolemus' independence of the Septuagint may be illustrated by a partial list of words which he uses but which are not recorded in the Greek version of Scripture at all:

ἄδολος	pure gold[50]
ἀποπατέω	pass with excrement[51]
δίκτυς	network[52]
καταστεγάζω	cover[53]
καταχρέομαι	consume[54]
παρεφθερμένος	corruptly, falsely[55]
προκομίζω	produce[56]
προσκλύζω	wash[57]
προσκρεμάννυμι	attached to[58]
τάφρος	trench[59]
ὑφίστημι	set under[60]
φερωνυμένος	named after[61]
φοινικοβάλανος	date-nut[62]

There are also a number of Hebrew words which Eupolemus rendered differently than did the Septuagint.[63] It is possible to explain this independence either that a) Eupolemus made a special effort to use a technical vocabulary divergent from that of the Greek translations of

---

49   Philo of Alexandria's degree of knowledge of Hebrew is often contested. See S. Sandmel, *Philo's Place in Judaism* (Cincinnati, Hebrew Union College Press, 1955), 11-13.

50   *P.E.,* IX, 34, 6, I, 543, 14 = 723 F 2a, 675, 23. For the use of the term, see Liddell-Scott-Jones, ad locum, who cite Eupolemus.

51   Ibid. 11, I, 543, 21 = 676, 19.

52   Ibid. 11, I, 543, 18 and 19 = 676, 15-16. A word not attested elsewhere: Mras, *Rh. M.,* 92 (1944), 235; Liddell-Scott-Jones-Barber (Suppl.).

53   Ibid. 8, I, 543, 4 f. = ibid. 676, 2.

54   Ibid. 16, I, 544, 8 = ibid. 677, 1.

55   Ibid. 13, I, 543, 24 = ibid. 676, 22. A rarely used term, cf. Liddell-Scott-Jones, ad verbum.

56   Ibid. 34, 4, I, 541, 18 f. = ibid. 675, 6.

57   Ibid. line 9 = ibid. line 6. Cf. Freudenthal, *Hellenistische Studien,* 228.

58   Ibid. line 18 = ibid. line 15.

59   Ibid. line 23 = ibid. line 21. Cf. LXX Mica 5:6(7), whose meaning is doubtful, but in the sense of trench.

60   Ibid. line 6 = ibid. line 3.

61   Ibid. line 25 f. = ibid. line 23.

62   Ibid. 34, 17, I, 544, 14 = ibid. 677, 8.

63   Thus the word ברוש , which Eupolemus and modern translations render as cypress, LXX uses either κέδρος or πεύκη. See Freudenthal, ibid, 120.

Scripture; or that b) our Greek translations of either Kings or Chronicles were not known to him. The former is unlikely in view of Eupolemus' rather slavish following of the Greek Pentateuch and the Book of Joshua. The latter may perhaps account for the freedom with which the author alters historical traditions.

The question of Eupolemus' use of other than the Hexateuch or the historical books of the Bible, may be disposed of briefly. Freudenthal cites Ps. 83:7-9 as Eupolemus' source for the list of nations allegedly conquered by David;[64] and Song of Songs 4:4 as the origin of Solomonic shields in Fragment 3;[65] Gutman has added the play on the word *shalom* (peace) and the name Solomon in Ps. 72:7 and Eupolemus' εἰρήνη.[66] If Eupolemus did use Song of Songs, however, he did not use the Greek version, since the Greek wording and the historian's wording of this verse diverge. The same is true of the two lists of the Davidic conquests. But not only is there no trace of the Greek versions in Eupolemus, it is quite doubtful that Eupolemus necessarily depended on any of these biblical texts. The lists of Ps. 83:7-9 and Eupolemus are based on differing historical realities. The former referred to the lists of ancient nations; the latter related to the geographic conditions of the contemporary world. And it is quite likely that use of the cipher in the two texts is coincidental. It is certain, however, that Eupolemus utilized the Book of Jeremiah, though it is impossible to say whether he used the Greek or Hebrew version of this work.

Eupolemus stands between the author of Chronicles and Josephus in his method of using Scripture. For the Chronicler the Book of Kings was the literary model, which he either abbreviated or expanded by adding from other sources, or rewrote in consonance with the contemporary religious outlook. Using the Greek Bible as his primary source, despite his embellishments, Josephus was faithful to the canonized tradition. In other words, supposing the biblical books were lost, it would be possible to reconstruct to a large extent Josephus' Hebrew sources. This would not be the case, however, if the Book of Kings had not survived and only the Chronicles remained. In this respect Eupolemus is certainly closer to the Chronicler than to Josephus. His contraction of the stories of Moses, Joshua, Samuel and Saul, giving only a few words to each, resembled the list of generations in the early chapters of I Chronicles. His own contribution, partly based on the sources, but mostly invented, was the chronological schemes. Although he wrote centuries after the author of Kings, the Chronicler attempted to imitate the historical style of his model. Josephus, however, recast the material in an

---

64 Freudenthal, ibid., 114 f.; Y. Gutman, *The Beginnings of the Jewish-Hellenistic Literature,* II, 85.

65 Freudenthal, ibid., 114; Gutman, ibid., II, 94.

66 Gutman, ibid., II, 85, cites also Ps. 72:10, where the kings of Tarshish, the islands Sheba and Seba are said to have brought tribute to the prince (Solomon?).

attempt to write standard Hellenistic history. Other Graeco-Jewish writers, discussed in the next chapter, in many respects anticipated Josephus. Eupolemus did not. His syntax and sentence formation left more of the Hebraic literary structure intact than did that of any other Hellenistic writer.

Are there traces of the Apocryphal works in Eupolemus? In the nineteenth century Ewald conjectured that Eupolemus' version of the Solomonic correspondence was taken from a lost apocryphon.[67] Attaching historical significance to this alleged exchange of letters, Gutman writes: "There is no doubt that Eupolemus constructed the letters between Solomon and the king of Egypt on the basis of popular tradition . . . , which fused Jewish and Egyptian legends."[68] The assertions of Ewald and Gutman are difficult to disprove. However, unless reliable sources for the content of the correspondence can be found, the presumption that Eupolemus manufactured it must stand. Indeed, Freudenthal believed that Eupolemus borrowed some phrases from the Letter of Aristeas for the wording of Vaphres' message to Solomon.[69] This, however, is correctly denied by Meecham and Walter.[70] The accounts concerning preservation of the ark in Eupolemus and in II Maccabees, on the one hand, and those of Eupolemus and the Lives of the Prophets, on the other, belong to a different category. Here interdependence cannot be doubted. Yet, Eupolemus must be regarded as the source rather than the recipient of these traditions.[71]   Even so, the possibility, though unverifiable, that Eupolemus had access to an apocryphon of Jeremiah should not be entirely excluded.

As far as we know, Eupolemus was the first Graeco-Jewish author to make extensive use of classical and Hellenistic historians. Certainly, the mendacious Ctesias, who invented the name of Astibares, allegedly the sixth king of Media, appears in Eupolemus at the head of a Median army as a conqueror of Judaea in 586.[72] It is possible that Ctesias' fictional histories, exceedingly popular as the source of exotic accounts, inspired some of the stories found in Eupolemus' fragments. Less certain but quite probable is Eupolemus' use of Herodotus, whose accounts of Egypt and the disposition of Xerxes' Persian

---

67   Ewald, *History of Israel* III, 225, note. Cf. Gutman, ibid. II, 85 f.

68   Gutman, *Beginnings of Jewish-Hellenistic Literature,* II, 88. He treats Eupolemus' account, with some anachronistic or similar passages excepted, as if they were historical, but does not explain now these traditions were preserved.

69   Freudenthal, *Hell. St.,* 110, comparing Aristeas 42, 46, with Eupolemus, in *P.E.,* IX, 32 = 723 F 2a, 674, 6-14.

70   H. G. Meecham, *The Letter of Aristeas* (Manchester, Manchester University Press, 1935), 327 f.; Walter, forthcoming publication. Cf. also P. Wendland, *Die Hellenistisch-Römische Kultur* (Tübingen, 1912), 198, n. 2; Gutman, *Beginnings of Jewish-Hellenistic Literature,* II, 86.

71   Cf. D. Th. Schermann, *Propheten- und Apostellegenden* (Leipzig, 1907), 87f., who assumes Eupolemus to have been the source of both the II Macc. and the Vita of Jeremiah.

72   Ctesias, in Diodorus, II, 34, 1-6 = *FGrH* 688 F 5.

army seem to reappear in the fragments.[73] Among the other likely sources of Eupolemus are, as noted above, Euhemerus, Hecataeus of Abdera, and the Babylonian, Egyptian, and Phoenician historians who addressed themselves to the Greek-reading world.[74]

Unlike Josephus, who noted what he had taken from heathen histories, Eupolemus supposedly felt no need to bolster the Judaeïc historical tradition with the names of pagan writers. This failure to distinguish between Jewish and heathen sources sometimes makes it difficult to trace the origin of certain traditions reported by Eupolemus, such as Solomon's age upon his accession to the crown, which ultimately found their way into some manuscripts of the Septuagint and rabbinic lore.

It is also important to recognize the source of Eupolemus' style. Failure to do so has resulted in an utterly negative evaluation of his use of the Greek language. Freudenthal, whose training in classics was matchless, gave this verdict: "The style of these [Eupolemus'] letters is much inferior to even the worst passages of Josephus' *Jewish Antiquities*. Eupolemus' style is as faulty and as tasteless as it is false, the vocabulary very limited, the sentence structure clumsy and confusing, almost incomprehensible."[75] In the context of classical literature this verdict does not appear to be too severe.

What needs to be noted, however, is that Eupolemus' language was not the literary Greek of Alexandria, which Josephus, apparently using assistants, tried to match;[76] but the specific kind of koine—Judaeo-Greek. The misuse of the conjecture καὶ,[77] the verb ποιέω,[78] ו the frequency of the compound verbs, or the abused objective ὅλος[79] are syntactically nearer to the Hebrew עשה וֹ and כל [80] than to their Greek equivalents. Another characteristic, as noted by Walter, is the use of the chiasmus.[81] All this must have sounded like pidgin Greek. Referring to the New Testament, Nietsche is said to have remarked irreverently that God did not know Greek. Nietsche failed to recognize that in the Gospels Jesus speaks Judaeo-Greek; and that this was a quite acceptable language compared to the primitive forms of this tongue as it appears in the fragments of Eupolemus. Only the Greek papyri may serve as comparative material for an analysis of Eupolemus' syntax.

    73   See above pp. 164; 234-35.

    74   Cf. Movers, *Die Phönizier*, II, 1 (Berlin, 1849), 141 f.; Freudenthal, *Hell. St.*, 111; Gutman, Beginnings of *Jewish-Hellenistic Literature*, II, 94.

    75   Freudenthal, *Hell. St.*, 109; cf. 105-30.

    76   *C. Apionem*, I, 50; cf. H. St. J. Thackeray, *Josephus: the Man and the Historian* (New York, Jewish Institute of Religion Press, 1929), 100-24.

    77   *P.E.* IX, 34, 15, I, 544, 3-5 = 723 F 2a, 676, 28-30.

    78   Ibid. 6, I, 542, 11-13 = ibid. 675, 20-22.

    79   Ibid. 11, I, 542, 19 = ibid. 676, 16.

    80   Ibid. 4, I, 541, 21-542, 2 = ibid. 675, 9-11.

    81   See Blass-Debrunner-Funk, *A Greek Grammar of the New Testament and Other Early Literature* (Chicago, University of Chicago Press, 1962), 1 f.

Unfortunately, these come almost exclusively from Egypt.[82] The Greek translations of Scripture frequently misused what was considered fair Greek idiom. This has been explained as a result of a wish to be faithful to the Semitic original. But this still does not account for the strong Hebrew flavor of Eupolemus' fragments. Only the presumed existence of a distinct Judaeo-Greek dialect renders Eupolemus' Greek tolerable.

As is befitting a Graeco-Palestinian author, Eupolemus appears to have been the most Jewish of the Jewish historians. Not only was his language more Graeco-Jewish than that of any other Hellenistic author, but the contents of his writings related more intimately to biblical historiography.[83] Although marvelously articulate, the Hellenic literary tradition did not favor accounts that described the detailed dimensions of the arts.[84] Herodotus often marveled at the spell of the ancient monuments, but it never occurred to him to describe them in detail.[85] The works of Phidias were universally admired, but we have no literary sketches of the Parthenon. Only the partial actual survival permits us to appreciate his artistic genius. The biblical tradition, however, as illustrated in the sections of Exodus, Kings, Chronicles and Ezekiel, found special satisfaction in cataloguing materials, builders, the minute dimensions of the temples, and their furnishings. No known ancient piece of writing, whether Greek or Barbarian, equaled or even came near to Josephus' marvelous descriptions of the Solomonic or Herodian Temples.[86] It is the concern for the architectural minutiae that makes the fragments of Eupolemus a bridge between biblical and Greek literature.

Eupolemus in describing the Solomonic Temple was more concerned with the value of the Temple's golden objects than with their art or holiness. In this respect he may be compared with his contemporary Callixenes of Rhodes, extracts of whose monograph *On Alexandria* are preserved in Athenaeus.[87] Callixenes described the enormous and most luxurious vessel that a Phoenician builder constructed for Ptolemy Philopator (222-204) and the quadrennial games of Ptolemy Philadelphus (285-246). He catalogued the

---

82   Cf. E. Norden, *Die antike Kunstprosa* (Leipzig, 1898); A. Deissmann, *Bible Studies* (Edinburgh, 1901); L. Mitteis and U. Wilcken, *Grundzüge und Chrestomatie der Papyruskunde* (Leipzig, 1912); P. F.-M. Abel, *Grammaire du grec biblique suivie d'un choix de papyrus* (Paris, 1927); *Corpus Papyrorum Judaicarum,* edited by Tcherikover-Fuks-Stern (Cambridge, Mass., Harvard University Press, 1957-64).

83   With the exception of Aristeas on Job (*P.E.* IX, 25 = 725 F 1), which was in fact a translation from the Syriac (LXX Job 42:17b-e).

84   Cf. J. Overbeck, *Die antiken Schriftequellen zur Geschichten der bildenden Künste bei den Griechen* (Leipzig, 1868); P. Friedländer, *Johannes von Gaza und Paulus Silentiarius* (Leipzig, 1912), 31-46.

85   Cf. *Herod.* II, 106; III 37.

86   *B.J.* V, 184-287; *A.J.* VIII, 63-98.

87   Athenaeus, Callixenes in V, 196A-203B; 203E-206C; *FGrH* 627 FF 1-5. Cf. Jacoby, in *R.E.,* X, (1919), 1751-54.

royal utensils which weighed about 10,000 talents of silver. Quoting from official reports, Callixenes listed the fabulous ornamentations of royal procession—the bowls, jewels, crowns, shields, statues, effigies of elephants, chariots mounted on columns—all made of gold. He does not tell us how many talents all these precious objects weighed. But he does report that the cost of the carnival borne by Ptolemy I Soter amounted to 2,239 talents and 50 minae.[88] A case could be made that the many parallels between Callixenes' itemization of the Ptolemaic gilded objects and Eupolemus' catalog of Solomonic sacred vessels shows interdependence. But whether the reports of the gaudyphallic symbols had inspired Eupolemus or whether the similarities are merely coincidental is an open question.

88   Athenaeus, V, 196A-203B = FGrH 627 F 2.

Chapter Eleven

THE GRAECO-PALESTINIAN LITERATURE

Our analysis of Eupolemus' fragments raises as many questions as it solves. Scholars have either ignored the incoherent Graeco-Jewish extracts, branded them as apologetic, addressed to the Gentile world and hence of no interest for the development of the mainstream of Judaism, or arbitrarily placed them all in the Diaspora, notably Alexandria. If this monograph proves anything, it shows that in one instance at least a Graeco-Jewish work was written in Jerusalem by a foremost priest and aide of Judah Maccabee. It is the contents of the fragments that give them a priestly identity. The assumption that Eupolemus the historian and Eupolemus the envoy of Judah were two different persons can no longer be justified.

Eupolemus' fragments reflect two cultures. We see a passionate interest in sacrificial Judaism and a continuation of the priestly biblical historiography on one hand, and a faulty replica of pagan Hellenistic book learning, on the other. Within the context of priestly Judaism, Eupolemus seems to fit best into the Sadducean faction. Josephus is the only other writer who ever practiced Sadducean customs, no matter how briefly. Should Eupolemus' fragments thus be regarded as the unique literary remnants of that sect? Do they confirm the view—often voiced but hardly documented—that the Sadducees, despite their conservative biblical exegesis, countenanced more of the pagan influences than did the other factions? How many of the attitudes, if any, implied in the fragments were shared by Judah Maccabee as well? These and similar interesting questions are worth raising even though the available evidence does not offer solutions.

The equally enigmatic problem of the existence of a Graeco-Jewish literary circle in Jerusalem is also worth considering. Until recently it has been taken for granted that the extant remnants of lost Greek works espousing Jewish views were the products of men living in Alexandria.[1] It has been assumed

---

1   E. Schürer, *Geschichte des jüdischen Volkes*, III[3], 420-716, and passim, gives a fair summary of the scholarly consensus in regard to the Alexandrian monopoly of the Graeco-Jewish literature. Though differing from Schürer in many respects, A. Schlatter, *Die Geschichte Israels*[2] (Calw and Stuttgart, 1906), is even more extreme in this, making Eupolemus an Egyptian Jew (p.101). The same view is repeated by P. Dalbert, *Der hellnistisch-jüdischen Missionsliteratur unter Ausschluss von Philo und Josephus* (Hamburg, 1954); as well as by the Hebrew-writing Y. Gutman, *The Beginnings of the Jewish-Hellenistic Literature* (Jerusalem, Mosad Bialik, 1958-63). Gutman goes so far as to say that Eupolemus was exiled from Jerusalem into Cyrene apparently during Menalaus' high priestly office (II, 77 f.).

that the Jews of Palestine, if they knew Greek at all, wrote either in Hebrew or in Aramaic. This presumption appeared justified in light of the unbroken chain of Semitic literary tradition in Palestine and Syria extending for millenia. Of the numerous nations conquered by the Macedonians, Palestine more than any other country continually presents a direct literary challenge to cultural Hellenism as well as to the use of the Greek language as such.

Reacting in opposition to this point of view, some scholars have now introduced the view that Palestine in general and Jerusalem in particular were thoroughly Hellenized regions. Sevenster, for instance, in dealing with the first Christian century, posits the theory that both Jesus and his brother James could compose in the smooth Greek style of, for instance, the epistle bearing the latter's name.[2] Hengel takes it for granted that almost everything that transpired in Palestine in the post-Alexandrian period was most profoundly influenced, if not inspired, by Hellenism. Dealing with the antecedents of the rabbinic literature, Lieberman also finds the talmudic sages deeply immersed in abstruse aspects of Greek literature.[3]

These and related discussions are important for the light they shed on the relationship between Hellenistic culture and the development of Christianity and rabbinic Judaism. We are more concerned, however, with a survey of the Palestinian Graeco-Jewish literary productions, as much as the fragmentary evidence permits. Eupolemus certainly was no unicum. There were other Graeco-Jewish or Graeco-Samaritan writers who may have lived in Jerusalem, Samaria, or in Tiberias, such as Pseudo-Hecataeus, Theodorus or Justus. Josephus' works are excluded from our theme since they are well-known, extant and they were composed outside of Palestine. But we are certainly interested in the extensive notes of the events he says were taken while he was a prisoner of the Romans in the years 67-70. Were they in Hebrew or Aramaic, as was his first version of the *Wars of Jews,* or were they written in Greek? Vespasian's *Memoirs* were probably composed in Latin, but the future emperor must have communicated with Josephus in Greek, and the latter no doubt had a hand in the official record of the war. Chronologically, Palestinian Graeco-Jewish literature begins during the period of the Diadochi, when Pseudo-Hecataeus wrote, and ends with Justus of Tiberias, whose works were composed in the last decade of the first Christian century.

A few words concerning the genre of works produced by priests of Eastern sanctuaries—to which the Septuagint and the Graeco-Jewish writings belong—

---

2   J. N. Sevenster, *Do You Know Greek: How Much Greek Could the First Jewish Christians Have Known:* (Leiden, E. L. Brill, 1968), passim, esp. 189-91.

3   M. Hengel, *Judentum und Hellenismus: Studien zu ihrer Begegnung unter besonderer Berücksichtigung Palästinas bis zur Mitte der 2.Jh. v. Chr.* (Tübingen, Mohr, 1969); S. Lieberman, *Hellenism in Jewish Palestine* (New York, The Jewish Theological Seminary, 1950). In his Introduction to the Hebrew edition (Jerusalem, Mosad Bialik, 1962), Lieberman moderated somewhat the hypothesis of the presence of Hellenistic culture in rabbinic literature.

may help focus the issue. Greek accounts of the barbarian peoples go back to the period of the logographers. In the sixth century B.C. Hecataeus of Miletus visited Asia and Egypt, where he interviewed the priests for his Researches (ἱστορίαν). Herodotus' work and the fifth century monographs on Egypt and Ethiopia by Hellanicus of Lesbos and Charon of Lampascus attest to the Greek fascination with alien anthropology.[4]

After the year 300 B.C. barbarian priests such as Berossus of Babylon and Manetho of Sebennystus composed accounts to tell the true dimensions of the glorious civilizations of their respective countries—Babylonia and Egypt. The priests of Tyre and Sidon, perhaps also in the first decades of the third century, or possibly somewhat later, published summaries of Phoenician records. They were the first to reveal to the world cuneiform and hieroglyphic texts.[5] At first the scholars of Alexandria—the intellectual center of the world—were fascinated, as attested in the foundation of the Museum, by the very existence of writings claiming to date back millenia prior to the oldest Greek literary traditions. The Alexandrian collectors had one weakness. They themselves did not control any of the foreign scripts. Neither were they impressed with the dry and matter-of-fact genealogical Greek style of the Barbarian chroniclers. For many, history had to be a source of enlightenment and entertainment as well as a search for truth; others preferred fiction to describing events as they were. Had the Gilgamesh epic been translated into Greek, it would have gained wide popularity as history. But the papyri rolls containing the dry writings of Berossus and Manetho gathered dust while the fictional romances of Onesicritus on the life in India

---

4   The sixth century B.C. Hecataeus of Miletes treated Asia and Africa under several subdivisions: Arabia and Phoenicia (*FGrH* 1 FF 271-88); East Asia (FF 288-99); Egypt (FF 300-28); Libya (329-59), best known by the influence on Herodotus, whose own history devotes much space to the East. Hellanicus, who flourished in second half of the fifth century, wrote histories of Egypt (*FGrH* 4 FF 53-55; 173-76 = 608a FF 1-7) and Persia (4 FF 59-63 = 687a FF 1-11). Charon of Lampascus, about 400 B.C., wrote on Crete, Libya, and Ethiopia (262 T 1; F 3a-b = 687b FF 1-6). Greek pre-Ctesian accounts of the Barbarians, however, were limited to regions where Hellenic settlements had been established so that bilingual Greeks were available to supply the (mis)information to traveling logographers.

5   Berossus, priest of Babylon's Temple Bell, wrote a three-book history of Babylonia to the period of Alexander, which he dedicated to Antiochus Soter I. He also transmitted Babylonian astronomy to the Hellenic world. His history is known chiefly through Alexander Polyhistor (*FGrH* 273), Josephus, and Eusebius. The most complete discussion of Berossus, although in need of revision, is by P. Schnabel, *Berossos* (Berlin 1923); (*FGrH* 680 TT 1-11; FF 1-20). Manetho of Sebennystus, the chief priest of Helipolis, also known primarily through Josephus and Eusebius, did for Egypt what Berossus had done for Babylonia. He is responsible for the dynastic divisions used by historians. Menander of Ephesos, the Phoenician historian, known primarily through Josephus, reputedly translated the native records for his Tyrian history (*A.J.* VIII, 144 = *FGrH* 783 T 3a-c).

and those of Ctesias on Persia and Assyria gained the almost exclusive attention of the reading public.[6]

Graeco-Jewish literature made its first appearance, according to tradition, in the so-called Septuagint translation of the Pentateuch during the reign of Ptolemy II Philadelphus (285-246 B.C.).[7] This statement is true if by Graeco-Jewish literature we mean a distinct and easily identifiable genre of writings. With the possible exception of ephemeral records, such as those that survive in papyri or official memoirs, all of the works written by Jews after this period show the Septuagint imprint. This is the case whether the works are translations from the Hebrew, historical writings such as the fragments of Demetrius the chronologist or Josephus, philosophical writings such as those of Aristobulus or Philo of Alexandria, epics by Ezekielus or Philo, or forgeries of the classical poets such as Pseudo-Homer, -Orpheus or -Euripides.[8] For clarity's sake the term Graeco-Jewish literature should not be applied to Greek accounts by pagans or to those by Jews if written prior to the appearance of the Septuagint.

Our allusion to the pre-Septuagint Graeco-Jewish writings does not refer to the alleged existence of such biblical translations, as claimed by the second century B.C. Aristobulus or more recently by Kahle.[9] It does refer to a unique first-person report of Jerusalem written about 300 B.C., extracts of which *Contra Apionem* I, 185-205, attributes to Hecataeus of Abdera (330-270). Because of the intrinsic significance of the report and because of the light it sheds on the history of literature, this fragment has inspired a vast

---

6   Among the Greek accounts of the East, the ones dealing with Egypt are the most interesting, perhaps because of the uniqueness of her civilization, but also because she was not touched by the romanceers such as Onesicritus or Ctesias. On Onesicritus, who piloted Alexander's boat on the Indus, see 134 FF 1-39; T.S. Brown, *Onesicritus: A Study in Hellenistic Historiography* (Berkeley and Los Angeles, University of California Press, 1949). The fragments of Ctesias (*FGrH* 688 F 1-74) await a good commentary.

7   Although the statement rests on the questionable letter of Aristeas (9 ff. and passim), or sources dependent on it, circumstantial evidence as to the king's interest in foreign records makes it quite likely that the author repeated here a reliable report.

8   For the Graeco-Jewish writers, see above . As to the hexametric forgeries, see now N. Walter, *Der Thoraussleger Aristobulos* (Berlin, Akademie-Verlag, 1964), 151-261.

9   Aristobulus in Eusebius, *P.E.*, XII, 12: P. Kahle, *The Cairo Geniza*[2] (New York, Praeger, 1959), 211-14. Kahle dates the LXX about 100, roughly about the same time of the Letter of Aristeas, which appeared soon after the translation was allegedly completed for "propaganda is made for something contemporary" (p. 211). This, however, does not assure us that the translation had been just recently made. For the issue whether the Greek was as reliable as the Hebrew text, was alive centuries after the translation itself had been completed. Aristeas may, moreover, be rehashing issues that were alive a long time but which he merely paraphrased, as is the case with the problem of the Ptolemy's treatment of the Jews after 312 B.C. (Aristeas, 12-28). Furthermore, Aristobulus, who flourished during the reign of Ptolemy (176-150), speaks of the official translation with a clear reference to Ptolemy Philadephus (*P.E.*, XII, 12), though, as noted, he, like Kahle, albeit in a different context, speaks of pre-LXX translation.

number of learned papers. The main issue debated by the experts has been whether Josephus was here quoting the pagan Hecataeus, who in fact had written about the Jews, or whether he was actually citing one of the Jewish-authored works written under the pseudonym of Hecataeus. If the former, the passage is genuine and dates from the Diadochi period; if the latter, it is a forgery of the second or first century B.C.[10] The agreement underlying both sides of the argument is that if the extracts were taken from an eyewitness report, they must have been written by a heathen, since Graeco-Jewish writings allegedly appeared only in the post-Septuagint period.

But is this presumption justified? It has been shown that native priests such as Manetho, Berossus, and others wrote up their national histories for the Greek world within half a century after the Macedonian conquest. Is it not possible that a Jerusalem priest did the same for the Jews? I believe that it can be shown that Josephus was quoting a pre-Septuagint Graeco-Jewish work here. The text from which Josephus quotes, it would seem, had originally been part of an eyewitness report intended for Ptolemy I, the founder of the Macedonian dynasty in Egypt. When the name of the reporter had been forgotten, however, the account was attributed to the contemporary Hecataeus. In other words, the passages quoted in *Contra Apionem,* I, 185-205, had originally been part of a monograph written by a native priest, similar to the ones produced by Berossus and Manetho, but different from them in that whereas Berossus and Manetho concerned themselves with the antiquities of Babylonia or Egypt, the theme of this one was contemporary Jerusalem.

In addition to the passage under discussion, we must introduce six more texts under the heading of Pseudo-Hecataeus:

1. *Contra Apionem,* I, 183-205 (cf. Aristeas, 83-120).
2. *Contra Apionem,* I, 213 f.
3. *Contra Apionem,* II, 43-47 (cf. *A.J.,* XII, 3-8 and Aristeas, 12-27).
4. Letter of Aristeas, 31.

---

10 Among the scholars who regard *C. Apionem,* I, 185-205 belonging to Hecataeus are: A. Elter, *De gnomologiorum graecorum historiae atque origine commentartio* (Bonn, 1893-95), 247-54; A. Schlatter, *Geschichte Israels,* 22; P. Wendland, in E. Kautzsch (ed.), *Die Apokryphen und Pseudepigraphen des Alten Testaments* (Tübingen, 1900), 1 f.; M. Engers, "De Hecataei Abderitae fragmentis," *Mnemosyne,* N.S. 51 (1923), 232 f.; H. Lewy, "Hekataios von Abdera...," *The Jews in the Graeco-Roman World* (Tel Aviv, 1961), 303 f. [in Hebrew]; Y. Gutman, *Beginnings of Jewish-Hellenistic Literature,* I, 70 f. [in Hebrew]. Of those who regard this text as Pseudo-Hecataean are: H. Willrich, *Judaica,* (Göttingen, 1900), 86-102; E. Schürer, *Geschichte des jüdischen Volkes*[4], III, 605-08; Th. Reinach, *Textes d'auteurs grecs et romains relatifs au Judaïsme* (Paris, 1895), 227-35; F. Jacoby, *FGrH,* IIIa, 61-75; B. Schaller, "Hekataios von Abdera über die Juden: Zur Frage der Echtheit und der Datierung," *ZNW,* 24 (1963), 15-31; N. Walter, *Der Thoraausleger Aristobulos,* 189-94.

5. *Jewish Antiquities,* I, 159.
6. Clement of Alexandria, *Stromata,* V, 113, 1-2.
7. Herennius Philo, in Origen, *Against Celsius,* I, 15,

The most characteristic of these remarkably varied texts is perhaps No. 6. Hecataeus' *On Abraham* quotes Orpheus, Sophocles, Euripides, Plato, and Heraclitus as indirectly affirming the veracity of the Pentateuch.[11] It was suspected by Elter that these quotations were Christian forgeries.[12] But their Jewish origin is assured since Aristobulus, who flourished in Alexandria during the Maccabean rebellion, cited them.[13] Their antiquity does not diminish the probability that Nos. 5-6, which quote Hecataeus' *On Abraham,* referred to a double pseudograph: falsely attributing pseudoclassical passages to Hecataeus. The first to raise questions about Hecataeus' pro-Jewish statements was the second century A.D. Herennius Philo of Byblos (No. 7), an expert in such matters, since he evidently manufactured mythological texts and ascribed them to the allegedly pre-Trojan Sanchuniathon.[14]

Also pseudographical, according to scholarly consensus, was the claim if the Letter of Aristeas (No. 4), repeated by Josephus (No. 3), that Hecataeus had commented on the holiness of the Law. This citation assures us that the pseudograph (Nos. 6-7) antedated the Letter of Aristeas, now generally placed, after Elias Bickerman, as written between 145 and 127 B.C. The question remains whether the fragments of Pseudo-Hecataeus, cited in Nos. 3-4, come from a pseudograph the same as or different from Nos. 6-7. The basis of the problem is that the citations of Clement (No. 6-7) appears to come from an alleged collection of poetic quotations dealing with creation, idolatry, and Abraham; the one of Josephus (Nos. 3-4) from a prose work

---

11   For the purpose of this discussion, the body of the falsified poetry is treated as a unit. But the Pythagorean, Orphic and Stoic elements as well as the complex literary history from the pre-Aristobulan beginnings to the Christian versions of the pseudo-pagan affirmations of the biblical beliefs should not be forgotten. For the Orphic fragments, see Otto Kern, [ed.] *Orphicorum Fragmenta* (Berlin, 1922); for the latest discussion of this subject, see Walter, *Der Thoraausleger Aristobulos,* 202-61.

12   Elter (note 10), 197-203.

13   They are said to have been quoted, and undoubtedly were, by Aristobulus in Eusebius, *P.E.,* XIII, 11, 3; 12; alluded to in the Letter of Aristeas, 16 (Ζῆνα καὶ Δία) XIII. 12, 7, meaning, as explained by Walter (*Thoraausleger,*101) that Zeus may be rendered as *Theos.* Other passages—that the philosophers agree that God must be addressed in a pious manner (Aristeas, 234 f. = *P.E.* XIII, 12, 8); that Jewish law reflects piety and justice (ibid. 131, 278 = ibid. XIII, 12, 8, II, 195, 9-11). Cf. also Walter, ibid. 99-103—also show dependence on Aristobulus.

14   Origines, *C. Celsium,* I, 15.   On Philo of Byblos' Sanchuniathon, *P.E.,* I, 9 ff. = *FGrH* 790 FF 1-4. For a recent view that rehabilitates Philo of Byblos' testimony, see Otto Eissfeldt, *Ras Schamara und Sanchunjaton* (Halle, 1939); cf. Speyer, *Die literarische Fälschung im Altertum,* 157 f.

concerned with the position of Alexandrian Jews in Ptolemaic Egypt. The cogent answer apparently is, as proposed by Walter, that we label the prose fragments as the product of Pseudo-Hecataeus I and that those written in meter as Pseudo-Hecataeus II.

The text which has confounded the expert, however, is No. 1. On the premise that it contains material which closely resembles the passage of Hecataeus quoted in Diodorus, XL, 3, and on the basis of erroneous statements which supposedly only a heathen author would have made, some scholars (Wendland, Schlatter, Lewy, Tcherikover) posit that the quotations in *Contra Apionem*, I, 185-205, come essentially from the genuine Hecataeus. Another group of critics (Schürer, Stein, Walter), however, because of the author's self-identification as a Jewish patriot, have argued that it was taken from the same Pseudo-Hecataeus as was *Contra Apionem*, II, 44-48 (No. 3), the author of an account on Ptolemaic Palestine. Thus although scholars differ as to whether or not there were two authors, called for convenience Pseudo-Hecataeus I and Pseudo-Hecataeus II, they do generally agree that Nos. 1 and 3 represent quotations from the same forged source.

A close analysis of the two fragments shows, however, as suggested by Jacoby, that both groups of critics are partly right.[15] Certainly, *Contra Apionem*, I, 183-205 (No. 1) cannot be ascribed to the pagan Hecataeus, since the extract was apparently taken from a work written by a priest of Jerusalem.[16] On the other hand, it is rather unlikely that the same priest would have also authored the fragment cited in *Contra Apionem*, II, 44-47 (No. 3), because a) No. 1 was taken from a work written by an eyewitness, while No. 3 was not;[17] b) No. 1's theme was Judaea, and No. 3's the citizenship rights of the Alexandrian Jews;[18] and c) No. 1 described Ptolemy I Lagus as kindly and humane, but No. 3 attributed kindly acts to Ptolemy II Philadelphus in contrast to his father's cruel treatment of prisoners.[19] These

15   Even some of the scholars who regard *C. Apionem*, II, 185-205, (No. 1) as genuine by Hecataean, such as Lewy (note 10), admit that *C. Apionem*, II, 43-47 (No. 3) belongs to Ps.-Hecataeus, as indicated by the presumption that the Samaritan state was by now under Judaean tutelage, as well as its dependence on Aristeas' account of Philadelphus' translation. Jacoby (*FGrH*, IIIa, 61-74), however, regards both of these fragments as Pseudo-Hecataean, but attributes them to two different authors.

16   Note *C. Apionem*, I, 188, where the reporter inserts the population of the priests; the technical information concerning the Temple's furniture (198 f.), in which only a priest would be interested.

17   See below, pp. 266 f.

18   Cf. *C. Apionem*, I, 189, with II, 44. No. 1 appears to have been unaware of the existence of Alexandrian Jewry or, for that matter, of Alexandria as such.

19   Ibid. I, 186, "Ptolemy's humanity and kindliness;" II, 44, stresses Ptolemy's self-interest. Cf. Aristeas 13, characterizes Ptolemy's "good fortune and prowess." The source of No. 3 appears to have been Agatharchides, mentioned by Josephus in *C. Apionem*, I, 205-12 (*FGrH* 86 F 20), as well as in *J.A.*, XII, 5. Agatharchides' account of Ptolemy's entrance into Jerusalem on a Sabbath day apparently referred to a later period than that reported in No. 1.

and other considerations, discussed below, indicate that No. 1 must be dated during the period of Ptolemy Lagus, and perhaps as early as the last decade of the fourth century B.C., when Persian rule was still a living memory. No. 3, however, was an imitation of No. 1, made during the second half of the second century, sometime after the composition of the Letter of Aristeas. Certainly, Aristeas 12-27, 31, 86-120 is an embellishment and falsification of No. 1.

If so, the seven texts listed above should be rearranged as follows:[20]

PSEUDO-HECATAEUS I (circa 300 B.C.)

1. *Contra Apionem,* I, 183-205.
1a. Letter of Aristeas, 83-120.
2. *Contra Apionem,* I, 213 f.

PSEUDO-HECATAEUS II (After Aristeas, before Josephus).

3. *Contra Apionem,* II, 43-47.
3a. *A.J.* XII, 3-8.
3b. Letter of Aristeas, 12-27.
4. Letter of Aristeas, 31.

PSEUDO-HECATAEUS III (before Aristobulus).

5. *Jewish Antiquities,* I, 159.
6. Clement of Alexandria, *Stromata,* V, 113-1-2.
7. Herennius Philo, in Origen, *Contra Celsium,* I, 15b.

PSEUDO-HECATAEUS I

If our analysis of the sources is correct, the extracts from the work labeled Pseudo-Hecataeus I are of paramount significance. They appear to be the oldest remnants of a Greek treatise written by a Jew. At least in five instances the author uses the first person to identify himself with Judaea, the subject of his work:

1. [Ezekias] "having been closely in touch with us" ($\dot{\eta}\mu\hat{\iota}\nu$).[21]
2. "Our people's ($\dot{\eta}\mu\hat{\omega}\nu\ \tau\grave{o}\ \acute{e}\theta\nu o\varsigma$) vast population."[22]

---

20   See N. Walter's arrangement of the Testimonia and Fragmenta (*Der Thora-ausleger Aristobulos,* 188). He attributes the prose writings to Ps.-Hecataeus I, but the poetry to Ps.-Hecataeus II.

21   *C. Apionem,* I, 189 = *FGrH* 264 F 21. the enigmatic statement, perhaps quoted out of context, implies an official relationship between the author and the authorities. Would this be the only assertion using first person, it could be taken as a report of the governor.

22   Ibid. I, 194. See next note.

3. "Many of our (ἡμῶν) people have been deported to Babylon."[23]

4. "When I myself (ἐμοῦ) was on the march to the Red Sea."[24]

5. "An escort of Jewish cavalry who accompanied us" (τις . . .παραπεμπτόν των ἡμᾶς).[25]

Of course the first person might have been used as a fictive device, as in the case of the author of the Letter of Aristeas. But there is quite a difference between Pseudo-Hecataeus I and the Letter of Aristeas. The latter shows no respect for facts, having assembled the account apparently from sources only half-understood by the author. The former, with perhaps an exceptional lapsus calami, discussed below, seems to have been written by some expert in priestly law and well informed as to the conditions of the country during the Persian occupation. The non-historicity of his account used to be deducted from the fact that Josephus' lists of postexilic priests do not mention a high priest named Ezekias.[26] But a coin of the late Persian period now confirms the existence of a high priest by this name.[27] The opinion of Willrich, followed by Jacoby, that the author used Ezekias to disguise the personality of Onias, the founder of the Jewish shrine in Heliopolis, is thus discredited.[28] The numismatic recovery of the High Priest Ezekias harmonizes with the general impression that the quotes of *Contra Apionem*, I, 183-205, from a lost treatise were factual.

We can now proceed with an analysis of the contents. Since he was quoting from a widely read book, Josephus offers only sketchy bits from various parts of the treatise, which makes its reconstruction problematical.[29] Josephus does suggest, however, that he was quoting from the introductory section, if not the first sentence, of the book: "In this time Ptolemy the son of Lagus,

23   Ibid. I, 194. Becker, cited by Niese, proposed to change from the first person to αὐτῶν "their," which Thackeray (Loeb Classical Library) correctly rejects, but for the wrong reason attributing the first-person pronoun to Josephus. This emendation, or rejection of traditional wording advocated by Niese, would require the same treatment for the other pronouns.

24   Ibid. I, 201.

25   Ibid. I, 201.

26   See *J.A.,* XX, 224-58, and L. H. Feldman's notes in the Loeb Classical Library edition (1965).

27   A. Reifenberg, *Ancient Jewish Coins*[4] (Jerusalem, Rubin Mass, 1965) Plate I, No. 2. O. R. Sellers, *The Citadel of Beth-Zur* (Philadelphia, 1933), 73, read also the name of *Yehoh* (Yehohanan) on the same coin, but as Reifenberg (p. 9) points out, quoting Sukenik, this should be read as *Yehud,* the formal name of the country under the Persians.

28   H. Willrich, *Judaica,* 101, 106-08; F. Jacoby, *FGrH* IIIa, 62, 21-30. Based on this presumption, Jacoby offers a "*Terminus post,* der sehr gut zum character und der warscheinlichen Tendenz des buches passt. Es ist sehr denkbar, dass sein verfasser palaestinensischer Jude, etwa aus der umgebung des Onias, und selbs priester war" (lines 26-29).

29   Cf. *C. Apionem,* I, 183; 205; *FGrH* 264 F 21, IIIa, 66, 20 ff.

defeated Demetrius son of Antigonus surnamed Poliorcetes, in a battle near Gaza."[30] It would seem that the author dealt with the period of Ptolemy Soter, with allusions to the Persian or Alexandrian era to illumine the current conditions of Judaea.

At that time a migration of Palestinian Jews to Egypt and Phoenicia was taking place with High Priest Ezekias making certain that Jewish civil rights were recorded in writing.[31] The author may have been an acquaintance of Ezekias, since he knew his age (66 years old),[32] although such information could have been public knowledge. He also praises the high priest as an intellectual and an able speaker, suggesting an eyewitness account. He was well enough informed to report that the high priest supervised some 1,500 priests, who assisted him in administering the realm.[33] The personality of Ezekias and his relations with Ptolemy Lagus were found in the first part of the treatise.

Another part of the book,[34] Josephus says, dealt with the obstinacy with which the Jews observed their laws. This, aside from the purely descriptive subject matter, was Pseudo-Hecataeus I's main theme. The treatise was richly illustrated with examples and anecdotes. "The frequent abuses of the Persian kings and satraps," says the author, "failed to shake their determination; for these laws, naked and defenseless, they face tortures and death in its most terrible forms, rather than repudiate the faith of their forefathers."[35] Willrich and Jacoby argue that the passage could have referred only to the persecution of Antiochus IV, and not to the Persians, whose religious tolerance was blameless.[36] But the fragment does not say that the Jewish religion was proscribed by the Persians any more than it was by Alexander; it says only that there were "frequent abuses" ($\pi\rho o\pi\eta\lambda\alpha\kappa\iota\zeta|\acute{o}\mu\epsilon\nu o\iota\ \pi o\lambda\lambda\acute{\alpha}\kappa\iota\varsigma$)[37]

---

30   Ibid. I, 185. Josephus says that the mention of the battle of Gaza, which took place in 312 B.C., dates Hecataeus. But Josephus' reasoning holds for Pseudo-Hecataeus as well.

31   Ibid. I, 186; 189, 194. The migration of the Jews is placed after Alexander's death, rather than before. In I, 186 the reference is certainly to the settlement of Alexandria. But 194 also mentions migrations to Phoenicia, on account of the chaotic conditions in Syria.

32   Ibid. I, 189. Since the date of the report seems to have been between 312 and 300, Ezechias must have been born between 378 and 366 B.C. His coin (n. 27) attests then that he held office before 332.

33   Ibid. I, 188. See Thackeray's note *b*. ad locum.

34   Ibid. I, 190; cf. 186, 194, 195, 197, 200, 201 for Josephus' formula here to indicate different sections of the book, which is rather unusual in Josephus. The indications are that Pseudo-Hecataeus I, mistakenly assumed by Josephus to have been a heathen, was an extremely rich source for the practice of Jewish laws, but was too detailed to be quoted in toto.

35   Ibid. I, 191.

36   Willrich, *Judaica*, 92-94; Jacoby, *FGrH*, IIIa, 72, 14-20.

37   *C. Apionem*, I, 191. Certainly, the incident connected with Bel's construction must have illustrated a common problem of Jewish mercenaries serving an occupying power.

which there undoubtedly were even in the Persian period. There is no reason to doubt that, despite the formal religious tolerance, the orders of the authorities often came into conflict with the requirements of Jewish religious law.

Josephus quotes two of the many anecdotes that the unknown author must have told at length. The first relates that Alexander had ordered his soldiers to restore the Temple of Bel in Babylon,[38] but that the Jewish soldiers refused. They were first heavily fined, but Alexander finally remitted the fine and freed them from such tasks in the future.[39] This story reminds us that the Jews insisted that the conquerors abstain from building idolatrous altars, and even destroyed those erected by the Persians, thus incurring the wrath of the satraps. In other words, the root of the conflict was the unwillingness of the Jews to permit their overlords to worship as they pleased. The peroration is therefore strange: "For this they deserve admiration."[40] This sentence proves, contrary to Lewy and others, the Jewish authorship of the fragment.[41] For the author of this fragment the Persian occupation was still a fresh experience, rather than, as scholarly consensus maintains, something remote as it would have been for someone who lived in the second or the first century B.C.

Josephus tells the second anecdote towards the end of the extracts, after having quoted the treatise's ethnic statistics, perhaps because he found it in the last part of the book, or possibly because he wanted to close with a good story. A Jewish soldier in Alexander's army named Mosollamus, described as "very intelligent" and "the best bowman, whether among the Greeks or Barbarians," killed a sacred bird used by a mantis for predicting the future. Asked how he dared to shoot something so sacred, he retorted: "Had it been gifted with divination, it would not have come to this spot for fear of the arrow of Mossolamus the Jew."[42] Fictional or not, the story's Euhemeristic flavor as well as its ethnic boasting reveals something of the author's mind.

About half of the extracts reports the ethnic and cultic characteristics of Judaea:

Judaea's area	3,000,000 arurae
Judaea's population	not given
Jerusalem's circumference	50 stadia
Jerusalem's population	120,000
Number of Judaean priests	1,500
Temple's enclosure	5 plethra long and 100 cubit wide

38 Alexander's alleged futile attempt to rebuild the Babylonian temple is also recorded in Arrian, VII, 17; Strabo, XVI, 1, 5.

39 *C. Apionem*, I, 192 f.

40 Ibid. I, 193.

41 See Lewy, *ZNW*, 31 (1932), 124-26.

42 *C. Apionem*, I, 201-05.

This table may be misleading, because for Pseudo-Hecataeus I's statistics do not intrude into the main narrative. Thus the account introduces the description of the country by a boast of "our" [Judaea's] vast population despite the "many myriads" deported by the Persians to Babylon and the myriads more who left after Alexander's death.[43] The slip that the Persians, rather than the Babylonians, were the ones who deported Jews to Babylon has been taken by Lewy to prove that the author was an uninformed pagan.[44] If so, this is the only passage to contradict the evidence of all the rest of the abstracts. Interestingly, however, the author of II Macc. 1:19, certainly a Jew, makes a similar lapsus.[45] There is every reason to believe that a Jew could have made such an error, especially since the author devoted a great deal of attention to Persian affairs. Certainly, the description of Judaea's soil as most fertile and beautiful tends to confirm Jewish authorship.

The description of the Temple seems to reflect a priestly piety.[46] More space is devoted to it, in Josephus' extracts, and perhaps in the original work, than to the accounts of Jerusalem and Judaea combined. Technical information, such as that the altar was built of "heaped up stones, unhewn and unwrought," alluding to Exod. 20:25, indicates the priestly basis of the narrative. There is a feeling of quiet pride as well as of conviction in the reports that no statue, votive offering, or trace of a plant was to be found in the precinct of the Temple; or in the account of the priestly rites and abstention from wine while in the sanctuary.[47]

How factual was Pseudo-Hecataeus' information? The answer hinges on which of the items one wishes to stress. He embarrassingly gives 50 stades (roughly 30,000 feet) as the compass of the city. Aristeas and Timochares, a Hellenistic historian cited by Alexander Polyhistor, mentioned 40, Josephus 33, and another view in Alexander Polyhistor, 27.[48] The smallest number was probably the most accurate one in the fourth century B.C. The other verifiable numbers, however, seem quite authentic. Certainly, 3,000,000 arurae

---

43   Ibid, I, 194.
44   Lewy, *ZNW*, 31 (1932), 126 f.
45   See above, p. 236.
46   First suggested by Jacoby, *FGrH*, IIIa, 62. See note 28.
47   *C. Apionem*, I, 199. Lewy (*ZNW*, 31 1932 128 f.) also points out that the location of the Temple "nearly in the middle of the city" (I, 198), when in fact it was in the east, proves that the writer was not an eyewitness, but that he was mechanically reproducing the Greek tradition as to where sanctuaries were supposed to be placed. In the Jewish version, however, the Temple was located in the middle of the world, not to say of Jerusalem (Tanhuma, *Kedoshim*, 10), no matter where physically found. Ps.-Hecataeus, though, seems to have been aware of its actual situation because he modifies it by "nearly" (μάλιστα).
48   See the preceding note. Ibid. I. 197; Aristeas, 105; Timochares, in *P.E.*, IX, 35 = *FGrH* 165 F 1; Josephus, *B.J.*, V. 159; the author of the *Measurements of Syria*, in *P.E.*, IX, 36 = *FGrH*, Anonymous (Xenophon?), 849 F 1.

or 825,000 hectars was a fair estimate of Judaea's area.[49] The number 120,000 for Jerusalem's population may or may not be an exaggeration. If an exaggeration, it is by far more reasonable than the census during Nero's time, reported in Josephus, of 2,700,000 souls who partook of the paschal lamb.[50] A fair verdict would seem to be that in view of the tendency of the ancients to exaggerate, Pseudo-Hecataeus I's account, if not what would be by modern standards considered accurate, was quite moderate and generally reliable.[51]

As to Pseudo-Hecataeus' sources, the account was primarily that of an eye-witness. Probably a friend of the high priest and a priest himself, he no doubt had access to the Temple's records. This may have been the basis of the statement that 1,500 priests administered the realm.[52] It is interesting that his characterization of Ptolemy Lagus, as pointed out by Willrich,[53] seems to echo that of Diodorus:

Diodorus, XIX, 86,3	Pseudo-Hecataeus I (*C. Apionem,* I, 186)
For indeed that prince [Ptolemy] was exceptionally gentle and forgiving and inclined towards deeds of kindness. It was this very thing that most increased his power and made many people desire to share his friendship.	Many of the inhabitants [of Judaea], hearing of his kindness and humanity, desired to accompany him to Egypt and to associate themselves with his realm.

Unfortunately, little is known about Diodorus' source for this text, though the names of Duris of Samos, Hieronymus of Cardia, and Cleitarchus of Alexandria have sometimes been proposed.[54] But Pseudo-Hecataeus' main

49   Aristeas, 116, apparently using here Pseudo-Hecataeus, says the area was 60,000,000 arurae, a twentyfold increase of his source.

50   *B.J.* VI, 423-27. Cf. Tosefta Pesahim, IV, 15, p. 166 (Lieberman); Bab. Pesahim, 64b.

51   This is also true of the description of the Temple and its furniture (*C. Apionem,* I, 198), such as the dimensions of the altar and lampstand. The embarrassingly fantastic amounts of gold talens given by Eupolemus, are not to be found in this text.

52   Citing Nehemia 7:39-42, which lists 4,289 returning priests, Reinach (ad locum) regards the Pseudo-Hecataeus I was referring to the priests who actually administered the realm. An interesting problem is the proportion of priests to the general population. Cf. J. Jeremias, "Einwohnerzahl Jerusalems zur Zeit Jesu," *Zeitschrift der deutschen morgenländischen Gesellschaft,* 66 (1943), 24-31; *Jerusalem in the Time of Jesus* (Philadelphia, Fortress Press, 1969), 77-84; S. Baron, *A Social and Religious History of the Jews* (Philadelphia, Jewish Publication Society, 1958), I, 168.

53   Willrich, *Juden und Griechen vor der Makkäbaischen Erhebung* (Göttingen, 1895), 26. Cf. also Willrich, *R.E.,* VIII (1913), 1554 ff.

54   Willrich, *Juden und Griechen,* 26 f., assumes that Hieronymus of Cardia (*FGrH* 154) was here the source of the genuine Hecataeus; however, as pointed out by Jacoby (*FGrH,* IIIa, 70, 20 f.). This is chronologically impossible. Hecataeus is older than Hieronymus. On Hieronymus, see Diod. XVIII, 42, 1 = *FGrH* 154 T 3; see also TT 4-6; II D, pp. 544-47, especially 544 f. As to Duris, *FGrH* 76 FF 16-21; 110, 120 f., Cleitarchus wrote a work on Alexander (137 FF 1-52) but did not reach this period.

model seems to have been the genuine Hecataeus, which accounts for some of the similar mannerisms in composition and vocabulary.[55]

Agetharchides of Cnidus, who flourished in the middle of the second century B.C., offers a divergent characterization of Ptolemy Lagus. Whereas Pseudo-Hecataeus I and Diodorus' source described him as one who gained the heart of men by kindness, Agartharchides said that the king had exploited the Jewish superstition of the Sabbath to forcibly make himself master of Jerusalem.[56] It is difficult to decide whether this report is historical or whether it was inspired by the clash between Antiochus IV and the Hasmoneans.[57] In 312, after his victory over Demetrius, according to Diodorus, Ptolemy destroyed the cities of Ace (Acca), Joppe, Samaria, and Gaza before retreating to Egypt.[58] Since Jerusalem is not mentioned in the reports, nothing is known of the Judaean situation during the wars among the Diadochi. But perhaps, inspired by Agatharchides, Jewish writers—Pseudo-Hecataeus II, the Letter of Aristeas, Josephus—drew a dark picture of Ptolemy Lagus.[59] Clearly, his son Ptolemy II Philadelphus, who is said to have freed the remnants of the 100,000 Jews enslaved by his father, and more importantly, who sponsored the translation of the Law, became the Jewish favorite among the Macedonian kings. Pseudo-Hecataeus I, however, had depicted an exceedingly positive evaluation of Ptolemy Lagus, which he surely would not have done if the exploitation of the Sabbath to gain entry into the holy city had been known to him.

What seems to have been the object of Pseudo-Hecataues' account? Writing after 312 B.C., the author, for whom the Persian occupation was still a living memory, appears to have been elated by the prospects of the Macedonian occupation. He put great thrust in Ptolemy Lagus' "kindliness and humanity." In fact it seems that the writer's purpose may have been to make sure

---

55   Cf. Hecataeus, in Diod. XL, 3, 4-5 with the Pseudo-Hecataeus' cultic description in *C.Apionem*, I, 199. The ideology and attitude are divergent, but the descriptive approach is the same. For other details, see Jacoby, *FGrH* IIIa, 62, 12-21; 65, 11 ff.

56   Agatharchides, in *C. Apionem*, I, 209-11; *A.J.*, XII, 4 f. = *FGrH* 86 F 20a-b, is known chiefly from Diodorus, Athenaeus, and Photius. Although many writers treated Jewish history before him, he seems to have been the first who made a study of Jewish law. For the possible date, see Willrich, *Juden und Griechen*, 23, who times it in 312. See note 58.

57   Appian, *Syriacus Liber*, 50, referring to Pompey's and Titus' forcible entries into Jerusalem, adds: "This city had already been destroyed by Ptolemy, the first king of Egypt." But this is a late tradition, based on the subsequent fate of Jerusalem, going back perhaps no further than Agatharchides.

58   Diod. XIX, 93, 7. See notes 56 f. Reinach, on *C. Apionem*, I, 210, citing Diodorus, disputes Diodorus' date of 312. Another conceivable year is 302, when Ptolemy reconquered Coele-Syria (Diod. XX, 113, 1).

59   Aristeas, 12-28; *C. Apionem*, I, 43-46; A.J. XII, 3-5. Josephus, *C. Apionem*, I, 183-212, tabulates Pseudo-Hecataeus and Agatharchides together, without any awareness that the two accounts apparently diverged.

that Ptolemy would treat the Jews fairly. Hence the flattering remark about the victorious general and the not so subtle hints that a public display of idolatrous altars should be avoided. The account of the military and religious significance of Jerusalem was also apparently intended for Ptolemy's eyes.[60] Pseudo-Hecataeus I, moreover, seems to have attempted to counter some of the disparaging remarks about the Jews made by Hecataeus. The latter, though sympathetic to or even sometimes enthusiastic about Judaism on the whole, felt compelled to criticize Moses for introducing a way of life supposedly hostile to other nations.[61] Hecataeus, moreover, despite his admiration of the Mosaic institutions, could not remove entirely from his account the sneering and condescension towards barbarian customs present in Greek writers. Pseudo-Hecataeus I, however, on the contrary, being a Jew, defends this selfisolation of the Jews, explaining that it stemmed from their abhorrence of idolatry, for which, he adds, "they deserve admiration."[62]

The early dating of Pseudo-Hecataeus I solves a puzzling aspect of his fragments. Other Graeco-Jewish writers without exception show a heavy verbal dependence on the Septuagint. The fact that our fragment in its description of the Temple does not show any trace of such technical terminology offers additional evidence that, if written by a Jew, it must antedate the Greek translation of the Pentateuch.

To summarize, *Contra Apionem* I, 183-205, offers excerpts of a treatise which, in Josephus' concluding words, "any who wish to pursue the subject can *easily* read the book." It is difficult to know what Josephus exactly meant by easily: that he owned a copy, that it could be located in the museums of Alexandria and Rome, or that the book was popular with many Greeks and Romans? Josephus, however, never doubted that its author was Hecataeus of Abdera, "at once a philosopher and a highly competent man of affairs, who rose to fame under King Alexander, and was afterwards associated with Ptolemy, the son of Lagus" (183). But Josephus was mistaken. A Jew, not a pagan, probably a priest of Jerusalem who flourished in the last decades of the fourth century, had authored this popular book. As a priest he was acquainted with High Priest Ezekias, whose term of office fell during the fall of the Persian empire. But the author of the treatise, here labeled as Pseudo-Hecataeus I, evidently abandoned his priestly garments to serve together with another Judaean named Mosollamus (Meshulam) in a Jewish contingent of Alexander's army marching towards the Red Sea (201). Pseudo-Hecataeus I may then be regarded as the first Graeco-Palestinian writer, an analogue of the Babylonian Berossus and the Egyptian Manetho.

---

60 *C. Apionem,* I, 185-204 = Ps.-Hecataeus, 264 F 21; cf. Jacoby, *FGrH,* IIIa, 64 f.

61 Hectaeus in Diod. (Phot. *Bibl.* 240), XL, 3, 4 = 264 F 6.

62 C. Apionem, I, 193 = 264 F 21.

JUDAEAN PART IN THE MAKING OF THE SEPTUAGINT

The preceding section suggests that pagan inquisitiveness into the nature of Jerusalem's hierocratic state and priestly attempts to explain Judaism to the Greek-reading world antedated the appearance of the so-called Septuagint. But the tremendous significance of the publication of the Septuagint, certainly, cannot be overestimated. Here we are only concerned insofar as it gave birth to the peculiar Graeco-Jewish and, ultimately, the Christian literatures. Interest in the East in general and especially in the region that was rapidly becoming a buffer state between two empires explains the origin of the Greek translation of the Pentateuch. Modern savants now presume that it was the need of the Alexandrian Jewish community for intelligible Scriptures which inspired the Greek translation of the Law.[63] Ancient testimony, however, notably recorded in the fictive Letter of Aristeas, maintained that the first and sole impetus had come from the outside world. In view of the concurrent opening of the Babylonian, Egyptian, and Phoenician writings to Greek audiences, there is no reason to accept a modern dogmatism that entirely rejects the reports of the ancients.[64]

The author of the Letter of Aristeas claims that the translators were priests brought from Jerusalem for the specific job. Not only were these priests bilingual, the romance says, but the king requested that Eleazar, said to have been the high priest: "Choose elders of exemplary life who possess skill in the law and ability to translate, six from each tribe. . ."[65] The men chosen possessed a phenomenal knowledge of Greek culture: "They had not only acquired proficiency in the literature of the Jews, but had bestowed no slight study on that of the Greeks also. They were, therefore, well qualified to be sent on embassies and performed this office whenever there was need."[66] In

---

63   O. Stählin, "Die hellenistisch-jüdische Literatur," in Christ, *Griechischer Literaturgeschichte,* II, 1[6] (Munich, 1921), 542; Eissfeldt, *Einleitung in das Alte Testament*[3], 819 f., who give more references.

64   See, for example, P. Kahle, *The Cairo Geniza* [2] 209 f.: "Today there can be *no doubt* that the Greek translation of the Law was not made by the order of a Ptolemaic king, but that it became a necessity for the Jewish communities in Egypt in view of the great number of their Greek-speaking members who no longer understood Hebrew. The translation was *not* made by Palestinian Jews, but by Jews who were familiar with the Greek language as spoken in Egypt" (emphasis added). This statement, summarizing the schoalrly consensus, is as challengeable as are some of the tales recorded in the Letter of Aristeas. If the Egyptian Jewish community could no longer understand Hebrew, how could it have produced the scholars to translate the text, especially the technical sections of Leviticus, on the whole accurately: Would not a rendition for Greek-reading Jews have been modeled after the literary works of the time. Note the dialect used by the Letter of Aristeas or Philo.

65   Aristeas, 39; *A.J.,* XII, 49.

66   Aristeas, 120. Josephus' paraphrase omits this section. Is it because it seemed even to him unrealistic in his day?

conclusion the author depicts the gratitude of the Alexandrian Jews to the messengers of the high priest for the excellent performance.[67]

There is no doubt that these assertions are fictional or highly exaggerated. But whether we accept the view that the Letter of Aristeas was addressed to pagan audiences or, as proposed by Tcherikover, was for the Jewish community, it must have had some factual basis.[68] Effective propaganda always is a mixture of fact and fiction. Moreover, a rejection of Aristeas does not prove that the translators were Alexandrian Jews. Like those of Babylon and Heliopolis, a handful of Jerusalem's priests may have known Greek, and as such may have participated in the Greek translation of the Law.[69]

Aside from the question of the homeland of the translators, there is also a problem of the origin of the dialect used for the rendition of the Pentateuch. Some scholars have stressed the Semitic flavor of the Septuagint; others, the bond between the biblical Greek and the papyrological departures from standard Greek. The fact remains, however, that none of the contemporary pagan literature of Alexandria, or anywhere else for that matter, was written with a syntax and vocabulary similar to that of the Septuagint.[70]

Semiticists delight in pointing out the translators' occasional misreadings of the Hebrew. But considering the absence of lexica and grammars in antiquity as well as the inherent difficulties of nonvoweled scripts, the translators display a remarkable mastery of the Hebrew language. Is it believable that the Alexandrian Jews were completely at ease in the technical intricacies of biblical priestly texts? If the answer is positive, the next question must be why did they not render the Torah into a Greek used by other writers of the period? Certainly, men such as Aristobulus, the founder of the biblical school of exegesis, Ezekielus the epic poet, and Philo, although tremendously influenced by the Septuagint, used the standard literary conventions of the time. Conceivably, Egypt's Jews lived in what may be labeled as ancient ghettos apart from the learned culture of the day. The Septuagint's dialect might then be regarded as a forerunner of the seventeenth century Yiddish *Ze'einah U-re'einah*. The Jewish papyrological remains of Egypt's Jewry,

---

67   Aristeas, 308-11; *A.J.*, XII, 108 f., the community decided that the text not be altered.

68   Eissfeldt, *Einleitung in das Alte Testament*[3], 819 f.; Kahle, *Cairo Geniza*[2], 214-17; Tcherikover, "The Ideology of the Letter of Aristeas," *Harvard Theological Review*, 51 (1958), 59-85.

69   See above, pp. 259-62.

70   The consensus in H. B. Swete, *Introduction to the Old Testament in Greek*, 20 f.: Kahle, *Cairo Geniza*, 214 f. For a contrary view, see E. Bickerman, "The Septuagint as a Translation," *Proceedings of the American Academy for Jewish Research*, 28 (1959), 1-39, esp. 12 ff.; M. Hengel, *Judentum und Helenismus*, 189 f. (see his note 343 for further references). Cf. R. Hanhart, "Fragen um die Entstehung der LXX," *Vetus Testamentum*, 12 (1962), 139-62.

however, seem to contradict the conclusion that there is a parallel between Egypt's ancient Jewry and that of medieval Western Europe. Independent of the claims of the Letter of Aristeas, then, the internal evidence of the Greek translation suggests that the men who rendered it were at home in two cultures. But the fact that they used what has been called Judaeo-Greek suggests either that they were ignorant of or not at home in the literary conventions of the time, or that they were consciously avoiding them. The indication seems to be that, even if it is granted that the translators were Alexandrian Jews, they nevertheless were more at home with the Hebrew culture of Jerusalem than with the Alexandrian literary tradition.[71]

It follows that neither the ancient view which saw the Greek translation as a Palestinian-priestly product nor the modern hypothesis which has labeled it as made in the Diaspora is without serious difficulty. A reasonable solution may be that the Septuagint represented a work of collaboration between the two main centers of third century Judaism.[72] In other words, Jews born in Jerusalem who migrated to Alexandria (and in some cases vice versa) were the savants who rendered the Hebrew Scriptures into Judaeo-Greek. The Letter of Aristeas' account may after all contain a grain of truth, which its author embellished by claiming that the Palestinian scholars were guests of the king and ambassadors of Jerusalem's high priest. The evidence available, though meager, as to the identity of the biblical translators—the prologue of Ecclesiasticus and the colophon of Esther—supports this view.

The first biblical translator whose identity is known, is the grandon of Ben Sira, who by his own testimony migrated from Jerusalem to Alexandria in 132 B.C. Simon Ben Sira had written a work quite similar both in style and language to that of Proverbs, called the Wisdom of Jesus (!) the Son of Sira, or otherwise known as Ecclesiasticus. Using hexameters and a tortuous Greek, the grandson first apologizes for his grandfather's daring to add another work beside the Law and the Prophets. He then asks the reader's indulgence for his own shortcomings in rendering the Hebrew into the Greek. He explains that even the translations of the Pentateuch and the other biblical books often

---

71   See previous note. See also Z. Frankel, *Vorstudien zu der Septuaginta* (Lepizig, 1841); *Über den Einfluss der palästinischen Exeqese auf die alexandrinische Hermeneutik* (Leipzig, 1851); R. Marcus, "Jewish and Greek Elements in the Septuagint," in *L. Ginzberg Jubilee Volume* English Section (New York, 1945), 227-45. Although Frankel denied that the Palestinian Jews had a share in the translation (*Vorstudien ze der Septuaginta*, 40 n. *g.*), he argued that the Targum Onkelos served as the basis of the Greek Version (*Über den Einfluss*, 229 f., and passim).

72   P. Kahle, *The Cairo Geniza*[2], 214 f., who ascribes the origin of the Septuagint to a Bible translation commissioned by the Alexandrian Jewish community, adds: "The commission entrusted with the revision of the Greek Bible consisted of experts, mainly Jewish scholars from Egypt, but there may have been one or more Hebrew scholars from Palestine." Whence Kahle gets the proportion is difficult to say.

suffered from the same failure to bring out the meanings of the original.[73] As to his identity, he says: "In the 38th year of King Euergetes I came to Egypt spending some time there, I found an opportunity for no little instruction. It seemed highly necessary that I should devote some pains and labor for the translation of this book. For I have used the time with great watchfulness and skill in order to complete and publish the book for those who are living abroad. . ."[74]

It is clear that he regarded himself primarily as a citizen of Jerusalem residing in Alexandria for a short while. Unfortunately, the vagueness of the Greek does not offer any clue as to the length of his stay in Egypt. Despite his diligence he still felt that the product was not an adequate reproduction of the original, partly because of his own inadequacy and partly because no satisfactory rendition from the Hebrew into the Greek seemed possible.

Until recently, the loss of the original Hebrew made it impossible to pass definite judgement on the accuracy of the translation. However, the partial recovery of the original at the turn of the century and the more recent finds of fragments at Massada confirm the suspicion that although he was the grandson of Ben Sira and a native of Palestine, his knowledge of Hebrew thus assured, he misread quite a number of words.[75] This suggests that the basic presumption which ascribes the misunderstanding of Hebrew terms in the Septuagint to the fact that the translators were from Alexandria needs revision. These men seem to have been professionals and their expertise depended on the training they received rather than on their place of origin.

Nevertheless, it seems significant that Ben Sira's grandson boasts that he was a native of Jerusalem. Significant too is the fact that neither Ben Sira nor his grandson mentions his tribal origin. The Greek text of 50:27 phrases the self-identification: "Jesus the son of Sirach, Son of Eleazar, the Jerusalemite." The Hebrew text, however, including the colophon, names the author "Simon, the son of Jesus, son of Eleazar, son of Sira," and lacks a place of origin altogether. Since it seems superfluous, it is likely that the grandson added Ben Sira's place of origin, of which he also boasts in the prologue. Although the Sinaiticus Manuscript concludes, instead of with "Jerusalemite," with "priest and Solemite," on the basis of which some scholars, ancient and modern, have indeed identified Ben Sira as a priest, this view should be rejected. Had he been of priestly descent, the grandson would have mentioned the distinguished pedigree in his prologue. The main point,

---

73   See now H. J. Cadbury, "The Grandson of Ben Sira," *HThR,* 48 (1955), 219-25; P. Auvray, "Notes sur le prologue de l'Ecclesiastique" in Robert et Feuillet, *Introduction a la Bible,* I (1957), 281-87; Kahle, *Cairo Geniza,* 215-28.

74   RSV translation.

75   See M. Z. Segal, *Sefer Ben Sira Hashalem*[2] (Jerusalem, Mosad Bialik, 1957), 61; Y. Yadin, *The Ben Sira Scroll from Masada* (Jerusalem, the Israel Exploration Society and the Shrine of the Book, 1965).

however, is that the Greek translation of Ben Sira was produced by one residing in Egypt but who was born and reared in Jerusalem.

The second witness that identifies a Greek translator of a Hebrew book also ascribes it to a native of Jerusalem. The colophon of the Book of Esther offers the following provenance: "In the fourth year of the reign of Ptolemy and Cleopatra, Dositheus, who said he was a priest and Levite, and Ptolemy his son, brought the preceding letter of Purim, which they said was genuine and was translated by Lysimachus the son of Ptolemy, one of the residents of Jerusalem."[76] The cautionary wording of the testimony and the fact that the Greek version contains extensive additions which are missing in the Hebrew seems to justify suspicion of the reliability of the evidence. But whether reliable or not, it does show that the translator's residence in Jerusalem was regarded as enhancing the authenticity of the text. This colophon, especially if unauthentic, and I believe it is, shows that the Greek translations of Hebrew texts were usually produced in Jerusalem. According to Hengel, the same may be said of the Greek Additions to the Book of Esther.[77]

Equally worth noting is the priestly pedigree boasted by the witnesses who brought the text to the Diaspora, evidently Egypt. The colophon seems to suggest that priestly ancestry added to the truthfulness of the testimony. But it implies in addition that priests were involved in the trading of such manuscripts. Josephus, let us recall, repeatedly boasts that his own priestly pedigree assures the veracity of his works: "I, Josephus, the son of Matthias, a priest from Jerusalem." Following the Septuagint tradition, Josephus labels his own work as a "translation' ($\mu\epsilon\theta\,\epsilon\rho\mu\eta\nu\epsilon\upsilon\mu\acute{\epsilon}\nu o\varsigma$), rather than as a subjective reworking of the biblical historical books, because the rendition of a sacred text into Greek was considered a hallowed task worthy only of men of distinguished ancestry.

It becomes clear then that the putative attribution of the Greek Bible exclusively to "Alexandrian" translators is misleading, if not false. The priests of Jerusalem, some of whom were imported and some of whom resided in Egypt, seem to have had an important share in the formation of the Greek text. It is likely that Lysimachus of Jerusalem, to whom the Greek Esther is attributed, and Ben Sira's grandson, who translated Ecclesiasticus, were

    76   RSV translation. See E. Bickerman, "The Colophon of the Book of Esther," *JBL* 63 (1944), 339-62, who takes the text to mean Levite, as a proper name. Ths view is rightly rejected by Kahle, *Cairo Geniza*[2], 213, n. 1.

    77   On the Additions to the Book of Esther, see Eissfeldt, (*Einleitung in das Alte Testament*[3], 800-03), who dates them in the middle of the second century B.C. (803). See M. Hengel, *Judentum und Hellenismus,* 187, n. 334, who disputes Hautsch's claim (*R.E.* II, 1600 f.) that the Additions were produced in Alexandria. Hengel's proof that they were a product of Jerusalem is that Josephus (*A.J.* XI, 184-296) had used them in his paraphrase of Esther; this is not convincing, however. The identification of Haman as a "Macedonian" (Est. 8:12k) was more likely to have been in Palestine rather than in Egypt or Antioch, where it would have aroused a reaction from the royal house.

typical; and that the work was usually done by men who had resided both in Jerusalem and in Egypt.

In addition to the Greek Esther, two other Greek versions of Apocryphal books may have been written in Jerusalem: the I Esdras and the Greek Daniel. Scholars have long noted the literary and ideological similarities among the three works "which may suggest that all three were translated by the same hand" (N. Turner, in *Interpreter's Dictionary of the Bible,* II, 142a). Whether or not one agrees with this view, it is difficult to deny that the Greek translators-authors of I Esdras, Daniel, and Esther belong to the same literary traditions. If the Greek Esther was a product of Palestinian Greek translation, it follows that the same is likely for the I Esdras and Daniel. Moreover, as has been shown above, the phrasing of the royal correspondence in Eupolemus and I Esdras show signs of definite interdependence. The interdependence would be more easily explainable if, like Eupolemus, I Esdras represents a Greek literary school of Jerusalem during the second century B.C.

Eupolemus must be viewed as an example of this Palestinian Septuagint tradition. The fragments of an aide to Judah Maccabee illustrate similar Palestinian Graeco-biblical productions, a possible example of which is the Additions to the Book of Esther and Daniel. Present evidence, however, does not support the conclusion of Hengel that all biblical translations into Greek were produced in Palestine.[78] Exciting evidence for this claim would seem to be the Greek papyri of the Twelve Minor Prophets, remnants of which were found in the fourth cave of Qumran.[79] Wherever the renditions from Hebrew into Greek were made, in Palestine or in the Diaspora, they were modeled after the Law. Language alone is therefore no substitute for historical tradition. But an analysis of the dialect and content combined may sometimes serve as a guide. We have believable testimony that Eupolemus worked in Jerusalem while Aristobulus wrote in Alexandria. Except for the translators of the Books of Esther and Ecclesiasticus, no such evidence, however, is available in regard to the other Graeco-Jewish writers.

---

78   Hengel, ibid., 186-90. As proof Hengel cites the two letters prefixed to II Macc. (1:1-9; 1:10-2:18), the translation of the I Maccabees (citing Bickerman, *Gott der Makkabäer* (Berlin, Schocken, 1937), 145; *JBL,* 63 1944, 357, and the Greek elements of poleis such as Sidon, Tyre, Gadara, and Ashkelon. For the evidence from Qumran, see next note.

79   M. Baillet, J. T. Milik, and R. de Vaux (eds.), *Discoveries in the Judaean Desert of Jordan* (Oxford, Clarendon Press, 1962), III, 142 ff.; R. W. Shehahan, "The Biblical scrolls from Qumran; and the Text of the Old Testament," *Biblical Archaeologist* 28 (1965), 87-100; Kahle, *Cairo Geniza*[2], 226-28; Eissfeldt, *Einleitung in das A.T.*[3], 960 f. Of interest is Volume V of the *Discoveries . . .* (ed. by J. M. Allegro), Fragment 4Q (186, pp. 88-90), which combines sometimes in part a cryptic cipher with the proto-Hebraic and Greek scripts. Note John Strugnell's announcement of the forthcoming publication of the cryptic alphabets in 4Q (*Revue de Qumrân,* 26 [1970], 220).

THE GRAECO-BIBLICAL PALESTINIAN TRADITION

As has been shown above, Demetrius the chronographer, who flourished during the reign of Ptolemy IV (222-05 B.C.), was the first Graeco-Jewish writer clearly dependent on the Septuagint text.[80] Was he a native of Palestine or of the Diaspora? His Alexandrian origin has been taken for granted, no doubt because Alexandria was believed to have been the exclusive home of the Graeco-Jewish literary tradition. Demetrius' datings ended with the reign of Ptolemy IV, which suggests a link with Egypt.[81] But since Palestine during his time was an Egyptian province, Demetrius' use of Ptolemaic chronology would have been natural even if he were born in Jerusalem. And we no longer subscribe to the hypothesis that Alexandria had a monopoly on the production of Graeco-Jewish texts.

Ever since Freudenthal, it has been assumed that Demetrius' style reflected the hermeneutic methods prevailing in the pagan culture. As an example of this indebtedness, Freudenthal cited Demetrius' rhetorical question and answer ($\overset{?}{\alpha}\pi o\rho\iota\alpha\iota\,\kappa\alpha\iota\,\lambda\upsilon\sigma\epsilon\iota\varsigma$), which it has been said ultimately became one of the chief devices of midrashic hermeneutics.[82] The absence in Demetrius, however, of any other rhetorical usage or technical vocabulary suggests that his use of the question and answer was not necessarily borrowed from a Greek manual of rules. As employed by Demetrius, the question and answer device is at least as old as the Pentateuch. Moreover, Demetrius' chronology seems to stem from a most thorough knowledge of Scripture alone, without any reference to synchronism with Egyptian or Alexandrian chronological systems. In this respect Demetrius hardly differs from the Book of Jubilees. Both exceedingly advance their chronological schemes far beyond those of biblical narrative by adding the years from creation, although Jubilees depended on the Hebrew text of the Pentateuch and Demetrius on the Septuagint. Demetrius, it is true, went a step further in his chronography by dividing the history of the world into epochs, totalling up the periods from Adam to the deluge, from Abraham's birth to Jacob's arrival into Egypt, and culminating with the date of the exodus. Although writing independently

---

80   Aside from the papyri (see previous note), Demetrius' use of a Septuagint text is the only independent evidence supporting the Aristeas' contention that the Greek translation existed during the middle of the third century B.C. For Demetrius' use of the LXX, see Freudenthal, *Hell. St.,* 36, note; 43, 49.

81   Clement, *Stromata,* I, 141, 2 = *FGrH* 722 F 6.

82   Freudenthal, *Hell. St.,* 77. Gutman, *Beginnings of Jewish-Hellenistic Litera-ture,* I, 138 f., maintains that Sosibius of Lacone, whom he dates during Ptolemy I and II, the author of a commentary on Alcman, Homer and chronography, was influenced by Demetrius. But the chronographer and commentator of Alcman was probably a different person from his namesake called the "confuter" ($\lambda\upsilon\tau\kappa\acute{o}\varsigma$). See C. Wachsmuth, *Einleitung in das Altes Geschichte* (Leipzig, 1895), 138 n. 1; Jacoby *FGrH* 595 F 26, IIIb (Commentary), 635 f.

from each other and for different purposes, both the author of Jubilees and Demetrius presuppose a schematic chronology of the world. The two biblical chronographers have this in common: they ignore completely the chronology of the world outside the Jewish horizon.[83]

Demetrius' presentation of nonchronological subject matter follows the narrative of the Greek text strictly, with generous sprinklings of what may be called midrashic explanations. A good example is his summary of Gen. 32:23-33: "But while going to Chanaan an angel of God wrestled with him [Jacob]. And he touched the broad part of Jacob's thigh, which was benumbed and became lame. Wherefore the sinew on the thigh of cattle is not eaten. And the angel said to him that from now his name should no longer be called Jacob but Israel."[84] Except for shortening and reorganizing the material, the vocabulary and the phrasing are almost strictly those of the Septuagint. But Demetrius does change the biblical "man" (32:26) into "angel of God."[85] Contrary to the Mishnaic tradition, which applies the commandment to all animals, Demetrius seems to restrict the prohibition against eating the sinew of the thigh to cattle only. Interestingly enough, Demetrius' omission of the Scriptural note that the abstention referred to the sons of Israel appears to presuppose that he was writing for a Jewish audience.

Most ingenious are some of Demetrius' insights into textual problems: Joseph failed to communicate the news of his elevation to high office to his father for nine years because he and his family had the lowly occupation of shepherds.[86] At the banquet Joseph gave five portions to Benjamin (Gen. 45:22) and he took two portions for himself to show that the offspring of Rachel was equal in status to the seven children of Jacob by Leah.[87] Another embellishment, as has been mentioned above, was the claim that Zipporah, Moses' wife, identical with the Cushite woman (Num. 12:1), was allegedly a sixth generation descendant of Abraham.[88] In some instances, as in the description of Moses' slaying of the Egyptian, Demetrius merely paraphrased

---

83 See above, pp. 89-104.

84 *P.E.*, IX, 21, 7 = 722 F 1.

85 Cf. 32:29. See Gutman, *Beginnings,* who cites Hos. 12:5: "He strove with the Angel," as the possible basis of Demetrius' interpretation, but wonders whether Hosea was already translated at that time or whether Demetrius knew Hebrew.

86 *P.E.*, IX, 21, 13 = 722 F 1. Alluding to Gen. 46:34, Demetrius explains the difference between shepherds, whose status in Egypt was low, and cattleraisers, the occupation Joseph found to be acceptable to Pharaoh. Freudenthal, 45, argues that Demetrius, on the basis of the scriptural allusion, concluded with "for every shepherd is an abomination for the Egyptian," which Alexander Polihistor abbreviated.

87 *P.E.*, IX, 21, 14 = 722 F 1. Freudenthal, followed by Jacoby, emends the numbers "seven" to "six," and "two" to "one."

88 Ibid. IX, 29, 1 f. = ibid. 722 F 2.

the biblical text.[89] But Alexander Polyhistor preferred to quote those passages that displayed Demetrius' midrashic insights.

Demetrius certainly possessed a remarkable knowledge of Scripture. The embellishments are sometimes apologetical. But this apology was not addressed to the Gentile world. He wrote for those who already knew enough of the Bible to be bothered by episodes that raised doubts concerning the probability of the story. It is noteworthy that the questions raised by Demetrius touch upon texts of the Joseph story or the exodus, sections containing intrinsic human interest.

Like its contents, the structure of Demetrius' work hardly reflects the Hellenistic literary tradition of Alexandria. The dialect was that of the Septuagint. The structure of the work never assumed any shape and lacked an outline, except that of the biblical narrative. Demetrius intermingled chronology and diverse comments without any hiatus. As has been noted above, Demetrius' chronography does not betray any dependence on that of Alexandria at a time when this discipline reached its zenith in antiquity. His repetition of the statement of Gen. 46:34 that there was a class distinction between shepherds and cattleraisers hardly qualifies him as an expert on Egypt's popular religion. From an exegetical point of view, Demetrius seems to have been closer to the authors of Jubilees or Genesis Apocryphon than to Hellenistic hermeneutics. But he lacked their common sense and sophistication. His only link with Alexandria was his use of the Septuagint. But if this metropolis is no longer regarded as the exclusive home of the Greek translations of all biblical books, there is hardly a reason to place Demetrius in Egypt. The possibility that he was a Palestinian should not be excluded.[90]

The epic compositions of Philo, sometimes called the Elder, Theodotus, and Ezekielus provide sharp contrast to Demetrius' shapeless prose. Of the three poets whose fragments survive, Philo is especially significant for this study. He appears to have been a native of Jerusalem.[91] Only twenty-four

---

89   Ibid., IX, 29, 14, I, 536, 22 f. = 722 F 4. "Demetrius reported . . . exactly as did the 'Holy Book.' " This appears to be the oldest known reference to the Holy Book (ἱερὰ βιβλία).

90   Did Demetrius know Hebrew? See above note 85, which is not conclusive. The transcription of the locative as Ἐφραθα (to Efrath) or Λουζα (to Luz) is no proof of ignorance as the LXX of Gen. 35:6 and 35:16 similarly transcribe the words. However, his departure from the LXX translation of חמושים (Exod. 13:18) as "armed" rather than "the fifth," does seem to suggest independent knowledge of the Hebrew.

91   On Philo's home, see G. Karpeles, *Geschichte der jüdischen Literatur* (Berlin, 1886), I, 236. Whether Philo, the author of the epic and known from Eusebius (*P.E.*, IX, 20= 729 F 1' IX, 37 = F 2' IX, 24 = F 2), and Philo, mentioned in *C. Apionem* (I, 218 = 729 T 1) and Clement (Strom. I, 141 = 729 T 2), are the same or not is difficult to decide. Jacoby was not sure, but grouped the epicist and the "Elder" together. Laqueur, "Philon" No. 46. *R.E.* [1941], cols. 51 f., maintains that they must be regarded as two different writers.

lines remain of his work *On Jerusalem,* which is said to have consisted of more than fourteen books. Because an epic of such length seemed excessively prolific, Freudenthal emended the text to reduce the number of books to four.[92] The first book depicted God's covenant with Abraham (circumcision), whereas the fourth (or the fourteenth, according to the manuscripts), described Joseph in Egypt. This was still quite a lengthy epic, since there is good reason to believe that the poem continued at least to the Israelites' entry into Canaan, if not to David's conquest of Jerusalem.

Whatever the length of the original epic, the remaining lines of his work are mostly unintelligible. It has been suggested that Philo's obscurity was deliberate.[93] This is not acceptable since the meaning of some lines is quite clear, indicating that the author wished to be understood. The unintelligibility must then be ascribed partly to the ravages of times, but chiefly, as suggested by Karpeles, to the fact that Philo's command of the Greek language was limited. That Philo was born or resided in Jerusalem, the city of which he sang, as claimed by Karpeles, is quite plausible.[94] His ill-constructed hexameters may be compared with Eupolemus' vulgar prose. From his mention of the high priest and his concern with ritual, it may be conjectured that, like Equpolemus, Philo the epicist belonged to the highest echelons of the priestly class, who attempted to spread the glory of the holy city and its sanctuary in the tongue of Yawan.

On a higher literary level than Philo's *Jerusalem* is the epic on the foundation of Shechem by a certain Theodotus.[95] We do not know whether or not the two poets were intended to be contentious, but they certainly appear to reflect the bitter rivalry between the Jews and Samaritans. As II Chr. 3:1 had claimed, Philo evidently asserted that Abraham bound Isaac in one of Jerusalem's hills.[96] Philo, like other Graeco-Jewish writers, boasted of Jerusalem's marvelous water supply brought into the Temple from a considerable distance.[97]

---

92 *P.E.* IX, 24 = 729 F 3, quotes from the "14th book of *On Jerusalem.*" Freudenthal, *Hell. St.,* 100, 129, labels the number as "unglaublich," emended it to 10. Jacoby, in app. crit. IIIC, 691, 4, would reduce the number further by reading "first" (cf. F 1). Cf. Gutman, *Beginnings of the Jewish-Hellenistic Literature,* I, 223, n. 2; see also Mras, app. crit. to the text listed in preceding note.

93 A. Ludwich, *De Philonis carmine graeco-judaico* (Königsberg, 1900), 3 f.; Stählin, *Hellenistisch-jüdische Literatur,* 607.

94 See note 91. Cf. also Freudenthal, *Hell. St.,* 100; Hengel, *Judentum und Hellenismus,* 190, n. 344.

95 Schürer, *Geschichte des jüdischen Volkes* III[4], 499 f.; see Freudenthal, *Hell. St.,* 99 f.; A. Ludwich, *De Theodoti carmine graeco-judaico* (Königsberg, 1899); Stählin, ibid., 607; Gutman, *Beginnings of Jewish-Hellenistic Literature,* I, 245-61.

96 See Gutman, ibid., I, 237 f.

97 *P.E.,* IX, 37, = 729 F 2.

The fragment of forty-seven lines by Theodotus opens with a similar theme of Shechem:

> Rich was the land, well watered, browsed by goats,
> Not far from the field to city was the road
> No leafy copse the weary wanderer found:
> Yet from it two strong mountains close at hand,
> With grass and forest trees abounding, rise.
> Midway a narrow path runs up the vale,
> Beneath whose farther slope the *sacred town*
> Of Sikimia mid sparkling streams is seen
> Deep down the mountain's side, around whose base
> E'en from the summit runs the well-built wall.[98]

Jerusalem is not directly named, but the contrast between its desert location and nature's favors to Shechem seem to permeate every one of Theodotus' lines.

Theodotus then proceeds, after an interjection by Alexander Polyhistor, to retell the story of Dinah's rape as recorded in Gen. 35. But he mentions first Jacob's arrival in the region ruled by Emmor and his son Sychem. Digressing, Theodotus recounts Jacob's journey to "Syria," the kingdom of Laban. Jacob's eleven sons were wise and brave, according to the poet, and Dinah was fair and eye-catching. Jacob's refusal to forego the decree ordained by God to Abraham compels the Shechemites to undergo the rite of circumcision. Alleging that since God had promised the ten nations to Abraham's seed and since Shechem had violated the elementary rules of hospitality, Symeon persuaded Levi to avenge their sister's shame. The fragment concludes with a hair-raising depiction of how Symeon cut off Emmor's head and Levi's sword pierced Shechem's shoulders, as their other brothers then joined in the pillage of the town.[99]

Unlike Philo, Theodotus was a genuine poet, as far as we can tell, perhaps the greatest writer of the Hellenistic biblical authors. Freudenthal identified Theodotus as a Samaritan a) by the theme of his epic; b) because he calls Shechem a holy city; and c) because Sicimius is said to have been the son of Hermes, indicating the Samaritan tendency to be syncretistic. The last proof ought to be rejected since syncretism was probably as common among some segments of the Jews as it was among the Samaritan rivals.[100] There is, moreover, an indication which suggests that Theodotus was a Jew rather than

---

98   Ibid., IX, 22, 1 = 732 F 1. I have used E. H. Gifford's translation in the Oxford, 1903, edition. Possibly the title of Theodotus' work was simply *On Jacob,* as indicated in the heading of Mras' edition (I, 512, 11).

99   Ibid., IX, 22, 2-12, = 732 F 1.

100   Freudenthal, *Hell. St.,* 99 f.; Gutman, *Beginnings of Jewish-Hellenistic Literature,* I, 246 f. Schürer, *Geschichte,* III⁴, 499 f.; J. A. Montgomery, *The Samaritans,* Bohlen Lectures (1906). Quite probably, as A. Ludwich, *De Theodoti fragmenta,* 5, suggested Σικίμιου τοῦ Ἑρμοῦ should read ...Ἐμμώρ i.e., Shechem the son of Hamor, there is no syncretism at all.

a Samaritan. His epic is named by Alexander Polyhistor *On the Jews,* a rather unlikely title for a Samaritan.[101] This is, however, not enough to negate the overwhelming evidence in support of the Northern origin of Theodotus. A heathen, Alexander Polyhistor could not differentiate between the rival claims of Jerusalem and Shechem; for him all those who claimed to be Hebrews were Jews. The title of Theodotus' work *On the Jews* should be interpreted as a description of its contents, but as proposed by Jacoby, the real name was *On the Foundation of Shechem,* or perhaps *On Jacob.*

There is no conclusive evidence that Theodotus might not have lived in Alexandria or for that matter in some other place of the Diaspora.[102] Chances are, however, that he was a native of the town whose glory he so ably depicted. Several motives of his epic—Abraham's legacy, the divine intervention and the role of the two brothers—appear to be curiously interdependent with the Testament of Levi, certainly the work of a Palestinian.[103] The Homeric hexameters of Philo and Theodotus may perhaps be taken to mirror the relative artistic achievement of the respective Greek-writing elements of the two Palestinian capitals.

Ezekielus is labeled by Alexander Polyhistor as "a tragic poet." None of his tragedies have survived, however, except for the two hundred and sixty-nine lines of his play *The Exodus.*[104] Because it is one of the few remaining specimens of Hellenistic drama, Ezekielus' work is of significance for the history of world literature. This uniqueness of Ezekielus has made him the subject of a relatively large number of studies.[105] Here it is necessary to deal with only one problem—the poet's homeland. In the nineteenth century, because of the flourishing theater in the Ptolemaic court, no one ever questioned that Ezekielus was a native of Alexandria.[106] This view has been challenged by Kuiper and Gutman. The former finds it unbelievable that a poet trained in Alexandria would have placed Zipporah's homeland (Midian) in Libya. This plus the poet's use of Hebrew convinced Kuiper that Ezekielus,

---

101   A. Ludwich, ibid., 5; Stählin, *Hellenistisch-jüdische Literatur,* 607; Gutman, *Beginnings of Jewish-Hellenistic Literature,* I, 246, deny that Theodotus was a Samaritan.

102   Josephus, *A.J.* (XIII, 74-79) reports that Jews and Samaritans quarreled in Alexandria during the reign of Ptolemy Philometor.

103   Cf. Test. Levi 6:3-7 with *P.E.,* IX, 22, 9-12; Gutmann, ibid., I, 255 f.

104   J. Wieneke, *Ezechielis Iudaei poetae Alexandrini fabulae quae inscribitur* ΕΞΑΓΩΓΗ *fragmenta* (Monasterii Westafalorum, 931); Mras, *P.E.,* IX, 28-29; English translation by Gifford in edition of *P.E.,* III, 1, 467-75.

105   See the detailed commentary by Gutman, *Beginnings of jewish-Hellenistic Literature,* II, 9-58 [in Hebrew]; the literature cited by Wieneke (preceding note, pp. viii-x); J. Strugnell, "Notes on the Text and Metre of Ezekiel the Tragedian's Exagoge," *HThR,* 60 (1967), 449-57.

106   See Schürer, *Geschichte des jüdischen Volkes,* III⁴, 500-03; Stählin, 607 f.

as Theodotus presumably, was a Samaritan.[107] But the same evidence persuaded Gutman that the dramatist lived in Libya, that is to say Cyrene, which, incidentally, would link Ezekielus with Maccabean historian Jason of Cyrene.[108] However, as pointed out by Wieneke, ancient poets were notoriously ignorant of geography. There is no reason to question the scholarly consensus that our dramatist actually resided in Alexandria.[109] But the appelation Ezekielus at a time when the Jews of Alexandria generally bore Greek names, plus the poet's unusual expertise in Jewish lore, suggest that he may have been born in Jerusalem.

It should not be forgotten that, with the exception of Eupolemus and Ben Sira's grandson, and perhaps Pseudo-Hecataeus, the locations of the men under consideration so far are strictly speculative. What is certain, however, is the absence of syncretism in the remnants of these Graeco-Jewish historians and poets. The main characteristic of the Alexandrian school of biblical exegesis, as far as we can tell from the fragments of Aristobulus, the Letter of Aristeas, and Philo of Alexandria, is an apparent tendency to allegorize or rationalize the tradition to make Scripture more palatable to a somewhat more sophisticated audience.[110] This hermeneutic school may be contrasted with that of Palestine which, in all of its varied manifestations, retained the literal meaning of the Hebrew text. The Palestinian writers were never embarrassed by Scripture's miraculous tales or anthropomorphisms. On the contrary; the authors of the Books of Enoch and Jubilees, Genesis Apocryphon, as well as the rabbis, all tended, if anything, to pile up new miracles in addition to those recounted in Scripture. By this scale the hermeneutics that underlie the writings of Demetrius, Eupolemus, and the poets belonged to a "Palestinian" school.[111] Thus even if we assume, as we

---

107   K. Kuiper, "De Exechiele poeta Iudaico," *Mnemosyne,* 28 (1900). 237-80, esp. 274 ff.; *REJ,* 46 (1903), 48-75, 161-77. M. Hadas, *Hellenistic Culture; Fusion and Diffusion* (New York, Columbia University Press, 1959), 100, admits that Exekielus might have lived in Palestine, which is branded by M. Hengel, *Judentum und Hellenismus,* 190, n. 344, as sheer speculation.

108   Gutman, *Beginnings,* 66-69 [in Hebrew]. Gutman finds it inconceivable that a drama depicting the drowning of the Egyptians would have been shown in Egypt, which he says should be replaced by Libya, because of line 60 (Wieneke; Mras, *P.E.,* I, p. 527, 17), where Graeco-Jewish literature flourished.

109   Stählin, 608; Wieneke, 124-26.

110   Aristobulus, in *P.E.,* XIII, 10, 1-17 = Walter F 2; XIII, 12, 1-16 = Walter FF 3-5. Aristeas, 131, 132, 171, 234, 278; cf. Walter, *Der Thoraausleger Aristobulos,* 99-103, and passim.

111   Note, for example, Josephus' ambiguous remarks concerning miracles. Sometimes, as in the miracle of the quails in the desert (*A.J.,* III, 25) of Exod. 16:13, he explained things by natural causes; more often, however, like the Sinaitic miracles, he comments: "Of these happenings each of my readers may think as he will; for my part, I am constrained to report them as they are recorded in the sacred books" (ibid. III, 81; cf. IV, 158 and passim). What is remarkable is Josephus' oblivion or ignorance of the allegorical school of Alexandria. This is another indication that Alexandrian-Jewish

may, that Demetrius and Ezekielus resided in Alexandria, we still must grant that among certain elements of the Diaspora Jews, the influence of the Palestinian midrash outweighed the intellectual currents of their immediate surroundings.

SYNCRETISTIC BIBLICAL HISTORY

In contrast to the writings whose inspiration is traceable either to the Jerusalem school or the Alexandrian school of biblical exegesis, a number of Graeco-Jewish fragments mirror a conscious attempt to fuse biblical traditions with the beliefs and ideas of the neighboring peoples. Pagan cultures contributed significantly to almost every shade of Jewish opinion, if sometimes only negatively. What distinguished the writings of Pseudo-Eupolemus, Artapanus, and sections of the·Sibylline Oracles, however, was the apparent conscious and free fusion of Jewish and pagan myths, often with ascriptions to Moses himself. In other words, if allegorical exegesis of Scripture appealed to the Euhemeristically inclined intellectuals, the universalists favored syncretistic exegesis.

A writer named Pseudo-Eupolemus seems to have been the first to identify pagan deities with the names of patriarchs listed in the beginning of Genesis. Pseudo-Eupolemus, a name coined by Freudenthal, is the presumed author of the syncretistic fragment dealing with Abraham, which Eusebius, quoting Alexander Polyhistor, ascribed to Eupolemus.[112] Since the writings of the latter make it clear that their author was a Jew and that he was almost certainly a native of Jerusalem, he could not have been at the same time the author of a text proclaiming Mount Gerizin as the site of a sacred shrine in the days of Abraham.[113] Evidently a Samaritan, Pseudo-Eupolemus must be counted among the earliest biblical historians writing in Greek. His pro-Phoenician and anti-Egyptian stance as well as his type of embellishments of ancient history suggest that Pseudo-Eupolemus was a native of Samaria.[114] Whether Pseudo-Eupolemus' account of the patriarchs served as the source of or was in any way related to the epic works of his fellow-Samaritan Theodotus is an open question.

---

exegesis was rather isolated from other segments of the Diaspora, not to mention Palestine.

112   Pseudo-Eupolemus, *P.E.*, IX, 17, 1-8 = 724 F 1. *P.E.*, IX, 18, 2, quotes an "Anonymous" author who seemed remarkably similar to Pseudo-Eupolemus. Freudenthal, *Hell. St.*, 82-103, esp. 91 (724 F 2), identified the two. See also my "Pseudo-Eupolemus' Two Greek Fragments on the Life of Abraham," *HUCA* 34 (1963), 83-113, esp. 83 f. But N. Walter, "Zu Pseudo-Eupolemos," *Klio*, 43-45 (1965), 282-90, may be right in rejecting Freudenthal's identification. If so, the Anonymous must be regarded as having flourished later than the Pseudo-Eupolemus.

113   *P.E.*, IX, 17, 5 = 724 F 1, 679, 1. See Freudenthal, ibid., 85 ff., Wacholder, ibid., esp. 106 f.

114   Wacholder, ibid., esp. 85-87; Walter (n. 112), 283 f.; Hengel, *Judentum und Hellenismus*, 162.

Pseudo-Eupolemus appears to have been a firm believer in the tenets of the Bible, including God's election of Abraham; he even added new miracles not recorded in Scripture.[115] But for Pseudo-Eupolemus, Abraham was more than the patriarch of Yahweh's chosen clan. Abraham was also the father of civilization. Commanded by God to leave his native Babylonia, Abraham introduced the sciences, especially astrology, to Phoenicia and Egypt.[116] Noah of Genesis equalled Belus of Babylonia and Enoch was the one called Atlas by the Greeks. Pseudo-Eupolemus took for granted the Euhemeristic view of polytheism, using it to support the authenticity of the biblical account of early civilization. He fused the writings of Hesiod and Berossus into the story of Genesis. The Torah recorded the story of the Hebrew people, but if properly understood, it related also the story of the neighboring cultures of Phoenicia, Egypt, and even Greece.[117]

In addition to Pseudo-Eupolemus' Euhemeristic tendencies and his use of Hellenistic texts, his link with the Palestinian Hebrew and Aramaic literature should not be forgotten. Abraham spread the knowledge of the sciences to the Phoenicians and Egyptians, but Abraham, says Pseudo-Eupolemus, credited Enoch as the man who first discovered the sciences. Enoch, in his turn, had been instructed by the angels of God. Here Pseudo-Eupolemus' link with the astronomical visions of Enoch in Jubilees is unmistakable.[118]

Unmistakable as well is the nexus between Pseudo-Eupolemus and the Genesis Apocryphon, a partially deciphered copper scroll recently discovered in Qumran. The Book of Enoch, Genesis Apocryphon, and Pseudo-Eupolemus all make Enoch the fountain of human knowledge, with the last two works also reporting that Abraham transmitted Enoch's teachings to the Egyptians. When Sarah was taken to the Egyptian palace, both the Genesis Apocryphon and Pseudo-Eupolemus know that the pharaoh "was not able to have sexual intercourse with her."[119]

---

115   *P.E.,* IX, 17, 7 I, 503, 20, = 724 F 1.

116   *P.E.,* IX, 17, 9 - 723 F 1. See Wacholder, ibid., 100-04; cf. L. H. Feldman, "Abraham the Greek Philosopher in Josephus," *Transactions and Proceedings of the American Philological Association.* 99 (1968), 143-56.

117   See Freudenthal, *Hell. St.,* 94; Wacholder, ibid., 89-94. Feldman, ibid., 155, n. 44, questions the evidence of Pseudo-Eupolemus' dependence on Berossus: "But the very element in common is the assertion that Abraham was versed in astronomy, and Pseudo-Eupolemus might have independently arrived at such a view from the association of Abraham with Chaldaea." Here Feldman disregards the fact that the presumed interdependence rests on the common vocabulary as it does on the similarity of the ideas. Cf. P. Schnabel, *Berossos und die babylonisch-hellenistische Literatur* (Berlin, 1923), 67-69.

118   For the Enochite traditions see R. H. Charles, "Introduction to the Book of Enoch," (*The Apocrypha and Pseudepigrapha of the Old Testament,* Oxford, 1915), II, 177-85.

119   Cf. I Enoch, Chapters 6-16, 23-36, 62-90; Jubilees 6:17-32, some of whose traditions probably lie behind Pseudo-Eupolemus' claim that Enoch was the first to have discovered astrology (*P.E.,* IX, 17 9 = 724 F 1). See also, Wacholder, *HUCA,* 34 (1963),

Assuming that Pseudo-Eupolemus must have lived in Alexandria, Vermès asks whether Genesis Apocryphon "was influenced by Hellenistic Judaism or did Jewish writers of the Greek Diaspora adopt and partly modify Palestinian traditions?" His answer is that "the literature of Hellenistic Judaism was built upon a Palestinian tradition."[120] In the light of our supposition, however, that Pseudo-Eupolemus wrote in Samaria, the presence of Enochite traditions in Graeco-Palestinian writers is less puzzling. The traces of a Greek literary tradition, in Palestine, as exemplified in the writings of Pseudo-Hecataeus, Eupolemus, Theophilus and Theodotus, dispense of the dichotomy usually drawn between the Judaean sources and those of the Diaspora. We know of barely a handful of historians and Hebrew-Greek translators. There is no doubt that their number was small and their audience quite restricted to the highest echelons of the priestly classes. The presumption that the Palestinian Graeco-Jewish writers were priests rests upon the analogy with men such as Berossus the high priest of Babylon and Manetho the high priest of Sebennystus, from outside Palestine; and with Eupolemus of the priestly clan Hakkos, as well as, from a later period, Josephus the priest.

We have no direct evidence that Pseudo-Eupolemus belonged to the priestly clan. But the fact is that, in contrast to Gen. 14:18, which either gives parity to Melchizedek's dual role as king and priest or stresses the former, Pseudo-Eupolemus goes out of his way to point out that Abraham was paying tribute primarily to the shrine of "Argerizin" and its chief priest.[121] This shift of emphasis may suggest that Pseudo-Eupolemus was himself a priest tracing the Samaritan priesthood back to Melchizedek. Is it then correct to regard Pseudo-Eupolemus as an antecedent of the Christian tradition, reported in the epistle to the Hebrews, which ranks Melchizedek above Abraham? And conversely, should this Epistle be regarded as influenced by Samaritan Hellenistic theology?[122]

95-97; "How Long did Abram Stay in Egypt?" *HUCA*, 35 (1964), 43-56. Cf. the wording of Gen. Apocryphon, Col. II, 19-21 with Eupolemus, in *P.E.* IX, 17, 9, I, 504, 8 f.; Col. XX, 17 with Pseudo-Eupolemus, *P.E.* IX, 17, 7, I, 503, 20. See now also J. A. Fritzmyer, S.J., *The Genesis Apocryphon of Cave I* (Rome, Pontifical Institute, 1966), Col. XIX (p. 52 f.) 25: "And I [Abram] read to them [the Egyptians] the Book of the words of Enoch." Pseudo-Eupolemus' statement (*P.E.* IX. 17, 8) that Abraham brought the Enochite legacy to Egypt is now directly supported only in Genesis Apocryphon; although both Josephus (*A.J.*, I, 156); Philo, (*Abraham*, 69-72); cf. S. Sandmel, *Philo's Place in Judaism; A Study in Conceptions of Abraham in Jewish Literature* (Cincinnati, Hebrew Union College Press, 1956) 181, n. 228.

120   G. Vermès, *Scripture and Tradition in Judaism* (Leiden, Brill, 1961), 124.

121   ξενισθῆναι τε αὐτὸν ὑπὸ πόλεως ἱερὸν Ἀργαριξίν, ὃ εἶναι μεθερμηνευόμενον ὄρος ὑψίστου (*P.E.*, IX, 17, 5, I, 503, 15 f.).

122   Cf. Ps. 76:3; 110:4; Gen. Apocryphon XXII, 14 f.; Heb. 5:6, 10; 6:20; 7:1, 10-11, 15, 17.

Freudenthal has ascribed Pseudo-Eupolemus' syncretistic tendencies to the fact that he was a Samaritan. Theodotus the poet and Cleodomus-Malchus displayed similar unorthodox views, Freudenthal says, because they belonged to the same sect.[123] But there is little reason to maintain that the Samaritans were more affected by the Hellenizing elements than were the Judaeans. The Tobiad clan, for example, whose connections extended from Transjordan to Jerusalem, came under strong assimilationist influence. Possibly the syncretistic literary trends reflected views favored by the class of priests who supported Antiochus IV's Hellenization of Palestine. In this respect there was practically no difference between Samaria and Jerusalem.[124] In both places sophisticated priests seem to have represented a significant but tiny minority of the ruling circles. On the basis of fragments of Theodotus and Pseudo-Eupolemus, however, there seems to be some reason to believe that the Samaritan Graeco-biblical literature reached a higher stage than did its Judaean couterpart.

As has been shown, there is a definite link between the Enochite works—Enoch, Jubilees, Genesis Apocryphon—and Pseudo-Eupolemus. Equally interesting is the relationship between Pseudo-Eupolemus and some sections of the Sibylline Oracles. Two passages illustrate this nexus. First, Or. Sib. III, 97-158 retells the story of the tower of Babel as if it were a battle between God and the rebellious Titans, who after the destruction of the tower fought among themselves, ultimately dispersing among the peoples of the earth. Like Pseudo-Eupolemus, Or. Sib. III, 97-104 claims that some of the giants who survived the catastrophe founded the first city, naming it Babylon. There is good reason to believe that the author of this Sibyl borrowed the Euhemeristic colorings as well as the particulars of the tower from syncretistic accounts, which he embellished with Hesiod's description of the battle between Kronos and the Titans.[125]

Second, Or. Sib. III, 218-36 begins: "There is a city . . . down in the land of Ur of the Chaldees from which comes a race of the most righteous men [Abraham and his progeny], who ever give themselves up to sound counsel and fair deeds. For they search not the circling of course of the sun and the

---

123   See Frankel, *Über den Einfluss,* 242-54; Freudenthal, *Hell. St.,* 99-103. Cf. B. Hullin, 6a; A. Spiro, "Samaritans, Tobiads and Juhadites . . . ," *Proceedings of the American Academy for Jewish Research,* 20 (1951), 279-355.

124   Cf. E. Bickerman, *Gott der Makkabäer,* 59-65; Tcherikover, *Hellenistic Civilization and the Jews* (Philadelphia, The Jewish Publication Society, 1959), 152-203. For a different view, see I. Heinemann, "Wer veranlasste den Glaubenzwang der Makkabäerzeit?" *MGWJ,* 82 (1938), 145-72.

125   See J. Geffcken, *Die Oracula Sibyllina* (Leipzig, 1902), on III, 97, p. 53, who in addition to (Pseudo-) Eupolemus, cites the ancient parallels. For more details and literature, see Wacholder, *HUCA,* 34 (1963), 90-93; Hengel, *Judentum und Hellenismus,* 162-64.

moon ... nor do study the predictions of Chaldean astrology nor do they astronomize, for all these things are prone to deceive ... But these diligently practice justice and virtue; and not covetousness which is the source of myriad ills to mortal men, of war and desperate famine."[126] Scholars have rightly interpreted this passage as a criticism of Pseudo-Eupolemus' account of Abraham, which made of him an astrologist and warrior.[127] Although other writers, such as Josephus and Philo, also attributed to the patriarch the knowledge of astronomy, the introductory words of this passage recall the words of Pseudo-Eupolemus: "In the Babylonian city of Camarina, which some call Urie, and which in translation is the city of the Chaldeans, Abraham was born ... By the command of God he went to Phoenicia, teaching them the changes of the sun and the moon."[128] In fact the Sibyll's criticism seems to be almost a point by point refutation of the remnant of Pseudo-Eupolemus. The antiquity of this criticism is attested by the fact that Alexander Polyhistor, who flourished in the first half of the first century B.C., quotes an excerpt of this Sibylline text.[129]

Although the criticism seems to have been directed primarily at Pseudo-Eupolemus, it was applicable to, and perhaps primarily intended for, the entire genre of Enochite works, which regarded astrology and astronomy as the queen of the sciences and attributed their discovery to the patriarchs. To be sure, these works had ascribed the discovery of astrology to Enoch. But as pointed out by the Genesis Apocryphon as well as by Pseudo-Eupolemus, after Sarah was freed Abraham introduced this Enochite science to the Egyptians.

It is unfortunate that we know nothing about the man who criticized the ascriptions of astrology to Abraham. Whoever he was, it is unlikely that he lived in the Diaspora, since as far as we know, outside of Palestine, Judaean traditions were often ignored or reinterpreted, but not directly criticized. It may be presumed, therefore, that the author who attacked the Enochite traditions was a Palestinian. It is possible, however, that the Greek critic was merely echoing Judaean objections to Enochite traditions.

The Sibyll's criticism of the Enochite texts—the righteous man is too busy practicing justice to be watching the stars or making war—raises the question

---

126   The translation is by R. H. Charles in *Apocrypha and Pseudepigrapha*, II, 382 f.

127   See Geffcken, on line III, 218, "Polemik gegen Eupolemos bei Alexander Polyhistor"; Charles: "The lacuna is to be filled with 'Camarina,' which Eupolemus gives as the ancient name of Ur" Wacholder, *HUCA*, 34 (1963), 99-101.

128   *P.E.*, IX, 17, 3-4 = 724 F 1. It seems paradoxical that Or. Sibyll. III, 97-157, on the one hand, enlarges upon the syncretistic elements of Genesis, but that III, 218-36, on the other hand, condemns the ascription of scientific interest to Abraham.

129   Josephus, *A.J.*, I, 118; Euseb. *Chronica* (Arm., ed. Karst) = *FGrH* 273 F 79a = Berossus 680 F 4, pp. 682 f.

whether we may conjecture that the author of the Sibylline Hexameters (III, 218-36) was perhaps acquainted with the Dead Sea Scrolls. R.H. Charles has already noted that some Essene views seem to have been stressed by the Jewish Sibyll. The requirements to wash the entire body with ever-running water, hands heavenward (Or. Sibyll. IV, 165), or to rise early to cleanse one's flesh (III, 591-95), may be interpreted to coincide with Josephus' description of the Essene mode of living.[130] Furthermore, passages attributed to the Erytherean Sibyll appear to echo some of the apocalyptic oracles of the Dead Sea Scrolls.

War Between the Sons of Light ...	*Oracula Sibyllina*
When the mighty hand of God will be raised against Belial and against all those whose lot is with his kingdom (18:1).	The threatened vengeance of the Almighty God draws near; and fiery energy comes through the swelling surge to earth and burns up Beliar and the overweening men (III, 71-73).

Do these and similar parallels prove an Esseean origin of certain sections of the Jewish Sibyll?

Although not conclusive, the evidence does point to a positive answer. It might be argued that ablutions were a common practice among many segments of the population, but there is no doubt that the Essenes were among the most zealous observers of ritual purity. Certainly, this purity referred primarily to the Temple's priest, rather than to the Diaspora. Likewise, the Qumran writers were the only ones who identified Belial (Beliar) with Satan.[131] The allusion to the Enochite texts, however, suggests an acquaintance with the lore popular among the Essenes. Of interest also is Ps. 151, until recently only partly preserved in the Syriac and the Greek, which shows that Orphic motives gained some popularity among the members of the Qumran sect. Thus David, like Orpheus, was a sweet singer whose music tamed the wild beasts.[132]

The presence of a Judaean Orphic tradition in Ps. 151 tends to further blur the traditional dichotomy between the Greek-reading Jews of the Diaspora and the Semitic literature of Palestine. This piece of evidence is supplemental to the writings of the Judaean Eupolemus, the Samaritan Pseudo-Eupolemus,

---

130   Cf. Josephus, *B.J.*, II, 129; 1QS III, 4-9.

131   Or. Sibyll. II, 167; III, 63-67, 1QS I, 19, 23-24; II, 4-5; Damascus Scroll IV, 12-18; IQM I, 5.

132   11 Q Ps. 151:1-3; cf. J. A. Sanders, *Discoveries*, IV, pp. 54-60. Cf. Artapanus, who makes Orpheus a disciple of Moses (in *P.E.*, IX, 27, 4 = 726 F 3). See also the Pseudo-Orphic texts sometimes associated with Aristobulus and Pseudo-Hecataeus III: Clement Alexandrinus, *Stromata*, V, 78, 4; 123, 1-24, 1: 126, 5-127, 2; Eusebius, *P. E.* XIII, 12,5; Ps.-Justin, 15. For a recent review of the Judaeo-Orphic tradition, see Walter, *Der Thoraausleger Aritobulos,* 202-61.

and the epic poets, Philo and Theodotus representing, respectively, Jerusalem and Shechem. It should be made clear, however, that most, if not all, of these Graeco-Palestinian writers were only superficially touched by Hellenism. They wrote in Greek as diplomats of the nineteenth century sometimes composed in French. Although many of the claims made in the Letter of Aristeas are sheer fiction, the tradition that Palestinian Jews had a significant share in the making of the Septuagint is historical. But the oldest Graeco-Palestinian literary work was that of Pseudo-Hecataeus, dating back to the end of the fourth or the beginning of the third century B.C. This unknown Jewish writer used a foreign tongue because he wanted to present the priestly view of Judaism to the Greek world. The conflicts with the Persian satraps had shown that pagan occupational forces were completely unaware of the Jewish sensitivity to idolatry. The priests of Jerusalem were aware that the symbiosis of Jews and Macedonians required a constant presentation of the Judaean position vis-à-vis their internal or external adversaries.

POLITICAL WRITINGS

The legendary figure of Alexander the Great captured the hearts of the ancient and medieval storytellers. The Hebrew Alexander found his way into the Megillat Ta'anit, talmudic and midrashic texts.[133] The Graeco-Jewish Alexander was important enough to be incorporated into some versions of the so-called Pseudo-Callisthenes, an ancient-medieval romance.[134] *Antiquities,* XI, 304-5; 313-47, has preserved sections of one of the oldest Graeco-Palestinian novella, evidently dating from before the destruction of the Samaritan shrine by John Hyrcanus (134-104) and after Simon the Hasmonean's accession to the high priesthood in 143 B.C.[135] It celebrated Alexander's visit to Jerusalem, a visit that never actually occurred.[136]

The Palestinian origin of this novella becomes clear because, unlike the novellas produced in the Diaspora which concerned themselves with Jewish civil rights in general, this one interwove the legendary visit of Alexander with

133 Megillat Ta'anit, ed. by H. Lichtenstein, *HUCA,* 8/9 (1931-32), 339-40; B. Yoma, 69a; Yosephon, II, 6. Cf. I, Levi, "La legende d'Alexandre dans le Talmud et le Midrasch," *Revue des Études Juives,* 7 (1883), 78-93; R. Marcus, in Volume VI of *Josephus,* 512-32.

134 See C. Mueller's edition, *Scriptores Rerum Alexandri Magni* (Paris, 1846), II, 24; W. Kroll, *Historia Alexandri Magni* (Berlin, 1926); *R.E.* X (1919), 1722 f.

135 Cf. A. Büchler, "La relation de Joséphe concernant Alexandre le Grand," *REJ,* 34 (1898), 1-26; R. Marcus, in *Josephus* (see n. 133).

136 I. Abrahams, *Campaigns in Palestine from Alexander the Great* (London, 1927), defends the historicity of the account.

the dispute between the Judaeans and the Samaritans.[137] The remnants summarized by Josephus suggest, as Büchler noted, that the Jewish version was a retort to an earlier Samaritan publication which claimed that Alexander had authorized the foundation of a shrine on Mount Gerizim.[138] This rivalry inspired the publication of Greek pamphlets that rehashed the arguments for or against Samaritan statehood.

More damaging from the Jewish point of view was the allegation, supported in part by Neh. 13:28, that Menasses, a brother of Jerusalem's high priest during the reign of Darius III, who had married the Samaritan chieftain's daughter, became the first high priest of the newly-founded shrine.[139] The Jewish version supposedly did not dispute these basic claims, but responded that the Samaritans were the first who approached Alexander, soon after his defeat of Darius, inciting him against the rebellion-prone Jewish state. Moreover, because the high priest of Jerusalem had rebuffed his suggestion that the Jews revolt against the Persians, Alexander allegedly marched to destroy Jerusalem. Expecting the worst, the people of the city were praying, but Jaddus, the high priest, had a dream telling him not to be afraid. As Jaddus and Alexander met, it was the king who prostrated himself before the high priest, to the amazement of the onlookers. Alexander is said to have told that while in Macedonia he had seen the high priest in a dream, promising him divine guidance in the forthcoming war against Darius. Alexander then sacrificed at the Temple on the spot where Daniel had prophesied the Greek victory over the Persians (Dan. 8:21). Afterwards, Alexander granted the Jews the right to observe their ancestral laws, freed them from tribute during the sabbatical years when the land was idle, and gladly promised to permit the Jews of Media and Persia to observe their religious practices. When leaving Jerusalem, Alexander refused the same privileges to the Samaritans, since they were unwilling to declare themselves Jews.[140]

A mere glance at Josephus' summary would seem to suggest that the Graeco-Jewish source concerned itself almost exclusively with the Macedonian's adjudication of Palestinian affairs. This is misleading. For *Antiquities,* XI, 304-05, in giving the background of Alexander's conquests, concludes with the familiar Josephean phrase "as has been related elsewhere," when in

---

137   For a Diaspora version see F. Pfister, "Eine jüdische Gründungs-geschichte Alexandrias, mit einem Anhang über Alexanders Besuch in Jerusalem," *Sitzungsberichte der Heidelberger Akademie der Wissenschaften,* Phil.-hist. Klasse B (1914), Abt. 11.

138   A. Büchler, *REJ,* 36 (1898), 1-26, quoted in part by Marcus in *Josephus* (LCL), VI, 532. For a different analysis of the sources claiming that Josephus utilized here a single anti-Samaritan composition, see B Motzo, "Una fonte sacerdotale antisamaritana di Giuseppe," *Saggi do storia e letterature giudeo-ellenistica* (Florence, 1924).

139   *A.J.,* XI, 306-13.

140   *A.J.,* XI, 329-45.

fact the historian never dealt with this subject. This Josephean formula usually means that the historian's source treated the matter at length, and he saw no purpose in repeating. If so, the Graeco-Jewish account of Alexander dealt at some length with the Macedonian conquest of Persia. Josephus, however, felt no need to describe the details of the battle at Granicus, and the conquests of Ionia, Caria, and Pamphylia. *Antiquities,* XI, 306-12, digressing into the origin of the schism, was not part of the treatise dealing with Alexander. For *Antiquities,* XI, 313-14, "Now about this time Darius heard that Alexander had crossed the Hellespont and defeated the satraps in a battle at the Granicus . . . "retells the war from the Persian point of view, paralleling closely the lines 304-05. It becomes quite probable that the digression, relating the genesis of the Samaritan shrine, was that of the source, rather than Josephus' own.[141] It is clear that the author of the treatise intended to relate how the mighty Persian empire fell, and that Providence saved the Jewish people from an impending catastrophe. As such this work was but part of the world-wide literature which converted Alexander into a legendary figure.

Another Graeco-Palestinian work, dating from the pre-Maccabean period, was the saga of the Tobiads. The Tobiad treatise was no doubt typical of the heroic period of the Diadochi in which personality traits were given a greater role than national or religious motives. It was also a sign of the extent of Hellenization that the wealthiest men of Judaea employed skilled craftsmen to spread their fame. *Antiquities,* XII, 154-236, records the saga of the Tobiads.[142]

For the purpose of analyzing the Graeco-Jewish treatise that lies behind the Tobiad sage, Josephus' account must be divided into three parts: 1) The introductory section (154-59), which abridges the source and intermingles extraneous material; 2) the middle section, a relatively close paraphrase of the saga (160-222); and 3) the concluding section (223-36), only peripherally related to the treatise. In this study we are only concerned with section 2.

The middle section of the Tobiad saga recounts the adventures of Joseph, the son of Tobias (or the Tobiad), and Joseph's son Hyrcanus in the Ptolemaic court: it tells how a local boy won the favors of Ptolemy and Cleopatra by sheer wit, and became the chief tax farmer of Syria and Palestine. As has been pointed out, the story was essentially fiction, written chiefly for amuse-

---

141   *A.J.,* XI, 306-12, was taken from the same source as XI, 297-303. Line 306 appears to be contiguous to 303.

142   For Tobiads, see A. Büchler, *Die Tobiaden und die Oniaden* (VI Jahresbericht der Israelitisch-Theologischen Lehranstalt in Wein, [Vienna, 1899]); Mozzo, *Saggi,* 186-206; Marcus' notes to *Josephus* (LCL), XII, 154-236; V. Tcherikover, *Hellenistic Civilization,* 127-42; V. Tcherikover and A. Fuks, *Corpus Papyrorum Judaicarum,* I (Cambridge, Mass., Harvard University Press, 1957), 115-46.

ment.[143] Religious practices, such as the problem of observing dietary laws at the royal banquets, are ignored as the tale relates the style of high living in the world's metropolis. Yet there seems to be no doubt that the author of this saga was a Palestinian Jew writing for other Jews.[144]

Although the main concern of the treatise appears to have been personal achievement, a more serious purpose also emerges. The villain of the story is the high priest Onias, described as "small-minded and passionately fond of money," who refused to pay the customary tribute to the king. Joseph the Tobiad, however, had a reputation for uprightness.[145] In other words the former was the enemy of the people; the latter, their protector. In Egypt Joseph excused Onias' incompetence as the result of old age. At the taxfarming auction Joseph doubled the nearest bid, but gave no security, except his own word, which the king surprisingly accepted. The anecdote of the drunken Joseph having intercourse with a dancing girl of Alexandria, who miracuously turns out to be his brother's daughter, and who gives birth to Hyrcanus; as well as the accounts of Hyrcanus' own escapades, reflect the cosmopolitan-minded men of rustic Palestine, whose inspiration came from the easy living of Alexandria, rather than from the austere priestly Jerusalem.[146] It was to these people that the author of the Tobiad romance addressed himself.

The Tobiads were not unique in having court biographers to spread their fame. I Macc. 16:23 says: "The rest of the acts of John (Hyrcanus I, 135-104) and the wars and the brave deeds which he did, and the building of the walls which he built, and his achievements, behold, they are written in the chronicles ($\beta\iota\beta\lambda\iota\alpha$ $\dot{\eta}\mu\epsilon\rho\tilde{\omega}\nu$) of his high priesthood, from the time that he became high priest after his father."[147] It is doubtful, however, that an anti-Hellenist like John Hyrcanus would have composed his day-to-day records in Greek. This objection does not apply to his successors Aristobulus (104-103), who was a phil-Hellenist, and to Alexander Jannaeus (103-76), whose coins contain inscriptions in both Hebrew and Greek.[148]

Herod I (37-4 B.C.) did everything on a large scale. Among the galaxy of foreign courtiers, whose task was to spread the king's alleged love of Hellenic culture, were counted names such as Julius Eurycles and Nicolaus of Damascus. Eurycles had been the tyrant of Cythera and the famous builder of

---

143   For the fictional elements, see H. Willrich, *Juden und Griechen,* 91-106; for the historical elements, Tcherikover, *Hellenistic Civilization and the Jews,* 127-42; cf. H. C. Butler and E. Littman, in *Publications of the Princeton University Archaeological Expedition to Syria in 1904-05* (Princeton, 1907).

144   Perhaps the author was one of the teachers mentioned in *A.J.,* XII, 191.

145   *A.J.,* XII, 192.

146   *A.J.,* XII, 175-89.

147   I. Macc. 16:23 f. = *FGrH* 736 T 1.

148   A. Reifenberg, *Ancient Jewish Coins,* 14, 41.

Corinthian baths before he became Herod's confidant, informing on his son's plot to slay their father. Nicolaus had been the tutor of Cleopatra's children and composed a biography of Augustus. He dedicated *The Collection of Exotic Customs* to Herod and while in Jerusalem wrote a world history consisting of 144 books.[149] That such a work could have been written in Jerusalem gives us a glimpse of the immense library collected for the king. Nicolaus was a heathen and his work hardly falls under the topic of ·Graeco-Jewish literature. Nevertheless, it is clear that Herod attempted to make Jerusalem a Greek literary center.[150]

Herod, who sometimes dabbled in philosophy and rhetoric, published royal accounts of major events, copies of which he no doubt sent to Augustus. Josephus, for example, reports that he saw two divergent reports of the incidents leading to the execution of Hyrcanus II. He attributes one to King Herod's Memoirs (*Hypomnemata*), which claimed that the former Hasmonean king and high priest was guilty of high treason. He ascribes to "others" the report that the king's case was based on perjured testimony and manufactured evidence.[151] Herod's Memoirs were certainly written in Greek. We do not know, however, whether he or some of his aides authored them. Neither can it be said whether the anti-Herodian source, used by Josephus, was also in Greek or in the vernacular, though the former is quite likely. Scholars have plausibly suggested that Josephus was not privy to Herod's *Memoirs,* but had found the citations in Nicolaus of Damascus' history.[152]

The question of the possible identify of this anonymous account is intriguing. Josephus infrequently mentions his source, but when he does he never alludes to it with such mysterious phrases as he uses here.[153] A possible explanation is that Josephus himself did not know the identity of the

149   Nicolaos Damascenus, *FGrH,* 90 TT 1-14; FF 1-143. Cf. Wacholder, *Nicolaus of Damascus* (Berkeley and Los Angeles, University of California Press, 1962); A. Schalit, *König Herodes* (Berlin, Walter de Gruyter Co., 1969), index.

150   J. von Destinon, *Die Quellen des Flavius Josephus* (Kiel, 1892); G. Hölscher, *Die Quellen des Josephus für die Zeit vom Exil bis zum jüdischen Kriege* (Leipzig, 1904), 17-36; Wacholder, *Nicolaus of Damascus,* 58-64.

151   *A.J.,* XV, 164-74 = *FGrH* 226 F 1, esp. 174; "we [Josephus] have written about these matters as they are found in the *Hypomnemata* of King Herod. But other sources (τοὶς δ ἄλλοις οὐ κατὰ τοῦτα συμφωνεῖ) do not agree with this account, for they hold . . ." Cf. 90 F 135, p. 422, that which records Herod's interest in philosophy, rhetoric and historiography; W. Otto, "Herodes," I No. 14, *R.E.,* Suppl. II (1913), 1; Schürer, *Geschichte des jüdischen Volkes,* I³, 48; Schalit, *König Herodes,* 413.

152   See Schürer, *Geschichte des jüdischen Volke,* I³, 48. Otto's theory (*R.E.,* Suppl. II, 7-10), which posits a "middle source" which reworked Nicolaus' account that Josephus utilized (cf. *A.J.,* XVI, 183-93), is not acceptable. Also to be rejected is supposedly anti-Herodian "Anonymous" of *A.J.,* XVI, 189, which in fact is Josephus himself. Cf. my *Nicolaus of Damascus,* 6; 92 f.

153   *A.J.,* XV, 174-78.

source. Perhaps it was circulated anonymously during Herod's reign. Conceivably, it was composed by one of the king's own courtiers who was present during the alleged dialogue between Herod and Hyrcanus. But the possibility remains that it, like Herod's own account, was a plausible but fictional reconstruction of the events.

The anonymous anti-Herodian source could not, however, have been a certain Ptolemy, whose multi-volume biography is quoted by the second century philologist Ammonius: "The Idumaeans and the Judaeans are not the same, as Ptolemy says in the first book of *On Herod the King*. The Judaeans were the natives of the country; the Idumaeans, however, were originally not Judaeans, but Phoenicians and Syrians, conquered by them [i.e. Judaeans] they were forced to be circumcised and became united in regard of custom [nation], thus having adopted the name laws they are called Judaeans."[154] Since several writers were named Ptolemy, J. G. Vossius identified this author with Ptolemy of Mendes in Egypt or with the brother of Nicolaus of Damascus; C. Mueller with the king's procurator; E. Schürer with Ptolemy of Askalon, often cited by Anmmonius.[155] Jacoby points out cogently, however, that with such an abundance of possibilities there is nothing decisive about choosing one over the others.[156] Ptolemy's biography of Herod, as suggested by the title, was most likely favorably disposed to his subject; and was not anonymous. It could not have been the anti-Herodian source allegedly used by Josephus.[157] There is good reason, however, to posit that Ptolemy was a Herodian Jew—hence the classification of the Idumaeans with the Phoenicians and Syrians, in contrast to the Judaeans who are labeled natives.

JUSTUS OF TIBERIAS

It is perhaps paradoxical that the last two Graeco-Palestinian writers participated in and recorded the events of the anti-Roman revolt of 66-73. The writings and aristocratic backgrounds of Josephus, the son of Matthias of Jerusalem, and Justus, the son of Pistus of Tiberias, were quite similar. Josephus belonged to the most exclusive priestly clan of Joiarib; his father had been named after the founder of the Hasmonean dynasty. Although he complained that his Greek was quite inadequate, Josephus' education was considered sufficient to send him at the age of twenty-six as a member of an

---

154   *FGrH* 199 F 1. Ammonius, *De adfinium vocabulorum differentia*, s.v. Ἰδ ουμαῖοι.

155   J. G. Vossius, *De historicis graecis,* ed. Westermann, 226; C. Mueller, *FGH,* III (Paris, 1883), 348, note; E. Schürer, *Geschichte des jüdischen Volkes,* I³, 48; Otto, *R.E.,* Suppl. II, 4; A. Schalit, *König Herodes,* 677 f., following Otto.

156   Jacoby, *FGrH* 199 F 1, commentary in IID, 625 f.

157   So G. Hölscher, *Die Quellen des Josephus,* 57; "Iosephos." *R.E.,* IX (1916), 1981. Cf. Jacoby, *FGrH,* IID, 625 f.

embassy to plead the freedom for jailed fellow priests. The next time he came to Rome was as a privileged prisoner to march in Titus' triumphal celebration of Jerusalem's conquest. In Rome, patronized by the Flavian emperors, Josephus devoted himself to eulogizing the past of a people he had helped defeat.[158]

By Josephus' own admission, Justus' family played a leading role in the history of Tiberias. Unfortunately, all our information about Justus comes from Josephus' hostile *Vita,* a diatribe attached to the *Antiquities*; written as a self-defense, self-contradictory, confusing, and often unreliable.[159] Thus *Vita,* 88, charges that Pistus and his son Justus sided with John of Gischala, the Galilean leader of the zealots, who demanded a stronger anti-Roman action than that provided by Josephus.[160] According to *Vita,* 32-39, however, Pistus and Justus led Tiberias' third faction which opposed either the majority of the leading citizens who wished to retain allegiance to Rome, or the minority who favored war. The third faction, if we disregard the account's invective hurled at Pistus and Justus, seems to have urged that the city act to defend Tiberias' self-interest and become again the capital of Galilee as it had been when founded by Herod Antipas. There is nothing in this long statement to corroborate the charge that Justus or his father was anti-Roman. *Vita,* 41, reports that Justus led a group that burned the villages belonging to the Greek cities of Gadara, Hippos, and Scythopolis. As pointed out by Luther, Stählin, and Jacoby, this action was not directed against

---

158   *Vita,* 1-16; passim. The immense literature on Josephus has recently been assembled by H. Schreckenberg, *Bibliographie zu Josehpus* (Leiden, Brill, 1968). But Josephus has not received an evaluation that he deserves.

159   *Vita,* 32-42, and passim. For an attempt to find Justus' influence in the evolution of Josephus' nationalistic feelings from his pro-Roman stand of the *Bellum* to his alleged Jewish patriotism of the *Anitquities* and *Vita,* see R. Laqueur, *Der Jüdische Hitoriker Flavius Josephus* (Giessen, 1920). In fact, *A.J.,* XX, 258-68, seems to be related to the *Vita,* though Laqueur (p. 5) maintains that the *Antiquities* contains two epilogues, one written for the first and the other for the second edition. The first conclusion contained XX, 258 plus 267-68; the second edition, because of the appearance of Justus' work, replaced it with a conclusion 259-66 plus *Vita.* Laqueur's hypothesis is made unlikely by XX, 267, the promise to rewrite the *Bellum,* no doubt because of Justus' work that severely criticized Josephus; it could not therefore have been, as Laqueur maintains, part of the first conclusion. Laqueur's hypothesis is, furthermore, premised on a faulty chronology, believing that Justus published his history of the war after 93-94, subsequent to the first appearance of the *Antiquities.* In fact, it was written about the year 90 (*Vita,* 359). The appearance of two conclusions to the *Antiquities* (XX, 258-59; 267) must be ascribed to Josephus' typical incoherence in the *Antiquities,* examples of which are the chronological divergences (cf. *A.J.* I, 82; VIII, 61-62; X, 143-48) or the crossreferences to his own works that are unverifiable (cf. H. Petersen, "Real and Alleged Literary Projects in Josephus," *AJPh,* 79 1958, 259-74; L. H. Feldman, on *A.J.,* XX, 267 n.b.; 268 n. d.).

160   Repeated in Vita, 175; 274-79 .

Rome but against Tiberias' Gentile neighbors who had refused to draw a distinction between pro- and anti-Roman Jews.[161]

Completely unjustified is the view which brands Josephus a traitor to his people but commends Justus as the zealot.[162] For Justus left Tiberias when the city was taken over by Josephus, to join King Agrippa II, who spent the war years in Berytus (Beirut). Justus' brother, sister, and possibly his sister's husband were slain by Josephus' followers, evidently because they had remained faithful to the pro-Roman Jewish king.[163]

As an active participant in the turmoil preceding the revolt and as Agrippa II's secretary, Justus was uniquely qualified to write about the Judaeo-Roman war.[164] Although this conflict occurred on the frontiers of the state, it aroused tremendous interest throughout the Roman Empire. Writing shortly after 75, Josephus mentions quite a number of works that described the war between the Romans and the Jews: "Of these [writers], some having taken no part in the action, have collected from hearsay casual and contradictory stories which they have then edited in a rhetorical style; while others, who witnessed the events, have either from flattery of the Romans or from the hatred of the Jews, misrepresented the facts, their writings exhibiting alternately invective or encomium, but nowhere *historical accuracy*."[165]

Josephus' introductory remarks were no doubt sincere and perhaps accurate, as far as they went. Even Justus would perhaps find little fault with them. An exception might be: "historical accuracy"; did Josephus' own *History of the Jewish War Against the Romans* live up to this ideal? In about the year 90, after working twenty years, Justus published *The Jewish War Against Vespasian*. It catalogued Josephus' misdeeds and incompetence as an anti-Roman Galilean general and his errors and self-seeking falsifications as a historian.

By now Domitian's reign of terror was in full swing, and Josephus was perhaps afraid that the emperor might be aroused to review the dossier against him. In the year 94, having completed the *Jewish Antiquities,* Josephus felt compelled to attach his *Vita* which not only retorted to Justus' attacks, but also gave quite a different version of Josephus' role as a Jewish

---

161   H. Luther, *Josephus und Justus of Tiberias* (Halle, 1910), 40-49; Jacoby, *R.E.,* X, 1341-43; Stählin, *Hellenistisch-jüdische Literatur,* 601 f.

162   Cf. H. Graetz, *Geschichte der Juden.* (Leipzig, 1906), III[5], 480; Schlatter, *Geschichter Israels*[2], 276; Wachsmuth, *Einleitung in das Studium der Alten Geschichte,* 498. Schürer, *Geschichte des jüdischen Volkes* I[3], 59 f., makes Justus an unwilling participant in the rebellion, which, as pointed out by Luther, p. 35, hardly agrees with the facts.

163   See *Vita,* 186; cf. 176 f.; *B.J,* IV, 18; 68.

164   Josephus (*Vita,* 358) argues that Justus could not have written accurately about what happened in Jerusalem, a front he never saw. This is true, but Agrippa II's court must have kept in close touch with events in the Holy City.

165   *B.J.,* Proem.

general. Almost every sentence of the *Vita* may be understood either as an attack on, or a defense against, Justus. Josephus' boast about his Hasmonean pedigree seems to have been intended as a contrast to Justus' links with the descendants of Herod (1-6). Josephus apparently points out that his expertise in Judaica was superior not only to that of his rival, but also to that of anyone else (7-13). The epilogue to the *Jewish Antiquities* indirectly admits that in Greek style he could not match the Tiberian author, highly praised in the *Vita*. But this was because of inadequate opportunities to receive a good Hellenic education in Jerusalem, in contrast no doubt to conditions in Agrippa II's Tiberias. Even so, his education was sufficient for him to have been dispatched as an ambassador to Rome, which incidentally showed that even as a young man he was a favorite of the Roman authorities (13-16). The remainder of the *Vita* (17-413), except for the concluding lines (414-30), consists of a defense of Josephus' actions and a counterattack against Justus.[166]

From Josephus' invective against his adversaries—Pistus had a strain of madness; his son Justus was a clever demagogue[167] —it is sometimes difficult to decide which of the two tended to be more truthful. According to *Vita* 341-43, the emperor urged Agrippa II to condemn Justus to death for his hostile action against the Greek Decapolis. But from what we know of the Jewish king's character, the statement of *Vita* 410, asserting that Agrippa II violated orders by concealing Justus, seems unbelievable.[168]

A conclusive judgment is difficult concerning the relative veracity of the rival histories. But certainly Josephus' own defense of his account hardly inspires confidence because: a) Vespasian's and Titus' *Memoirs* supported his version;[169] · b) King Agrippa II wrote sixty-two letters commending his *Bellum;*[170] and c) the king was in Galilee while Justus had fled the country.[171] Point a) shows only that Josephus utilized, or perhaps better, helped write, the official record, but does not attest to its accuracy. Point b) confirms that the king was pleased with the description of himself in *Bellum*.

---

166   *Vita*, 424 f., relates the fate of Jonathan of Cyrene, who had slandered Josephus, and was put to death by Vespasian. Was Josephus suggesting that the same fate may happen to Justus: cf. 425.

167   *Vita*, 34; 40.

168   Cf. also *Vita*, 355; 425.

169   *Vita*, 342; 358. Cf. 363, *C. Apionem*, I, 49 f.

170   *Vita*, 363-66. In fact, Agrippa II seems to have been less satisfied than the *Bellum* intimates. The first of the king's two letters (365), quoted by Josephus, merely said that Josephus' *Bellum* dealt better with the subject than any of the predecessors who had written about the war. In the second letter Agrippa II promises to tell Josephus what was not generally known, apparently even by Josephus himself. Since Justus was the king's secretary, it may be presumed that his history of the war was more in consonance with Agrippa's position.

171   *Vita*, 357; cf. 49; 181.

Josephus himself negates point c) by admitting that he often omitted incidents that might have embarrassed certain people, as moderation was even more incumbent upon the historian than veracity.[172] Josephus also naively argues that Justus was less truthful because it took him twenty years longer to complete his work.[173] All this, however, does not really prove the converse, that Justus was more reliable than Josephus. But it does suggest, as is indicated below, that Justus was more typical of a first century Greek historian than was Josephus. This is especially apparent in Justus' rather objective treatment of Agrippa II in contrast to Josephus' admitted whitewashing of his contemporaries.

Perhaps emulating Josephus, Justus also wrote a history of the Jewish people. The ninth century patriarch of Constantinople, Photius says: "I have read the Chronicle of Justus of Tiberius, which is entitled: *The Jewish Kings Arranged in Genealogical Tables*. He was a native of Tiberias in the Gailiee. Beginning his history with Moses, he concluded it with the death of Agrippa, the seventh of the Herodian dynasty, the last king of the Jews. He [Agrippa] received the realm under Claudius, that Nero enlarged, and was made even larger by Vespasian. He died in the third year of Trajan" (A.D. 100).[174] Photius' last sentence has caused much scholarly controversy. In the last sections of his *Jewish Antiquities,* dated by the author in 93-94, as well as in the *Vita* Josephus makes it clear that Agrippa was already dead.[175] Of the various proposals to reconcile Josephus with Photius, the one that seems reasonable is that Photius confused the date of Justus' publication of his *Chronicle,* mentioned in the introduction, with the date of Agrippa II's death. The king certainly died in 93, as his coins attest.[176]

If so, Justus' history began with Moses and ended with the year 93. Photius describes it as "written in the most concise style, mentioning only the most essential facts."[177] Little else is known about this work. Of its three extant fragments, one tells an unhistorical anecdote of an abortive attempt by Plato to defend Socrates, in which he was shouted down by the judges.[178]

---

172   *Vita,* 339. Joephus defends his omission in the *Bellum* of Justus' supposedly anti-Roman role in the *Bellum.*

173   *Vita,* 360.

174   Photius, *Bibl.* 33 = Iustus von Tiberias, *FGrH* 734 T 2.

175   *A.J.,* XVII, 28; XX, 145, mentioning Agrippa II's incestual relations with Berenice; XX, 211-12; 267 dates the conclusion of the *Antiquities* in the year 93-94, alluding to Justus' work. See also *Vita,* 362, 365 f.

176   See Schürer, *Geschichte des jüdischen Volkes,* III³, 597-600, who defends Photius' date of 100; Luther, *Justus,* 54-63; Reifenberg, *Ancient Jewish Coins,* 25-27; L. H. Feldman, on *A.J.* XX, 145 (LCL), "perhaps," citing more monographic literature.

177   Photius, *Bibl.* 33 = 734 T 2, p. 695, 21 f.

178   Diog., *Laertius,* II, 41 = 734 F 1. Schlatter, *Geschichte Israels*², 276, posits that either Justus wrote several histories of the world or that Photius saw only an abridged version of the more extensive Jewish history.

This remnant does not quite conform with Photius' epithets concerning the Chronicle's conciseness.

The remaining two fragments of Justus' history synchronize the date of the exodus with contemporary Attic and Egyptian kings, which, as shown above, also present problems of interpretation.[179] There is no doubt, however, that a major part of Justus' work was devoted to genealogy and chronography—subjects rather neglected by Josephus. In this field Justus made a deep imprint.[180] Although the Christian writers lamented the fact that despite being a Galilean, Justus had failed to mention Jesus, they nonetheless dated Christ's coming by his chronographic lists. The remnants of the third century Jerusalem-born Sextus Julius Africanus, quoted by Eusebius and Syncellus, show Justus to have been the father of Christian biblical chronography. It would seem, as noted by Gutschmid and Wachsmuth, that Africanus' five-book *Chronography* reproduced large chunks of Justus' work.[181]

Of immense interest is Africanus' treatment of Herod I, since it appears to have been based neither on Josephus nor on the Jewish or Christian tradition.[182] It lacks the venomous hate that fills the Christian or Jewish writings on Herod; and it uses a topography placing Antipatris in the Lydian plain and giving Gabinii as the name of Samaria before Herod changed it again to Sabaste[183] —quite divergent from that of Josephus. Yet there is no doubt that the fragment was based on a writer who was quite familiar with Herodian history. This plus the integrated synchronism suggests that parts of the preserved Africanus followed Justus.

If so, Justus treated Herod more harshly but more fairly than did Josephus. The latter depended either on the pro-Herodian Nicolaus of Damascus or on an anti-Herodian source, discussed above. Both historians, for

---

179 See above, pp. 123-24.

180 Euseb., *Chron* ... p. 7b (Helm) = 734 F 2; Africanus, in Syncellus, *Chron.*, III, p. 116 = 734 F 3.

181 For the fragments of Africanus, see Migne, *P.G.*, X, 63-94; M. J. Routh, *Reliquiae Sacra*[2] (Oxford, 1846), II, 238-309. For Africanus' dependence on Justus, see A. von Gutschmid, *Kleine Schriften*, IV (Leipzig, 1893), 350, who maintains that the early Church Fathers had preferred Justus to Josephus, before the latter gained wide popularity, evidently thanks to Eusebius. See also K. Wachsmuth, *Einleitung*, 438; H. Gelzer, *Sextus Julius Africanus und die Byzantische Chronologie* (Leipzig, 1880) I, 4, 20, 188, 207, 265; W. Speyer, *Die Fälschung im heidnischen und christlichen Altertum* (Munich, 1971), 69, 76 f., 110, 153, 181, 240.

182 Gelzer, ibid., I, 258-61, defends Africanus' tradition that, contrary to Josephus (*B.J.*,I, 181; *A.J.*, XIV, 121), who makes an Idumaean of Atipater the father of Herod,(who) traces Antipater to Askalon (Euseb., *Hist. Eccl.*, I, 7, 11; Syncellus, Paris, 1652, pp. 296), allegedly recorded by Justus (p. 265).

183 Africanus in Syncellus (Paris, 1652), 308 f.; cf. *B.J.* I, 99, 417 (Antipatris), but Gabinii is not attested in Josephus.

example, record Antigonus' mutilation of Hyrcanus II to make him legally unfit for the office of high priest. But Josephus mentions Antigonus' cruelty, whereas Justus notes his kindness in sparing Hyrcanus' life, apparently contrasting Antigonus' action with Herod's subsequent murder of Hyrcanus. Cleopatra, an unpopular name in Roman history, is a much closer ally of Herod in the fragment of Africanus, than in Josephus, who describes the mutual antagonism between the two rulers. Josephus makes Herod a faithful ally of Antony at Actium. Justus, via Africanus, however, says that Herod entrusted two sets of letters to his messengers, one pledging fealty to Antony, the other to Augustus, with orders to hand over the appropriate message to the victor. Although no doubt apocryphal, this anecdote offers a pithy sketch of Herod's character.[184]

The fragments of Justus' works indicate how radically Graeco-Palestinian historiography had changed since the days of Eupolemus. The Graeco-Jewish dialect of the Septuagint was still very much alive at the end of the first Christian century. But the Tiberian *paidea* that Justus received in the courts of Herod Antipas and Agrippa II was the cosmopolitan Greek of Antioch or Alexandria. Josephus, writing in Rome, with the help of Greek assistants, virtually admits his own linguistic inferiority.[185] Justus, as has been noted, wrote "with extreme conciseness, giving the most essential facts."[186] This was in sharp contrast to Josephus' diffuse style. But both Justus and Josephus departed completely from the Graeco-Jewish of the Septuagint. Josephus evidently took as his paradigm the teachings of Dionysius of Halicarnassus (30-8 B.C.) on how to imitate the classical rhetoricians and historians. Justus, however, became part of the chronographic school initiated by Eratosthenes of Cyrene, and continued by Apollodorus of Athens, Castor of Rhodes, and Ptolemy of Mendes. Herod, it would seem, was the first to replace Jerusalem's Graeco-Jewish dialect with the standard literary style of the Greek world. Agrippa II's court patronized men who were culturally, if not ethnically Hellenized.[187]

In some respects, however, the Graeco-Jewish historiographic tradition profoundly influenced the writings of both Josephus and Justus. Josephus' conception of Abraham hardly differed from Pseudo-Eupolemus' depiction of the patriarch. His lengthy descriptions of the Solomonic and Herodian temples reflected the Jewish literary tradition of repeating detailed dimension of religious structures, a practice unknown in antiquity. Reading Josephus one feels that Jerusalem was in some way the center of the world.[188]

184   Africanus in Syncellus, 307-09.

185   *A.J.,* XX, 262-66; *Vita,* 40; *C. Apionem,* I, 50.

186   Photius, *Bibl.,* 33 = 734 T 2, p. 695, 21 f.

187   See Walter Otto, "Herodes" No. 24, *R.E.,* Suppl. II, 168-91; Rosenberg, "M. Iulius Agrippa (II)," *R.E.,* X (1917), 146-50.

188   Cf. Feldman, *AJPh,* 99 (1968), 143-56; P. Friedländer, *Johannes von Gaza,* 41 f. On Josephus' view of Jewish history, see his introductory sections of *B.J.* (esp. I, 1) and *A.J.* (esp. I, 10-17), as well as the tenor of *C. Apionem.*

In some respects, however, Justus appears to have been closer to Graeco-Jewish historiography. One of his works—*On the Judaean Kings*—apparently modeled after Demetrius' chronographic work *On the Kings of Judaea,* was written at the end of the third century B.C. As attested by Africanus, Justus' chronology, like that of Demetrius and perhaps Eupolemus, but unlike that of Josephus, followed the Septuagint. It is even possible that Justus' work was directly based on the chronographies of his predecessors. There is a tradition, possibly accurate, that Justus composed commentaries on the Bible.[189] Unlike Josephus who addressed himself to the Graeco-Roman public, Justus followed the tradition established by Demetrius and Eupolemus of writing for fellow Jews. For it is rather unbelievable that chronological tables of Jewish kings were designed to attract any readers in the pagan world.

Almost nothing is known of the Graeco-Palestinian writers whose vestiges have been traced in this study. Justus of Tiberias and Eupolemus of Jerusalem. however, are exceptions. The available information about these historians sheds considerable light on the remnants of their works as well as on the Graeco-Palestinian literary milieu. Their patrons were men whose rise and fall reflected the vicissitudes of fortune. Eupolemus introduced the Romans to Palestinian politics; the dire consequences were witnessed by Justus. Eupolemus and Justus were moderates, respectively, apparently reflecting the views of significant factions. Descendants of distinguished families, whose fathers served as diplomats, the sons attempted to continue the ancestral traditions while inexorable forces raged. A member of a priestly clan that officiated in the Temple, Eupolemus sided with Judah Maccabee, but there is good reason to assume that he was not a member of the Hasideans, described in the First and Second Maccabees. The fact that a man with a relatively cosmopolitan outlook such as Eupolemus was attracted to the rebels shows the excesses of the Hellenizers who had sided with the Seleucids. Justus' father and brothers were faithful servants of the house of Herod, possibly members of the Herodian faction, who are mentioned in Mark 3:6. Like most moderates, he opposed the rebellion against Rome, but almost lost his life because the Romans condemned him for fighting their anti-Jewish allies. With Justus of Tiberias, and especially with the death of his patron, Agrippa II in A.D. 93, the Graeco-Palestinian literary tradition ended.

The earliest indication of such a tradition are the remnants of a description

189   Jerome, *De viris illustr.,* 14 = 734 T 1: "Justus Tiberiensis, de provincia Galilaea, conatus est et ipse Judaicarum rerum historiam texere, et quosdam commentarios de Scripturis componere." Schürer, *Geschichte des jüdischen Volkes,* I[3], 59, questions the authenticity of this tradition, as it is recorded only in Jerome. But this is hardly convincing in view of the sad state of preservation of Justus' works.

of Judaea and its people that was apparently intended for the Diadochi, written by a former priest of Jerusalem who had joined Alexander's army in its march to Egypt. Under the Ptolemies, a number of Jerusalem's priests wrote anti-Samaritan tracts and collaborated with Alexandrian Jews in the production of Greek translations of Hebrew sacred texts. Judah Maccabee, according to II Macc. 2:13-15, distributed a large number of such books to the Greek Diaspora, one of which may have been Eupolemus' history. But Jerusalem's circle who wrote or read Greek must have been rather small. The situation changed temporarily, first, in the years 167-64 B.C., when Jerusalem became a *polis* and was renamed Antioch; and second, when Herod attempted to make the Holy City a major center of Greek learning. Under the Herodians, the use of the Greek language became a symbol of Roman oppression, a feeling that was sharply intensified during the war against Rome in the years of 66-70. But the older and more significant tradition that utilized the Greek language to spread the virtues of Judaism survived the fall of Jerusalem. Each in his own way, Josephus and Justus present a fitting epitaph of a once significant but now lost chapter of Judaeo-Greek culture.

THE FRAGMENTS OF EUPOLEMUS

(*FGrH* 723)

TESTIMONIES

1 I Macc. 8:17: And Judah chose Eupolemus son of John son Accos and Jason the son of Eleazer, and sent them to Rome to conclude a treaty of friendship and alliance, to remove the yoke from them, for it was clear that the kingdom of the Greeks was reducing Israel to slavery. And they journeyed to Rome, though the way was very long, and entering the Senate house they said: "Judah the Maccabee and his brothers and people of Judaea have sent us to you to establish an alliance and peace with you so that we may be enrolled as your allies and friends." They (the Romans) found the proposal pleasing, and this is the copy of the letter which they wrote in answer, on brass tablets, and sent back to Jerusalem to remain there among them as a memorial of peace and alliance (text of treaty: 23-32).

1a II Macc. 4:11: And he (Antiochus) set aside the royal privileges established for the Jews through John the father of Eupolemus, who negotiated a treaty of friendship and alliance with the Romans.

1b Josephus, *A.J.,* XII, 415: Accordingly, he (Judah) sent to Rome his friends Eupolemus son of Joannes, and Jason son of Eleazar, and through them requested the Romans to become his allies and friends, and to write to Demetrius that he should not make war on the Jews 416. When the envoys sent by Judah came to Rome, the senate received them and, after they had spoken about their mission, agreed to the alliance. It also made a decree concerning this and sent a copy to Judaea, while the original was engraved on bronze tablets and deposited in the Capitol. (text of treaty: 417-19)

2 Eusebius, *Historia Ecclesiastica,* VI, 13, 7: He (Clement of Alexandria) mentions . . . Philo (729 F T 2; F 4), Aristobulus, Josephus, Demetrius (722 F 3) and Eupolemus, Jewish writers all of them, show that Moses and the Jewish people went back further in their origins than the Greeks.

3 *Contra Apionem,* I, 218: But Demetrius [Pahlereus] (722 T 1), Philo the Elder (729), and Eupolemus do not go far astray from the truth, and may be excused (for any error) on the ground of their inability to follow the meaning of our writings accurately.

FRAGMENTS

1   a) Eusebius, *Praeparatio Evangelica,* IX, 25, 4: And concerning

Moses the same author (Alexander Polyhistor) again brings forward many things that are worth hearing: Eupolemus says that Moses was the first wise man; and he handed over the- letters to the Jews first, the Phoenicians received them from the Jews, the Greeks from the Phoenicians. Moses was also the first who wrote laws for the Jews.

b) Clement Alexandrinus, *Stromata*, I, 153, 4: Eupolemus, in his *Kings of Judaea,* says that Moses was the first wise man; and that he first taught writing to the Jews; the Phoenicians received it from the Jews, the Greeks from the Phoenicians.

2   a) Clement Al., *Strom.,* I, 130, 3: Alexander who is surnamed Polyhistor in his work On the Jews (273 F 19b), records certain letter of Solomon, some to Uaphres the king of Egypt, others to the king of Tyre in Phoenicia, and their letters to him. According to these letters, Uaphres sent 80,000 Egyptian men to build the Temple; the other king sent an equal number of men together with a Tyrian architect, whose mother was a Jewess of the tribe of [David] (Dan), whose name as written there, was Hyperon (see App. Crit.).

b) Euseb. *P.E.,* 9, 30: Eupolemus, in *On the Prophecy of Elias,* says: Moses prophesied for forty years; then Jesus the son of Naue, thirty years. He lived 110 years, having pitched the holy tabernacle in Shilo. Afterwards Samuel became prophet; then, by God's wish, Saulus was chosen king by Samuel, who (Saulus) died after a reign of 21 years. Then his son David succeeded him to the reign. He subdued the Syrians who live on the shores of the Euphrates and in the region of Commagene and the Assyrians of Galadene, and the Phoenicians. He also led an army against the Idumaeans and the Ammonites and Moabites and the Ituraeans and the Nabataeans and the Nabdaeans. Again he made an expedition against Suron the king of Tyre and Phoenicia, whom he compelled to pay tribute to the Jews. But with Uaphres the king of Egypt he made an alliance of friendship. But when David wished to build a temple for God, he asked God to show him a worthy place for the altar. Whereupon an angel appeared to him standing on top of the place, where the altar (abomination?) is standing in Jerusalem, and commanded him not to build the temple himself for he was defiled with human blood and many years of warfare. The name of the angel was Dianathan [Nathan] . (*An alternate translation:* It [the message] came to him [David] in the name [of the angel] through Nathan). And he (the angel? Nathan?) commanded him to entrust the building to his son. But that he himself should make ready to prepare the things needed to build---gold, silver, brass, (precious?)`stones, cypress and cedar wood. Upon hearing this, David built a fleet in Elana, an Arabian city; and he sent miners to the island of Urphe, which lies in the Red Sea and which contains gold mines. And the miners transported the mined gold from there to Judaea. After a rule of forty years he handed over the realm to his son Solomon, then twelve years old, in the presence of Eli, the high priest, and the twelve heads of the tribes. And he also handed over to him the gold and the silver and the brass and the (precious?) stone and cypress and cedar wood. Then David died and Solomon took over the realm. He then wrote a letter to Uaphres, the King of Egypt, the letter copied below:

King Solomon to Uaphres, the king of Egypt, father's friend, greetings!

Know that with the help of the Most High God, I have received the kingdom from my father David, who commanded me to build a temple to God, the maker of the heavens and the earth, and at once to write to you to send me some men of your people who will assist me till all things needed will have been completed, as I was commanded.

King Uaphres to the Great King Solomon, greetings!

As soon as we read your letter we rejoiced very much. I and my entire administration have set aside a feast day in honor of your succession to the kingdom, after such kindly man and one recognized by so mighty a God.

As to the matter you have written to me concerning the peoples who are under me, I have sent you 80,000 men. How many and wherefrom they come I am explaining to you: from the Sethroitic (Sebrithitic) nome, 10,000 men; from the Medesians and Sebennytic, 20,000 men each, and from the nomes of Busiris, Leontopolis and Athribitus, 10,000 men from each, Give due consideration for their food supply and for all other things so that they be well disciplined, and that they be brought back to their own country as soon as they are free from their tasks.

King Solomon to Suron, the king of Tyre and Sidon and Phoenicia, his father's friend, Greetings!

Know that by help of God the Most High, I have received the kingdom from David my father. He commanded me to build a temple to God, who had made the heavens and the earth; and immediately to write to you that you send me some of your people who will be assisting me till every requirement of God will be completed, as I have been commanded.

I have also written to Galilee and to Samaria and to Moabitis and to Ammonitis and to Galaditis to supply them (the workers) with their needs from the produce land: 10,000 cors of wheat monthly (a cor is six artabae) and 10,000 cors of wine (a liquid cor is ten measures), oil and other things shall be supplied from Judaea, slaughtered animals to supply meat from Arabia.

Suron to the Great King Solomon, greetings!

Blessed be God, the maker of the heavens and the earth, who chose a kind man and the son of a kind man. Upon reading your letter I rejoiced greatly and I praised God that you have succeeded to the kingdom.

As to your writing me concerning my people, I am sending you 80,000 Tyrians and Phoenicians; and I am also sending you a Tyrian man whose mother was Jewish of the tribe of (David) [Dan] . Whatever you shall ask him under the heavens, concerning architecture, he will guide you and will do the work. As to the necessities and the servants that I have sent you, you will do well to command the local governors that they supply the necessary provisions.

But Solomon, with his father's friends, passed through the Mount Libanus, and together with the Sidonians and the Tyrians transported the timber, which his father had cut, by sea to Joppe and from there by land to Jerusalem.

And he began to build the temple of God at the age of thirteen. And the work was done by the above-mentioned nations; and the twelve Jewish tribes supplied the 160,00 with all their needs, one tribe each month.

He laid the foundations of the temple of God, sixty cubits its length and sixty cubits its width, but the width of the building and of the foundation was ten cubits wide. Thus he was commanded by Nathan, the prophet of God. And he built alternately a course of stone and a layer of cypress wood, bonding the two courses together with bronze clamps of a talent weight. Having built it thus he boarded the inside wall with cedar and cypress wood so that the stone walls were not visible. He overlaid the naos with gold on the inside by casting golden bricks row by row, five cubits long, fastening them to the walls with silver nails, weighing a talent, in the shape of a breast, four in number.

Thus he covered it with gold from the floor to the ceiling; and the ceiling he made with gold; but the roof he made of bronze tiles, having smeltered the bronze and cast it into molds.

He also made two pillars and covered them with pure gold, a finger thick. The pillars were of the same height as the temple, the width of each pillar was ten cubits in circumference; and he set one of the pillars on the right side of the house, the other on the left. He made also ten lampstands of gold, each weighting ten talents, having taken as a model the lampstand made by Moses in the tent of the testimony. He placed some of the lampstands at the right of the shrine, others at the left. He also made seventy lamps of gold, so that each lampstand had seven lamps. He also built the gates of the temple adorning them with gold and silver and he paneled them with cedar and cypress wood. He also made, in the northern portion of the temple, a porch, and he supported it with forty-eight pillars of brass.

He also built a bronze laver, twenty cubits long, twenty cubits wide and five cubits high, extending a brim around the base a cubit long, projecting to the outside, so that the priests may stand upon it when they dip their feet and wash their hands. He also made the twelve legs of the laver of cast oxen, the height of a man, and he attached them to the lower part of the laver, at the right of the altar.

He also made a bronze platform, two cubits high around the laver, so that the king may stand upon it when praying, that he would be seen by the Jewish people. He also built an altar twenty-five cubits by twenty-five cubits and twelve cubits high.

He also made two bronze ringlike lattices, and he set them upon contrivances, which rose above the temple twenty cubits, and they cast a shadow over the entire sanctuary. And upon each network he hung four hundred bronze bells of a talent weight. And he made the entire network so that the bells would toll and frighten away the birds, that none would settle upon the temple nor nest in the panels of the gates and porches nor pollute the temple with their dung. He also surrounded the city of Jerusalem with walls, towers and trenches. He also built a palace for himself.

The shrine was first called the temple of Solomon, but later, because of the temple, was falsely named Jerusalem, but by the Greeks it was called Hierosolyma.

When he had completed the Temple and walls of the city, he went to Selom and offered a sacrifice to God, a burnt-offering of 1,000 oxen. Then he took the tabernacle and the altar and the vessels, which Moses had made, and he carried them to Jerusalem and he placed them in the house. And the ark and the golden altar and the lampstand and the table and the other vessels he also placed there, as the prophet commanded him. But he offered there a myriad offering to God, 2,000 sheep, 3,500 oxen.

But the total weight of gold expended on the two pillars and the Temple was 4,600,000 talents; silver for the nails and the other vessels he had expended 1,232 talents; bronze for the columns, the laver, and the porch, 18,050 talents. Then Solomon sent back the Egyptians and the Phoenicians to their respective countries, after having given to each man ten golden shekels, a shekel equals a talent. And to Vaphres, the king of Egypt, he sent 10,000 measures of oil, 1,000 artabae of date-nuts, 100 vessels of honey and spices. But to Suron of Tyre he sent a pillar of gold, which was set up in Tyre in the Temple of Zeus.

THEOPHILUS

(*FGrH* 733 F 1)

(Eus. *P.E.,* IX, 34, 19: Theophilus says that Solomon sent the surplus gold to the king of Tyre, who made a lifesize likeness of his daughter and he adorned the golden column of the statue with a covering.)

EUPOLEMUS

(*FGrH* 723)

3   Eus. *P.E.,* IX, 34, 20: Eupolemus says that Solomon made also 1,000 shields, each of them weighed 500 shekels of gold. But he lived fifty-two years, forty of which he reigned in peace.

4   Eus. *P.E.,* IX, 39: Besides this Polyhistor makes mention of Jeremiah's prophecy (273 F 19a), it would be most unreasonable for us to pass over this in silence; let this also be put down:

Then Jonachim, in whose reign the prophet Jeremiah prophesied. Sent by

God, he caught the Jews sacrificing to the golden idol named Baal. He warned them of the forthcoming calamity, but Jonachim attempted to burn him alive. But he said that with this wood they shall cook dishes for the Babylonians and that as captives they shall dig canals in the Tigris and Euphrates.

But when Nebuchadnezzar, the king of the Babylonians, heard the prophecy of Jeremiah, he summoned Antibares, the king of the Medes, to join him in an expedition. After having taken with him Babylonians and Medes, he gathered 180,000 foot soldiers, 120,000 cavalry and 10,000 chariots. He subdued first Samaritis, Galilee, Scythopolis, and the Jews who lived in Galaaditis. Then he conquered Jerusalem and he took captive the king of the Jews, Jonachim. But the gold, the silver, and the brass of the temple he sent to Babylon as tribute. Except the ark and the tablets; these Jeremiah retained.

5 Clem. Al., *Strom.,* I, 141, 4 (Philo, 729 T 2): Yet in a similar work Eupolemus says that the total number of years from Adam until the fifth year of King Demetrius (158/7), of Ptolemy XII (159/8), the king of Egypt, is 5149 years; from the time that Moses brought the Jews out from Egypt, on the beforehand appointed day, a total of [two] thousand five hundred and eighty. But from that time to the time of the Gnaius Dometian and Asinius, the consuls in Rome, make 120 years.

APPENDIX B

THE FRAGMENT(S) OF PSEUDO–EUPOLEMUS (ANONYMOUS)

FGrH 724

F 1, Eusebius, *Praeparatio Evangelica*, IX, 17:

(This is what Josephus writes [AJ, I, 158 ff.]). And with this agrees Alexander Polyhistor, a man of great understanding and great learning and very well known among those Greeks who have not acquired the fruits of education in a superficial manner. For in his treatise *On the Jews,* he records the history of Abraham as follows, word by word.

Eupolemus in his *On the Jews* [of Assyria] says the city of Babylon (of Assyria) was first founded by those who had escaped the flood. They were the giants who built the tower recorded in history. But when the tower was ruined by the act of God, the giants dispersed over the whole earth. In the tenth generation, he (Eupolemus) says, in a Babylonian city of Camarina, which some call Urie, and which is in translation the city of the Chaldaeans. In the thirteenth generation, Abraham was born, who surpassed all men in nobility and wisdom, who also discovered the Chaldaean [science?] , and who on account of his piety was well-pleasing to God. By the command of God this man went to Phoenicia to dwell there and he pleased the king by teaching the Phoenicians the changes of the sun and moon and all things of that kind. But later the Armenians marched against the Phoenicians, and being victorious they took captive his nephew; Abraham together with his servants came to the rescue, overcame the captors, and made their wives and children prisoners. But when the ambassadors came to Abraham to ransom for money the prisoners, he chose not to take advantage of the unfortunates, but after providing food for his servants he restored the booty.

Being entertained as a guest by the temple of the city of Argarizin, which may be translated as the Mount of the Most High, he (Abraham) received gifts from Melchizedek, who was its priest of God and its king.

But there being a famine (in Phoenicia), Abraham and his whole household departed to Egypt and settled there. The king of the Egyptians married his wife, having been told by Abraham that she was his sister. But Eupolemus related even more extraordinary things, that the king was unable to have intercourse with her and that his people and household were perishing. The diviners having been summoned, they said that the woman was not a widow. Thus the king of the Egyptians learned that she was Abraham's wife and he restored her to her husband. And Abraham lived with the Egyptian priests in Heliopolis, teaching them many things. And he introduced astrology and other sciences to them, saying that the Babylonians and he himself discovered them, but he traced the discovery to Enoch. And he (Enoch) was the first to

313

discover astrology, not the Egyptians. The Babylonians say that the first (giant) was Belus, who is Kronos, who begat Belus and Cham. He (Cham) had a son named Chanaan, the father of the Phoenicians. His son was Chum, who is called by the Greeks Asbolus, the father of the Ethiopians and brother of Metsraeim, the father of the Egyptians. The Greeks say that Atlas discovered astrology, Atlas being the same as Enoch. And Enoch had a son Methusalah, who learned all things through the angels of God, and thus we gained our knowledge.

F 2 (Eusebius, *P.E.,* IX, 18, 2): In an Anonymous work we find that Abraham traced his ancestry to the giants. Their dwellings in Babylonia were destroyed by the gods on account of their impiety, as one of them, Belus, escaping death, settled in Babylon, and having built a tower he ruled over it, which was named Belus after its builder Belus. And that Habramos, trained in the science of astrology, came first to Phoenicia and taught astrology to the Phoenicians and subsequently departed for Egypt.

INDEX

INDEX

I. PASSAGES

BIBLE

Genesis

4:18-19; 22	162-63
5:3-31	98
5:5; 10:15-19	163
11:10-25	98
12:4	101
14:18-22	162-63
14:18	208, 289
14:19	161-63
15:5	76
17:16	100
21:5	100-01
21:6	95
22:2	249
22:14	208
23:1; 25:1-6	100
25:3	101-03
25:20	100
25:26	101
32:23-33	281
ch. 35	284
35:6	282
36:33	58
43:34	281
45:22; 46:34	281
47:9	101
49:10	210

Exodus

1:3	106
2:16-21 (LXX)	101
3:1	101
7:1	62
7:7	243
12:40	98, 101-04, 123 (LXX)
13:18	59, 282
15:22-27	95
16:18	286
20:25	195, 270
25:3-7	147
25:8	141
25:9	181
25:22	141
25:31-40	184-86
25:40	181, 184-86, 247
26:31	249
26:32	180
27:1	185
28:1	152

29:46	141
30:3	191, 244
30:13	216
30:17-21	193, 244
32:1-20	229
35:29-40:21	212
37:24	184-86
38:2	214-15
38:24-31	214-15
39:3 (LXX)	216

Leviticus

5:15	216
10:1-20	152
25:23	90

Numbers

3:2-4, 26-61	152
3:47	216
8:4	185
10:29	101
11:25-29	62
12:1	281
14:23-33	65, 108
14:34	243
18:23	90
21:1	100
22:22	143
34:10-12	132

Deuteronomy

11:30	210
17:18	194
27:5-6	146, 195
34:7	243

Joshua

5:13	143
8:31	146, 195
14:7	65, 108, 243
15:7	108
18:1	210, 247-48, 243 (LXX)
24:9	65
24:29	107, 243

Judges

3:19	210

I Samuel

1:1	243
1:2, 3; 3:10	210
4:3	210
8:1-14	244
Ch. 9	243
13:1	65, 243
14:3	210

II Samuel

5:9	208
5:11-12	158
5:17-25	132
6:2	212
ch. 7	142, 244
8:2-14	132
8:15	208
9:15, 28; 11:27	208
12:1-25	144
12:24-25	109
13:38; 14:28; 15:7; 21:1	109
22:9	244
ch. 24	139, 142, 244
24:1	143
24:8	109
24:15-16	143

I Kings

chs. 1-2	145, 157-58, 249
2:11	244
2:12 (LXX)	57-58, 108-10, 154-55, 244-45, 250
2:27	152
2:46g (LXX)	224
3:3-4	209-13
3:4	213
3:11	171
ch. 4	164
5:3-4	165
5:4-5	224
5:6-8	244
5:15-32	171
5:15	134
5:16-23	158-59, 244
5:17-32	171
5:21	170
5:24-32	158
5:25-26	216

5:25	165	16:14-15	195
5:28-29	163	16:17	191
5:29	165-66	17:2; 18:9	101
chs. 6-9	85	22:8	153
chs. 6-7	251-58	25:16-17	181-83, 197
6:1	102 (LXX), 108, 171		

Isaiah

6:3	175-79, 244, 251	5:10	166
6:5	176		

Jeremiah

6:7	146, 251		
6:10	251	2:8, 23	228
6:15-18	178, 244	3:16	237
6:15 (LXX)	179-81	7:9	228
6:20 (LXX)	179-81	7:12	210
6:35-7:1	203	11:11-14	228
6:36	178	12:16; 19:5	228
7:1-12	245	22:18-19	227
7:2-27	131	ch. 26	229
7:6-7	188	26:1	227
7:12-50	158	26:6	210
7:12	178	26:11	228
7:12 (LXX)	179	26:36; 32:29, 35	228
7:15-22	181-83	39:14; 40:4	237
7:17-18, 20	197	43:8-44:30	137
7:23-26	190-93	44:30	136, 137
7:27-39	190-93, 196, 244	51:11, 28	230
		52:25	228
7:31 (LXX)	187-90, 244, 250-51	52:20-23	181-83
		52:22	197
7:42	197		

Ezekiel

7:43-44 (LXX)	188		
7:48		chs. 40-46	187
7:49	184-86, 244	40:1-49	141
		40:45-46	144
7:50	244	41:23-25	187
7:51	180	43:19	144
8:1-9	212	44:15	153
8:13	213	45:1-8	90
8:9	85	45:14	166
8:22-23	141	48:1-29	90
8:22	194		
9:2	210		

Hosea

9:11	218, 244		
9:15-19	203	12:5	281
9:26-28	147-48, 244	12:54	62
10:16-17	124-25, 245		

Amos

11:1	222		
11:42	245	3:7	144
14:25-26	135		

Micah

II Kings

		5:3 (LXX)	252
1:2	194		

Zechariah

11:14	194		
24:1-17	227-30, 245	4:14	184, 254
25:1-19	228		

Malachi

3:23-24	22

Psalms

72:7, 10	254
76:3	289
78:60	210
78:69-72	141
83(82):7-9	134, 135, 244, 254
84:4(3)	200

Proverbs

22:29	203

Job

18:8	197
42:17b (LXX)	59, 257

Song of Songs

4:4	224

Esther

2:6	233
8:12k (LXX)	278
8:12q (LXX)	159

Daniel

7:25	24
8:21	299
9:1	233
10:21	237
11:1-45	137
11:30-32	140-41
12:11	140-41

Ezra

2:59-63	9
2:61	8-9
3:7	244
5:8	178
6:3-12	11
6:3	174
6:17	154

Nehemiah

3:4, 21	8-9
7:39-42	271
7:62-63	8
7:63-65	9
8:4	194, 244
8:17-9:37	40
9:4	194
13:28	294

I Chronicles

1:32 (LXX, A)	101
2:11	159
4:12-13	197
5:27-41	152
8:2	218
9:15-16	224-25
14:1	135
18:3	132
21:15	139
16:39-40	210
18:1-11	244
ch. 21	139, 142
21:29	210
ch. 22	145
22:1	139
22:3(2)	147
22:5	108, 154
22:8	142, 244
22:14	214-15
chs. 23-27	109
24:7, 10	8-9
chs. 28-29	151-52
28:1	154, 244
28:22	152
29:1-9	146
29:1	108, 154
29:4	147, 214-15
29:6, 24	154
29:29	144

II Chronicles

Chs. 1-7	85
1:2-6	209-11
2:2-9	158-59
2:9	165-66
2:10-11	170
2:11	161-63
2:15	244
2:16-17	163, 244
3:1	283
3:2	171
3:4-7	244
3:4	175-79, 244, 252
3:5	180-81
3:8-9	179-81
3:14	249
3:15	182-83
3:16	252
3:17	182-83
3:57	180
4:1	195-96, 244
4:2-5	190-93, 244
4:4-7	184-86, 247

4:12-13	181-83
4:12, 14	252
4:22	244
5:2-9	212
5:2	180
5:10	85
6:2	100, 245
6:12-13	245
6:13	194
7:5	213, 245
8:17-18	147
8:17	148, 158
9:21	158
9:29	144
ch. 17	142
22:2-4	146
22:14-16	180
23:13	194
29:9	146
29:25	144
35:3	241
36:5-10	227-30
36:11-21	228
36:20	236

APOCRYPHA

I Esdras

5:38	8-9
6:8, 13	160
6:24	178-79
7:8	154
8:16-17, 20, 25	160

Tobit

1:14	233
8:5	162
14:14	233

Judith

2:5	234
2:7, 15, 48	136
4:8	154
11:14; 16:8	154

Ecclesiasticus

Prologue	12, 277
44:16	75
48:10	23
49:6-7	228
49:14	75
50:1-21	12
50:27	277

Baruch

6:7-10	241

Bel

3	166

I Maccabees

1:11-15	30
1:24	141
1:16	30
1:19	12, 236
1:21-23	215
1:21	185
1:41-53	31
1:47	140-41
1:49-55	140-41
2:1	8
2:19	19
2:23-25	141
2:42-48	30
2:45	141
3:1-9	30
3:38-4:25	30
4:7	14
4:26-61	30
4:38-59	141
4:42-47	195
4:44-46	23, 213
4:47	146
4:49	40
4:50	185
4:56	195
4:57	187
ch. 5	130
5:1	141
5:13	133
5:68	141
6:1-17	30
6:7	141
6:18-63	30
ch. 7	30
7:36	141
7:47-49	30
ch. 8	31
8:1-16	35-37
8:9-10	36
8:17	1, 5-6, 8, 12
8:17-30	16-17, 36-38
9:22	29, 31, 27
9:37	134
9:73; 10:1	32
10:20-21	153
12:6-23	50, 51
12:6	154
12:31	134
13:49-52	208
ch. 14	32
14:20-41	34
14:41	23
14:47	34
16:23-24	28

318

II Maccabees

1:1-9	39
1:10-2:18	39-40, 237-42
1:10	39-40, 154
1:19	270
2:1	40
2:4-8	245
2:4-5	39-40
2:18	39
2:13-15	306
2:23-32	28
chs. 3-5	38
3:6-14	215
3:36	159
4:7-5:17	153
4:11	1, 10, 14, 137, 205
4:44	154
6:1-6	31
6:1-4	140-41
6:12-17	29
7:3	229
8:8-36	30
chs. 9-11	30
9:19-21	229
10:2	140
10:10	29
11:27-34	153
11:27	154
chs. 12-15	30
13:7-8	153
14:7	154
14:33	252
15:28-36	30
15:37-39	28

SECTARIAN WRITINGS

II Baruch

7:24	23

Enoch

12:3-5; 15:1	75
12:3	72
18:2	75
40:7; 53:3; 56:1; 62:11; 63:1	143
69:9	75
89:52; 93:8	23

Vita

Jeremiah	237-42

Jubilees

1:1	74

1:27	141
3:28	74
4:17-19	72, 75
6:17-32	288
10:35	233
25:21	141

Martyrdom of Isaiah

2:11	23

Psalms of Solomon

17:29	23

QUMRAN LITERATURE

Genesis Apocryphon

II, 19-21	289
II, 22-26; XIX, 25	75
XXI, 15-18	138
XXII, 14-15	289

Damascus Document

I, 1	24
II, 6	143, 146
III, 21-IV, 5	153
IV, 12-18	292
V, 5	153

Thanksgiving Hymn (1QH)

IV, 6	143

War Scroll (1QM)

I, 5	292
XVIII, 1	292

Manual of Discipline (1QS)

I, 19, 23-24	292
I, 24; II, 3	153
II, 4-5	292
V, 2, 9; IX, 14	153

Copper Scroll (3Q15)

	215

Testament of the XII Patriarchs

Symeon

5:4	75

Levi

6:3-7	285
10:5; 14:1; 16:1	75

JUDAEO-GREEK LITERATURE

Aristeas *(FGrH 725)*

F 1	4-5, 7, 47, 58, 274-76

Letter of Aristeas

12-28	262, 272
31	87
39	275
42	168-69, 158
83-120	263, 173
89	60
105	270
116	271
120	275
131-32	236
171	286
234; 278	286
308-11	274-75

Aristobulus
(see General Index)

Artapanus *(FGrH 726)*

	46, 48, 53, 81-83, 86-87, 104-06

Cleodomus-Malchus *(FGrH 727)*

F 1	44, 46, 48

Demetrius *(FGrH 722)*

	46, 280-82
FF 1-2	115-16
F 2	100-04
F 5	47, 59, 95, 100-04
F 6	61

Eupolemus *(FGrH 723)*

T 1	1, 5-6, 8, 12, 16-17, 36-38, 137, 205

T 2	72	VII, 196	109	XVIII, 259-60	57
T 3	1-3, 52, 56-57, 116, 218	VII, 215	215	XVIII, 312	216
		VII, 422-32	164	XX, 145	302
		VIII, 2	154	XX, 184-89	251
F 1	21-24, 47, 59, 65, 71-96, 112	VIII, 10-12	131	XX, 211-12	302
		VIII, 50-54	158	XX, 220-21	188
		VIII, 57	165-67	XX, 224-40	52
		VIII, 61-62	64, 176-79, 299	XX, 236-37	164, 211
F 2	47, 129-225			XX, 237	154
				XX, 238	153
F 4	6, 40-44, 47, 71-96, 280	VIII, 63-98	257	XX, 258-68	299
		VIII, 74	187	XX, 262-66	304
		VIII, 79-80	191	XX, 267	302
F 5	48, 62, 78, 85, 227-42	VIII, 85	252		

Ezekielus

(see General Index)

Herod *(FGrH 236)*

		VIII, 88	195-96	**Jewish War**	
		VIII, 91-98	188	Proem	300
		VIII, 98	187	I, 33	164
		VIII, 104-49	158	I, 61	215
		VIII, 144	261	I, 68	62
F 1	297-98	VIII, 163	148	I, 99	303
		VIII, 164	149	IV, 18	300
		VIII, 211	154	V, 25	195-96

Jason of Cyrene
(FGrH 182)
(see General Index)

		X, 84	236	V, 143	204
		X, 95	229	V, 184-287	257
		X, 99	236	V, 185	188
		X, 143-48	299	V, 224	198-201
		X, 143	108	V, 194	11

Josephus
Jewish Antiquities

		XI, 184-296	278	V, 201-06	187
		XI, 304-5	293-95	V, 225	195
		XI, 313-47	293-95	V, 438	207-08
		XII, 3-8	263	VI, 423-27	271
I, 17	28	XII, 4-5	272	VI, 435-42	64
I, 24	44	XII, 38-39	211	VI, 438	207-08
I, 82-88	98	XII, 49	274	VI, 439	60
I, 82	299	XII, 63-98	173	VII, 148-49	186
I, 93-95	56	XII, 108-09	275	VII, 421-25	211
I, 94	95	XII, 136	205		
I, 118	51, 54-55, 291	XII, 138-53	10, 39	*Against Apion*	
		XII, 147-52	11		
I, 118	115	XII, 154-236	52, 295	I, 38	74-75
I, 148-50	98	XII, 160-222	295-96	I, 50	304
I, 156	289	XII, 174-78	57	I, 86-90	125
I, 158	264-66	XII, 353	140	I, 94, 102-03	94
I, 180	207-08	XII, 387-88	164	I, 106-27	158
I, 181	303	XII, 414-19	35, 52	I, 106	3, 88
I, 238-41	46, 48	XII, 415	1	I, 109	219
I, 240-41	53-54	XIII, 45	153	I, 116-26	219-23
I, 417	303	XIII, 62-73	164	I, 133-37	236
II, 129	292	XIII, 74-79	285	I, 172-74	206
II, 228-37	76	XIII, 171-73	144	I, 174	207-08
II, 232-53	52	XIII, 208	208	I, 179	205
III, 25, 81	286	XIII, 249	215	I, 183-204	235-36
III, 102-183	173	XIII, 297	84	I, 183-85	87
III, 195	216	XIV, 121	303	I, 186-205	87, 186, 263-73
III, 321	166-67	XIV, 233	18		
IV, 68	300	XV, 164-74	297-98	I, 209-11	272
IV, 320-26	64	XV, 274-78	297-98	I, 213-14	263-73
V, 130	203	XV, 314	166-67	I, 216	218
V, 361	153	XV, 417	11	I, 218	1-3, 52, 56-57, 116, 218
VI, 378	108	XVI, 179	215		
VII, 67	207-08	XVII, 28	302	I, 227-32	94
VII, 68	64	XVIII, 85-86	241	I, 304-11	94, 95
VII, 77-78	181-83	XVIII, 257-59	119	I, 311	206-07

II, 16-20	94, 95
II, 17	127
II, 43-47	263-66
II, 79-96	93
II, 154-56	83-84
II, 184-87	89
II, 216	5

Life

13-413	301
32-39	299
40	304
41, 88, 172	299
176-77	300
191	84
196	300
274-99	299
358	300
362, 365-66	302

Justus (FGrH 734)

T 1	305
T 2	25, 33, 56
T 3	191, 299-302
FF 1-6	24-27

Philo
On Abraham

| 13 | 76 |
| 69-72 | 289 |

The Worse Attacks for the Better

| 169, 175 | 76 |

On the Giants

| 56 | 76 |

Allegorical Interpretations

| II, 87 | 76 |

Life of Moses

| | 21-22, 76 |
| I, 2 | 76 |

Philo the Elder (FGrH 729)

| TT 1-2 (see Eupolemus T 3; F 4) | |
| FF 1-3 | 46, 47, 48, 205, 282-84 |

Ptolemy (FGrH 199)

| F 1 | 43 |

Pseudo-Eupolemus (FGrH 724)

| FF 1-2 | 46, 104-06, 135, 162-63, 205-06, 286-93 |

Pseudo-Hecataeus (FGrH 264)

| T 7; FF 21-22 | 186, 198, 235-36 |
| T 8 | 264-66 |

Pseudo-Philo

VIII, 8, 11	58
XXI, 6	107
XXII, 8	210

Sibylline Oracles

II, 63-67, 167	292
III, 1-96	53
III, 71-73	292
III, 97-104	55, 290-91
III, 106-60	105-06
III, 168	135
III, 175-78	35
III, 218-36	290-91
III, 591-95	292
IV, 115-27	207

Theodotus (FGrH 732)

| F 1 | 5, 7, 46, 218, 283-85 |

Theophilus (FGrH 733)

| F | 5, 7, 48, 110, 243, 289 |

Timochares (FGrH 16 5)

| F 1 | 47, 270 |

TALMUDIC LITERATURE

Megillat Ta'anit

| V | 208, 239-40, 293 |

MISHNAH
Berakhot

| I, 4 | 170 |
| IX, 5 | 161 |

Eruvin

| III, 4 | 4 |

Megillah

I, 11	210
II, 11	78
VII, 8	194
IX, 13	58
X, 1	161

Avot

| I, 2 | 12 |
| V, 6 | 155 |

Zevahim

| XIV, 4-8 | 210 |

Menahot

| XIII, 10 | 164 |

Tamid

| III, 6 | 193 |

Middot

III, 1	195-96
IV, 1-2	187
IV, 6	195, 198-201

Kelim

| I, 8 | 11 |
| I, 6-9 | 141 |

Niddah

| V, 6 | 155 |

Yadayyim

| IV, 3 | 165 |
| IV, 4 | 101 |

TOSEPHTA
Hallah

| II, 11 | 138 |

Terumah

| II, 12 | 138 |

Pesahim

IV, 15   271

Shekalim

II, 18   242
III, 18   213
VI, 1   242

Sotah

XIII, 1   213, 242

Qiddushin

V, 4   101
XIII, 22-23   228

Yadayyim

II, 16   165

BABYLONIAN TALMUD

Shabbat

13a   24
55a   143
90a   199

Pesahim

54a   141
64b   271
94a   24
112a   24

Yoma

52b; 53b   242
53b   213
69b   293
82a   155

Megillah

28b   24

Ta'anit

5b   109

Mo'ed Katan

9a   199
28a   109

Ketuvot

50a   155

Nazir

5a   58, 109

Sotah

48b   146
49b   58

Gittin

8a   138

Qiddushin

80b   24

Bava Qamma

82b   58

Sanhedrin

21b   78
69b   109
92a   24
94a   24
97a   23, 99

Avodah Zarah

5b   24
9a   23, 24, 99
18a   229

Zevahim

58b-59a   193

Menahot

28b   185
29a   184, 185
74b   58
107a   199

Hullin

106a   192

Arakhin

6a   199

Temurah

14b-15a   109
15b   58

Tamid

32a   24

PALESTINIAN TALMUD

Berakhot

IV, 7b   109
I, 8, 3d   170
IX, 14c   161
IV, 8, 60a   138

Shevi'it

VI, 1, 36d   138

Bikkurim

II, 64c   109
IV, 3   185
VI, 1, 49c   213, 242

Yoma

I, 1, 38c   228

Ta'aniyyot

IV, 67c   109

Megillah

II, 11, 71b   78

MIDRASHIM

Mekhilta d'Rabbi Ishmael

Pisha 2   185

Sifra

Mezora' 77a   192

Sifre Numbers

61   185

Sifre Deuteronomy

357   58, 108, 154

Melekhet Hamishkan

VII   213, 242
X   184

Genesis Rabbah

I, 4   141
VIII, 2   218
LVI   208
LXIX, 17   141
LXXXV   4

| XCVI, 4 | 218 |
| C | 58, 109, 154 |

Leviticus Rabbah

| XXVIII, 2 | 137 |

Numbers Rabbah

| XIV, 1 | 203 |
| XIX, 3 | 168 |

Songs Rabbah

| 1:5 | 203 |

Ecclesiastes Rabbah

| 7:23 | 168 |

Seder Olam Rabbah

12	107
14	57-58, 108-10, 154
30	23

Midrash Tadshe

| | 74-75, 108 |

Pesiqta d'Rav Kahana

| I, 60 | 168, 216 |
| I, 104 | 185 |

Pesiqta Rabbati

| 59b | 168 |

Pirke d'Rabbi Eliezer

| 11 | 159 |

Seder Eliyyahu Rabbah

| 6 | 23 |

Tanhuma

Wa'ra 8 (Buber)	218
Wa'ra 9 (Buber)	16
Kedoshim 10	270

Chronicle of Jerahmeel

| LXXVII, 9 | 241 |

NEW TESTAMENT

Matthew

| 11:14; 16:14 | 23 |
| 26:16 | 174 |

Luke

| 1:17 | 23 |
| 12:42 | 155 |

John

| 10:23 | 188 |
| 21:25 | 29 |

Acts

3:11; 5:12	188
13:21	108
23:8	143

I Corinthians

| 9:13 | 174 |

Hebrews

| 5:6, 10; 6:20; 7:1; 10-11, 15, 17 | 289 |
| 7:1-2 | 207 |

Revelation

| 16:16 | 205 |

CHRISTIAN WRITINGS

Chronicon Paschali

| 68 | 73 |

Clement of Alexandria
Stromata

I, 69	60
I, 72	4-5, 61, 65
I, 101	43, 122
I, 102	122
I, 109	62, 64
I, 113	63, 144
I, 114	63-64, 221
I, 125	99
I, 130	150
I, 141	6, 40-44, 280
I, 147	60, 63, 64
I, 150	60, 65, 68
I, 150	106

I, 153	21-24, 59, 65, 71-96, 112
I, 154	65, 129
V, 78	27, 65, 292
V, 107	27
V, 113-14	60
V, 113	64-66
V, 126-27	27
V, 131	87
VI, 132	64

Epiphanius
Measures and Weights

| III, 12 | 123 |
| XXII | 74 |

Eusebius
Ecclesiastical History

I, 6	2, 67
VI, 13	72
VII, 32	4

Ecclesiastical Preparation

VIII, 9	37, 239-40
VIII, 10-17	4-5
IX, 6	9, 68
IX, 17	21-24, 46, 135, 162, 287-93
IX, 18	2, 46, 80-81, 104-06, 135, 162
IX, 19-21	46
IX, 22	5, 46, 283-85
IX, 23	46, 80-81
IX, 24	25, 47, 205, 283-85
IX, 25	47
IX, 26	71-96, 112
IX, 27	47, 53, 80-81, 86-87, 129
IX, 28-29	47, 59, 95, 100-04, 246
IX, 30-34	47, 58, 62, 247-58
IX, 30	21-24

IX, 30, 1-3	129-31				
IX, 30, 3-4	132-39				
IX, 30, 5	72				
IX, 30, 5-6	139-44				
IX, 30, 6-7	145-50				
IX, 30, 8	151-55				
IX, 31-34	155-70				
IX, 32, 2	227-30				
IX, 34, 4	170-72				
IX, 34, 4-5	175-81				
IX, 34, 6-7	181-83				
IX, 34, 7-8	183-86				
IX, 34, 8	186-87				
IX, 34, 9	187-90				
IX, 34, 10	190-96				
IX, 34, 11	196-202				
IX, 34, 12-13	203-208				
IX, 34, 14-16	208-13				
XI, 34, 15	34, 40, 143				
IX, 34, 16	213-15				
IX, 34, 17	215-16				
IX, 34, 18-19	47, 85, 217-24				
IX, 34, 20	47, 224-25				
IX, 35-36	47, 173, 270				
IX, 37	48, 88-90, 283-85				
IX, 38	48				
IX, 39, 2-5	48, 62, 227-42				
IX, 39, 2	227-29				
IX, 39, 3	229-30				
IX, 39, 4	230-34				
IX, 39, 5	78, 85, 234-42				
IX, 42	1, 2				
X, 10	115-17				
X, 12, 8	122, 262				
XIII, 10	286				
XIII, 12	27, 59, 286, 292				
XV, 1	74				

Jerome
De viris illustribus

14	305
38	42, 68

Origin
Against Celsus

I, 15	264-66
I, 23, 26, V, 41	88

PseudoJustin
Admonition to the Gentiles

8	116-18
9	43, 67, 122
15	59
37	55

Unity of God

2	59

Tatian
Oration to the Greeks

5	34
37	64, 67, 220-21
38	122, 126, 127

ANCIENT PAGAN LITERATURE

Abydenus
(FGrH 685)

	45, 53-54, 55
F 4	51, 55, 115-16
F 5	232

Acusilaus
(FGrH 2)

F 23	116

Aelian
Varia Historia

IX, 26	148

Agatharchides
(FGrH 86)

F 20	172

Alexander Polyhistor
(FGrH 273)

TT 1-3	45, 261
F 20	49
F 79	51, 115-24, 291
F 101	115-24
F 102	53-54, 117-29
F 121	37, 49, 50, 204

Anaximander
(FGrH 9)

F 3	79

Anticlidus
(FGrH 140)

F 11	79

Apion
(FGrH 616)

T 1	127
TT 4; 15	94
T 6	119
FF 2-3	125
F 4	126

Apollodorus
(FGrH 144)

FF 83-86	113
F 165	79

Apollonius Molon
(FGrH 728)

F 1	49, 95

Appian
Syria

50	272

Arrian

VII, 16	269

Aristotle

F 105 (Rose)	79

Athenian Constitution

1-13	84

Berossus
(FGrH 680)

T 7	55
FF 1; 3	45, 53
F 4	45, 53, 56, 114, 115
F 8	236
F 32	114

Callixenes
(FGrH 627)

FF 1-5	257

Castor
(FGrH 250)

F 6   116
F 14   114-27

Censorinus
De die natali

21   118-19

Cephalion
(FGrH 93)

F 1   123

Claudius Iolaus
(FGrH 788)

F 3   204

Ctesias
(FGrH 688)

                   104, 262
TT 1-19   231
F 5   255

Diodorus

I, 1-3; 7-9   87
I, 7-9
I, 12; 16   80
I, 17   87
I, 27   86, 91
I, 28-29   80, 89
I, 43   86-87
I, 45; 65; 79   125
I, 94   86, 90-91
I, 95   125
II, 1-28   104
II, 1   115
II, 23-32   232
II, 23   123
II, 32, 5-34, 6   231
II, 34   255
III, 67   81
V, 57   81
V, 74   79
XVIII, 42   271
XIX, 86   271
XIX, 93   292
XXXI, 19   134
XXXIV, 1-4   93
XL, 3   81-91,
                   94, 89,
                   114, 265,
                   272

Diogenes Laertius

I, 40   77, 83
II, 41   302

Dionysius of Halicarnassus

Roman Antiquities

I, 74   127

Dionysius of Miletus
(FGrH 687)

F 1   79

Dionysius Periegetes
(Mueller I)

160   148

Dius *(FGrH 785)*

F 1   219-23

Eratosthenes
(FGrH 241)

                   103

Euhemerus
(FGrH 63)

                   87
F 3   149

Glaucus
(FGrH 674)

F 7

Hecataeus of Abdera
(FGrH 264)

T 7   264-66
FF 1;3   90-91
F 6   88-91, 94,
                   114, 205,
                   265, 272
F 25   80, 86, 94

Hecataeus of Miletus
(FGrH 1)

                   261
F 20   79

Hellanicus
(FGrH 4)

                   261
F 47   116

Hermogenes
(FGrH 795)

F 2   119

Herodotus

I, 16   231
I, 46   246
I, 65-66   84
I, 73-75   231, 234
I, 103,   231
107-08, 119,
127-30, 139
I, 161-71   164
I, 173   206
II, 17   164
II, 44   219-23
II, 104   80,88
II, 105   82
II, 106; III, 37   257
IV, 87   82
V, 58   79, 81
V, 89   82
VI, 94-101   234
VII, 63   82
VII, 98   136
VIII, 113;   234
IX, 32

Hesiod
Theogony

                   104
421   115

Hieronymus
(FGrH 154 T 3)

                   271

Homer
Iliad

VI, 184, 206   206

Odyssey

V, 283   206

Justin

XXXVI, 2,   88
11-16
XXXVI, 3, 9   18

Laetus
(FGrH 784)

F 1   64

Leon *(FGrH 659)*

                   87
T 2   86
F 7   88

Lydus
De mensibus

IV, 53   86

Lysimachus
(FGrH 621)

                      94, 95,
                      125-27
F 1   206-07

Malalas

V, 7   123

Manetho
(FGrH 609)

T 7   94
FF 2-3   105, 135,
                      136
8-9   94
F 10   94, 95

Marmor Parium
(FGrH 339)

A 1; II B   116-18

Martialis

VII, 55; IX, 94   206

Menander
(FGrH 783)

F 1   64, 11-26,
                      219-23,
                      261

Nicolaus
(FGrH 90)

T 2   43,
                      239-40
FF 1-6   104, 231
F 2   123
F 72   95

Pausanias

VIII, 116   206
X, 12, 9   55

Philochorus
(FGrH 328)

F 92   116-18

Philo of Byblos
(FGrH 790)

                      220, 222
F 9   264-66
F 38

Polybius

XII, 11, 1   113
XVI   205

Polybius *(FGrH 256)*

F 33   116, 205

Porphyry

On Abstinence

II, 26   92, 193
FF 33;40   124

Posidonius
(FGrH 87)

F 67   222
F 69   93
F 70   91, 94,
                      114
F 109   93

Pseudo-Apollodorus
(FGrH 244)

F 83   115-24

Ptolemy of Mendes
(FGrH 611)

T 1   43
F 1   119-27

Strabo

IX, 1, 18   115
XII, 8, 13   119
XII, 3, 37, 85   206
XVI, 1, 5   269

XIV, 3, 10   148
XVI, 2, 34-35   93
XVI, 4, 4   148
XVII, 1, 20; 40   164

Suetonius
On Letters

20   43

Tacitus
Annals

XI, 14   81

Histories

V, 2, 5   206
V, 3, 1   126

Teucrus *(FGrH 274)*

T 1   114, 124

Thallus *(FGrH 256)*

F 7   116-23

Thrasyllus
(FGrH 253)

F 1   120-22

Thucydides

II, 15, 1   116

Timaeus *(FGrH 566)*

F 60   127
130   84

Timagenes *(FGrH 88)*

FF 4-6   114

Zeno *(FGrH 533)*

F 1   81

II. GENERAL

Aaron 62-152-55

Abiather 152-55

Achias of 81-82
 Salmon

Acts of Judah 29-32, 35-37

Adam 25, 37, 50, 51, 53, 71,
 72, 75, 98-106, 111-28,
 130, 283-93

Africanus, Sex- 43-44, 50, 55, 64, 98-
 tus Julius 100, 112, 120-27, 303-06

Agatharchides 272
 of Cnidos

Agrippa II 56, 300-06

Ahasuerus 233-34

Alcimus 154

Alcman 280

Alexander 88, 268, 293-95

Alexander 3, 21-25, 37, 44-55, 60,
 Polyhistor 65, 69, 106, 113, 114-
 125, 129-31, 227, 226,
 247, 285

Angelology 143-44

Antiochus III 10-11, 14, 16, 36, 205

Antiochus IV 14, 37, 39, 93, 135, 215,
 Epiphanes 239

Antipater son 20, 35
 of Jason

Apion 43, 44, 63, 93, 113,
 116-23

Apollodorus 113

Apollonius 9, 46, 49, 63, 88, 93
 Molon

Arabia 79, 145-50, 165

Aristarchus 56

Aristeas, 4-5, 7, 58, 274-76
 historian

Aristeas, 4-5, 7, 58, 60, 103, 255,
 Letter of 262-67, 274-76

Aristobulus, 296
 King of Judaea

Aristobulus, 4-5, 7, 39, 52, 55-56, 59,
 writer 68, 238-42, 262

Aristophanes 218

Aristotle 88

Artapanus 46, 53, 68, 73, 80-81,
 87, 96, 105-6, 129,
 286-93

Asinius Pollio 6, 41-44

Assyrians 231-36

Astibares 223, 230-36

Astyages 231-36

Atlas 2, 87, 104

Atthis 115

Baal 227-30

Babylon 79, 104, 115-17, 227-42

Bar Kochba 139

Barzillai 8-9

Belial 292

Belus 79, 89, 104, 121-24

Belochus 121-27

Berossus 103, 107, 113, 115-17,
 232, 262, 288

Bias of Priene 77

Bocchoris 125-27

Bolus
 Democritus 106

Cadmus 79, 81, 79

Callixenes of 257-58
 Rhodes

Caesar, Julius 51

Castor 54, 63, 114-17

Cassian, Julius 40-44, 63, 120

Charon of 261
 Lampascus

Cecrops 116-24

Cedrenus, 68, 73, 74
 Georgius

Chenephres 105

Church 57-70, 98-100, 106, 108
 Fathers

Cicero 51, 91, 93

Chilon of 77
 Sparta

Cleitarchus 28, 271

Cleobolus of 77
 Mindos

Cleodomus- 7, 44, 46, 53-55, 95
 Malchus

Commagene 19, 131-39, 248

Conon 218

Ctesias 13, 104-05, 107, 110,
 245-46, 255-56

Cyaxares 231-36

Danaüs 79, 89

Daniel, Book of 23, 97, 124

Darius I 86

Darius III 294

David 2, 32, 61-63, 66, 129-50,
 155-70, 246, 248, 283,
 292

Dead Sea
 Scrolls,
 see Qumran

Demeter 88

Demetrius I 6, 15, 17, 41-44, 246
 Soter

Demetrius II 6, 41-44
 Nicator

Demetrius, 2-4, 24-25, 34, 46, 52,
 writer 55-56, 66-68, 96-128,
 247, 280-82

Demetrius of 2-3
 Phaleron

Democritus 96

Deucalion 115-24

Dicaearchus 77

Didymus 56

Dionysius of   63, 304
  Halicarnassus
Dius   110-11, 113, 136,
                   218-23
Dositheus   278
Dura-Europos   58-59, 185

Elath   145-50, 165
Eleazar,   152-55
  descendants of
Eli   22-23, 130, 151-55, 211,
                   248
Elijah   21-24, 58, 129, 248
Enoch   2, 71, 75-6, 87, 96, 104,
                   119, 288-93
Eratosthenes   63, 103-04, 113-15,
                   117-18, 219
Erymanthe   55
Essenes   292-93
Euhemerus   74, 85, 87, 88, 115-16,
                   149-550, 218, 256, 269,
                   287-93
Eurycles   296-97
Ezekias, priest   266-73
Ezekiel   183, 200-01
Ezekielus   65, 73, 262, 285-87
Ezra   239

Fannius Strabo   18

Gabriel   74
Galilee   34, 155, 164-65, 234-36
Gaulanitis   132-35
Genesis   13, 103, 107, 130, 137,
  Apocryphon   282, 286
Georgius   68, 73-74
  Hamartolus
Gibeon   210-13
Gilead   34, 131-39, 155, 164-65,
                   234-36

Hakkos   8-9, 20-21, 37, 153
Hasidim   15
Hasmoneans   19-20, 23, 38
Hecataeus of   13, 79, 80-82, 85-96,
  Abdera   256
Hecataeus of   78, 81, 261
  Miletus
Hellanicus   115, 60, 261
Hellenism   10, 12-14, 14, 38, 58,
                   61-96, 245, 259-60
Heracles   15, 44, 79, 210-11
Hermes   80-81
Hermes   81
  Trismegistus
Hermogenes   218
Herod   19, 67, 232, 296-98,
                   303-06
Herod   299
  Antipas
Herodotus   13, 79, 81, 88, 89, 92,
                   107, 234-35, 246, 255-56

Hesiod   60, 115, 288, 290
Hilkiah   153
Hippolytus   98-99
Hiram   110-111, 132-50, 215-23
Historiography   181, 257, 259-62
  Phoenician   219-23
  Priestly   148-53, 213-15
Homer   56, 58-60, 84, 206-08
Hyksos   94, 117
Hypsicrates   221-23

Inachus   63, 116-27
Isaac   49, 100
Ithamar,   152-55
  descendants of
Ituraeans   131-39, 148, 248

Jacob   100-02, 281, 284
Jason,   15, 16, 32, 153
  High Priest
Jason of Cyrene   4, 7, 15, 20, 28, 34-39
Jason son of   1, 16, 20
  Eleazar
Jehoiachin   227-30, 248
Jeremiah   23, 39-40, 78, 85, 204-08,
                   227-42
Jerusalem   87, 89-90, 93, 110-11,
                   139-49, 185, 227-42, 248,
                   269-70, 283-85
Jesus   23, 98, 303-06
Job   58
John, father   8, 10-12, 16, 19, 36, 39,
  of Eupolemus   144
John
  Hyrcanus I   27, 28, 215, 295-96
John
  Hyrcanus II   297-98, 304-06
Joiarib   8-9
Jonathan, the   20, 32, 153
  Hasmonean
Jonathan of   301
  Cyrene
Jose ben   57
  Halaphta
Joseph   80, 100-01, 281, 283
Josephus   19, 21, 25, 28, 34, 36,
                   43, 44, 52-57, 60, 63-64,
                   83-84, 97, 110, 126, 127,
                   147, 219-20, 247-48,
                   260, 262, 290-306
Joshua   22, 51, 64, 107-08, 129-31,
                   211, 248, 254
Jubilees, Book   13, 34, 74, 102, 106, 130,
  of   282
Judaea   34, 89-91, 132-50, 165,
                   293-95, 269-70
Judaeophobia   88, 92, 94, 114, 125-28,
                   206
Judah Maccabee   5, 7, 9, 16, 19, 20, 25, 29, ·
                   32, 35, 68, 84, 106, 111,
                   238, 259, 305, 306
Judah Hanasi   139

Judas, historian 98-99
Justus of   43, 56, 60, 63-64, 67,
  Tiberias   123-27, 243, 260,
                   298-306

Keturah   50, 100-01
Kohat   101-02, 103
Kronos   104, 149, 290

Laetus   64, 220-23
Laosthenidas   81
Law, origin of   71, 83-85
Leon of Pella   87-88
Leontopolis   156-63
Linus   48, 79, 81
Liturgy   169-70
Lycurgus   83, 94
Lyncaeus   88
Lysimachus,   93, 195-97
  historian
Lysimachus,   12, 278
  translator

Manetho   13-16, 94-96, 103, 107,
                   113, 120-21, 135, 263
Melchizedek   162-63
Menander   64, 110-11, 113, 136,
                   256, 219-23
Menorah   183-86
Merrhís   105
Midrash   171-72
Minos of Crete   86
Mnaseas   218
Mochus   220
Moab   34, 131-39, 155, 164-65,
                   235-36
Moses   25, 44, 49, 51, 54, 60,
                   63-66, 68, 71-96,
                   106-26, 129-31, 144,
                   183-86, 204, 242, 246,
                   254, 281-83
Musaeus   80

Nabataea   19, 34, 148, 131-39,
                   165, 248
Nabdaeans   132-39
Nathan   61, 63, 65, 139-44,
                   176-77
Nebuchadnezzar   78, 230-42
Neco   67-68
Nehemiah   39-40
Neo-Pythagore-   45, 50
  ans
Nicanor   19, 31-32
Nicolaus   19, 21, 43-44, 95, 128,
                   131-32, 296, 303
Nimrod   104
Ninus   104, 114-27
Noah   55, 99, 103-04, 117-24
Numenius,   106
  philosopher
Numenius, son   20-21, 35
  of Antiochus

Ogygus   43, 115-24
Onias IV   211, 249, 296
Ophir   145-50, 248
Orpheus   27, 80, 292

Pharisees   84, 144
Philo   44, 52, 56, 58, 66, 247,
                   253, 291
Philo the   2-3, 7, 46, 52, 55-56, 62,
  Elder   64, 66-67, 68, 99-100,
                   111-114, 262, 282-84,
                   285
Philochorus   115
Phoenicia   34, 71, 77-83, 106,
                   131-39, 215-23
Plato   48, 59, 60, 68, 95, 106
Plutarch   93
Polybius   20, 21, 205, 124-27
Pompey   20, 50, 93
Pompeius   95
  Trogus
Porphyry   93, 124
Posidonius   85-86, 87, 91, 93, 95, 237
Pseudo-   114, 116-28
  Apollodrus
Pseudo-   293-95
  Callisthenes
Pseudo-   60
  Democritus
Pseudo-   3, 7, 22, 46, 71, 87,
  Eupolemus   104-06, 135, 162-63.
                   205-06, 286-93
Pseudo-   262, 263-66
  Euripides
Pseudo-   60, 195, 235-36, 262-73,
  Hecataeus   289, 292
Pseudo-   60
  Heraclitus
Pseudo-Hesiod   27, 262
Pseudo-Homer   27, 60, 262
Pseudo-Justin   15, 27, 59
Pseudo-Linus   27
Pseudo-   262, 264-66
  Orpheus
Pseudo-   264-66
  Sophocles
Ptolemy Lagus   264-63
Ptolemy   9
  Philadelphus
Ptolemy IV   99, 111
  Philopator
Ptolemy VI   6, 41-44
  Philometor
Ptolemy VII E   41-42
  Euergetes
Ptolemy VIII   6, 40-44
  Euergetes Physco
  Physcon
Ptolemy of   43
  Askalon
Ptolemy of   40-44, 63, 65, 73, 113,
  Mendes   118-21
Pythagoras   77

Qumran texts	8-9, 56, 137, 143, 177, 292-93
Rome	16-20, 36-38, 50, 299-303, 305-06
Sadducees	84, 143-44, 259
Samaria	111, 165, 234-7, 293-95
Samaritans	78, 112, 155, 205-06, 241-43, 283-95
Samuel	22, 108-09, 129-31, 144, 211, 248, 254
Sanchuniathon	67, 220-21, 223,264
Satan	139, 292
Saul	65-66, 107-09, 129-31, 248
Semiramis	48, 124
Sennacherib	101, 187
Septuaginta	62-63, 82, 87, 91-92, 102, 111-113, 136, 262-98
Shechem	283-85
Shiloh	23,34,62,153-55, 185, 209-13
Simon, Hasmonean	20, 23
Simon, Oniad	14
Solomon	15,58,61,64,71,85,107-11, 130, 151-225, 246-48
Sparta	20, 50, 37, 51
Strabo	91,92, 93-94, 116, 127
Suron	132-50, 155-70, 215-23, 248, 249
Syria	19, 50-51, 78-80, 82, 115, 125, 130-39 240
Tabernacle	147-50, 245
Tacitus	91, 93, 123
Temple of Jerusalem:	
accounts of	173-75, 245-58
altar	194-96, 249, 319-44
area of	269-71
expenditures	213-15
king's platform	193-94
lamps	183-86
laver	190-93
name	204-08
pillars	181-83
scarecrow	196-201
site of	139-44
supplies	145-50
Herodian	90, 187-90, 195-96, 257
Zerubabel's	175-201, 249-58, 270
Thales	77
Thallus	124-27, 218
Theodotus	5, 7, 46, 221-23, 283-85 287, 289-90
Theophilus	5, 7, 15, 243, 289
Theophilus of Antioch	59, 217-23
Theophrastus	92, 93, 124
Thrasyllus	113, 120-24
Thucydides	33, 116
Timarchus	18, 63, 113
Timochares	47, 270
Titans	104, 115, 290
Tobiads	9-10, 290, 295-96
Tyre	110-11, 150, , 215-23
Udaeus	37, 50
Vaphres	111, 164, 215-23, 249,255
Varro	93, 113, 118-19, 120-21, 132-50 115-70
Vespasian	299-303
Xisuthrus	55, 114-27
Zabdaeans	134
Zadokites	25, 63, 130-33, 151-55
Zerubabel	183, 249
Zeus	15, 140-44, 215-23
Zipporah	100-101, 281, 285
Zopyrion	218
Zoroaster	86
Zurvan	24

III. MODERN AUTHORS

Abel, F.M.	2, 8, 28, 39, 237, 239, 257
Abrahams, I.	293
Abramson, Sheraga	9
Africa, Thomas	28
Albeck, Ch.	168
Albright, W.F.	110, 219, 220
Altaner, Berthold	59
Allegro, John	279
Anderson, B.N.	86
Auvray, P.	277
Baer, S.	107
Barber, G.L.	94
Baron, Salo	271
Bévenot, H.	2, 39
Bernays, J.	93
Bickerman, Elias	12, 14, 28, 31, 37-39 95, 140, 208, 239, 264-275, 278, 279, 290
Bidez, J.	96
Blank, S.H.	77
Bloch, H.	52

Bosse, A.   97, 126
Brown, T.S.   84, 262
Büchler,   10, 293-95
  Adolf
Bueddinger, M.   126
Burrows, M.   205
Busink, Th. A.   138, 172-200, 204, 208, 249
Butler, R. C.   9

Charles, R. H.   7, 75, 288, 291-92
Cadbury, H.J.   277
Christ,   43, 60
  Wilhelm
Cowley, A.   86, 211
Cramer, I.N.   68
Cross, F.N.   78
Cruice, P.M.   27
Cumont, F.   96
Curtis, E.L.   194

Dahlmann   118
Dalbert, P.   25, 70, 84, 115, 146 161
Dancy, J.C.   1
Daniel,   141
  Suzanne
Deissmann, A.   257
Denis,   24, 45, 47, 48, 59,
  Albert-Marie   70, 146
Destinon,   98-99, 297
  Justus
De Vries, S.J.   102
Diels   45, 77, 220
Dihle   43, 44
Diringer,   78, 79, 82, 83
  David
Drews, R.   104
Dubbenstein, W.   37

Eissfeldt, Otto   40, 78, 117, 160, 264, 274, 275, 279
Elter, A.   27, 263
Engers, M.   263
Ewald, H.   40, 52, 55, 159, 167, 255
Exler E.   39, 157-70

Favaloro, G.   32-34
Feldman, L.H.   76, 267, 288, 297, 302, 204
Festugiere, A. J.   75
Fitzmyer J. A.   75, 138, 289
Flusser, David   75
Freedman, N. D.   78
Frankel, Z.   276
Freudenthal,   2-4, 6, 12, 21, 27,
  Jacob   28, 53-55, 69-71, 73, 102, 106, 108-9, 112, 130, 131, 134, 136, 142, 147-49, 156,

  157, 158, 162, 166, 168-69, 171-72, 175-76, 184, 194, 204, 205, 209, 210, 211-12, 215, 224, 238, 247, 248, 249, 250, 252, 254, 256, 280, 281, 283
Frey, Jean   10, 11
  Baptiste
Friedländer,   257, 304
  Paul
Friedmann (Ish-   24
  Shalom), M.

Gager, John   76, 92, 85, 86, 88, 90, 95
Gardner, Alan   79
Gaster, Moses   52, 101
Gaster, T. H.   143
Geiger,   29
  Abraham
Geisau, H.   50
Geffcken, J.   290, 291
Gelzer, H.   23, 43, 54, 56, 67, 94, 114-27, 304
Gerleman, G.   252
Giblet, G.   70, 146, 175, 204, 209, 289
Gifford, E. H.   284
Ginzberg,   199, 218, 223, 228
  Louis
Glueck, Nelson   149
Graetz,   6, 17, 99, 300
  Heinrich
Greenfield, J. C.   132
Grimm, C. L.   11, 17, 19, 28, 36, 38, 40, 140, 236, 239
Grintz, Y. M.   136
Guthrie, W.   77
Gutman, Y.   6, 37, 61, 80, 90, 104, 105, 118, 138, 157, 163, 211, 254, 280, 285
Gutschmid,   41-45, 69-70, 113, 120,
  Alfred   125, 126, 206, 219, 221, 303
Gutmann,   59
  Joseph
Guttmann,   144
  Alexander

Hadas, Moses   5, 286
Hahn, S.   98
Hanhart, R.   275
Harkavy,   194
  Abraham
Heinemann, I.   44, 76, 88, 91, 92,
Hengel M.   37, 38, 239, 260, 275, 277, 278, 279, 283, 290
Hody, H.   1
Hölscher,   53
  Gustav

Jacoby, Felix 2, 3-4, 7, 22, 42, 43, 50, 51, 54-55, 56, 63, 66, 69-70, 79-80, 81-82, 85, 87, 88, 89, 90-96, 100, 112, 113, 114-27, 169, 190, 194-95, 220, 263, 265, 267, 270, 272, 280, 283, 298, 299

Jaeger, W. 89-92, 92, 93
Jastrow, Marcus 4
Jeremias, J. 271

Kahle, Paul 91, 262, 274, 276, 279
Karpeles, G. 282
Katzenstein, 110
  H. J.
Kautzsch, E. 7
Kittel, R. 57
Klein, Samuel 9
König, E. 32
Koetschau, P. 42
Kolbe, W. 5, 239
Kraeling, C. H. 59
Krauss, Samuel 2
Kroll, W. 293
Kugler, F. 29, 110
Kuhlmey, Carl 1-3, 6,.21, 42, 69, 134, 136, 142, 156, 157, 194, 210, 231
Kuiper, K. 285-86
Kutscher, E. J. 136

Laqueur, 85, 95, 125, 220, 239,
  Richard 282, 299
Lewy, H. 235-36, 263, 265, 269
Levi, I. 293
Lichtenstein, 30, 293
  Hans
Lieberman, Saul 58, 199-200, 260
Linton, O. 97, 106
Littmann, E. 9, 296
Ludwich, A. 5, 283, 284, 284
Luther, H. 56, 123, 299-300

Mandelbaum, M. 168
Marcus, Ralph 10, 17, 37, 108, 144, 207, 276, 293
Margulies, M. 168
Mazar, B. 304
Meecham, 169-70, 255
  Henry
Meyer, Eduard 11, 29, 31, 38-39, 95, 125
Milik, J. T. 215, 279
Momingliano, 10, 50
  Armand
Montgomery,
  A. J.
Movers, F. 137, 157, 219, 222, 256
Motzo, B. 294

Mras, C. 44-52, 59, 66, 70, 115, 157, 183, 184, 190, 195-96, 215, 251, 252, 283, 285
Mueller, Carl 6, 41, 54, 70, 105, 126, 293, 298
Müller, I. G. 235-36
Murray, 149
  Margaret

Nestle, P. 57
Niebuhr, M. 6, 41, 53-54, 232
Niese, B. 5, 7, 29, 39, 48, 98, 207, 239, 267
Nikiprowetzky, 37, 51
  V.
Nock, A. D. 59
Norden, E. 51, 92, 257

Oppenheim, L. 183, 232
Otto, Walter 304
Overbeck, J. 257

Pape, W, 4
Parker, Richard 37
Parsons, L. A. 68
Peretti, A. 35
Peterson, H. 299
Pfeifer, R. H. 2, 17, 75, 160
Pfister, F. 294
Potscher, W. 124
Preisigke, F. 4
Pritchard, J.B 77, 103, 183, 210

Rabin Ch. 153
Rahlfs, Alfred 57, 188
Ratner, B. 154
Rauch, J. 27
Reifenberg, A. 267, 296
Reinach, 2, 90, 128, 218, 235-
  Théodore 36, 263, 271
Reinhardt, I. 87, 96, 120
Reitzenstein, R. 81
Riessler, P.
Rist, M. 75
Ritschl, F. 17
Roberts, C. H. 232
Roth, O. 17-18
Routh, M.H. 303
Rowley, 233
  H.H.
Rudolph, 8, 143, 152, 172,
  Wilhelm 194, 214, 218, 248, 249
Ryckmans, G. 149

Sanders, J. A. 292
Sandmel, 5, 76, 253, 289
  Samuel
Scaliger, J. J. 68, 136
Schalit, 46, 297
  Abraham
Schaller, B. 263

Schermann, Th. -24, 40, 137, 255,

Schlatter, A. 4, 29, 42, 52, 259, 263, 265

Schnabel, Paul 45, 55, 288

Schreckenberg, H. 299

Schunck, Klaus-Dietrich 29-30

Schürer, Emil 2, 17, 22, 35, 42, 55-56 69, 80, 118, 119, 146, 169, 263, 284, 285, 297, 298, 300, 302, 305,

Schwartz, Eduard 45, 54, 82, 85, 103, 114, 154, 238-42

Segal. S. Z. 277

Sellers, O. R. 167, 267

Sevenster, N. 260

Shehahan, R. W. 279

Smith, G. A. 165

Speyer, Wolfgang 88, 264, 303

Spiro, Abram 78, 130, 146, 210-11, 290

Spoerri, W. 85

Stahlin, O. 53, 60, 102, 112, 169, 283, 285-86, 299-300

Starcky, Jean 2, 28, 37, 39, 40, 239, 240

Stein, E. 52

Stendahl, K. 97

Stern, M. 10, 167

Strugnell, John 48, 62, 73, 90, 113, 142, 143, 279, 285

Sukenik, E. 59

Sundberg, A.C. 144

Susemihl, F. 42

Swete, H.B. 102, 249, 275

Täubler, E. 17

Tcherikover, Victor 10, 12, 38, 265, 275, 290, 295

Tedesche, S. 15, 28

Thackeray, H. St. J. 98, 218, 256, 268

Tonneau, R. M. 68, 74

Torrey, Charles 160

Tramontano, R. 5, 169

Turner, N. 2, 279

Tur-Sinai, N. T. 78, 82-83

Unger, F. G. 45, 120

Valckaner, L. 5, 27, 61

Vermes, G. 76, 289

Vincent 189

Vossius, J. G. 198

Vossius, I. 2, 43, 68

Wachsmuth, C. 44, 123, 280, 300,303,

Walter, Nikolaus 1, 2, 3, 5, 7, 13, 27, 40, 42, 44, 46, 52, 54, 55, 60, 61, 71, 73, 87, 104, 108, 120, 133, 134, 152, 156, 161, 167, 171, 176, 184, 194-95, 196, 236, 250, 251, 262, 268-73, 286, 287, 304

Weill, R. 123

Weitzmann, Kurt 58

Wellhausen, Julius 17

Wendland, Paul 5, 169, 255, 265

Wieneke, J. 47, 246, 285, 286

Wilamowitz, U. 63

Wilcken, U. 257

Willrich, Hugo 1, 11, 30, 31, 80, 164, 239-40, 267, 268, 271

Wiseman, J. 228, 232, 235

Wolfson, H. 66

Yadin, Y. 78, 177, 201, 277

Yeivin, S. 78

Zaehner, R. C. 24

Zeitlin, Solomon 15, 28, 34, 240

Zimmern, H. 77

Zöcker, Otto 29